# Linux® Command
# Line and Shell Scripting
# Bible

# Linux® Command Line and Shell Scripting
## BIBLE

Richard Blum

Christine Bresnahan

WILEY

**Linux® Command Line and Shell Scripting Bible**

Copyright © 2021 by John Wiley & Sons, Inc., Indianapolis, Indiana

Published simultaneously in Canada and the United Kingdom

ISBN: 978-1-119-70091-3
ISBN: 978-1-119-70094-4 (ebk)
ISBN: 978-1-119-70093-7 (ebk)

For general information on our other products and services please contact our Customer Care Department within the United States at (877) 762-2974, outside the United States at (317) 572-3993 or fax (317) 572-4002.

Wiley publishes in a variety of print and electronic formats and by print-on-demand. Some material included with standard print versions of this book may not be included in e-books or in print-on-demand. If this book refers to media such as a CD or DVD that is not included in the version you purchased, you may download this material at booksupport.wiley.com. For more information about Wiley products, visit www.wiley.com.

**Library of Congress Control Number:** 2020949805

SKY10087017_100724

*To the Lord God Almighty, "in whom are hidden all the treasures of wisdom and knowledge."*

*— Colossians 2:3*

# About the Authors

**Richard Blum** has worked in the IT industry for more than 30 years as both a systems and a network administrator. During that time, he's had the opportunity to work with lots of different computer products, including Windows, NetWare, Cisco, Avaya, different flavors of UNIX, and of course, Linux. Over the years he's also volunteered for several nonprofit organizations to help support small networks that had little financial support. Rich is the author of many Linux-based books for total Linux geeks and teaches online courses in Linux and web programming. When he's not busy being a computer nerd, Rich enjoys playing piano and bass guitar and spending time with his wife, Barbara, and their two daughters, Katie Jane and Jessica.

**Christine Bresnahan** started working with computers more than 30 years ago in the IT industry as a systems administrator. Christine is an adjunct professor at Ivy Tech Community College, where she teaches Linux certification and Python programming classes. She also writes books and produces instructional resources for the classroom. During her downtime, Christine enjoys spending time with her husband and family, hiking, and gardening.

# About the Technical Editor

Jason W. Eckert is an experienced technical trainer, consultant, and best-selling author in the technology industry. With 45 industry certifications, 25 published textbooks, and over 30 years of technology and programming experience, Jason brings his expertise to every class that he teaches at triOS College. For more information about him, visit jasoneckert.net.

# Acknowledgments

First, all glory and praise go to God, who through His Son, Jesus Christ, makes all things possible and gives us the gift of eternal life.

Many thanks go to the fantastic team of people at John Wiley & Sons for their outstanding work on this project. Thanks to Kenyon Brown, the acquisitions editor, for offering us the opportunity to work on this book. Also thanks to Patrick Walsh, the project editor, for keeping things on track and making this book more presentable. Thanks, Pat, for all your hard work and diligence. The technical editor, Jason Eckert, did a wonderful job of double-checking all the work in the book, plus making suggestions to improve the content. Thanks to Saravanan Dakshinamurthy and his team for their endless patience and diligence to make our work readable. We would also like to thank Carole Jelen at Waterside Productions, Inc., for arranging this opportunity for us, and for helping us out in our writing careers.

Christine would like to thank her husband, Timothy, for his encouragement, patience, and willingness to listen, even when he has no idea what she is talking about. Rich would like to thank his wife, Barbara, for the life-sustaining baked goods she readily prepared to help him keep up his energy while writing!

# Contents at a Glance

## Contents at a Glance

# Contents

# Contents

# Contents

# Contents

# Contents

# Contents

# Contents

## Part IV: Creating and Managing Practical Scripts    679

### Chapter 24: Writing Simple Script Utilities . . . . . . . . . . . . . . . . . . . . . . . . . . . . 681

# Contents

# Introduction

Welcome to the fourth edition of *Linux Command Line and Shell Scripting Bible*. Like all books in the *Bible* series, you can expect to find both hands-on tutorials and real-world information, as well as reference and background information that provides a context for what you are learning. This book is a fairly comprehensive resource on the Linux command line and shell commands. By the time you have completed *Linux Command Line and Shell Scripting Bible*, you will be well prepared to write your own shell scripts that can automate practically any task on your Linux system.

## Who Should Read This Book

If you're a systems administrator in a Linux environment, you'll benefit greatly by knowing how to write shell scripts. The book doesn't walk you through the process of setting up a Linux system, but after you have it running, you'll want to start automating some of the routine administrative tasks. That's where shell scripting comes in, and that's where this book helps you out. This book demonstrates how to automate any administrative task using shell scripts, from monitoring system statistics and data files to generating reports for your boss.

If you're a home Linux enthusiast, you'll also benefit from *Linux Command Line and Shell Scripting Bible*. Nowadays, it's easy to get lost in the graphical world of prebuilt widgets. Most desktop Linux distributions try their best to hide the Linux system from the typical user. However, sometimes you must know what's going on under the hood. This book shows you how to access the Linux command-line prompt and what to do when you get there. Often, performing simple tasks, such as file management, can be done more quickly from the command line than from a fancy graphical interface. You can use a wealth of commands from the command line, and this book shows you how to use them.

## How This Book Is Organized

This book leads you through the basics of the Linux command line and into more complicated topics, such as creating your own shell scripts. The book is divided into four parts, each one building on the previous parts.

Part I assumes that you either have a Linux system running or are looking into getting a Linux system. Chapter 1, "Starting with Linux Shells," describes the parts of a total Linux system and shows how the shell fits in. After describing the basics of the Linux system, this part continues with the following:

- Using a terminal emulation package to access the shell (Chapter 2)
- Introducing the basic shell commands (Chapter 3)
- Using more advanced shell commands to peek at system information (Chapter 4)
- Understanding what the shell is used for (Chapter 5)
- Working with shell variables to manipulate data (Chapter 6)
- Understanding the Linux filesystem and security (Chapter 7)
- Working with Linux filesystems from the command line (Chapter 8)
- Installing and updating software from the command line (Chapter 9)
- Using the Linux editors to start writing shell scripts (Chapter 10)

In Part II, you begin writing shell scripts. As you go through the chapters, you'll do the following:

- Learn how to create and run shell scripts (Chapter 11)
- Alter the program flow in a shell script (Chapter 12)
- Iterate through code sections (Chapter 13)
- Handle data from the user in your scripts (Chapter 14)
- See different methods for storing and displaying data from your script (Chapter 15)
- Control how and when your shell scripts run on the system (Chapter 16)

Part III dives into more advanced areas of shell script programming, including these things:

- Creating your own functions to use in all your scripts (Chapter 17)
- Utilizing the Linux graphical desktop for interacting with your script users (Chapter 18)
- Using advanced Linux commands to filter and parse data files (Chapter 19)
- Using regular expressions to define data (Chapter 20)
- Learning advanced methods of manipulating data in your scripts (Chapter 21)
- Working with advanced features of scripting to generate reports from raw data (Chapter 22)
- Modifying your shell scripts to run in other Linux shells (Chapter 23)

The last section of the book, Part IV, demonstrates how to use shell scripts in real-world environments. In this part, you will learn these things:

- How to put all the scripting features together to write your own scripts (Chapter 24)
- How to organize and track your script versions using the popular git software (Chapter 25)

## Conventions and features

You will find many different organizational and typographical features throughout this book designed to help you get the most out of the information.

### Tips and warnings

Whenever the authors want to bring something important to your attention, the information appears in a Warning.

**WARNING**

This information is important and is set off in a separate paragraph with a special icon. Warnings provide information about things to watch out for, whether simply inconvenient or potentially hazardous to your data or systems.

For additional items of interest that relate to the chapter text, the authors use Tip.

**TIP**

Tips provide additional, ancillary information that is helpful, but somewhat outside of the current presentation of information.

# Minimum Requirements

*Linux Command Line and Shell Scripting Bible* doesn't focus on any specific Linux distribution, so you can follow along in the book using any Linux system you have available. The bulk of the book references the Bash shell, which is the default shell for most Linux systems.

# Where to Go from Here

After you've finished reading *Linux Command Line and Shell Scripting Bible*, you're well on your way to incorporating Linux commands in your daily Linux work. In the ever-changing world of Linux, it's always a good idea to stay in touch with new developments. Often, Linux distributions change, adding new features and removing older ones. To keep your knowledge of Linux fresh, always stay well informed. Find a good Linux forum site and monitor what's happening in the Linux world. Many popular Linux news sites, such as Slashdot and DistroWatch, provide up-to-the-minute information about new advances in Linux.

# Part I

# The Linux Command Line

**IN THIS PART**

# Starting with Linux Shells

B efore you can dive into working with the Linux command line and shells, it's a good idea to first understand what Linux is, where it came from, and how it works. This chapter walks you through what Linux is and explains where the shell and command line fit in the overall Linux picture.

## Investigating Linux

If you've never worked with Linux before, you may be confused as to why there are so many different versions of it available. We're sure that you've heard various terms such as distribution, LiveDVD, and GNU when looking at Linux packages and been confused. Wading through the world of Linux for the first time can be a tricky experience. This chapter takes some of the mystery out of the Linux system before you start working on commands and scripts.

For starters, four main parts make up a Linux system:

- The Linux kernel
- The GNU utilities
- A graphical desktop environment
- Application software

Each of these four parts has a specific job in the Linux system. Each one of the parts by itself isn't very useful. Figure 1-1 shows a basic diagram of how the parts fit together to create the overall Linux system.

**FIGURE 1-1**

The Linux system

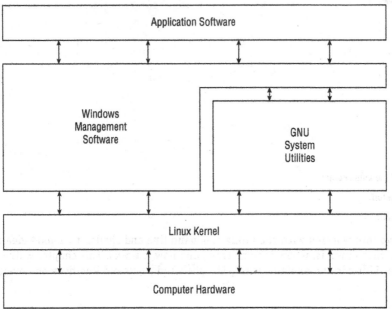

This section describes these four main parts in detail and gives you an overview of how they work together to create a complete Linux system.

## Looking into the Linux kernel

The core of the Linux system is the *kernel*. The kernel controls all the hardware and software on the computer system, allocating hardware when necessary and executing software when required.

If you've been following the Linux world at all, no doubt you've heard the name Linus Torvalds. Linus is the person responsible for creating the first Linux kernel software while he was a student at the University of Helsinki. He intended it to be a copy of the Unix system, at the time a popular operating system used at many universities.

After developing the Linux kernel, Linus released it to the Internet community and solicited suggestions for improving it. This simple process started a revolution in the world of computer operating systems. Soon Linus was receiving suggestions from students as well as professional programmers from around the world.

Allowing anyone to change programming code in the kernel would result in complete chaos. To simplify things, Linus acted as a central point for all improvement suggestions. It was ultimately Linus's decision whether or not to incorporate suggested code in the kernel. This same concept is still in place with the Linux kernel code, except that instead of just Linus controlling the kernel code, a team of developers has taken on the task.

The kernel is primarily responsible for four main functions:

- System memory management
- Software program management
- Hardware management
- Filesystem management

The following sections explore each of these functions in more detail.

### System memory management

One of the primary functions of the operating system kernel is memory management. Not only does the kernel manage the physical memory available on the server, but it can also create and manage virtual memory, or memory that does not actually exist.

It does this by using space on the hard disk, called the *swap space*. The kernel swaps the contents of virtual memory locations back and forth from the swap space to the actual physical memory. This allows the system to think there is more memory available than what physically exists (shown in Figure 1-2).

**FIGURE 1-2**

The Linux system memory map

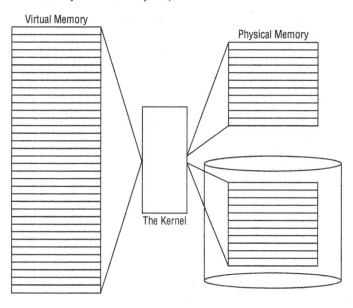

The memory locations are grouped into blocks called *pages*. The kernel locates each page of memory in either the physical memory or the swap space. The kernel then maintains a table of the memory pages that indicates which pages are in physical memory and which pages are swapped out to disk.

The kernel keeps track of which memory pages are in use and automatically copies memory pages that have not been accessed for a period of time to the swap space area (called *swapping out*), even if other memory is available. When a program wants to access a memory page that has been swapped out, the kernel must make room for it in physical memory by swapping out a different memory page, and swap in the required page from the swap space. Obviously, this process takes time and can slow down a running process. The process of swapping out memory pages for running applications continues for as long as the Linux system is running.

### Software program management

The Linux operating system calls a running program a *process*. A process can run in the foreground, displaying output on a display, or it can run in the background, behind the scenes. The kernel controls how the Linux system manages all the processes running on the system.

The kernel creates the first process, called the *init process*, to start all other processes on the system. When the kernel starts, it loads the init process into virtual memory. As the kernel starts each additional process, it gives the process a unique area in virtual memory to store the data and code that the process uses.

A few different types of init process implementations are available in Linux, but these days the two most popular are:

- **SysVinit:** The *SysVinit (SysV)* initialization method, the original method used by Linux, was based on the Unix System V initialization method. Though it is not used by many Linux distributions these days, you still may find it around in older Linux distributions.
- **Systemd:** The *systemd* initialization method, created in 2010, has become the most popular initialization and process management system used by Linux distributions.

The SysVinit initialization method used a concept called *runlevels* to determine what processes to start. The runlevel defines the state of the running Linux system and what processes should run in each state. Table 1-1 shows the different runlevels associated with the SysVinit initialization method.

**TABLE 1-1  The SysVinit Runlevels**

| Runlevel | Description |
| --- | --- |
| 0 | Shut down the system |
| 1 | Single-user mode used for system maintenance |

| Runlevel | Description |
|----------|-------------|
| 2 | Multi-user mode without networking services enabled |
| 3 | Multi-user mode with networking services enabled |
| 4 | Custom |
| 5 | Multi-user mode with GUI available |
| 6 | Reboot the system |

The /etc/inittab file defines the default runlevel for a system. The processes that start for specific runlevels are defined in subdirectories of the /etc/rc.d directory. You can view the current runlevel at any time using the runlevel command:

```
$ runlevel
N 5
$
```

The systemd initialization method became popular because it has the ability to start processes based on different events:

- When the system boots
- When a particular hardware device is connected
- When a service is started
- When a network connection is established
- When a timer has expired

The systemd method determines what processes to run by linking events to *unit files*. Each unit file defines the programs to start when the specified event occurs. The systemctl program allows you to start, stop, and list the unit files currently running on the system.

The systemd method groups unit files together into *targets*. A target defines a specific running state of the Linux system, similar to the SysVinit runlevel concept. At system startup, the default.target unit defines all the unit files to start. You can view the current default target using the systemctl command:

```
$ systemctl get-default
graphical.target
$
```

The graphical.target unit file defines the processes to start when a multi-user graphical environment is running, similar to the old SysVinit runlevel 5.

> **NOTE**
>
> In Chapter 4, "More Bash Shell Commands," you'll see how to use the ps command to view the processes currently running on the Linux system.

### Hardware management

Still another responsibility for the kernel is hardware management. Any device that the Linux system must communicate with needs driver code inserted inside the kernel code. The driver code allows the kernel to pass data back and forth to the device, acting as an intermediary between applications and the hardware. Two methods are used for inserting device driver code in the Linux kernel:

- Drivers compiled in the kernel
- Driver modules added to the kernel

Previously, the only way to insert device driver code was to recompile the kernel. Each time you added a new device to the system, you had to recompile the kernel code. This process became even more inefficient as Linux kernels supported more hardware. Fortunately, Linux developers devised a better method to insert driver code into the running kernel.

Programmers developed the concept of kernel modules to allow you to insert driver code into a running kernel without having to recompile the kernel. Also, a kernel module could be removed from the kernel when the device was finished being used. This greatly simplified and expanded using hardware with Linux.

The Linux system identifies hardware devices as special files, called *device files*. There are three classifications of device files:

- Character
- Block
- Network

Character device files are for devices that can handle data only one character at a time. Most types of modems and terminals are created as character files. Block files are for devices that can handle data in large blocks at a time, such as disk drives.

The network file types are used for devices that use packets to send and receive data. This includes network cards and a special loopback device that allows the Linux system to communicate with itself using common network programming protocols.

Linux creates special files, called *nodes*, for each device on the system. All communication with the device is performed through the device node. Each node has a unique number pair that identifies it to the Linux kernel. The number pair includes a major and a minor device number. Similar devices are grouped into the same major device number. The minor device number is used to identify a specific device within the major device group.

### Filesystem management

Unlike some other operating systems, the Linux kernel can support different types of filesystems to read and write data to and from hard drives. Besides having over a dozen filesystems of its own, Linux can read and write to and from filesystems used by other operating systems, such as Microsoft Windows. The kernel must be compiled with support for all types of filesystems that the system will use. Table 1-2 lists the standard filesystems that a Linux system can use to read and write data.

TABLE 1-2    **Linux Filesystems**

| Filesystem | Description |
| --- | --- |
| ext | Linux extended filesystem — the original Linux filesystem |
| ext2 | Second extended filesystem; provided advanced features over ext |
| ext3 | Third extended filesystem; supports journaling |
| ext4 | Fourth extended filesystem; supports advanced journaling |
| btrfs | A newer, high-performance filesystem that supports journaling and large files |
| exfat | The extended Windows filesystem, used mainly for SD cards and USB sticks |
| hpfs | OS/2 high-performance filesystem |
| jfs | IBM's journaling filesystem |
| iso9660 | ISO 9660 filesystem (CD-ROMs) |
| minix | MINIX filesystem |
| msdos | Microsoft FAT16 |
| ncp | NetWare filesystem |
| nfs | Network File System |
| ntfs | Support for Microsoft NT filesystem |
| proc | Access to system information |
| smb | Samba SMB filesystem for network access |
| sysv | Older Unix filesystem |
| ufs | BSD filesystem |
| umsdos | Unix-like filesystem that resides on top of msdos |
| vfat | Windows 95 filesystem (FAT32) |
| XFS | High-performance 64-bit journaling filesystem |

Any hard drive that a Linux server accesses must be formatted using one of the filesystem types listed in Table 1-2.

The Linux kernel interfaces with each filesystem using the Virtual File System (VFS). This provides a standard interface for the kernel to communicate with any type of filesystem. VFS caches information in memory as each filesystem is mounted and used.

## The GNU utilities

Besides having a kernel to control hardware devices, a computer operating system needs utilities to perform standard functions, such as controlling files and programs. Although Linus created the Linux system kernel, he had no system utilities to run on it. Fortunately for him, at the same time he was working, a group of people were working together on the

Internet trying to develop a standard set of computer system utilities that mimicked the popular Unix operating system.

The GNU organization (GNU stands for GNU's Not Unix) developed a complete set of Unix utilities but had no kernel system to run them on. These utilities were developed under a software philosophy called open source software (OSS).

The concept of OSS allows programmers to develop software and then release it to the world with no licensing fees attached. Anyone can use, modify, or incorporate the software into their own system without having to pay a license fee. Uniting Linus's Linux kernel with the GNU operating system utilities created a complete, functional, free operating system.

Although the bundling of the Linux kernel and GNU utilities is often just called Linux, you will see some Linux purists on the Internet refer to it as the GNU/Linux system to give credit to the GNU organization for its contributions to the cause.

### The core GNU utilities

The GNU project was mainly designed for Unix system administrators to have a Unix-like environment available. This focus resulted in the project porting many common Unix system command-line utilities. The core bundle of utilities supplied for Linux systems is called the *coreutils* package.

The GNU coreutils package consists of three parts:

- Utilities for handling files
- Utilities for manipulating text
- Utilities for managing processes

Each of these three main groups of utilities contains several utility programs that are invaluable to the Linux system administrator and programmer. This book covers each of the utilities contained in the GNU coreutils package in detail.

### The shell

The GNU/Linux shell is a special interactive utility. It provides a way for users to start programs, manage files on the filesystem, and manage processes running on the Linux system. The core of the shell is the command prompt. The command prompt is the interactive part of the shell. It allows you to enter text commands, and then it interprets the commands and executes them in the kernel.

The shell contains a set of internal commands that you use to control tasks such as copying files, moving files, renaming files, displaying the programs currently running on the system, and stopping programs running on the system. Besides the internal commands, the shell allows you to enter the name of a program at the command prompt. The shell passes the program name off to the kernel to start it.

You can also group shell commands into files to execute as a program. Those files are called *shell scripts*. Any command that you can execute from the command line can be placed in a shell script and run as a group of commands. This provides great flexibility in creating utilities for commonly run commands or processes that require several commands grouped together.

Quite a few Linux shells are available to use on a Linux system. Different shells have different characteristics, some being more useful for creating scripts and some being more useful for managing processes. The default shell used in all Linux distributions is the Bash shell. The Bash shell was developed by the GNU project as a replacement for the standard Unix shell, called the Bourne shell (after its creator). The Bash shell name is a play on this wording, referred to as the "Bourne again shell."

In addition to the Bash shell, we will cover several other popular shells in this book. Table 1-3 lists the different shells we will examine.

**TABLE 1-3  Linux Shells**

| Shell | Description |
| --- | --- |
| ash | A simple, lightweight shell that runs in low-memory environments but has full compatibility with the Bash shell |
| korn | A programming shell compatible with the Bourne shell but supporting advanced programming features like associative arrays and floating-point arithmetic |
| tcsh | A shell that incorporates elements from the C programming language into shell scripts |
| zsh | An advanced shell that incorporates features from Bash, tcsh, and korn, providing advanced programming features, shared history files, and themed prompts |

Most Linux distributions include more than one shell, although usually they pick one of them to be the default. If your Linux distribution includes multiple shells, feel free to experiment with different shells and see which one fits your needs.

## The Linux desktop environment

In the early days of Linux (the early 1990s), all that was available was a simple text interface to the Linux operating system. This text interface allowed administrators to start programs, control program operations, and move files around on the system.

With the popularity of Microsoft Windows, computer users expected more than the old text interface to work with. This spurred more development in the OSS community, and the Linux graphical desktops emerged.

Linux is famous for being able to do things in more than one way, and no place is this more relevant than in graphical desktops. In Linux you can choose from a plethora of graphical desktops. The following sections describe a few popular ones.

### The X Window software

Two basic elements control your video environment — the video card in your PC and your monitor. To display fancy graphics on your computer, the Linux software needs to know how to talk to both of them. The X Window software is the core element in presenting graphics.

The X Window software is a low-level program that works directly with the video card and monitor in the PC and controls how Linux applications can present fancy windows and graphics on your computer.

Linux isn't the only operating system that uses X Window; versions have been written for many different operating systems. In the Linux world, a few software packages can implement it. Two X Window packages are most commonly used in Linux:

- X.org
- Wayland

The X.org package is the older of the two, based on the original Unix X Window System version 11 (often called X11). More Linux distributions are migrating to the newer Wayland software, which is more secure and easier to maintain.

When you first install a Linux distribution, it attempts to detect your video card and monitor, and it then creates an X Window configuration file that contains the required information. During installation you may notice a time when the installation program scans your monitor for supported video modes. Sometimes this causes your monitor to go blank for a few seconds. Because lots of different types of video cards and monitors are out there, this process can take a little while to complete.

The core X Window software produces a graphical display environment but nothing else. Although this is fine for running individual applications, it is not too useful for day-to-day computer use. There is no desktop environment allowing users to manipulate files or launch programs. To do that, you need a desktop environment on top of the X Window system software.

### The KDE Plasma desktop

The K Desktop Environment (KDE) was first released in 1996 as an open source project to produce a graphical desktop similar to the Microsoft Windows environment. The KDE desktop incorporates all the features you are probably familiar with if you are a Windows user. Figure 1-3 shows the current version, called KDE Plasma, running in the openSUSE Linux distribution.

The KDE Plasma desktop allows you to place both application and file icons in a special area on the desktop. If you single-click an application icon, the Linux system starts the application. If you single-click a file icon, the KDE desktop attempts to determine what application to start to handle the file.

**FIGURE 1-3**

The KDE Plasma desktop on an openSUSE Linux system

The bar at the bottom of the desktop is called the Panel. The Panel consists of four parts:

- **The K menu:** Much like the Windows Start menu, the K menu contains links to start installed applications.
- **Program shortcuts:** These are quick links to start applications directly from the Panel.
- **The taskbar:** The taskbar shows icons for applications currently running on the desktop.
- **Applets:** These are small applications that have an icon in the Panel that can often change depending on information from the application.

All of the Panel features are similar to what you would find in Windows. In addition to the desktop features, the KDE project has produced a wide assortment of applications that run in the KDE environment.

## The GNOME desktop

The GNU Network Object Model Environment (GNOME) is another popular Linux desktop environment. First released in 1999, GNOME has become the default desktop environment for many Linux distributions (the most popular being Red Hat Linux).

**NOTE**

The GNOME desktop underwent a radical change with version 3, released in 2011. It departed from the standard look and feel of most desktops using standard menu bars and taskbars to make the interface more user-friendly across multiple platforms, such as tablets and mobile phones. This change led to controversy (see the "Other desktops" section), but slowly many Linux enthusiasts accepted the new look and feel of the GNOME 3 desktop.

Figure 1-4 shows the standard GNOME desktop used in the Ubuntu Linux distribution.

**FIGURE 1-4**

A GNOME 3 desktop on an Ubuntu Linux system

The GNOME 3 desktop cleans up the desktop interface by reducing the available menus to just three:

- **Activities:** Displays favorites, as well as any running application icons
- **Calendar:** Shows the current date/time, along with any system notification messages
- **System:** Shows network connections, system settings, and options to restart the system

The GNOME 3 desktop was designed to work on multiple types of devices, so you won't find a lot of menus. To launch applications, you must search for them using the Activities Overview, which is a search feature on the Activities menu.

Not to be outdone by KDE, the GNOME developers have also produced a host of graphical applications that integrate with the GNOME desktop.

### Other desktops

One of the main features of Linux is choice, and nowhere is that more evident than in the graphical desktop world. There are a plethora of different types of graphical desktops available in the Linux world. If you're not happy with the default desktop in your Linux distribution, it usually doesn't take much effort to change it to something else!

When the GNOME desktop project radically changed its interface in version 3, many Linux developers who preferred the look and feel of GNOME version 2 created spin-off versions based on GNOME 2. Of these, two became somewhat popular:

- **Cinnamon:** The Cinnamon desktop was developed in 2011 by the Linux Mint distribution in an attempt to continue development of the original GNOME 2 desktop. It's now available as an option in several Linux distributions, including Ubuntu Fedora and openSUSE.
- **MATE:** The MATE desktop was also developed in 2011 by an Arch Linux user who disliked the switch to GNOME 3. It incorporates a few features of GNOME 3 (such as replacing the taskbar) but maintains the overall look and feel of GNOME 2.

Figure 1-5 shows the Cinnamon desktop as it appears in the Linux Mint distribution.

The downside to these fancy graphical desktop environments is that they require a fair amount of system resources to operate properly. In the early days of Linux, a hallmark and selling feature of Linux was its ability to operate on older, less powerful PCs that the newer Microsoft desktop products couldn't run on. However, with the popularity of KDE Plasma and GNOME 3 desktops, this has changed, since it takes just as much memory to run a KDE Plasma or GNOME 3 desktop as it does to run the latest Microsoft desktop environment.

If you have an older PC, don't be discouraged. The Linux developers have banded together to take Linux back to its roots. They've created several low memory–oriented graphical desktop applications that provide basic features that run perfectly fine on older PCs.

Although these graphical desktops don't have all that many applications designed around them, they still run many basic graphical applications that support features such as word processing, spreadsheets, databases, drawing, and, of course, multimedia support.

Table 1-4 shows some of the smaller Linux graphical desktop environments that can be used on lower-powered PCs and laptops.

**FIGURE 1-5**

The Cinnamon desktop from Linux Mint

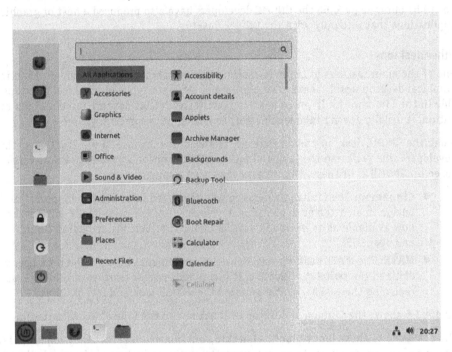

**TABLE 1-4  Other Linux Graphical Desktops**

| Desktop | Description |
|---|---|
| Fluxbox | A bare-bones desktop that doesn't include a Panel, only a pop-up menu to launch applications |
| Xfce | A desktop that's similar to the GNOME 2 desktop but with less graphics for low-memory environments |
| JWM | Joe's Window Manager, a very lightweight desktop ideal for low-memory and low–disk space environments |
| fvwm | Supports some advanced desktop features such as virtual desktops and Panels, but runs in low-memory environments |
| fvwm95 | Derived from fvwm but made to look like a Windows 95 desktop |

These graphical desktop environments are not as fancy as the KDE Plasma and GNOME 3 desktops, but they provide basic graphical functionality just fine. Figure 1-6 shows what the Xfce desktop used in the MX Linux distribution looks like.

**FIGURE 1-6**

The Xfce desktop as seen in the MX Linux distribution

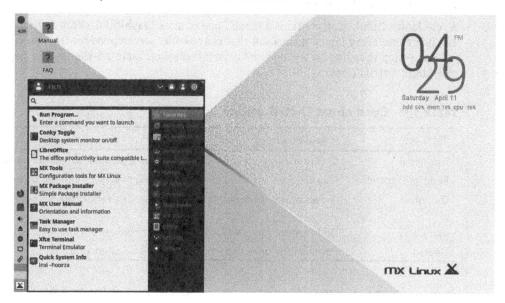

If you are using an older PC, try a Linux distribution that uses one of these desktops and see what happens. You may be pleasantly surprised.

## Examining Linux Distributions

Now that you have seen the four main components required for a complete Linux system, you may be wondering how you are going to get them all together to make a Linux system. Fortunately, there are people who have already done that for you.

A complete Linux system package is called a *distribution*. Numerous Linux distributions are available to meet just about any computing requirement you could have. Most distributions are customized for a specific user group, such as business users, multimedia enthusiasts, software developers, or average home users. Each customized distribution includes the software packages required to support specialized functions, such as audio- and video-editing software for multimedia enthusiasts, or compilers and integrated development environments (IDEs) for software developers.

The different Linux distributions are often divided into two categories:

- Full-core Linux distributions
- Specialized distributions

The following sections describe these types of Linux distributions and show examples in each category.

## Core Linux distributions

A core Linux distribution contains a kernel, one or more graphical desktop environments, and just about every Linux application that is available, precompiled for the kernel. It provides one-stop shopping for a complete Linux installation. Table 1-5 shows some popular core Linux distributions.

**TABLE 1-5**   **Core Linux Distributions**

| Distribution | Description |
| --- | --- |
| Slackware · | One of the original Linux distribution sets; popular with Linux geeks |
| Red Hat Enterprise | A commercial business distribution used mainly for Internet servers |
| Gentoo | A distribution designed for advanced Linux users, containing only Linux source code |
| openSUSE | Different distributions for business and home use |
| Debian | Popular with Linux experts and commercial Linux products |

In the early days of Linux, a distribution was released as a set of floppy disks. You had to download groups of files and then copy them onto disks. It would usually take 20 or more disks to make an entire distribution! Needless to say, this was a painful experience.

Nowadays, Linux distributions are released as an *ISO image file*. The ISO image file is a complete disk image of a DVD as a single file. You use a software application to either burn the ISO image file onto a DVD or create a bootable USB stick. You then just boot your workstation from the DVD or USB stick to install Linux. This makes installing Linux much easier.

However, beginners still often run into problems when they install one of the core Linux distributions. To cover just about any situation in which someone might want to use Linux, a single distribution has to include lots of application software. They include everything from high-end Internet database servers to common games.

Although having lots of options available in a distribution is great for Linux geeks, it can become a nightmare for beginning Linux users. Most core distributions ask a series of questions during the installation process to determine which applications to load by default, what hardware is connected to the PC, and how to configure the hardware. Beginners often find these questions confusing. As a result, they often either load way too many programs on their computer or don't load enough and later discover that their computer won't do what they want it to.

Fortunately for beginners, there's a much simpler way to install Linux.

### Specialized Linux distributions

A new subgroup of Linux distributions has started to appear. These are typically based on one of the main distributions but contain only a subset of applications that would make sense for a specific area of use.

In addition to providing specialized software (such as only office products for business users), customized Linux distributions attempt to help beginning Linux users by autodetecting and autoconfiguring common hardware devices. This makes installing Linux a much more enjoyable process.

Table 1-6 shows some of the specialized Linux distributions available and what they specialize in.

**TABLE 1-6**  **Specialized Linux Distributions**

| Distribution | Description |
| --- | --- |
| Fedora | A free distribution built from the Red Hat Enterprise Linux source code |
| Ubuntu | A free distribution for school and home use |
| MX Linux | A free distribution for home use |
| Linux Mint | A free distribution for home entertainment use |
| Puppy Linux | A free small distribution that runs well on older PCs |

That's just a small sampling of specialized Linux distributions. There are literally hundreds of specialized Linux distributions, and more are popping up all the time on the Internet. No matter your specialty, you'll probably find a Linux distribution made for you.

Many of the specialized Linux distributions are based on the Debian Linux distribution. They use the same installation files as Debian but package only a small fraction of a full-blown Debian system.

> **NOTE**
>
> Most Linux distributions also have a LiveDVD version available. The LiveDVD version is a self-contained ISO image file that you can burn onto a DVD (or USB stick) to boot up a running Linux system directly, without having to install it on your hard drive. Depending on the distribution, the LiveDVD contains either a small subset of applications or, in the case of specialized distributions, the entire system. The benefit of the LiveDVD is that you can test it with your system hardware before going through the trouble of installing the system.

# Summary

This chapter discussed the Linux system and the basics of how it works. The Linux kernel is the core of the system, controlling how memory, programs, and hardware all interact with one another. The GNU utilities are also an important piece in the Linux system. The Linux shell, which is the main focus of this book, is part of the GNU core utilities. The chapter also discussed the final piece of a Linux system, the Linux desktop environment. Things have changed over the years, and Linux now supports several graphical desktop environments.

The chapter also discussed the various Linux distributions. A Linux distribution bundles the various parts of a Linux system into a simple package that you can easily install on your PC. The Linux distribution world consists of full-blown Linux distributions that include just about every application imaginable, as well as specialized Linux distributions that only include applications focused on a special function. The Linux LiveDVD craze has created another group of Linux distributions that allow you to easily test-drive Linux without even having to install it on your hard drive.

In the next chapter, we look at what you need to start your command-line and shell scripting experience. You'll see what you have to do to get to the Linux shell utility from your fancy graphical desktop environment. These days, that's not always an easy thing.

# Getting to the Shell

I n the old days of Linux, system administrators, programmers, and system users all sat at something called a Linux console terminal entering shell commands and viewing text output. These days, with graphical desktop environments, it's getting harder to find a shell prompt on the system in order to enter shell commands. This chapter discusses what is required to reach a command-line environment. And it walks you through a few terminal emulation packages you may run into in the various Linux distributions.

## Reaching the Command Line

Before the days of graphical desktops, the only way to interact with a Unix system was through a text *command-line interface (CLI)* provided by the shell. The CLI allowed text input only and could display only text and rudimentary graphics output.

Because of these restrictions, output devices were not very fancy. Often, you needed only a simple dumb terminal to interact with the Unix system. A dumb terminal was usually nothing more than a monitor and keyboard connected to the Unix system via a communication cable (usually a multi-wire serial cable). This simple combination provided an easy way to enter text data into the Unix system and view text results.

As you well know, things are significantly different in today's Linux environment. Just about every Linux desktop distribution uses some type of graphical desktop environment. However, to enter shell commands, you still need a text display to access the shell's CLI. The problem now is getting to one. Sometimes finding a way to get a CLI in a Linux distribution is not an easy task.

## Console terminals

One way to get to a CLI is to access the Linux system via text mode. This provides nothing more than a simple shell CLI on the monitor, just like the days before graphical desktops. This mode is called the *Linux console* because it emulates the old days of a hard-wired console terminal and is a direct interface to the Linux system.

When the Linux system starts, it automatically creates several *virtual consoles*. A virtual console is a terminal session that runs in Linux system memory. Instead of having several dumb terminals connected to the computer, most Linux distributions start five or six (or sometimes even more) virtual consoles that you can access from a single computer keyboard and monitor.

## Graphical terminals

The alternative to using a virtual console terminal is to use a *terminal emulation package* from within the Linux graphical desktop environment. A terminal emulation package simulates working on a console terminal but within a desktop graphical window. Figure 2-1 shows an example of a terminal emulator running in a Linux graphical desktop environment.

**FIGURE 2-1**

A simple terminal emulator running on a Linux desktop

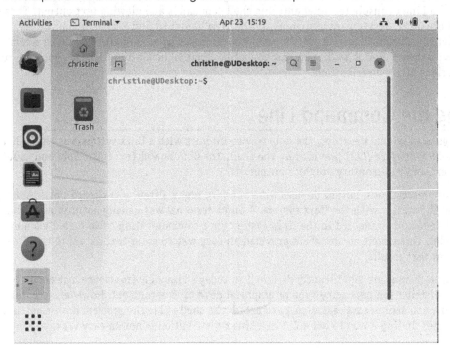

Graphical terminal emulation is responsible only for a portion of the Linux graphical experience. As a whole, the experience is accomplished through several components, including graphical terminal emulation software (called a *client*). Table 2-1 shows the different components in the Linux graphical desktop environment.

**TABLE 2-1  Graphical Interface Elements**

| Name | Examples | Description |
| --- | --- | --- |
| Client | Graphical terminal emulator, desktop environment (GNOME Shell, KDE Plasma), network browser | An application that requests graphical services |
| Display Server | Wayland, X Window System | Element that manages the display (screen) and the input devices (keyboard, mouse, touch screen) |
| Window Manager | Mutter, Metacity, Kwin | Element that adds borders to windows and provides features to move and manage windows |
| Widgets Library | Plasmoids, Cinnamon Spices | Element that adds menus and appearance items for desktop environment clients |

For dealing with the command line from the desktop, the focus is on the graphical terminal emulator. You can think of graphical terminal emulators as CLI terminals *in* the graphical user interface (GUI) and virtual console terminals as CLI terminals *outside* the GUI. Understanding the various terminals and their features can enhance your command-line experience.

## Accessing CLI via a Linux Console Terminal

In the early days of Linux, when you booted up your system you would see a login prompt on your monitor, and that's all. As mentioned earlier, this is called the Linux console. It was the only place you could enter commands for the system.

Even though several virtual consoles are created at boot time, many Linux desktop distributions switch to a graphical environment after the boot sequence completes. This provides the user with a graphical login and desktop experience. For these systems, accessing a virtual console is done manually.

On most Linux distributions, you can access one of the Linux virtual consoles using a simple keystroke combination. Usually, you must hold down the Ctrl+Alt key combination and then press a function key (F1 through F7) for the virtual console you want to use. Function key F2 produces virtual console 2, key F3 produces virtual console 3, key F4 produces virtual console 4, and so on.

> **NOTE**
> Linux distributions typically use the Ctrl+Alt key combination with F1, F7, or F8 to reach the graphical interface. Ubuntu and CentOS both use F1. However, it is best to test and see where your distribution puts the graphical interface, especially on older distribution versions.

Text mode virtual consoles use the whole screen and start with the text login screen displayed. An example of a text login screen from a virtual console is shown in Figure 2-2.

Notice in Figure 2-2 the word `tty2` at the end of the first text line. The `2` in `tty2` indicates that it is virtual console 2 and was reached by pressing the Ctrl+Alt+F2 key sequence. `tty` stands for teletypewriter. *Teletypewriter* is an old term, indicating a machine used for sending messages.

**FIGURE 2-2**

Linux virtual console login screen

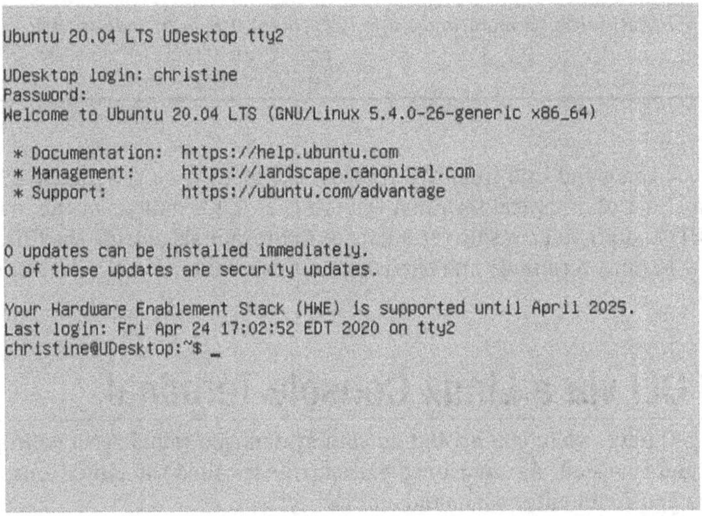
Ubuntu 20.04 LTS UDesktop tty2
UDesktop login: christine
Password:
Welcome to Ubuntu 20.04 LTS (GNU/Linux 5.4.0-26-generic x86_64)
* Documentation: https://help.ubuntu.com
* Management: https://landscape.canonical.com
* Support: https://ubuntu.com/advantage
0 updates can be installed immediately.
0 of these updates are security updates.
Your Hardware Enablement Stack (HWE) is supported until April 2025.
Last login: Fri Apr 24 17:02:52 EDT 2020 on tty2
christine@UDesktop:~$ _

> **NOTE**
> Not all Linux distributions show the virtual console's `tty` number at the login screen. If you are logged into a virtual console, you can enter the command `tty` and press Enter to see what virtual console you are currently using. Entering commands is covered in Chapter 3, "Basic Bash Shell Commands."

You log into a console terminal by entering your user ID after the login: prompt and typing your password after the Password: prompt. If you have never logged in this way before, be aware that typing your password is a different experience than it is in a graphical environment. In a graphical environment, you may see dots or asterisks indicating the password characters as you type. However, at the virtual console, *nothing* is displayed when you type your password.

> **NOTE**
>
> Keep in mind that, within the Linux virtual console, you do not have the ability to run *any* graphical programs.

After logging into a virtual console, you are taken to the Linux CLI, and you can switch to another virtual console without losing your current active session. You can switch between all the virtual consoles, with multiple active sessions running. This feature provides a great deal of flexibility while you work at the CLI.

Additional flexibility deals with the virtual console's appearance. Even though it is a text mode console terminal, you can modify the text and background colors.

For example, it may be easier on your eyes to set the background of the terminal to white and the text to black. After you have logged in, you can accomplish this modification in a couple of ways. One way is to type in the command **setterm --inversescreen on** and press the Enter key, as shown in Figure 2-3. Notice in the figure that the --inversescreen feature is being turned on using the option on. You can also turn it off using the off option.

**FIGURE 2-3**

Linux virtual console with inversescreen being turned on

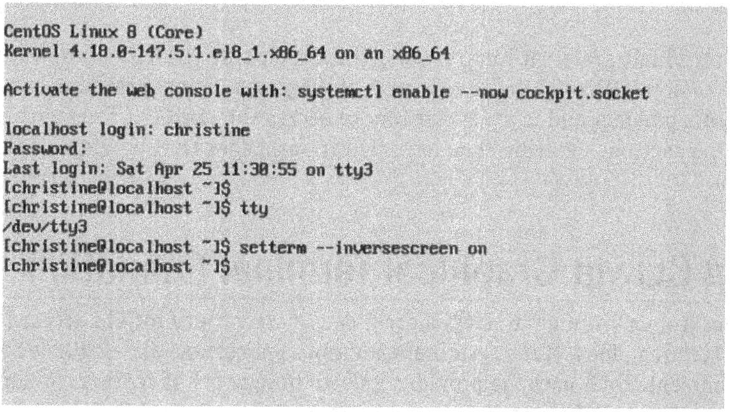

```
CentOS Linux 8 (Core)
Kernel 4.18.0-147.5.1.el8_1.x86_64 on an x86_64

Activate the web console with: systemctl enable --now cockpit.socket

localhost login: christine
Password:
Last login: Sat Apr 25 11:30:55 on tty3
[christine@localhost ~]$
[christine@localhost ~]$ tty
/dev/tty3
[christine@localhost ~]$ setterm --inversescreen on
[christine@localhost ~]$
```

Another way is to type two commands, one after the other. Type `setterm --background white` and press Enter, and then type `setterm --foreground black` and press Enter. Be careful because, when you change your terminal background first, it may be hard to see the commands you are typing.

With the commands in the preceding paragraph, you are not turning features on and off, as with `--inversescreen`. Instead, you have a choice of eight colors. The choices are `black`, `red`, `green`, `yellow`, `blue`, `magenta`, `cyan`, and `white` (which looks gray on some distributions). You can get rather creative with your plain text mode console terminals. Table 2-2 shows some options you can use with the `setterm` command to help improve your console terminal's readability or appearance.

**TABLE 2-2** `setterm` **Options for Foreground and Background Appearance**

| Option | Parameter Choices | Description |
|---|---|---|
| `--background` | `black`, `red`, `green`, `yellow`, `blue`, `magenta`, `cyan`, or `white` | Changes the terminal's background color to the one specified |
| `--foreground` | `black`, `red`, `green`, `yellow`, `blue`, `magenta`, `cyan`, or `white` | Changes the terminal's foreground color, specifically text, to the one specified |
| `--inversescreen` | on or off | Switches the background color to the foreground color and the foreground color to the background color |
| `--reset` | None | Changes the terminal appearance back to its default setting and clears the screen |
| `--store` | None | Sets the current terminal's foreground and background colors as the values to be used for `--reset` |

Virtual console terminals are great for accessing the CLI outside the GUI. However, sometimes, you need to access the CLI and run graphical programs. Using a terminal emulation package solves this problem and is a popular way to access the shell CLI from within the GUI. The following sections describe common software packages that provide graphical terminal emulation.

## Accessing CLI via Graphical Terminal Emulation

The graphical desktop environment offers a great deal more variety for CLI access than the virtual console terminal does. Many terminal emulator applications are available for the graphical environment. Each package provides its own unique set of features and options. Some popular graphical terminal emulator applications are shown in Table 2-3 along with their websites.

**TABLE 2-3    Popular Graphical Terminal Emulator Packages**

| Name | Website |
| --- | --- |
| Alacritty | github.com/alacritty/alacritty |
| cool-retro-term | github.com/Swordfish90/cool-retro-term |
| GNOME Terminal | wiki.gnome.org/Apps/Terminal |
| Guake | guake-project.org |
| Konsole | konsole.kde.org |
| kitty | sw.kovidgoyal.net/kitty |
| rxvt-unicode | software.schmorp.de/pkg/rxvt-unicode.html |
| Sakura | pleyades.net/david/projects/sakura |
| st | st.suckless.org |
| Terminator | gnometerminator.blogspot.com |
| Terminology | enlightenment.org/about-terminology.md |
| Termite | github.com/thestinger/termite |
| Tilda | github.com/lanoxx/tilda |
| xterm | invisible-island.net/xterm |
| Xfce4-terminal | docs.xfce.org/apps/terminal/start |
| Yakuake | kde.org/applications/system/org.kde.yakuake |

Although many graphical terminal emulator applications are available, the focus in this chapter is on three. Installed in different Linux distributions by default, they are GNOME Terminal, Konsole Terminal, and xterm.

# Using the GNOME Terminal Emulator

GNOME Terminal is the GNOME Shell desktop environment's default terminal emulator. Many distributions, such as Red Hat Enterprise Linux (RHEL), CentOS, and Ubuntu, use the GNOME Shell desktop environment by default, and therefore use GNOME Terminal by default. It is fairly easy to use and a good terminal emulator for individuals who are new to Linux. This section walks you through the various parts of accessing, configuring, and using GNOME Terminal.

## Accessing GNOME Terminal

In the GNOME Shell desktop environment, accessing the GNOME Terminal is fairly straightforward. Click on the Activities icon in the upper-right corner of the desktop window. When the search bar appears, click within the bar to access it and type **terminal**. The results of these actions are shown in Figure 2-4.

**FIGURE 2-4**

Finding GNOME Terminal in GNOME Shell

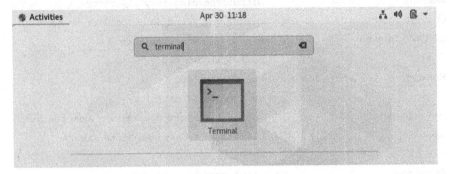

Notice in the previous figure that the GNOME Terminal application icon is named Terminal. Click the icon to open the terminal emulator. An open GNOME Terminal application on a CentOS distribution is shown in Figure 2-5.

**FIGURE 2-5**

GNOME Terminal on CentOS

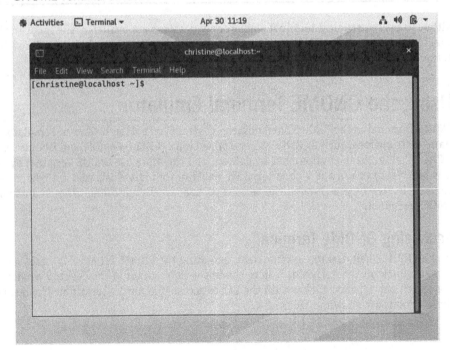

When you are done using the terminal emulator application, you close it just like other desktop windows: by clicking the x in the window's upper-right corner.

The GNOME Terminal application's appearance may vary between Linux distributions. For example, in Figure 2-6, GNOME Terminal is shown on an Ubuntu GNOME Shell desktop environment.

**FIGURE 2-6**

GNOME Terminal on Ubuntu

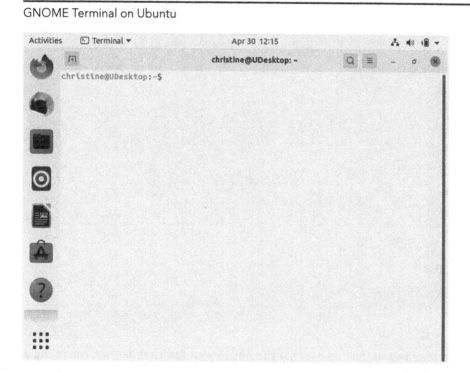

Notice that the appearance of the GNOME Terminal application in Figure 2-6 is different compared to Figure 2-5. This is typically due to the application's default configuration (covered later in this chapter) and the various features a Linux distribution has in its GUI windows.

**TIP**

If you are using a different desktop environment than GNOME Shell (and have GNOME Terminal installed), be aware that you may not have a search feature. In these cases, use the environment's menu system to look for GNOME Terminal. It is typically named Terminal.

On many distributions, the first time you launch the GNOME Terminal application, its terminal emulator icon will appear in your GNOME Shell Favorites bar. Hovering over the icon with your mouse will show the terminal emulator's name, as shown in Figure 2-7.

**FIGURE 2-7**

GNOME Terminal icon in the Favorites bar

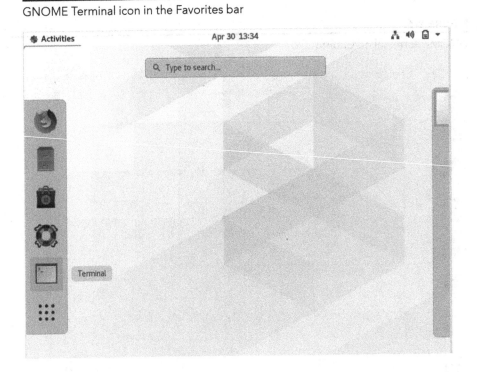

If for some reason the icon does not show up in your Favorites bar, you can set up a keyboard shortcut to launch it. This approach is handy for those who don't care for using a mouse, and it allows faster access to the CLI.

**TIP**

GNOME Shell on the Ubuntu distribution already has a keystroke shortcut for opening the GNOME terminal emulator: Ctrl+Alt+T.

To create a keyboard shortcut, you'll need to access the Keyboard Shortcuts window within Keyboard Settings. To accomplish this quickly, click the Activities icon in the upper-right corner of the GNOME Shell desktop window. When the search bar appears, click within the bar to access it, and type **Keyboard Shortcuts**. The results of these actions are shown in Figure 2-8.

**FIGURE 2-8**

Reaching the Keyboard Shortcuts window

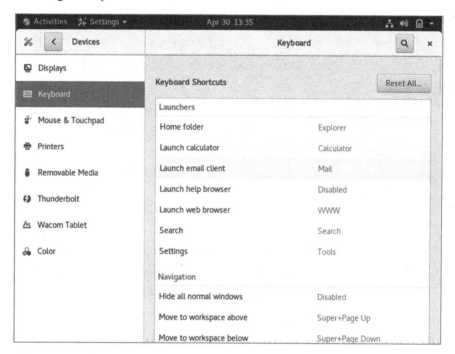

Once you are in the Keyboard Shortcuts window, scroll down to reach the + button, which is all the way at the bottom. Clicking this button opens a dialog box, where you can name your new shortcut, provide the command to open the application, and set the shortcut's keystrokes, as shown in Figure 2-9.

It is important to use the correct command name in order to properly launch the GNOME terminal emulator, so type **gnome-terminal** in the Command field, as shown in Figure 2-9. When you are all done setting up your new shortcut, click the Add button in the window. Now you can quickly launch the GNOME Terminal by just using the keystroke combination you specified.

Several configuration options are provided by menus and shortcut keys in the application, which you can apply after you get the GNOME terminal emulation started. Understanding these options can enhance your GNOME Terminal CLI experience.

**FIGURE 2-9**

Creating a keyboard shortcut

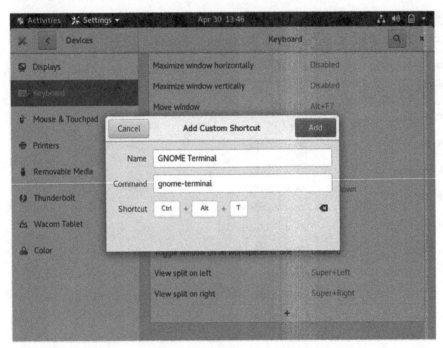

## The menu bar

The GNOME Terminal menu bar contains the configuration and customization options you need to make your GNOME Terminal just the way you want it. The following tables briefly describe the configuration options in the menu bar and shortcut keys associated with them.

> **TIP**
>
> If the GNOME Terminal window does not display its menu bar, right-click in the terminal emulator session area, and click Show Menubar in the drop-down menu.

Table 2-4 shows the configuration options available within the GNOME Terminal File menu system. The File menu item contains items to create and manage your overall CLI terminal sessions.

**TABLE 2-4   The File Menu**

| Name | Shortcut Key | Description |
|------|--------------|-------------|
| New Tab | Shift+Ctrl+T | Starts a new shell session in a new tab in the existing GNOME Terminal window |
| New Window | Shift+Ctrl+N | Starts a new shell session in a new GNOME Terminal window |
| Close Tab | Shift+Ctrl+W | Closes the current tab in the GNOME Terminal window |
| Close Window | Shift+Ctrl+Q | Closes the current GNOME Terminal window |

Notice that, as in a network browser, you can open new tabs within the GNOME Terminal session to start a whole new CLI session. Each tab session is considered to be an independent CLI session.

**TIP**

You don't always have to click through the menu to reach options in the File menu. Some of the File menu selections are also available by right-clicking in the terminal emulator session area.

The Edit menu contains items, shown in Table 2-5, for handling text within the tabs. You can copy and paste text anywhere within the session window.

**TABLE 2-5   The Edit Menu**

| Name | Shortcut Key | Description |
|------|--------------|-------------|
| Copy | Shift+Ctrl+C | Copies selected text to the GNOME clipboard |
| Copy as HTML | None | Copies selected text, along with its font and color, to the GNOME clipboard |
| Paste | Shift+Ctrl+V | Pastes text from the GNOME clipboard into a session |
| Select All | None | Selects output in the entire scrollback buffer |
| Preferences | None | Edits the current session profile |

Copying and pasting commands in the terminal is useful if you are lacking in keyboarding skills. Thus, the keyboard shortcuts for the GNOME Terminal Copy and Paste functions are worth memorizing.

**NOTE**

As you read through these GNOME Terminal menu options, keep in mind that your Linux distribution's GNOME Terminal may have slightly different menu options available. This is because several Linux distributions use older versions of GNOME Terminal. You can find the version number by clicking Help in the menu bar and selecting About from the drop-down menu.

The View menu, shown in Table 2-6, contains items for controlling how the CLI session windows appear. These options can be helpful for individuals with visual impairment.

**TABLE 2-6  The View Menu**

| Name | Shortcut Key | Description |
| --- | --- | --- |
| Show Menubar | None | Toggles on/off the menu bar display |
| Full Screen | F11 | Toggles on/off the terminal window filling the entire desktop |
| Zoom In | Ctrl++ | Enlarges the font size in the window incrementally |
| Normal Size | Ctrl+0 | Returns the font size to default |
| Zoom Out | Ctrl+- | Reduces the font size in the window incrementally |

Be aware that if you toggle off the menu bar display, the session's menu bar disappears. However, you can easily get the menu bar to display again by right-clicking in any terminal session window and selecting the Show Menubar option.

The Search menu, shown in Table 2-7, contains items for conducting simple searches within the terminal session. These searches are similar to ones you may have conducted in a network browser or word processor.

**TABLE 2-7  The Search Menu**

| Name | Shortcut Key | Description |
| --- | --- | --- |
| Find | Shift+Ctrl+F | Opens Find window to provide designated text search options |
| Find Next | Shift+Ctrl+G | Searches forward from current terminal session location for designated text |
| Find Previous | Shift+Ctrl+H | Searches backward from current terminal session location for designated text |
| Clear Highlight | Shift+Ctrl+J | Removes highlighting of found text |

The Terminal menu, shown in Table 2-8, contains options for controlling the terminal emulation session features. There are no shortcut keys to access these items.

**TABLE 2-8** **The Terminal Menu**

| Name | Description |
|------|-------------|
| Read-Only | Toggles on/off the terminal session accepting keyboard strokes; it does *not* enable/disable keyboard shortcuts |
| Reset | Sends reset terminal session control code |
| Reset and Clear | Sends reset terminal session control code and clears terminal session screen |
| 80x24 | Adjusts the current terminal window size to 80 columns wide by 24 rows high |
| 80x43 | Changes the current terminal window size to 80 columns wide by 43 rows high |
| 132x24 | Adjusts the current terminal window size to 130 columns wide by 24 rows high |
| 130x43 | Changes the current terminal window size to 130 columns wide by 43 rows high |

The Reset option is extremely useful. One day, you may accidentally cause your terminal session to display random characters and symbols. When this occurs, the text is unreadable. It is typically caused by displaying a nontext file to the screen. You can quickly get the terminal session back to normal by selecting Reset or Reset And Clear.

> **NOTE**
> Keep in mind that when you adjust your terminal's size, such as by using the 80x24 setting in the Terminal menu, the actual size is determined by factors such as the character font in use. It's a good idea to play around with the different settings to find a size that suits your taste.

The Tabs menu, shown in Table 2-9, provides items for controlling the location of the tabs and selecting which tab is active. This menu displays *only* when you have more than one tab session open.

**TABLE 2-9** **The Tabs Menu**

| Name | Shortcut Key | Description |
|------|-------------|-------------|
| Previous Tab | Ctrl+Page Up | Makes the previous tab in the list active |
| Next Tab | Ctrl+Page Down | Makes the next tab in the list active |
| Move Terminal Left | Shift+Ctrl+Page Up | Shuffles the current tab in front of the previous tab |
| Move Terminal Right | Shift+Ctrl+Page Down | Shuffles the current tab in front of the next tab |
| Detach Terminal | None | Removes the tab and starts a new GNOME Terminal window using this tab session |

2

Finally, the Help menu contains two menu options:

- Contents provides a full GNOME Terminal manual so that you can research individual GNOME Terminal items and features.
- About shows you the current GNOME Terminal application version that's running.

Besides the GNOME terminal emulator package, another commonly used package is Konsole. In many ways, Konsole is similar to GNOME Terminal. However, enough differences exist to warrant its own section.

# Using the Konsole Terminal Emulator

The KDE project created its own terminal emulation package called *Konsole*. The Konsole application incorporates basic terminal emulation features, along with more advanced ones expected from a graphical application. This section describes Konsole features and shows you how to use them.

## Accessing Konsole

The Konsole application is the default terminal emulator for the KDE desktop environment, Plasma. You can easily access it via the KDE environment's menu system. In other desktop environments, accessing Konsole is typically done via search features.

In the KDE desktop environment (Plasma), you start the Konsole terminal emulator by clicking the icon labeled Application Launcher in the lower-left corner of the screen. Then click Applications ⇨ System ⇨ Terminal (Konsole).

> **NOTE**
> You may see two or more terminal menu options within the Plasma menu environment. If you do, the Terminal menu option with the word Konsole beneath it is the Konsole terminal emulator application.

In the GNOME Shell desktop environment, the Konsole application is typically not installed by default. If Konsole has been installed, you can access it via the GNOME Shell search feature. Click the Activities icon in the upper-right corner of the desktop window. When the search bar appears, click your mouse within the bar to access it, and type **konsole**. If the terminal emulator is available on your system, you will see the Konsole icon displayed.

> **NOTE**
> You may not have the Konsole terminal emulation package installed on your system. If you would like to install it, see Chapter 9, "Installing Software," to learn how to install software via the command line.

Click the Konsole icon with your mouse to open the terminal emulator. An open Konsole application on an Ubuntu distribution is shown in Figure 2-10.

**FIGURE 2-10**

The Konsole terminal emulator

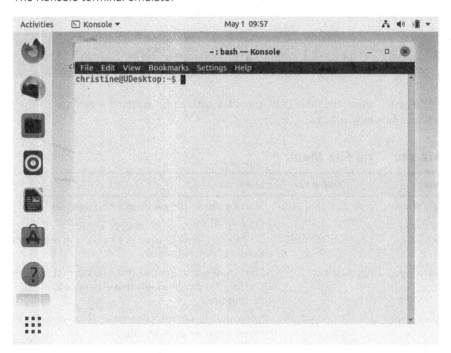

Remember that, in most desktop environments, you can create a keyboard shortcut to access applications such as Konsole. The command you need to type for the shortcut in order to start up the Konsole terminal emulator is **konsole**. Also, if the Konsole application is installed, you can start it from another terminal emulator by typing **konsole** and pressing Enter.

**TIP**

In the Plasma desktop environment, the Konsole terminal emulator application already has a default keyboard shortcut: Ctrl+Alt+T.

The Konsole terminal emulator, similar to GNOME Terminal, has several configuration options provided by menus and shortcut keys. The following section describes these various features.

## The menu bar

The Konsole menu bar contains the configuration and customization options you need to easily view and change features in your terminal emulation session. The following tables briefly describe the menu options and associated shortcut keys.

**TIP**

If the Konsole menu bar is not currently displayed, you can press Ctrl+Shift+M to enable it.

The File menu, shown in Table 2-10, provides options for starting a new tab in the current window or in a new window.

**TABLE 2-10** **The File Menu**

| Name | Shortcut Key | Description |
| --- | --- | --- |
| New Window | Ctrl+Shift+N | Starts a new shell session in a new Konsole Terminal window |
| New Tab | Ctrl+Shift+T | Starts a new shell session in a new tab in the existing Konsole Terminal window |
| Clone Tab | None | Starts a new shell session in a new tab in the existing Konsole Terminal window that attempts to duplicate the current tab |
| Save Output As | Ctrl+Shift+S | Saves the current tab's output in its scrollback buffer as either a text or an HTML file |
| Print Screen | Ctrl+Shift+P | Prints the current tab's displayed text |
| Open File Manager | None | Opens the default file browser application |
| Close Session | Ctrl+Shift+W | Closes the current tab session |
| Close Window | Ctrl+Shift+Q | Closes the current Konsole window |

Notice that Konsole offers two handy options for saving information from your shell session: Save Output As and Print Screen. The Print Screen function allows you to print the displayed text to a system printer or save it as a PDF file.

**NOTE**

As you read through these Konsole menu options, keep in mind that your Linux distribution's Konsole application may have very different menu options available. This is because some Linux distributions have kept older versions of the Konsole terminal emulation package.

The Edit menu, shown in Table 2-11, provides options for handling text in the session. Also, managing tab names is in this options list.

**TABLE 2-11** **The Edit Menu**

| Name | Shortcut Key | Description |
|---|---|---|
| Copy | Ctrl+Shift+C | Copies selected text to the Konsole clipboard |
| Paste | Ctrl+Shift+V | Pastes text from the Konsole clipboard into a session |
| Select All | None | Selects all the text in the current tab |
| Copy Input To | None | Starts/stops session input copies to chosen additional sessions |
| Send Signal | None | Sends the selected signal from the drop-down menu to the current tab's shell process or other process |
| Rename Tab | Ctrl+Alt+S | Modifies session tab title bar setting |
| ZModem Upload | Ctrl+Alt+U | Starts the process of uploading a selected file, if the ZMODEM file transfer protocol is supported |
| Find | Ctrl+Shift+F | Opens the Find window to provide scrollback buffer text search options |
| Find Next | F3 | Finds the next text match in more recent scrollback buffer history |
| Find Previous | Shift+F3 | Finds the next text match in older scrollback buffer history |

Konsole provides an excellent method for tracking what function is taking place in each tab session. Using the Rename Tab option, you can name a tab to match its current task. This helps in tracking which open tab session is performing what job.

**NOTE**

Konsole retains a history, formally called a *scrollback buffer*, for each tab. The history contains output text that has scrolled out of the terminal viewing area. By default, the last 1,000 lines in the scrollback buffer are retained. You can scroll back through the scrollback buffer by simply using the scrollbar in the viewing area. Also, you can scroll back line by line by pressing the Shift+Up Arrow or scroll back a page (24 lines) at a time by pressing Shift+Page Up.

The View menu, shown in Table 2-12, contains items for controlling individual session views in the Konsole Terminal window. In addition, options are available that aid in monitoring terminal session activity.

**TABLE 2-12  The View Menu**

| Name | Shortcut Key | Description |
| --- | --- | --- |
| Split View | None | Controls a multiple tab session display within the current Konsole window |
| Detach Current Tab | Ctrl+Shift+L | Removes a tab session and starts a new Konsole window using this tab session |
| Detach Current View | Ctrl+Shift+H | Removes the current tab session's view and starts a new Konsole window with it |
| Monitor for Silence | Ctrl+Shift+I | Toggles on/off a special message when no activity is occurring in the tab session |
| Monitor for Activity | Ctrl+Shift+A | Toggles on/off a special message when activity starts occurring in the tab session |
| Read-only | None | Toggles on/off the terminal session accepting keyboard strokes; does not enable/disable keyboard shortcuts |
| Enlarge Font | Ctrl++ | Enlarges the font size in the window incrementally |
| Reset Font Size | Ctrl+Alt+0 | Returns the font size to default |
| Shrink Font | Ctrl+- | Reduces the font size in the window incrementally |
| Set Encoding | None | Selects the character set used to send and display characters |
| Clear Scrollback | None | Removes the text in the current session's scrollback buffer |
| Clear Scrollback and Reset | Ctrl+Shift+K | Removes the text in the current session's scrollback buffer and resets the terminal window |
| Full Screen Mode | F11 | Toggles on/off the terminal window filling the entire monitor display area |

The Monitor for Silence option is used for indicating tab silence. Tab silence occurs when no new text appears in the current tab session for about seven seconds. This allows you to switch to another tab while waiting for the application's output to stop.

**TIP**
The Konsole application provides a simple menu when you right-click in the active session area. Several menu items are available in this easy-to-access menu.

The Bookmarks menu options, shown in Table 2-13, provide a way to manage *bookmarks* set in the Konsole window. A bookmark enables you to save your active session's directory location and then easily return there in either the same session or a new session.

TABLE 2-13 **The Bookmarks Menu**

| Name | Shortcut Key | Description |
|---|---|---|
| Add Bookmark | Ctrl+Shift+B | Creates a new bookmark at the current directory location |
| Bookmark Tabs as Folder | None | Creates a new bookmark for all current terminal tab sessions |
| New Bookmark Folder | None | Creates a new bookmark storage folder |
| Edit Bookmarks | None | Edits existing bookmarks |

The Settings menu, shown in Table 2-14, allows you to customize and manage your profiles. Profiles allow a user to automate the running of commands, set up the session's appearance, configure the scrollback buffer, and so on. Also, within the Settings menu you can add a little more functionality to your shell sessions.

TABLE 2-14 **The Settings Menu**

| Name | Shortcut | Key Description |
|---|---|---|
| Edit Current Profile | None | Opens the Edit Profile window to provide profile configuration options |
| Switch Profile | None | Applies to the current tab a selected profile |
| Manage Profiles | None | Opens the Manage Profiles window to provide profile management options |
| Show Menubar | Ctrl+Shift+M | Toggles on/off menu bar display |
| Configure Keyboard Shortcuts | None | Creates Konsole command keyboard shortcuts |
| Configure Notifications | None | Creates custom Konsole notifications |
| Configure Konsole | Ctrl+Shift+, | Configures many Konsole features |

Configure Notifications allows you to associate specific events that can occur within a session with different actions, such as playing a sound. When one of the events occurs, the defined action (or actions) is taken.

The Help menu, shown in Table 2-15, provides the full Konsole handbook (if KDE handbooks were installed in your Linux distribution) and the standard About Konsole dialog box.

**TABLE 2-15** **The Help Menu**

| Name | Shortcut Key | Description |
|---|---|---|
| Konsole Handbook | None | Contains the full Konsole Handbook |
| What's This? | Shift+F1 | Contains help messages for terminal widgets |
| Report Bug | None | Opens the Submit Bug Report form |
| Donate | None | Opens the KDE donation page within a web browser |
| Switch Application Language | None | Opens the Switch Application Language form |
| About Konsole | None | Displays information about the Konsole application, including its current version |
| About KDE | None | Displays information about the KDE desktop environment |

Rather extensive documentation is provided to help you use the Konsole terminal emulator package within the Help menu. The Bug Report form to submit to the Konsole developers when you encounter a program bug is handy.

The Konsole terminal emulator package is young compared to another popular package, xterm. In the next section, we explore the "old-timer" xterm.

# Using the xterm Terminal Emulator

The oldest and most basic of terminal emulation packages is *xterm*. The xterm package has been around since before the original days of X Window, a historically popular display server, and it's still included by default in some distributions, such as openSUSE.

xterm is a full terminal emulation package, but it doesn't require many resources (such as memory) to operate. Because of this, the xterm package is still popular in Linux distributions designed to run on older hardware.

Although it doesn't offer many fancy features, the xterm package does one thing extremely well: it emulates older terminals, such as the Digital Equipment Corporation (DEC) VT102, VT220, and Tektronix 4014 terminals. For the VT102 and VT220 terminals, xterm can even emulate the VT series of color control codes, allowing you to use color in your scripts.

> **NOTE**
>
> The DEC VT102 and VT220 were dumb text terminals popular for connecting to Unix systems in the 1980s and early 1990s. A VT102/VT220 could display text and display rudimentary graphics using block mode graphics. This style of terminal access is still used in many business environments today, thus keeping VT102/VT220 emulation popular.

Figure 2-11 shows what the basic xterm display looks like running on a CentOS distribution's GNOME Shell environment, where it had to be manually installed. You can see that it is very basic.

**FIGURE 2-11**

The xterm terminal

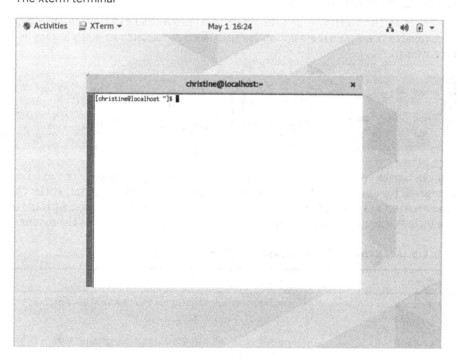

The xterm terminal emulator can be tricky to find these days. Often, it is not included in a desktop environment graphical menu arrangement.

## Accessing xterm

In the KDE desktop environment (Plasma), you can access xterm by clicking the Application Launcher icon in the lower-left corner of the screen. Then click Applications ⇨ System ⇨ standard terminal emulator for the X Window system (xterm).

Once the xterm package is installed, you can access it via the GNOME Shell search feature. Click the Activities icon in the upper-right corner of the desktop window. When the search bar appears, click within the bar to access it and type **xterm**, and you'll see the Konsole icon displayed. Also, remember that you can create your own keyboard shortcut to start up xterm.

The xterm package allows you to set individual features using command-line parameters. The following sections discuss these features and how to change them.

## Command-line parameters

The list of xterm command-line parameters is extensive. You can control lots of features to customize the terminal emulation features, such as enabling or disabling individual VT emulations.

> **NOTE**
>
> xterm has a huge number of configuration options — so many that they cannot all be covered here. Extensive documentation is available via the Bash manual. Accessing the Bash manual is covered in Chapter 3. In addition, the xterm development team provides some excellent help on its website: invisible-island.net/xterm.

You can invoke certain configuration options by adding a parameter to the xterm command. For example, to have the xterm emulate a DEC VT100 terminal, at the CLI type the command **xterm -ti vt100** and press Enter. Table 2-16 shows some parameters you can include when invoking the xterm terminal emulator software from the command line.

**TABLE 2-16   xterm Command-Line Parameters**

| Parameter | Description |
|-----------|-------------|
| -bg *color* | Specifies the color to use for the terminal background |
| -fb *font* | Sets the font to use for bold text |
| -fg *color* | Specifies the color to use for the foreground text |
| -fn *font* | Sets the font to use for text |
| -fw *font* | Specifies the font to use for wide text |
| -lf *filename* | Sets the filename to use for screen logging |
| -ms *color* | Specifies the color used for the text cursor |
| -name | Sets the name of the application that appears in the title bar |
| -ti *terminal* | Specifies the terminal type to emulate |

Some xterm command-line parameters use a plus sign (+) or minus sign (-) to signify how a feature is set. A plus sign may turn a feature on, whereas a minus sign turns it off. However, the opposite can be true as well. A plus sign may disable a feature, whereas a minus sign enables it, such as when using the bc parameter. Table 2-17 lists some of the more common features you can set using the +/- command-line parameters.

**TABLE 2-17    xterm +/- Command-Line Parameters**

| Parameter | Description |
| --- | --- |
| ah | Enables/disables highlighted text cursor |
| aw | Enables/disables auto-line-wrap |
| bc | Enables/disables text cursor blinking |
| cm | Enables/disables recognition of ANSI color change control codes |
| fullscreen | Enables/disables full-screen mode |
| j | Enables/disables jump scrolling |
| l | Enables/disables logging screen data to a log file |
| mb | Enables/disables margin bell |
| rv | Enables/disables reverse video colors |
| t | Enables/disables Tektronix mode |

It is important to note that not all implementations of xterm support all these command-line parameters. You can determine which parameters your xterm implements by using the -help parameter when you start xterm on your system.

> **NOTE**
>
> If xterm appeals to you but you'd like to use a more modern terminal emulation application, consider trying the rxvt-unicode package. It is available to install via most distributions' standard repositories (covered in Chapter 9), uses little RAM, and is very fast. Find out more at software.schmorp.de/pkg/rxvt-unicode.html.

Now that you have been introduced to three terminal emulator packages, the big question is, which is the best terminal emulator to use? There is no definite answer to that question. Which terminal emulator package you use depends on your individual needs and desires. But it is great to have so many choices.

## Summary

To start learning Linux command-line commands, you need access to a CLI. In the world of graphical interfaces, this can sometimes be challenging. This chapter discussed various interfaces you should consider to get to the Linux command line.

First, this chapter discussed the difference between accessing the CLI via a virtual console terminal (a terminal outside the GUI) and a graphical terminal emulation package (a terminal inside the GUI). We took a brief look at the basic differences between these two access methods.

Next, we explored in detail accessing the CLI via a virtual console terminal, including specifics on how to change console terminal configuration options such as background color.

After looking at virtual console terminals, the chapter traveled through accessing the CLI via a graphical terminal emulator. Primarily, we covered three types of terminal emulators: GNOME Terminal, Konsole, and xterm.

This chapter also covered the GNOME Shell desktop project's GNOME terminal emulation package. GNOME Terminal is typically installed by default on the GNOME Shell desktop environment. It provides convenient ways to set many terminal features through menu options and shortcut keys.

We also discussed the KDE desktop project's Konsole terminal emulation package. The Konsole application is typically installed by default on the KDE desktop environment (Plasma). It provides several nice features, such as the ability to monitor a terminal for silence.

Finally, we explored the xterm terminal emulator package. xterm was the first terminal emulator available for Linux. It can emulate older terminal hardware such as the VT and Tektronix terminals.

In the next chapter, we'll start looking at the Linux command-line commands. We'll walk you through the commands necessary to navigate around the Linux filesystem and to create, delete, and manipulate files.

# Basic Bash Shell Commands

## IN THIS CHAPTER

Interacting with the shell

Using the Bash manual

Traversing the filesystem

Listing files and directories

Managing files and directories

Viewing file contents

The default shell used in many Linux distributions is the GNU Bash shell. This chapter describes the basic features available in the Bash shell, such as the Bash manual, command-line completion, and how to display a file's contents. We will walk you through how to work with Linux files and directories using the basic commands provided by the Bash shell. If you're already comfortable with the basics in the Linux environment, feel free to skip this chapter and go to Chapter 4, "More Bash Shell Commands," to see more advanced commands.

## Starting the Shell

The GNU Bash shell is a program that provides interactive access to the Linux system. It runs as a regular program and is normally started whenever a user logs into a terminal. The shell that the system starts depends on your user ID configuration.

The /etc/passwd file contains a list of all the system user accounts, along with basic configuration information about each user. Here's a sample entry from an /etc/passwd file:

```
christine:x:1001:1001::/home/christine:/bin/bash
```

Every entry has seven data fields, separated by colons (:). The system uses the data in these fields to assign specific features for the user. Most of these entries are discussed in more detail in Chapter 7, "Understanding Linux File Permissions." For now, just pay attention to the last field, which specifies the user's shell program.

In the earlier /etc/passwd sample entry, the user christine has /bin/bash set as their default shell program. This means when christine logs into the Linux system, the GNU Bash shell program is automatically started.

Although the Bash shell program is automatically started at login, whether a shell command-line interface (CLI) is presented depends on which login method is used. If you use a virtual console terminal to log in, the CLI prompt is automatically presented, and you can begin to type shell commands. However, if you log into the Linux system via a graphical desktop environment, you need to start a graphical terminal emulator to access the shell CLI prompt.

## Using the Shell Prompt

After you start a terminal emulation package or log into a Linux virtual console, you get access to the shell CLI *prompt*. The prompt is your gateway to the shell. This is the place where you enter shell commands.

The default prompt symbol for the Bash shell is the dollar sign ($). This symbol indicates that the shell is waiting for you to enter text. Different Linux distributions use different formats for the prompt. On this Ubuntu Linux system, the shell prompt looks like this:

```
christine@UDesktop:~$
```

On the CentOS Linux system, it looks like this:

```
[christine@localhost ~]$
```

Besides acting as your access point to the shell, the prompt can provide additional helpful information. In the two preceding examples, the current user ID name, christine, is shown in the prompt. Also, the name of the system is shown, UDesktop on the Ubuntu system and localhost on the CentOS machine. You'll learn later in this chapter about additional items shown in the prompt.

The shell prompt is not static. It can be changed to suit your needs. Chapter 6, "Using Linux Environment Variables," covers the shell CLI prompt configuration.

Think of the shell CLI prompt as a helpmate, assisting you with your Linux system, giving you helpful insights, and letting you know when the shell is ready for new commands. Another helpful item in the shell is the Bash manual.

## Interacting with the Bash Manual

Most Linux distributions include an online manual for looking up information on shell commands, as well as lots of other GNU utilities included in the distribution. You should become familiar with the manual, because it's invaluable for working with commands, especially when you're trying to figure out various command-line parameters.

The man command provides access to the manual pages stored on the Linux system. Entering the man command followed by a specific command name provides that utility's manual entry. Figure 3-1 shows an example of looking up the hostname command's manual pages. This page was reached by typing the command **man hostname.**

**FIGURE 3-1**

Manual pages for the hostname command

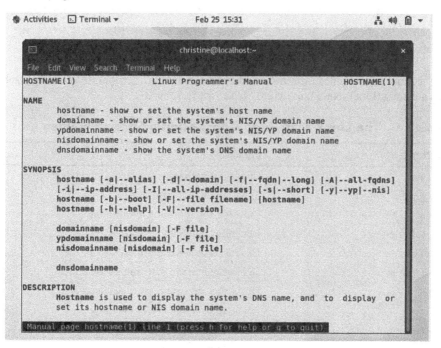

Notice the hostname command's DESCRIPTION paragraph in Figure 3-1. It is rather sparse and full of technical jargon. The Bash manual is not a step-by-step guide but instead a quick reference.

> **TIP**
>
> If you are new to the Bash shell, you may find that the man pages are not very helpful at first. However, get into the habit of using them, especially to read the first paragraph or two of a command's DESCRIPTION section. Eventually, you will learn the technical lingo, and the man pages will become more helpful to you.

When you use the man command to view a command's manual, the information is displayed with something called a *pager*. A pager is a utility that allows you to view text a page (or a line) at a time. Thus, you can page through the man pages by pressing the spacebar, or you can go line by line using the Enter key. In addition, you can use the arrow keys to scroll forward and backward through the man information (assuming that your terminal emulation package supports the arrow key functions).

When you are finished with the man pages, press the Q key to quit. When you leave the man pages, you receive a shell CLI prompt, indicating the shell is waiting for your next command.

> **TIP**
>
> The Bash manual even has reference information on itself. Type man man to see information concerning the man pages.

The manual page divides information about a command into separate sections. Each section has a conventional naming standard, as shown in Table 3-1.

**TABLE 3-1**   **The Linux Man Page Conventional Section Names**

| Section | Description |
| --- | --- |
| Name | Displays command name and a short description |
| Synopsis | Shows command syntax |
| Configuration | Provides configuration information |
| Description | Describes command generally |
| Options | Describes command option(s) |
| Exit Status | Defines command exit status indicator(s) |
| Return Value | Describes command return value(s) |
| Errors | Provides command error messages |
| Environment | Describes environment variable(s) used |
| Files | Defines files used by command |

| Section | Description |
| --- | --- |
| Versions | Describes command version information |
| Conforming To | Provides standards followed |
| Notes | Describes additional helpful command material |
| Bugs | Provides the location to report found bugs |
| Example | Shows command use examples |
| Authors | Provides information on command developers |
| Copyright | Defines command code copyright status |
| See Also | Refers to similar available commands |

Not every command's man page has all the section names described in Table 3-1. Also, some commands have section names that are not listed in the conventional standard.

In a command's synopsis section, you can find out how the command should be entered at the shell prompt. Many commands use a basic pattern:

```
COMMAND-NAME [OPTION] ... [ARGUMENT] ...
```

In the command's pattern structure,

- *COMMAND-NAME* is the name of the command used to run the desired program.
- *[OPTION]*s are additional items added to modify the command's behavior. There are typically many *OPTION*s (also called *switches*) you can add. The brackets ([]) indicate that *OPTION*s are not required, and the three dots (...) show that you can use more than one *OPTION* at a time.
- *[ARGUMENT]* is typically an item you pass to the command to let the program know you want it to operate on that item. You can see that it too is not required due to the brackets, and you can pass multiple *ARGUMENT*s to the program.

**TIP**

If you want to use more than one command option, often you can squish them together. For example, to use the options -a and -b, you type **-ab**.

Many commands were written by different individuals, so you'll find the way to use them varies as well. Thus, the command's synopsis section within its man page is a great place to find the proper syntax in order to get things done with the command.

**TIP**

If you can't remember a command's name, you can search the man pages using keywords. The syntax is man -k *keyword*. For example, to find commands dealing with the terminals, you type **man -k terminal**.

In addition to the conventionally named sections for a man page, there are man page section areas. Each section area has an assigned number, starting at 1 and going to 9; they are listed in Table 3-2.

**TABLE 3-2    The Linux Man Page Section Areas**

| Section Number | Area Contents |
|---|---|
| 1 | Executable programs or shell commands |
| 2 | System calls |
| 3 | Library calls |
| 4 | Special files |
| 5 | File formats and conventions |
| 6 | Games |
| 7 | Overviews, conventions, and miscellaneous |
| 8 | Super user and system administration commands |
| 9 | Kernel routines |

Typically, the man utility provides the lowest numbered content area for the command. For example, looking back to Figure 3-1 where the command man  hostname was entered, notice that in the upper-left and upper-right display corners, the word HOSTNAME is followed by a number in parentheses, (1). This means the man pages displayed are coming from content area 1 (executable programs or shell commands).

> **NOTE**
> Your Linux system may include a few nonstandard section numbers in its man pages. For example, 1p is the section covering Portable Operating System Interface (POSIX) commands and 3n is for network functions.

Occasionally, a command has the same name as a special file or overview section in the man pages, and thus the name is listed in multiple section content areas. For example, the man pages for hostname contain information on the command as well as an overview section on system hostnames. Typically by default, the man information for the lowest section number is displayed. Such was the case in Figure 3-1, where the hostname man pages from section 1 was automatically chosen. To get around the default section search order, type **man** *section# topicname*. Thus, to see the hostname overview man pages in section 7, type **man  7  hostname**.

You can also step through an introduction to the various section content areas by typing **man  1  intro** to read about section 1, **man  2  intro** to read about section 2, **man  3 intro** to read about section 3, and so on.

The man pages are not the only reference. There are also the information pages called info pages. You can learn about the info pages by typing **info info**.

Built-in commands, which are covered in Chapter 5, "Understanding the Shell," have their own special resource called the help pages. For more information on using help pages, type **help help**. (See a pattern here?)

In addition, most commands accept the -h or --help option. For example, you can type **hostname --help** to see a brief help screen.

Obviously, several helpful resources are available for reference. However, many basic shell concepts still need detailed explanation. In the next section, we cover navigating through the Linux filesystem.

# Navigating the Filesystem

When you log into the system and reach the shell command prompt, you are usually placed in your home directory. Often, you want to explore other areas in the Linux system besides just your home directory. This section describes how to do that using shell commands. To start, you need to take a tour of just what the Linux filesystem looks like so you know where you are going.

## Looking at the Linux filesystem

If you're new to the Linux system, you may be confused by how it references files and directories, especially if you're used to the way the Microsoft Windows operating system does that. Before exploring the Linux system, it helps to have an understanding of how it's laid out.

The first difference you'll notice is that Linux does not use drive letters in pathnames. In the Windows world, the partitions on physical drives installed on the computer determine the pathname of the file. Windows assigns a letter to each physical disk drive partition, and each one contains its own directory structure for accessing files stored on it.

For example, in Windows you may be used to seeing the file paths such as

```
C:\Users\Rich\Documents\test.doc
```

The Windows file path tells you exactly which physical disk partition contains the file named test.doc. For example, if you saved test.doc on a flash drive, designated by the letter E, the file path would be E:\test.doc. This path indicates that the file is located at the root of the drive assigned the letter E.

This is not the method used by Linux. Linux stores files within a single directory structure, called a *virtual directory*. The virtual directory contains file paths from all the storage devices installed on the computer, merged into a single directory structure.

The Linux virtual directory structure contains a single base directory, called the *root*. Directories and files beneath the root directory are listed based on the directory path used to get to them, similar to the way Windows does it.

> **TIP**
>
> You'll notice that Linux uses a forward slash (/) instead of a backward slash (\) to denote directories in file paths. The backslash character in Linux denotes an escape character and causes all sorts of problems when you use it in a file path. This may take some getting used to if you're coming from a Windows environment.

In Linux, as depicted in Figure 3-2, you will see file paths similar to this:

```
/home/rich/Documents/test.doc
```

**FIGURE 3-2**

A Linux virtual directory file path

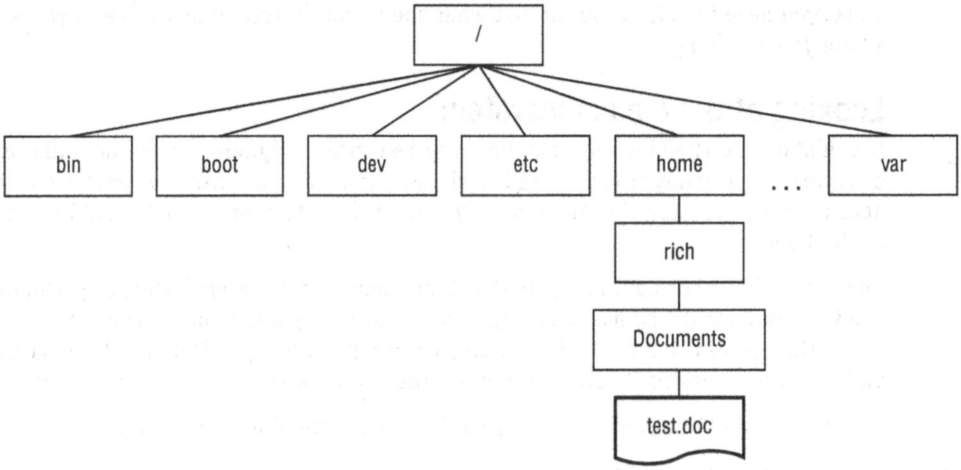

This indicates that the file `test.doc` is in the directory `Documents`, under the directory `rich`, which is contained in the directory `home`. Notice that the path doesn't provide any information as to which physical disk the file is stored on.

The tricky part about the Linux virtual directory is how it incorporates each storage device. The first hard drive installed in a Linux system is called the *root drive*. The root drive contains the virtual directory core. Everything else builds from there.

On the root drive, Linux can use special directories as *mount points*. Mount points are directories in the virtual directory where you can assign additional storage devices. Linux causes files and directories to appear within these mount point directories, even though they are physically stored on a different drive.

Often system files are physically stored on the root drive. User files are typically stored on a separate drive or drives, as shown in Figure 3-3.

**FIGURE 3-3**

The Linux file structure

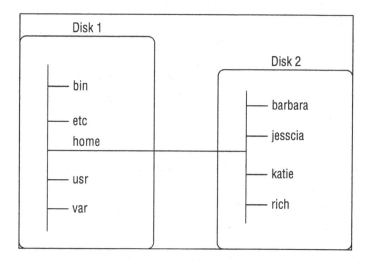

Figure 3-3 shows two hard drives on the computer. One hard drive (Disk 1) is associated with the root of the virtual directory. Other hard drives can be mounted anywhere in the virtual directory structure. In this example, the second hard drive (Disk 2) is mounted at the location /home, which is where the user directories are located.

The Linux filesystem structure originally evolved from the Unix file structure. In a Linux filesystem, common directory names are used for common functions. Table 3-3 lists some common Linux virtual top-level directory names and their contents.

**TABLE 3-3   Common Linux Directory Names**

| Directory | Usage |
| --- | --- |
| / | Root of the virtual directory, where normally, no files are placed |
| /bin | Binary directory, where many GNU user-level utilities are stored |
| /boot | Boot directory, where boot files are stored |
| /dev | Device directory, where Linux creates device nodes |
| /etc | System configuration files directory |
| /home | Home directory, where Linux creates user directories, which are optional |
| /lib | Library directory, where system and application library files are stored |
| /libname | Library directory(ies), where alternative format system and application library files are stored, which is optional |
| /media | Media directory, a common place for mount points used for removable media |
| /mnt | Mount directory, a common place used for temporarily mounting filesystems |
| /opt | Optional directory, where third-party software packages are stored |
| /proc | Process directory, where current kernel, system, and process information is stored |
| /root | Root user's home directory, which is optional |
| /run | Run directory, where runtime data is held during system operation |
| /sbin | System binary directory, where many GNU admin-level utilities are stored |
| /srv | Service directory, where local services store their files |
| /sys | System directory, where devices, drivers, and some kernel feature information is stored |
| /tmp | Temporary directory, where temporary work files can be created and destroyed |
| /usr | User directory, a secondary directory hierarchy |
| /var | Variable directory, for files that change frequently, such as log files |

On the CentOS Linux system, the root virtual directory typically has these top-level directories within it:

```
bin   dev  home  lib64   mnt  proc  run   srv  tmp  var
boot  etc  lib   media   opt  root  sbin  sys  usr
```

The /usr directory deserves some special attention, because it is a secondary directory grouping, containing read-only files that are sharable. You'll often find user commands, source code files, games, and so on. Here is an example of the /usr directory on a CentOS system:

```
bin  games  include  lib  lib64  libexec  local  sbin  share  src  tmp
```

The common Linux directory names are based on the Filesystem Hierarchy Standard (FHS). Many Linux distributions maintain compliance with FHS. Therefore, you should be able to easily find files on any FHS-compliant Linux systems.

> **NOTE**
>
> The FHS is occasionally updated. You may find that some Linux distributions are still using an older FHS standard, whereas other distributions only partially implement the current standard. To keep up to date on the FHS standard, visit its official home at `refspecs.linuxfoundation.org/fhs.shtml`.

When you log into your system and reach a shell CLI prompt, your session starts in your home directory. Your home directory is a unique directory assigned to your user account. When a user account is created, the system normally assigns a unique directory for the account (see Chapter 7).

You can move around the virtual directory using a graphical interface. However, to move around the virtual directory from a CLI prompt, you need to learn to use the cd command.

## Traversing directories

You use the change directory command (cd) to move your shell session to another directory in the Linux filesystem. The cd command syntax is pretty simple: cd *destination*.

The cd command may take a single argument, *destination*, which specifies the directory name you want to go to. If you don't specify a destination on the cd command, it takes you to your home directory.

The *destination* argument can be expressed using two different methods. One method is using an absolute directory reference. The other method uses a relative directory reference.

The following sections describe each of these methods. The differences between these two methods are important to understand as you traverse the filesystem.

### Using absolute directory references

You can reference a directory name within the virtual directory system using an *absolute directory reference*. The absolute directory reference defines exactly where the directory is in the virtual directory structure, starting at the root. Think of the absolute directory reference as the full name for a directory.

An absolute directory reference always begins with a forward slash (/), indicating the virtual directory system's root. Thus, to reference user binaries, contained within the usr directory's bin subdirectory, you would use

```
/usr/bin
```

3

With the absolute directory reference, there's no doubt as to exactly where you want to go. To move to a specific location in the filesystem using the absolute directory reference, you just specify the full pathname in the cd command:

```
[christine@localhost ~]$ cd /usr/bin
[christine@localhost bin]$
```

Notice in the preceding example that the prompt originally had a tilde (~) in it. After the change to a new directory occurred, the tilde was replaced by bin. This is where a CLI prompt can help you keep track of where you are in the virtual directory structure. The tilde indicates that your shell session is located in your home directory. After you move out of your home directory, the partial directory reference is shown in the prompt (if the prompt has been configured to do so).

> **NOTE**
>
> If your shell CLI prompt does not show your shell session's current location, then it has not been configured to do so. Chapter 6 discusses CLI prompt configuration, if you desire modifications to your CLI prompt.

If your prompt has not been configured to show the shell session's current absolute directory location, then you can display the location via a shell command. The pwd command displays the shell session's current directory location, which is called the *present working directory* or *current working directory*. An example of using the pwd command is shown here:

```
[christine@localhost bin]$ pwd
/usr/bin
[christine@localhost bin]$
```

> **TIP**
>
> It is a good habit to use the pwd command whenever you change to a new present working directory. Because many shell commands operate on the present working directory, you always want to make sure you are in the correct directory before issuing a command.

You can move to any level within the entire Linux virtual directory structure from any level using the absolute directory reference:

```
[christine@localhost bin]$ cd /var/log
[christine@localhost log]$ pwd
/var/log
[christine@localhost log]$
```

You can also quickly jump to your home directory from any level within the Linux virtual directory structure:

```
[christine@localhost log]$ cd
[christine@localhost ~]$ pwd
/home/christine
[christine@localhost ~]$
```

However, if you're just working within your own home directory structure, often using absolute directory references can get tedious. For example, if you're already in the directory /home/christine, it seems somewhat cumbersome to have to type the command

```
cd /home/christine/Documents
```

just to get to your Documents directory. Fortunately, there's a simpler solution.

### Using relative directory references

*Relative directory references* allow you to specify a destination directory reference relative to your current location. A relative directory reference doesn't start with a forward slash (/).

Instead, a relative directory reference starts with either a directory name (if you're traversing to a directory under your current directory) or a special character. For example, if you are in your home directory and want to move to your Documents subdirectory, you can use the cd command along with a relative directory reference:

```
[christine@localhost ~]$ pwd
/home/christine
[christine@localhost ~]$ cd Documents
[christine@localhost Documents]$ pwd
/home/christine/Documents
[christine@localhost Documents]$
```

In the preceding example, note that no forward slash (/) was used. Instead, a relative directory reference was used and the present work directory was changed from /home/christine to /home/christine/Documents, with much less typing.

3

> **TIP**
>
> If you are new to the command line and the Linux directory structure, it is recommended that you stick with absolute directory references for a while. After you become more familiar with the directory layout, switch to using relative directory references.

You can use a relative directory reference with the cd command in any directory containing subdirectories. You can also use a special character to indicate a relative directory location.

The two special characters used for relative directory references are:

- The single dot (.) to represent the current directory
- The double dot (..) to represent the parent directory

You *can* use the single dot, but it doesn't make sense to use it with the cd command. Later in the chapter, you will see how another command uses the single dot for relative directory references effectively.

The double-dot character is extremely handy when trying to traverse a directory hierarchy. For example, if you are in the Documents directory under your home directory and need to go to your Downloads directory, also under your home directory, you can do this:

```
[christine@localhost Documents]$ pwd
/home/christine/Documents
[christine@localhost Documents]$ cd ../Downloads
[christine@localhost Downloads]$ pwd
/home/christine/Downloads
[christine@localhost Downloads]$
```

The double-dot character takes you back up one level to your home directory; then the /Downloads portion of the command takes you back down into the Downloads directory. You can use as many double-dot characters as necessary to move around. For example, if you are in your home directory (/home/christine) and want to go to the /etc directory, you could type the following:

```
[christine@localhost ~]$ cd ../../etc
[christine@localhost etc]$ pwd
/etc
[christine@localhost etc]$
```

Of course, in a case like this, you actually have to do more typing rather than just typing the absolute directory reference, /etc. Thus, use a relative directory reference only if it makes sense to do so.

> **NOTE**
> It's helpful to have a long informative shell CLI prompt, as used in this chapter section. However, for clarity purposes, a simple $ prompt is used in the rest of the book's examples.

Now that you know how to traverse the directory system and confirm your present working directory, you can start to explore what's contained within the various directories. The next section takes you through the process of looking at files within the directory structure.

## Listing Files and Directories

To see what files are available on the system, use the list command (ls). This section describes the ls command and options available to format the information it can display.

## Displaying a basic listing

The ls command at its most basic form displays the files and directories located in your current directory:

```
$ ls
Desktop     Downloads   my_script   Public      test_file
Documents   Music       Pictures    Templates   Videos
$
```

Notice that the ls command produces the listing in alphabetical order (in columns rather than rows). If you're using a terminal emulator that supports color, the ls command may also show different types of entries in different colors. The LS_COLORS environment variable controls this feature. (Environment variables are covered in Chapter 6. Different Linux distributions set this environment variable depending on the capabilities of the terminal emulator.

If you don't have a color terminal emulator, you can use the -F parameter with the ls command to easily distinguish files from directories. Using the -F parameter produces the following output:

```
$ ls -F
Desktop/     Downloads/   my_script*   Public/      test_file
Documents/   Music/       Pictures/    Templates/   Videos/
$
```

The -F parameter flags the directories with a forward slash (/), to help identify them in the listing. Similarly, it marks executable files (like the my _ script file in the preceding code) with an asterisk (*), to help you more easily find files that can be run on the system.

The basic ls command can be somewhat misleading. It shows the files and directories contained in the current directory, but not necessarily all of them. Linux often uses *hidden files* to store configuration information. In Linux, hidden files are files with filenames starting with a period (.). These files don't appear in the default ls listing. Thus, they are called hidden files.

To display hidden files along with normal files and directories, use the -a parameter. Here is an example of using the -a parameter with the ls command:

```
$ ls -a
.               .bash_profile  Desktop     .ICEauthority  my_script  Templates
..              .bashrc        Documents   .local         Pictures   test_file
.bash_history   .cache         Downloads   .mozilla       .pki       Videos
.bash_logout    .config        .esd_auth   Music          Public
$
```

All the files beginning with a period, hidden files, are now shown. Notice that four files begin with .bash. These are hidden files that are used by the Bash shell environment and are covered in detail in Chapter 6.

The -R parameter is another option the ls command can use. Called the recursive option, it shows files that are contained within subdirectories in the current directory. If you have lots of subdirectories, this can be quite a long listing. Here's a simple example of what the -R parameter produces. The -F option was tacked on to help you see the file types:

```
$ ls -F -R
.:
Desktop/      Downloads/   my_script*   Public/      test_file
Documents/    Music/       Pictures/    Templates/   Videos/

./Desktop:

./Documents:

./Downloads:

./Music:
ILoveLinux.mp3*

./Pictures:

./Public:

./Templates:

./Videos:
$
```

Notice that the -R parameter shows the contents of the current directory, which are the files from a user's home directory shown in earlier examples. It also shows each subdirectory in the user's home directory and their contents. The only subdirectory containing a file is the Music subdirectory, and it contains the executable file ILoveLinux.mp3.

**TIP**

Option parameters don't have to be entered separately as shown in the previous example: ls -F -R. They can often be combined as follows: ls -FR.

In the previous example, there were no subdirectories within subdirectories. If there had been further subdirectories, the -R parameter would have continued to traverse those as well. As you can imagine, for large directory structures, this can become quite a long listing.

## Displaying a long listing

In the basic listings, the `ls` command doesn't produce much information about each file. For listing additional information, another popular parameter is -l. The -l parameter produces a long listing format, providing more information about each file in the directory:

```
$ ls -l
total 8
drwxr-xr-x. 2 christine christine  6 Feb 20 14:23 Desktop
drwxr-xr-x. 2 christine christine  6 Feb 20 14:23 Documents
drwxr-xr-x. 2 christine christine  6 Feb 20 14:23 Downloads
drwxr-xr-x. 2 christine christine 28 Feb 29 15:42 Music
-rwxrw-r--. 1 christine christine 74 Feb 29 15:49 my_script
drwxr-xr-x. 2 christine christine  6 Feb 20 14:23 Pictures
drwxr-xr-x. 2 christine christine  6 Feb 20 14:23 Public
drwxr-xr-x. 2 christine christine  6 Feb 20 14:23 Templates
-rw-rw-r--. 1 christine christine 74 Feb 29 15:50 test_file
drwxr-xr-x. 2 christine christine  6 Feb 20 14:23 Videos
$
```

The long listing format lists each file and directory on a single line. Along with the filename, the listing shows additional useful information. The first line in the output shows the total number of allocated blocks for the files within the directory (8). After that, each line contains the following information about each file (or directory):

- The file type — such as directory (d), file (-), linked file (l), character device (c), or block device (b)
- The file permissions (see Chapter 7)
- The number of file hard links (see the section "Linking Files" in this chapter).
- The file owner username
- The file primary group name
- The file byte size
- The last time the file was modified
- The filename or directory name

The -l parameter is a powerful tool to have. Armed with this parameter, you can see most of the information you need for any file or directory.

> **TIP**
>
> If you want to view the long listing for only one file, simply tack on the file's name to your `ls -l` command. However, if you want to see such a listing for a directory, and not its contents, you'll not only need to add its name to the command, but add the `-d` switch, as in: `ls -ld Directory-Name`.

The `ls` command has lots of parameters that can come in handy as you do file management. If you type **man ls** at the shell prompt, you see several pages of available parameters for you to use to modify the `ls` command output.

Don't forget that you can also combine many of the parameters. You can often find a parameter combination that not only displays the desired output, but is also easy to remember, such as ls -alF.

## Filtering listing output

As you've seen in the examples, by default the ls command lists all the non-hidden directory files. Sometimes, this can be overkill, especially when you're just looking for information on a few files.

Fortunately, the ls command also provides a way for you to define a filter on the command line. It uses the filter to determine which files or directories it should display in the output.

Before using the filter command, let's create some files to play with via the touch command (covered in the next section). If the file already exists, the command won't hurt the file:

```
$ touch my_script my_scrapt my_file
$ touch fall fell fill full
$ ls
Desktop    Downloads  fell  full  my_file   my_script  Public     test_file
Documents  fall       fill  Music my_scrapt Pictures   Templates  Videos
$
```

The filter works as a simple text-matching string. Include the filter after any command line parameters you want to use:

```
$ ls -l my_script
-rwxrw-r--. 1 christine christine 74 Feb 29 16:12 my_script
$
```

When you specify the name of a specific file as the filter, the ls command only shows that file's information. Sometimes, you might not know the exact filename you're looking for. The ls command also recognizes standard wildcard characters and uses them to match patterns within the filter:

■ A question mark (?) to represent one character

■ An asterisk (*) to represent any number of characters

The question mark can be used to replace exactly one character anywhere in the filter string. For example:

```
$ ls -l my_scr?pt
-rw-rw-r--. 1 christine christine  0 Feb 29 16:12 my_scrapt
-rwxrw-r--. 1 christine christine 74 Feb 29 16:12 my_script
$
```

The filter my_scr?pt matched two files in the directory. Similarly, the asterisk can be used to match zero or more characters:

```
$ ls -l my*
-rw-rw-r--. 1 christine christine  0 Feb 29 16:12 my_file
-rw-rw-r--. 1 christine christine  0 Feb 29 16:12 my_scrapt
-rwxrw-r--. 1 christine christine 74 Feb 29 16:12 my_script
$
```

Using the asterisk finds three different files, starting with the name my. As with the question mark, you can place the asterisks anywhere in the filter:

```
$ ls -l my_s*t
-rw-rw-r--. 1 christine christine  0 Feb 29 16:12 my_scrapt
-rwxrw-r--. 1 christine christine 74 Feb 29 16:12 my_script
$
```

Using the asterisk and question mark in the filter is called *file globbing*. File globbing is the process of pattern matching using wildcards. The wildcards are officially called *metacharacter wildcards*. You can use more metacharacter wildcards for file globbing than just the asterisk and question mark. You can also use brackets:

```
$ touch my_scrypt
$ ls -l my_scr[ay]pt
-rw-rw-r--. 1 christine christine 0 Feb 29 16:12 my_scrapt
-rw-rw-r--. 1 christine christine 0 Feb 29 16:18 my_scrypt
$
```

In this example, we used the brackets along with two potential choices for a single character in that position, a or y. The brackets represent a single character position and give you multiple options for file globbing. You can list choices of characters, as shown in the preceding example, and you can specify a range of characters, such as an alphabetic range [a-i]:

```
$ ls f*ll
fall  fell  fill  full
$ ls f[a-i]ll
fall  fell  fill
$
```

Also, you can specify what should *not* be included in the pattern match by using the exclamation point (!):

```
$ ls -l f[!a]ll
-rw-rw-r--. 1 christine christine 0 Feb 29 16:12 fell
-rw-rw-r--. 1 christine christine 0 Feb 29 16:12 fill
-rw-rw-r--. 1 christine christine 0 Feb 29 16:12 full
$
```

File globbing is a powerful feature when searching for files. It can also be used with other shell commands besides ls. You'll find out more about this later in the chapter.

# Handling Files

The shell provides many file manipulation commands on the Linux filesystem. This section walks you through the basic shell commands you need to handle files.

## Creating files

Every once in a while you run into a situation where you need to create an empty file. For example, sometimes applications expect a log file to be present before they can write to it. In these situations, you can use the touch command to easily create an empty file:

```
$ touch test_one
$ ls -l test_one
-rw-rw-r--. 1 christine christine 0 Feb 29 17:24 test_one
$
```

The touch command creates the new file you specify and assigns your username as the file owner. Notice in the preceding example that the file size is zero because the touch command just created an empty file.

The touch command can also be used to change the modification time. This is done without changing the file contents:

```
$ ls -l test_one
-rw-rw-r--. 1 christine christine 0 Feb 29 17:24 test_one
$ touch test_one
$ ls -l test_one
-rw-rw-r--. 1 christine christine 0 Feb 29 17:26 test_one
$
```

The modification time of test_one is now updated to 17:26 from the original time, 17:24.

Creating empty files and altering file time stamps is not something you will do on a Linux system daily. However, copying files is an action you will do often while using the shell.

## Copying files

Copying files and directories from one location in the filesystem to another is a common practice for system administrators. The cp command provides this feature.

In its most basic form, the cp command uses two parameters — the source object and the destination object: cp *source destination*.

When both the *source* and *destination* parameters are filenames, the cp command copies the source file to a new destination file. The new file acts like a brand-new file, with an updated modification time:

```
$ cp test_one test_two
$ ls -l test_one test_two
```

```
-rw-rw-r--. 1 christine christine 0 Feb 29 17:26 test_one
-rw-rw-r--. 1 christine christine 0 Feb 29 17:46 test_two
$
```

The new file `test_two` shows a different modification time than the `test_one` file. If the destination file already exists, the `cp` command may not prompt you to this fact. It is best to add the `-i` option to force the shell to ask whether you want to overwrite a file:

```
$ ls -l test_one test_two
-rw-rw-r--. 1 christine christine 0 Feb 29 17:26 test_one
-rw-rw-r--. 1 christine christine 0 Feb 29 17:46 test_two
$
$ cp -i test_one test_two
cp: overwrite 'test_two'? n
$
```

If you don't answer `y`, the file copy does not proceed. You can also copy a file into a preexisting directory:

```
$ cp -i test_one /home/christine/Documents/
$
$ ls -l /home/christine/Documents/
total 0
-rw-rw-r--. 1 christine christine 0 Feb 29 17:48 test_one
$
```

The new file is now under the `Documents` directory, using the same filename as the original.

> **NOTE**
> The preceding example uses a trailing forward slash (`/`) on the destination directory name. Using the slash indicates `Documents` is a directory and not a file. This is helpful for clarity purposes and is important when copying single files. If the forward slash is not used and the subdirectory `/home/christine/Documents` does not exist, a file named `Documents` is created within the current directory and no error message is displayed. That is problematic, so use a trailing forward slash on your destination directory names.

This last example used an absolute directory reference, but you can just as easily use a relative directory reference:

```
$ cp -i test_two Documents/
$ ls -l Documents/
total 0
-rw-rw-r--. 1 christine christine 0 Feb 29 17:48 test_one
-rw-rw-r--. 1 christine christine 0 Feb 29 17:51 test_two
$
```

Earlier in this chapter, you read about the special symbols that can be used in relative directory references. One of them, the single dot (.), is great to use with the `cp` command. Remember that the single dot represents your current working directory. If you need to copy a file with a long source object name to your current working directory, the single dot can simplify the task:

```
$ cp /etc/NetworkManager/NetworkManager.conf .
$ ls *.conf
NetworkManager.conf
$
```

It's hard to see that single dot! If you look closely, you'll see it at the end of the first example code line. Using the single dot symbol is much easier than typing a full destination object name when you have long source object names.

The `-R` parameter is a powerful `cp` command option. It allows you to recursively copy the contents of an entire directory in one command:

```
$ ls -l Documents/
total 0
-rw-rw-r--. 1 christine christine 0 Feb 29 17:48 test_one
-rw-rw-r--. 1 christine christine 0 Feb 29 17:51 test_two
$
$ cp -R Documents/ NewDocuments/
$ ls -l NewDocuments/
total 0
-rw-rw-r--. 1 christine christine 0 Feb 29 17:55 test_one
-rw-rw-r--. 1 christine christine 0 Feb 29 17:55 test_two
$
```

The directory NewDocuments did not exist prior to the `cp -R` command. It was created with the `cp -R` command, and the entire Documents directory's contents were copied into it. Notice that all the files in the new NewDocuments directory have new dates associated with them. Now NewDocuments is a complete copy of the Documents directory.

> **TIP**
>
> There are many more `cp` command parameters than those described here. Remember that you can see all the different parameters available for the `cp` command by typing `man cp`.

You can also use wildcard metacharacters in your `cp` commands:

```
$ ls
Desktop    fall  full   my_scrapt  NetworkManager.conf  Public     test_one
Documents  fell  Music  my_script  NewDocuments         Templates  test_two
```

```
Downloads  fill  my_file  my_scrypt  Pictures          test_file  Videos
$
$ cp my* NewDocuments/
$ ls NewDocuments/
my_file  my_scrapt  my_script  my_scrypt  test_one  test_two
$
```

This command copied any files that started with my to NewDocuments. Now the directory contains six files instead of just two.

When copying files, another shell feature can help you besides the single dot and wildcard metacharacters. It is called command-line completion.

## Using command-line completion

When working at the command line, you can easily mistype a command, directory name, or filename. In fact, the longer a directory reference or filename, the greater the chance you will mistype it.

This is where *command-line completion* (also called *tab completion*) can be a lifesaver. Tab completion allows you to start typing a filename or directory name, and then press the tab key to have the shell complete it for you:

```
$ touch really_ridiculously_long_file_name
$
$ cp really_ridiculously_long_file_name NewDocuments/
$ ls NewDocuments/
my_file    my_script  really_ridiculously_long_file_name  test_two
my_scrapt  my_scrypt  test_one
$
```

After creating a file with a very long name in the preceding example, we typed the command **cp really** and pressed the Tab key, and the shell autocompleted the rest of the filename for us! Of course, the destination directory had to be typed, but still tab completion saved the command from several potential typographical errors.

The trick to using command-line completion is to give the shell enough filename characters so it can distinguish the desired file from other files. For example, if another filename started with really, pressing the Tab key would not autocomplete the filename. Instead, you would hear a beep. If this happens, you can press the Tab key again, and the shell shows you all the filenames starting with really. This feature allows you to see what needs to be typed for tab completion to work properly.

## Linking files

Linking files is a great option available in the Linux filesystem. If you need to maintain two (or more) copies of the same file on the system, instead of having separate physical

3

copies, you can use one physical copy and multiple virtual copies, called links. A *link* is a placeholder in a directory that points to the real location of the file. Two types of file links are available in Linux:

- A symbolic link
- A hard link

A *symbolic link*, also called a *soft link*, is simply a physical file that *points* to another file somewhere in the virtual directory structure. The two symbolically linked together files do not share the same contents.

To create a symbolic link, the original file must already exist. We then use the `ln` command with the `-s` option to create the symbolic link:

```
$ ls -l test_file
-rw-rw-r--. 1 christine christine 74 Feb 29 15:50 test_file
$
$ ln -s test_file slink_test_file
$
$ ls -l *test_file
lrwxrwxrwx. 1 christine christine  9 Mar  4 09:46 slink_test_file -> test_file
-rw-rw-r--. 1 christine christine 74 Feb 29 15:50 test_file
$
```

In the preceding example, notice that the name of the symbolic link, slink_test_file, is listed second in the `ln` command. The —> symbol displayed after the symbolic link file's name in its long listing (`ls -l`) shows that it is symbolically linked to the file test_file.

Also note the symbolic link's file size versus the data file's file size. The symbolic link, slink_test_file, is only 9 bytes, whereas the test_file is 74 bytes. This is because slink_test_file is only *pointing* to test_file. They do not share contents and are two physically separate files.

Another way to tell that these linked files are separate physical files is by viewing their *inode* numbers. The inode number of a file or directory is a unique identification number that the kernel assigns to each object in the filesystem. To view a file or directory's inode number, add the `-i` parameter to the `ls` command:

```
$ ls -i *test_file
1415020 slink_test_file  1415523 test_file
$
```

The example shows that the test file's inode number is 1415523, whereas the slink_test_file inode number is different (it is 1415020). Thus, they are different files.

A *hard link* creates a separate virtual file that contains information about the original file and where to locate it. However, the two files are actually the same physical file. To create a hard link, again the original file must preexist, except that this time no parameter is needed on the ln command:

```
$ ls -l *test_one
-rw-rw-r--. 1 christine christine 0 Feb 29 17:26 test_one
$
$ ln test_one hlink_test_one
$
$ ls -li *test_one
1415016 -rw-rw-r--. 2 christine christine 0 Feb 29 17:26 hlink_test_one
1415016 -rw-rw-r--. 2 christine christine 0 Feb 29 17:26 test_one
$
```

In the preceding example, after creating the hard link file, we used the ls -li command to show both the inode numbers and a long listing for the *test_one. Notice that both files, which are hard-linked together, share the same inode number. This is because they are physically the same file. Their file size is exactly the same as well.

> **NOTE**
>
> You can only create a hard link between files on the same physical medium. To create a link between files under separate physical mediums, you must use a symbolic link.

You may find symbolic and hard links difficult concepts. Fortunately, renaming files, the topic of our next section, is a great deal easier to understand.

## Renaming files

In the Linux world, renaming files is called *moving files*. The mv command is available to move both files and directories to another location or a new name:

```
$ ls -li f?ll
1414976 -rw-rw-r--. 1 christine christine 0 Feb 29 16:12 fall
1415004 -rw-rw-r--. 1 christine christine 0 Feb 29 16:12 fell
1415005 -rw-rw-r--. 1 christine christine 0 Feb 29 16:12 fill
1415011 -rw-rw-r--. 1 christine christine 0 Feb 29 16:12 full
$
$ mv fall fzll
$
$ ls -li f?ll
1415004 -rw-rw-r--. 1 christine christine 0 Feb 29 16:12 fell
1415005 -rw-rw-r--. 1 christine christine 0 Feb 29 16:12 fill
1415011 -rw-rw-r--. 1 christine christine 0 Feb 29 16:12 full
1414976 -rw-rw-r--. 1 christine christine 0 Feb 29 16:12 fzll
$
```

3

Notice that moving the file changed the name from `fall` to `fzll` but it kept the same inode number and time stamp value. This is because `mv` affects only a file's name.

You can also use `mv` to change a file's location:

```
$ ls -li /home/christine/fzll
1414976 -rw-rw-r--. 1 christine christine 0 Feb 29 16:12 /home/christine/fzll
$
$ ls -li /home/christine/NewDocuments/fzll
ls: cannot access '/home/christine/NewDocuments/fzll': No such file or directory
$
$ mv /home/christine/fzll /home/christine/NewDocuments/
$
$ ls -li /home/christine/NewDocuments/fzll
1414976 -rw-rw-r--. 1 christine christine 0 Feb 29 16:12
/home/christine/NewDocuments/fzll
$
$ ls -li /home/christine/fzll
ls: cannot access '/home/christine/fzll': No such file or directory
$
```

In the preceding example, we moved the file `fzll` from /home/christine to /home/christine/NewDocuments using the `mv` command. Again, there were no changes to the file's inode number or time stamp value.

> **TIP**
>
> Like the `cp` command, you can use the `-i` option on the `mv` command. Thus, you are asked before the command attempts to overwrite any preexisting files.

The only change was to the file's location. The `fzll` file no longer exists in /home/christine, because a copy of it was not left in its original location, as the `cp` command would have done.

You can use the `mv` command to move a file's location and rename it, all in one easy step:

```
$ ls -li NewDocuments/fzll
1414976 -rw-rw-r--. 1 christine christine 0 Feb 29 16:12 NewDocuments/fzll
$
$ mv /home/christine/NewDocuments/fzll /home/christine/fall
$
$ ls -li /home/christine/fall
1414976 -rw-rw-r--. 1 christine christine 0 Feb 29 16:12 /home/christine/fall
```

```
$
$ ls -li /home/christine/NewDocuments/fzll
ls: cannot access '/home/christine/NewDocuments/fzll': No such file or directory
$
```

For this example, we moved the file `fzll` from a subdirectory, `NewDocuments`, to the home directory, `/home/christine`, and renamed it `fall`. Neither the timestamp value nor the inode number changed. Only the location and name were altered.

You can also use the `mv` command to move entire directories and their contents:

```
$ ls NewDocuments
my_file    my_script   really_ridiculously_long_file_name   test_two
my_scrapt  my_scrypt   test_one
$
$ mv NewDocuments OldDocuments
$
$ ls NewDocuments
ls: cannot access 'NewDocuments': No such file or directory
$
$ ls OldDocuments
my_file    my_script   really_ridiculously_long_file_name   test_two
my_scrapt  my_scrypt   test_one
$
```

The directory's entire contents are unchanged. The only thing that changes is the name of the directory.

Once you know how to rename. . .err. . .*move* files with the `mv` command, you realize how simple it is to accomplish. Another easy, but potentially dangerous, task is deleting files.

## Deleting files

Most likely at some point you'll want to be able to delete existing files. Whether it's to clean up a filesystem or to remove temporary work data, you always have opportunities to delete files.

In the Linux world, deleting is called *removing*. The command to remove files in the Bash shell is `rm`. The basic form of the `rm` command is simple:

```
$ rm -i fall
rm: remove regular empty file 'fall'? y
$ ls fall
ls: cannot access 'fall': No such file or directory
$
```

Notice that the `-i` command parameter prompts you to make sure that you're serious about removing the file. The shell has no recycle bin or trashcan. After you remove a file, it's gone forever. Therefore, a good habit is to always tack on the `-i` parameter to the `rm` command.

You can also use wildcard metacharacters to remove groups of files. However, again, use that -i option to protect yourself:

```
$ rm -i f?ll
rm: remove regular empty file 'fell'? y
rm: remove regular empty file 'fill'? y
rm: remove regular empty file 'full'? y
$ ls f?ll
ls: cannot access 'f?ll': No such file or directory
$
```

One other feature of the rm command, if you're removing lots of files and don't want to be bothered with the prompt, is to use the -f parameter to force the removal. Just be careful!

# Managing Directories

Linux has a few commands that work for both files and directories (such as the cp command) and some that work only for directories. To create a new directory, you need to use a specific command, which is covered in this section. Removing directories can get interesting, so that is covered in this section as well.

## Creating directories

Creating a new directory in Linux is easy — just use the mkdir command:

```
$ mkdir New_Dir
$ ls -ld New_Dir
drwxrwxr-x. 2 christine christine 6 Mar  6 14:40 New_Dir
$
```

The system creates a new directory named New_Dir. Notice in the new directory's long listing that the directory's record begins with a d. This indicates that New_Dir is a directory.

Occasionally, you may need to create directories and subdirectories in "bulk." To do this, add the -p option to the mkdir command as shown here:

```
$ mkdir -p New_Dir/SubDir/UnderDir
$ ls -R New_Dir
New_Dir:
SubDir

New_Dir/SubDir:
UnderDir

New_Dir/SubDir/UnderDir:
$
```

The -p option on the mkdir command makes any missing *parent directories* as needed. A parent directory is a directory that contains other directories at the next level down the directory tree.

Of course, after you make something, you need to know how to delete it. This is especially useful if you created a directory in the wrong location.

## Deleting directories

Removing directories can be tricky, and for good reason. There are lots of opportunities for bad things to happen when you start deleting directories. The shell tries to protect us from accidental catastrophes as much as possible.

The basic command for removing a directory is rmdir:

```
$ mkdir Wrong_Dir
$ touch Wrong_Dir/newfile
$
$ rmdir Wrong_Dir/
rmdir: failed to remove 'Wrong_Dir/': Directory not empty
$
```

By default, the rmdir command works only for removing *empty* directories. Because we created a file, newfile, in the Wrong _ Dir directory, the rmdir command refuses to remove it.

To use rmdir to remove this directory, we must remove the file first. Then we can use the rmdir command on the now empty directory:

```
$ rm -i Wrong_Dir/newfile
rm: remove regular empty file 'Wrong_Dir/newfile'? y
$ rmdir Wrong_Dir/
$ ls Wrong_Dir
ls: cannot access 'Wrong_Dir': No such file or directory
$
```

The rmdir has no -i option to ask if you want to remove the directory. This is one reason it is helpful that rmdir removes only empty directories.

You can also use the rm command on entire nonempty directories. Using the -r option allows the command to descend into the directory, remove the files, and then remove the directory itself:

```
$ mkdir TestDir
$ touch TestDir/fileone TestDir/filetwo
$ ls TestDir
fileone   filetwo
$ rm -ir TestDir
```

```
rm: descend into directory 'TestDir'? y
rm: remove regular empty file 'TestDir/fileone'? y
rm: remove regular empty file 'TestDir/filetwo'? y
rm: remove directory 'TestDir'? y
$ ls TestDir
ls: cannot access 'TestDir': No such file or directory
$
```

This also works for descending into multiple subdirectories and is especially useful when you have lots of directories and files to delete:

```
$ touch New_Dir/testfile
$ ls -FR New_Dir
New_Dir:
SubDir/   testfile

New_Dir/SubDir:
UnderDir/

New_Dir/SubDir/UnderDir:
$
$ rm -iR New_Dir
rm: descend into directory 'New_Dir'? y
rm: descend into directory 'New_Dir/SubDir'? y
rm: remove directory 'New_Dir/SubDir/UnderDir'? y
rm: remove directory 'New_Dir/SubDir'? y
rm: remove regular empty file 'New_Dir/testfile'? y
rm: remove directory 'New_Dir'? y
$
```

Although this works, it's somewhat awkward. Notice that you still must verify each and every file that gets removed. For a directory with lots of files and subdirectories, this can become tedious.

> **NOTE**
>
> For the `rm` command, the `-r` parameter and the `-R` parameter work exactly the same — it recursively traverses through the directory removing files. It is unusual for a shell command to have different cased parameters with the same function.

The ultimate solution for quickly deleting a directory tree is the `rm -rf` command. It gives no warnings and no messages, and it just deletes the directory specified and all its contents. This, of course, is an extremely dangerous tool to have. Use it sparingly, and only after triple checking to make sure that you're doing exactly what you want to do!

In the last few sections, we looked at managing both files and directories. So far we've covered everything you need to know about files, except for how to peek inside them.

# Viewing File Contents

You can use several commands for looking inside files without having to pull out a text editor utility (see Chapter 10, "Working with Editors"). This section demonstrates a few of those commands.

## Viewing the file type

Before you go charging off trying to display a file, you need to get a handle on what type of file it is. If you attempt to display a binary file, you may get lots of gibberish on your screen and possibly even lock up your terminal emulator.

The file command is a handy little utility to have around. It can peek inside a file and determine just what kind of file it is:

```
$ file .bashrc
.bashrc: ASCII text
$
```

The file in the preceding example is a text file. The file command determined not only that the file contains text but also the character code format of the text file, ASCII.

This following example shows a file that is simply a directory. Thus, the file command gives you another method to distinguish a directory:

```
$ file Documents
Documents/: directory
$
```

This third file command example shows a file that is a symbolic link. Note that the file command even tells you to which file it is symbolically linked:

```
$ file slink_test_file
slink_test_file: symbolic link to test_file
$
```

The following example shows what the file command returns for a script file. Although the file is ASCII text, because it's a script file, you can execute (run) it on the system:

```
$ file my_script
my_script: Bourne-Again shell script, ASCII text executable
$
```

The final example is a binary executable program. The file command determines the platform that the program was compiled for and what types of libraries it requires. This is an especially handy feature if you have a binary executable program from an unknown source:

```
$ file /usr/bin/ls
/usr/bin/ls: ELF 64-bit LSB shared object, x86-64, version 1 (SYSV),
dynamically linked, interpreter /lib64/ld-linux-x86-64.so.2,
for GNU/Linux 3.2.0, [...]
$
```

3

Now that you know a quick method for viewing a file's type, you can start displaying and viewing files.

## Viewing the whole file

If you have a large text file on your hands, you may want to be able to see what's inside it. Linux has three different commands that can help you here.

### Using the *cat* command

The `cat` command is a handy tool for displaying all the data inside a text file:

```
$ cat test_file
Hello World
Hello World again
Hello World a third time
How are you World?

$
```

Nothing too exciting, just the contents of the text file. However, the `cat` command has a few parameters that can help you out.

The -n parameter numbers all the lines for you:

```
$ cat -n test_file
     1  Hello World
     2  Hello World again
     3  Hello World a third time
     4  How are you World?
     5
$
```

That feature will come in handy when you're examining scripts. If you just want to number the lines that have text in them, the -b parameter is for you:

```
$ cat -b test_file
     1  Hello World
     2  Hello World again
     3  Hello World a third time
     4  How are you World?

$
```

For large files, the `cat` command can be somewhat annoying. The text in the file just quickly scrolls off the display without stopping. Fortunately, we have a simple way to solve this problem.

### Using the *more* command

The main drawback of the `cat` command is that you can't control what's happening after you start it. To solve that problem, developers created the `more` command. The `more` command displays a text file but stops after it displays each page of data. We typed the command **more /etc/profile** to produce the sample more screen shown in Figure 3-4.

**FIGURE 3-4**

Using the more command to display a text file

```
# /etc/profile

# System wide environment and startup programs, for login setup
# Functions and aliases go in /etc/bashrc

# It's NOT a good idea to change this file unless you know what you
# are doing. It's much better to create a custom.sh shell script in
# /etc/profile.d/ to make custom changes to your environment, as this
# will prevent the need for merging in future updates.

pathmunge () {
    case ":${PATH}:" in
        *:"$1":*)
            ;;
        *)
            if [ "$2" = "after" ] ; then
                PATH=$PATH:$1
            else
                PATH=$1:$PATH
            fi
    esac
}
--More--(29%)
```

Notice at the bottom of the screen in Figure 3-4 that the more command displays a tag showing that you're still in the more application and how far along (29%) in the text file you are. This is the prompt for the more command.

**TIP**

If you're following along with the examples, and your Linux system does not have the /etc/profile file or it's rather short, try using more on the /etc/passwd file instead. Type **more /etc/passwd** and press Enter at your shell prompt.

The more command is a pager utility. Earlier in this chapter we discussed that a pager utility displays selected Bash manual pages when you use the man command. Similarly to navigating through the man pages, you can use more to navigate through a text file by pressing the spacebar, or you can go forward line by line using the Enter key. When you are finished navigating through the file using more, type **q** to quit.

The more command allows some rudimentary movement through the text file. For more advanced features, try the less command.

3

### Using the *less* command

From its name, it sounds like it shouldn't be as advanced as the more command. However, the less command name is actually a play on words and is an advanced version of the more command (the less command name comes from the phrase "less is more"). It provides several very handy features for scrolling both forward and backward through a text file, as well as some pretty advanced searching capabilities.

The less command can also display a file's contents before it finishes reading the entire file. The cat and more commands cannot do this.

The less command operates much the same as the more command, displaying one screen of text from a file at a time. It supports the same command set as the more command, plus many more options.

> **TIP**
>
> To see all the options available for the less command, view its man pages by typing man less. You can do the same for the more command to see the reference material concerning its various options.

One set of features is that the less command recognizes the up and down arrow keys as well as the Page Up and Page Down keys (assuming that you're using a properly defined terminal). This gives you full control when viewing a file.

> **NOTE**
>
> The less utility is typically the pager service used for the man pages. Thus, the more you learn about less, the easier it will be for you to navigate through various commands' man pages.

## Viewing parts of a file

Often the data you want to view is located either right at the top or buried at the bottom of a text file. If the information is at the top of a large file, you still need to wait for the cat or more command to load the entire file before you can view it. If the information is located at the bottom of a file (such as a log file), you need to wade through thousands of lines of text just to get to the last few entries. Fortunately, Linux has specialized commands to solve both of these problems.

### Using the *tail* command

The tail command displays the last lines in a file (the file's "tail"). By default, it shows the last 10 lines in the file.

For these examples, we created a text file containing 15 text lines. It is displayed here in its entirety using the cat command:

```
$ cat log_file
line1
```

```
line2
line3
line4
Hello World - line5
line6
line7
line8
line9
Hello again World - line10
line11
line12
line13
line14
Last Line - line15
$
```

Now that you have seen the entire text file, you can see the effect of using `tail` to view the file's last 10 lines:

```
$ tail log_file
line6
line7
line8
line9
Hello again World - line10
line11
line12
line13
line14
Last Line - line15
$
```

You can change the number of lines shown using `tail` by including the -n parameter. In this example, only the last two lines of the file are displayed, by adding -n 2 to the `tail` command:

```
$ tail -n 2 log_file
line14
Last Line - line15
$
```

The -f parameter is a pretty cool feature of the `tail` command. It allows you to peek inside a file as the file is being used by other processes. The `tail` command stays active and continues to display new lines as they appear in the text file. This is a great way to monitor the system log files in real-time mode.

### Using the *head* command

The head command does what you'd expect; it displays a file's first group of lines (the file's "head"). By default, it displays the first 10 lines of text:

```
$ head log_file
line1
line2
line3
line4
Hello World - line5
line6
line7
line8
line9
Hello again World - line10
$
```

Similar to the tail command, the head command supports the -n parameter so that you can alter what's displayed. Both commands also allow you to simply type a dash along with the number of lines to display, as shown here:

```
$ head -3 log_file
line1
line2
line3
$
```

Usually the beginning of a file doesn't change, so the head command doesn't support the -f parameter feature as the tail command does. The head command is a handy way to just peek at the beginning of a file.

## Summary

This chapter covered the basics of working with the Linux filesystem from a shell prompt. We began with a discussion of the Bash shell and showed you how to interact with the shell. The CLI uses a prompt string to indicate when it's ready for you to enter commands.

The shell provides a wealth of utilities you can use to create and manipulate files. Before you start playing with files, you should understand how Linux stores them. This chapter discussed the basics of the Linux virtual directory and showed you how Linux references storage media devices. After describing the Linux filesystem, we walked you through using the cd command to move around the virtual directory.

After showing you how to get to a directory, we demonstrated how to use the ls command to list the files and subdirectories. Lots of parameters can customize the output of the ls command. You can obtain information on both files and directories by using this command.

The `touch` command is useful for creating empty files and for changing the access or modification times on an existing file. We also discussed using the `cp` command to copy existing files from one location to another. We walked you through the process of linking files instead of copying them, providing an easy way to have the same file in two locations without making a separate copy. The `ln` command provides this linking ability.

Next, you learned how to rename files (called *moving*) in Linux using the `mv` command and how to delete files (called *removing*) using the `rm` command. We also showed you how to perform the same tasks with directories, using the `mkdir` and `rmdir` commands.

Finally, this chapter closed with a discussion on viewing the contents of files. The `cat`, `more`, and `less` commands provide easy methods for viewing the entire contents of a file, whereas the `tail` and `head` commands are great for peeking inside a file to just see a small portion of it.

The next chapter continues the discussion on Bash shell commands. We'll look at more advanced administrator commands that come in handy as you administer your Linux system.

3

# More Bash Shell Commands

## IN THIS CHAPTER

C hapter 3, "Basic Bash Shell Commands," covered the basics of rummaging through the Linux filesystem and working with the files and directories. File and directory management is a major feature of the Linux shell; however, we should look at some more things before we start our script programming. This chapter digs into the Linux system management commands, showing you how to peek inside your Linux system using command-line commands. After that, it shows you a few handy commands that you can use to work with data files on the system.

## Monitoring Programs

One of the toughest jobs of being a Linux system administrator is keeping track of what's running on the system — especially now, when graphical desktops take a handful of programs just to produce a single desktop. There are always a lot of programs running on the system.

Fortunately, a few command-line tools are available that can help make life easier for you. This section covers a few of the basic tools you'll need to know to manage programs on your Linux system.

### Peeking at the processes

When a program runs on the system, it's referred to as a *process*. To examine these processes, you must become familiar with the ps command, the Swiss Army knife of utilities. It can produce lots of information about all the programs running on your system.

Unfortunately, with this robustness comes complexity — in the form of numerous parameters — making the ps command probably one of the most difficult commands to master. Most system administrators find a subset of these parameters that provide the information they want and then stick with using only those.

That said, however, the basic ps command doesn't provide all that much information:

```
$ ps
   PID TTY          TIME CMD
  3081 pts/0    00:00:00 bash
  3209 pts/0    00:00:00 ps
$
```

Not too exciting. By default the ps command shows only the processes that belong to the current user and that are running on the current terminal. In this case, we only had our Bash shell running (remember, the shell is just another program running on the system) and, of course, the ps command itself.

The basic output shows the process ID (PID) of the programs, the terminal (TTY) that they are running from, and the CPU time the process has used.

The GNU ps command that's used in Linux systems supports three different types of command-line parameters:

- Unix-style parameters, which are preceded by a dash
- BSD-style parameters, which are not preceded by a dash
- GNU long parameters, which are preceded by a double dash

The following sections examine the three different parameter types and show examples of how they work.

### Unix-style parameters

The Unix-style parameters originated with the original ps command that ran on the AT&T Unix systems invented by Bell Labs. These parameters are shown in Table 4-1.

**TABLE 4-1  The ps Command Unix Parameters**

| Parameter | Description |
|---|---|
| -A | Show all processes. |
| -N | Show the opposite of the specified parameters. |
| -a | Show all processes except session headers and processes without a terminal. |
| -d | Show all processes except session headers. |
| -e | Show all processes. |
| -C *cmslist* | Show processes contained in the list *cmdlist*. |
| -G *grplist* | Show processes with a group ID listed in *grplist*. |
| -U *userlist* | Show processes owned by a user ID listed in *userlist*. |
| -g *grplist* | Show processes by session or by group ID contained in *grplist*. |
| -p *pidlist* | Show processes with PIDs in the list *pidlist*. |
| -s *sesslist* | Show processes with a session ID in the list *sesslist*. |
| -t *ttylist* | Show processes with a terminal ID in the list *ttylist*. |
| -u *userlist* | Show processes by an effective user ID in the list *userlist*. |
| -F | Use extra full output. |
| -O *format* | Display specific columns in the list *format*, along with the default columns. |
| -M | Display security information about the process. |
| -c | Show additional scheduler information about the process. |
| -f | Display a full format listing. |
| -j | Show job information. |
| -l | Display a long listing. |
| -o *format* | Display only specific columns listed in *format*. |
| -y | Don't show process flags. |
| -Z | Display the security context information. |
| -H | Display processes in a hierarchical format (showing parent processes). |
| -n *namelist* | Define the values to display in the WCHAN output column. |
| -w | Use wide output format, for unlimited width displays. |
| -L | Show process threads. |
| -V | Display the version of ps. |

4

That's a lot of parameters, and remember, there are still more! The key to using the ps command is not to memorize all the available parameters but only those you find most useful. Most Linux system administrators have their own sets of commonly used parameters that they remember for extracting pertinent information. For example, if you need to see everything running on the system, use the -ef parameter combination (the ps command lets you combine parameters like this):

```
$ ps -ef
UID          PID    PPID  C STIME TTY          TIME CMD
root           1       0  0 12:14 ?        00:00:02 /sbin/init splash
root           2       0  0 12:14 ?        00:00:00 [kthreadd]
root           3       2  0 12:14 ?        00:00:00 [rcu_gp]
root           4       2  0 12:14 ?        00:00:00 [rcu_par_gp]
root           5       2  0 12:14 ?        00:00:00
[kworker/0:0-events]
root           6       2  0 12:14 ?        00:00:00
[kworker/0:0H-kblockd]
root           7       2  0 12:14 ?        00:00:00
[kworker/0:1-events]
...
rich        2209    1438  0 12:17 ?        00:00:01 /usr/libexec/
gnome-terminal-
rich        2221    2209  0 12:17 pts/0    00:00:00 bash
rich        2325    2221  0 12:20 pts/0    00:00:00 ps -ef
$
```

Quite a few lines have been cut from the output to save space, but as you can see, lots of processes run on a Linux system. This example uses two parameters: the -e parameter, which shows all of the processes running on the system, and the -f parameter, which expands the output to show a few useful columns of information:

- **UID:** The user responsible for launching the process
- **PID:** The process ID of the process
- **PPID:** The PID of the parent process (if a process is started by another process)
- **C:** Processor utilization over the lifetime of the process
- **STIME:** The system time when the process started
- **TTY:** The terminal device from which the process was launched
- **TIME:** The cumulative CPU time required to run the process
- **CMD:** The name of the program that was started

This produces a reasonable amount of information, which is what many system administrators would like to see. For even more information, you can use the -l parameter, which produces the long format output:

```
$ ps -l
F S   UID PID  PPID  C PRI  NI ADDR SZ WCHAN    TTY          TIME CMD
0 S   500 3081 3080  0  80   0 -  1173 do_wai pts/0    00:00:00
bash
```

```
0 R  500 4463 3081 1 80  0 - 1116 -     pts/0  00:00:00  ps
$
```

Notice the extra columns that appear when you use the -1 parameter:

- **F:** System flags assigned to the process by the kernel
- **S:** The state of the process (O = running on processor; S = sleeping; R = runnable, waiting to run; Z = zombie, process terminated but parent not available; T = process stopped)
- **PRI:** The priority of the process (higher numbers mean lower priority)
- **NI:** The nice value, used for determining priorities
- **ADDR:** The memory address of the process
- **SZ:** Approximate amount of swap space required if the process was swapped out
- **WCHAN:** Address of the kernel function where the process is sleeping

### BSD-style parameters

Now that you've seen the Unix parameters, let's take a look at the BSD-style parameters. The Berkeley Software Distribution (BSD) was a version of Unix developed at (of course) the University of California, Berkeley. It had many subtle differences from the AT&T Unix system, thus sparking many Unix wars over the years. The BSD version of the ps command parameters are shown in Table 4-2.

**TABLE 4-2   The ps Command BSD Parameters**

| Parameter | Description |
| --- | --- |
| T | Show all processes associated with this terminal. |
| a | Show all processes associated with any terminal. |
| g | Show all processes, including session headers. |
| r | Show only running processes. |
| x | Show all processes, even those without a terminal device assigned. |
| U *userlist* | Show processes owned by a user ID listed in *userlist*. |
| p *pidlist* | Show processes with a PID listed in *pidlist*. |
| t *ttylist* | Show processes associated with a terminal listed in *ttylist*. |
| O *format* | List specific columns in *format* to display along with the standard columns. |
| X | Display data in the register format. |
| Z | Include security information in the output. |
| j | Show job information. |
| l | Use the long format. |
| o *format* | Display only columns specified in *format*. |
| s | Use the signal format. |

*Continues*

4

89

**TABLE 4.2** *(continued)*

| Parameter | Description |
|---|---|
| u | Use the user-oriented format. |
| v | Use the virtual memory format. |
| N *namelist* | Define the values to use in the WCHAN column. |
| O *order* | Define the order in which to display the information columns. |
| S | Sum numerical information, such as CPU and memory usage, for child processes into the parent process. |
| c | Display the true command name (the name of the program used to start the process). |
| e | Display any environment variables used by the command. |
| f | Display processes in a hierarchical format, showing which processes started which processes. |
| h | Don't display the header information. |
| k *sort* | Define the column(s) to use for sorting the output. |
| n | Use numeric values for user and group IDs, along with WCHAN information. |
| w | Produce wide output for wider terminals. |
| H | Display threads as if they were processes. |
| m | Display threads after their processes. |
| L | List all format specifiers. |
| V | Display the version of ps. |

As you can see, a lot of overlap exists between the Unix and BSD types of parameters. Most of the information you can get from one you can also get from the other. Most of the time, you choose a parameter type based on which format you're more comfortable with (for example, if you were used to a BSD environment before using Linux).

When you use the BSD-style parameters, the ps command automatically changes the output to simulate the BSD format. Here's an example using the l parameter:

```
$ ps l
$ ps l
F   UID     PID    PPID PRI  NI    VSZ    RSS WCHAN   STAT TTY
TIME COMMAND
4   1000    1491    1415 20    0 163992   6580 poll_s Ssl+ tty2
0:00 /usr/li
4   1000    1496    1491 20    0 225176  58712 ep_pol S1+  tty2
0:05 /usr/li
0   1000    1538    1491 20    0 192844  15768 poll_s S1+  tty2
0:00 /usr/li
```

```
0  1000    2221    2209  20   0  10608  4740 do_wai Ss
pts/0       0:00 bash
0  1000    2410    2221  20   0  11396  1156 -      R+
pts/0       0:00 ps l
$
```

Notice that while many of the output columns are the same as when we used the Unix-style parameters, there are a few different ones:

- **VSZ:** The size in kilobytes of the process in memory
- **RSS:** The physical memory that a process has used that isn't swapped out
- **STAT:** A multicharacter state code representing the current process state

Many system administrators like the BSD-style l parameter because it produces a more detailed state code for processes (the STAT column). The multicharacter code defines exactly what's happening with the process more precisely than the single-character Unix-style output.

The first character uses the same values as the Unix-style S output column, showing when a process is sleeping, running, or waiting. The following characters further define the process's status:

- **<:** The process is running at high priority.
- **N:** The process is running at low priority.
- **L:** The process has pages locked in memory.
- **s:** The process is a session leader.
- **l:** The process is multithreaded.
- **+:** The process is running in the foreground.

From the simple example shown previously, you can see that the bash command is sleeping, but it is a session leader (it's the main process in my session), whereas the ps command is running in the foreground on the system.

### The GNU long parameters

Finally, the GNU developers put their own touches on the new, improved ps command by adding a few more options to the parameter mix. Some of the GNU long parameters copy existing Unix- or BSD-style parameters, whereas others provide new features. Table 4-3 lists the available GNU long parameters.

4

**TABLE 4-3** **The ps Command GNU Parameters**

| Parameter | Description |
| --- | --- |
| --deselect | Show all processes except those listed in the command line. |
| --Group grplist | Show processes whose group ID is listed in grplist. |
| --User userlist | Show processes whose user ID is listed in userlist. |
| --group grplist | Show processes whose effective group ID is listed in grplist. |
| --pid pidlist | Show processes whose process ID is listed in pidlist. |
| --ppid pidlist | Show processes whose parent process ID is listed in pidlist. |
| --sid sidlist | Show processes whose session ID is listed in sidlist. |
| --tty ttylist | Show processes whose terminal device ID is listed in ttylist. |
| --user userlist | Show processes whose effective user ID is listed in userlist. |
| --format format | Display only columns specified in the format. |
| --context | Display additional security information. |
| --cols n | Set screen width to n columns. |
| --columns n | Set screen width to n columns. |
| --cumulative | Include stopped child process information. |
| --forest | Display processes in a hierarchical listing showing parent processes. |
| --headers | Repeat column headers on each page of output. |
| --no-headers | Don't display column headers. |
| --lines n | Set the screen height to n lines. |
| --rows n | Set the screen height to n rows. |
| --sort order | Define the column(s) to use for sorting the output. |
| --width n | Set the screen width to n columns. |
| --help | Display the help information. |
| --info | Display debugging information. |
| --version | Display the version of the ps program. |

You can combine GNU long parameters with either Unix- or BSD-style parameters to customize your display. One cool feature of GNU long parameters that we really like is the --forest parameter. It displays the hierarchical process information but uses ASCII characters to draw cute charts:

```
    1981 ?          00:00:00 sshd
    3078 ?          00:00:00  \_ sshd
    3080 ?          00:00:00      \_ sshd
    3081 pts/0      00:00:00          \_ bash
   16676 pts/0      00:00:00              \_ ps
```

This format makes tracing child and parent processes a snap!

## Real-time process monitoring

The ps command is great for gleaning information about processes running on the system, but it has one drawback. The ps command can display information for only a specific point in time. If you're trying to find trends about processes that are frequently swapped in and out of memory, it's hard to do that with the ps command.

Instead, the top command can solve this problem. The top command displays process information similarly to the ps command, but it does so in real-time mode. Figure 4-1 is a snapshot of the top command in action.

**FIGURE 4-1**

The output of the top command while it is running

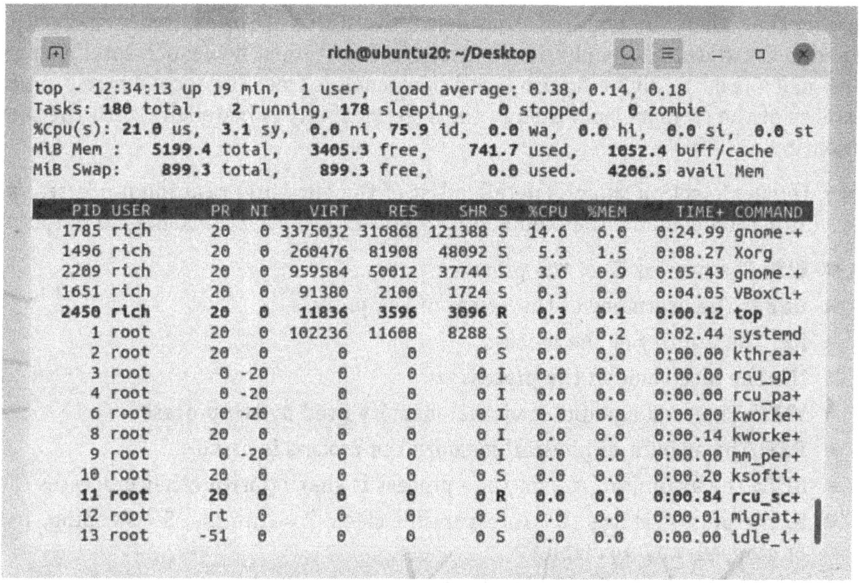

The first section of the output shows general system information. The first line shows the current time, how long the system has been up, the number of users logged in, and the load average on the system.

The load average appears as three numbers, the 1-minute, 5-minute, and 15-minute load averages. The higher the values, the more load the system is experiencing. It's not uncommon for the 1-minute load value to be high for short bursts of activity. If the 15-minute load value is high, your system may be in trouble.

4

The second line shows general process information (called *tasks* in top): how many processes are running, sleeping, stopped, and zombie (have finished but their parent process hasn't responded).

The next line shows general CPU information. The top display breaks down the CPU utilization into several categories depending on the owner of the process (user versus system processes) and the state of the processes (running, idle, or waiting).

Following that, there are two lines that detail the status of the system memory. The first line shows the status of the physical memory in the system, how much total memory there is, how much is currently being used, and how much is free. The second memory line shows the status of the swap memory area in the system (if any is installed), with the same information.

Finally, the next section shows a detailed list of the currently running processes, with some information columns that should look familiar from the ps command output:

- **PID:** The process ID of the process
- **USER:** The username of the owner of the process
- **PR:** The priority of the process
- **NI:** The nice value of the process
- **VIRT:** The total amount of virtual memory used by the process
- **RES:** The amount of physical memory the process is using
- **SHR:** The amount of memory the process is sharing with other processes
- **S:** The process status (D = interruptible sleep, R = running, S = sleeping, T = traced or stopped, or Z = zombie)
- **%CPU:** The share of CPU time that the process is using
- **%MEM:** The share of available physical memory the process is using
- **TIME+:** The total CPU time the process has used since starting
- **COMMAND:** The command-line name of the process (program started)

By default, when you start top it sorts the processes based on the %CPU value. You can change the sort order by using one of several interactive commands while top is running. Each interactive command is a single character you can press while top is running that changes the behavior of the program. Pressing F allows you to select the field to use to sort the output, and pressing d allows you to change the polling interval. Press q to exit the top display. You have lots of control over the output of the top command. Using this tool, you can often find offending processes that have taken over your system. Of course, once you find one, the next job is to stop it, which brings us to the next topic.

## Stopping processes

A crucial part of being a system administrator is knowing when and how to stop a process. Sometimes a process gets hung up and just needs a gentle nudge to either get going again or stop. Other times, a process runs away with the CPU and refuses to give it up. In both cases, you need a command that will allow you to control a process. Linux follows the Unix method of interprocess communication.

In Linux, processes communicate with each other using *signals*. A process signal is a predefined message that processes recognize and may choose to ignore or act on. The developers program how a process handles signals. Most well-written applications have the ability to receive and act on the standard Unix process signals. These signals are shown in Table 4-4.

**TABLE 4-4   Linux Process Signals**

| Signal | Name | Description |
| --- | --- | --- |
| 1 | HUP | Hang up. |
| 2 | INT | Interrupt. |
| 3 | QUIT | Stop running. |
| 9 | KILL | Unconditionally terminate. |
| 11 | SEGV | Segment violation. |
| 15 | TERM | Terminate if possible. |
| 17 | STOP | Stop unconditionally but don't terminate. |
| 18 | TSTP | Stop or pause but continue to run in background. |
| 19 | CONT | Resume execution after STOP or TSTP. |

A few different commands are available in Linux that allow you to send process signals to running processes. This section discusses the two most common ones: kill and pkill.

### The kill command

The kill command allows you to send signals to processes based on their PIDs. By default, the kill command sends a TERM signal to all the PIDs listed on the command line. Unfortunately, you can use only the process PID instead of its command name, making the kill command difficult to use sometimes.

4

To send a process signal, you must either be the owner of the process or be logged in as the root user:

```
$ kill 3940
-bash: kill: (3940) - Operation not permitted
$
```

The TERM signal tells the process to stop running. Unfortunately, if you have a runaway process, most likely it will ignore the request. When you need to get forceful, the -s parameter allows you to specify other signals (using either their name or their signal number).

As you can see from the following example, no output is associated with the kill command:

```
# kill -s HUP 3940
#
```

To see if the command was effective, you'll have to perform another ps or top command to see if the offending process stopped.

### The pkill command

The pkill command is a powerful way to stop processes by using their names rather than the PID numbers. The pkill command allows you to use wildcard characters as well, making it a very useful tool when you've got a system that's gone awry:

```
# pkill http*
#
```

This example will kill all the processes that start with http, such as the httpd services for the Apache Web Server.

> **CAUTION**
>
> Be extremely careful using the pkill command when logged in as the root user. It's easy to get carried away with wildcard characters and accidentally stop important system processes. This could lead to a damaged filesystem.

# Monitoring Disk Space

Another important task of the system administrator is to keep track of the disk usage on the system. Whether you're running a simple Linux desktop or a large Linux server, you'll need to know how much space you have for your applications.

A few command-line commands are available that can help you manage the media environment on your Linux system. This section describes the core commands you'll likely run into during your system administration duties.

## Mounting media

As discussed in Chapter 3, the Linux filesystem combines all media disks into a single virtual directory. Before you can use a new media disk on your system, you need to place it in the virtual directory. This task is called *mounting*.

In today's graphical desktop world, most Linux distributions have the ability to automatically mount specific types of *removable media*. A removable media device is a medium that (obviously) can be easily removed from the PC, such as DVDs and USB memory sticks.

If you're not using a distribution that automatically mounts and unmounts removable media, you'll have to do it yourself. This section describes the Linux command-line commands that help you manage your removable media devices.

### The *mount* command

Oddly enough, the command used to mount media is called mount. By default, the mount command displays a list of media devices currently mounted on the system. However, the newer version of the kernel mounts lots of virtual filesystems for management purposes, besides your standard storage devices. This can make the default output of the mount command very cluttered and confusing. If you know the filesystem type used for your drive partitions, you can filter that out using

```
$ mount -t ext4
/dev/sda5 on / type ext4 (rw,relatime,errors=remount-ro)
$ mount -t vfat
/dev/sda2 on /boot/efi type vfat
(rw,relatime,fmask=0077,dmask=0077,codepage=437,iocharset=iso88591,
shortname=mixed,errors=remount-ro)
/dev/sdb1 on /media/rich/54A1-7D7D type vfat
(rw,nosuid,nodev,relatime,uid=1000,gid=1000,fmask=0022,dmask=0022,
codepage=437,
iocharset=iso8859-1,shortname=mixed,showexec,utf8,flush,
errors=remountro,uhelper=udisks2)
$
```

The mount command provides four pieces of information:

- The device filename of the media
- The mount point in the virtual directory where the media is mounted
- The filesystem type
- The access status of the mounted media

The last entry in the preceding example is a USB memory stick that the GNOME desktop automatically mounted at the /media/rich/54A1-7D7D mount point. The vfat filesystem type shows that it was formatted for a Microsoft Windows PC.

4

To manually mount a media device in the virtual directory, you'll need to be logged in as the root user, or use the `sudo` command to run the command as the root user. The following is the basic command for manually mounting a media device:

```
mount -t type device directory
```

The `type` parameter defines the filesystem type the disk was formatted under. Linux recognizes numerous filesystem types. If you share removable media devices with your Windows PCs, the types you're most likely to run into are:

- **vfat:** Windows FAT32 filesystem with support for long filenames
- **ntfs:** Windows advanced filesystem used in Windows NT and later operating systems
- **exfat:** Windows filesystem optimized for removable media
- **iso9660:** The standard CD-ROM and DVD filesystem

Most USB memory sticks are formatted using the vfat filesystem. If you need to mount a data CD or DVD, you'll have to use the iso9660 filesystem type.

The next two parameters define the location of the device file for the media device and the location in the virtual directory for the mount point. For example, to manually mount the USB memory stick at device /dev/sdb1 at location /media/disk, you'd use the following command:

```
mount -t vfat /dev/sdb1 /media/disk
```

Once a media device is mounted in the virtual directory, the root user will have full access to the device, but access by other users will be restricted. You can control who has access to the device using directory permissions (discussed in Chapter 7, "Understanding Linux File Permissions").

In case you need to use some of the more exotic features of the `mount` command, the available parameters are shown in Table 4-5.

**TABLE 4-5** The `mount` **Command Parameters**

| Parameter | Description |
| --- | --- |
| -a | Mount all filesystems specified in the /etc/fstab file. |
| -f | Causes the mount command to simulate mounting a device but not actually mount it. |
| -F | When used with the -a parameter, mounts all filesystems at the same time. |
| -v | Verbose mode; explains all the steps required to mount the device. |
| -i | Don't use any filesystem helper files under /sbin/mount.filesystem. |
| -l | Add the filesystem labels automatically for ext2, ext3, ext4, or XFS filesystems. |
| -n | Mount the device without registering it in the /etc/mtab mounted device file. |
| -p num | For encrypted mounting, read the passphrase from the file descriptor num. |
| -s | Ignore mount options not supported by the filesystem. |

| Parameter | Description |
|---|---|
| -r | Mount the device as read-only. |
| -w | Mount the device as read-write (the default). |
| -L label | Mount the device with the specified label. |
| -U uuid | Mount the device with the specified uuid. |
| -o | When used with the -a parameter, limits the set of filesystems applied. |
| -o | Add specific options to the filesystem. |

The -o option allows you to mount the filesystem with a comma-separated list of additional options. The popular options to use are as follows:

- ro: Mount as read-only.
- rw: Mount as read-write.
- user: Allow an ordinary user to mount the filesystem.
- check=none: Mount the filesystem without performing an integrity check.
- loop: Mount a file.

### The *umount* command

To remove a removable media device, you should never just remove it from the system. Instead, you should always *unmount* it first.

**TIP**

Linux doesn't allow you to eject a mounted CD or DVD. If you ever have trouble removing a CD or DVD from the drive, most likely it means it is still mounted in the virtual directory. Unmount it first, and then try to eject it.

The command used to unmount devices is umount (yes, there's no "n" in the command, which gets confusing sometimes). The format for the umount command is pretty simple:

```
umount [directory | device ]
```

The umount command gives you the choice of defining the media device by either its device location or its mounted directory name. If any program has a file open on a device, the system won't let you unmount it.

```
# umount /home/rich/mnt
umount: /home/rich/mnt: device is busy
umount: /home/rich/mnt: device is busy
# cd /home/rich
# umount /home/rich/mnt
# ls -l mnt
total 0
#
```

4

In this example, the command prompt was still in a directory within the filesystem structure, so the umount command couldn't unmount the image file. Once the command prompt was moved out of the image file filesystem, the umount command was able to successfully unmount the image file.

## Using the *df* command

Sometimes you need to see how much disk space is available on an individual device. The df command allows you to easily see what's happening on all the mounted disks:

```
$ df -t ext4 -t vfat
Filesystem       1K-blocks       Used Available Use% Mounted on
/dev/sda5        19475088     7326256 11136508  40% /
/dev/sda2          524272           4   524268   1% /boot/efi
/dev/sdb1          983552      247264   736288  26% /media/
rich/54A1-7D7D
$
```

The df command shows each mounted filesystem that contains data. Similar to the mount command, the df command shows any of the virtual filesystems mounted by the kernel, so we've filtered those out from the listing by specifying the filesystem type using the -t options. The command displays the following:

- The device location of the device
- How many 1024-byte blocks of data it can hold
- How many 1024-byte blocks are used
- How many 1024-byte blocks are available
- The amount of used space as a percentage
- The mount point where the device is mounted

A few different command-line parameters are available with the df command, most of which you'll never use. One popular parameter is -h, which shows the disk space in human-readable form, usually as an M for megabytes or a G for gigabytes:

```
$ df -h
Filesystem          Size  Used Avail Use% Mounted on
/dev/sda5           19G   7.0G   11G  40% /
/dev/sda2           512M  4.0K  512M   1% /boot/efi
/dev/sdb1           961M  242M  720M  26% /media/rich/54A1-7D7D
$
```

Now instead of having to decode those ugly block numbers, all of the disk sizes are shown using "normal" sizes. The df command is invaluable in troubleshooting disk space problems on the system.

> **NOTE**
>
> Remember that the Linux system always has processes that handle files running in the background. The values from the df command reflect what the Linux system thinks are the current values at that point in time. It's possible that you have a process running that has created or deleted a file but has not released the file yet. This value is not included in the free space calculation.

## Using the *du* command

With the df command, it is easy to see when a disk is running out of space. The next problem for the system administrator is to know what to do when that happens.

Another useful command to help you out is the du command. The du command shows the disk usage for a specific directory (by default, the current directory). This is a quick way to determine if you have any obvious disk hogs on the system.

By default, the du command displays all the files, directories, and subdirectories under the current directory, and it shows how many disk blocks each file or directory takes. For a standard-sized directory, this can be quite a listing. Here's a partial listing of using the du command:

```
$ du
484      ./.gstreamer-0.10
8        ./Templates
8        ./Download
8        ./.ccache/7/0
24       ./.ccache/7
368      ./.ccache/a/d
384      ./.ccache/a
424      ./.ccache
8        ./Public
8        ./.gphpedit/plugins
32       ./.gphpedit
72       ./.gconfd
128      ./.nautilus/metafiles
384      ./.nautilus
8        ./Videos
8        ./Music
16       ./.config/gtk-2.0
40       ./.config
8        ./Documents
```

The number at the left of each line is the number of disk blocks that each file or directory takes. Notice that the listing starts at the bottom of a directory and works its way up through the files and subdirectories contained within the directory.

4

The du command by itself can be somewhat useless. It's nice to be able to see how much disk space each individual file and directory takes up, but it can be meaningless when you have to wade through pages and pages of information before you find what you're looking for.

You can use the following command-line parameters with the du command to make things a little more legible:

- -c: Produce a grand total of all the files listed.
- -h: Print sizes in human-readable form, using K for kilobyte, M for megabyte, and G for gigabyte.
- -s: Summarize each argument.

The next step for the system administrator is to use some file-handling commands for manipulating large amounts of data. That's exactly what the next section covers.

# Working with Data Files

When you have a large amount of data, it's often difficult to handle the information and make it useful. As you saw with the du command in the previous section, it's easy to get data overload when working with system commands.

The Linux system provides several command-line tools to help you manage large amounts of data. This section covers the basic commands that every system administrator — as well as any everyday Linux user — should know to make their lives easier.

## Sorting data

One popular function that comes in handy when working with large amounts of data is the sort command. The sort command does what it says — it sorts data.

By default, the sort command sorts the data lines in a text file using standard sorting rules for the language you specify as the default for the session:

```
$ cat file1
one
two
three
four
five
$ sort file1
five
four
one
three
two
$
```

Pretty simple. However, things aren't always as easy as they appear. Take a look at this example:

```
$ cat file2
1
2
100
45
3
10
145
75
$ sort file2
1
10
100
145
2
3
45
75
$
```

If you were expecting the numbers to sort in numerical order, you were disappointed. By default, the sort command interprets numbers as characters and performs a standard character sort, producing output that might not be what you want. To solve this problem, use the -n parameter, which tells the sort command to recognize numbers as numbers instead of characters and to sort them based on their numerical values:

```
$ sort -n file2
1
2
3
10
45
75
100
145
$
```

Now, that's much better! Another parameter that's commonly used is -M, the month sort. Linux log files usually contain a time stamp at the beginning of the line to indicate when the event occurred:

```
Apr 13 07:10:09 testbox smartd[2718]: Device: /dev/sda, opened
```

If you sort a file that uses time stamp dates using the default sort, you'll get something like this:

```
$ sort file3
Apr
```

```
Aug
Dec
Feb
Jan
Jul
Jun
Mar
May
Nov
Oct
Sep
$
```

Not exactly what you wanted. If you use the -M parameter, the sort command recognizes the three-character-month nomenclature and sorts appropriately:

```
$ sort -M file3
Jan
Feb
Mar
Apr
May
Jun
Jul
Aug
Sep
Oct
Nov
Dec
$
```

Table 4-6 shows other handy sort parameters you can use.

**TABLE 4-6  The sort Command Parameters**

| Single Dash | Double Dash | Description |
| --- | --- | --- |
| -b | --ignore-leading-blanks | Ignore leading blanks when sorting. |
| -C | --check=quiet | Don't sort, but don't report if data is out of sort order. |
| -c | --check | Don't sort, but check if the input data is already sorted. Report if not sorted. |
| -d | --dictionary-order | Consider only blanks and alphanumeric characters; don't consider special characters. |
| -f | --ignore-case | By default, sort orders capitalized letters first. This parameter ignores case. |
| -g | --general-numeric-sort | Use general numerical value to sort. |

| Single Dash | Double Dash | Description |
|---|---|---|
| -i | --ignore-nonprinting | Ignore nonprintable characters in the sort. |
| -k | --key=POS1[,POS2] | Sort based on position POS1 and end at POS2 if specified. |
| -M | --month-sort | Sort by month order using three-character month names. |
| -m | --merge | Merge two already sorted data files. |
| -n | --numeric-sort | Sort by string numerical value. |
| -o | --output=file | Write results to file specified. |
| -R | --random-sort | Sort by a random hash of keys. |
|  | --random-source=FILE | Specify the file for random bytes used by the -R parameter. |
| -r | --reverse | Reverse the sort order (descending instead of ascending). |
| -S | --buffer-size=SIZE | Specify the amount of memory to use. |
| -s | --stable | Disable last-resort comparison. |
| -T | --temporary-direction=DIR | Specify a location to store temporary working files. |
| -t | --field-separator=SEP | Specify the character used to distinguish key positions. |
| -u | --unique | With the -c parameter, check for strict ordering; without the -c parameter, output only the first occurrence of two similar lines. |
| -z | --zero-terminated | End all lines with a NULL character instead of a new line. |

The -k and -t parameters are handy when sorting data that uses fields, such as the /etc/passwd file. Use the -t parameter to specify the field separator character, and use the -k parameter to specify which field to sort on. For example, to sort the password file based on numerical user ID, just do this:

```
$ sort -t ':' -k 3 -n /etc/passwd
root:x:0:0:root:/root:/bin/bash
bin:x:1:1:bin:/bin:/sbin/nologin
daemon:x:2:2:daemon:/sbin:/sbin/nologin
adm:x:3:4:adm:/var/adm:/sbin/nologin
lp:x:4:7:lp:/var/spool/lpd:/sbin/nologin
sync:x:5:0:sync:/sbin:/bin/sync
shutdown:x:6:0:shutdown:/sbin:/sbin/shutdown
halt:x:7:0:halt:/sbin:/sbin/halt
mail:x:8:12:mail:/var/spool/mail:/sbin/nologin
```

4

```
news:x:9:13:news:/etc/news:
uucp:x:10:14:uucp:/var/spool/uucp:/sbin/nologin
operator:x:11:0:operator:/root:/sbin/nologin
games:x:12:100:games:/usr/games:/sbin/nologin
gopher:x:13:30:gopher:/var/gopher:/sbin/nologin
ftp:x:14:50:FTP User:/var/ftp:/sbin/nologin
```

Now the data is perfectly sorted based on the third field, which is the numerical user ID value.

The -n parameter is great for sorting numerical outputs, such as the output of the du command:

```
$ du -sh * | sort -nr
1008k   mrtg-2.9.29.tar.gz
972k    bldg1
888k    fbs2.pdf
760k    Printtest
680k    rsync-2.6.6.tar.gz
660k    code
516k    fig1001.tiff
496k    test
496k    php-common-4.0.4pl1-6mdk.i586.rpm
448k    MesaGLUT-6.5.1.tar.gz
400k    plp
```

Notice that the -r option also sorts the values in descending order so that you can easily see what files are taking up the most space in your directory.

> **NOTE**
>
> The pipe command (|) used in this example redirects the output of the du command to the sort command. That's discussed in more detail in Chapter 11, "Basic Script Building."

## Searching for data

Often in a large file, you have to look for a specific line of data buried somewhere in the middle of the file. Instead of manually scrolling through the entire file, you can let the grep command search for you. The command-line format for the grep command is

```
grep [options] pattern [file]
```

The grep command searches either the input or the file you specify for lines that contain characters that match the specified pattern. The output from grep is the lines that contain the matching pattern.

Here are two simple examples of using the grep command with the file1 file used in the "Sorting Data" section:

```
$ grep three file1
three
```

```
$ grep t file1
two
three
$
```

The first example searches the file `file1` for text matching the pattern *three*. The grep command produces the line that contains the matching pattern. The next example searches the file `file1` for the text matching the pattern *t*. In this case, two lines matched the specified pattern, and both are displayed.

Because of the popularity of the grep command, it has undergone lots of development changes over its lifetime. Many features have been added to the grep command. If you look over the man pages for the grep command, you'll see how versatile it is.

If you want to reverse the search (output lines that don't match the pattern), use the -v parameter:

```
$ grep -v t file1
one
four
five
$
```

If you need to find the line numbers where the matching patterns are found, use the -n parameter:

```
$ grep -n t file1
2:two
3:three
$
```

If you just need to see a count of how many lines contain the matching pattern, use the -c parameter:

```
$ grep -c t file1
2
$
```

If you need to specify more than one matching pattern, use the -e parameter to specify each individual pattern:

```
$ grep -e t -e f file1
two
three
four
five
$
```

This example outputs lines that contain either the string t or the string f.

By default, the grep command uses basic Unix-style regular expressions to match patterns. A Unix-style regular expression uses special characters to define how to look for matching

4

patterns. For a more detailed explanation of regular expressions, see Chapter 20, "Regular Expressions."

Here's a simple example of using a regular expression in a grep search:

```
$ grep [tf] file1
two
three
four
five
$
```

The square brackets in the regular expression indicate that grep should look for matches that contain either a *t* or an *f* character. Without the regular expression, grep would search for text that would match the string tf.

The egrep command is an offshoot of grep, which allows you to specify POSIX extended regular expressions, which contain more characters for specifying the matching pattern (again, see Chapter 20 for more details). The fgrep command is another version that allows you to specify matching patterns as a list of fixed-string values, separated by newline characters. This allows you to place a list of strings in a file and then use that list in the fgrep command to search for the strings in a larger file.

## Compressing data

If you've done any work in the Microsoft Windows world, no doubt you've used zip files. It became such a popular feature that Microsoft eventually incorporated it into the Windows operating system starting with XP. The zip utility allows you to easily compress large files (both text and executable) into smaller files that take up less space.

Linux contains several file compression utilities. Although this may sound great, it often leads to confusion and chaos when trying to download files. Table 4-7 lists the file compression utilities available for Linux.

### TABLE 4-7  Linux File Compression Utilities

| Utility | File Extension | Description |
| --- | --- | --- |
| bzip2 | .bz2 | Uses the Burrows–Wheeler block sorting text compression algorithm and Huffman coding |
| com-press | .Z | Original Unix file compression utility; starting to fade away into obscurity |
| gzip | .gz | The GNU Project's compression utility; uses Lempel–Ziv–Welch coding |
| xz | .xz | A general-purpose compression utility gaining in popularity |
| zip | .zip | The Unix version of the PKZIP program for Windows |

The compress file compression utility is not often found on Linux systems. If you download a file with a .Z extension, you can usually install the compress package (called ncompress in many Linux distributions) using the software installation methods discussed in Chapter 9, "Installing Software," and then uncompress the file with the uncompress command. The gzip utility is the most popular compression tool used in Linux.

The gzip package is a creation of the GNU Project in their attempt to create a free version of the original Unix compress utility. This package includes these files:

- gzip for compressing files
- gzcat for displaying the contents of compressed text files
- gunzip for uncompressing files

These utilities work the same way as the bzip2 utilities:

```
$ gzip myprog
$ ls -l my*
-rwxrwxr-x 1 rich rich 2197 2007-09-13 11:29 myprog.gz
$
```

The gzip command compresses the file you specify on the command line. You can also specify more than one filename or even use wildcard characters to compress multiple files at once:

```
$ gzip my*
$ ls -l my*
-rwxr--r--    1 rich     rich          103 Sep   6 13:43 myprog.c.gz
-rwxr-xr-x    1 rich     rich         5178 Sep   6 13:43 myprog.gz
-rwxr--r--    1 rich     rich           59 Sep   6 13:46 myscript.gz
-rwxr--r--    1 rich     rich           60 Sep   6 13:44 myscript2.gz
$
```

The gzip command compresses every file in the directory that matches the wildcard pattern.

## Archiving data

Although the zip command works great for compressing and archiving data into a single file, it's not the standard utility used in the Unix and Linux worlds. By far the most popular archiving tool used in Unix and Linux is the tar command.

The tar command was originally used to write files to a tape device for archiving. However, it can also write the output to a file, which has become a popular way to archive data in Linux.

Here is the format of the tar command:

```
tar function [options] object1 object2 ...
```

The function parameter defines what the tar command should do, as shown in Table 4-8.

4

**TABLE 4-8** **The tar Command Functions**

| Function | Long Name | Description |
|---|---|---|
| -A | --concatenate | Append an existing tar archive file to another existing tar archive file. |
| -c | --create | Create a new tar archive file. |
| -d | --diff | Check the differences between a tar archive file and the filesystem. |
| | --delete | Delete from an existing tar archive file. |
| -r | --append | Append files to the end of an existing tar archive file. |
| -t | --list | List the contents of an existing tar archive file. |
| -u | --update | Append files to an existing tar archive file that are newer than a file with the same name in the existing archive. |
| -x | --extract | Extract files from an existing archive file. |

Each function uses *options* to define a specific behavior for the tar archive file. Table 4-9 lists the common options that you can use with the tar command.

**TABLE 4-9** **The tar Command Options**

| Option | Description |
|---|---|
| -C *dir* | Change to the specified directory. |
| -f *file* | Output results to file (or device) *file*. |
| -j | Redirect output to the bzip2 command for compression. |
| -J | Redirect output to the xz command for compression. |
| -p | Preserve all file permissions. |
| -v | List files as they are processed. |
| -z | Redirect the output to the gzip command for compression. |
| -Z | Redirect the output to the compress command for compression. |

These options are usually combined to create the following scenarios. First, you'll want to create an archive file using this command:

```
tar -cvf test.tar test/ test2/
```

This command creates an archive file called test.tar containing the contents of both the test directory and the test2 directory. Next, the command

```
tar -tf test.tar
```

lists (but doesn't extract) the contents of the tar file `test.tar`. Finally, the command

```
tar -xvf test.tar
```

extracts the contents of the tar file `test.tar`. If the tar file was created from a directory structure, the entire directory structure is re-created starting at the current directory.

As you can see, using the `tar` command is a simple way to create archive files of entire directory structures. This is a common method for distributing source code files for open source applications in the Linux world.

> **TIP**
>
> If you download open source software, often you'll see filenames that end in `.tgz`. These are gzipped tar files, and they can be extracted using the command `tar -zxvf` `filename.tgz`.

## Summary

This chapter discussed some of the more advanced `bash` commands used by Linux system administrators and programmers. The `ps` and `top` commands are vital in determining the status of the system, allowing you to see what applications are running and how many resources they are consuming.

In this day of removable media, another popular topic for system administrators is mounting storage devices. The `mount` command allows you to mount a physical storage device into the Linux virtual directory structure. To remove the device, you use the `umount` command.

Finally, we discussed various utilities used for handling data. The `sort` utility easily sorts large data files to help you organize data, and the `grep` utility allows you to quickly scan through large data files looking for specific information. A few file compression utilities are available in Linux, including `gzip` and `zip`. Each one allows you to compress large files to help save space on your filesystem. The Linux `tar` utility is a popular way to archive directory structures into a single file that can easily be ported to another system.

The next chapter discusses Linux environment variables. Environment variables allow you to access information about the system from your scripts, as well as provide a convenient way to store data within your scripts.

4

# Understanding the Shell

N ow that you know a few shell basics, such as reaching the shell and rudimentary commands, it's time to explore the actual shell process. To understand it, you need to know how it operates in different circumstances.

A shell is not just a CLI. It is a complicated interactive running program. Entering commands and using the shell to run scripts can raise some interesting and confusing issues. Understanding the shell process and its relationships helps you resolve these issues or avoid them altogether.

This chapter takes you through learning about the shell process and how it operates in various situations. We'll explore how subshells are created as well as the relationship to their parent shell. The different commands that create child processes are examined along with those that don't (built-in commands). We also cover some shell tips and tricks you can try to make your CLI experience more productive.

## Investigating Shell Types

The shell program that the system starts, when you log into the system, depends on your user ID configuration. In the /etc/passwd file, the user ID has its default shell program listed in field #7 of its entry. This default shell program is started when the user either logs into a virtual console terminal or starts a terminal emulator in the GUI.

In the following example, the user christine has the GNU Bash shell as their default shell program:

```
$ cat /etc/passwd
[...]
christine:x:1001:1001::/home/christine:/bin/bash
$
```

The Bash shell program (bash) typically resides in the /usr/bin directory on modern Linux systems. However, on your Linux system you may find it in the /bin directory. The which bash command can help here by providing the directory and filename to use for the Bash shell:

```
$ which bash
/usr/bin/bash
$
```

A long listing reveals that the bash file (the Bash shell) is an executable program via the trailing asterisk (*) on the file's name:

```
$ ls -1F /usr/bin/bash
-rwxr-xr-x. 1 root root 1219248 Nov  8 11:30 /usr/bin/bash*
$
```

> **NOTE**
> Typically on modern Linux systems, the /bin directory is symbolically linked to the /usr/bin/ directory, which is why the user christine has /bin/bash listed as their default shell program, but the Bash shell program actually resides in the /usr/bin/ directory. Symbolic (soft) links were covered in Chapter 3, "Basic Bash Shell Commands."

Several other shell programs are on this particular Linux system. They include tcsh, which is based on the original C shell:

```
$ which tcsh
/usr/bin/tcsh
$ ls -1F /usr/bin/tcsh
-rwxr-xr-x. 1 root root 465200 May 14  2019 /usr/bin/tcsh*
$
```

Another shell on this system is zsh, which is a more elaborate version of the Bash shell. It also has a few tcsh features as well as other elements:

```
$ which zsh
/usr/bin/zsh
$ ls -1F /usr/bin/zsh
-rwxr-xr-x. 1 root root 879872 May 11  2019 /usr/bin/zsh*
$
```

**TIP**

If you don't find some of these shells on your Linux system, you may be able to install them. Chapter 9, "Installing Software," can help you accomplish this task.

A soft link (see Chapter 3) of the C shell points to the tcsh shell:

```
$ which csh
/usr/bin/csh
$ ls -lF /usr/bin/csh
lrwxrwxrwx. 1 root root 4 May 14  2019 /usr/bin/csh -> tcsh*
$
```

On Debian-based Linux systems, such as Ubuntu, you often find dash, which is a version of the Ash shell:

```
$ which dash
/usr/bin/dash
$ ls -lF /usr/bin/dash
-rwxr-xr-x 1 root root 129816 Jul 18  2019 /usr/bin/dash*
$
```

**NOTE**

A brief description of various shells was included in Chapter 1, "Starting with Linux Shells." You may be interested in learning even more about shells other than the GNU Bash shell. Additional alternative shell information is in Chapter 23, "Working with Alternative Shells."

On most Linux systems, you'll find the various installed shells that can be used as the user's default shell within the /etc/shells file, as shown here:

```
$ cat /etc/shells
/bin/sh
/bin/bash
/usr/bin/sh
/usr/bin/bash
/bin/csh
/bin/tcsh
/usr/bin/csh
/usr/bin/tcsh
/usr/bin/zsh
/bin/zsh
$
```

5

A user can set any of these different shell programs on this system as their shell. However, due to its popularity, it is rare to use any other shell instead of Bash as an account's default interactive shell. The *default interactive shell*, also called a *login shell*, starts whenever a user logs into a virtual console terminal or starts a terminal emulator in the GUI.

Another shell, sh, is the *default system shell*. The default system shell is used for system shell scripts, such as those needed at startup.

Often, you see a distribution with its default system shell (sh) pointing to the Bash shell using a soft link. An example of this is shown here on a CentOS distribution:

```
$ which sh
/usr/bin/sh
$ ls -l /usr/bin/sh
lrwxrwxrwx. 1 root root 4 Nov  8 11:30 /usr/bin/sh -> bash
$
```

However, be aware that on some distributions, the default system shell is linked differently, such as on this Ubuntu distribution:

```
$ which sh
/usr/bin/sh
$ ls -l /usr/bin/sh
lrwxrwxrwx 1 root root 4 Mar 10 18:43 /usr/bin/sh -> dash
$
```

In this case, the default system shell, /usr/bin/sh, points to the Dash shell, instead of the Bash shell.

You are not forced to stick with your default interactive shell. You can start any shell available on your distribution simply by typing its name. However, there's no fanfare or message displayed to indicate what shell you are currently using. But help is available from the $0 variable. The command echo $0 will display the name of your current shell, providing the needed reference.

With our handy $0 variable, we'll display the shell we are currently using, start the Dash shell by typing the command **dash**, and show the new shell's name via echo $0 again:

```
$ echo $0
-bash
$
$ dash
$
$ echo $0
dash
$
```

The $ prompt is a CLI prompt for the Dash shell. You can leave the Dash shell program (and the Bash shell for that matter) by typing the command **exit**:

```
$ echo $0
dash
$ exit
$ echo $0
-bash
$
```

Jumping back and forth through the various shells seems simple, but there is more to the action happening behind the scenes. To understand this process, the next section explores the relationship between a login shell program and a newly started shell program.

# Exploring Parent and Child Shell Relationships

The default interactive shell (login shell) that starts when a user logs into a virtual console terminal or starts a terminal emulator in the GUI is a *parent shell*. As you have read so far in this book, a parent shell process provides a CLI prompt and waits for commands to be entered.

When the bash command (or other shell program name) is entered at the CLI prompt, a new shell program is created. This is a *child shell*. A child shell also has a CLI prompt and waits for commands to be entered.

5

Because you do not see any relevant messages when you type **bash** and spawn a child shell, another command can help bring clarity. The ps command was covered in Chapter 4, "More Bash Shell Commands." Using this with the -f option before and after entering a child shell is useful:

```
$ ps -f
UID         PID   PPID  C STIME TTY          TIME CMD
christi+   6160   6156  0 11:01 pts/1    00:00:00 -bash
christi+   7141   6160  0 12:51 pts/1    00:00:00 ps -f
$
$ bash
$
$ ps -f
UID         PID   PPID  C STIME TTY          TIME CMD
christi+   6160   6156  0 11:01 pts/1    00:00:00 -bash
christi+   7142   6160  0 12:52 pts/1    00:00:00 bash
christi+   7164   7142  0 12:52 pts/1    00:00:00 ps -f
$
```

The first use of ps -f shows two processes. One process has a process ID of 6160 (second column) and is running the Bash shell program (last column). The second process (process ID 7141) is the actual ps -f command running.

> **NOTE**
>
> A *process* is a running program. The Bash shell is a program, and when it runs, it is a process. A running shell is simply one type of process. Therefore, when reading about running a Bash shell, you often see the word "shell" and the word "process" used interchangeably.

In the previous example, after the command bash is entered, a child shell is created. The second ps -f is executed from within the child shell. From this display, you can see that *two* Bash shell programs are running. The first Bash shell program, the parent shell process, has the original process ID (PID) of 6160. The second Bash shell program, the child shell process, has a PID of 7142. Note that the child shell has a parent process ID (PPID) of 6160, denoting that the parent shell process is its parent. Figure 5-1 diagrams this relationship.

**FIGURE 5-1**

Parent and child Bash shell processes

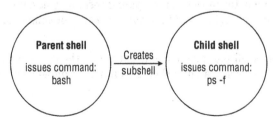

When a child shell process is spawned, only some of the parent's environment is copied to the child's shell environment. This can cause problems with items such as variables. How to prevent such problems is covered in Chapter 6, "Using Linux Environment Variables."

A child shell is also called a *subshell*. A subshell can be created from a parent shell, and a subshell can be created from another subshell:

```
$ ps -f
UID         PID   PPID  C STIME TTY          TIME CMD
christi+   7650   7649  0 16:01 pts/0     00:00:00 -bash
christi+   7686   7650  0 16:02 pts/0     00:00:00 ps -f
$
$ bash
$ bash
$ bash
$
$ ps --forest
  PID TTY          TIME CMD
 7650 pts/0     00:00:00 bash
 7687 pts/0     00:00:00  \_ bash
 7709 pts/0     00:00:00      \_ bash
 7731 pts/0     00:00:00          \_ bash
 7753 pts/0     00:00:00              \_ ps
$
```

In the preceding example, the bash command was entered three times. Effectively, this created three subshells. The ps --forest command shows the nesting of these subshells. Figure 5-2 also shows this subshell nesting.

The ps -f command can be useful in subshell nesting, because it displays who is whose parent via the PPID column:

```
$ ps -f
UID         PID   PPID  C STIME TTY          TIME CMD
christi+   7650   7649  0 16:01 pts/0     00:00:00 -bash
christi+   7687   7650  0 16:02 pts/0     00:00:00 bash
christi+   7709   7687  0 16:02 pts/0     00:00:00 bash
christi+   7731   7709  0 16:02 pts/0     00:00:00 bash
christi+   7781   7731  0 16:04 pts/0     00:00:00 ps -f
$
```

The Bash shell program can use command-line options to modify the shell's start. Table 5-1 lists a few of these available switches to use with the bash command.

**FIGURE 5-2**

Subshell nesting

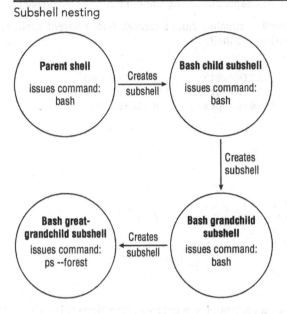

**TABLE 5-1** **The bash Command-Line Options**

| Option | Description |
| --- | --- |
| -c *string* | Reads commands from *string* and processes them |
| -i | Starts an interactive shell, allowing input from the user |
| -l | Acts as if invoked as a login shell |
| -r | Starts a restricted shell, limiting the user to the default directory |
| -s | Reads commands from the standard input |

You can find more help on the bash command and even more command-line parameters by typing **man bash**. The bash --help command provides additional assistance as well.

**TIP**

If you'd like to see the version of the Bash shell, just type bash --version at the command line. This won't create a subshell, but instead displays the current version of your system's GNU Bash shell program.

You can gracefully exit out of each subshell by entering the **exit** command:

```
$ ps -f
UID        PID  PPID  C STIME TTY         TIME CMD
```

120

```
christi+   7650   7649   0 16:01 pts/0    00:00:00 -bash
christi+   7687   7650   0 16:02 pts/0    00:00:00 bash
christi+   7709   7687   0 16:02 pts/0    00:00:00 bash
christi+   7731   7709   0 16:02 pts/0    00:00:00 bash
christi+   8080   7731   0 16:35 pts/0    00:00:00 ps -f
$
$ exit
exit
$
$ ps --forest
  PID TTY          TIME CMD
 7650 pts/0    00:00:00 bash
 7687 pts/0    00:00:00  \_ bash
 7709 pts/0    00:00:00      \_ bash
 8081 pts/0    00:00:00          \_ ps
$
$ exit
exit
$ exit
exit
$
$ ps --forest
  PID TTY          TIME CMD
 7650 pts/0    00:00:00 bash
 8082 pts/0    00:00:00  \_ ps
$
```

Not only does the `exit` command allow you to leave child subshells, but you can log out of your current virtual console terminal or terminal emulation software as well. Just type **exit** in the parent shell, and you gracefully exit the CLI.

Also, a subshell is sometimes created when you run a shell script. You learn more about that topic in Chapter 11. Next we'll cover how a subshell is spawned using a process list.

## Looking at process lists

On a single line, you can designate a list of commands to be run one after another. This is done by entering a command list using a semicolon (;) between the commands:

```
$ pwd ; ls test* ; cd /etc ; pwd ; cd ; pwd ; ls my*
/home/christine
test_file   test_one   test_two
/etc
/home/christine
my_file   my_scrapt   my_script   my_scrypt
$
```

In the preceding example, the commands all executed one after another with no problems. However, while using commands in this manner is called a list, it is not a *process*

121

*list.* For a command list to be considered a process list, the commands must be encased in parentheses:

```
$ (pwd ; ls test* ; cd /etc ; pwd ; cd ; pwd ; ls my*)
/home/christine
test_file   test_one   test_two
/etc
/home/christine
my_file  my_scrapt  my_script  my_scrypt
$
```

Though the parentheses addition may not appear to be a big difference, they do cause a very different effect. Adding parentheses and turning the command list into a process list created a subshell to execute the commands.

> **NOTE**
>
> A process list is a *command grouping* type. Another command grouping type puts the commands between curly brackets and ends the command list with a semicolon (;). The syntax is as follows: { command; }. Using curly brackets for command grouping does *not* create a subshell as a process list does.

To indicate if a subshell was spawned, a command using an environment variable is needed here. (Environment variables are covered in detail in Chapter 6). The command needed is echo $BASH_SUBSHELL. If it returns 0, then there is no subshell. If it returns 1 or more, a subshell was created.

First, the example using just a command list is executed with the echo $BASH_SUBSHELL tacked onto the end:

```
$ pwd ; ls test* ; cd /etc ; pwd ; cd ; pwd ; ls my* ; echo $BASH_SUBSHELL
/home/christine
test_file   test_one   test_two
/etc
/home/christine
my_file  my_scrapt  my_script  my_scrypt
0
$
```

At the very end of the commands' output, you can see the number zero (0) is displayed. This indicates a subshell was not created to execute these commands.

The results are different using a process list. The list is executed with echo $BASH_SUBSHELL tacked onto the end:

```
$ (pwd ; ls test* ; cd /etc ; pwd ; cd ; pwd ; ls my* ; echo $BASH_SUBSHELL)
/home/christine
test_file   test_one   test_two
```

```
/etc
/home/christine
my_file  my_scrapt  my_script  my_scrypt
1
$
```

In this case, the number one (1) displayed at the output's end. This indicates a subshell was indeed created and used for executing these commands.

Thus, a process list is a command grouping enclosed with parentheses, which creates a subshell to execute the command(s). You can even create a grandchild subshell by embedding parentheses within a process list:

```
$ (pwd ; echo $BASH_SUBSHELL)
/home/christine
1
$ (pwd ; (echo $BASH_SUBSHELL))
/home/christine
2
$
```

Notice in the first process list, the number one (1) is displayed, indicating a child subshell as you would expect. However, in the example's second process list, additional parentheses were included around the echo $BASH_SUBSHELL command. These additional parentheses caused a grandchild subshell to be created for the command's execution. Thus, a number two (2) was displayed, indicating a subshell within a subshell.

Subshells are often used for multiprocessing in shell scripts. However, entering a subshell is an expensive method. (In this situation, *expensive* means that more resources, such as memory and processing power, are consumed.) It can also significantly slow down completion of the task. Subshell issues exist also for an interactive CLI shell session, which is not truly multiprocessing, because the terminal gets tied up with the subshell's I/O.

## Creatively using subshells

At the interactive shell CLI, you have more productive ways to use subshells. Process lists, co-processes, and pipes (covered in Chapter 11) all use subshells. Each can be used effectively within the interactive shell.

One productive subshell method in the interactive shell uses background mode. Before we discuss how to use background mode and subshells together, you need to understand background mode.

### Investigating background mode

Running a command in background mode allows the command to be processed and frees up your CLI for other use. A classic command to demonstrate background mode is the sleep command.

5

**123**

The sleep command accepts as a parameter the number of seconds you want the process to wait (sleep). This command is often used to introduce pauses in shell scripts. The command sleep 10 causes the session to pause for 10 seconds and then return a shell CLI prompt:

```
$ sleep 10
$
```

To put a command into background mode, the & character is tacked onto its end. Putting the sleep command into background mode allows a little investigation with the ps command:

```
$ sleep 3000&
[1] 2542
$
$ ps -f
UID         PID  PPID  C STIME TTY          TIME CMD
christi+   2356  2352  0 13:27 pts/0    00:00:00 -bash
christi+   2542  2356  0 13:44 pts/0    00:00:00 sleep 3000
christi+   2543  2356  0 13:44 pts/0    00:00:00 ps -f
$
```

The sleep command was told to sleep for 3000 seconds (50 minutes) in the background (&). When it was put into the background, two informational items were displayed before the shell CLI prompt was returned. The first informational item is the background job's number (1) displayed in brackets. The second item is the background job's process ID (2542).

The ps command was used to display the various processes. Notice that the sleep 3000 command is listed. Also note that its PID in the second column is the same PID displayed when the command went into the background, 2542.

In addition to the ps command, you can use the jobs command to display background job information. The jobs command displays your processes (jobs) currently running in background mode:

```
$ jobs
[1]+  Running                 sleep 3000 &
$
```

The jobs command shows the job number (1) in brackets. It also displays the job's current status (Running) as well as the command itself (sleep 3000 &).

You can see even more information by using the -1 (lowercase L) parameter on the jobs command. The -1 parameter displays the command's PID in addition to the other information:

```
$ jobs -1
[1]+  2542 Running             sleep 3000 &
$
```

> **TIP**
>
> When you have more than one background process running, there is some additional helpful information to show which background job was started last. The most recently started job has a plus sign (+) next to its job number in the `jobs` command's display. And the second newest process will have a minus sign (–) to provide you with additional information.

When the background job is finished, its completion status is displayed the next time you press the Enter key at the command line:

```
$
[1]+   Done                    sleep 3000
$
```

Background mode is very handy. And it provides a method for creating useful subshells at the CLI.

### Putting process lists into the background

By placing process lists into the background, you can do large amounts of multiprocessing within a subshell. A side benefit is that your terminal is not tied up with the subshell's I/O.

As stated earlier, a process list is a command or series of commands executed within a subshell. Using a process list including `sleep` commands and displaying the BASH_SUBSHELL variable operates as you would expect:

```
$ (sleep 2 ; echo $BASH_SUBSHELL ; sleep 2)
1
$
```

In the preceding example, a two-second pause occurs, the number one (1) is displayed indicating a single subshell level (child shell), and then another two-second pause occurs before the prompt returns. Nothing too dramatic here.

Putting the same process list into background mode can cause a slightly different effect with command output:

```
$ (sleep 2 ; echo $BASH_SUBSHELL ; sleep 2)&
[1] 2553
$ 1

[1]+   Done                    ( sleep 2; echo $BASH_SUBSHELL; sleep 2 )
$
```

Putting the process list into the background causes a job number and process ID to appear, and the prompt returns. However, the odd event is that the displayed number one (1), indicating a single-level subshell, is displayed next to the prompt! Don't let this confuse you. Simply press the Enter key, and you get another prompt back.

5

Using a process list in background mode is one creative method for using subshells at the CLI. This allows you to be more productive with fewer keystrokes.

Of course, the process list of `sleep` and `echo` commands are just for example purposes. Creating backup files with `tar` (see Chapter 4) is a more practical example of using background process lists effectively:

```
$ (tar -cf Doc.tar Documents ; tar -cf Music.tar Music)&
[1] 2567
$
$ ls *.tar
Doc.tar  Music.tar
[1]+ Done                       ( tar -cf Doc.tar Documents;
 tar -cf Music.tar Music )
$
```

Putting a process list in background mode is not the only way to use subshells creatively at the CLI. Co-processing is another method.

### Looking at co-processing

Co-processing does two things at the same time. It spawns a subshell in background mode and it executes a command within that subshell.

To perform co-processing, the `coproc` command is used along with the command to be executed in the subshell:

```
$ coproc sleep 10
[1] 2689
$
```

Co-processing performs almost identically to putting a command in background mode, except for the fact that it creates a subshell. You'll notice that when the `coproc` command and its parameters were entered, a background job was started. The background job number (1) and process ID (2689) were displayed on the screen.

The `jobs` command allows you to display the co-processing status:

```
$ jobs
[1]+ Running                    coproc COPROC sleep 10 &
$
```

From the preceding example, you can see that the background command executing in the subshell is `coproc COPROC sleep 10`. COPROC is a name given to the process by the `coproc` command. You can set the name yourself by using extended syntax for the command:

```
$ coproc My_Job { sleep 10; }
[1] 2706
$
```

```
$ jobs
[1]+  Running                 coproc My_Job { sleep 10; } &
$
```

By using the extended syntax, the co-processing name was set to My_Job. Be careful here, because the extended syntax is a little tricky. Make sure you place a space after the first curly bracket ({) and before the start of your command. Also, the command must end with a semicolon (;). And you must put a space after the semicolon and before the closing curly bracket (}).

> **NOTE**
> Co-processing allows you to get very fancy and send/receive information to the process running in the subshell. The only time you need to name a co-process is when you have multiple co-processes running and you need to communicate with them all. Otherwise, just let the coproc command set the name to the default, COPROC.

You can be really clever and combine co-processing with process lists, creating nested subshells. Just type your process list and put the command coproc in front of it:

```
$ coproc ( sleep 10; sleep 2 )
[1] 2750
$
$ jobs
[1]+  Running                 coproc COPROC ( sleep 10; sleep 2 ) &
$
$ ps --forest
  PID TTY          TIME CMD
 2367 pts/0    00:00:00 bash
 2750 pts/0    00:00:00  \_ bash
 2751 pts/0    00:00:00  |   \_ sleep
 2752 pts/0    00:00:00  \_ ps
$
```

Just remember that spawning a subshell can be expensive and slow. Creating nested subshells is even more so!

Using subshells can provide flexibility as well as convenience. Understanding their behavior is important in order to reach these goals. Command actions are also important to understand. In the next section, the behavior differences between built-in and external commands are explored.

# Understanding External and Built-In Commands

While learning about the GNU Bash shell, you likely have heard the term *built-in command*. It is important to understand both shell built-in and non–built-in (external) commands. Built-in commands and non–built-in commands operate very differently.

5

## Looking at external commands

An *external command*, sometimes called a filesystem command, is a program that exists outside of the Bash shell. In other words, it is not built into the shell program. An external command program is typically located in /bin, /usr/bin, /sbin, or /usr/sbin directories.

The ps command is an external command. You can find its filename by using both the which and the type commands:

```
$ which ps
/usr/bin/ps
$
$ type ps
ps is /usr/bin/ps
$
$ ls -l /usr/bin/ps
-rwxr-xr-x. 1 root root 142216 May 11  2019 /usr/bin/ps
$
```

Whenever an external command is executed, a child process is created. This action is termed *forking*. Conveniently, the external command ps displays its current parent as well as its own forked child processes:

```
$ ps -f
UID         PID  PPID  C STIME TTY          TIME CMD
christi+   2367  2363  0 10:47 pts/0    00:00:00 -bash
christi+   4242  2367  0 13:48 pts/0    00:00:00 ps -f
$
```

Because it is an external command, when the ps command executes, a child process is created. In this case, the ps command's PID is 4242 and the parent PID is 2367. The Bash shell process, which in this case is the parent process, has a PID of 2367. Figure 5-3 illustrates the forking that occurs when an external command is executed.

**FIGURE 5-3**

External command forking

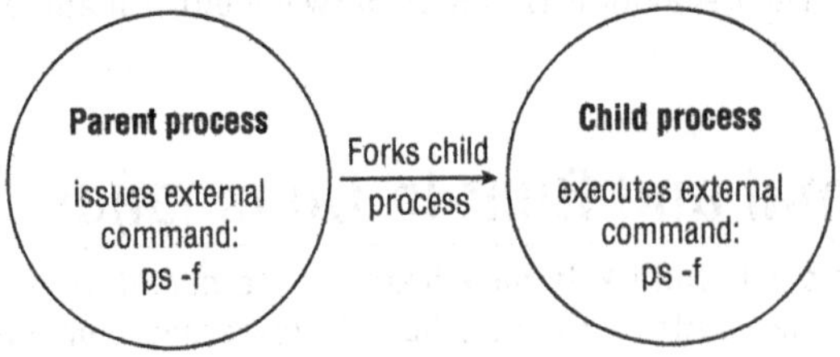

Whenever a process must fork, it takes time and effort to set up the new child process's environment. Thus, external commands can be a little expensive.

---

**NOTE**

If you fork a child process or create a subshell, you can still communicate with it via signaling, which is extremely helpful in both the command line and in writing shell scripts. *Signaling* allows process communication via signals. Signals and signaling are covered in Chapter 16, "Script Control."

---

When using a built-in command, no forking is required. Therefore, built-in commands are less expensive.

## Looking at built-in commands

*Built-in commands* are different in that they do not need a child process to execute. They were compiled into the shell, and thus are part of the shell's toolkit. No external program file exists to run them.

Both the cd and exit commands are built into the Bash shell. You can tell a command is built-in by using the type command:

```
$ type cd
cd is a shell builtin
$
$ type exit
exit is a shell builtin
$
```

Because they do not need to fork a child process to execute or open a program file, built-in commands are faster and more efficient. A list of GNU Bash shell built-in commands is provided in Appendix A.

Be aware that some commands have multiple flavors. For example, both echo and pwd have a built-in command flavor as well as an external command flavor. These flavors are slightly different. To see multiple flavors for commands, use the -a option on the type command:

```
$ type -a echo
echo is a shell builtin
echo is /usr/bin/echo
$
$ which echo
/usr/bin/echo
$
$ type -a pwd
pwd is a shell builtin
pwd is /usr/bin/pwd
```

5

```
$
$ which pwd
/usr/bin/pwd
$
```

Using the type -a command shows both types (built-in and external) for each of the two commands. Note that the which command shows only the external command file.

> **TIP**
>
> To use the external command for a command that has multiple flavors, directly reference the file. For example, to use the pwd external command, type */usr/bin/pwd*.

### Using the *history* command

The Bash shell keeps track of the most recent commands you have used. You can recall these commands and even reuse them. A helpful built-in command that lets you explore and manage these previously issued commands is the history command.

To see a list of recently used commands, type the history command with no options:

```
$ history
    1  ps -f
    2  pwd
    3  ls
    4  coproc ( sleep 10; sleep 2 )
    5  jobs
    6  ps --forest
    7  ls
    8  ps -f
    9  pwd
   10  ls -l /usr/bin/ps
   11  history
   12  cd /etc
   13  pwd
   14  ls
   15  cd
   16  type -a pwd
   17  which pwd
   18  type -a echo
   19  which echo
   20  ls
 [...]
$
```

In this example, the listing is snipped and only the first 20 commands are shown. Typically, the last 1,000 commands are kept in history. That's a lot of commands!

**TIP**

You can set the number of commands to keep in the Bash history. To do so, you need to modify an environment variable called HISTSIZE (see Chapter 6).

You can recall and reuse the last command in your history list. This can save time and typing. To recall and reuse your last command, type !! and press the Enter key:

```
$ ps --forest
  PID TTY          TIME CMD
 2367 pts/0    00:00:00 bash
 5240 pts/0    00:00:00  \_ ps
$
$ !!
ps --forest
  PID TTY          TIME CMD
 2367 pts/0    00:00:00 bash
 5241 pts/0    00:00:00  \_ ps
$
```

When !! was entered, the Bash shell first displayed the command it was recalling from the shell's history. And after the command was displayed, it was executed.

Command history is kept in the hidden .bash_history file, which is located in each user's home directory:

```
$ pwd
/home/christine
$
$ ls .bash_history
.bash_history
$
```

Be aware that during your CLI session, the bash command history is stored in memory. It is only written out into the history file when the shell is exited:

```
$ history
    1  ps -f
    2  pwd
[...]
   38  exit
   39  history
   40  ps --forest
   41  ps --forest
   42  pwd
   43  ls .bash_history
   44  history
```

```
$
$ cat .bash_history
ps -f
pwd
[...]
ls
history
exit
$
```

Notice that when the history command is run, the last commands displayed do not match final commands in the .bash_history file. There were six additional commands issued, which are not recorded in the history file.

You can force the command history to be written to the .bash_history file without leaving a shell session. In order to impose this write, use the -a option on the history command:

```
$ history -a
$
$ history
    1  ps -f
    2  pwd
[...]
   38  exit
   39  history
   40  ps --forest
   41  ps --forest
   42  pwd
   43  ls .bash_history
   44  history
   45  cat .bash_history
   46  history -a
   47  history
$
$ cat .bash_history
ps -f
pwd
[...]
exit
history
ps --forest
ps --forest
pwd
ls .bash_history
history
cat .bash_history
history -a
$
```

Notice that contents from both the `history` command and the .bash_history file match, except for the very last command listed (the `history` command), because it came after the `history -a` command was issued.

You can recall any command from the history list. Just enter an exclamation point and the command's number from the history list:

```
$ history
    1  ps -f
    2  pwd
[...]
   39  history
   40  cat .bash_history
   41  ps --forest
   42  pwd
   43  ps -f
   44  history
   45  cat .bash_history
   46  history -a
   47  history
   48  cat .bash_history
   49  history
$
$ !42
pwd
/home/christine
$
```

Command number 42 was pulled from the history list. Notice that similar to executing the last command in history, the Bash shell first displays the command it is recalling from the shell's history. After the command is displayed, it is executed.

5

Using Bash shell command history can be a great timesaver. You can do even more with the built-in `history` command. Be sure to view the Bash manual pages for `history` by typing **man history**.

### Using command aliases

The `alias` command is another useful built-in shell command. A *command alias* allows you to create an alias name for common commands (along with their parameters) to help keep your typing to a minimum.

Most likely, your Linux distribution has already set some common command aliases for you. To see a list of the active aliases, use the `alias` command along with the -p parameter:

```
$ alias -p
[...]
alias l='ls -CF'
alias la='ls -A'
alias ll='ls -alF'
alias ls='ls --color=auto'
$
```

Notice that, on this Ubuntu Linux distribution, an alias is used to override the standard ls command. It automatically provides the --color=auto parameter, which will cause the ls command to use color coding (for example, directories may be shown in blue), if the terminal supports colorization. The LS_COLORS environment variable controls the color codes used (environment variables are covered in Chapter 6).

> **TIP**
>
> When jumping between various distributions, be cautious using color coding to help you determine which listed name is a directory and which is a file. Because color codes are not standardized, it's best to use the `ls -F` command to see the file's type code instead.

You can create your own aliases using the `alias` command:

```
$ alias li='ls -i'
$
$ li
34665652 Desktop            1415018 NetworkManager.conf
 1414976 Doc.tar           50350618 OldDocuments
34665653 Documents          1414981 Pictures
51693739 Downloads         16789591 Public
 1415016 hlink_test_one     1415019 really_ridiculously_long_file_name
 1415021 log_file           1415020 slink_test_file
51693757 Music              1415551 Templates
 1414978 Music.tar          1415523 test_file
 1415525 my_file            1415016 test_one
 1415524 my_scrapt          1415017 test_two
```

```
1415519 my_script        16789592 Videos
1415015 my_scrypt
$
```

After you define an alias value, you can use it at any time in your shell, including in shell scripts. Be aware that because command aliases are built-in commands, an alias is valid only for the shell process in which it is defined:

```
$ alias li='ls -i'
$
$ bash
$ li
bash: li: command not found...
$
$ exit
exit
$
$ li
34665652 Desktop          1415018 NetworkManager.conf
 1414976 Doc.tar          50350618 OldDocuments
[...]
1415524 my_scrapt        1415017 test_two
 1415519 my_script       16789592 Videos
 1415015 my_scrypt
$
```

**TIP**

If needed, you can turn off an alias by typing `unalias alias-name` at the command line. Keep in mind, if the alias wasn't set by you, it will be turned back on the next time you log into the system. You can modify your environment files to permanently disable an alias. Environment files are covered in Chapter 6.

Fortunately, you can make an alias value permanent across subshells. The next chapter covers how to do that, along with environment variables.

## Summary

This chapter discussed the complicated interactive program, the GNU Bash shell. We covered understanding the shell process and its relationships, including how subshells are spawned and their relationship to the parent shell. We also explored commands that create child processes and commands that don't.

The default interactive shell is normally started whenever a user logs into a terminal. The shell that the system starts depends on a user ID configuration. Typically, it is /usr/bin/bash. The default system shell, /usr/bin/sh, is used for system shell scripts, such as those needed at startup.

5

A subshell or child shell can be spawned using the bash command. They are also created when a process list or the coproc command is used. Using subshells at the command line can allow for creative and productive use of the CLI. Subshells can be nested, spawning grandchild shells and great-grandchild shells. Creating a subshell is an expensive process because a new environment for the shell must be created as well.

Finally, we looked at two different types of shell commands: built-in and external commands. External commands create a child process with a new environment, but a built-in command does not. This causes external commands to be more expensive to use. Because a new environment is not needed, built-in commands are more efficient and not affected by any environment changes.

Shells, subshells, processes, and forked processes are all affected by environment variables. How the variables affect and can be used within these different contexts is explored in the next chapter.

# Using Linux Environment Variables

## IN THIS CHAPTER

L inux environment variables help define your Linux shell experience. Many programs and scripts use environment variables to obtain system information and store temporary data as well as configuration information. Environment variables are set in lots of places on the Linux system, and it's helpful to know their locations.

This chapter walks you through the world of Linux environment variables, showing where they are, how to use them, and even how to create your own. The chapter concludes with how to use variable arrays.

## Exploring Environment Variables

The Bash shell uses a feature called *environment variables* to store information about the shell session and the working environment (thus the name environment variables). This feature also allows you to store data in memory that can be easily accessed by any program or script running from the shell. It is a handy way to store needed persistent data.

There are two environment variable types in the Bash shell:

- Global variables
- Local variables

This section describes each type of environment variable and shows how to view and use them.

## Looking at global environment variables

Global environment variables are visible from the shell session and from any spawned child subshells. Local variables are available only in the shell that creates them. This fact makes global environment variables useful in applications that create child subshells, which require parent shell information.

The Linux system sets several global environment variables when you start your Bash session. (For more details about what variables are started at that time, see the "Locating System Environment Variables" section later in this chapter.) The system environment variables almost always use all capital letters to differentiate them from user-defined variables.

To view global environment variables, use the env or the printenv command:

```
$ printenv
[...]
USER=christine
[...]
PWD=/home/christine
HOME=/home/christine
[...]
TERM=xterm
SHELL=/bin/bash
[...]
HISTSIZE=1000
[...]
$
```

So many global environment variables get set for the Bash shell that the display had to be snipped. Not only are many set during the login process, but how you log in can affect which ones are set as well.

To display an individual environment variable's value, you can use the printenv command, but not the env command:

```
$ printenv HOME
/home/christine
```

```
$
$ env HOME
env: 'HOME': No such file or directory
$
```

You can also use the `echo` command to display a variable's value. When referencing an environment variable in this case, you must place a dollar sign ($) before the environment variable name:

```
$ echo $HOME
/home/christine
$
```

Using the dollar sign along with the variable name does more than just display its current definition when used with the `echo` command. The dollar sign before a variable name allows the variable to be passed as a parameter to various other commands:

```
$ ls $HOME
Desktop          Music        NetworkManager.conf                       Templates
Doc.tar          Music.tar    OldDocuments                              test_file
Documents        my_file      Pictures                                  test_one
Downloads        my_scrapt    Public                                    test_two
hlink_test_one   my_script    really_ridiculously_long_file_name  Videos
log_file         my_scrypt    slink_test_file
$
```

As mentioned earlier, global environment variables are also available to any process's subshells:

```
$ bash
$ ps -f
UID          PID   PPID  C STIME TTY          TIME CMD
christi+     2770  2766  0 11:19 pts/0    00:00:00 -bash
christi+     2981  2770  4 11:37 pts/0    00:00:00 bash
christi+     3003  2981  0 11:37 pts/0    00:00:00 ps -f
$
$ echo $HOME
/home/christine
$ exit
exit
$
```

In this example, after spawning a subshell using the `bash` command, the HOME environment variable's current value is shown. It is set to the exact same value, /home/christine, as it was in the parent shell.

## Looking at local environment variables

*Local environment variables*, as their name implies, can be seen only in the local process in which they are defined. Even though they are local, they are just as important as global environment variables. In fact, the Linux system also defines standard local environment variables for you by default. However, you can also define your own local variables. These, as you would assume, are called *user-defined local variables*.

Trying to see the local variables list is a little tricky at the CLI. Unfortunately, there isn't a command that displays only these variables. The `set` command displays all variables defined for a specific process, including both local and global environment variables as well as user-defined variables:

```
$ set
BASH=/bin/bash
[...]
HOME=/home/christine
[...]
PWD=/home/christine
[...]
SHELL=/bin/bash
[...]
TERM=xterm
[...]
USER=christine
[...]
colors=/home/christine/.dircolors
my_variable='Hello World'
[...]
_command ()
{
[...]
$
```

All the global environment variables displayed using the `env` or `printenv` command appear in the `set` command's output. The additional environment variables are the local environment and user-defined variables. Also included in the `set` command's output are local shell functions, such as the _ command function listed in the previous display. Shell functions are covered in Chapter 17, "Creating Functions."

> **NOTE**
>
> The differences between the commands `env`, `printenv`, and `set` are subtle. The `set` command displays global and local environment variables, user-defined variables, and local functions. It also sorts the display alphabetically. The `env` and `printenv` are different from `set` in that they do not sort the variables, nor do they include local environment variables, local user-defined variables, or local shell functions. Used in this context, `env` and `printenv` produce duplicate listings. However, the `env` command has additional functionality that `printenv` does not have, making it the slightly more powerful command.

# Setting User-Defined Variables

You can set your own variables directly from the Bash shell. This section shows you how to create your own variables and reference them from an interactive shell or shell script program.

## Setting local user-defined variables

After you start a Bash shell (or spawn a shell script), you're allowed to create local user-defined variables that are visible within your shell process. You can assign either a numeric or a string value to an environment variable by assigning the variable to a value using the equal sign:

```
$ my_variable=Hello
$ echo $my_variable
Hello
$
```

That was simple! Now, any time you need to reference the my_variable user-defined variable's value, just reference it by the name $my_variable.

If you need to assign a string value that contains spaces, you must use a single or double quotation mark to delineate the beginning and the end of the string:

```
$ my_variable=Hello World
bash: World: command not found...
$
$ my_variable="Hello World"
$ echo $my_variable
Hello World
$
```

Without the quotation marks, the Bash shell assumes that the next word (World) is another command to process. Notice that for the local variable you defined, you used lowercase letters, whereas the system environment variables you've seen so far have all used uppercase letters.

> **TIP**
>
> The standard Bash shell convention is for all environment variables to use uppercase letters. If you are creating a local variable for yourself and your own shell scripts, use lowercase letters. Variables are case sensitive. By keeping your user-defined local variables lowercase, you avoid the potential disaster of redefining a system environment variable.

It's extremely important that you not use spaces between the variable name, the equal sign, and the value. If you put any spaces in the assignment, the Bash shell interprets the value as a separate command:

```
$ my_variable = "Hello World"
bash: my_variable: command not found...
$
```

After you set a local variable, it's available for use anywhere within your shell process. However, if you spawn another shell, it's not available in the child shell:

```
$ my_variable="Hello World"
$
$ bash
$ echo $my_variable

$ exit
exit
$ echo $my_variable
Hello World
$
```

In this example, a child shell was spawned via the bash command. The user-defined my_variable was not available in the child shell. This is demonstrated by the blank line returned after the echo $my_variable command. After the child shell was exited and returned to the original shell, the local variable was available.

Similarly, if you set a local variable in a child process, after you leave the child process, the local variable is no longer available:

```
$ echo $my_child_variable

$ bash
$ my_child_variable="Hello Little World"
$ echo $my_child_variable
Hello Little World
$ exit
exit
$ echo $my_child_variable

$
```

The local variable set within the child shell doesn't exist after a return to the parent shell. You can change this behavior by turning your local user-defined variable into a global variable.

## Setting global environment variables

Global environment variables are visible from any child processes created by the parent process that sets the variable. The method used to create a global environment variable is to first create a local variable and then export it to the global environment.

This is done by using the export command and the variable name (minus the dollar sign):

```
$ my_variable="I am Global now"
$
$ export my_variable
$
$ echo $my_variable
```

```
I am Global now
$ bash
$ echo $my_variable
I am Global now
$ exit
exit
$ echo $my_variable
I am Global now
$
```

After defining and exporting the local variable my_variable, a child shell was started by the bash command. The child shell was able to properly display the my_variable variable's value. The variable kept its value, because the export command made it global.

Changing a global environment variable within a child shell does not affect the variable's value in the parent shell:

```
$ export my_variable="I am Global now"
$ echo $my_variable
I am Global now
$
$ bash
$ echo $my_variable
I am Global now
$ my_variable="Null"
$ echo $my_variable
Null
$ exit
exit
$
$ echo $my_variable
I am Global now
$
```

After defining and exporting the variable my_variable, a subshell was started by the bash command. The subshell properly displayed the value of the my_variable global environment variable. The variable's value was then changed by the child shell. However, the variable's value was modified only within the child shell, and not in the parent's shell environment.

A child shell cannot even use the export command to change the parent shell's global variable's value:

```
$ echo $my_variable
I am Global now
```

```
$
$ bash
$ export my_variable="Null"
$ echo $my_variable
Null
$ exit
exit
$
$ echo $my_variable
I am Global now
$
```

Even though the child shell redefined and exported the variable my_variable, the parent shell's my_variable variable kept its original value.

# Removing Environment Variables

Of course, if you can create a new environment variable, it makes sense that you can also remove an existing environment variable. You can do this with the unset command. When referencing the environment variable in the unset command, remember not to use the dollar sign:

```
$ my_variable="I am going to be removed"
$ echo $my_variable
I am going to be removed
$
$ unset my_variable
$ echo $my_variable

$
```

> **TIP**
>
> It can be confusing to remember when to use and when not to use the dollar sign with environment variables. Just remember this: If you are doing anything *with* the variable, use the dollar sign. If you are doing anything *to* the variable, *don't* use the dollar sign. The exception to this rule is using printenv to display a variable's value.

When dealing with global environment variables, things get a little tricky. If you're in a child process and unset a global environment variable, it applies only to the child process. The global environment variable is still available in the parent process:

```
$ export my_variable="I am Global now"
$ echo $my_variable
I am Global now
$
$ bash
$ echo $my_variable
```

```
I am Global now
$ unset my_variable
$ echo $my_variable

$ exit
exit
$ echo $my_variable
I am Global now
$
```

Just as with modifying a variable, you cannot unset it in a child shell and have the variable be unset in the parent's shell.

# Uncovering Default Shell Environment Variables

The Bash shell uses specific environment variables by default to define the system environment. You can always count on these variables being set or available to be set on your Linux system. Because the Bash shell is a derivative of the original Unix Bourne shell, it also includes environment variables originally defined in that shell.

Table 6-1 shows the environment variables that the Bash shell provides that are compatible with the original Unix Bourne shell.

**TABLE 6-1  The Bash Shell Bourne Variables**

| Variable | Description |
| --- | --- |
| CDPATH | A colon-separated list of directories used as a search path for the cd command |
| HOME | The current user's home directory |
| IFS | A list of characters that separate fields used by the shell to split text strings |
| MAIL | The filename for the current user's mailbox (the Bash shell checks this file for new mail) |
| MAILPATH | A colon-separated list of multiple filenames for the current user's mailbox (the Bash shell checks each file in this list for new mail) |
| OPTARG | The value of the last option argument processed by the getopt command |
| OPTIND | The index value of the last option argument processed by the getopt command |
| PATH | A colon-separated list of directories where the shell looks for commands |
| PS1 | The primary shell command-line interface's prompt string |
| PS2 | The secondary shell command-line interface's prompt string |

Besides the default Bourne environment variables, the Bash shell also provides several variables of its own, as shown in Table 6-2.

TABLE 6-2   **The Bash Shell Environment Variables**

| Variable | Description |
| --- | --- |
| BASH | The full pathname to execute the current instance of the Bash shell |
| BASH_ALIASES | An associative array of currently set aliases |
| BASH_ARGC | A variable array that contains the number of parameters being passed to a subroutine or shell script |
| BASH_ARCV | A variable array that contains the parameters being passed to a subroutine or shell script |
| BASH_ARCV0 | A variable that contains the name of either the shell or, if used within a script, the shell script's name |
| BASH_CMDS | An associative array of locations of commands the shell has executed |
| BASH_COMMAND | The shell command currently being or about to be executed |
| BASH_COMPAT | A value designating the shell's compatibility level |
| BASH_ENV | When set, each Bash script attempts to execute a startup file defined by this variable before running. |
| BASH_EXECUTION_STRING | The command(s) passed using the bash command's -c option |
| BASH_LINENO | A variable array containing the source code line number of the currently executing shell function |
| BASH_LOADABLE_PATH | A colon-separated list of directories where the shell looks for dynamically loadable built-ins |
| BASH_REMATCH | A read-only variable array containing patterns and their sub-patterns for positive matches using the regular expression comparison operator, =~ |
| BASH_SOURCE | A variable array containing the source code filename of the currently executing shell function |
| BASH_SUBSHELL | The current nesting level of a subshell environment (the initial value is 0) |
| BASH_VERSINFO | A variable array that contains the individual major and minor version numbers of the current instance of the Bash shell |
| BASH_VERSION | The version number of the current instance of the Bash shell |
| BASH_XTRACEFD | If set to a valid file descriptor (0,1,2), trace output generated from the 'set -x' debugging option can be redirected. This is often used to separate trace output into a file. |
| BASHOPTS | A list of Bash shell options that are currently enabled |
| BASHPID | Process ID of the current Bash process |
| CHILD_MAX | A setting that controls the number of exited child status values for the shell to track |

6

| Variable | Description |
|---|---|
| COLUMNS | Contains the terminal width of the terminal used for the current instance of the Bash shell |
| COMP_CWORD | An index into the variable COMP_WORDS, which contains the current cursor position |
| COMP_LINE | The current command line |
| COMP_POINT | The index of the current cursor position relative to the beginning of the current command |
| COMP_KEY | The final key used to invoke the current completion of a shell function |
| COMP_TYPE | An integer value representing the type of completion attempted that caused a completion shell function to be invoked |
| COMP_WORDBREAKS | The Readline library word separator characters for performing word completion |
| COMP_WORDS | An array variable that contains the individual words on the current command line |
| COMPREPLY | An array variable that contains the possible completion codes generated by a shell function |
| COPROC | An array variable that holds an unnamed coprocess's I/O file descriptors |
| DIRSTACK | An array variable that contains the current contents of the directory stack |
| EMACS | Indicates the emacs shell buffer is executing and line editing is disabled, when set to 't' |
| EPOCHREALTIME | Contains the number of seconds since the Unix Epoch (00:00:00 UTC on 1 January 1970) with micro-seconds included |
| EPOCHSECONDS | Contains the number of seconds since the Unix Epoch (00:00:00 UTC on 1 January 1970) without micro-seconds |
| ENV | When set, executes the startup file defined before a Bash shell script runs (it is used only when the Bash shell has been invoked in POSIX mode) |
| EUID | The numeric effective user ID of the current user |
| EXECIGNORE | A colon-separated list of filters that determine executable files to ignore (such as shared library files), when employing PATH in a search |
| FCEDIT | The default editor used by the fc command |
| FIGNORE | A colon-separated list of suffixes to ignore when performing file-name completion |
| FUNCNAME | The name of the currently executing shell function |

*Continues*

**TABLE 6.2**   *(continued)*

| Variable | Description |
|---|---|
| FUNCNEST | Sets the maximum allowed function nesting level, when set to a number greater than 0 (if it is exceeded, the current command aborts) |
| GLOBIGNORE | A colon-separated list of patterns defining the set of filenames to be ignored by filename expansion |
| GROUPS | A variable array containing the list of groups of which the current user is a member |
| histchars | Up to three characters, which control history expansion |
| HISTCMD | The history number of the current command |
| HISTCONTROL | Controls what commands are entered in the shell history list |
| HISTFILE | The name of the file in which to save the shell history list (.bash_history by default) |
| HISTFILESIZE | The maximum number of lines to save in the history file |
| HISTIGNORE | A colon-separated list of patterns used to decide which commands are ignored for the history file |
| HISTSIZE | The maximum number of commands stored in the history file |
| HISTTIMEFORMAT | Used as a formatting string to print each command's time stamp in Bash history, if set and not null |
| HOSTFILE | Contains the name of the file that should be read when the shell needs to complete a hostname |
| HOSTNAME | The name of the current host |
| HOSTTYPE | A string describing the machine the Bash shell is running on |
| IGNOREEOF | The number of consecutive EOF characters the shell must receive before exiting (if this value doesn't exist, the default is 1) |
| INPUTRC | The name of the Readline initialization file (the default is .inputrc) |
| INSIDE_EMACS | Set only when process is running in an Emacs editor shell buffer and can disable line editing (disablement of line editing also depends on the value in the TERM variable) |
| LANG | The locale category for the shell |
| LC_ALL | Overrides the LANG variable, defining a locale category |
| LC_COLLATE | Sets the collation order used when sorting string values |
| LC_CTYPE | Determines the interpretation of characters used in filename expansion and pattern matching |
| LC_MESSAGES | Determines the locale setting used when interpreting double-quoted strings preceded by a dollar sign |
| LC_NUMERIC | Determines the locale setting used when formatting numbers |

| Variable | Description |
| --- | --- |
| LC_TIME | Determines the locale setting used when formatting data and time |
| LINENO | The line number in a script currently executing |
| LINES | Defines the number of lines available on the terminal |
| MACHTYPE | A string defining the system type in cpu-company-system format |
| MAILCHECK | How often (in seconds) the shell should check for new mail (the default is 60) |
| MAPFILE | An array variable that holds read-in text from the mapfile command when no array variable name is given |
| OLDPWD | The previous working directory used in the shell |
| OPTERR | If set to 1, the Bash shell displays errors generated by the getopts command. |
| OSTYPE | A string defining the operating system the shell is running on |
| PIPESTATUS | A variable array containing a list of exit status values from the processes in the foreground process |
| POSIXLY_CORRECT | If set, Bash starts in POSIX mode. |
| PPID | The process ID (PID) of the Bash shell's parent process |
| PROMPT_COMMAND | If set, the command to execute before displaying the primary prompt |
| PROMPT_DIRTRIM | An integer used to indicate the number of trailing directory names to display when using the \w and \W prompt string escapes (the directory names removed are replaced with one set of ellipses) |
| PS0 | If set, contents are displayed by the interactive shell after the command is entered but before command is executed. |
| PS3 | The prompt to use for the select command |
| PS4 | The prompt displayed before the command line is echoed if the Bash -x parameter is used |
| PWD | The current working directory |
| RANDOM | Returns a random number between 0 and 32767 (assigning a value to this variable seeds the pseudo-random number generator) |
| READLINE_LINE | Readline buffer contents when using bind -x command |
| READLINE_POINT | Readline buffer content insertion point's current position when using bind -x command |
| REPLY | The default variable for the read command |
| SECONDS | The number of seconds since the shell was started (assigning a value resets the timer to the value) |
| SHELL | The full pathname to the Bash shell |
| SHELLOPTS | A colon-separated list of enabled Bash shell options |

*Continues*

**TABLE 6.2** *(continued)*

| Variable | Description |
|---|---|
| SHLVL | Indicates the shell level, incremented by one each time a new Bash shell is started |
| TIMEFORMAT | A format specifying how the shell displays time values |
| TMOUT | The value of how long (in seconds) the select and read commands should wait for input (the default of 0 indicates to wait indefinitely) |
| TMPDIR | Directory name where the Bash shell creates temporary files for its use |
| UID | The numeric real user ID of the current user |

You may notice that not all default environment variables are shown when the set command is used. When not in use, a default environment variable is not required to contain a value.

> **NOTE**
> Whether or not a default environment variable is in use on your system sometimes depends on the version of the Bash shell running. For example, EPOCHREALTIME is only available on Bash shell version 5 and above. You can view your Bash shell's version number by typing bash --version and pressing Enter at the CLI.

## Setting the *PATH* Environment Variable

When you enter an external command (see Chapter 5, "Understanding the Shell") in the shell CLI, the shell must search the system to find the program. The PATH environment variable defines the directories it searches looking for commands and programs. On this Ubuntu Linux system, the PATH environment variable looks like this:

```
$ echo $PATH
/usr/local/sbin:/usr/local/bin:/usr/sbin:/usr/bin:
/sbin:/bin:/usr/games:/usr/local/games:/snap/bin
$
```

The directories in the PATH are separated by colons. And this shows that there are nine directories where the shell looks for commands and programs.

If a command's or program's location is not included in the PATH variable, the shell cannot find it without an absolute directory reference. If the shell cannot find the command or program, it produces an error message:

```
$ myprog
myprog: command not found
$
```

The problem is that sometimes applications place their executable programs in directories that aren't in the PATH environment variable. The trick is to ensure your PATH environment variable includes all the directories where your applications reside.

You can add new search directories to the existing PATH environment variable without having to rebuild it from scratch. The individual directories listed in the PATH are separated by colons. All you need to do is reference the original PATH value, add a colon (:), and type in the new directory using an absolute directory reference. On a CentOS Linux system, it looks something like this:

```
$ ls /home/christine/Scripts/
myprog
$ echo $PATH
/home/christine/.local/bin:/home/christine/bin:/usr/local/bin:/usr/
bin:/usr/local/sbin:/usr/sbin
$
$ PATH=$PATH:/home/christine/Scripts
$
$ myprog
The factorial of 5 is 120
$
```

By adding the directory to the PATH environment variable, you can now execute your program from *anywhere* in the virtual directory structure:

```
$ cd /etc
$ myprog
The factorial of 5 is 120
$
```

Changes to the PATH variable last only until you exit the system or the system reboots. The changes are not persistent. In the next section, you see how you can make changes to environment variables permanent.

# Locating System Environment Variables

The Linux system uses environment variables for many purposes. You know now how to modify system environment variables and create your own variables. The trick is in how these environment variables are made persistent.

When you start a Bash shell by logging into the Linux system, by default Bash checks several files for commands. These files are called *startup files* or *environment files*. Which startup files Bash processes depends on the method you use to start the Bash shell. You can start a Bash shell in three ways:

- As a default login shell at login time
- As an interactive shell that is started by spawning a subshell
- As a noninteractive shell to run a script

The following sections describe the startup files the Bash shell executes in each of these startup methods.

## Understanding the login shell process

When you log into the Linux system, the Bash shell starts as a *login shell*. The login shell typically looks for five different startup files to process commands from:

- /etc/profile
- $HOME/.bash_profile
- $HOME/.bashrc
- $HOME/.bash_login
- $HOME/.profile

The /etc/profile file is the main default startup file for the Bash shell on the system. All users on the system execute this startup file when they log in.

> **NOTE**
>
> Be aware that some Linux distributions use pluggable authentication modules (PAM). In this case, before the Bash shell is started, PAM files are processed, including ones that may contain environment variables. PAM file examples include the /etc/environment file and the $HOME/.pam_environment file. Find more information about PAM at www.linux-pam.org.

The other four startup files are specific for each user, located in the home ($HOME) directory, and can be customized for an individual user's requirements. Let's look more closely at these files.

### Viewing the */etc/profile* file

The /etc/profile file is the main default startup file for the Bash shell. Whenever you log into the Linux system, Bash executes the commands in the /etc/profile startup file first. Different Linux distributions place different commands in this file. On this Ubuntu Linux system, the file looks like this:

```
$ cat /etc/profile
# /etc/profile: system-wide .profile file for the Bourne
shell (sh(1))
# and Bourne compatible shells (bash(1), ksh(1), ash(1), ...).

if [ "${PS1-}" ]; then
  if [ "${BASH-}" ] && [ "$BASH" != "/bin/sh" ]; then
    # The file bash.bashrc already sets the default PS1.
    # PS1='\h:\w\$ '
    if [ -f /etc/bash.bashrc ]; then
      . /etc/bash.bashrc
    fi
  else
    if [ "`id -u`" -eq 0 ]; then
      PS1='# '
    else
      PS1='$ '
    fi
  fi
fi

if [ -d /etc/profile.d ]; then
  for i in /etc/profile.d/*.sh; do
    if [ -r $i ]; then
      . $i
    fi
  done
  unset i
fi
$
```

Most of the commands and syntax you see in this file are covered in more detail in Chapter 12, "Using Structure Commands," and later chapters. Each distribution's /etc/profile file has different settings and commands. For example, notice that a file is mentioned in this Ubuntu distribution's /etc/profile file, called /etc/bash.bashrc. It contains system environment variables.

However, in this next CentOS distribution's /etc/profile file listed, no /etc/bash .bashrc file is called. Also note that it sets and exports some system environment variables (HISTSIZE; HOSTNAME) within itself:

```
$ cat /etc/profile
# /etc/profile

# System wide environment and startup programs, for login setup
# Functions and aliases go in /etc/bashrc
```

```
# It's NOT a good idea to change this file unless you know what you
# are doing. It's much better to create a custom.sh shell script in
# /etc/profile.d/ to make custom changes to your environment, as this
# will prevent the need for merging in future updates.

pathmunge () {
    case ":${PATH}:" in
        *:"$1":*)
            ;;
        *)
            if [ "$2" = "after" ] ; then
                PATH=$PATH:$1
            else
                PATH=$1:$PATH
            fi
    esac
}


if [ -x /usr/bin/id ]; then
    if [ -z "$EUID" ]; then
        # ksh workaround
        EUID=`id -u`
        UID=`id -ru`
    fi
    USER="`id -un`"
    LOGNAME=$USER
    MAIL="/var/spool/mail/$USER"
fi

# Path manipulation
if [ "$EUID" = "0" ]; then
    pathmunge /usr/sbin
    pathmunge /usr/local/sbin
else
    pathmunge /usr/local/sbin after
    pathmunge /usr/sbin after
fi

HOSTNAME=`/usr/bin/hostname 2>/dev/null`
HISTSIZE=1000
if [ "$HISTCONTROL" = "ignorespace" ] ; then
    export HISTCONTROL=ignoreboth
else
    export HISTCONTROL=ignoredups
fi

export PATH USER LOGNAME MAIL HOSTNAME HISTSIZE HISTCONTROL
```

```
# By default, we want umask to get set. This sets it for login shell
# Current threshold for system reserved uid/gids is 200
# You could check uidgid reservation validity in
# /usr/share/doc/setup-*/uidgid file
if [ $UID -gt 199 ] && [ "`id -gn`" = "`id -un`" ]; then
    umask 002
else
    umask 022
fi

for i in /etc/profile.d/*.sh /etc/profile.d/sh.local ; do
    if [ -r "$i" ]; then
        if [ "${-#*i}" != "$-" ]; then
            . "$i"
        else
            . "$i" >/dev/null
        fi
    fi
done

unset i
unset -f pathmunge

if [ -n "${BASH_VERSION-}" ] ; then
        if [ -f /etc/bashrc ] ; then
                # Bash login shells run only /etc/profile
                # Bash non-login shells run only /etc/bashrc
                # Check for double sourcing is done in /etc/bashrc.
                . /etc/bashrc
        fi
fi
$
```

Both distributions' /etc/profile files use a certain feature. It is a for statement that iterates through any files located in the /etc/profile.d directory. (for statements are discussed in detail in Chapter 13, "More Structured Commands.") This provides a place for the Linux system to place application-specific and/or administrator-customized startup files that are executed by the shell when you log in. On this Ubuntu Linux system, the following files are in the /etc/profile.d directory:

```
$ ls /etc/profile.d
01-locale-fix.sh  bash_completion.sh     gawk.csh   Z97-byobu.sh
apps-bin-path.sh  cedilla-portuguese.sh  gawk.sh
$
```

You can see that this CentOS system has quite a few more files in /etc/profile.d:

```
$ ls /etc/profile.d
bash_completion.sh  colorxzgrep.csh  flatpak.sh  less.csh  vim.sh
colorgrep.csh       colorxzgrep.sh   gawk.csh    less.sh   vte.sh
```

```
colorgrep.sh      colorzgrep.csh   gawk.sh     PackageKit.sh  which2.csh
colorls.csh       colorzgrep.sh    lang.csh    sh.local       which2.sh
colorls.sh        csh.local        lang.sh     vim.csh
$
```

Notice that several files are related to specific applications on the system. Most applications create two startup files — one for the Bash shell (using the .sh extension) and one for the C shell (using the .csh extension).

### Viewing the *$HOME* startup files

The remaining startup files are all used for the same function — to provide a user-specific startup file for defining user-specific environment variables. Most Linux distributions use only one or two of these four startup files:

- $HOME/.bash_profile
- $HOME/.bashrc
- $HOME/.bash_login
- $HOME/.profile

Notice that all four files start with a dot, making them hidden files (they don't appear in a normal ls command listing). Because they are in the user's $HOME directory, each user can edit the files and add their own environment variables that are active for every Bash shell session they start.

**NOTE**

Environment files are one area where Linux distributions vary greatly. Not every $HOME file listed in this section exists for every user. For example, some users may have only the $HOME/.bash_profile file. This is normal.

The first file found in the following ordered list is run, and the rest are ignored:

```
$HOME/.bash_profile
$HOME/.bash_login
$HOME/.profile
```

Notice that $HOME/.bashrc is not in this list. This is because it is typically run from one of the other files.

**TIP**

Remember that $HOME represents a user's home directory. Also, the tilde (~) is used to represent a user's home directory.

156

This CentOS Linux system contains the following in the .bash_profile file:

```
$ cat $HOME/.bash_profile
# .bash_profile

# Get the aliases and functions
if [ -f ~/.bashrc ]; then
        . ~/.bashrc
fi

# User specific environment and startup programs
$
```

The .bash_profile startup file first checks to see if the startup file, .bashrc, is present in the $HOME directory. If it's there, the startup file executes the commands in it.

## Understanding the interactive shell process

If you start a Bash shell without logging into a system (if you just type **bash** at a CLI prompt, for example), you start what's called an *interactive shell*. The interactive shell, like the login shell, provides a CLI prompt for you to enter commands.

If Bash is started as an interactive shell, it doesn't process the /etc/profile file. Instead, it checks only for the .bashrc file in the user's $HOME directory.

On this Linux CentOS distribution, the file looks like this:

```
$ cat $HOME/.bashrc
# .bashrc

# Source global definitions
if [ -f /etc/bashrc ]; then
        . /etc/bashrc
fi

# User specific environment
PATH="$HOME/.local/bin:$HOME/bin:$PATH"
export PATH
# Uncomment the following line if you don't like systemctl's
auto-paging feature:
# export SYSTEMD_PAGER=

# User specific aliases and functions
$
```

The .bashrc file does two things. First, it checks for a common bashrc file in the /etc directory. Second, it provides a place for the user to enter personal command aliases (discussed in Chapter 5) and script functions (described in Chapter 17).

## Understanding the noninteractive shell process

The last type of shell is a *noninteractive subshell*. This is the shell where the system can start to execute a shell script. This is different in that there isn't a CLI prompt to worry about. However, you may want to run specific startup commands each time you start a script on your system.

> **TIP**
>
> Scripts can be executed in different ways. Only some execution methods start a subshell. You'll learn about the different shell execution methods in Chapter 11.

To accommodate that situation, the Bash shell provides the BASH_ENV environment variable. When the shell starts a noninteractive subshell process, it checks this environment variable for the startup file name to execute. If one is present, the shell executes the file's commands, which typically include variables set for the shell scripts.

On this CentOS Linux distribution, this environment value is not set by default. When a variable is not set, the `printenv` command simply returns the CLI prompt:

```
$ printenv BASH_ENV
$
```

On this Ubuntu distribution, the BASH_ENV variable isn't set either. Remember that, when a variable is not set, the `echo` command displays a blank line and returns the CLI prompt:

```
$ echo $BASH_ENV

$
```

So if the BASH_ENV variable isn't set, how do the shell scripts get their environment variables? Remember that some shell script execution methods start a subshell, also called a child shell (see Chapter 5). A child shell inherits its parent shell's exported variables.

For example, if the parent shell was a login shell and had variables set and exported in the /etc/profile file, /etc/profile.d/*.sh files, and the $HOME/.bashrc file, the child shell for the script inherits these exported variables.

> **TIP**
>
> Any variables set, but not exported, by the parent shell are local variables. Local variables are *not* inherited by a subshell.

For scripts that do not start a subshell, the variables are already available in the current shell. Thus, even if BASH _ ENV is not set, both the current shell's local and global variables are present to be used.

## Making environment variables persistent

Now that you know your way around the various shell process types and their various environment files, locating the permanent environment variables is much easier. You can also set your own permanent global or local variables using these files.

For global environment variables (those variables needed by all the users on a Linux system), it may be tempting to put new or modified variable settings in /etc/profile, but this is a bad idea. The file could be changed when your distribution is upgraded, and you would lose all the customized variable settings.

It is a better idea to create a file ending with .sh in the /etc/profile.d/ directory. In that file, place all your new or modified global environment variable settings.

On most distributions, the best place to store an individual user's persistent Bash shell variables is in the $HOME/.bashrc file. This is true for all shell process types. However, if the BASH_ENV variable is set, keep in mind that unless it points to $HOME/.bashrc, you may need to store a user's variables for noninteractive shell types elsewhere.

> **NOTE**
>
> User environment variables for graphical interface elements, such as the GUI client, may need to be set in different configuration files than where Bash shell environment variables are set.

Recall from Chapter 5 that the command alias settings are also not persistent. You can also store your personal alias settings in the $HOME/.bashrc startup file to make them permanent.

# Learning about Variable Arrays

A really cool feature of environment variables is that they can be used as *arrays*. An array is a variable that can hold multiple values. Values can be referenced either individually or as a whole for the entire array.

To set multiple values for an environment variable, just list them in parentheses, with values separated by spaces:

```
$ mytest=(zero one two three four)
$
```

Not much excitement there. If you try to display the array as a normal environment variable, you'll be disappointed:

```
$ echo $mytest
zero
$
```

Only the first value in the array appears. To reference an individual array element, you must use a numerical index value, which represents its place in the array. The numeric value is enclosed in square brackets, and everything after the dollar sign is encased by curly brackets:

```
$ echo ${mytest[2]}
two
$
```

To display an entire array variable, you use the asterisk wildcard character as the index value:

```
$ echo ${mytest[*]}
zero one two three four
$
```

You can also change the value of an individual index position:

```
$ mytest[2]=seven
$ echo ${mytest[2]}
seven
$
```

You can even use the unset command to remove an individual value within the array, but be careful, because this gets tricky. Consider this example:

```
$ unset mytest[2]
$ echo ${mytest[*]}
zero one three four
$
$ echo ${mytest[2]}

$ echo ${mytest[3]}
three
$
```

This example uses the unset command to remove the value at index value 2. When you display the array, it appears that the other index values just dropped down one. However, if you specifically display the data at index value 2, you see that that location is empty.

You can remove the entire array just by using the array name in the unset command:

```
$ unset mytest
$ echo ${mytest[*]}

$
```

Sometimes variable arrays just complicate matters, so they're often not used in shell script programming. They're not very portable to other shell environments, which is a downside if you do lots of shell programming for different shells. Some Bash system environment variables use arrays (such as BASH_VERSINFO), but overall you probably won't run into them very often.

## Summary

This chapter examined the world of Linux environment variables. Global environment variables can be accessed from any child shell spawned by the parent shell in which they're defined. Local environment variables can be accessed only from the process in which they're defined.

The Linux system uses both global and local environment variables to store information about the system environment. You can access this information from the shell command-line interface, as well as within shell scripts. The Bash shell uses the system environment variables defined in the original Unix Bourne shell, as well as lots of new environment variables. The PATH environment variable defines the search pattern the Bash shell takes to find an executable command. You can modify the PATH environment variable to add your own directories.

You can also create global and local environment variables for your own use. After you create an environment variable, it's accessible for the entire duration of your shell session.

The Bash shell executes several startup files when it starts up. These startup files can contain environment variable definitions to set standard environment variables for each Bash session. When you log into the Linux system, the Bash shell accesses the /etc/profile startup file and local startup files for each user. Users can customize these files to include environment variables and startup scripts for their own use.

Finally, we discussed the use of environment variable arrays. These environment variables can contain multiple values in a single variable. You can access the values either individually by referencing an index value or as a whole by referencing the entire environment variable array name.

The next chapter dives into the world of Linux file permissions. This is possibly the most difficult topic for novice Linux users. However, to write good shell scripts, you need to understand how file permissions work and be able to use them on your Linux system.

# Understanding Linux File Permissions

N o system is complete without some form of security. A mechanism must be available to protect files from unauthorized viewing or modification. The Linux system follows the Unix method of file permissions, allowing individual users and groups access to files based on a set of security settings for each file and directory. This chapter discusses how to use the Linux file security system to protect data when necessary and share data when desired.

## Exploring Linux Security

The core of the Linux security system is the *user account*. Each individual who accesses a Linux system should have a unique user account assigned. What permissions users have to objects on the system depends on the user account they log in with.

User permissions are tracked using a *user ID* (often called a UID), which is assigned to an account when it's created. The UID is a numerical value, unique for each user. However, you don't log into a Linux system using your UID. Instead, you use a *login name*. The login name is an alphanumeric text string of eight characters or fewer that the user uses to log into the system (along with an associated password).

The Linux system uses special files and utilities to track and manage user accounts on the system. Before we can discuss file permissions, we need to examine how Linux handles user accounts. This section describes the files and utilities required for user accounts so that you can understand how to use them when working with file permissions.

## The /etc/passwd file

The Linux system uses a special file to match the login name to a corresponding UID value. This file is the /etc/passwd file. The /etc/passwd file contains several pieces of information about the user. Here's what a typical /etc/passwd file looks like on a Linux system:

```
$ cat /etc/passwd
root:x:0:0:root:/root:/bin/bash
bin:x:1:1:bin:/bin:/sbin/nologin
daemon:x:2:2:daemon:/sbin:/sbin/nologin
adm:x:3:4:adm:/var/adm:/sbin/nologin
lp:x:4:7:lp:/var/spool/lpd:/sbin/nologin
sync:x:5:0:sync:/sbin:/bin/sync
shutdown:x:6:0:shutdown:/sbin:/sbin/shutdown
halt:x:7:0:halt:/sbin:/sbin/halt
...
rich:x:500:500:Rich Blum:/home/rich:/bin/bash
mama:x:501:501:Mama:/home/mama:/bin/bash
katie:x:502:502:katie:/home/katie:/bin/bash
jessica:x:503:503:Jessica:/home/jessica:/bin/bash
mysql:x:27:27:MySQL Server:/var/lib/mysql:/bin/bash
$
```

The list can be very long, so we've truncated the file from our system. The root user account is the administrator for the Linux system and is always assigned UID 0. As you can see, the Linux system creates lots of user accounts for various functions that aren't actual users. These are called *system accounts*. A system account is a special account that services running on the system use to gain access to resources on the system. All services that run in background mode need to be logged into the Linux system under a system user account.

Before security became a big issue, these services often just logged in using the root user account. Unfortunately, if an unauthorized person broke into one of these services, they instantly gained access to the system as the root user. To prevent this, now just about every service that runs in the background on a Linux server has its own user account to log in with. This way, if a troublemaker does compromise a service, they still can't necessarily get access to the whole system.

Linux reserves UIDs below 500 for system accounts. Some services even require specific UIDs to work properly. When you create accounts for normal users, most Linux systems assign the first available UID starting at 500 (although this is not necessarily true for all Linux distributions, such as Ubuntu, which starts at 1000).

You probably noticed that the /etc/passwd file contains lots more than just the login name and UID for the user. The fields of the /etc/passwd file contain the following information:

- The login username
- The password for the user

- The numerical UID of the user account
- The numerical group ID (GID) of the user's primary group
- A text description of the user account (called the comment field)
- The location of the $HOME directory for the user
- The default shell for the user

The password field in the /etc/passwd file is set to an *x*. This doesn't mean that all the user accounts have the same password. In the old days of Linux, the /etc/passwd file contained an encrypted version of the user's password. However, since lots of programs need to access the /etc/passwd file for user information, this became somewhat of a security problem. With the advent of software that could easily decrypt encrypted passwords, the bad folks had a field day trying to break user passwords stored in the /etc/passwd file. Linux developers needed to rethink that policy.

Now, most Linux systems hold user passwords in a separate file (called the *shadow* file, located at /etc/shadow). Only special programs (such as the login program) are allowed access to this file.

As you can see, the /etc/passwd file is a standard text file. You can use any text editor to manually perform user management functions (such as adding, modifying, or removing user accounts) directly in the /etc/passwd file. However, this is an extremely dangerous practice. If the /etc/passwd file becomes corrupted, the system won't be able to read it, and it will prevent anyone (even the root user) from logging in. Instead, it's safer to use the standard Linux user management utilities to perform all user management functions.

## The /etc/shadow file

The /etc/shadow file provides more control over how the Linux system manages passwords. Only the root user has access to the /etc/shadow file, making it more secure than the /etc/passwd file.

The /etc/shadow file contains one record for each user account on the system. A record looks like this:

```
rich:$1$.FfcK0ns$f1UgiyHQ25wrB/hykCn020:11627:0:99999:7:::
```

Each /etc/shadow file record includes nine fields:

- The login name corresponding to the login name in the /etc/passwd file
- The encrypted password
- The day the password was last changed, depicted as the number of days since January 1, 1970
- The minimum number of days before the password can be changed
- The number of days before the password must be changed
- The number of days before password expiration that the user is warned to change the password
- The number of days after a password expires before the account will be disabled

- The date (stored as the number of days since January 1, 1970) since the user account was disabled
- A field reserved for future use

Using the shadow password system, the Linux system has much finer control over user passwords. It can control how often a user must change their password and when to disable the account if the password hasn't been changed.

## Adding a new user

The primary tool used to add new users to your Linux system is useradd. This command provides an easy way to create a new user account and set up the user's $HOME directory structure all at once. The useradd command uses a combination of system default values and command-line parameters to define a user account. To see the system default values used on your Linux distribution, enter the **useradd** command with the **-D** parameter:

```
# useradd -D
GROUP=100
HOME=/home
INACTIVE=-1
EXPIRE=
SHELL=/bin/bash
SKEL=/etc/skel
CREATE_MAIL_SPOOL=yes
#
```

> **NOTE**
> The default values for the useradd command are set using the /etc/default/useradd file. Also, further security settings are defined in the /etc/login.defs file. You can tweak these files to change the default security behavior on your Linux system.

The -D parameter shows what defaults the useradd command uses if you don't specify them in the command line when creating a new user account. This example shows the following default values:

- The new user will be added to a common group with group ID 100.
- The new user will have a HOME account created in the directory /home/*loginname*.
- The account will not be disabled when the password expires.
- The new account will not be set to expire at a set date.
- The new account will use the bash shell as the default shell.
- The system will copy the contents of the /etc/skel directory to the user's $HOME directory.
- The system will create a file in the mail directory for the user account to receive mail.

The useradd command allows an administrator to create a default $HOME directory con-figuration and then uses that as a template to create the new user's $HOME directory. This allows you to place default files for the system in every new user's $HOME directory auto-matically. In the Ubuntu Linux system, the /etc/skel directory has the following files:

```
$ ls -al /etc/skel
total 32
drwxr-xr-x   2 root root  4096 2010-04-29 08:26 .
drwxr-xr-x 135 root root 12288 2010-09-23 18:49 ..
-rw-r--r--   1 root root   220 2010-04-18 21:51 .bash_logout
-rw-r--r--   1 root root  3103 2010-04-18 21:51 .bashrc
-rw-r--r--   1 root root   179 2010-03-26 08:31 examples.desktop
-rw-r--r--   1 root root   675 2010-04-18 21:51 .profile
$
```

You should recognize these files from Chapter 6, "Using Linux Environment Variables." These are the standard startup files for the Bash shell environment. The system automati-cally copies these default files into every user's $HOME directory you create.

You can test this by creating a new user account using the default system parameters and then looking at the $HOME directory for the new user:

```
# useradd -m test
# ls -al /home/test
total 24
drwxr-xr-x 2 test test 4096 2010-09-23 19:01 .
drwxr-xr-x 4 root root 4096 2010-09-23 19:01 ..
-rw-r--r-- 1 test test  220 2010-04-18 21:51 .bash_logout
-rw-r--r-- 1 test test 3103 2010-04-18 21:51 .bashrc
-rw-r--r-- 1 test test  179 2010-03-26 08:31 examples.desktop
-rw-r--r-- 1 test test  675 2010-04-18 21:51 .profile
#
```

For many Linux distributions the useradd command doesn't create a $HOME directory by default, but the -m command-line option tells it to create the $HOME directory. You can change that behavior within the /etc/login.defs file. As you can see in the example, the useradd command created the new $HOME directory, using the files contained in the /etc/skel directory.

> **NOTE**
>
> To run the user account administration commands in this chapter, you need to either be logged in as the special root user account or use the sudo command to run the commands as the root user account.

If you want to override a default value or behavior when creating a new user, you can do that with command-line parameters. These are shown in Table 7-1.

TABLE 7-1   **The useradd Command-Line Parameters**

| Parameter | Description |
|---|---|
| -c *comment* | Add text to the new user's comment field. |
| -d *home _ dir* | Specify a different name for the home directory other than the login name. |
| -e *expire_date* | Specify a date, in YYYY-MM-DD format, when the account will expire. |
| -f *inactive_days* | Specify the number of days after a password expires when the account will be disabled. A value of 0 disables the account as soon as the password expires; a value of -1 disables this feature. |
| -g *initial_group* | Specify the group name or GID of the user's login group. |
| -G *group* . . . | Specify one or more supplementary groups the user belongs to. |
| -k | Copy the /etc/skel directory contents into the user's $HOME directory (must use -m as well). |
| -m | Create the user's $HOME directory. |
| -M | Don't create a user's $HOME directory (used if the default setting is to create one). |
| -n | Create a new group using the same name as the user's login name. |
| -r | Create a system account. |
| -p *passwd* | Specify a default password for the user account. |
| -s *shell* | Specify the default login shell. |
| -u *uid* | Specify a unique UID for the account. |

As you can see, you can override all the system default values when creating a new user account just by using command-line parameters. However, if you find yourself having to override a value all the time, it's easier to just change the system default value.

You can change the system default new user values by using the -D parameter, along with a parameter representing the value you need to change. These parameters are shown in Table 7-2.

TABLE 7-2   **The useradd Change Default Values Parameters**

| Parameter | Description |
|---|---|
| -b *default_home* | Change the location where users' home directories are created. |
| -e *expiration_date* | Change the expiration date on new accounts. |
| -f *inactive* | Change the number of days after a password has expired before the account is disabled. |
| -g *group* | Change the default group name or GID used. |
| -s *shell* | Change the default login shell. |

Changing the default values is a snap:

```
# useradd -D -s /bin/tsch
# useradd -D
GROUP=100
HOME=/home
INACTIVE=-1
EXPIRE=
SHELL=/bin/tsch
SKEL=/etc/skel
CREATE_MAIL_SPOOL=yes
#
```

Now, the useradd command will use the tsch shell as the default login shell for all new user accounts you create.

## Removing a user

If you want to remove a user from the system, the userdel command is what you need. By default, the userdel command removes only the user information from the /etc/passwd and /etc/shadow files. It doesn't remove any files the account owns on the system.

If you use the -r parameter, userdel will remove the user's $HOME directory, along with the user's mail directory. However, there may still be other files owned by the deleted user account on the system. This can be a problem in some environments.

Here's an example of using the userdel command to remove an existing user account:

```
# userdel -r test
# ls -al /home/test
ls: cannot access /home/test: No such file or directory
#
```

After using the -r parameter, the user's old /home/test directory no longer exists.

**CAUTION**

Be careful when using the -r parameter in an environment with lots of users. You never know if a user had important files stored in their $HOME directory that are used by someone else or another program. Always check before removing a user's $HOME directory!

## Modifying a user

Linux provides a few utilities for modifying the information for existing user accounts. Table 7-3 shows these utilities.

TABLE 7-3  **User Account Modification Utilities**

| Command | Description |
|---|---|
| usermod | Edits user account fields, and specifies primary and secondary group membership |
| passwd | Changes the password for an existing user |
| chpasswd | Reads a file of login name and password pairs, and updates the passwords |
| chage | Changes the password's expiration date |
| chfn | Changes the user account's comment information |
| chsh | Changes the user account's default shell |

Each utility provides a specific function for changing information about user accounts. The following sections describe each of these utilities.

### usermod

The usermod command is the most robust of the user account modification utilities. It provides options for changing most of the fields in the /etc/passwd file. To do that, you just need to use the command-line parameter that corresponds to the value you want to change. The parameters are mostly the same as the useradd parameters (such as -c to change the comment field, -e to change the expiration date, and -g to change the default login group). However, a few additional parameters might come in handy:

- -l to change the login name of the user account
- -L to lock the account so the user can't log in
- -p to change the password for the account
- -U to unlock the account so that the user can log in

The -L parameter is especially handy. Use it to lock an account so that a user can't log in without having to remove the account and the user's data. To return the account to normal, just use the -U parameter.

### passwd and chpasswd

A quick way to change just the password for a user is the passwd command:

```
# passwd test
Changing password for user test.
New UNIX password:
Retype new UNIX password:
passwd: all authentication tokens updated successfully.
#
```

If you just use the passwd command by itself, it will change your own password. Any user in the system can change their own password, but only the root user can change someone else's password.

The -e option is a handy way to force a user to change the password on the next login. This allows you to set the user's password to a simple value and then force them to change it to something harder that they can remember.

If you ever need to do a mass password change for lots of users on the system, the chpasswd command can be a lifesaver. The chpasswd command reads a list of login name and password pairs (colon-separated) from the standard input, automatically encrypts the password, and sets it for the user account. You can also use the redirection command to redirect a file of *username:password* pairs into the command:

```
# chpasswd < users.txt
#
```

### chsh, chfn, and chage

The chsh, chfn, and chage utilities are used for specific account modification functions. The chsh command allows you to quickly change the default login shell for a user. You must use the full pathname for the shell and not just the shell name:

```
#  chsh -s /bin/csh test
Changing shell for test.
Shell changed.
#
```

The chfn command provides a standard method for storing information in the comments field in the /etc/passwd file. Instead of just inserting random text, such as names or nicknames, or even just leaving the comment field blank, the chfn command uses specific information used in the Unix finger command to store information in the comment field. The finger command allows you to easily find information about people on your Linux system:

```
# finger rich
Login: rich                             Name: Rich Blum
Directory: /home/rich                   Shell: /bin/bash
On since Thu Sep 20 18:03 (EDT) on pts/0 from 192.168.1.2
No mail.
No Plan.
#
```

> **NOTE**
>
> Because of security concerns, most Linux distributions don't install the finger command by default. Be aware that installing it may open your system to attack vulnerabilities.

If you use the chfn command with no parameters, it queries you for the appropriate values to enter in the comment field:

```
# chfn test
Changing finger information for test.
Name []: Ima Test
```

```
Office []: Director of Technology
Office Phone []: (123)555-1234
Home Phone []: (123)555-9876

Finger information changed.
# finger test
Login: test                              Name: Ima Test
Directory: /home/test                    Shell: /bin/csh
Office: Director of Technology           Office Phone: (123)555-1234
Home Phone: (123)555-9876
Never logged in.
No mail.
No Plan.
#
```

If you now check the entry in the /etc/passwd file, it looks like this:

```
# grep test /etc/passwd
test:x:504:504:Ima Test,Director of Technology,(123)555-
1234,(123)555-9876:/home/test:/bin/csh
#
```

All of the finger information is neatly stored away in the /etc/passwd file entry.

Finally, the chage command helps you manage the password aging process for user accounts. There are several parameters to set individual values, as shown in Table 7-4.

### TABLE 7-4   The chage Command Parameters

| Parameter | Description |
|-----------|-------------|
| -d | Set the number of days since the password was last changed. |
| -E | Set the date the password will expire. |
| -I | Set the number of days of inactivity after the password expires to lock the account. |
| -m | Set the minimum number of days between password changes. |
| -M | Set the maximum number of days the password is valid. |
| -W | Set the number of days before the password expires that a warning message appears. |

The chage date values can be expressed using one of two methods:

- A date in YYYY-MM-DD format
- A numerical value representing the number of days since January 1, 1970

One neat feature of the chage command is that it allows you to set an expiration date for an account. Using this feature, you can create temporary user accounts that automatically expire on a set date, without your having to remember to delete them! Expired accounts are similar to locked accounts. The account still exists, but the user can't log in with it.

# Using Linux Groups

User accounts are great for controlling security for individual users, but they aren't so good at allowing groups of users to share resources. To accomplish this, the Linux system uses another security concept, called *groups*.

Group permissions allow multiple users to share a common set of permissions for an object on the system, such as a file, directory, or device (more on that later in the "Decoding File Permissions" section).

Linux distributions differ somewhat on how they handle default group memberships. Some Linux distributions create just one group that contains all the user accounts as members. You need to be careful if your Linux distribution does this, because your files may be readable by all other users on the system. Other distributions create a separate user account for each user to provide a little more security.

Each group has a unique GID, which, like UIDs, is a unique numerical value on the system. Along with the GID, each group has a unique group name. There are a few group utilities you can use to create and manage your own groups on the Linux system. This section discusses how group information is stored and how to use the group utilities to create new groups and modify existing groups.

## The /etc/group file

Just like user accounts, group information is stored in a file on the system. The /etc/group file contains information about each group used on the system. Here are a few examples from a typical /etc/group file on a Linux system:

```
root:x:0:root
bin:x:1:root,bin,daemon
daemon:x:2:root,bin,daemon
sys:x:3:root,bin,adm
adm:x:4:root,adm,daemon
rich:x:500:
mama:x:501:
katie:x:502:
jessica:x:503:
mysql:x:27:
test:x:504:
```

Like UIDs, GIDs are assigned using a special format. Groups used for system accounts are assigned GIDs below 500, and user groups are assigned GIDs starting at 500. The /etc/group file uses four fields:

- The group name
- The group password
- The GID
- The list of user accounts that belong to the group

The group password allows a non-group member to temporarily become a member of the group by using the password. This feature is not used all that commonly, but it does exist.

Since the /etc/group file is a standard text file, you can manually edit the file to add and modify group memberships. However, be careful that you don't make any typos or you could corrupt the file and cause problems for your system. Instead, it's safer to use the usermod command (discussed earlier in the "Exploring Linux Security" section) to add a user account to a group. Before you can add users to different groups, you must create the groups.

> **NOTE**
> The list of user accounts is somewhat misleading. You'll notice that there are several groups in the list that don't have any users listed. This isn't because they don't have any members. When a user account uses a group as the primary group in the /etc/passwd file, the user account doesn't appear in the /etc/group file as a member. This has caused confusion for more than one system administrator over the years!

## Creating new groups

The groupadd command allows you to create new groups on your system:

```
# /usr/sbin/groupadd shared
# tail /etc/group
haldaemon:x:68:
xfs:x:43:
gdm:x:42:
rich:x:500:
mama:x:501:
katie:x:502:
jessica:x:503:
mysql:x:27:
test:x:504:
shared:x:505:
#
```

When you create a new group, no users are assigned to it by default. The groupadd command doesn't provide an option for adding user accounts to the group. Instead, to add new users, use the usermod command:

```
# /usr/sbin/usermod -G shared rich
# /usr/sbin/usermod -G shared test
```

```
# tail /etc/group
haldaemon:x:68:
xfs:x:43:
gdm:x:42:
rich:x:500:
mama:x:501:
katie:x:502:
jessica:x:503:
mysql:x:27:
test:x:504:
shared:x:505:rich, test
#
```

The shared group now has two members, test and rich. The -G parameter in usermod appends the new group to the list of groups for the user account.

> **NOTE**
>
> If you change the user groups for an account that is currently logged into the system, the user will have to log out, then back in for the group changes to take effect.

> **CAUTION**
>
> Be careful when assigning groups for user accounts. If you use the -g parameter, the group name you specify replaces the primary group assigned to the user account in the /etc/passwd file. The -G parameter adds the group to the list of groups the user belongs to, keeping the primary group intact.

## Modifying groups

As you can see from the /etc/group file, there isn't too much information about a group for you to modify. The groupmod command allows you to change the GID (using the -g parameter) or the group name (using the -n parameter) of an existing group:

```
# groupmod -n sharing shared
# tail /etc/group
haldaemon:x:68:
xfs:x:43:
gdm:x:42:
rich:x:500:
mama:x:501:
katie:x:502:
jessica:x:503:
mysql:x:27:
test:x:504:
sharing:x:505:test,rich
#
```

When changing the name of a group, the GID and group members remain the same and only the group name changes. Because all security permissions are based on the GID, you can change the name of a group as often as you wish without adversely affecting file security.

# Decoding File Permissions

Now that you know about users and groups, it's time to decode the cryptic file permissions you've seen when using the ls command. This section describes how to decipher the permissions and where they come from.

## Using file permission symbols

As you'll recall from Chapter 3, "Basic Bash Shell Commands," the ls command allows you to see the file permissions for files, directories, and devices on the Linux system:

```
$ ls -l
total 68
-rw-rw-r-- 1 rich rich   50 2010-09-13 07:49 file1.gz
-rw-rw-r-- 1 rich rich   23 2010-09-13 07:50 file2
-rw-rw-r-- 1 rich rich   48 2010-09-13 07:56 file3
-rw-rw-r-- 1 rich rich   34 2010-09-13 08:59 file4
-rwxrwxr-x 1 rich rich 4882 2010-09-18 13:58 myprog
-rw-rw-r-- 1 rich rich  237 2010-09-18 13:58 myprog.c
drwxrwxr-x 2 rich rich 4096 2010-09-03 15:12 test1
drwxrwxr-x 2 rich rich 4096 2010-09-03 15:12 test2
$
```

The first field in the output listing is a code that describes the permissions for the files and directories. The first character in the field defines the type of the object:

- - for files
- d for directories
- l for links
- c for character devices
- b for block devices
- p for named pipes
- s for network sockets

After that, there are three sets of three characters. Each set of three characters defines an access permission triplet:

- r for read permission for the object
- w for write permission for the object
- x for execute permission for the object

If a permission is denied, a dash appears in the location. The three sets relate to the three levels of security for the object:

- The owner of the object
- The group that owns the object
- Everyone else on the system

This is broken down in Figure 7-1.

**FIGURE 7-1**

The Linux file permissions

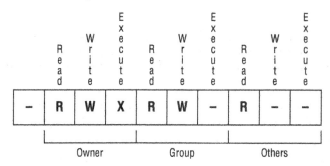

The easiest way to discuss this is to take an example and decode the file permissions one by one:

```
-rwxrwxr-x 1 rich rich 4882 2010-09-18 13:58 myprog
```

The file `myprog` has the following sets of permissions:

- `rwx` for the file owner (set to the login name rich)
- `rwx` for the file group owner (set to the group name rich)
- `r-x` for everyone else on the system

These permissions indicate that the user login name rich can read, write, and execute the file (considered full permissions). Likewise, members in the group rich can also read, write, and execute the file. However, anyone else not in the rich group can only read and execute the file; the *w* is replaced with a dash, indicating that write permissions are not assigned to this security level.

## Default file permissions

You may be wondering about where these file permissions come from. The answer is *umask*. The umask command sets the default permissions for any file or directory you create:

```
$ touch newfile
$ ls -al newfile
-rw-r--r--    1 rich      rich              0 Sep 20 19:16 newfile
$
```

The touch command created the file using the default permissions assigned to my user account. The umask command shows and sets the default permissions:

```
$ umask
0022
$
```

Unfortunately, the umask command setting isn't overtly clear, and trying to understand exactly how it works makes things even muddier. The first digit represents a special security feature assigned to the file. We'll talk more about that later on in this chapter in the "Sharing Files" section.

The next three digits represent the octal values of the umask for a file or directory. To understand how umask works, you first need to understand octal mode security settings.

Octal mode security settings take the three rwx permission values and convert them into a 3-bit binary value, represented by a single octal value. In the binary representation, each position is a binary bit. Thus, if the read permission is the only permission set, the value becomes r--, relating to a binary value of 100, indicating the octal value of 4. Table 7-5 shows the possible combinations you'll run into.

**TABLE 7-5    Linux File Permission Codes**

| Permissions | Binary | Octal | Description |
|---|---|---|---|
| --- | 000 | 0 | No permissions |
| --x | 001 | 1 | Execute-only permission |
| -w- | 010 | 2 | Write-only permission |
| -wx | 011 | 3 | Write and execute permissions |
| r-- | 100 | 4 | Read-only permission |
| r-x | 101 | 5 | Read and execute permissions |
| rw- | 110 | 6 | Read and write permissions |
| rwx | 111 | 7 | Read, write, and execute permissions |

Octal mode takes the octal permissions and lists three of them in order for the three security levels (user, group, and everyone). Thus, the octal mode value 664 represents read and write permissions for the user and group but read-only permission for everyone else.

Now that you know about octal mode permissions, the umask value becomes even more confusing. The octal mode shown for the default umask on my Linux system is 0022, but the file I created had an octal mode permission of 644. How did that happen?

The umask value is just that, a mask. It masks out the permissions you don't want to give to the security level. Now we have to dive into some octal arithmetic to figure out the rest of the story.

The umask value is subtracted from the full permission set for an object. The full permission for a file is mode 666 (read/write permission for all), but for a directory it's 777 (read/write/execute permission for all).

Thus, in the example, the file starts out with permissions 666, and the umask of 022 is applied, leaving a file permission of 644.

The umask value is normally set in the /etc/profile startup file (see Chapter 6). You can specify a different default umask setting using the umask command:

```
$ umask 026
$ touch newfile2
$ ls -l newfile2
-rw-r-----    1 rich      rich             0 Sep 20 19:46 newfile2
$
```

When we set the umask value to 026, the default file permissions became 640, so the new file is now restricted to read-only for the group members, and everyone else on the system has no permissions to the file.

The umask value also applies to making new directories:

```
$ mkdir newdir
$ ls -l
drwxr-x--x    2 rich      rich          4096 Sep 20 20:11 newdir/
$
```

Because the default permissions for a directory are 777, the resulting permissions from the umask are different from those of a new file. The 026 umask value is subtracted from 777, leaving the 751 directory permission setting.

# Changing Security Settings

If you've already created a file or directory and need to change the security settings on it, a few different utilities for this purpose are available in Linux. This section shows you how to change the existing permissions, the default owner, and the default group settings for a file or directory.

## Changing permissions

The `chmod` command allows you to change the security settings for files and directories. The format of the `chmod` command is

```
chmod options mode file
```

The *mode* parameter allows you to set the security settings using either octal or symbolic mode. The octal mode settings are pretty straightforward; just use the standard three-digit octal code you want the file to have:

```
$ chmod 760 newfile
$ ls -l newfile
-rwxrw----    1 rich     rich               0 Sep 20 19:16 newfile
$
```

The octal file permissions are automatically applied to the file indicated. The symbolic mode permissions are not so easy to implement.

Instead of using the normal string of three sets of three characters, the `chmod` command takes a different approach. The following is the format for specifying a permission in symbolic mode:

```
[ugoa...][[+-=][rwxXstugo...]
```

Makes perfectly good sense, doesn't it? The first group of characters defines to whom the new permissions apply:

- u for the user
- g for the group
- o for others (everyone else)
- a for all of the above

Next, a symbol is used to indicate whether you want to add the permission to the existing permissions (+), subtract the permission from the existing permissions (–), or set the permissions to the value (=).

Finally, the third symbol is the permission used for the setting. You may notice that there are more than the normal `rwx` values here. The additional settings are as follows:

- X to assign execute permissions only if the object is a directory or if it already had execute permissions
- s to set the SUID or SGID on execution
- t to set the sticky bit
- u to set the permissions to the owner's permissions
- g to set the permissions to the group's permissions
- o to set the permissions to the others' permissions

Using these permissions looks like this:

```
$ chmod o+r newfile
$ ls -l newfile
-rwxrw-r--    1 rich      rich            0 Sep 20 19:16 newfile
$
```

The o+r entry adds the read permission to whatever permissions the everyone security level already had.

```
$ chmod u-x newfile
$ ls -l newfile
-rw-rw-r--    1 rich      rich            0 Sep 20 19:16 newfile
$
```

The u-x entry removes the execute permission that the user already had. Note that the settings for the ls command indicate if a file has execution permissions by adding an asterisk to the filename.

The *options* parameters provide a few additional features to augment the behavior of the chmod command. The -R parameter performs the file and directory changes recursively. You can use wildcard characters for the filename specified, changing the permissions on multiple files with just one command.

## Changing ownership

Sometimes you need to change the owner of a file, such as when someone leaves an organization or a developer creates an application that needs to be owned by a system account when it's in production. Linux provides two commands for doing that. The chown command makes it easy to change the owner of a file, and the chgrp command allows you to change the default group of a file.

The format of the chown command is

```
chown options owner[.group] file
```

You can specify either the login name or the numeric UID for the new owner of the file:

```
# chown dan newfile
# ls -l newfile
-rw-rw-r--    1 dan       rich            0 Sep 20 19:16 newfile
#
```

Simple. The chown command also allows you to change both the user and group of a file:

```
# chown dan.shared newfile
# ls -l newfile
-rw-rw-r--    1 dan       shared          0 Sep 20 19:16 newfile
#
```

If you really want to get tricky, you can just change the default group for a file:

```
# chown .rich newfile
# ls -l newfile
-rw-rw-r--    1 dan       rich           0 Sep 20 19:16 newfile
#
```

Finally, if your Linux system uses individual group names that match user login names, you can change both with just one entry:

```
# chown test. newfile
# ls -l newfile
-rw-rw-r--    1 test      test           0 Sep 20 19:16 newfile
#
```

The chown command uses a few different *options* parameters. The -R parameter allows you to make changes recursively through subdirectories and files, using a wildcard character. The -h parameter also changes the ownership of any files that are symbolically linked to the file.

> **NOTE**
>
> Only the root user can change the owner of a file. Any user can change the default group of a file, but the user must be a member of the groups the file is changed from and to.

The chgrp command provides an easy way to change just the default group for a file or directory:

```
$ chgrp shared newfile
$ ls -l newfile
-rw-rw-r--    1 rich      shared         0 Sep 20 19:16 newfile
$
```

Now any member in the shared group can write to the file. This is one way to share files on a Linux system. However, sharing files among a group of people on the system can get tricky. The next section discusses how to do this.

## Sharing Files

As you've probably already figured out, creating groups is the way to share access to files on the Linux system. However, for a complete file-sharing environment, things are more complicated.

As you've already seen in the "Decoding File Permissions" section, when you create a new file, Linux assigns the file permissions of the new file using your default UID and GID. To allow others access to the file, you need to either change the security permissions for the everyone security group or assign the file a different default group that contains other users.

This can be a pain in a large environment if you want to create and share documents among several people. Fortunately, there's a simple solution for this problem.

Linux stores three additional bits of information for each file and directory:

- **The set user ID (SUID):** When a file is executed by a user, the program runs under the permissions of the file owner.
- **The set group ID (SGID):** For a file, the program runs under the permissions of the file group. For a directory, new files created in the directory use the directory group as the default group.
- **The sticky bit:** When applied to a directory, only file owners can delete or rename the files in the directory.

The SGID bit is important for sharing files. By enabling the SGID bit, you can force all new files created in a shared directory to be owned by the directory's group and now the individual user's group.

The SGID is set using the chmod command. It's added to the beginning of the standard three-digit octal value (making a four-digit octal value), or you can use the symbol s in symbolic mode.

If you're using octal mode, you'll need to know the arrangement of the bits, shown in Table 7-6.

**TABLE 7-6   The chmod SUID, SGID, and Sticky Bit Octal Values**

| Binary | Octal | Description |
|--------|-------|-------------|
| 000 | 0 | All bits are cleared. |
| 001 | 1 | The sticky bit is set. |
| 010 | 2 | The SGID bit is set. |
| 011 | 3 | The SGID and sticky bits are set. |
| 100 | 4 | The SUID bit is set. |
| 101 | 5 | The SUID and sticky bits are set. |
| 110 | 6 | The SUID and SGID bits are set. |
| 111 | 7 | All bits are set. |

So, to create a shared directory that always sets the directory group for all new files, all you need to do is set the SGID bit for the directory:

```
$ mkdir testdir
$ ls -l
drwxrwxr-x    2 rich      rich          4096 Sep 20 23:12 testdir/
$ chgrp shared testdir
$ chmod g+s testdir
```

```
$ ls -l
drwxrwsr-x    2 rich      shared      4096 Sep 20 23:12 testdir/
$ umask 002
$ cd testdir
$ touch testfile
$ ls -l
total 0
-rw-rw-r--    1 rich      shared         0 Sep 20 23:13 testfile
$
```

The first step is to create a directory that you want to share using the mkdir command. Next, the chgrp command is used to change the default group for the directory to a group that contains the members who need to share files. Finally, the SGID bit is set for the directory to ensure that any files created in the directory use the shared group name as the default group.

For this environment to work properly, all of the group members need to have their umask values set to make files writable by group members. In the preceding example, the umask is changed to 002 so that the files are writable by the group.

After all that's done, any member of the group can go to the shared directory and create a new file. As expected, the new file uses the default group of the directory, not the user account's default group. Now any user in the shared group can access this file.

## Access Control Lists

The basic Linux method of permissions has one drawback in that it's somewhat limited. You can assign permissions for a file or directory only to a single group or user account. In a complex business environment with different groups of people needing different permissions to files and directories, that doesn't work.

Linux developers have devised a more advanced method of file and directory security called an *access control list (ACL)*. The ACL allows you to specify a list of multiple user or groups, and the permissions that are assigned to them. Just like the basic security method, ACL permissions use the same read, write, and execute permission bits but can now be assigned to multiple users and groups.

To use the ACL feature in Linux, you use the setfacl and getfacl commands. The getfacl command allows you to view the ACLs assigned to a file or directory:

```
$ touch test
$ ls -l
total 0
-rw-r----- 1 rich rich 0 Apr 19 17:33 test
$ getfacl test
# file: test
```

```
# owner: rich
# group: rich
user::rw-
group::r--
other::---
$
```

If you've only assigned basic security permissions to the file, those still appear in the get-facl output, as shown in this example.

To assign permissions for additional users or groups, you use the setfacl command:

```
setfacl [options] rule filenames
```

The setfacl command allows you to modify the permissions assigned to a file or directory using the -m option, or remove specific permissions using the -x option. You define the *rule* with three formats:

```
u[ser]:uid:perms
g[roup]:gid:perms
o[ther]::perms
```

To assign permissions for additional user accounts, use the user format; for additional groups, use the group format; and for others, use the other format. For the uid or gid values, you can use either the numerical user ID or group ID, or the names. Here's an example:

```
$ setfacl -m g:sales:rw test
$ ls -l
total 0
-rw-rw----+ 1 rich rich 0 Apr 19 17:33 test
$
```

This example adds read and write permissions for the sales group to the test file. Notice that there's no output from the setfacl command. When you list the file, only the standard owner, group, and other permissions are shown, but note that there's a plus sign (+) added to the permissions list. This indicates that the file has additional ACLs applied to it. To view the additional ACLs, use the getfacl command again:

```
$ getfacl test
# file: test
# owner: rich
# group: rich
user::rw-
group::r--
group:sales:rw-
mask::rw-
other::---
$
```

The `getfacl` output now shows that there are permissions assigned to two groups. The default file group (`rich`) is assigned read permissions, but now the `sales` group has read and write permissions to the file. To remove the permissions, use the `-x` option:

```
$ setfacl -x g:sales test
$ getfacl test
# file: test
# owner: rich
# group: rich
user::rw-
group::r--
mask::r--
other::---

$
```

Linux also allows you to set a default ACL on a directory that is automatically inherited by any file created in the directory. This feature is called inheritance.

To create a default ACL on a directory, start the rule with `d:` followed by the normal rule definition. That looks like this:

```
$ sudo setfacl -m d:g:sales:rw /sales
```

This example assigns the read and write permissions to the `sales` group for the `/sales` directory. Now all files created in that folder will automatically be assigned read and write permissions for the `sales` group.

## Summary

This chapter discussed the command-line commands you need to know to manage the Linux security on your system. Linux uses a system of user IDs and group IDs to protect access to files, directories, and devices. Linux stores information about user accounts in the /etc/passwd file and information about groups in the /etc/group file. Each user is assigned a unique numeric user ID, along with a text login name to identify the user in the system. Groups are also assigned unique numerical group IDs, and text group names. A group can contain one or more users allowed shared access to system resources.

Several commands are available for managing user accounts and groups. The useradd command allows you to create new user accounts, and the groupadd command allows you to create new group accounts. To modify an existing user account, use the usermod command. Similarly, the groupmod command is used to modify group account information.

Linux uses a complicated system of bits to determine access permissions for files and directories. Each file contains three security levels of protection: the file's owner, a default group that has access to the file, and a level for everyone else on the system. Each security level is defined by three access bits: read, write, and execute. The combination of three bits is often referred to by the symbols `rwx`, for read, write, and execute. If a permission is denied, its symbol is replaced with a dash (such as `r--` for read-only permission).

The symbolic permissions are often referred to as octal values, with the three bits combined into one octal value and three octal values representing the three security levels. The `umask` command is used to set the default security settings for files and directories created on the system. The system administrator normally sets a default umask value in the `/etc/profile` file, but you can use the `umask` command to change your umask value at any time.

The `chmod` command is used to change security settings for files and directories. Only the file's owner can change permissions for a file or directory. However, the root user can change the security settings for any file or directory on the system. The `chown` and `chgrp` commands can be used to change the default owner and group of the file.

The chapter also discussed how to use the set GID bit to create a shared directory. The SGID bit forces any new files or directories created in a directory to use the default group name of the parent directory, not that of the user who created them. This provides an easy way to share files between users on the system.

Finally, the chapter provided a primer on using the Linux ACL feature to assign more detailed and advanced permissions to files and directories. The `getfacl` and `setfacl` commands provide access to this feature.

Now that you're up to speed with file permissions, it's time to take a closer look at how to work with the actual filesystem in Linux. The next chapter shows you how to create new partitions in Linux from the command line and then how to format the new partitions so that they can be used in the Linux virtual directory.

7

# Managing Filesystems

W hen you're working with your Linux system, one of the decisions you'll need to make is what filesystem to use for the storage devices. Most Linux distributions provide a default filesystem for you at installation time, and most beginning Linux users just use it without giving the topic another thought.

Although using the default filesystem isn't necessarily a bad thing, sometimes it helps to know the other options available to you. This chapter discusses the different filesystem options you have available in the Linux world and shows you how to create and manage them from the Linux command line.

## Exploring Linux Filesystems

Chapter 3, "Basic Bash Shell Commands," discussed how Linux uses a *filesystem* to store files and folders on a storage device. The filesystem provides a way for Linux to bridge the gap between the ones and zeroes stored in the hard drive and the files and folders you work with in your applications.

Linux supports several types of filesystems to manage files and folders. Each filesystem implements the virtual directory structure on storage devices using slightly different features. This section walks you through the strengths and weaknesses of common filesystems used in the Linux environment as well as some history regarding them.

## Exploring the Linux filesystem evolution

The original Linux system used a simple filesystem that mimicked the functionality of the Unix filesystem. This section discusses its improvements through time.

### Looking at the ext filesystem

The original filesystem introduced with the Linux operating system was called the *extended filesystem* (or just *ext* for short). It provided a basic Unix-like filesystem for Linux, using virtual directories to handle physical devices and storing data in fixed-length blocks on the physical devices.

The ext filesystem used a system called *inodes* to track information about the files stored in the virtual directory. The inode system created a separate table on each physical device, called the *inode table*, to store file information. Each stored file in the virtual directory had an entry in the inode table. The *extended* part of the name comes from the additional data that it tracked on each file, which consisted of these items:

- The filename
- The file size
- The owner of the file
- The group the file belongs to
- Access permissions for the file
- Pointers to each disk block that contains data from the file

Linux referenced each inode in the inode table using a unique number (called the inode number), assigned by the filesystem as data files were created. The filesystem used the inode number to identify the file rather than having to use the full filename and path.

### Looking at the ext2 filesystem

The original ext filesystem had quite a few limitations, such as restraining files to only 2 GB in size. Not too long after Linux was first introduced, the ext filesystem was upgraded to create the second extended filesystem, called *ext2*.

The ext2 filesystem maintained the same ext filesystem structure but expanded its abilities:

- Created, modified, and last accessed time values for files were added to the inode table.
- The maximum file size allowed was increased to 2 TB, and then later to 32 TB.
- Disk blocks were allocated in groups when a file was saved.

The ext2 filesystem too had limitations. If something happened to the system between a file being stored and the inode table being updated, a potential result was losing the file's data location on the disk. The ext2 filesystem was notorious for experiencing these corruptions due to system crashes and power outages. And it wasn't long before developers were exploring a different avenue of Linux filesystems.

# Digging into journaling filesystems

*Journaling filesystems* provide a new level of safety to the Linux system. Instead of writing data directly to the storage device and then updating the inode table, journaling filesystems write file changes into a temporary file (called the *journal*) first. After data is successfully written to the storage device and the inode table, the journal entry is deleted.

If the system should crash or suffer a power outage before the data can be written to the storage device, the journaling filesystem reads through the journal file and processes any uncommitted data.

Linux commonly uses three different methods of journaling, each with different levels of protection. These are shown in Table 8-1.

**TABLE 8-1   Journaling Filesystem Methods**

| Method | Description |
| --- | --- |
| Data mode | Both inode and file data are journaled. Low risk of losing data, but poor performance |
| Ordered mode | Only inode data is written to the journal, but not removed until file data is successfully written. Good compromise between performance and safety |
| Writeback mode | Only inode data is written to the journal; no control over when the file data is written. Higher risk of losing data but still better than not using journaling |

8

The data mode journaling method is by far the safest for protecting data, but it is also the slowest. All the data written to a storage device must be written twice, once to the journal and again to the actual storage device. This can cause poor performance, especially for systems that do lots of data writing.

Over the years, a few different journaling filesystems have appeared in Linux. The following sections briefly describe the popular Linux journaling filesystems available.

## Looking at the ext3 filesystem

The *ext3* filesystem is a descendant of ext2 that supports files up to 2 TB, with a total file system size of 32 TB. By default, it uses the ordered mode method of journaling, but the other modes are available via command-line options. It doesn't provide any recovery from accidental file deletion or allow data compression by default.

## Looking at the ext4 filesystem

A still popular descendant of ext3, the *ext4* filesystem supports files up to 16 tebibytes (TiB), with a total file system size of 1 exbibyte (EiB). By default, it uses the ordered mode method of journaling, but the other modes are available via command-line options. It supports encryption, compression, and unlimited subdirectories within a single directory. Old ext2 and ext3 filesystems can be mounted as if they were ext4 to improve their performance.

### Looking at the JFS filesystem

Possibly one of the oldest journaling filesystems around, the *Journaled File System* (*JFS*) was developed by IBM in 1990 for its AIX (Advanced Interactive Executive) flavor of Unix. However, it wasn't until its second version that it was ported to the Linux environment.

> **NOTE**
> The official IBM name of the second version of the JFS filesystem is JFS2, but most Linux systems refer to it as just JFS.

The JFS filesystem uses the ordered journaling method, storing only the inode table data in the journal and not removing it until the actual file data is written to the storage device.

### Looking at ReiserFS

In 2001, Hans Reiser created the first journaling filesystem for Linux, called *ReiserFS*, which provides features now found in both ext3 and ext4. Linux has dropped support for the most recent version, Reiser4.

### Looking at XFS

The *X File System* (*XFS*) was created by Silicon Graphics for their (now defunct) advanced graphical workstations. The filesystem provided some advanced high-performance features that make it still popular in Linux.

The XFS filesystem uses the writeback mode of journaling, which provides high performance but does introduce an amount of risk because the actual data isn't stored in the journal file.

## Understanding the volume-managing filesystems

With journaling, you must choose between safety and performance. Although data mode journaling provides the highest safety, performance suffers because both inode and data are journaled. With writeback mode journaling, performance is acceptable but safety is compromised.

For filesystems, an alternative to journaling is a technique called *copy-on-write (COW)*. COW offers both safety and performance via *snapshots*. For modifying data, a *clone* or *writable snapshot* is used. Instead of writing modified data over current data, the modified data is put in a new filesystem location.

> **NOTE**
> A true COW system modifies the old data only when the data modification is completed. If old data is never overwritten, the proper term to call this action is a redirect-on-write (ROW). However, typically ROWs are simply called COWs.

Though disk sizes have grown significantly over the years, the need for more space is constant. *Storage pools*, which are created from one or more disks or disk partitions, provide the ability to create what appears to be a single disk, called a *volume*. Using these storage pools allows volumes to be grown as needed, providing flexibility and a lot less downtime.

Filesystems with COW, snapshot, and volume-management features are gaining in popularity. Two of the most popular, Btrfs and ZFS, are briefly reviewed in the following sections as well as a newcomer, Stratis.

### Looking at the ZFS filesystem

The *ZFS* filesystem was initially released in 2005 by Sun Microsystems for the OpenSolaris operating system. It began being ported to Linux in 2008 and was finally available for Linux production use in 2012.

ZFS is a stable filesystem that competes well against Resier4, Btrfs, and ext4. It boasts data integrity verification along with automatic repair, provides a maximum file size of 16 exabytes, and has a 256 quadrillion Zettabytes maximum storage size. That's one large filesystem!

Unfortunately, its biggest detractor is that ZFS does not have a GNU General Public License (GPL) and thus cannot be included in the Linux kernel. Fortunately, most Linux distributions provide a way for it to be installed.

### Looking at the Btrfs filesystem

The *Btrfs* filesystem (typically pronounced *butter-fs*) is also called the B-tree filesystem. Oracle started development on Btrfs in 2007. It was based on many of Reiser4's features but offered improvements in reliability. Over time, additional developers joined in and helped Btrfs quickly rise toward the top of the popular filesystems list. This popularity is due to stability and ease of use, as well as the ability to dynamically resize a mounted filesystem.

While the openSUSE Linux distribution established Btrfs as its default filesystem, in 2017 Red Hat deprecated it, meaning that it would no longer support the filesystem (as of RHEL version 8 and beyond). Unfortunately, for those organizations who are married to RHEL, it means that Btrfs is not the filesystem of choice.

### Looking at the Stratis filesystem

When Red Hat deprecated Btrfs, the decision was made to create a new filesystem, *Stratis*. But you cannot accurately call Stratis a filesystem using the standard definition. Instead, it provides more of a management perspective. The storage pools it maintains are made up of one or more XFS filesystems. And it also offers COW functionality like the more traditional volume-management filesystems, such as ZFS and Btrfs. The terms "ease of use" and "advanced storage features" are often used to describe it, but at this point, it's too early to tell how close to those concepts Stratis performs.

> **NOTE**
> XFS in recent years has been improving its COW offerings. For example, it now has an `always_cow` mode, which causes XFS to not overwrite original data when it is modified.

Stratis was first offered for inspection in Fedora 29 (released in 2018), and it is considered to be a technological preview feature in RHEL v8. This means that Stratis is not yet intended for use in a production environment. You've been warned.

# Working with Filesystems

Linux provides a few utilities that make it easier to work with filesystems from the command line. You can add new filesystems or change existing filesystems from the comfort of your own keyboard. This section walks you through the commands for managing filesystems from a command-line environment.

## Creating partitions

To start out, you need to create a *partition* on the storage device to contain the filesystem. The partition can be an entire disk or a subset of a disk that will contain a portion of the virtual directory.

Several utilities are available that can help you organize and manage partitions. The three CLI programs we'll focus on in this section are:

- `fdisk`
- `gdisk`
- GNU `parted`

Sometimes, the hardest part of creating a new disk partition is trying to find the physical disk on your Linux system. Linux uses a standard format for assigning device names to hard drives, and you need to be familiar with the format before partitioning a drive:

- SATA drives and SCSI drives: Linux uses /dev/sdx, where x is a letter based on the order in which the drive is detected (a for the first drive, b for the second, and so on)
- SSD NVMe drives: The device name format is /dev/nvmeNn#, where N is a number based on the order in which the drive is detected, starting at 0. And the # is the number assigned to the drive's namespace structure, starting at 1.
- IDE drives: Linux uses /dev/hdx, where x is a letter based on the order in which the drive is detected (a for the first drive, b for the second, and so on).

Once you have the correct drive name, you can consider which partitioning tool to use. The following sections take a look at three choices.

### Looking at the *fdisk* utility

The *fdisk* utility is an older but powerful tool for creating and managing partitions on any drive. However, fdisk handles only disks up to 2 TB in size. If you have a disk larger than that, you can use either the gdisk or the GNU parted utility instead.

> **TIP**
>
> If this is the first time you're partitioning the storage device, fdisk gives you a warning that a partition table is not on the device.

The `fdisk` command is an interactive program that allows you to enter commands to walk through the steps of partitioning a hard drive. To start the `fdisk` utility, you need to specify the device name of the storage device you want to partition, and you need to have super user privileges (be logged in as the root user or use the `sudo` command).

```
# whoami
root
# fdisk /dev/sda

Welcome to fdisk (util-linux 2.32.1).
Changes will remain in memory only, until you decide to write them.
Be careful before using the write command.


Command (m for help):
```

The `fdisk` program uses its own command line that allows you to submit commands to work with the drive partitions. Table 8-2 shows the common commands you have available with which to work.

**TABLE 8-2** **Common `fdisk` Commands**

| Command | Description |
|---|---|
| a | Toggle a bootable flag. |
| b | Edit bad disk label. |
| c | Toggle the DOS compatibility flag. |
| d | Delete a partition. |
| g | Create a new empty GPT partition table. |
| G | Create an IRIX (SGI) partition table. |
| l | List known partition types. |
| m | Print this menu. |
| n | Add a new partition. |
| o | Create a new empty DOS partition table. |
| p | Print the partition table. |
| q | Quit without saving changes. |
| s | Create a new empty Sun disk label. |
| t | Change a partition's system ID. |
| u | Change display/entry units. |
| v | Verify the partition table. |
| w | Write table to disk and exit. |
| x | Extra functionality (experts only). |

8

The p command displays the current partition scheme on the selected drive:

```
Command (m for help): p
Disk /dev/sda: 20 GiB, 21474836480 bytes, 41943040 sectors
Units: sectors of 1 * 512 = 512 bytes
Sector size (logical/physical): 512 bytes / 512 bytes
I/O size (minimum/optimal): 512 bytes / 512 bytes
Disklabel type: dos
Disk identifier: 0x8a136eb4

Device     Boot   Start      End  Sectors Size Id Type
/dev/sda1  *       2048  2099199  2097152  1G 83 Linux
/dev/sda2       2099200 41943039 39843840 19G 8e Linux LVM

Command (m for help):
```

In this example, the /dev/sda drive is sectioned into two partitions, sda1 and sda2. The first partition is allocated about 1 GB of space (shown in the Size column), while the second is allocated a little over 19 GB of space.

The fdisk command is somewhat rudimentary in that it doesn't allow you to alter the size of an existing partition; all you can do is delete the existing partition and rebuild it from scratch.

> **TIP**
>
> Some distributions and older distribution versions do not automatically inform your Linux system of a new partition after it is made. In this case, you need to use either the `partprobe` or the `hdparm` command (see their man pages), or reboot your system so that it reads the updated partition table.

If you make any changes to the drive partitions, you must exit using the w command to write the changes to the drive. To quit without making any modifications, use the q command:

```
Command (m for help): q
#
```

The following example makes a new partition on the /dev/sdb drive to use in the "Creating a Filesystem" section later in this chapter:

```
$ sudo fdisk /dev/sdb
[sudo] password for christine:
[...]
Command (m for help): n
Partition type
   p   primary (0 primary, 0 extended, 4 free)
   e   extended (container for logical partitions)
Select (default p): p
Partition number (1-4, default 1): 1
```

```
First sector (2048-4194303, default 2048):
Last sector, +sectors or +size{K,M,G,T,P} (2048-4194303,
default 4194303):

Created a new partition 1 of type 'Linux' and of size 2 GiB.

Command (m for help): w
The partition table has been altered.
Calling ioctl() to re-read partition table.
Syncing disks.

$
```

Now a new disk partition, /dev/sdb1, is ready for formatting. Be aware when creating a new disk partition with fdisk, you don't have to type in any information. Instead, just press Enter to accept the displayed defaults.

## Working with *gdisk*

If you're working with drives that use the GUID Partition Table (GPT) indexing method, you can use the *gdisk* program:

```
$ sudo gdisk /dev/sda
[sudo] password for christine:
GPT fdisk (gdisk) version 1.0.3

Partition table scan:
  MBR: MBR only
  BSD: not present
  APM: not present
  GPT: not present

*****************************************************************
Found invalid GPT and valid MBR; converting MBR to GPT format
in memory. THIS OPERATION IS POTENTIALLY DESTRUCTIVE! Exit by
typing 'q' if you don't want to convert your MBR partitions
to GPT format!
*****************************************************************
[...]
Command (? for help): q
$
```

The gdisk program identifies the type of formatting used on the drive. If the drive doesn't currently use the GPT method, gdisk offers you the option to convert it to a GPT drive.

**WARNING**
Be careful with converting the drive method specified for your drive. The method you select must be compatible with the system firmware (BIOS or UEFI). If not, your drive will not be able to boot.

The gdisk program also uses its own command prompt, allowing you to enter commands to manipulate the drive layout, as shown in Table 8-3.

**TABLE 8-3** **Common gdisk Commands**

| Command | Description |
| --- | --- |
| b | Back up GPT data to a file. |
| c | Change a partition's name. |
| d | Delete a partition. |
| i | Show detailed information on a partition. |
| l | List known partition types. |
| n | Add a new partition. |
| o | Create a new empty GUID partition table (GPT). |
| p | Print the partition table. |
| q | Quit without saving changes. |
| r | Recovery and transformation options (experts only). |
| s | Sort partitions. |
| t | Change a partition's type code. |
| v | Verify disk. |
| w | Write table to disk and exit. |
| x | Extra functionality (experts only). |
| ? | Print this menu. |

You'll notice that many of the gdisk commands are similar to those in the fdisk program, making it easier to switch between the two programs.

## The GNU *parted* command

The GNU *parted* program provides yet another command-line interface for working with drive partitions. Unlike the fdisk and gdisk programs, the commands within this utility are more word-like:

```
$ sudo parted
GNU Parted 3.2
Using /dev/sda
Welcome to GNU Parted! Type 'help' to view a list of commands.
(parted) print
Model: ATA VBOX HARDDISK (scsi)
Disk /dev/sda: 21.5GB
Sector size (logical/physical): 512B/512B
```

```
Partition Table: msdos
Disk Flags:

Number  Start   End     Size    Type     File system  Flags
 1      1049kB  1075MB  1074MB  primary  ext4         boot
 2      1075MB  21.5GB  20.4GB  primary               lvm

(parted) quit
$
```

One of the selling features of the parted program is that it allows you to modify existing partition sizes, so you can easily shrink or grow partitions on the drive.

## Creating a filesystem

Before you can store data on the partition, you must format it with a filesystem so that Linux can use it. Each filesystem type uses its own command-line program to format partitions. Table 8-4 lists the utilities used for the filesystems discussed in this chapter.

**TABLE 8-4    Command-Line Programs to Create Filesystems**

| Utility | Purpose |
|---|---|
| mkefs | Creates an ext filesystem. |
| mke2fs | Creates an ext2 filesystem. |
| mkfs.ext3 | Creates an ext3 filesystem. |
| mkfs.ext4 | Creates an ext4 filesystem. |
| mkreiserfs | Creates a ReiserFS filesystem. |
| jfs _ mkfs | Creates a JFS filesystem. |
| mkfs.xfs | Creates an XFS filesystem. |
| mkfs.zfs | Creates a ZFS filesystem. |
| mkfs.btrfs | Creates a Btrfs filesystem. |

Not all filesystem utilities are installed by default. To determine whether you have a particular filesystem utility, use the type command:

```
$ type mkfs.ext4
mkfs.ext4 is /usr/sbin/mkfs.ext4
$
$ type mkfs.btrfs
-bash: type: mkfs.btrfs: not found
$
```

The preceding example shows that the mkfs.ext4 utility is available. However, the Btrfs utility is not.

All the filesystem commands allow you to create a default filesystem with just the simple command with no options, but you'll need to have super user privileges:

```
$ sudo mkfs.ext4 /dev/sdb1
[sudo] password for christine:
mke2fs 1.44.6 (5-Mar-2019)
Creating filesystem with 524032 4k blocks and 131072 inodes
[...]
Creating journal (8192 blocks): done
Writing superblocks and filesystem accounting information: done
$
```

The new filesystem uses the ext4 filesystem type, which is a journaling filesystem in Linux. Notice that part of the creation process was to create the new journal.

After you create the filesystem for a partition, the next step is to mount it on a virtual directory mount point so that you can store data there. You can mount the new filesystem anywhere in your virtual directory where you need the extra space.

```
$ mkdir /home/christine/part
$
$ sudo mount -t ext4 /dev/sdb1 /home/christine/part
[sudo] password for christine:
$
$ lsblk -f /dev/sdb
NAME    FSTYPE LABEL UUID       MOUNTPOINT
sdb
⌐sdb1 ext4          a8d1d[...]  /home/christine/part
$
```

The mkdir command (Chapter 3) creates the mount point in the virtual directory, and the mount command adds the new hard drive partition to the mount point. The -t option on the mount command indicates what filesystem type, ext4, you are mounting. And the lsblk -f command allows you to see the newly formatted and mounted partition.

Now that the filesystem is mounted within the virtual directory system, it can start to be used on a regular basis. Unfortunately, with regular use comes the potential for serious problems, such as filesystem corruption. The next section looks at how to deal with these issues.

## Checking and repairing a filesystem

Even with modern filesystems, things can go wrong if power is unexpectedly lost or if a wayward application locks up the system while file access is in progress. Fortunately, some command-line tools are available to help you attempt to restore the filesystem back to order.

Each filesystem has its own recovery command for interacting with the filesystem. That has the potential of getting ugly, because more and more filesystems are available in the Linux environment, making for lots of individual commands you have to know. Fortunately, a common front-end program can determine the filesystem on the storage device and use the appropriate filesystem recovery command based on the filesystem being recovered.

The *fsck* command is used to check and repair most Linux filesystem types, including ones discussed earlier in this chapter. The format of the command is

```
fsck options filesystem
```

You can list multiple *filesystem* entries on the command line to check. Filesystems are referenced using several methods, such as the device name or its mount point in the virtual directory. However, the device must be unmounted before you use fsck on it.

The fsck command uses the /etc/fstab file to automatically determine the filesystem on a storage device that's normally mounted on the system. If the storage device isn't normally mounted (e.g., if you just created a filesystem on a new storage device), you need to use the -t command-line option to specify the filesystem type. Table 8-5 lists the other commonly used command-line options available.

**TABLE 8-5** **The `fsck` Commonly Used Command-Line Options**

| Option | Description |
|--------|-------------|
| -a | Automatically repairs the filesystem if errors are detected. |
| -A | Checks all the filesystems listed in the /etc/fstab file. |
| -N | Doesn't run the check; only displays what checks would be performed. |
| -r | Prompts to fix if errors found. |
| -R | Skips the root filesystem if using the -A option. |
| -t | Specifies the filesystem type to check. |
| -V | Produces verbose output during the checks. |
| -y | Automatically repairs the filesystem if errors detected. |

You may notice that some of the command-line options are redundant. That's part of the problem of trying to implement a common front end for multiple commands. Some of the individual filesystem repair commands have additional options that can be used.

---

**TIP**

You run the `fsck` command only on *unmounted* filesystems. For most filesystems, just unmount the filesystem to check it, and then remount it when you're finished. However, because the root filesystem contains all the core Linux commands and log files, you can't unmount it on a running system.

This is a time when having a Linux Live CD, DVD, or USB comes in handy! Just boot your system with the Linux Live media, and then run the `fsck` command on the root filesystem.

---

This chapter has showed you how to handle filesystems contained in physical storage devices. Linux also provides a few ways to create logical storage devices for filesystems. The next section examines how you can use a logical storage device for your filesystems.

# Managing Logical Volumes

Data has a habit of increasing. If you create your filesystems using standard partitions on hard drives, trying to add space to an existing filesystem can be somewhat of a painful experience. If no more space is available on that hard drive, you're stuck having to get a larger hard drive and manually moving the existing filesystem to the new drive.

What would come in handy is a way to dynamically add more space to an existing filesystem by just adding a partition from another hard drive to the existing filesystem. The Linux *Logical Volume Management* or *Manager (LVM)* allows you to do just that. It provides an easy way for you to manipulate disk space on a Linux system without having to rebuild entire filesystems. This section covers logical volumes and various terms, and offers practical steps for setting them up.

## Exploring LVM layout

LVM allows multiple partitions to be grouped together and used as a single partition for formatting, mounting on the Linux virtual directory structure, storing data, and so on. You can also add partitions to a logical volume as your data needs grow.

LVM has three primary parts, covered in the next few sections. Each part plays an important role in creating and maintaining logical volumes.

### Physical volume

A *physical volume (PV)* is created using the LVM's `pvcreate` command. This utility designates an unused disk partition (or whole drive) to be used by LVM. The LVM structures, a volume label, and metadata are added to the partition during this process.

### Volume group

A *volume group (VG)* is created using the LVM's `vgcreate` command, which adds PVs to a storage pool. This storage pool is used in turn to build various logical volumes.

You can have multiple volume groups. When you use the command to add a PV(s) to a VG, volume group metadata is added to the PV during this process.

A disk's partition, designated as a PV, can only belong to a single VG. However, a disk's other partitions, also designated as PVs, can belong to other VGs.

### Logical volume

A *logical volume (LV)* is created using the LVM's `lvcreate` command. This is the final object in logical volume creation. An LV consists of storage space chunks from a VG pool. It can be formatted with a filesystem, mounted, and used just like a typical disk partition.

While you can have multiple VGs, each LV is created from only one designated VG. However, you can have multiple LVs sharing a single VG. You can resize (grow or reduce) an LV using the appropriate LVM commands. This feature adds a great deal of flexibility to your data storage management.

There are many ways to divide up and manage your data storage media using LVM. Next, we'll dive into the details of creating and managing these volumes.

## Understanding the LVM in Linux

The `lvm` utility is an interactive utility for creating and managing LVs. If not installed, you can install it via the `lvm2` package (see Chapter 9). You do not need to enter the `lvm` utility to access the various LVM tools. Instead, you can access the tools directly at the CLI, as covered in this section.

8

> **NOTE**
>
> The 2 in `lvm2` or LVM2 refers to version 2 of LVM. It adds some additional features and an improved design over LVM version 1 (lvm1). We're using LVM2 in this chapter.

To set up a logical volume for the first time:

1. Create physical volumes.
2. Create a volume group.
3. Create a logical volume.
4. Format the logical volume.
5. Mount the logical volume.

Important considerations are involved in the first three steps of setting up your logical volume. Each decision you make in the early steps will determine how flexible and easy it is to manage your LVs.

### Create the PVs

Before designating drives as PVs, ensure that they are partitioned and currently unused. You designate the partitions as a PV using the pvcreate command along with super user privileges:

```
$ lsblk
NAME          MAJ:MIN RM  SIZE RO TYPE MOUNTPOINT
[...]
sdb            8:16  0     2G  0 disk
 └sdb1         8:17  0     2G  0 part
sdc            8:32  0     1G  0 disk
 └sdc1         8:33  0 1023M  0 part
sdd            8:48  0     1G  0 disk
 └sdd1         8:49  0 1023M  0 part
sde            8:64  0     1G  0 disk
 └sde1         8:65  0 1023M  0 part
sr0           11:0   1 1024M  0 rom
$
$ sudo pvcreate /dev/sdc1 /dev/sdd1 /dev/sde1
[sudo] password for christine:
  Physical volume "/dev/sdc1" successfully created.
  Physical volume "/dev/sdd1" successfully created.
  Physical volume "/dev/sde1" successfully created.
$
```

It's wise to set up more than one PV. The whole point of LVM is having additional storage media to add on the fly to your LVs. Once you have PVs set up, create a VG.

### Create a VG

Any PV can be added to a volume group. The command to use is vgcreate.

> **TIP**
>
> You can designate more than one PV during the VG creation process. If you need to add PVs to a VG at a later time, use the vgextend command.

Common practice names the first VG vg00, and the next one vg01, and so on. However, it's your choice what to name your volume group. Because many distributions set up LVM during installation for the virtual directory structure's root (/), it's a good idea to check for any current VGs on your system using the vgdisplay command:

```
$ sudo vgdisplay
  --- Volume group ---
  VG Name               c1
  System ID
  Format                lvm2
[...]
$
```

Notice in the preceding example that a VG named c1 is already set up. Thus, we're safe to use the vg00 name for our first volume group:

```
$ sudo vgcreate vg00 /dev/sdc1 /dev/sdd1
  Volume group "vg00" successfully created
$
```

In the preceding example, only two of our PVs were used to create VG vg00: /dev/sdc1 and /dev/sdd1. Now that our VG storage pool contains at least one PV, we can create an LV.

### Create an LV

To create a logical volume, use the lvcreate command. The resulting storage volume's size is set using the -L option, which uses space from the designated VG storage pool:

```
$ sudo lvcreate -L 1g -v vg00
[sudo] password for christine:
  Archiving volume group "vg00" metadata (seqno 1).
  Creating logical volume lvol0
[...]
  Logical volume "lvol0" created.
$
```

Notice that the first LV from this VG's default name is lvol0. Its full device pathname is /dev/vg00/lvol0.

> **NOTE**
>
> If for some reason a VG does not have enough partition space to give to the LV for the designated size, the lvcreate command will not make the LV. Instead, you will receive an insufficient free space error message.

Once the LV is created, use the lvdisplay command to show its information. Notice that the full pathname is used to designate the logical volume to the command:

```
$ sudo lvdisplay /dev/vg00/lvol0
[sudo] password for christine:
```

```
     --- Logical volume ---
    LV Path                /dev/vg00/lvol0
    LV Name                lvol0
    VG Name                vg00
   [...]
    LV Size                1.00 GiB
   [...]
    $
```

Besides the lvdisplay command, you can use the lvs and the lvscan commands to display information on all your systems' LVs. It's nice to have options.

## Using the Linux LVM

Once your LV is created, treat it as if it is a regular partition. Of course, it is different in that you can grow or shrink this partition on the fly as needed. But before you can do any of that, you'll need to attach your LV to the virtual directory structure.

### Format and mount an LV

With your LV, there is nothing special you have to do in order to make a filesystem on it and then mount it to the virtual directory structure:

```
$ sudo mkfs.ext4 /dev/vg00/lvol0
[sudo] password for christine:
[...]
Writing inode tables: done
Creating journal (8192 blocks): done
Writing superblocks and filesystem accounting information: done

$ mkdir my_LV
$ sudo mount -t ext4 /dev/vg00/lvol0 my_LV
$ ls my_LV
lost+found
$
```

Now that all the various LVM parts are created and the LV is attached to your virtual directory structure, you can use it as needed. Keep in mind that you'll want to add a record to the /etc/fstab file so that your new LV is mounted automatically when the system boots.

### Growing or shrinking your VGs and LVs

The time comes when you need to increase a VG's or LV's size. It may be due to increasing data on the volume, or it could be a new application being installed. However, you may want to shrink a VG or LV. If you don't have access to a fancy graphical interface for handling these activities on your Linux LVM environment, all is not lost. Table 8-6 lists the common commands that are available to accomplish these tasks.

**TABLE 8-6** **The Growing and Shrinking LVM Commands**

| Command | Function |
|---------|----------|
| vgextend | Adds physical volumes to a volume group. |
| vgreduce | Removes physical volumes from a volume group. |
| lvextend | Increases the size of a logical volume. |
| lvreduce | Decreases the size of a logical volume. |

Using these command-line programs, you have more control over your Linux LVM environment. Be sure to consult their man pages for additional details.

**TIP**

To see all the various LVM commands available, type `lvm help` at the CLI and press Enter.

Using the various command-line programs we covered, you have full control over your Linux LVM environment. And you gain the added flexibility LVM provides.

# Summary

8

Working with storage devices in Linux requires that you know a bit about filesystems. Knowing how to create and work with filesystems from the command line can come in handy as you work on Linux systems. This chapter discussed how to handle filesystems from the Linux command line.

Before you can install a filesystem on a storage device, you must first prepare the drive. The fdisk, gdisk, and parted commands are used to partition storage devices to get them ready for the filesystem. When you partition the storage device, you must define what type of filesystem will be used on it.

After you partition a storage device, you can use one of several filesystems for the partition. Popular Linux filesystems include journaling or volume-managing features, making them less prone to errors and problems.

One limiting factor in creating filesystems directly on a storage device partition is that you can't easily change the size of the filesystem if you run out of disk space. However, Linux supports logical volume management, a method of creating virtual partitions across multiple storage devices, which allows you to easily expand an existing filesystem without having to completely rebuild it.

Now that you've seen the core Linux command-line commands, it's close to the time to start creating some shell script programs. However, before you start coding, we need to discuss another element: installing software. If you plan to write shell scripts, you need an environment in which to create your masterpieces. The next chapter discusses how to install and manage software packages from the command line in different Linux environments.

# Installing Software

I n the old days of Linux, installing software could be a painful experience. Fortunately, the Linux developers have made life a little easier for us by bundling software into prebuilt packages that are much easier to install. However, there's still a little work on our part to get the software packages installed, especially if you want to do so from the command line. This chapter takes a look at the various package management systems available in Linux and the command-line tools used for software installation, management, and removal.

## Exploring Package Management

Before diving into the world of Linux software package management, this chapter goes through a few of the basics. Each of the major Linux distributions utilizes some form of package management system to control installing software applications and libraries. A *package management system* uses a database that keeps track of the following:

- What software packages are installed on the Linux system
- What files have been installed for each package
- Versions of each of the software packages installed

Software packages are stored on servers, called *repositories*, and are accessed across the Internet via package management system utilities running on your local Linux system. You can use these utilities to search for new software packages or even updates to software packages already installed on the system.

A software package will often have *dependencies*, or other packages that must be installed first for the software to run properly. The package management system utilities will detect these dependencies and offer to install any additionally needed software packages before installing the desired package.

The downside to a package management system is that there isn't a single standard utility. Whereas all the Bash shell commands discussed so far in this book will work no matter which Linux distribution you use, this is not true with software package management.

The package management system utilities and their associated commands are vastly different between the various Linux distributions. The two primary package management system base utilities commonly used in the Linux world are *dpkg* and *rpm*.

Debian-based distributions such as Ubuntu and Linux Mint use, at the base of their package management system utilities, the dpkg command. This command interacts directly with the package management system on the Linux system and is used for installing, managing, and removing software packages.

The Red Hat–based distributions, such as Fedora, CentOS, and openSUSE, use the rpm command at the base of their package management system. Similar to the dpkg command, the rpm command can list installed packages, install new packages, and remove existing software.

Note that these two commands are the core of their respective package management system, not the entire package management system itself. Many Linux distributions that use the dpkg or rpm methods have built additional specialty package management system utilities upon these base commands to make your life much easier. The following sections walk through various package management system utility commands you'll run into in the popular Linux distributions.

## Inspecting the Debian-Based Systems

The dpkg command is at the core of the Debian-based family of package management system tools. It provides options to install, update, and remove DEB package files on your Linux system.

The dpkg command assumes you have the DEB package file either downloaded onto your local Linux system or available as a URL. More often than not, that isn't the case. Usually you'll want to install an application package from the repository for your Linux distribution. To do that, you'll use the Advanced Package Tool (APT) suite of tools:

- apt-cache
- apt-get
- apt

The apt command is essentially a front end for both the apt-cache and apt-get commands. The nice thing about APT is that you don't need to remember which tool to use when—it covers everything you need to do with package management. The basic format for the apt command is

```
apt [options] command
```

The *command* defines the action for apt to take. If needed, you can specify one or more *options* to fine-tune what happens. This section looks at how to use the APT command-line tool to work with the software packages on your Linux system.

## Managing packages with *apt*

A common task faced by Linux system administrators is to determine what packages are already installed on the system. The apt list command displays all the packages available in the repository, but by adding the --installed option you can limit the output to only those packages already installed on your system:

```
$ apt --installed list
Listing... Done
accountsservice/focal,now 0.6.55-0ubuntu11 amd64 [installed,automatic]
acl/focal,now 2.2.53-6 amd64 [installed,automatic]
acpi-support/focal,now 0.143 amd64 [installed,automatic]
acpid/focal,now 1:2.0.32-1ubuntu1 amd64 [installed,automatic]
adduser/focal,focal,now 3.118ubuntu2 all [installed,automatic]
adwaita-icon-theme/focal,focal,now 3.36.0-1ubuntu1 all [installed,automatic]
aisleriot/focal,now 1:3.22.9-1 amd64 [installed,automatic]
alsa-base/focal,focal,now 1.0.25+dfsg-0ubuntu5 all [installed,automatic]
alsa-topology-conf/focal,focal,now 1.2.2-1 all [installed,automatic]
alsa-ucm-conf/focal,focal,now 1.2.2-1 all [installed,automatic]
...
$
```

As you can guess, the list of installed packages will be very long, so we've abbreviated the output to show just a sample of what the output looks like. Next to the package name is additional information about the package, such as the version name, and whether the package is installed and flagged for automatic upgrades.

If you already know the packages on your system and want to quickly display detailed information about a particular package, use the show command:

```
apt show package_name
```

Here's an example of displaying the details of the package zsh:

```
$ apt show zsh
Package: zsh
Version: 5.8-3ubuntu1
Priority: optional
Section: shells
Origin: Ubuntu
Maintainer: Ubuntu Developers <ubuntu-devel-discuss@lists.ubuntu.com>
```

```
Original-Maintainer: Debian Zsh Maintainers <pkg-zsh-devel@lists.alioth
.debian.org>
Bugs: https://bugs.launchpad.net/ubuntu/+filebug
Installed-Size: 2,390 kB
Depends: zsh-common (= 5.8-3ubuntu1), libc6 (>= 2.29), libcap2 (>= 1:2.10),
libtinfo6 (>= 6)
Recommends: libgdbm6 (>= 1.16), libncursesw6 (>= 6), libpcre3
Suggests: zsh-doc
Homepage: https://www.zsh.org/
Download-Size: 707 kB
APT-Sources: http://us.archive.ubuntu.com/ubuntu focal/main amd64 Packages
Description: shell with lots of features
 Zsh is a UNIX command interpreter (shell) usable as an
 interactive login shell and as a shell script command
 processor. Of the standard shells, zsh most closely resembles
 ksh but includes many enhancements. Zsh has command-line editing,
 built-in spelling correction, programmable command completion,
 shell functions (with autoloading), a history mechanism, and a
 host of other features.

$
```

> **NOTE**
>
> The apt show command does not indicate that the package is installed on the system. It shows only detailed package information from the software repository.

One detail you cannot get with apt is a listing of all the files associated with a particular software package. To get this list, you will need to go to the dpkg command itself:

```
dpkg -L package_name
```

Here's an example of using dpkg to list all the files installed as part of the acl package:

```
$ dpkg -L acl
/.
/bin
/bin/chacl
/bin/getfacl
/bin/setfacl
/usr
/usr/share
/usr/share/doc
/usr/share/doc/acl
/usr/share/doc/acl/copyright
/usr/share/man
/usr/share/man/man1
/usr/share/man/man1/chacl.1.gz
/usr/share/man/man1/getfacl.1.gz
/usr/share/man/man1/setfacl.1.gz
```

```
/usr/share/man/man5
/usr/share/man/man5/acl.5.gz
/usr/share/doc/acl/changelog.Debian.gz
$
```

You can also do the reverse — find what package a particular file belongs to:

```
dpkg --search absolute_file_name
```

Note that you need to use an absolute file reference for this to work:

```
$ dpkg --search /bin/getfacl
acl: /bin/getfacl
$
```

The output shows the getfacl file was installed as part of the acl package.

## Installing software packages with *apt*

Now that you know more about listing software package information on your system, this section walks you through a software package installation. First, you'll want to determine the package name to install. How do you find a particular software package? Use apt with the search command:

```
apt search package_name
```

The beauty of the search command is that you do not need to insert wildcards around *package_name*. Wildcards are implied. By default, the search command displays packages that contain the search term in either the package name or the package description, which can be misleading at times. If you want to limit the output to only package names, include the --names-only option:

```
$ apt --names-only search zsh
Sorting... Done
Full Text Search... Done
fizsh/focal,focal 1.0.9-1 all
   Friendly Interactive ZSHell

zsh/focal 5.8-3ubuntu1 amd64
   shell with lots of features

zsh-antigen/focal,focal 2.2.3-2 all
   manage your zsh plugins

zsh-autosuggestions/focal,focal 0.6.4-1 all
   Fish-like fast/unobtrusive autosuggestions for zsh

zsh-common/focal,focal 5.8-3ubuntu1 all
   architecture independent files for Zsh

zsh-dev/focal 5.8-3ubuntu1 amd64
   shell with lots of features (development files)
```

9

```
zsh-doc/focal,focal 5.8-3ubuntu1 all
   zsh documentation - info/HTML format

zsh-static/focal 5.8-3ubuntu1 amd64
   shell with lots of features (static link)

zsh-syntax-highlighting/focal,focal 0.6.0-3 all
   Fish shell like syntax highlighting for zsh

zsh-theme-powerlevel9k/focal,focal 0.6.7-2 all
   powerlevel9k is a theme for zsh which uses powerline fonts

zshdb/focal,focal 1.1.2-1 all
   debugger for Z-Shell scripts

$
```

Once you find the package you'd like to install, installing it using apt is as easy as this:

```
apt install package_name
```

The output will show basic information about the package and ask if you want to proceed with the installation:

```
$ sudo apt install zsh
[sudo] password for rich:
Reading package lists... Done
Building dependency tree
Reading state information... Done
The following additional packages will be installed:
   zsh-common
Suggested packages:
   zsh-doc
The following NEW packages will be installed:
   zsh zsh-common
0 upgraded, 2 newly installed, 0 to remove and 56 not upgraded.
Need to get 4,450 kB of archives.
After this operation, 18.0 MB of additional disk space will be used.
Do you want to continue? [Y/n] y
Get:1 http://us.archive.ubuntu.com/ubuntu focal/main amd64 zsh-common all
5.8-3ubuntu1 [3,744 kB]
Get:2 http://us.archive.ubuntu.com/ubuntu focal/main amd64 zsh amd64
5.8-3ubuntu1 [707 kB]
Fetched 4,450 kB in 4s (1,039 kB/s)
Selecting previously unselected package zsh-common.
(Reading database ... 179515 files and directories currently installed.)
Preparing to unpack .../zsh-common_5.8-3ubuntu1_all.deb ...
Unpacking zsh-common (5.8-3ubuntu1) ...
Selecting previously unselected package zsh.
```

```
Preparing to unpack .../zsh_5.8-3ubuntu1_amd64.deb ...
Unpacking zsh (5.8-3ubuntu1) ...
Setting up zsh-common (5.8-3ubuntu1) ...
Setting up zsh (5.8-3ubuntu1) ...
Processing triggers for man-db (2.9.1-1) ...
$
```

> **NOTE**
>
> Before the `apt` command in the preceding listing, the `sudo` command is used. The `sudo` command allows you to run a command as the root user. You can use the `sudo` command to run administrative tasks, such as installing software.

To check if the installation processed properly, just use the `list` command with the `--installed` option again. You should see the package appear, indicating that it is installed.

Notice that when installing the requested package, `apt` asked to install other packages as well. This is because `apt` automatically resolves any necessary package dependencies for us and installs the needed additional library and software packages. This is a wonderful feature included in many package management systems.

## Upgrading software with *apt*

While `apt` helps protect you from problems installing software, trying to coordinate a multiple-package update with dependencies can get tricky. To safely upgrade all the software packages on a system with any new versions in the repository, use the upgrade command:

```
apt upgrade
```

Notice that this command doesn't take any software package names as an argument. That's because the `upgrade` option will upgrade all the installed packages to the most recent version available in the repository, which is safer for system stabilization.

Here's a sample output from running the `apt upgrade` command:

```
$
$ sudo apt upgrade
Reading package lists... Done
Building dependency tree
Reading state information... Done
Calculating upgrade... Done
The following NEW packages will be installed:
  binutils binutils-common binutils-x86-64-linux-gnu build-essential dpkg-dev
  fakeroot g++ g++-9 gcc gcc-9 libalgorithm-diff-perl
  libalgorithm-diff-xs-perl libalgorithm-merge-perl libasan5 libatomic1
  libbinutils libc-dev-bin libc6-dev libcrypt-dev libctf-nobfd0 libctf0
  libfakeroot libgcc-9-dev libitm1 liblsan0 libquadmath0 libstdc++-9-dev
  libtsan0 libubsan1 linux-libc-dev make manpages-dev
```

9

```
The following packages will be upgraded:
  chromium-codecs-ffmpeg-extra eog file-roller fonts-opensymbol gedit
  gedit-common girl.2-gnomedesktop-3.0 glib-networking glib-networking-common
  glib-networking-services gnome-control-center gnome-control-center-data
  gnome-control-center-faces gnome-desktop3-data gnome-initial-setup
  libgnome-desktop-3-19 libjuh-java libjurt-java libnautilus-extension1a
  libnetplan0 libreoffice-base-core libreoffice-calc libreoffice-common
  libreoffice-core libreoffice-draw libreoffice-gnome libreoffice-gtk3
  libreoffice-help-common libreoffice-help-en-us libreoffice-impress
  libreoffice-math libreoffice-ogltrans libreoffice-pdfimport
  libreoffice-style-breeze libreoffice-style-colibre
  libreoffice-style-elementary libreoffice-style-tango libreoffice-writer
  libridl-java libuno-cppu3 libuno-cppuhelpergcc3-3 libuno-purpenvhelpergcc3-3
  libuno-sal3 libuno-salhelpergcc3-3 libunoloader-java nautilus nautilus-data
  netplan.io python3-distupgrade python3-uno thermald ubuntu-drivers-common
  ubuntu-release-upgrader-core ubuntu-release-upgrader-gtk uno-libs-private
  ure
56 upgraded, 32 newly installed, 0 to remove and 0 not upgraded.
Need to get 133 MB of archives.
After this operation, 143 MB of additional disk space will be used.
Do you want to continue? [Y/n]
```

In the output, notice that apt lists the packages that will be upgraded, but also any new packages that are required to be installed because of upgrades.

The upgrade command won't remove any packages as part of the upgrade process. If a package needs to be removed as part of an upgrade, use the command

```
apt full-upgrade
```

Although this may seem like an odd thing, sometimes it's required to remove packages to keep things synchronized between distribution upgrades.

> **NOTE**
>
> Obviously, running apt's upgrade option is something you should do on a regular basis to keep your system up to date. However, it is especially important to run it after a fresh distribution installation. Usually there are lots of security patches and updates that have been released since the last full release of a distribution.

## Uninstalling software with *apt*

Getting rid of software packages with apt is as easy as installing and upgrading them. The only real choice you have to make is whether or not to keep the software's data and configuration files around afterward.

To remove a software package, but not the data and configuration files, use apt's remove command. To remove a software package and the related data and configuration files, use the purge option:

```
$ sudo apt purge zsh
Reading package lists... Done
Building dependency tree
Reading state information... Done
The following package was automatically installed and is no longer required:
  zsh-common
Use 'sudo apt autoremove' to remove it.
The following packages will be REMOVED:
  zsh*
0 upgraded, 0 newly installed, 1 to remove and 56 not upgraded.
After this operation, 2,390 kB disk space will be freed.
Do you want to continue? [Y/n] y
(Reading database ... 180985 files and directories currently installed.)
Removing zsh (5.8-3ubuntu1) ...
Processing triggers for man-db (2.9.1-1) ...
(Reading database ... 180928 files and directories currently installed.)
Purging configuration files for zsh (5.8-3ubuntu1) ...
$
```

Notice, though, as part of the purge output apt warns us that the zsh-common package that was installed as a dependency wasn't removed automatically, just in case it might be required for some other package. If you're sure the dependency package isn't required by anything else, you can remove it using the autoremove command:

```
$ sudo apt autoremove
Reading package lists... Done
Building dependency tree
Reading state information... Done
The following packages will be REMOVED:
  zsh-common
0 upgraded, 0 newly installed, 1 to remove and 56 not upgraded.
After this operation, 15.6 MB disk space will be freed.
Do you want to continue? [Y/n] y
(Reading database ... 180928 files and directories currently
installed.)
Removing zsh-common (5.8-3ubuntu1) ...
Processing triggers for man-db (2.9.1-1) ...
$
```

The autoremove command will check for all packages that are marked as dependencies and no longer required.

9

## The *apt* repositories

The default software repository locations for apt are set up for you when you install your Linux distribution. The repository locations are stored in the file /etc/apt/ sources.list.

In many cases, you will never need to add/remove a software repository, so you won't need to touch this file. However, apt will only pull software from these repositories. Also, when searching for software to install or update, apt will only check these repositories. If you need to include some additional software repositories for your package management system, this is the place to do it.

> **TIP**
>
> The Linux distribution developers work hard to make sure package versions added to the repositories don't conflict with one another. Usually it's safest to upgrade or install a software package from the repository. Even if a newer version is available elsewhere, you may want to hold off installing it until that version is available in your Linux distribution's repository.

The following is an example of a sources.list file from an Ubuntu system:

```
$ cat /etc/apt/sources.list
#deb cdrom:[Ubuntu 20.04 LTS _Focal Fossa_ - Release amd64 (20200423)]/ focal
main restricted

# See http://help.ubuntu.com/community/UpgradeNotes for how to upgrade to
# newer versions of the distribution.
deb http://us.archive.ubuntu.com/ubuntu/ focal main restricted
# deb-src http://us.archive.ubuntu.com/ubuntu/ focal main restricted

## Major bug fix updates produced after the final release of the
## distribution.
deb http://us.archive.ubuntu.com/ubuntu/ focal-updates main restricted
# deb-src http://us.archive.ubuntu.com/ubuntu/ focal-updates main restricted

## N.B. software from this repository is ENTIRELY UNSUPPORTED by the Ubuntu
## team. Also, please note that software in universe WILL NOT receive any
## review or updates from the Ubuntu security team.
deb http://us.archive.ubuntu.com/ubuntu/ focal universe
# deb-src http://us.archive.ubuntu.com/ubuntu/ focal universe
deb http://us.archive.ubuntu.com/ubuntu/ focal-updates universe
# deb-src http://us.archive.ubuntu.com/ubuntu/ focal-updates universe

## N.B. software from this repository is ENTIRELY UNSUPPORTED by the Ubuntu
## team, and may not be under a free licence. Please satisfy yourself as to
## your rights to use the software. Also, please note that software in
## multiverse WILL NOT receive any review or updates from the Ubuntu
## security team.
```

```
deb http://us.archive.ubuntu.com/ubuntu/ focal multiverse
# deb-src http://us.archive.ubuntu.com/ubuntu/ focal multiverse
deb http://us.archive.ubuntu.com/ubuntu/ focal-updates multiverse
# deb-src http://us.archive.ubuntu.com/ubuntu/ focal-updates multiverse

## N.B. software from this repository may not have been tested as
## extensively as that contained in the main release, although it includes
## newer versions of some applications which may provide useful features.
## Also, please note that software in backports WILL NOT receive any review
## or updates from the Ubuntu security team.
deb http://us.archive.ubuntu.com/ubuntu/ focal-backports main restricted
universe multiverse
# deb-src http://us.archive.ubuntu.com/ubuntu/ focal-backports main
restricted universe multiverse

## Uncomment the following two lines to add software from Canonical's
## 'partner' repository.
## This software is not part of Ubuntu, but is offered by Canonical and the
## respective vendors as a service to Ubuntu users.
# deb http://archive.canonical.com/ubuntu focal partner
# deb-src http://archive.canonical.com/ubuntu focal partner

deb http://security.ubuntu.com/ubuntu focal-security main restricted
# deb-src http://security.ubuntu.com/ubuntu focal-security main restricted
deb http://security.ubuntu.com/ubuntu focal-security universe
# deb-src http://security.ubuntu.com/ubuntu focal-security universe
deb http://security.ubuntu.com/ubuntu focal-security multiverse
# deb-src http://security.ubuntu.com/ubuntu focal-security multiverse

# This system was installed using small removable media
# (e.g. netinst, live or single CD). The matching "deb cdrom"
# entries were disabled at the end of the installation process.
# For information about how to configure apt package sources,
# see the sources.list(5) manual.
$
```

First, notice that the file is full of helpful comments and warnings. The repository sources specified use the following structure:

```
deb (or deb-src) address  distribution_name  package_type_list
```

The deb or deb-src value indicates the software package type. The deb value indicates it is a source of compiled programs, whereas the deb-src value indicates it is a source of source code.

The address entry is the software repository's web address. The distribution_name entry is the name of this particular software repository's distribution version. In the example, the distribution name is focal. This does not necessarily mean that the distribution you are running is Ubuntu's Focal Fossa; it just means the Linux distribution is using the

9

Ubuntu Focal Fossa software repositories. For example, in Linux Mint's `sources.list` file, you will see a mix of Linux Mint and Ubuntu software repositories.

Finally, the `package_type_list` entry may be more than one word and indicates what type of packages the repository has in it. For example, you may see values such as `main`, `restricted`, `universe`, or `partner`.

When you need to add a software repository to your sources file, you can try to wing it yourself, but that more than likely will cause problems. Often, software repository sites or various package developer sites will have an exact line of text that you can copy from their website and paste into your `sources.list` file. It's best to choose the safer route and just copy/paste.

The front-end interface, `apt`, provides intelligent command-line options for working with the Debian-based `dpkg` utility. Now it's time to take a look at the Red Hat–based distributions' `rpm` utility and its various front-end interfaces.

# The Red Hat–Based Systems

Like the Debian-based distributions, the Red Hat–based systems have several different front-end tools available. The common ones are:

- `yum`: Used in Red Hat, CentOS, and Fedora
- `zypper`: Used in openSUSE
- `dnf`: An updated version of `yum` with some additional features

These front ends are all based on the `rpm` command-line tool. The following section discusses how to manage software packages using these various `rpm`-based tools. The focus will be on `dnf`, but the other packages use similar commands and formats.

## Listing installed packages

To find out what is currently installed on your system, at the shell prompt type the following command:

```
dnf list installed
```

The information will probably whiz by you on the display screen, so it's best to redirect the installed software listing into a file. You can then use the `more` or `less` command (or a GUI editor) to look at the list in a controlled manner.

```
dnf list installed > installed_software
```

To find out detailed information for a particular software package, `dnf` really shines. Not only will it give you a very verbose description of the package, but with another simple command, you can see whether the package is installed:

```
$ dnf list xterm
Last metadata expiration check: 0:05:17 ago on Sat 16 May 2020 12:10:24 PM EDT.
```

```
Available Packages
xterm.x86_64                        351-1.fc31                              updates

$ dnf list installed xterm
Error: No matching Packages to list

$ dnf list installed bash
Installed Packages
Bash.x86_64                         5.0.11-1.fc31                           @updates
$
```

Finally, if you need to find out what software package provides a particular file on your filesystem, the versatile dnf can do that, too! Just enter the command

```
dnf provides file_name
```

Here's an example of trying to find what software provided the file /usr/bin/gzip:

```
$ dnf provides /usr/bin/gzip
Last metadata expiration check: 0:12:06 ago on Sat 16 May 2020 12:10:24 PM EDT.
gzip-1.10-1.fc31.x86_64 : The GNU data compression program
Repo        : @System
Matched from:
Filename    : /usr/bin/gzip

gzip-1.10-1.fc31.x86_64 : The GNU data compression program
Repo        : fedora
Matched from:
Filename    : /usr/bin/gzip

$
```

dnf checked two separate repositories: the local system and the default fedora repository.

## Installing software with *dnf*

Installation of a software package using dnf is incredibly easy. The following is the basic command for installing a software package, all its needed libraries, and package dependencies from a repository:

```
dnf install package_name
```

Here's an example of installing the zsh package, which provides an alternative command-line shell:

```
$ sudo dnf install zsh
[sudo] password for rich:
Last metadata expiration check: 0:19:45 ago on Sat 16 May 2020 12:05:01 PM EDT.
Dependencies resolved.
```

9

```
================================================================================
 Package        Architecture    Version                   Repository      Size
================================================================================
Installing:
 zsh            x86_64          5.7.1-6.fc31              updates         2.9 M

Transaction Summary
================================================================================
Install  1 Package

Total download size: 2.9 M
Installed size: 7.4 M
Is this ok [y/N]:
Downloading Packages:
zsh-5.7.1-6.fc31.x86_64.rpm                      1.5 MB/s | 2.9 MB      00:01
--------------------------------------------------------------------------------
Total                                            1.0 MB/s | 2.9 MB      00:02
Running transaction check
Transaction check succeeded.
Running transaction test
Transaction test succeeded.
Running transaction
  Preparing        :                                                      1/1
  Installing       : zsh-5.7.1-6.fc31.x86_64                              1/1
  Running scriptlet: zsh-5.7.1-6.fc31.x86_64                              1/1
  Verifying        : zsh-5.7.1-6.fc31.x86_64                              1/1

Installed:
  zsh-5.7.1-6.fc31.x86_64

Complete!
$
```

> **NOTE**
> Before the `dnf` command in the preceding listing, the `sudo` command is used. This command allows you to switch to the root user to run the command. You should only switch to root user temporarily in order to run administrative tasks, such as installing and updating software.

You can begin to see that one of `dnf`'s strengths is that it uses very logical and user-friendly commands.

## Upgrading software with *dnf*

In most Linux distributions, when you're working away in the GUI, you get those nice little notification icons telling you a software upgrade to a new version is needed. Here at the command line, it takes a little more work.

To see the list of all the available upgrades for your installed packages, type the following command:

```
dnf list upgrades
```

It's always nice to get no response to this command because it means you have nothing to upgrade! However, if you do discover that a particular software package needs upgrading, then type in the following command:

```
dnf upgrade package_name
```

If you'd like to upgrade all the packages listed in the upgrade list, just enter the following command:

```
dnf upgrade
```

> **NOTE**
>
> One nice extra feature in `dnf` is the `upgrade-minimal` command. It upgrades a package to the latest bug fix or security patch version instead of the latest and greatest version.

## Uninstalling software with *dnf*

The `dnf` tool also provides an easy way to uninstall software you no longer want on your system:

```
dnf remove package_name
```

Unfortunately, as of this writing there isn't an option or command to remove the application files but keep any configuration or data files.

While life is considerably easier with package management system packages, it's not always problem free. Occasionally things do go wrong. Fortunately, there's help.

## Dealing with broken dependencies

Sometimes as multiple software packages get loaded, a software dependency for one package can get overwritten by the installation of another package. This is called a *broken dependency*.

If this should happen on your system, first try the following command:

```
dnf clean all
```

Then try to use the `upgrade` option in the `dnf` command. Sometimes, just cleaning up any misplaced files can help.

9

If that doesn't solve the problem, try the following command:

```
dnf repoquery --deplist package_name
```

This command displays all the package's library dependencies and what software package provides them. Once you know the libraries required for a package, you can then install them. Here's an example of determining the dependencies for the xterm package:

```
# dnf repoquery --deplist xterm

#
```

> **NOTE**
> The yum tool's upgrade command includes support for the --skip-broken option that skips over broken packages but tries to continue upgrading other packages. The dnf tool does this automatically.

## RPM repositories

Just like the apt systems, dnf has its software repositories set up at installation. For most purposes, these preinstalled repositories will work just fine for your needs. But if and when the time comes that you need to install software from a different repository, here are some things you will need to know.

> **TIP**
> A wise system administrator sticks with approved repositories. An approved repository is one that is sanctioned by the distribution's official site. If you start adding unapproved repositories, you lose the guarantee of stability. And you will be heading into broken dependencies territory.

To see what repositories you are currently pulling software from, type the following command:

```
dnf repolist
```

If you don't find a repository you need software from, then you will need to do a little configuration file editing. There are two places where the dnf repository definitions can be located:

- In the /etc/dnf/dnf.conf configuration file
- As separate files in the /etc/yum.repos.d directory

Good repository sites such as rpmfusion.org will lay out all the steps necessary to use them. Sometimes these repository sites will offer an RPM file that you can download and install. The installation of the RPM file will do all the repository setup work for you. Now that's convenient!

# Managing Software Using Containers

Although package management systems have certainly made software installation in the Linux world much easier, they do have their drawbacks. To start with, as you've already seen in this chapter, there are multiple competing package management systems. So for application developers to distribute an application that can be installed in all Linux distributions, they must create multiple versions to distribute.

But there's even more complexity than that. Every application has some type of library functions that it depends on to run. When developers create a Linux application, they must take into consideration what library files are available in most Linux distributions, and not only that, but also what versions of the library files. Although package management systems can track dependencies, as you can guess, this can quickly turn into a nightmare for software developers trying to get their applications working in most Linux distributions.

With cloud computing came a new paradigm in how applications can be packaged: *application containers*. An application container creates an environment where all the files required for an application to run are bundled together, including runtime library files. The developer can then release the application container as a single package and be guaranteed that it'll run just fine on any Linux system.

Though still relatively new, several competing application container standards are starting to emerge. The following sections take a look at two of the more popular ones: snap and flatpak.

## Using snap containers

Canonical, the creators of the Ubuntu Linux distribution, have developed an application container format called *snap*. The snap packaging system bundles all the files required for an application into a single snap distribution file. The snapd application runs in the background, and you use the snap command-line tool to query the snap database to display installed snap packages, as well as to install, upgrade, and remove snap packages.

To check whether snap is running on your system, use the snap version command:

```
$ snap version
snap    2.44.3+20.04
snapd   2.44.3+20.04
series  16
ubuntu  20.04
kernel  5.4.0-31-generic
$
```

If snap is running, you can see a list of the currently installed snap applications by using the snap list command:

```
$ snap list
Name            Version         Rev   Tracking        Publisher     Notes
core            16-2.44.3       9066  latest/stable   canonical✓    core
```

```
core18              20200427                      1754  latest/stable    canonical✓    base
gimp                2.10.18                        273  latest/stable    snapcrafters  -
gnome-3-28-1804     3.28.0-16-g27c9498.27c9        116  latest/stable    canonical✓    -
gnome-3-34-1804     0+git.3009fc7                   33  latest/stable/... canonical✓    -
gtk-common-themes   0.1-36-gc75f853               1506  latest/stable/... canonical✓    -
gtk2-common-themes  0.1                              9  latest/stable    canonical✓    -
snap-store          3.36.0-74-ga164ec9             433  latest/stable/... canonical✓    -
snapd               2.44.3                        7264  latest/stable    canonical✓    snapd
$
```

To search the snap repository for new applications, use the `snap find` command:

```
$ snap find solitaire
Name                   Version  Publisher  Notes  Summary
solitaire              1.0      1bsyl      -      usual Solitaire card game,
  as known as Patience or Klondike
kmahjongg              20.04.1  kde✓       -      Mahjong Solitaire
kshisen                19.08.0  kde✓       -      Shisen-Sho Mahjongg-like TileGame
kpat                   20.04.0  kde✓       -      Solitaire card game
freecell-solitaire     1.0      1bsyl      -      FreeCell Solitaire, card game
open-solitaire-classic 0.9.2    metasmug   -      Open-source implementation of the
classic solitaire game
spider-solitaire       1.0      1bsyl      -      Spider Solitaire card game
solvitaire             master   popey      -      solitaire (klondike & spider) in
your terminal
gnome-mahjongg         3.34.0   ken-vandine -     Match tiles and clear the board

$
```

To view more information about a snap application (snap for short), use the `snap info` command:

```
$ snap info solitaire
name:      solitaire
summary:   usual Solitaire card game, as known as Patience or Klondike
publisher: Sylvain Becker (1bsyl)
store-url: https://snapcraft.io/solitaire
contact:   sylvain.becker@gmail.com
license:   Proprietary
description: |
  This is the usual Solitaire card game. Also known as Patience
or Klondike.
snap-id: 0rnkesZh4jFy9oovDTvL661qVTW4iDdE
channels:
  latest/stable:    1.0 2017-05-17 (2) 11MB -
  latest/candidate: 1.0 2017-05-17 (2) 11MB -
  latest/beta:      1.0 2017-05-17 (2) 11MB -
```

```
    latest/edge:       1.0 2017-05-17 (2) 11MB -
$
```

To install a new snap, use the snap install command:

```
$ sudo snap install solitaire
[sudo] password for rich:
solitaire 1.0 from Sylvain Becker (1bsyl) installed
$
```

Notice that you must have root user privileges to install snap. In Ubuntu, that means using the sudo command.

> **NOTE**
>
> When you install a snap, the snapd program mounts it as a drive. You can see the new snap mount by using the mount command.

If you need to remove a snap, just use the snap remove command:

```
$ sudo snap remove solitaire
solitaire removed
$
```

As the snap is removed, you'll see some messages about the progress of the removal.

> **NOTE**
>
> Instead of removing a snap, you can just disable it without removing it. Just use the snap disable command. To reenable the snap, use the snap enable command.

## Using flatpak containers

The *flatpak* application container format was created as an independent open source project with no direct ties to any specific Linux distribution. That said, battle lines have already been drawn, with Red Hat, CentOS, and Fedora oriented toward using flatpak instead of Canonical's snap container format.

If you're using a Linux distribution that supports flatpak, you can list the installed application containers using the flatpak list command:

```
$ flatpak list
Name              Application ID                  Version     Branch    Installation
Platform          org.fedoraproject.Platform                  f32       system
$
```

To find an application in the flatpak repository, you use the flatpak search command:

```
$ flatpak search solitaire
Name          Description        Application ID        Version    Branch    Remotes
Aisleriot Solitaire              org.gnome.Aisleriot   stable     fedora
GNOME Mahjongg                   org.gnome.Mahjongg    3.32.0     stable    fedora
$
```

9

We edited out some of the information in the output to help simplify things. When working with a container you must use its Application ID value and not its name. To install the application, use the `flatpak install` command:

```
$ sudo flatpak install org.gnome.Aisleriot
Looking for matches...
Found similar ref(s) for 'org.gnome.Aisleriot' in remote 'fedora' (system).
Use this remote? [Y/n]: y

org.gnome.Aisleriot permissions:
    ipc      pulseaudio     wayland      x11      dri      file access [1]      dbus
access [2]

    [1] xdg-run/dconf, ~/.config/dconf:ro
    [2] ca.desrt.dconf, org.gnome.GConf


        ID                           Arch      Branch  Remote      Download
 1. [✓] org.gnome.Aisleriot         x86_64    stable  fedora      8.4 MB / 8.4 MB

Installation complete.
$
```

To check if the installation went well, you can use the `flatpak list` command again:

```
$ flatpak list
Name                 Application ID             Version  Branch       Installation
Platform             org.fedoraproject.Platform          f32          system
Aisleriot Solitaire  org.gnome.Aisleriot                 stable       system
$
```

And finally, to remove an application container, use the `flatpak uninstall` command:

```
$ sudo flatpak uninstall org.gnome.Aisleriot


        ID                           Arch      Branch
 1. [-] org.gnome.Aisleriot         x86_64    stable

Uninstall complete.
$
```

Using application containers is similar to using package management systems, but what goes on behind the scenes is fundamentally different. However, the end result is that you have an application installed on your Linux system that can be easily maintained and upgraded.

# Installing from Source Code

Before package management systems and application containers, open source application developers had to distribute their software as source code and allow users to compile the applications on their own systems. Source code packages were commonly released as *tarballs*. Chapter 4, "More Bash Shell Commands," discussed tarball packages — how to create them using the `tar` command-line command and how to unpack them.

If you develop or work with open source software source code much, there's a good chance you will still find software packed up as a tarball. This section walks you through the process of unpacking and installing a tarball software package.

For this example, the software package `sysstat` will be used. The sysstat utility is a very nice software package that provides a variety of system monitoring tools.

First, you will need to download the `sysstat` tarball to your Linux system. While you can often find the `sysstat` package available on different Linux sites, it's usually best to go straight to the source of the program. In this case, it's the website sebastien.godard. pagesperso-orange.fr.

When you click the Download link, you'll go to the page that contains the files for downloading. The current version as of this writing is 12.3.3, and the distribution filename is `sysstat-12.3.3.tar.xz`.

Click the link to download the file to your Linux system. Once you have downloaded the file, you can unpack it.

To unpack a software tarball, use the standard `tar` command:

```
$ tar -Jxvf sysstat-12.3.3.tar.xz
sysstat-12.3.3/
sysstat-12.3.3/pcp_stats.h
sysstat-12.3.3/rd_sensors.h
sysstat-12.3.3/xml/
sysstat-12.3.3/xml/sysstat.xsd
sysstat-12.3.3/xml/sysstat-3.9.dtd
sysstat-12.3.3/sa.h
sysstat-12.3.3/man/
sysstat-12.3.3/man/sadf.in
sysstat-12.3.3/man/mpstat.1
...
sysstat-12.3.3/pcp_stats.c
sysstat-12.3.3/pr_stats.h
sysstat-12.3.3/rd_stats.c
sysstat-12.3.3/pr_stats.c
sysstat-12.3.3/.travis.yml
sysstat-12.3.3/configure
$
```

9

Now that the tarball is unpacked and the files have neatly put themselves into a directory called sysstat-12.3.3, you can dive down into that directory and continue.

First, use the cd command to get into the new directory and then list the contents of the directory:

```
$ cd sysstat-12.3.3
$ ls
activity.c         images             pr_stats.h         sar.c
BUG_REPORT         INSTALL            raw_stats.c        sa_wrap.c
build              ioconf.c           raw_stats.h        svg_stats.c
CHANGES            ioconf.h           rd_sensors.c       svg_stats.h
cifsiostat.c       iostat.c           rd_sensors.h       sysconfig.in
cifsiostat.h       iostat.h           rd_stats.c         sysstat-12.3.3.lsm
common.c           json_stats.c       rd_stats.h         sysstat-12.3.3.spec
common.h           json_stats.h       README.md          sysstat.in
configure          Makefile.in        rndr_stats.c       sysstat.ioconf
configure.in       man                rndr_stats.h       sysstat.service.in
contrib            mpstat.c           sa1.in             sysstat.sysconfig.in
COPYING            mpstat.h           sa2.in             systest.c
count.c            nls                sa_common.c        systest.h
count.h            pcp_def_metrics.c  sa_conv.c          tapestat.c
CREDITS            pcp_def_metrics.h  sa_conv.h          tapestat.h
cron               pcp_stats.c        sadc.c             tests
do_test            pcp_stats.h        sadf.c             version.in
FAQ.md             pidstat.c          sadf.h             xml
format.c           pidstat.h          sadf_misc.c        xml_stats.c
iconfig            pr_stats.c         sa.h               xml_stats.h
$
```

In the directory listing, you should typically see a README or an INSTALL file. It is very important to read this file. In the file will be the instructions you will need to finish the software's installation.

Following the advice contained in the INSTALL file, the next step is to run the configure utility for your system. This checks your Linux system to ensure it has the proper library dependencies, in addition to the proper compiler to compile the source code:

```
$ ./configure
.
Check programs:
.
checking for gcc... gcc
checking whether the C compiler works... yes
checking for C compiler default output file name... a.out
checking for suffix of executables...
checking whether we are cross compiling... no
checking for suffix of object files... o
checking whether we are using the GNU C compiler... yes
checking whether gcc accepts -g... yes
```

```
...
config.status: creating man/cifsiostat.1
config.status: creating tests/variables
config.status: creating Makefile

    Sysstat version:          12.3.3
    Installation prefix:              /usr/local
    rc directory:             /etc
    Init directory:           /etc/init.d
    Systemd unit dir:                 /lib/systemd/system
    Configuration file:               /etc/sysconfig/sysstat
    Man pages directory:              ${datarootdir}/man
    Compiler:                 gcc
    Compiler flags:           -g -O2

$
```

If anything does go wrong, the configure step will display an error message explaining
what's missing.

> **NOTE**
>
> Most Linux utility programs are written using the C or C++ programming language. To compile them on your system,
> you will need the gcc package installed, as well as the make package. Most Linux desktop distributions don't
> install these by default. If the configure program shows an error that these parts are missing, consult your spe-
> cific Linux distribution docs on what packages you need to install.

The next stage is to build the various binary files using the make command. The make
command compiles the source code and then the linker to create the final executable files
for the package. As with the configure command, the make command produces lots of
output as it goes through the steps of compiling and linking all the source code files:

```
$ make
gcc -o sadc.o -c -g -O2 -Wall -Wstrict-prototypes -pipe -O2
  -DSA_DIR=\"/var/log/sa\" -DSADC_PATH=\"/usr/local/lib/sa/sadc\"
  -DHAVE_SYS_SYSMACROS_H -DHAVE_LINUX_SCHED_H -DHAVE_SYS_PARAM_H sadc.c
gcc -o act_sadc.o -c -g -O2 -Wall -Wstrict-prototypes -pipe -O2 -DSOURCE_SADC
  -DSA_DIR=\"/var/log/sa\" -DSADC_PATH=\"/usr/local/lib/sa/sadc\"
  -DHAVE_SYS_SYSMACROS_H -DHAVE_LINUX_SCHED_H -DHAVE_SYS_PARAM_H activity.c
gcc -o sa_wrap.o -c -g -O2 -Wall -Wstrict-prototypes -pipe -O2 -DSOURCE_SADC
  -DSA_DIR=\"/var/log/sa\" -DSADC_PATH=\"/usr/local/lib/sa/sadc\"
  -DHAVE_SYS_SYSMACROS_H -DHAVE_LINUX_SCHED_H -DHAVE_SYS_PARAM_H sa_wrap.c
gcc -o sa_common_sadc.o -c -g -O2 -Wall -Wstrict-prototypes -pipe -O2
-DSOURCE_SADC
  -DSA_DIR=\"/var/log/sa\" -DSADC_PATH=\"/usr/local/lib/sa/sadc\"
-DHAVE_SYS_SYSMACROS_H -DHAVE_LINUX_SCHED_H -DHAVE_SYS_PARAM_H sa_common.c
...
$
```

When make is finished, you'll have the actual sysstat software program available in the directory! However, it's somewhat inconvenient to have to run it from that directory. Instead, you'll want to install it in a common location on your Linux system. To do that, you'll need to log in as the root user account (or use the sudo command if your Linux distribution prefers), and then use the install option of the make command:

```
# make install
mkdir -p /usr/local/share/man/man1
mkdir -p /usr/local/share/man/man5
mkdir -p /usr/local/share/man/man8
rm -f /usr/local/share/man/man8/sa1.8*
install -m 644 -g man man/sa1.8 /usr/local/share/man/man8
rm -f /usr/local/share/man/man8/sa2.8*
install -m 644 -g man man/sa2.8 /usr/local/share/man/man8
rm -f /usr/local/share/man/man8/sadc.8*
...
install -m 644 -g man man/sadc.8 /usr/local/share/man/man8
install -m 644 FAQ /usr/local/share/doc/sysstat-12.3.3
install -m 644 *.lsm /usr/local/share/doc/sysstat-12.3.3
#
```

Now the sysstat package is installed on the system! Though not quite as easy as installing a software package via a package management system, installing software using tarballs is not that difficult.

# Summary

This chapter discussed how to work with a software package management system to install, update, or remove software from the command line. Most of the Linux distributions use fancy GUI tools for software package management, but you can also perform package management from the command line.

The Debian-based Linux distributions use the dpkg utility to interface with the package management system from the command line, and the apt-cache and apt-get utilities to interface with a common repository to easily download and install new software. A front end to these utilities is apt. It provides simple command-line options for working with software packages in the dpkg format.

The Red Hat–based Linux distributions are based on the rpm utility but use different front-end tools at the command line. Red Hat, CentOS, and Fedora use dnf for installing and managing software packages. The openSUSE distribution uses zypper for managing software.

Application containers are a relatively new player in software package management. An application container bundles all the files necessary for an application to run in one install-able package. This means the application doesn't rely on any external dependencies such as library files, and the container bundle can be installed in any Linux distribution and run.

Currently the two most popular container packages are snap, common in the Ubuntu Linux distribution, and flatpak, used in Red Hat Linux environments.

The chapter closed with a discussion on how to install software packages that are only distributed in source code tarballs. The `tar` command allows you to unpack the source code files from the tarball, and then `configure` and `make` allow you to build the final executable program from the source code.

The next chapter takes a look at the various editors available in Linux distributions. As you get ready to start working on shell scripts, it will come in handy to know what editors are available to use.

9

# Working with Editors

B efore you start your shell scripting career, it's wise to gain proficiency using at least one text editor in Linux. Using features such as searching, cutting, and pasting allows you to develop your shell scripts more quickly.

You have the choice of several editors. Many individuals find a particular editor whose functionality they love and use that one exclusively. This chapter provides a brief sampling of a few of the text editors you can employ in the Linux world.

## Visiting the vim Editor

The vi editor was one of the early editors used on Unix systems. It uses the console graphics mode to emulate a text-editing window, allowing you to see the lines of your file; move around within the file; and insert, edit, and replace text.

Although it is quite possibly the most complicated editor in the world (at least in the opinion of those who don't like it), vi provides many features that have made it a staple for programmers and system administrators for decades.

When the GNU Project ported the vi editor to the open source world, they chose to make some improvements to it. Because it extended the original vi editor found in the Unix world, the developers also renamed it "vi improved" or *vim*.

This section walks you through the basics of using the vim editor to edit your text shell script files.

## Checking your vim package

Before you begin your exploration of the vim editor, it's a good idea to understand what vim package your Linux system has installed. On some distributions, you will have the full vim package installed and an alias for the vi command, as shown on this CentOS distribution:

```
$ alias vi
alias vi='vim'
$
$ which vim
/usr/bin/vim
$
$ ls -l /usr/bin/vim
-rwxr-xr-x. 1 root root 3522560 Nov 11 14:08 /usr/bin/vim
$
```

Notice that the program file's long listing does not show any linked files (see Chapter 3, "Basic Bash Shell Commands," for more information on linked files). If the vim program is linked, it may be linked to a less than full-featured editor. Thus, it's a good idea to check for linked files.

On other distributions, you will find various flavors of the vim editor. Notice on this Ubuntu distribution that not only is there no alias for the vi command, but the /usr/bin/vi program file belongs to a series of file links:

```
$ alias vi
-bash: alias: vi: not found
$
$ which vi
/usr/bin/vi
$
$ ls -l /usr/bin/vi
lrwxrwxrwx 1 root root 20 Apr 23 14:33 /usr/bin/vi ->
 /etc/alternatives/vi
$
$ ls -l /etc/alternatives/vi
lrwxrwxrwx 1 root root 17 Apr 23 14:33 /etc/alternatives/vi ->
 /usr/bin/vim.tiny
$
$ readlink -f /usr/bin/vi
/usr/bin/vim.tiny
$
```

Thus, when the vi command is entered, the /usr/bin/vim.tiny program is executed. The vim.tiny program provides only a few vim editor features. If you are serious about trying out the vim editor and are using a distribution that uses a vim alternative, such as vim.tiny, consider installing the basic vim package for more vim features.

Software package management was covered in detail in Chapter 9, "Installing Software." Installing the basic vim package on this Ubuntu distribution is fairly straightforward:

```
$ sudo apt install vim
[sudo] password for christine:
[...]
The following additional packages will be installed:
  vim-runtime
Suggested packages:
  ctags vim-doc vim-scripts
The following NEW packages will be installed:
  vim vim-runtime
[...]
Do you want to continue? [Y/n] Y
[...]
Setting up vim (2:8.1.2269-1ubuntu5) ...
[...]
Processing triggers for man-db (2.9.1-1) ...
$
$ readlink -f /usr/bin/vi
/usr/bin/vim.basic
$
```

The basic vim editor is now installed on this Ubuntu distribution, and the /usr/bin/vi program file's link was automatically changed to point to /usr/bin/vim.basic. Thus, when the vi command is entered on this Ubuntu system, the basic vim editor is used instead of tiny vim.

## Exploring vim basics

The vim editor works with data in a memory buffer. To start the vim editor, just type the vim command (or vi if there's an alias or linked file) and the name of the file you want to edit:

```
$ vi myprog.c
```

If you start vim without a filename, or if the file doesn't exist, vim opens a new buffer area for editing. If you specify an existing file on the command line, vim reads the entire file's contents into a buffer area, where it is ready for editing, as shown in Figure 10-1.

10

**FIGURE 10-1**

The vim main window

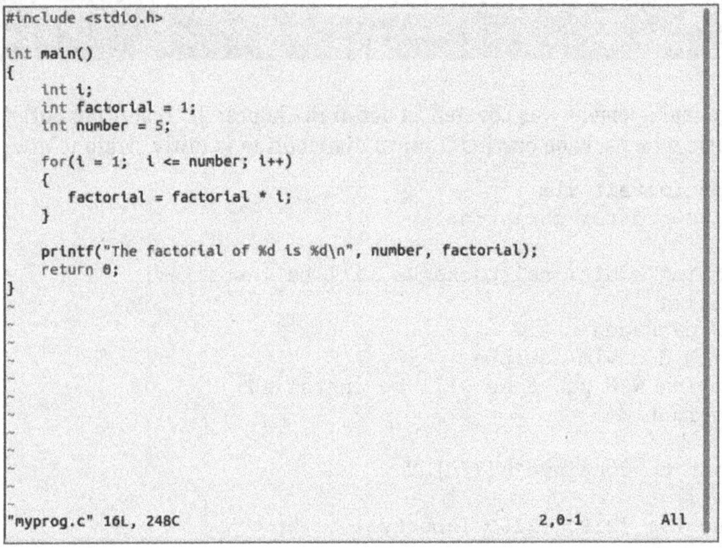

```
#include <stdio.h>

int main()
{
    int i;
    int factorial = 1;
    int number = 5;

    for(i = 1;  i <= number; i++)
    {
        factorial = factorial * i;
    }

    printf("The factorial of %d is %d\n", number, factorial);
    return 0;
}
~
~
~
~
~
~
~
~
~
~
"myprog.c" 16L, 248C                          2,0-1          All
```

The vim editor detects the terminal type for the session (see Chapter 2, "Getting to the Shell") and uses a full-screen mode to consume the entire console window for the editor area.

The initial vim edit window shows the contents of the file (if there are any) along with a message line at the bottom of the window. If the file contents don't take up the entire screen, vim places a tilde (~) on lines that are not part of the file (as shown in Figure 10-1).

The message line at the bottom indicates information about the edited file, depending on the file's status, and the default settings in your vim installation. If the file is new, the message [New File] appears.

The vim editor has three modes of operation:

- Command mode
- Ex mode
- Insert mode

When you first open a file (or start a new file) for editing, the vim editor enters *command* mode (sometimes called normal mode). In command mode, the vim editor interprets keystrokes as commands (more on those later).

In *insert* mode, vim places the letter, number, or symbol of the keys you type at the current cursor location in the buffer. To enter insert mode, enter i. To get out of insert mode and go back into command mode, press the Esc key on your keyboard.

In command mode, you can move the cursor around the text area by using the arrow keys (as long as your terminal type is detected properly by vim). If you happen to be on an unusual terminal connection that doesn't have the arrow keys defined, all hope is not lost. The vim editor include commands for moving the cursor:

- h to move left one character
- j to move down one line (the next line in the text)
- k to move up one line (the previous line in the text)
- l to move right one character

Moving around within large text files line by line can get tedious. Fortunately, vim provides a few commands to help speed things along:

- Press PageDown (or Ctrl+F) to move forward one screen of data.
- Press PageUp (or Ctrl+B) to move backward one screen of data.
- Enter G to move to the last line in the buffer.
- Enter *num* G to move to the line number *num* in the buffer.
- Enter *gg* to move to the first line in the buffer.

The vim editor has a special feature within command mode called *Ex mode*. This mode provides an interactive command line where you can enter additional commands to control the actions in vim. To get to Ex mode, press the colon key (:) in command mode. The cursor moves to the message line, and a colon (:) appears, waiting for you to enter a command.

Within the Ex mode are several commands for saving the buffer to the file and exiting vim:

- q to quit if no changes have been made to the buffer data
- q! to quit and discard any changes made to the buffer data
- w *filename* to save the file under a different filename
- wq to save the buffer data to the file and quit

After seeing just a few basic vim commands, you might understand why some people loathe the vim editor. To use vim to its fullest, you must know plenty of obscure commands. However, after you get a few of the basic vim commands down, you can quickly edit files directly from the command line, no matter what type of environment you're in. Due to its enormous functionality and despite its steep learning curve, the vim editor maintains its popularity. It is still considered one of the top 10 text editors.

**10**

## Editing data

While in command mode, the vim editor provides several commands for editing the data in the buffer. Table 10-1 lists some common editing commands for vim.

**TABLE 10-1** **vim Editing Commands**

| Command | Description |
| --- | --- |
| x | Deletes the character at the current cursor position. |
| dd | Deletes the line at the current cursor position. |
| dw | Deletes the word at the current cursor position. |
| d$ | Deletes to the end of the line from the current cursor position. |
| J | Deletes the line break at the end of the line at the current cursor position (joins lines). |
| u | Undoes the previous edit command. |
| a | Appends data after the current cursor position. |
| A | Appends data to the end of the line at the current cursor position. |
| r char | Replaces a single character at the current cursor position with char. |
| R text | Overwrites the data at the current cursor position with text, until you press Esc. |

Some of the editing commands also allow you to use a numeric modifier to indicate how many times to perform the command. For example, the command 2x deletes two characters, starting from the current cursor position, and the command 5dd deletes five lines, starting at the line from the current cursor position.

> **NOTE**
>
> Be careful when trying to use the keyboard Backspace or Delete key while in the vim editor's command mode. The vim editor usually recognizes the Delete key only as the functionality of the x command, deleting the character at the current cursor location. Usually, the vim editor doesn't recognize the Backspace key in command mode as a deleting action, but instead as a method to move the cursor back one space.

## Copying and pasting

A standard editor feature is the ability to cut or copy data and paste it elsewhere in the document. The vim editor provides a way to do this.

Cutting and pasting is relatively easy. You've already seen the commands in Table 10-1 that can remove data from the buffer. However, when vim removes data, it actually keeps it stored in a *separate* area. While in command mode, that data is retrievable by using the p command.

For example, use the dd command to delete a line of text, move the cursor to the buffer location where you want to place it, and then use the p command. The p command inserts the text after the line at the current cursor position. You can do this with any command that removes text while in command mode.

Copying text is a little bit trickier. The copy command in vim is y (for yank). You can use the same second character with y as with the d command (yw to yank a word, y$ to yank to the end of a line). After you yank the text, move the cursor to the location where you want to place the text and use the p command. The yanked text now appears at that location.

Yanking is tricky in that you can't see what happened because you're not affecting the text that you yank. You never know for sure what you yanked until you paste it somewhere. But there's another feature in vim that helps you out with yanking.

While in command mode, the *visual mode* highlights text as you move the cursor. You use visual mode to select text to yank for pasting. To enter visual mode, move the cursor to the location where you want to start yanking, and press v. Notice that the text at the cursor position is now highlighted. Next, move the cursor to cover the text you want to yank (you can even move down lines to yank more than one line of text). As you move the cursor, vim highlights the text in the yank area. After you've covered the text you want to copy, enter y to activate the yank command. Now that you have the text in the register, just move the cursor to where you want to paste and use the p command.

## Searching and substituting

You can easily search for data in the buffer using the vim search command. To enter a search string, press the forward slash (/) key. The cursor goes to the message line, and vim displays a forward slash. Enter the text you want to find, and press the Enter key. The vim editor responds with one of three actions:

- If the word appears after the current cursor location, it jumps to the first location where the text appears.
- If the word doesn't appear after the current cursor location, it wraps around the end of the file to the first location in the file where the text appears (and indicates this with a message).
- It produces an error message stating that the text was not found in the file.

If the word appears, to continue searching for the same word, press the forward slash character and then press the Enter key, or you can use n, which stands for next.

10

> **NOTE**
>
> Are you more familiar with writing scripts and programs on a Microsoft Windows platform with an integrated development environment (IDE)? If so, Microsoft's Visual Studio Code is available on Linux. (We'll wait a minute for you to reread that last sentence.) Yes, Microsoft offers Visual Studio for Linux. Find information for installing it on your particular Linux distribution at code.visualstudio.com/docs/setup/linux. If desired, you can add the VSCodeVim plugin to Visual Studio, and have all the vim commands at your fingertips.

The substitute command, performed within Ex mode, allows you to quickly replace (substitute) one word for another in the text. To get to the substitute command, you must be in command-line mode. The format for the substitute command is :s/*old*/*new*/. The vim editor jumps to the first occurrence of the text *old* and replaces it with the text *new*. You can make a few modifications to the substitute command to replace more than one occurrence of the text:

- :s/*old*/*new*/g to replace all occurrences of *old* in a line
- :*n*,*m*s/*old*/*new*/g to replace all occurrences of *old* between line numbers *n* and *m*
- :%s/*old*/*new*/g to replace all occurrences of *old* in the entire file
- :%s/*old*/*new*/gc to replace all occurrences of *old* in the entire file, but prompt for each occurrence

As you can see, for a console mode text editor, vim contains quite a few advanced features. Because nearly every Linux distribution includes it, it's a good idea to at least know the basics of the vim editor so that you can always edit scripts, no matter where you are or what you have available.

## Navigating the nano Editor

In contrast to vim, which is a complicated editor with powerful features, nano is a simple editor. For individuals who need a simple console mode text editor that is easy to navigate, nano is the tool to use. It's also a great text editor for those who are just starting on their Linux command-line adventure.

The nano text editor is a clone of the Unix systems' Pico editor. Although Pico also is a light and simple text editor, it is not licensed under the GPL. Not only is the nano text editor licensed under the GPL, it is also part of the GNU project.

The nano text editor is installed on most Linux distributions by default. Everything about the nano text editor is easy. To open a file at the command line with nano, enter

```
$ nano myprog.c
```

If you start nano without a filename, or if the file doesn't exist, nano simply opens a new buffer area for editing. If you specify an existing file on the command line, nano reads the entire contents of the file into a buffer area, where it is ready for editing, as shown in Figure 10-2.

**FIGURE 10-2**

The nano editor window

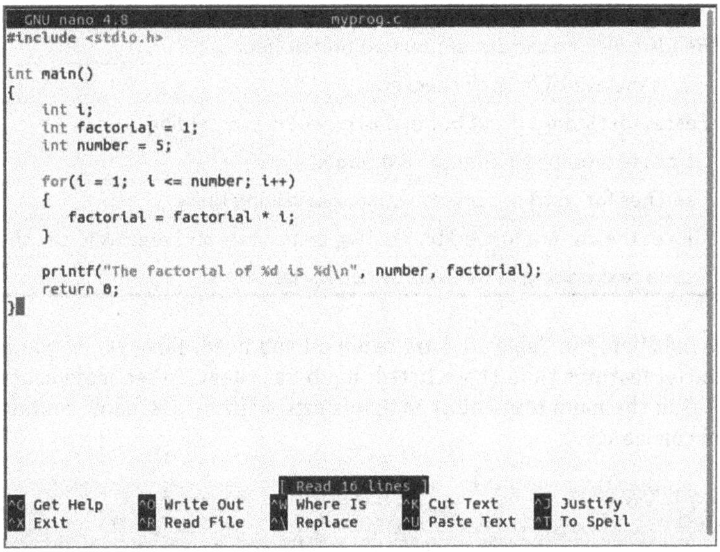

```
  GNU nano 4.8                      myprog.c
#include <stdio.h>

int main()
{
    int i;
    int factorial = 1;
    int number = 5;

    for(i = 1;  i <= number; i++)
    {
        factorial = factorial * i;
    }

    printf("The factorial of %d is %d\n", number, factorial);
    return 0;
}

                          [ Read 16 lines ]
^G Get Help    ^O Write Out   ^W Where Is    ^K Cut Text    ^J Justify
^X Exit        ^R Read File   ^\ Replace     ^U Paste Text  ^T To Spell
```

Notice that at the bottom of the nano editor window, various commands with brief descriptions are shown. These commands are the nano control commands. The caret (^) symbol shown represents the Ctrl key. Therefore, ^X stands for the keyboard sequence Ctrl+X.

> **TIP**
>
> Though the nano control commands list capital letters in the keyboard sequences, you can use either lowercase or uppercase characters for control commands.

Having most of the basic commands listed right in front of you is great — no need to memorize what control command does what. Table 10-2 presents the various nano control commands.

10

TABLE 10-2   **nano Control Commands**

| Command | Description |
| --- | --- |
| Ctrl+C | Displays the cursor's position within the text editing buffer. |
| Ctrl+G | Displays nano's main help window. |
| Ctrl+J | Justifies the current text paragraph. |
| Ctrl+K | Cuts the text line and stores it in cut buffer. |
| Ctrl+O | Writes out the current text editing buffer to a file. |
| Ctrl+R | Reads a file into the current text editing buffer. |
| Ctrl+T | Starts the available spell checker. |
| Ctrl+U | Pastes text stored in cut buffer and places in current line. |
| Ctrl+V | Scrolls text editing buffer to next page. |
| Ctrl+W | Searches for word or phrases within text editing buffer. |
| Ctrl+X | Closes the current text editing buffer, exits nano, and returns to the shell. |
| Ctrl+Y | Scrolls text editing buffer to previous page. |

The control commands listed in Table 10-2 are really all you need. However, if you desire more powerful control features than those listed, nano has them. To see more control commands, press Ctrl+G in the nano text editor to display its main help window containing additional control commands.

> **NOTE**
>
> Some of these additional commands available in nano are called Meta-key sequences. In the nano documentation, they are denoted by the letter M. For example, you'll find the key sequence to undo the last task denoted as M-U in the nano help system. But don't press the M key to accomplish this. Instead, M represents either the Esc, Alt, or Meta key, depending on your keyboard's configuration. Thus, you might press the Alt+U key combination to undo the last task within nano.

Even more features are available through command-line options to control the nano editor. Creating a backup file before editing is one nice selection. Type **man nano** to see these additional command-line options for starting nano.

The vim and nano text editors offer a choice between powerful and simple console mode text editors. However, neither offers the ability to use graphical features for editing. Some text editors can operate in both worlds, as explored in the next section.

## Exploring the Emacs Editor

The Emacs editor was an extremely popular editor for Digital Equipment Corporation (DEC) computers in the late 1970s. Developers liked it so much that they ported it to the Unix environment, and then to the Linux environment, where its official name is GNU Emacs. Though currently not as popular as vim, it still has its place in the world.

The Emacs editor started out life as a console editor, much like vim, but was migrated to the graphical world. The original console mode editor is still available, but it can use a graphical window to allow editing text in a graphical environment. Typically, when you start the Emacs editor from a command line, if the editor determines you have an available graphical session, it starts in graphical mode. If you don't, it starts in console mode.

This section describes both the console mode and graphical mode Emacs editors so that you'll know how to use either one if you want (or need) to.

## Checking your Emacs package

Many distributions do not come with the Emacs editor installed by default. You can check your Red Hat–based distribution by using the which and/or dnf list (use yum list on older versions of Red Hat-based distributions) command, as shown on this CentOS distribution:

```
$ which emacs
/usr/bin/which: no emacs in (/home/christine/.local/bin:
/home/christine/bin:/usr/local/bin:/usr/bin:/usr/local/sbin:
/usr/sbin)
$
$ dnf list emacs
[...]
Available Packages
emacs.x86_64[...]
$
```

The emacs editor package is not currently installed on this CentOS distribution. However, it is available to be installed. (For a more thorough discussion on displaying installed software, see Chapter 9.)

For a Debian-based distribution, check for the Emacs editor package by using the which and/or apt show command, as shown on this Ubuntu distribution:

```
$ which emacs
$
$ apt show emacs
Package: emacs
[...]
Description: GNU Emacs editor (metapackage)
 GNU Emacs is the extensible self-documenting text editor.
 This is a metapackage that will always depend on the latest
 recommended Emacs variant (currently emacs-gtk).

$
```

10

The which command operates a little differently here. When it does not find the installed command, it simply returns the Bash shell prompt. The emacs editor package for this Ubuntu distribution is available to be installed. The following shows the Emacs editor being installed on Ubuntu:

```
$ sudo apt install emacs
[sudo] password for christine:
Reading package lists... Done
[...]
Do you want to continue? [Y/n] Y
[...]
$
$ which emacs
/usr/bin/emacs
$
```

Now when the which command is used, it points to the emacs program file. The Emacs editor is ready for use on this Ubuntu distribution.

For the CentOS distribution, install the Emacs editor using the dnf install or yum install command:

```
$ sudo yum install emacs
[sudo] password for christine:
[...]
Dependencies resolved.
[...]
Is this ok [y/N]: Y
Downloading Packages:
[...]
Complete!
$
$ which emacs
/usr/bin/emacs
$
```

With the Emacs editor successfully installed on your Linux distribution, you can begin to explore its different features, starting with using it on the console.

## Using Emacs on the console

The console mode version of Emacs is another editor that uses lots of key commands to perform editing functions. The Emacs editor uses key combinations involving the Ctrl key and the Meta key. In most terminal emulator packages, the Meta key is mapped to the Alt key.

The official Emacs documents abbreviate the Ctrl key as C- and the Meta key as M-. Thus, the Ctrl+X key combination is shown in the document as C-x. This chapter section uses the Emacs' documentation format.

### Exploring the basics of Emacs

To edit a file using Emacs, from the command line, enter

```
$ emacs myprog.c
```

The Emacs console mode window appears and loads the file into the active buffer, as shown in Figure 10-3.

**FIGURE 10-3**

Editing a file using the Emacs editor in console mode

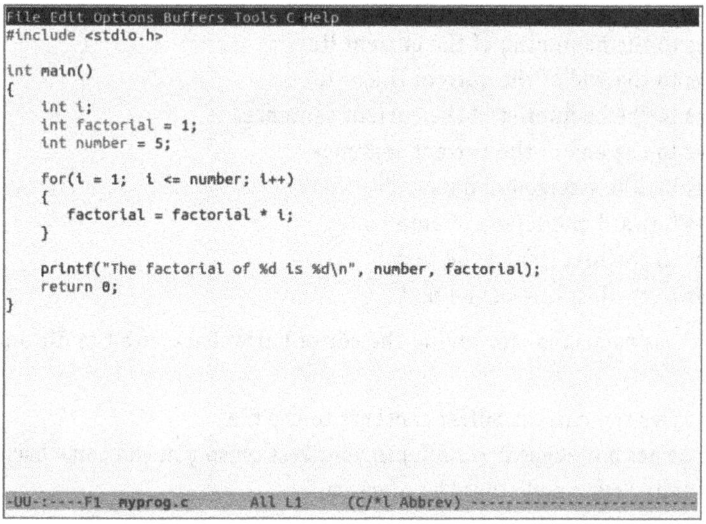

```
File Edit Options Buffers Tools C Help
#include <stdio.h>

int main()
{
    int i;
    int factorial = 1;
    int number = 5;

    for(i = 1;  i <= number; i++)
    {
        factorial = factorial * i;
    }

    printf("The factorial of %d is %d\n", number, factorial);
    return 0;
}
```
```
-UU-:----F1  myprog.c      All L1      (C/*l Abbrev) -----------------------------
```

You'll notice that the top of the console mode window shows a typical menu bar. Unfortunately, you can't use the menu bar in console mode, only in graphical mode.

> **NOTE**
>
> If you run Emacs in a graphical desktop environment, some commands in this section work differently than described. To use Emac's console mode in a graphical desktop environment, use the emacs -nw command. If you want to use Emacs's graphical features, see the section "Using Emacs in a GUI."

Unlike the vim editor, where you move into and out of insert mode and switch between entering commands and inserting text, the Emacs editor has only one mode. If you type a printable character, Emacs inserts it at the current cursor position. If you type a command, Emacs executes the command.

10

To move the cursor around the buffer area, you can use the arrow keys and the PageUp and PageDown keys, assuming that Emacs detected your terminal emulator correctly. If not, these commands move the cursor around:

- C-p moves up one line (the previous line in the text).
- C-b moves left (back) one character.
- C-f moves right (forward) one character.
- C-n moves down one line (the next line in the text).

The following commands make longer jumps within the text:

- M-f moves right (forward) to the next word.
- M-b moves left (backward) to the previous word.
- C-a moves to the beginning of the current line.
- C-e moves to the end of the current line.
- M-a moves to the beginning of the current sentence.
- M-e moves to the end of the current sentence.
- M-v moves back one screen of data.
- C-v moves forward one screen of data.
- M-< moves to the first line of the text.
- M-> moves to the last line of the text.

You should know these commands for saving the editor buffer back into the file and exiting Emacs:

- C-x C-s saves the current buffer contents to the file.
- C-z exits Emacs but keeps it running in your session so you can come back to it.
- C-x C-c exits Emacs and stops the program.

You'll notice that two of these features require two key combinations. The C-x command is called the *extend command*. This provides yet another whole set of commands to work with.

### Editing data

The Emacs editor is pretty robust about inserting and deleting text in the buffer. To insert text, just move the cursor to the location where you want to insert the text and start typing.

To delete text, Emacs uses the Backspace key to delete the character before the current cursor position and the Delete key to delete the character at the current cursor location.

The Emacs editor also has commands for cutting text. The Emacs documentation calls this *killing text*, but we'll stick with the friendlier *cutting* terminology.

The difference between deleting text and cutting text is that when you cut text, Emacs places it in a temporary area where you can retrieve it (see the next section, "Copying and Pasting"). Deleted text is gone forever.

These commands are for cutting text in the buffer:

- M-Backspace cuts the word before the current cursor position.
- M-d cuts the word after the current cursor position.
- C-k cuts from the current cursor position to the end of the line.
- M-k cuts from the current cursor position to the end of the sentence.

**TIP**

If you happen to make a mistake when cutting text, the C-/ command undoes the cut command and returns the data to the state it was in before you cut it.

The Emacs editor also includes a fancy way of mass-cutting text. Just move the cursor to the start of the area you want to cut, and press either the C-@ or C-spacebar keys. Then move the cursor to the end of the area you want to cut, and enter C-w. All the text between the two locations is cut.

### Copying and pasting

You've seen how to cut data from the Emacs buffer area; now it's time to see how to paste it somewhere else. Unfortunately, if you use the vim editor, this process may confuse you when you use the Emacs editor.

In an unfortunate coincidence, pasting data in Emacs is called *yanking*. In the vim editor, copying is called yanking, which is what makes this a difficult thing to remember if you happen to use both editors.

After you cut data using one of the cut commands, move the cursor to the location where you want to paste the data, and use the C-y command. This yanks the text out of the temporary area and pastes it at the current cursor position. The C-y command yanks the text from the last cut command. If you've performed multiple cut commands, you can cycle through them using the M-y command.

To copy text, just yank it back into the same location you cut it from and then move to the new location and use the C-y command again. You can yank text back as many times as you desire.

### Searching and replacing

Searching for text in the Emacs editor is done by using the C-s and C-r commands. The C-s command performs a forward search in the buffer area from the current cursor position to the end of the buffer, whereas the C-r command performs a backward search in the buffer area from the current cursor position to the start of the buffer.

When you enter either the C-s or the C-r command, a prompt appears in the bottom line, querying you for the text to search. You can perform two types of searches in Emacs.

In an *incremental* search, the Emacs editor performs the text search in real-time mode as you type the word. When you type the first letter, it highlights all the occurrences of that

**10**

letter in the buffer. When you type the second letter, it highlights all the occurrences of the two-letter combination in the text and so on until you complete the text you're searching for.

In a *non-incremental* search, press the Enter key after the C-s or C-r command. This locks the search query into the bottom line area and allows you to type the search text in full before searching.

To replace an existing text string with a new text string, you must use the M-x command. This command requires a text command, along with parameters.

The text command is replace-string. After typing the command, press the Enter key, and Emacs queries you for the existing text string. After entering that, press the Enter key again and Emacs queries you for the new replacement text string.

### Using buffers in Emacs

The Emacs editor allows you to edit multiple files at the same time by having multiple buffer areas. You can load files into a buffer and switch between buffers while editing.

To load a new file into a buffer while you're in Emacs, use the C-x C-f commands. This is the Emacs find-file mode, called *Dired*. It takes you to the bottom line in the window and allows you to enter the name of the file you want to start to edit. If you don't know the name or location of the file, just press the Enter key. This brings up a file browser in the edit window, as shown in Figure 10-4.

**FIGURE 10-4**

The Emacs file browser

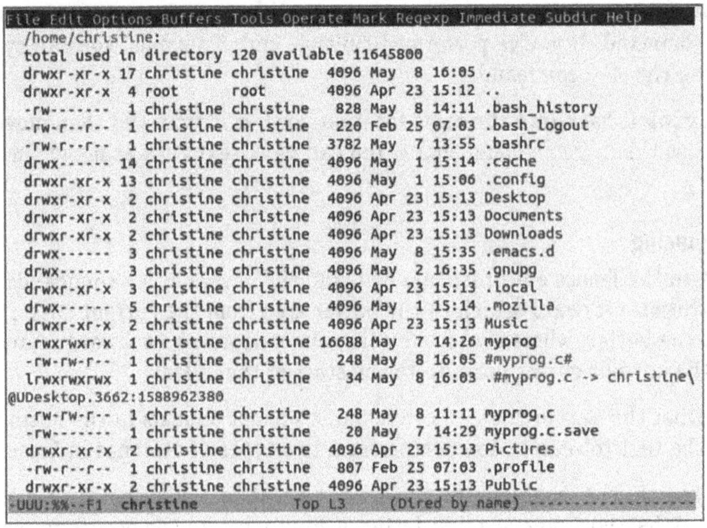

```
File Edit Options Buffers Tools Operate Mark Regexp Immediate Subdir Help
  /home/christine:
  total used in directory 120 available 11645800
  drwxr-xr-x 17 christine christine  4096 May  8 16:05 .
  drwxr-xr-x  4 root      root       4096 Apr 23 15:12 ..
  -rw-------  1 christine christine   828 May  8 14:11 .bash_history
  -rw-r--r--  1 christine christine   220 Feb 25 07:03 .bash_logout
  -rw-r--r--  1 christine christine  3782 May  7 13:55 .bashrc
  drwx------ 14 christine christine  4096 May  1 15:14 .cache
  drwxr-xr-x 13 christine christine  4096 May  1 15:06 .config
  drwxr-xr-x  2 christine christine  4096 Apr 23 15:13 Desktop
  drwxr-xr-x  2 christine christine  4096 Apr 23 15:13 Documents
  drwxr-xr-x  2 christine christine  4096 Apr 23 15:13 Downloads
  drwx------  3 christine christine  4096 May  8 15:35 .emacs.d
  drwx------  3 christine christine  4096 May  2 16:35 .gnupg
  drwxr-xr-x  3 christine christine  4096 Apr 23 15:13 .local
  drwx------  5 christine christine  4096 May  1 15:14 .mozilla
  drwxr-xr-x  2 christine christine  4096 Apr 23 15:13 Music
  -rwxrwxr-x  1 christine christine 16688 May  7 14:26 myprog
  -rw-rw-r--  1 christine christine   248 May  8 16:05 #myprog.c#
  lrwxrwxrwx  1 christine christine    34 May  8 16:03 .#myprog.c -> christine\
@UDesktop.3662:1588962380
  -rw-rw-r--  1 christine christine   248 May  8 11:11 myprog.c
  -rw-------  1 christine christine    20 May  7 14:29 myprog.c.save
  drwxr-xr-x  2 christine christine  4096 Apr 23 15:13 Pictures
  -rw-r--r--  1 christine christine   807 Feb 25 07:03 .profile
  drwxr-xr-x  2 christine christine  4096 Apr 23 15:13 Public
-UUU:%%--F1  christine      Top L3   (Dired by name) --------------------
```

From here, you can browse to the file you want to edit. To traverse up a directory level, go to the double dot entry and press the Enter key. To traverse down a directory, go to the directory entry and press Enter. When you've found the file you want to edit, press Enter and Emacs loads it into a new buffer area.

> **TIP**
>
> When you start the file browser in the edit window, you may decide you don't want to open a file. In this case, enter q to quit the file browser window.

You can list the active buffer areas by entering the C-x  C-b extended command combination. The Emacs editor splits the editor window and displays a list of buffers in the bottom window. Emacs provides two buffers in addition to your main editing buffer:

- A scratch area called scratch
- A message area called Messages

The scratch area allows you to enter LISP programming commands as well as enter notes to yourself. The messages area shows messages generated by Emacs while operating. If any errors occur while using Emacs, they appear in the messages area.

You can switch to a different buffer area in the window in two ways:

- Use C-x  C-b to open the buffer listing window. Use C-x  b and then type **\*Buffer List\*** to switch to that window. Use the arrow keys to move the cursor to the buffer area you want and press the Enter key.
- Use C-x  b to type in the name of the buffer area you want to switch to.

When you select the option to switch to the buffer listing window, Emacs opens the buffer area in a new window area. The Emacs editor allows you to have multiple windows open in a single session. The following section discusses how to manage multiple windows in Emacs.

### Using windows in console mode Emacs

The console mode Emacs editor was developed many years before the idea of graphical windows appeared. However, it was advanced for its time in that it could support multiple editing windows within the main Emacs window.

You can split the Emacs editing window into multiple windows by using one of two commands:

- C-x  2 splits the window horizontally into two windows.
- C-x  3 splits the window vertically into two windows.

To move from one window to another, use the C-x  o command. Notice that when you create a new window, Emacs uses the buffer area from the original window in the new window.

**10**

After you move into the new window, you can use the C-x  C-f command to load a new file or use one of the commands to switch to a different buffer area in the new window.

To close a window, move to it and use the C-x  0 (that's a zero) command. If you want to close all the windows except the one you're in, use the C-x  1 (that's a numerical one) command.

## Using Emacs in a GUI

If you use Emacs from a GUI environment (such as in the GNOME Shell desktop), it starts in graphical mode, as shown in Figure 10-5.

**FIGURE 10-5**

The Emacs graphical window

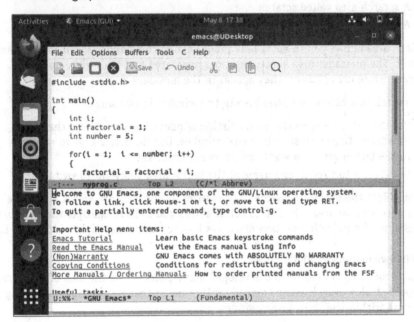

If you've already used Emacs in console mode, you should be fairly familiar with the graphical mode. All the key commands are available as menu bar items. The Emacs menu bar contains the following items:

- **File** allows you to open files in the window, create new windows, close windows, save buffers, and print buffers.

- **Edit** allows you to cut and copy selected text to the clipboard, paste clipboard data to the current cursor position, search for text, and replace text.
- **Options** provides settings for many more Emacs features, such as highlighting, word wrap, cursor type, and setting fonts.
- **Buffers** lists the current buffers available and allows you to easily switch between buffer areas.
- **Tools** provides access to the advanced features in Emacs, such as the command-line interface access, spell checking, comparing text between files (called diff), sending an email message, calendar, and the calculator.
- **C** allows advanced settings for highlighting C program syntax, compiling, running, and debugging the code.
- **Help** provides the Emacs manual online for access to help on specific Emacs functions.

The graphical Emacs window is an example of an older console application that made the migration to the graphical world. Now that many Linux distributions provide graphical desktops (even on servers that don't need them), graphical editors are becoming more commonplace. Popular Linux desktop environments (such as KDE Plasma and GNOME Shell) have also provided graphical text editors specifically for their environments, which are covered in the rest of this chapter.

# Exploring the KDE Family of Editors

If you're using a Linux distribution that uses the KDE Plasma desktop environment, you have a couple of options when it comes to text editors. The KDE project officially supports two popular text editors:

- **KWrite:** A single-screen text-editing package
- **Kate:** A full-featured, multiwindow text-editing package

Both of these editors are graphical text editors that contain many advanced features. The Kate editor also provides extra niceties not often found in standard text editors. This section describes each of the editors and shows some of the features you can use to help with your shell script editing.

## Looking at the KWrite editor

The basic editor for the KDE Plasma environment is KWrite. It provides simple word processing–style text editing, along with support for code syntax highlighting and editing. The default KWrite editing window is shown in Figure 10-6.

10

**FIGURE 10-6**

The default KWrite window editing a shell script program

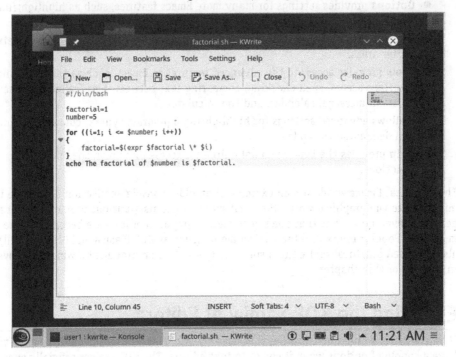

You can't tell from Figure 10-6, but the KWrite editor recognizes several types of programming languages and uses color coding to distinguish constants, functions, and comments. The KWrite editing window provides full cut and paste capabilities, using the mouse and the arrow keys. As with a word processor, you can highlight and cut (or copy) text anywhere in the buffer area and paste it at any other place.

> **TIP**
>
> Typically, KWrite is no longer installed by default on the KDE desktop environment. However, you can easily install it (see Chapter 9) on Plasma or other desktop environments, where available. The package name is `kwrite`.

To edit a file using KWrite, you can either select KWrite from the KDE menu system on your desktop (some Linux distributions even create a Panel icon for it) or start it from the command-line prompt:

```
$ kwrite factorial.sh
```

The `kwrite` command has several command-line parameters you can use to customize how it starts. Here are few of the more practical ones:

- `--stdin` causes KWrite to read data from the standard input device instead of a file.
- `--encoding` specifies a character encoding type to use for the file.
- `--line` specifies a line number in the file to start at in the editor window.
- `--column` specifies a column number in the file to start at in the editor window.

The KWrite editor provides both a menu bar and a toolbar at the top of the edit window, allowing you to select features and change the configuration settings of the KWrite editor.

The menu bar contains these items:

- **File** loads, saves, prints, and exports text from files.
- **Edit** manipulates text in the buffer area.
- **View** manages how the text appears in the editor window.
- **Bookmarks** handle pointers to return to specific locations in the text; this option may need to be enabled in the configurations.
- **Tools** contains specialized features to manipulate the text.
- **Settings** configures the way the editor handles text.
- **Help** gives you information about the editor and commands.

The Edit menu bar item provides commands for all your text-editing needs. Instead of having to remember cryptic key commands (which by the way, KWrite also supports), you can just select items in the Edit menu bar, as shown in Table 10-3.

**TABLE 10-3**   **The KWrite Edit Menu Items**

| Item | Description |
|---|---|
| Undo | Reverses the last action or operation. |
| Redo | Reverses the last undo action. |
| Cut | Deletes the selected text and places it in the clipboard. |
| Copy | Copies the selected text to the clipboard. |
| Paste | Inserts the current contents of the clipboard at the current cursor position. |
| Clipboard History | Displays portions of text recently copied to the clipboard from which you can select to paste. |
| Copy As HTML | Copies the selected text as HTML. |
| Select All | Selects all text in the editor. |
| Deselect | Deselects any text that is currently selected. |
| Block Selection Mode | Toggles on/off block selection mode which allows vertical text selection. |

*(Continues)*

**10**

**TABLE 10.3** *(continued)*

| Item | Description |
|---|---|
| Input Modes | Toggles between a normal and a vi-like editing mode. |
| Overwrite Mode | Toggles insert mode to overwrite mode, replacing text with new typed text instead of just inserting the new text. |
| Find | Produces the Find Text dialog box, which allows you to customize a text search. |
| Find Variants | Provides a submenu of various text searches — Find Next, Find Previous, Find Selected, and Find Selected Backwards. |
| Replace | Produces the Replace With dialog box, which allows you to customize a text search and replace. |
| Go To | Provides a submenu of various Go To choices — Move To Matching Bracket, Select To Matching Bracket, Move To Previous Modified Line, Move To Next Modified Line, Go To Line. |

The Find feature has two modes. Normal mode performs simple text searches and power searches. Replace mode lets you do advanced searching and replacing if necessary. You toggle between the two modes using the icon on the lower-right side of the window, as shown in Figure 10-7.

**FIGURE 10-7**

The KWrite Find section

The Find power mode allows you to search not only with words, but with a regular expression (discussed in Chapter 20, "Regular Expressions") for the search. You can use some other options to customize the search as well, indicating, for example, whether or not to perform a case-sensitive search or to look only for whole words instead of finding the text within words.

The Tools menu bar item provides several handy features for working with the text in the buffer area. Table 10-4 describes the tools available in KWrite.

**TABLE 10-4  The KWrite Tools**

| Tool | Description |
| --- | --- |
| Read Only Mode | Locks the text so that no changes can be made while in the editor. |
| Mode | Sets the file type arrangement for the text from a submenu selection. |
| Highlighting | Selects the text highlighting plan from a submenu selection. |
| Indentation | Sets the indentation style for the text from a submenu selection. |
| Encoding | Chooses the character set encoding used by the text. |
| End of Line | Switches the End of Line characters between Unix, Windows/DOS, and Macintosh. |
| Add Byte Order Mark | Toggles on/off setting a byte order mark (BOM) at the start of the text. |
| Scripts | Selects scripted actions from a submenu for quickly accomplishing such items as editing. |
| Invoke Code Completion | Displays a tooltip suggesting the code text to use at the cursor's location; autocompletion using the tip is selected by pressing Enter. |
| Word Completion | Performs autocompletion of the current typed text from a submenu selection. |
| Spelling | Starts and/or controls the spell-check program for the text. |
| Clean Indentation | Returns all paragraph indentation to the original settings. |
| Align | Forces the current line or the selected lines to return to the default indentation settings. |
| Toggle Comment | Turns the text line into a comment line using syntax based on the current mode selected. |
| Uppercase | Sets the selected text, or the character at the current cursor position, to uppercase. |
| Lowercase | Sets the selected text, or the character at the current cursor position, to lowercase. |
| Capitalize | Capitalizes the first letter of the selected text or the word at the current cursor position. |
| Join Lines | Combines the selected lines, or the line at the current cursor position and the next line, into one line. |
| Apply Word Wrap | Enables word wrapping in the text. If a line extends past the editor window edge, the line continues on the next line. |

10

There are lots of tools for this simple text editor! The Mode and Indentation tools are particularly nice to help you along if you are writing a script or program. The Mode's Script submenu is displayed in Figure 10-8.

**FIGURE 10-8**

The KWrite Tool Mode Script submenu

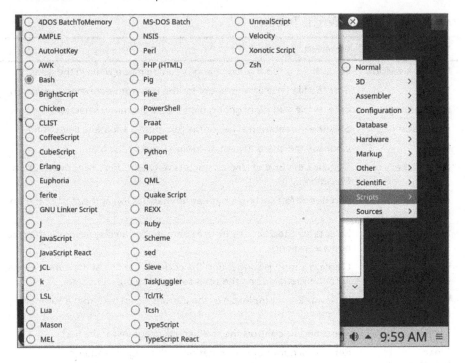

The Settings menu includes the Configure Editor dialog box, shown in Figure 10-9.

The Configuration dialog box uses icons on the left side for you to select the feature in KWrite to configure. When you select an icon, the right side of the dialog box shows the configuration settings for the feature.

The Appearance feature allows you to set several features that control how the text appears in the text editor window. You can enable word wrap, line count (great for programmers), and word count from here. With the Fonts & Colors feature, you can customize the complete color scheme for the editor, determining what colors to make each category of text in the program code. There are also several customizations you can choose, such as encoding and mode, so you don't have to set them via the menu system each time you open a file.

**FIGURE 10-9**

The KWrite Configure Editor dialog box

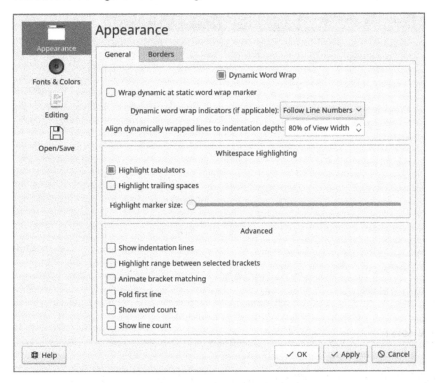

## Looking at the Kate editor

The Kate editor is the flagship editor for the KDE Project. It uses the same core text editor as the KWrite application (so most of those features are the same), but it incorporates lots of other features into a single package, including a multiple document interface (MDI).

> **TIP**
>
> If you find that the Kate editor has not been installed with your KDE desktop environment, you can easily install it (see Chapter 9). The package name that contains Kate is `kate` or `kdesdk`.

When you start the Kate editor from the Plasma menu system, you see the main Kate editor window, shown in Figure 10-10.

You'll notice the window looks very similar to the KWrite editing window shown previously in Figure 10-6. However, there are differences. For example, the left side frame shows the Documents icon. Clicking this icon opens a new interface called the Documents List, shown in Figure 10-11, which allows switching between open documents, creating new documents, and exploring other files to open.

**10**

**FIGURE 10-10**

The main Kate editing window

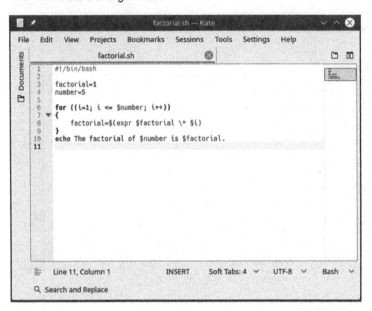

**FIGURE 10-11**

The Kate Documents List

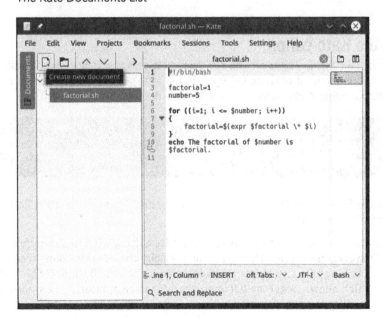

Kate also supports several external plugin applications, which can be activated in the Plugin Manager window, shown in Figure 10-12. You reach this feature by choosing Settings ⇨ Configure ⇨ Kate ⇨ Plugins. In this window, you can select various plugins to make your shell scripting environment more productive.

**FIGURE 10-12**

The Kate Plugin Manager

One great feature of the Kate editor is the built-in terminal plugin (`Terminal tool view`), which provides a terminal window, shown in Figure 10-13. The terminal icon at the bottom text editor's window starts the built-in terminal emulator in Kate (using the KDE Konsole terminal emulator is covered in Chapter 2, "Getting to the Shell").

**TIP**

If you don't see the terminal icon at the bottom of the Kate window, most likely you have not activated the `Terminal tool view` plugin. Once you have reached the Plugin Manager window (described earlier) and have selected the `Terminal tool view` plugin, be sure to click the Apply icon to activate this feature.

10

This terminal emulator feature horizontally splits the current editing window, creating a new window with Konsole running in it. You can now enter command-line commands, start programs, or check on system settings without having to leave the editor! To close the terminal window, just type **exit** at the command prompt.

**FIGURE 10-13**

The Kate built-in terminal window

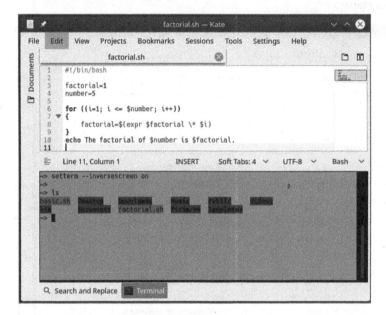

As you can tell from the terminal feature, Kate also supports multiple windows. The Window menu bar item (View) provides options to perform these tasks, such as the following:

- Create a new Kate window using the current session.
- Split the current window vertically to create a new window.
- Split the current window horizontally to create a new window.
- Close the current window.

The View menu also allows you to control the editor window's functionality such as displaying various tools, changing the font size, and showing nonprintable characters. Kate is rich in features.

> **NOTE**
>
> The Kate editor handles files in sessions. You can have multiple files open in a session, and you can have multiple sessions saved through the Sessions menu. When you start Kate, you can recall saved sessions. This allows you to easily manage files from multiple projects by using separate workspaces for each project.

To set the configuration settings in Kate, select Settings ⇨ Configure Kate. The Configuration dialog box, shown in Figure 10-14, appears. The Application settings area allows you to configure settings for the Kate items, such as controlling sessions (shown in Figure 10-14), the documents list, and the filesystem browser.

**FIGURE 10-14**

The Kate configuration dialog box

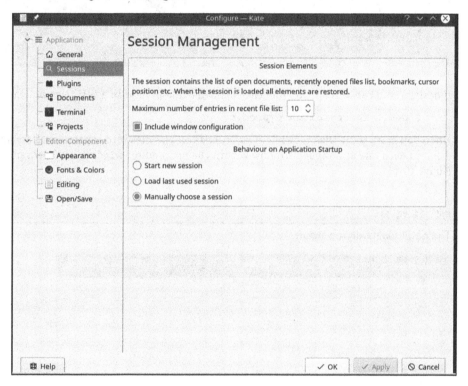

Kate and Kwrite work well side by side. Kate is a rich MDI editor that acts as an IDE, making it useful for creating and editing shell scripts. KWrite, on the other hand, launches quickly while providing nearly as much power as Kate so that you can make fast fixes to your scripts. Both editors have their place in the world.

# Exploring the GNOME Editor

If you're working on a Linux system with the GNOME Shell desktop environment, there's a graphical text editor that you can use as well. The gedit text editor is a basic text editor, with a few advanced features thrown in just for fun. This section walks you through the features of gedit and demonstrates how to use it for your shell script programming.

## Starting gedit

In the GNOME Shell desktop environment, accessing gedit is fairly straightforward. Click the Activities icon in the upper-right corner of the desktop window. When the search bar appears, click within the bar to access it, type **gedit** or **text editor**, and then click Text Editor.

> **TIP**
>
> If gedit is not installed by default on your desktop environment, you can easily install it (see Chapter 9). The package name is `gedit`. You should install the gedit plugins as well, because they provide powerful and advanced features. Their package name, as you might have already guessed, is `gedit-plugins`.

If desired, you can start gedit from the command-line prompt in a GUI terminal emulator:

```
$ gedit factorial.sh myprog.c
```

When you start gedit with multiple files, it loads all the files into separate buffers and displays each one as a tabbed window within the main editor window, as shown in Figure 10-15.

**FIGURE 10-15**

The gedit main editor window

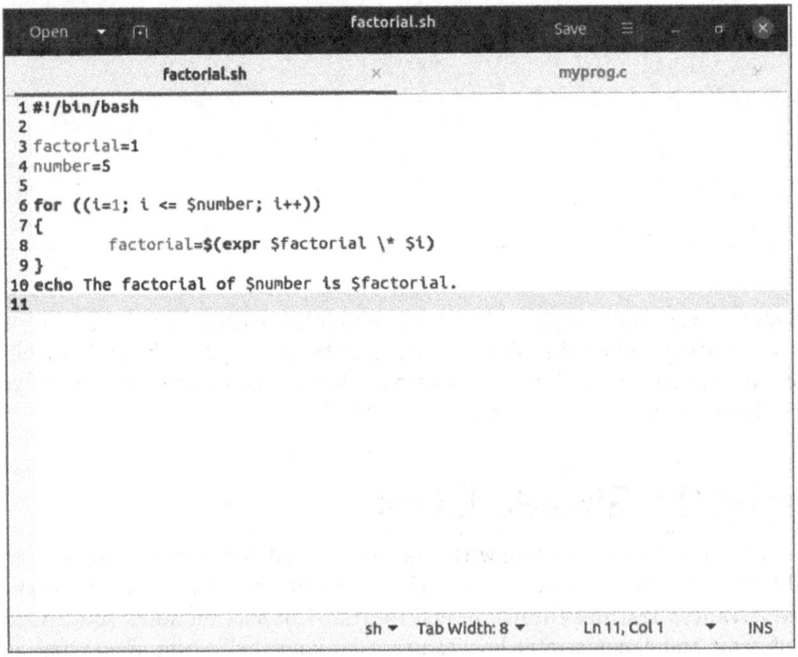

In Figure 10-15, the left frame in the gedit main editor window shows the documents you're currently editing. The right side shows the tabbed window that contains the buffer text of the second file. If you hover your mouse pointer over each tab, a dialog box appears, showing the full pathname of the file, the MIME type, and the character set encoding it uses.

**TIP**

You can quickly jump between the gedit tabs by clicking on the tab. If you prefer shortcut keys, pressing Ctrl+Alt+PageDown will put you into the tab buffer on the right. Pressing Ctrl+Alt+PageUp will take you to the left.

## Understanding basic gedit features

Modern versions of gedit don't use a menu bar. Instead, they use a menu system accessible through a collapsed menu icon (also called a hamburger button) in the title bar that allows you to control files, manage your editing session, configure settings, and so on, as shown in Figure 10-16.

**FIGURE 10-16**

The gedit menu system

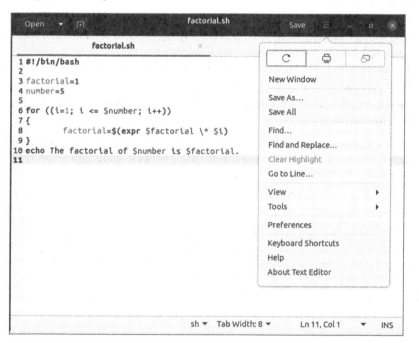

These menu items available are:

- **New Window** opens a new editing window instead of a tab.
- **Save As** saves the current buffered file to a new filename.
- **Save All** saves all the tabs' contents to disk.
- **Find** opens the Find Text dialog box, which allows you to customize a text search, and highlights the found text.
- **Find and Replace** displays the Find/Replace pop-up window, which allows you to customize a text search and replace.
- **Clear Highlight** removes the highlighting of found text.
- **Go to Line** opens the Go to Line dialog box, which moves the cursor to the entered line number of the text.
- **View** opens a submenu allowing the selection of displaying a Documents List/File Manager (Side Panel), Embedded Terminal (Bottom Panel), and syntax highlighting (Highlight Mode).
- **Tools** displays a submenu allowing the activation of a spell checker (Check Spelling), changing the spell checker's language (Set Language), highlights of misspellings (Highlight Misspelled Words), displaying text stats (Document Statistics), and selecting a particular date and time format for insertion (Insert Date And Time)
- **Preferences** opens a pop-up window providing customization of the gedit editor's operation, including such choices as displaying the line numbers, tab stops, text fonts and colors, and activated gedit plugins.
- **Keyboard Shortcuts** displays a brief list of available gedit keyboard shortcuts.
- **Help** provides access to the full gedit manual.
- **About Text Editor** shows information concerning the gedit version, description, website, and so on.

One item not on the menu is a basic save feature that lets you save the text in the current tab buffer with its original filename. That's because gedit conveniently provides a Save icon on the title bar (see Figure 10-16). Just a click on the icon and the file is saved. If you prefer to use the keyboard instead, the Ctrl+S shortcut provides the same function.

> **NOTE**
> Your Linux desktop environment may have an older or newer version of gedit than the one shown in these figures. In this case, your gedit text editor could have diverse options or even the same options, but they are available in slightly different menu locations. Consult your distribution's gedit Help menu for more assistance.

The Side Panel in gedit provides functionality similar to the Documents List in Kate. Access this feature by clicking the menu hamburger icon and then choosing View. When the View submenu appears, click the box next to Side Panel. These actions result in something similar to Figure 10-17.

**FIGURE 10-17**

The gedit Side Panel

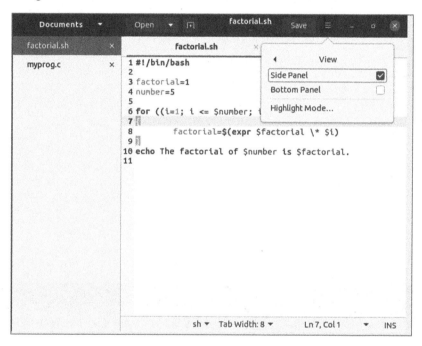

The gedit Side Panel provides quick switching between open documents. You can also switch to a file manager by clicking Documents and selecting File Browser, as shown in Figure 10-18.

Within the File Browser pane, you can look through various folders and find other files to edit. If desired, switch back to Documents by clicking File Browser and selecting Documents.

10

**FIGURE 10-18**

The gedit Side Panel's file manager

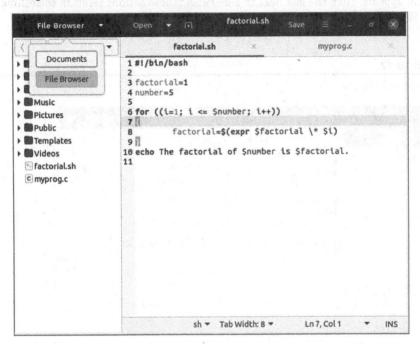

The File Browser is a gedit plugin. If for some reason you cannot reach the File Browser from the Side Panel, it may not be enabled or possibly not installed. You can always open files using the Ctrl+O keyboard shortcut, but the File Browser is a useful plugin. We cover more about the managing gedit plugins next.

## Managing plugins

The Plugins tab within the gedit Preferences window (shown in Figure 10-19) provides control over the plugins used in gedit. Plugins are separate programs that can interface with gedit to provide additional functionality.

**FIGURE 10-19**

The gedit Plugins tab

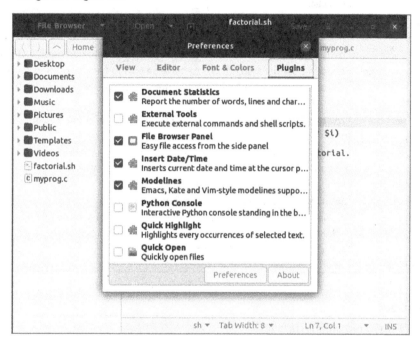

Typically only basic gedit plugins are installed by default. Table 10-5 describes the basic plugins that are currently available in the GNOME desktop's gedit application.

If desired, you can get additional useful features, such as an embedded terminal, by installing the plugins metapackage (see Chapter 9), as shown here on Ubuntu:

```
$ sudo apt install gedit-plugins
[sudo] password for christine:
[...]
0 upgraded, 29 newly installed, 0 to remove and 77 not upgraded.
Need to get 2,558 kB of archives.
After this operation, 13.6 MB of additional disk space will be used.
Do you want to continue? [Y/n] Y
[...]
Setting up gedit-plugins (3.36.2-1) ...
$
```

Once you have the additional plugins installed on your system, you'll see many additional choices on the Plugins tab within the gedit Preferences window, as shown in Figure 10-20.

10

**TABLE 10-5  The GNOME Desktop gedit Plugins**

| Plugin | Description |
|---|---|
| Document Statistics | Reports the number of words, lines, characters, and non-space characters. |
| External Tools | Provides a shell environment in the editor to execute commands and scripts. |
| File Browser Panel | Provides a simple file browser to make selecting files for editing easier. |
| Insert Date/Time | Inserts the current date and time in several formats at the current cursor position. |
| Modelines | Provides Emacs, Kate, and vim-style message lines at the bottom of the editor window. |
| Python Console | Provides an interactive console at the bottom of the editor window for entering commands using the Python programming language. |
| Quick Highlight | Highlights all the matching text of a selection. |
| Quick Open | Opens files directly in the gedit edit window. |
| Snippets | Allows you to store often-used pieces of text for easy retrieval anywhere in the text. |
| Sort | Quickly sorts the entire file or selected text. |
| Spell Checker | Provides dictionary spell checking for the text file. |

**FIGURE 10-20**

The gedit Plugins tab after installation

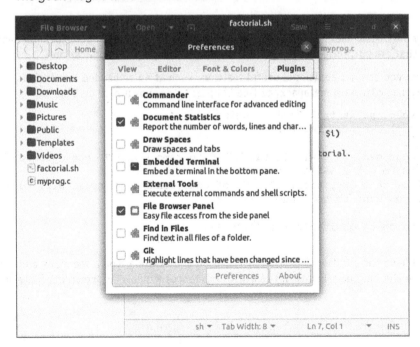

Plugins that are enabled show a check mark in the check box next to their name. Enabling a plugin does not start it. If you want to use, for example, the Embedded Terminal, you must enable it in the Preferences tab first. After that, you can access the plugin by clicking the menu hamburger icon and choosing View, and when the View submenu appears, clicking the box next to Bottom Panel to open the Embedded Terminal, as shown in Figure 10-21.

**FIGURE 10-21**

The gedit Embedded Terminal plugin

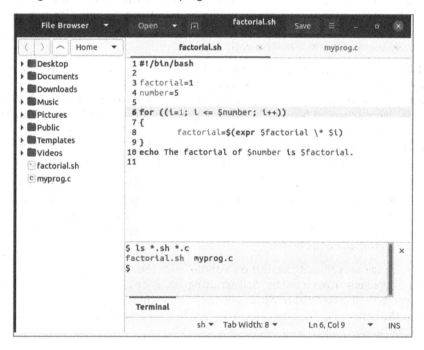

This chapter has covered just a few of the text editors available on Linux. If you find that the text editors described here don't meet your needs, you have options. Many more Linux editors are available, such as Geany, Sublime Text, Atom, Visual Studio Code, and Brackets, to name a few. All these editors can help you as you begin your Bash shell script writing journey.

# Summary

When it comes to creating shell scripts, you need some type of text editor. Several popular text editors are available for the Linux environment. The most popular editor in the Unix world, vi, has been ported to the Linux world as the vim editor. The vim editor provides simple text editing from the console, using a rudimentary full-screen graphical mode. The vim editor provides many advanced editor features, such as text searching and replacement.

Another editor that has been ported from the Unix world to Linux is the nano text editor. The vim editor can be rather complex, but the nano editor offers simplicity. The nano editor allows quick text editing in console mode.

Another popular Unix editor — Emacs — has also made its way to the Linux world. The Linux version of Emacs has both a console and a graphical mode, making it the bridge between the old world and the new. The Emacs editor provides multiple buffer areas, allowing you to edit multiple files simultaneously.

The KDE Project created two editors for use in the KDE Plasma desktop. The KWrite editor is a simple editor that provides basic text-editing features, along with a few advanced features, such as syntax highlighting for programming code and line numbering. The Kate editor provides more advanced features for programmers. One great feature in Kate is a built-in terminal window. You can open a command-line interface session directly in the Kate editor without having to open a separate terminal emulator window. The Kate editor also allows you to open multiple files, providing different windows for each opened file.

The GNOME Project also provides a graphical text editor for programmers. The gedit editor provides some advanced features such as code syntax highlighting and line numbering, but it was designed to be a bare-bones editor. To spruce up the gedit editor, developers created plugins, which expand the features available in gedit. Plugins include a spell-checker, a terminal emulator, and a file browser.

This wraps up the background chapters on working with the command line in Linux. The next part of the book dives into the shell scripting world. The next chapter starts off by showing you how to create a shell script file and how to run it on your Linux system. It also shows you the basics of shell scripts, allowing you to create simple programs by stringing multiple commands together into a script you can run.

# Part II

# Shell Scripting Basics

## IN THIS PART

# Basic Script Building

## IN THIS CHAPTER

Using multiple commands

Creating a script file

Displaying messages

Using variables

Redirecting input and output

Pipes

Performing math

Exiting the script

N ow that we've covered the basics of the Linux system and the command line, it's time to start coding. This chapter discusses the basics of writing shell scripts. You'll need to know these basic concepts before you can start writing your own shell script masterpieces.

## Using Multiple Commands

So far you've seen how to use the command-line interface (CLI) prompt of the shell to enter commands and view the command results. The key to shell scripts is the ability to enter multiple commands and process the results from each command, even possibly passing the results of one command to another. The shell allows you to chain commands together into a single step.

If you want to run two commands together, you can enter them on the same prompt line, separated with a semicolon:

```
$ date ; who
Mon Jun 01 15:36:09 EST 2020
Christine tty2         2020-06-01 15:26
Samantha tty3         2020-06-01 15:26
Timothy  tty1         2020-06-01 15:26
user     tty7         2020-06-01 14:03 (:0)
user     pts/0        2020-06-01 15:21 (:0.0)

$
```

Congratulations, you just wrote a shell script! This simple script uses just two Bash shell commands. The date command runs first, displaying the current date and time, followed by the output of the who command, showing who is currently logged on to the system. Using this technique, you can string together as many commands as you wish, up to the maximum command-line character count of 255 characters.

Although using this technique is fine for small scripts, it has a major drawback in that you have to enter the entire command at the command prompt every time you want to run it. Instead of having to manually enter the commands on a command line, you can combine them into a simple text file. When you need to run the commands, just simply run the text file.

## Creating a Script File

To place shell commands in a text file, first you'll need to use a text editor (see Chapter 10, "Working with Editors") to create a file, and then enter the commands into the file.

When creating a shell script file, you should specify the shell you are using in the first line of the file. The format for this is

```
#!/bin/bash
```

In a normal shell script line, the pound sign (#) is used as a comment line. A comment line in a shell script isn't processed by the shell. However, the first line of a shell script file is a special case, and the pound sign followed by the exclamation point tells the shell what shell to run the script under (yes, you can be using a Bash shell and run your script using another shell).

After indicating the shell, commands are entered onto each line of the file, followed by a carriage return. As mentioned, comments can be added by using the pound sign. An example looks like this:

```
#!/bin/bash
# This script displays the date and who's logged on
date
who
```

And that's all there is to it. You can use the semicolon and put both commands on the same line if you want to, but in a shell script, you can list commands on separate lines. The shell will process commands in the order in which they appear in the file.

Also notice that another line was included that starts with the pound symbol and adds a comment. Lines that start with the pound symbol (other than the first #! line) aren't interpreted by the shell. This is a great way to leave comments for yourself about what's happening in the script so that when you come back to it two years later you can easily remember what you did.

Save this script in a file called test1, and you are almost ready. There are still a couple of things to do before you can run your new shell script file.

If you try running the file now, you'll be somewhat disappointed to see this:

```
$ test1
bash: test1: command not found
$
```

The first hurdle to jump is getting the Bash shell to find your script file. If you remember from Chapter 6, "Using Linux Environment Variables," the shell uses an environment variable called PATH to find commands. A quick look at the PATH environment variable demonstrates our problem:

```
$ echo $PATH
/usr/kerberos/sbin:/usr/kerberos/bin:/usr/local/bin:/usr/bin
:/bin:/usr/local/sbin:/usr/sbin:/sbin:/home/user/bin $
```

The PATH environment variable is set to look for commands only in a handful of directories. To get the shell to find the test1 script, we need to do one of two things:

- Add the directory where our shell script file is located to the PATH environment variable.
- Use an absolute or relative file path to reference our shell script file in the prompt.

**TIP**

Some Linux distributions add the $HOME/bin directory to the PATH environment variable. This creates a place in every user's $HOME directory to place files where the shell can find them to execute.

For this example, we'll use the second method to tell the shell exactly where the script file is located. Remember that to reference a file in the current directory, you can use the single dot operator in the shell:

```
$ ./test1
bash: ./test1: Permission denied
$
```

Now the shell found the shell script file just fine, but there's another problem. The shell indicated that you don't have permission to execute the file. A quick look at the file permissions should show what's going on here:

```
$ ls -l test1
-rw-r--r--    1 user       user              73 Jun 02 15:36 test1
$
```

When the new test1 file was created, the umask value determined the default permission settings for the new file. Because the umask variable is set to 022 (see Chapter 7, "Understanding Linux File Permissions"), the system created the file with only read/write permissions for the file's owner.

The next step is to give the file owner permission to execute the file, using the chmod command (see Chapter 7):

```
$ chmod u+x test1
$ ./test1
Mon Jun 01 15:38:19 EST 2020
Christine tty2        2020-06-01 15:26
Samantha tty3        2020-06-01 15:26
Timothy  tty1        2020-06-01 15:26
user     tty7        2020-06-01 14:03 (:0)
user     pts/0       2020-06-01 15:21 (:0.0) $
```

Success! Now all the pieces are in the right places to execute the new shell script file.

# Displaying Messages

Most shell commands produce their own output, which is displayed on the console monitor where the script is running. Many times, however, you will want to add your own text messages to help the script user know what is happening within the script. You can do this with the echo command. The echo command can display a simple text string if you add the string following the command:

```
$ echo This is a test
This is a test
$
```

Notice that by default you don't need to use quotes to delineate the string you're displaying. However, sometimes this can get tricky if you are using quotes within your string:

```
$ echo Let's see if this'll work
Lets see if thisll work
$
```

The echo command uses either double or single quotes to delineate text strings. If you use them within your string, you need to use one type of quote within the text and the other type to delineate the string:

```
$ echo "This is a test to see if you're paying attention"
This is a test to see if you're paying attention
$ echo 'Rich says "scripting is easy".'
Rich says "scripting is easy".
$
```

Now all of the quotation marks appear properly in the output.

You can add echo statements anywhere in your shell scripts where you need to display additional information:

```
$ cat test1
#!/bin/bash
# This script displays the date and who's logged on
echo  The time and date are:
date
```

```
echo "Let's see who's logged into the system:"
who
$
```

When you run this script, it produces the following output:

```
$ ./test1
The time and date are:
Mon Jun 01 15:41:13 EST 2020
Let's see who's logged into the system:
Christine tty2           2020-06-01 15:26
Samantha tty3            2020-06-01 15:26
Timothy  tty1            2020-06-01 15:26
user     tty7            2020-06-01 14:03 (:0)
user     pts/0           2020-06-01 15:21 (:0.0)
$
```

That's nice, but what if you want to echo a text string on the same line as a command output? You can use the -n parameter for the echo statement to do that. Just change the first echo statement line to this:

```
echo -n "The time and date are: "
```

You'll need to use quotes around the string to ensure that there's a space at the end of the echoed string. The command output begins exactly where the string output stops. The output will now look like this:

```
$ ./test1
The time and date are: Mon Jun 01 15:42:23 EST 2020
Let's see who's logged into the system:
Christine tty2           2020-06-01 15:26
Samantha tty3            2020-02-01 15:26
Timothy  tty1            2020-06-01 15:26
user     tty7            2020-06-01 14:03 (:0)
user     pts/0           2020-06-01 15:21 (:0.0)
$
```

Perfect! The echo command is a crucial piece of shell scripts that interact with users. You'll find yourself using it in many situations, especially when you want to display the values of script variables. Let's look at that next.

# Using Variables

Just running individual commands from the shell script is useful, but doing so has its limitations. Often you'll want to incorporate other data in your shell commands to process information. You can do this by using *variables*. Variables allow you to temporarily store information within the shell script for use with other commands in the script. This section shows how to use variables in your shell scripts.

## Environment variables

You've already seen one type of Linux variable in action. Chapter 6 described the environment variables available in the Linux system. You can access these values from your shell scripts as well.

The shell maintains environment variables that track specific system information, such as the name of the system, the name of the user logged into the system, the user's system ID (called UID), the default home directory of the user, and the search path used by the shell to find programs. You can display a complete list of active environment variables available by using the set command:

```
$ set
BASH=/bin/bash
...
HOME=/home/Samantha
HOSTNAME=localhost.localdomain
HOSTTYPE=i386
IFS=$' \t\n'
IMSETTINGS_INTEGRATE_DESKTOP=yes
IMSETTINGS_MODULE=none
LANG=en_US.utf8
LESSOPEN='|/usr/bin/lesspipe.sh %s'
LINES=24
LOGNAME=Samantha
...
```

You can tap into these environment variables from within your scripts by using the environment variable's name preceded by a dollar sign. This is demonstrated in the following script:

```
$ cat test2
#!/bin/bash
# display user information from the system.
echo "User info for userid: $USER"
echo UID: $UID
echo HOME: $HOME
$
```

The $USER, $UID, and $HOME environment variables are used to display the pertinent information about the logged-in user. The output should look something like this:

```
$chmod u+x test2
$ ./test2
User info for userid: Samantha
UID: 1001
HOME: /home/Samantha
$ $
```

Notice that the environment variables in the `echo` commands are replaced by their current values when the script is run. Also notice that we were able to place the *$USER* system variable within the double quotation marks in the first string and that the shell script was still able to figure out what we meant. There is a drawback to using this method, however. Look at what happens in this example:

```
$ echo "The cost of the item is $15"
The cost of the item is 5
```

That is obviously not what was intended. Whenever the script sees a dollar sign within quotes, it assumes you're referencing a variable. In this example the script attempted to display the variable *$1* (which was not defined), and then the number 5. To display an actual dollar sign, you must precede it with a backslash character:

```
$ echo "The cost of the item is \$15"
The cost of the item is $15
```

That's better. The backslash allowed the shell script to interpret the dollar sign as an actual dollar sign, and not a variable. The next section shows how to create your own variables in your scripts.

> **NOTE**
>
> You may also see variables referenced using the format `${variable}`. The extra braces around the variable name are often used to help identify the variable name from the dollar sign.

## User variables

In addition to the environment variables, a shell script allows you to set and use your own variables within the script. Setting variables allows you to temporarily store data and use it throughout the script, making the shell script more like a real computer program.

User variables can be any text string of up to 20 letters, digits, or underscore characters. User variables are case sensitive, so the variable *Var1* is different from the variable *var1*. This little rule often gets novice script programmers in trouble.

Values are assigned to user variables using an equal sign. No spaces can appear between the variable, the equal sign, and the value (another trouble spot for novices). Here are a few examples of assigning values to user variables:

```
var1=10
var2=-57
var3=testing
var4="still more testing"
```

The shell script stores all variable values as text strings; it's up to the individual commands in the shell to determine the data type used for the variable value. Variables defined within the shell script maintain their values throughout the life of the shell script but are deleted when the shell script completes.

Just like system variables, user variables can be referenced using the dollar sign:

```
$ cat test3
#!/bin/bash
# testing variables
days=10
guest="Katie"
echo "$guest checked in $days days ago"
days=5
guest="Jessica"
echo "$guest checked in $days days ago"
$
```

Running the script produces the following output:

```
$ chmod u+x test3
$ ./test3
Katie checked in 10 days ago
Jessica checked in 5 days ago
$
```

Each time the variable is referenced, it produces the value currently assigned to it. It's important to remember that when referencing a variable value you use the dollar sign, but when referencing the variable to assign a value to it, you do not use the dollar sign. Here's an example of what we mean:

```
$ cat test4
#!/bin/bash
# assigning a variable value to another variable

value1=10
value2=$value1
echo The resulting value is $value2
$
```

When you use the value of the *value1* variable in the assignment statement, you must still use the dollar sign. This code produces the following output:

```
$ chmod u+x test4
$ ./test4
The resulting value is 10
$
```

If you forget the dollar sign, and make the *value2* assignment line look like

```
value2=value1
```

you get the following output:

```
$ ./test4
The resulting value is value1
$
```

Without the dollar sign, the shell interprets the variable name as a normal text string, which is most likely not what you wanted.

## Command substitution

One of the most useful features of shell scripts is the ability to extract information from the output of a command and assign it to a variable. Once you assign the output to a variable, you can use that value anywhere in your script. This comes in handy when you're processing data in your scripts.

There are two ways to assign the output of a command to a variable:

- The backtick character
- The $() format

Be careful with the backtick character — it is not the normal single quotation mark character you are used to using for strings. Because it is not used very often outside of shell scripts, you may not even know where to find it on your keyboard. You should become familiar with it, because it's a crucial component of many shell scripts. Hint: On a U.S. keyboard, it is usually on the same key as the tilde symbol (~).

Command substitution allows you to assign the output of a shell command to a variable. Though this doesn't seem like much, it is a major building block in script programming.

You must either surround the entire command-line command with the backtick characters:

```
testing=`date`
```

or use the $() format:

```
testing=$(date)
```

The shell runs the command within the command substitution characters and assigns the output to the variable testing. Notice that there aren't any spaces between the assignment equal sign and the command substitution character. Here's an example of creating a variable using the output from a normal shell command:

```
$ cat test5
#!/bin/bash
testing=$(date)
echo "The date and time are: " $testing
$
```

The variable testing receives the output from the date command, and it is used in the echo statement to display it. Running the shell script produces the following output:

```
$ chmod u+x test5
$ ./test5
The date and time are:  Mon Jun 01 15:45:25 EDT 2020
$
```

That's not all that exciting in this example (you could just as easily put the command in the echo statement), but once you capture the command output in a variable, you can do anything with it.

Here's a popular example of how command substitution is employed to capture the current date and use it to create a unique filename in a script:

```
#!/bin/bash
# copy the /usr/bin directory listing to a log file
today=$(date +%y%m%d)
ls /usr/bin -al > log.$today
```

The today variable is assigned the output of a formatted date command. This is a common technique used to extract date information for log filenames. The +%y%m%d format instructs the date command to display the date as a two-digit year, month, and day:

```
$ date +%y%m%d
200601
$
```

The script assigns the value to a variable, which is then used as part of a filename. The file itself contains the redirected output (discussed later in the "Redirecting Input and Output" section) of a directory listing. After running the script, you should see a new file in your directory:

```
-rw-r--r--    1 user      user            769 Jun 01 16:15 log.200601
```

The log file appears in the directory using the value of the $today variable as part of the filename. The contents of the log file are the directory listing from the /usr/bin directory. If the script is run the next day, the log filename will be log.200602, thus creating a new file for the new day.

> **WARNING**
>
> Command substitution creates what's called a *subshell* to run the enclosed command. A subshell is a separate child shell generated from the shell that's running the script. Because of that, any variables that you create in the script won't be available to commands running in the subshell.
>
> Subshells are also created if you run a command from the command prompt using the ./ path, but they aren't created if you just run the command without a path. However, if you use a built-in shell command, that doesn't generate a subshell. Be careful when running scripts from the command prompt!

# Redirecting Input and Output

There are times when you'd like to save the output from a command instead of just having it displayed on the monitor. The Bash shell provides a few different operators that allow you to *redirect* the output of a command to an alternative location (such as a file). Redirection can be used for input as well as output, redirecting a file to a command for input. This section describes what you need to do to use redirection in your shell scripts.

## Output redirection

The most basic type of redirection is sending output from a command to a file. The Bash shell uses the greater-than symbol (>) for this:

```
command > outputfile
```

Anything that would appear on the monitor from the command instead is stored in the output file specified:

```
$ date > test6
$ ls -l test6
-rw-r--r--    1 user      user               29 Jun 01 16:56 test6
$ cat test6
Mon Jun 01 16:56:58 EDT 2020
$
```

The redirect operator created the file test6 (using the default umask settings) and redirected the output from the date command to the test6 file. If the output file already exists, the redirect operator overwrites the existing file with the new file data:

```
$ who > test6
$ cat test6
rich      pts/0     Jun 01 16:55
$
```

Now the contents of the test6 file contain the output from the who command.

Sometimes, instead of overwriting the file's contents, you may need to append output from a command to an existing file — for example, if you're creating a log file to document an action on the system. In this situation, you can use the double greater-than symbol (>>) to append data:

```
$ date >> test6
$ cat test6
rich      pts/0     Jun 01 16:55
Mon Jun 01 17:02:14 EDT 2020
$
```

The test6 file still contains the original data from the who command processed earlier — plus now it contains the new output from the date command.

## Input redirection

Input redirection is the opposite of output redirection. Instead of taking the output of a command and redirecting it to a file, input redirection takes the content of a file and redirects it to a command.

The input redirection symbol is the less-than symbol (<):

```
command < inputfile
```

The easy way to remember this is that the command is always listed first in the command line, and the redirection symbol "points" to the way the data is flowing. The less-than symbol indicates that the data is flowing from the input file to the command.

Here's an example of using input redirection with the wc command:

```
$ wc < test6
      2      11      60
$
```

The wc command provides a count of text in the data. By default, it produces three values:

- The number of lines in the text
- The number of words in the text
- The number of bytes in the text

By redirecting a text file to the wc command, you can get a quick count of the lines, words, and bytes in the file. The example shows that there are 2 lines, 11 words, and 60 bytes in the test6 file.

There's another method of input redirection, called *inline input redirection*. This method allows you to specify the data for input redirection on the command line instead of in a file. This may seem somewhat odd at first, but there are a few applications for this process (such as those shown in the "Performing Math" section later).

The inline input redirection symbol is the double less-than symbol (<<). Besides this symbol, you must specify a text marker that delineates the beginning and end of the data used for input. You can use any string value for the text marker, but it must be the same at the beginning of the data and the end of the data:

```
command << marker
data
marker
```

When using inline input redirection on the command line, the shell will prompt for data using the secondary prompt, defined in the PS2 environment variable (see Chapter 6). Here's how this looks when you use it:

```
$ wc << EOF
> test string 1
> test string 2
> test string 3
> EOF
      3       9      42
$
```

The secondary prompt continues to prompt for more data until you enter the string value for the text marker. The wc command performs the line, word, and byte counts of the data supplied by the inline input redirection.

# Employing Pipes

There are times when you need to send the output of one command to the input of another command. This is possible using redirection, but somewhat clunky:

```
$ rpm -qa > rpm.list
$ sort < rpm.list
abattis-cantarell-fonts-0.0.25-1.el7.noarch
abrt-2.1.11-52.el7.centos.x86_64
abrt-addon-ccpp-2.1.11-52.el7.centos.x86_64
abrt-addon-kerneloops-2.1.11-52.el7.centos.x86_64
abrt-addon-pstoreoops-2.1.11-52.el7.centos.x86_64
abrt-addon-python-2.1.11-52.el7.centos.x86_64
abrt-addon-vmcore-2.1.11-52.el7.centos.x86_64
abrt-addon-xorg-2.1.11-52.el7.centos.x86_64
abrt-cli-2.1.11-52.el7.centos.x86_64
abrt-console-notification-2.1.11-52.el7.centos.x86_64
...
```

The rpm command manages the software packages installed on systems using the Red Hat Package Management system (RPM), such as the CentOS system as shown. When used with the -qa parameters, it produces a list of the existing packages installed, but not necessarily in any specific order. If you're looking for a specific package, or group of packages, it can be difficult to find it using the output of the rpm command.

Using the standard output redirection, the output was redirected from the rpm command to a file called rpm.list. After the command finished, the rpm.list file contained a list of all the installed software packages on this system. Next, input redirection was used to send the contents of the rpm.list file to the sort command to sort the package names alphabetically.

That was useful, but again, a somewhat clunky way of producing the information. Instead of redirecting the output of a command to a file, you can redirect the output to another command. This process is called *piping*.

Like the command substitution backtick (`` ` ``), the symbol for piping is not used often outside of shell scripting. The symbol is two vertical lines, one above the other. However, the pipe symbol often looks like a single vertical line in print (|). On a U.S. keyboard, it is usually on the same key as the backslash (\). The pipe is put between the commands to redirect the output from one to the other:

```
command1 | command2
```

Don't think of piping as running two commands back to back. The Linux system actually runs both commands at the same time, linking them together internally in the system. As the first command produces output, it's sent immediately to the second command. No intermediate files or buffer areas are used to transfer the data.

Now, using piping you can easily pipe the output of the rpm command directly to the sort command to produce your results:

```
$ rpm -qa | sort
abattis-cantarell-fonts-0.0.25-1.el7.noarch
abrt-2.1.11-52.el7.centos.x86_64
abrt-addon-ccpp-2.1.11-52.el7.centos.x86_64
abrt-addon-kerneloops-2.1.11-52.el7.centos.x86_64
abrt-addon-pstoreoops-2.1.11-52.el7.centos.x86_64
abrt-addon-python-2.1.11-52.el7.centos.x86_64
abrt-addon-vmcore-2.1.11-52.el7.centos.x86_64
abrt-addon-xorg-2.1.11-52.el7.centos.x86_64
abrt-cli-2.1.11-52.el7.centos.x86_64
abrt-console-notification-2.1.11-52.el7.centos.x86_64
...
```

Unless you're a (very) quick reader, you probably couldn't keep up with the output generated by this command. Because the piping feature operates in real time, as soon as the rpm command produces data, the sort command gets busy sorting it. By the time the rpm command finishes outputting data, the sort command already has the data sorted and starts displaying it on the monitor.

There's no limit to the number of pipes you can use in a command. You can continue piping the output of commands to other commands to refine your operation.

In this case, because the output of the sort command zooms by so quickly, you can use one of the text paging commands (such as less or more) to force the output to stop at every screen of data:

```
$ rpm -qa | sort | more
```

This command sequence runs the rpm command, pipes the output to the sort command, and then pipes that output to the more command to display the data, stopping after every screen of information. This now lets you pause and read what's on the display before continuing, as shown in Figure 11-1.

To get even fancier, you can use redirection along with piping to save your output to a file:

```
$ rpm -qa | sort > rpm.list
$ more rpm.list
abrt-1.1.14-1.fc14.i686
abrt-addon-ccpp-1.1.14-1.fc14.i686
abrt-addon-kerneloops-1.1.14-1.fc14.i686
abrt-addon-python-1.1.14-1.fc14.i686
abrt-desktop-1.1.14-1.fc14.i686
abrt-gui-1.1.14-1.fc14.i686
abrt-libs-1.1.14-1.fc14.i686
abrt-plugin-bugzilla-1.1.14-1.fc14.i686
abrt-plugin-logger-1.1.14-1.fc14.i686
abrt-plugin-runapp-1.1.14-1.fc14.i686
acl-2.2.49-8.fc14.i686
...
```

**FIGURE 11-1**

Using piping to send data to the more command

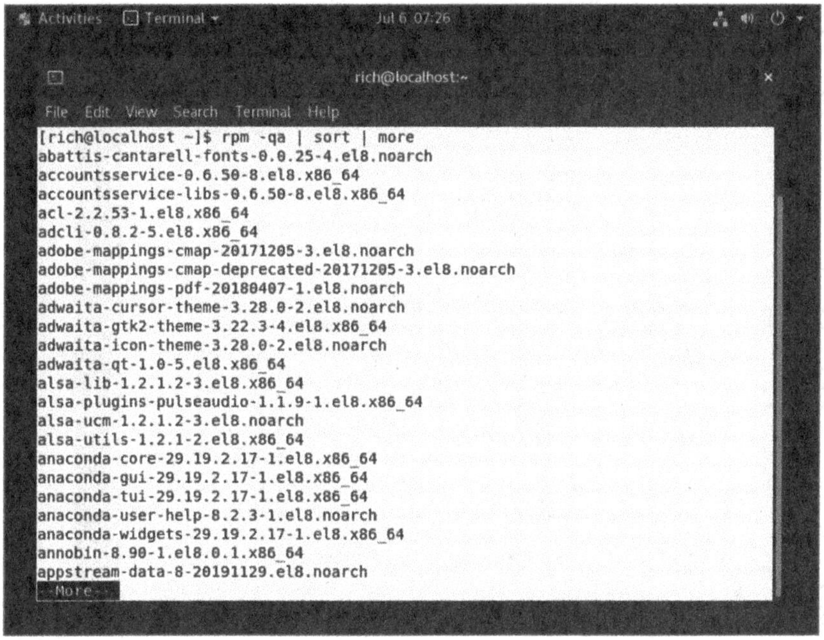

As expected, the data in the rpm.list file is now sorted!

By far one of the most popular uses is piping the results of commands that produce long output to the more command. This is especially common with the ls command, as shown in Figure 11-2.

The ls -1 command produces a long listing of all the files in the directory. For directories with lots of files, this can be quite a listing. By piping the output to the more command, you force the output to stop at the end of every screen of data.

# Performing Math

Another feature crucial to any programming language is the ability to manipulate numbers. Unfortunately, for shell scripts this process is a bit awkward. You have two ways to perform mathematical operations in your shell scripts.

**FIGURE 11-2**

Using the more command with the ls command

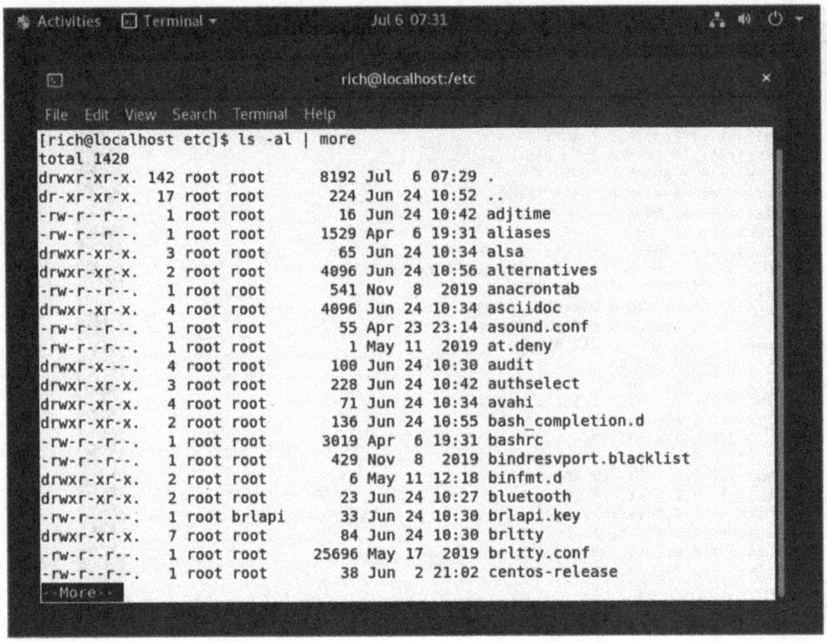

```
Activities    Terminal ▾              Jul 6 07:31

                          rich@localhost:/etc                        ×

File  Edit  View  Search  Terminal  Help
[rich@localhost etc]$ ls -al | more
total 1420
drwxr-xr-x. 142 root root      8192 Jul  6 07:29 .
dr-xr-xr-x.  17 root root       224 Jun 24 10:52 ..
-rw-r--r--.   1 root root        16 Jun 24 10:42 adjtime
-rw-r--r--.   1 root root      1529 Apr  6 19:31 aliases
drwxr-xr-x.   3 root root        65 Jun 24 10:34 alsa
drwxr-xr-x.   2 root root      4096 Jun 24 10:56 alternatives
-rw-r--r--.   1 root root       541 Nov  8  2019 anacrontab
drwxr-xr-x.   4 root root      4096 Jun 24 10:34 asciidoc
-rw-r--r--.   1 root root        55 Apr 23 23:14 asound.conf
-rw-r--r--.   1 root root         1 May 11  2019 at.deny
drwxr-x---.   4 root root       100 Jun 24 10:30 audit
drwxr-xr-x.   3 root root       228 Jun 24 10:42 authselect
drwxr-xr-x.   4 root root        71 Jun 24 10:34 avahi
drwxr-xr-x.   2 root root       136 Jun 24 10:55 bash_completion.d
-rw-r--r--.   1 root root      3019 Apr  6 19:31 bashrc
-rw-r--r--.   1 root root       429 Nov  8  2019 bindresvport.blacklist
drwxr-xr-x.   2 root root         6 May 11 12:18 binfmt.d
drwxr-xr-x.   2 root root        23 Jun 24 10:27 bluetooth
-rw-r-----.   1 root brlapi      33 Jun 24 10:30 brlapi.key
drwxr-xr-x.   7 root root        84 Jun 24 10:30 brltty
-rw-r--r--.   1 root root     25696 May 17  2019 brltty.conf
-rw-r--r--.   1 root root        38 Jun  2 21:02 centos-release
--More--
```

## The *expr* command

Originally, the Bourne shell provided a special command that was used for processing mathematical equations. The expr command allowed the processing of equations from the command line, but it is extremely clunky:

```
$ expr 1 + 5
6
```

The expr command recognizes a few different mathematical and string operators, shown in Table 11-1.

The standard operators work fine in the expr command, but the problem occurs when using them from a script or the command line. Many of the expr command operators have other meanings in the shell (such as the asterisk). Using them in the expr command produces odd results:

```
$ expr 5 * 2
expr: syntax error
$
```

### TABLE 11-1  The `expr` Command Operators

| Operator | Description |
|---|---|
| ARG1 \| ARG2 | Return ARG1 if neither argument is null or 0; otherwise, return ARG2. |
| ARG1 & ARG2 | Return ARG1 if neither argument is null or 0; otherwise, return 0. |
| ARG1 < ARG2 | Return 1 if ARG1 is less than ARG2; otherwise, return 0. |
| ARG1 <= ARG2 | Return 1 if ARG1 is less than or equal to ARG2; otherwise, return 0. |
| ARG1 = ARG2 | Return 1 if ARG1 is equal to ARG2; otherwise, return 0. |
| ARG1 != ARG2 | Return 1 if ARG1 is not equal to ARG2; otherwise, return 0. |
| ARG1 >= ARG2 | Return 1 if ARG1 is greater than or equal to ARG2; otherwise, return 0. |
| ARG1 > ARG2 | Return 1 if ARG1 is greater than ARG2; otherwise, return 0. |
| ARG1 + ARG2 | Return the arithmetic sum of ARG1 and ARG2. |
| ARG1 - ARG2 | Return the arithmetic difference of ARG1 and ARG2. |
| ARG1 * ARG2 | Return the arithmetic product of ARG1 and ARG2. |
| ARG1 / ARG2 | Return the arithmetic quotient of ARG1 divided by ARG2. |
| ARG1 % ARG2 | Return the arithmetic remainder of ARG1 divided by ARG2. |
| STRING : REGEXP | Return the pattern match if REGEXP matches a pattern in STRING. |
| match STRING REGEXP | Return the pattern match if REGEXP matches a pattern in STRING. |
| substr STRING POS LENGTH | Return the substring LENGTH characters in length, starting at position POS (starting at 1). |
| index STRING CHARS | Return position in STRING where CHARS is found; otherwise, return 0. |
| length STRING | Return the numeric length of the string STRING. |
| + TOKEN | Interpret TOKEN as a string, even if it's a keyword. |
| (EXPRESSION) | Return the value of EXPRESSION. |

To solve this problem, you need to use the shell escape character (the backslash) to identify any characters that may be misinterpreted by the shell before being passed to the `expr` command:

```
$ expr 5 \* 2
10
$
```

Now that's really starting to get ugly! Using the `expr` command in a shell script is equally cumbersome:

```
$ cat test6
#!/bin/bash
# An example of using the expr command
var1=10
```

*(Continues)*

(continued)
```
    var2=20
    var3=$(expr $var2 / $var1)
    echo The result is $var3
```

To assign the result of a mathematical equation to a variable, you have to use command substitution to extract the output from the `expr` command:

```
$ chmod u+x test6
$ ./test6
The result is 2
$
```

Fortunately, the Bash shell has an improvement for processing mathematical operators, as you will see in the next section.

## Using brackets

The Bash shell includes the `expr` command to stay compatible with the Bourne shell; however, it also provides a much easier way of performing mathematical equations. In Bash, when assigning a mathematical value to a variable, you can enclose the mathematical equation using a dollar sign and square brackets (`$[ operation ]`):

```
$ var1=$[1 + 5]
$ echo $var1
6
$ var2=$[$var1 * 2]
$ echo $var2
12
$
```

Using brackets makes shell math much easier than with the `expr` command. The same technique also works in shell scripts:

```
$ cat test7
#!/bin/bash
var1=100
var2=50
var3=45
var4=$[$var1 * ($var2 - $var3)]
echo The final result is $var4
$
```

Running this script produces the following output:

```
$ chmod u+x test7
$ ./test7
The final result is 500
$
```

Also, notice that when using the square brackets method for calculating equations you don't need to worry about the multiplication symbol, or any other characters, being misinterpreted by the shell. The shell knows that it's not a wildcard character because it is within the square brackets.

There's one major limitation to performing math in the Bash shell script. Take a look at this example:

```
$ cat test8
#!/bin/bash
var1=100
var2=45
var3=$[$var1 / $var2]
echo The final result is $var3
$
```

Now run it and see what happens:

```
$ chmod u+x test8
$ ./test8
The final result is 2
$
```

The Bash shell mathematical operators support only integer arithmetic. This is a huge limitation if you're trying to do any sort of real-world mathematical calculations.

---

**NOTE**

The z shell (zsh) provides full floating-point arithmetic operations. If you require floating-point calculations in your shell scripts, you might consider checking out the z shell (discussed in Chapter 23, "Working with Alternative Shells").

---

## A floating-point solution

There are several solutions for overcoming the Bash integer limitation. The most popular solution uses the built-in Bash calculator, called bc.

### The basics of *bc*

The Bash calculator is actually a programming language that allows you to enter floating-point expressions at a command line and then interprets the expressions, calculates them, and returns the result. The Bash calculator recognizes the following:

- Numbers (both integer and floating point)
- Variables (both simple variables and arrays)
- Comments (lines starting with a pound sign or the C language /* */ pair)
- Expressions
- Programming statements (such as if-then statements)
- Functions

You can access the Bash calculator from the shell prompt using the bc command:

```
$ bc
bc 1.06.95
Copyright 1991-1994, 1997, 1998, 2000, 2004, 2006 Free Software
Foundation, Inc.
This is free software with ABSOLUTELY NO WARRANTY.
For details type 'warranty'.
12 * 5.4
64.8
3.156 * (3 + 5)
25.248
quit
$
```

The example starts out by entering the expression 12 * 5.4. The Bash calculator returns the answer. Each subsequent expression entered into the calculator is evaluated, and the result is displayed. To exit the Bash calculator, you must enter quit.

The floating-point arithmetic is controlled by a built-in variable called *scale*. You must set this value to the desired number of decimal places you want in your answers or you won't get what you were looking for:

```
$ bc -q
3.44 / 5
0
scale=4
3.44 / 5
.6880
quit
$
```

The default value for the *scale* variable is 0. Before the *scale* value is set, the Bash calculator provides the answer to zero decimal places. After you set the *scale* variable value to 4, the Bash calculator displays the answer to four decimal places. The -q command-line parameter suppresses the lengthy welcome banner from the Bash calculator.

In addition to normal numbers, the Bash calculator understands variables:

```
$ bc -q
var1=10
var1 * 4
40
var2 = var1 / 5
print var2
2
quit
$
```

Once a variable value is defined, you can use the variable throughout the Bash calculator session. The print statement allows you to print variables and numbers.

### Using *bc* in scripts

Now you may be wondering how the Bash calculator is going to help you with floating-point arithmetic in your shell scripts. Do you remember your friend the backtick character? Yes, you can use the command substitution character to run a bc command and assign the output to a variable! The basic format to use is this:

```
variable=$(echo "options; expression" | bc)
```

The first portion, options, allows you to set variables. If you need to set more than one variable, separate them using the semicolon. The expression parameter defines the mathematical expression to evaluate using bc. Here's a quick example of doing this in a script:

```
$ cat test9
#!/bin/bash
var1=$(echo " scale=4; 3.44 / 5" | bc)
echo The answer is $var1
$
```

This example sets the scale variable to four decimal places and then specifies a specific calculation for the expression. Running this script produces the following output:

```
$ chmod u+x test9
$ ./test9
The answer is .6880
$
```

Now that's fancy! You aren't limited to just using numbers for the expression value. You can also use variables defined in the shell script:

```
$ cat test10
#!/bin/bash
var1=100
var2=45
var3=$(echo "scale=4; $var1 / $var2" | bc)
echo The answer for this is $var3
$
```

The script defines two variables, which are used within the expression sent to the bc command. Remember to use the dollar sign to signify the value for the variables and not the variables themselves. The output of this script is as follows:

```
$ ./test10
The answer for this is 2.2222
$
```

And of course, once a value is assigned to a variable, that variable can be used in yet another calculation:

```
$ cat test11
#!/bin/bash
var1=20
```

*(Continues)*

295

*(continued)*

```
var2=3.14159
var3=$(echo "scale=4; $var1 * $var1" | bc)
var4=$(echo "scale=4; $var3 * $var2" | bc)
echo The final result is $var4
$
```

This method works fine for short calculations, but sometimes you need to get more involved with your numbers. If you have more than just a couple of calculations, it gets confusing trying to list multiple expressions on the same command line.

There's a solution to this problem. The bc command recognizes input redirection, allowing you to redirect a file to the bc command for processing. However, this also can get confusing, since you'd need to store your expressions in a file.

The best method is to use inline input redirection, which allows you to redirect data directly from the command line. In the shell script, you assign the output to a variable:

```
variable=$(bc << EOF
options
statements
expressions
EOF
)
```

The EOF text string indicates the beginning and end of the inline redirection data. Remember that the command substitution characters are still needed to assign the output of the bc command to the variable.

Now you can place all of the individual Bash calculator elements on separate lines in the script file. Here's an example of using this technique in a script:

```
$ cat test12
#!/bin/bash

var1=10.46
var2=43.67
var3=33.2
var4=71

var5=$(bc << EOF
scale = 4
a1 = ( $var1 * $var2)
b1 = ($var3 * $var4)
a1 + b1
EOF
)

echo The final answer for this mess is $var5
$
```

Placing each option and expression on a separate line in your script makes things cleaner and easier to read and follow. The EOF string indicates the start and end of the data to redirect to the bc command. Of course, you need to use the command substitution characters to indicate the command to assign to the variable.

You'll also notice in this example that you can assign variables within the Bash calculator. It's important to remember that any variables created within the Bash calculator are valid only within the Bash calculator and can't be used in the shell script.

# Exiting the Script

So far in our sample scripts, we terminated things pretty abruptly. When we were done with our last command, we just ended the script. There's a more elegant way of completing things available to us.

Every command that runs in the shell uses an *exit status* to indicate to the shell that it's done processing. The exit status is an integer value between 0 and 255 that's passed by the command to the shell when the command finishes running. You can capture this value and use it in your scripts.

## Checking the exit status

Linux provides the $? special variable that holds the exit status value from the last command that executed. You must view or use the $? variable immediately after the command you want to check. It changes values to the exit status of the last command executed by the shell:

```
$ date
Mon Jun 01 16:01:30 EDT 2020
$ echo $?
0
$
```

By convention, the exit status of a command that successfully completes is 0. If a command completes with an error, then a positive integer value is placed in the exit status:

```
$ asdfg
-bash: asdfg: command not found
$ echo $?
127
$
```

The invalid command returns an exit status of 127. There's not much of a standard convention to Linux error exit status codes. However, there are a few guidelines you can use, as shown in Table 11-2.

**TABLE 11-2  Linux Exit Status Codes**

| Code | Description |
|------|-------------|
| 0 | Successful completion of the command |
| 1 | General unknown error |
| 2 | Misuse of shell command |
| 126 | The command can't execute |
| 127 | Command not found |
| 128 | Invalid exit argument |
| 128+x | Fatal error with Linux signal x |
| 130 | Command terminated with Ctrl+C |
| 255 | Exit status out of range |

An exit status value of 126 indicates that the user didn't have the proper permissions set to execute the command:

```
$ ./myprog.c
-bash: ./myprog.c: Permission denied
$ echo $?
126
$
```

Another common error you'll encounter occurs if you supply an invalid parameter to a command:

```
$ date %t
date: invalid date '%t'
$ echo $?
1
$
```

This generates the general exit status code of 1, indicating that an unknown error occurred in the command.

## The *exit* command

By default, your shell script will exit with the exit status of the last command in your script:

```
$ ./test6
The result is 2
$ echo $?
0
$
```

You can change that to return your own exit status code. The exit command allows you to specify an exit status when your script ends:

```
$ cat test13
#!/bin/bash
# testing the exit status
var1=10
var2=30
var3=$[ $var1 + var2 ]
echo The answer is $var3
exit 5
$
```

When you check the exit status of the script, you'll get the value used as the parameter of the exit command:

```
$ chmod u+x test13
$ ./test13
The answer is 40
$ echo $?
5
$
```

You can also use variables in the exit command parameter:

```
$ cat test14
#!/bin/bash
# testing the exit status
var1=10
var2=30
var3=$[ $var1 + var2 ]
exit $var3
$
```

When you run this command, it produces the following exit status:

```
$ chmod u+x test14
$ ./test14
$ echo $?
40
$
```

You should be careful with this feature, however — the exit status codes can only go up to 255. Watch what happens in this example:

```
$ cat test14b
#!/bin/bash
# testing the exit status
var1=10
var2=30
var3=$[ $var1 * var2 ]
echo The value is $var3
exit $var3
$
```

Now when you run it, you get the following:

```
$ ./test14b
The value is 300
$ echo $?
44
$
```

The exit status code is reduced to fit in the 0 to 255 range. The shell does this by using modulo arithmetic. The *modulo* of a value is the remainder after a division. The resulting number is the remainder of the specified number divided by 256. In the case of 300 (the result value), the remainder is 44, which is what appears as the exit status code.

In the next chapter, you'll see how you can use the if-then statement to check the error status returned by a command to see whether or not the command was successful.

# Working through a Practical Example

Now that you have the basics of shell scripting, we can try putting them together to create a useful script. For this example, we'll work on creating a shell script to calculate the number of days between two dates. For our example, we'll allow the user to specify the dates in any format that's recognized by the Linux date command.

First, we'll store the two specified dates in variables:

```
$date1="Jan 1, 2020"
$date2="May 1, 2020"
```

Performing date arithmetic is hard; you have to know which months have 28, 30, or 31 days, and you need to know what years are leap years. However, we can get some help from the date command.

The date command allows us to specify a specific date using the -d option (in any format), and then output the date in any other format that we define. To do our calculations, we'll make use of a Linux feature called the *epoch time*. The epoch time specifies the time as an integer value of the number of seconds since midnight, January 1, 1970 (it's an old Unix standard). Thus, to get the epoch time for January 1, 2020, you'd do this:

```
$date -d "Jan 1, 2020" +%s
1577854800
$
```

We'll use that method to get the epoch time for both dates, and then just subtract the two values to get the number of seconds between the two dates. From there, we can divide that value by the number of seconds in a day (60 seconds per minute, 60 minutes per hour, and 24 hours per day) to get the difference between the two dates in days.

We'll use the command substitution feature to capture the output of the date command in a variable:

```
$time1=$(date -d "$date1" +%s)
```

Once we have the epoch times for both dates, it's just a matter of using our new friend the expr command to calculate the differences (we could use the bc utility, but since we're working with integer values expr will work just fine for us).

So, putting that all together gives us this script:

```
$ cat mydate.sh
#!/bin/bash
# calculate the number of days between two dates
date1="Jan 1, 2020"
date2="May 1, 2020"

time1=$(date -d "$date1" +%s)
time2=$(date -d "$date2" +%s)

diff=$(expr $time2 - $time1)
secondsinday=$(expr 24 \* 60 \* 60)
days=$(expr $diff / $secondsinday)

echo "The difference between $date2 and $date1 is $days days"
$
```

Then it's just a matter of assigning the correct permissions and running the script:

```
$ chmod u+x mydate.sh
$ ./mydate.sh
The difference between May 1, 2020 and Jan 1, 2020 is 120 days
$
```

Now you can plug any dates into the variables (using just about any date format you need) and you should get the proper results!

# Summary

The Bash shell script allows you to string commands together into a script. The most basic way to create a script is to separate multiple commands on the command line using a semicolon. The shell executes each command in order, displaying the output of each command on the monitor.

You can also create a shell script file, placing multiple commands in the file for the shell to execute in order. The shell script file must define the shell used to run the script. This is done in the first line of the script file, using the #! symbol, followed by the full path of the shell.

Within the shell script you can reference environment variable values by using a dollar sign in front of the variable. You can also define your own variables for use within the script, and assign values and even the output of a command by using the backtick character or the $() format. The variable value can be used within the script by placing a dollar sign in front of the variable name.

The Bash shell allows you to redirect both the input and output of a command from the standard behavior. You can redirect the output of any command from the monitor display to a file by using the greater-than symbol, followed by the name of the file to capture the output. You can append output data to an existing file by using two greater-than symbols. The less-than symbol is used to redirect input to a command. You can redirect input from a file to a command.

The Linux pipe command (the broken bar symbol) allows you to redirect the output of a command directly to the input of another command. The Linux system runs both commands at the same time, sending the output of the first command to the input of the second command without using any redirect files.

The Bash shell provides a couple of ways for you to perform mathematical operations in your shell scripts. The expr command is a simple way to perform integer math. In the Bash shell, you can also perform basic math calculations by enclosing equations in square brackets, preceded by a dollar sign. To perform floating-point arithmetic, you need to use the bc calculator command, redirecting input from inline data and storing the output in a user variable.

Finally, we discussed how to use the exit status in your shell script. Every command that runs in the shell produces an exit status. The exit status is an integer value between 0 and 255 that indicates whether or not the command completed successfully, and if not, what the reason may have been. An exit status of 0 indicates that the command completed successfully. You can use the exit command in your shell script to declare a specific exit status upon the completion of your script.

So far in your shell scripts, things have proceeded in an orderly fashion from one command to the next. In the next chapter, you'll see how you can use some logic flow control to alter which commands are executed within the script.

# Using Structured Commands

## IN THIS CHAPTER

Working with the `if-then` statement

Nesting `if`s

Understanding the `test` command

Testing compound conditions

Using double brackets and parentheses

Looking at `case`

In Chapter 11, "Basic Script Building," the shell processed each individual command in the order in which it appeared within a shell script. Although this works out fine for sequential operations, many programs require some sort of logic flow control between the commands in the script.

There is a whole command class that allows the shell to skip over script sections based on tested conditions and alter the operation flow. These commands are generally referred to as *structured commands*.

Quite a few structured commands are available in the Bash shell, so we'll break them up into different chapters. In this chapter, we look at `if-then` and `case` statements.

## Working with the *if-then* Statement

The most basic type of structured command is the `if-then` statement. The `if-then` statement has the following format:

```
if command
then
    commands
fi
```

If you're using `if-then` statements in other programming languages, this format may be somewhat confusing. In other programming languages, the object after the `if` statement is an equation that is evaluated for a TRUE or FALSE value. That's not how the Bash shell `if` statement works.

The Bash shell if statement runs the command defined on the if line. If the exit status of the command (see Chapter 11) is zero (the command completed successfully), the commands listed under the then section are executed. If the exit status of the command is anything else, the then commands aren't executed, and the Bash shell moves on to the next command in the script. The fi statement sets the if-then statement's end.

Here's a simple example to demonstrate this concept:

```
$ cat test1.sh
#!/bin/bash
# testing the if statement
if pwd
then
      echo "It worked"
fi
$
```

This script uses the pwd command on the if line. If the command completes successfully, the echo statement should display the text string. When we run this script from the command line, we get these results:

```
$ ./test1.sh
/home/christine/scripts
It worked
$
```

The shell executed the pwd command listed on the if line. Because the exit status was zero, it also executed the echo statement listed in the then section.

Here's another example:

```
$ cat test2.sh
#!/bin/bash
# testing an incorrect command
if IamNotaCommand
then
      echo "It worked"
fi
echo "We are outside the if statement"
$
$ ./test2.sh
./test2.sh: line 3: IamNotaCommand: command not found
We are outside the if statement
$
```

In this example, we deliberately used a nonexistent command, IamNotaCommand, in the if statement line. Because this is an incorrect command, it produces an exit status that's non-zero. Thus, the Bash shell skips the echo statement in the then section. Also notice that the error message generated from running the command in the if statement still appears in the script's output. There may be times when you don't want an error statement to appear. Chapter 15, "Presenting Data," discusses how this can be avoided.

> **NOTE**
>
> You might see an alternative form of the `if-then` statement used in some scripts:
>
> ```
> if command; then
>     commands
> fi
> ```
>
> By putting a semicolon (;) at the end of the command to evaluate, you can include the `then` statement on the same line, which looks closer to how `if-then` statements are handled in some other programming languages.

You are not limited to just one command in the `then` section. You can list commands just as you do in the rest of the shell script. The Bash shell treats the commands as a block, executing *all* of them when the command in the `if` statement line returns a zero exit status or skipping all of them when the command returns a non-zero exit status:

```
$ cat test3.sh
#!/bin/bash
# testing multiple commands in the then block
#
testuser=christine
#
if grep $testuser /etc/passwd
then
        echo "This is my first command in the then block."
        echo "This is my second command in the then block."
        echo "I can even put in other commands besides echo:"
        ls /home/$testuser/*.sh
fi
echo "We are outside the if statement"
$
```

The `if` statement line uses the `grep` comment to search the /etc/passwd file to see if a specific username is currently used on the system. If there's a user with that logon name, the script displays some text and then lists the Bash scripts in the user's $HOME directory:

```
$ ./test3.sh
christine:x:1001:1001::/home/christine:/bin/bash
This is my first command in the then block.
This is my second command in the then block.
I can even put in other commands besides echo:
/home/christine/factorial.sh
We are outside the if statement
$
```

However, if you set the *testuser* variable to a user that doesn't exist on the system, *nothing* within the `then` code block executes:

```
$ cat test3.sh
#!/bin/bash
# testing multiple commands in the then block
#
testuser=NoSuchUser
#
if grep $testuser /etc/passwd
then
      echo "This is my first command in the then block."
      echo "This is my second command in the then block."
      echo "I can even put in other commands besides echo:"
      ls /home/$testuser/*.sh
fi
echo "We are outside the if statement"
$
$ ./test3.sh
We are outside the if statement
$
```

It's not all that exciting. It would be nice if we could display a little message saying that the username wasn't found on the system. Well, we can, using another feature of the if-then statement.

# Exploring the *if-then-else* Statement

In the if-then statement, you have only one option for whether a command is successful. If the command returns a non-zero exit status code, the Bash shell just moves on to the next command in the script. In this situation, it would be nice to be able to execute an alternate set of commands. That's exactly what the if-then-else statement is for.

The if-then-else statement provides another group of commands in the statement:

```
if command
then
    commands
else
    commands
fi
```

When the command in the if statement line returns with a zero exit status code, the commands listed in the then section are executed, just as in a normal if-then statement. When the command in the if statement line returns a non-zero exit status code, the Bash shell executes the commands in the else section.

Now you can copy and modify the test script to include an else section:

```
$ cp test3.sh test4.sh
$
$ nano test4.sh
```

```
$
$ cat test4.sh
#!/bin/bash
# testing the else section
#
testuser=NoSuchUser
#
if grep $testuser /etc/passwd
then
     echo "The script files in the home directory of $testuser are:"
     ls /home/$testuser/*.sh
     echo
else
     echo "The user $testuser does not exist on this system."
     echo
fi
echo "We are outside the if statement"
$
$ ./test4.sh
The user NoSuchUser does not exist on this system.

We are outside the if statement
$
```

That's more user-friendly. Just like the then section, the else section can contain multiple commands. The fi statement delineates the end of the else section.

# Nesting *ifs*

Sometimes, you must check for several situations in your script code. For these situations, you can nest the if-then statements.

To check if a logon name is not in the /etc/passwd file and yet a directory for that user still exists, use a nested if-then statement. In this case, the nested if-then statement is within the primary if-then-else statement's else code block:

```
$ cat test5.sh
#!/bin/bash
# testing nested ifs
#
testuser=NoSuchUser
#
if grep $testuser /etc/passwd
then
     echo "The user $testuser account exists on this system."
     echo
```

```
else
      echo "The user $testuser does not exist on this system."
      if  ls -d /home/$testuser/
      then
            echo "However, $testuser has a directory."
      fi
fi
echo "We are outside the nested if statements."

$ ls -d /home/NoSuchUser/
/home/NoSuchUser/
$
$ ./test5.sh
The user NoSuchUser does not exist on this system.
/home/NoSuchUser/
However, NoSuchUser has a directory.
We are outside the nested if statements.
$
```

The script correctly finds that although the login name has been removed from the /etc/
passwd file, the user's directory is still on the system. The problem with using this manner
of nested if-then statements in a script is that the code can get hard to read, and the
logic flow becomes difficult to follow.

> **NOTE**
>
> The ls command has some additional useful command options (and option combinations) we use in this chapter:
>
> - -d shows only the directory information, not the directory's contents.
> - -sh displays the file's size in a human-readable format.
> - -g shows the file's long listing minus the owner name.
> - -o displays the file's long listing minus the group name.
>
> The ls command was first covered in Chapter 3, "Basic Bash Shell Commands."

Instead of having to write separate if-then statements, you can use an alternative version of the else section called elif. The elif continues an else section with another
if-then statement:

```
if command1
then
    commands
elif command2
then
    more commands
fi
```

The elif statement line provides another command to evaluate, similar to the original if
statement line. If the exit status code from the elif command is zero, Bash executes the

commands in the second `then` statement section. Using this method of nesting provides cleaner code with an easier-to-follow logic flow:

```
$ cat test5.sh
#!/bin/bash
# testing nested ifs - using elif
#
testuser=NoSuchUser
#
if grep $testuser /etc/passwd
then
     echo "The user $testuser account exists on this system."
     echo
elif ls -d /home/$testuser/
     then
          echo "The user $testuser has a directory,"
          echo "even though $testuser doesn't have an account."
fi
echo "We are outside the nested if statements."
$
$ ./test5.sh
/home/NoSuchUser/
The user NoSuchUser has a directory,
even though NoSuchUser doesn't have an account.
We are outside the nested if statements.
$
```

The problem with this script is that if the account is gone as well as the directory, you get no notifications of these facts. You can fix this problem, and even take the script a step further by having it check for both a nonexistent user with a directory and a nonexistent user without a directory. You accomplish this by adding an `else` statement within the nested `elif`:

```
$ cat test5.sh
#!/bin/bash
# testing nested ifs - using elif and else
#
testuser=NoSuchUser
#
if grep $testuser /etc/passwd
then
     echo "The user $testuser account exists on this system."
     echo
elif ls -d /home/$testuser/
     then
          echo "The user $testuser has a directory,"
          echo "even though $testuser doesn't have an account."
     else
          echo "The user $testuser does not exist on this system,"
          echo "and no directory exists for the $testuser."
```

*(Continues)*

*(continued)*

```
        fi
        echo "We are outside the nested if statements."
        $
        $ ./test5.sh
        /home/NoSuchUser/
        The user NoSuchUser has a directory,
        even though NoSuchUser doesn't have an account.
        We are outside the nested if statements.
        $
        $ sudo rmdir /home/NoSuchUser/
        [sudo] password for christine:
        $
        $ ./test5.sh
        ls: cannot access '/home/NoSuchUser/': No such file or directory
        The user NoSuchUser does not exist on this system,
        and no directory exists for the NoSuchUser.
        We are outside the nested if statements.
        $
```

Before the /home/NoSuchUser directory was removed and the test script executed the elif statement, a zero exit status was returned. Thus, the statements within the elif's then code block were executed. After the /home/NoSuchUser directory was removed, a non-zero exit status was returned for the elif statement. This caused the statements in the else block within the elif block to be executed.

> **NOTE**
> Keep in mind that, with an elif statement, any else statements immediately following it are only for that elif code block. They are not part of a preceding if-then statement code block.

You can continue to string elif statements together, creating one huge if-then-elif conglomeration:

```
if command1
then
    command set 1
elif command2
then
    command set 2
elif command3
then
    command set 3
elif command4
then
    command set 4
fi
```

Each block of commands is executed depending on which command returns the zero exit status code. Remember that the Bash shell executes the if statements in order, and only the first one that returns a zero exit status results in the then section being executed.

Even though the code looks cleaner with elif statements, it still can be confusing to follow the script's logic. Later in the "Considering the case Command" section, you'll see how to use the case command instead of having to nest lots of if-then statements.

# Trying the *test* Command

So far, all you've seen in the if statement line are normal shell commands. You might be wondering if the Bash if-then statement has the ability to evaluate any condition other than a command's exit status code.

The answer is no, it can't. However, a neat utility available in the Bash shell helps you evaluate other things using the if-then statement.

The test command provides a way to test different conditions in an if-then statement. If the condition listed in the test command evaluates to TRUE, the test command exits with a zero exit status code. This makes the if-then statement behave in much the same way that if-then statements work in other programming languages. If the condition is false, the test command exits with a non-zero exit status code, which causes the if-then statement to exit.

The format of the test command is pretty simple:

```
test condition
```

The *condition* is a series of parameters and values that the test command evaluates. When used in an if-then statement, the test command looks like this:

```
if test condition
then
    commands
fi
```

If you leave out the *condition* portion of the test command statement, it exits with a non-zero exit status code (false) and triggers any else block statements:

```
$ cat test6.sh
#!/bin/bash
# testing the test command
#
if test
then
    echo "No expression returns a True"
else
    echo "No expression returns a False"
fi
```

*(Continues)*

311

*(continued)*

```
$
$ ./test6.sh
No expression returns a False
$
```

When you add in a condition, it is tested by the test command. For example, using the test command, you can determine whether a variable has content. A simple condition expression is needed to determine whether a variable has content:

```
$ cat test6.sh
#!/bin/bash
# testing if a variable has content
#
my_variable="Full"
#
if test $my_variable
then
        echo "The my_variable variable has content and returns a True."
        echo "The my_variable variable content is: $my_variable"
else
        echo "The my_variable variable doesn't have content,"
        echo "and returns a False."
fi
$
$ ./test6.sh
The my_variable variable has content and returns a True.
The my_variable variable content is: Full
$
```

The variable my_variable contains content (Full), so when the test command checks the condition, the exit status returns a zero. This triggers the statements in the then code block.

As you would suspect, the opposite occurs when the variable does not contain content:

```
$ cat test6.sh
#!/bin/bash
# testing if a variable has content
#
my_variable=""
#
if test $my_variable
then
        echo "The my_variable variable has content and returns a True."
        echo "The my_variable variable content is: $my_variable"
else
```

```
            echo "The my_variable variable doesn't have content,"
            echo "and returns a False."
    fi
    $
    $ ./test6.sh
    The my_variable variable doesn't have content,
    and returns a False.
    $
```

The Bash shell provides an alternative way of testing a condition without declaring the test command in an if-then statement:

```
    if [ condition ]
    then
        commands
    fi
```

The square brackets define the test condition. Be careful: you *must* have a space after the first bracket and a space before the last bracket, or you'll get an error message.

The test command and test conditions can evaluate three classes of conditions:

- Numeric comparisons
- String comparisons
- File comparisons

The next sections describe how to use each of these test classes in your if-then statements.

## Using numeric comparisons

The most common test evaluation method is to perform a comparison of two numeric values. Table 12-1 shows the list of condition parameters used for testing two values.

**TABLE 12-1** **The test Numeric Comparisons**

| Comparison | Description |
| --- | --- |
| n1 -eq n2 | Checks if n1 is equal to n2. |
| n1 -ge n2 | Checks if n1 is greater than or equal to n2. |
| n1 -gt n2 | Checks if n1 is greater than n2. |
| n1 -le n2 | Checks if n1 is less than or equal to n2. |
| n1 -lt n2 | Checks if n1 is less than n2. |
| n1 -ne n2 | Checks if n1 is not equal to n2. |

The numeric test conditions can be used to evaluate both numbers and variables. Here's an example of doing that:

```
$ cat numeric_test.sh
#!/bin/bash
# Using numeric test evaluations
#
value1=10
value2=11
#
if [ $value1 -gt 5 ]
then
      echo "The test value $value1 is greater than 5."
fi
#
if [ $value1 -eq $value2 ]
then
      echo "The values are equal."
else
      echo "The values are different."
fi
$
```

The first test condition:

```
if [ $value1 -gt 5 ]
```

tests if the value of the variable value1 is greater than 5. The second test condition:

```
if [ $value1 -eq $value2 ]
```

tests if the value of the variable value1 is equal to the value of the variable value2. Both numeric test conditions evaluate as expected:

```
$ ./numeric_test.sh
The test value 10 is greater than 5
The values are different
$
```

> **WARNING**
>
> For test conditions, the only numbers the Bash shell can handle are integers. Although you can use floating-point values for commands, such as `echo`, they will not work properly in test conditions.

## Using string comparisons

Test conditions also allow you to perform comparisons on string values. Performing comparisons on strings can get tricky, as you'll see. Table 12-2 shows the comparison functions you can use to evaluate two string values.

**TABLE 12-2  The test String Comparisons**

| Comparison | Description |
| --- | --- |
| str1 = str2 | Checks if str1 is the same as string str2. |
| str1 != str2 | Checks if str1 is not the same as str2. |
| str1 < str2 | Checks if str1 is less than str2. |
| str1 > str2 | Checks if str1 is greater than str2. |
| -n str1 | Checks if str1 has a length greater than zero. |
| -z str1 | Checks if str1 has a length of zero. |

The following sections describe the different string comparisons available.

### Looking at string equality

The equal and not equal conditions are fairly self-explanatory with strings. It's pretty easy to know whether two string values are the same or not:

```
$ cat string_test.sh
#!/bin/bash
# Using string test evaluations
#
testuser=christine
#
if [ $testuser = christine ]
then
      echo "The testuser variable contains: christine"
else
      echo "The testuser variable contains: $testuser"
fi
$
$ ./string_test.sh
The testuser variable contains: christine
$
```

Also, using the not equals string comparison allows you to determine whether or not two strings have the same value:

```
$ cat string_not_test.sh
#!/bin/bash
# Using string test not equal evaluations
#
testuser=rich
#
if [ $testuser != christine ]
then
      echo "The testuser variable does NOT contain: christine"
```

*(Continues)*

(continued)
```
    else
        echo "The testuser variable contains: christine"
    fi
    $
    $ ./string_not_test.sh
    The testuser variable does NOT contain: christine
    $
```

Keep in mind that the test comparison takes all punctuation and capitalization into account when comparing strings for equality.

## Looking at string order

Trying to determine if one string is less than or greater than another is where things start getting tricky. Two problems often plague shell programmers when they're trying to use the greater-than or less-than features of test conditions:

- The greater-than and less-than symbols must be escaped, or the shell uses them as redirection symbols, with the string values as filenames.
- The greater-than and less-than order is not the same as that used with the sort command.

The first item can result in a huge problem that often goes undetected when programming your scripts. Here's an example of what sometimes happens to novice shell script programmers:

```
$ cat bad_string_comparison.sh
#!/bin/bash
# Misusing string comparisons
#
string1=soccer
string2=zorbfootball
#
if [ $string1 > $string2 ]
then
        echo "$string1 is greater than $string2"
else
        echo "$string1 is less than $string2"
fi
$
$ ./bad_string_comparison.sh
soccer is greater than zorbfootball
$
$ ls z*
zorbfootball
$
```

By just using the greater-than symbol itself in the script, no errors are generated, but the results are wrong. The script interpreted the greater-than symbol as an output redirection (see Chapter 15). Thus, it created a file called zorbfootball. Because the redirection completed successfully, the test condition returns a zero exit status code, which the `if` statement evaluates as though things completed successfully!

To fix this problem, you need to properly escape the greater-than symbol using the backslash (\):

```
$ cat good_string_comparison.sh
#!/bin/bash
# Properly using string comparisons
#
string1=soccer
string2=zorbfootball
#
if [ $string1 \> $string2 ]
then
     echo "$string1 is greater than $string2"
else
     echo "$string1 is less than $string2"
fi
$
$ rm -i zorbfootball
rm: remove regular empty file 'zorbfootball'? y
$
$ ./good_string_comparison.sh
soccer is less than zorbfootball
$
$ ls z*
ls: cannot access 'z*': No such file or directory
$
```

Now that answer is more along the lines of what you would expect from the string comparison.

> **NOTE**
> The string `soccer` is less than the string `zorbfootball`, because test comparisons use each character's Unicode numeric value. Lowercase `s` equates to 115, whereas `z` is 122. Thus, `s` is less than `z`, and therefore, `soccer` is less than `zorbfootball`.

The second issue is a little more subtle, and you may not even run across it unless you are working with uppercase and lowercase letters. The `sort` command handles uppercase letters opposite to the way the `test` conditions consider them:

```
$ cat SportsFile.txt
Soccer
soccer
$
$ sort SportsFile.txt
soccer
```

*(Continues)*

*(continued)*

```
Soccer
$
$ cat sort_order_comparison.sh
#!/bin/bash
# Testing string sort order
#
string1=Soccer
string2=soccer
#
if [ $string1 \> $string2 ]
then
     echo "$string1 is greater than $string2"
else
     echo "$string1 is less than $string2"
fi
$
$
$ ./sort_order_comparison.sh
Soccer is less than soccer
$
```

Capitalized letters are treated as less than lowercase letters in test comparisons. However, the sort command does the opposite. When you put the same strings in a file and use the sort command, the lowercase letters appear first. This is due to different ordering techniques.

Test comparisons use standard Unicode ordering, using each character's Unicode numeric value to determine the sort order. The sort command uses the sorting order defined for the system locale language settings. For the English language, the locale settings specify that lowercase letters appear before uppercase letters in sorted order.

> **NOTE**
> The test command and test expressions use the standard mathematical comparison symbols for string comparisons and text codes for numerical comparisons. This is a subtle feature that many programmers manage to get reversed. If you use the mathematical comparison symbols for numeric values, the shell interprets them as string values and may not produce the correct results.

### Looking at string size

The -n and -z comparisons are handy when you're trying to evaluate whether a variable contains data:

```
$ cat variable_content_eval.sh
#!/bin/bash
# Testing string length
#
string1=Soccer
string2=''
#
```

```
    if [ -n $string1 ]
    then
        echo "The string '$string1' is NOT empty"
    else
        echo "The string '$string1' IS empty"
    fi
    #
    if [ -z $string2 ]
    then
        echo "The string '$string2' IS empty"
    else
        echo "The string '$string2' is NOT empty"
    fi
    #
    if [ -z $string3 ]
    then
        echo "The string '$string3' IS empty"
    else
        echo "The string '$string3' is NOT empty"
    fi
    $
    $ ./variable_content_eval.sh
    The string 'Soccer' is NOT empty
    The string '' IS empty
    The string '' IS empty
    $
```

This example creates two string variables. The string1 variable contains a string, and the string2 variable is created as an empty string. The following comparisons are made:

```
    if [ -n $string1 ]
```

The preceding code determines whether the string1 variable is non-zero in length, which it is, so its then section is processed.

```
    if [ -z $string2 ]
```

This preceding code determines whether the string2 variable is zero in length, which it is, so its then section is processed.

```
    if [ -z $string3 ]
```

The preceding code determines whether the string3 variable is zero in length. This variable was never defined in the shell script, so it indicates that the string length is still zero, even though it wasn't defined.

**WARNING**

Empty and uninitialized variables can have catastrophic effects on your shell script tests. If you're not sure of the contents of a variable, it's always best to test if the variable contains a value using -n or -z before using it in a numeric or string comparison.

## Using file comparisons

The last category of test comparisons includes quite possibly the most powerful and most used comparisons in shell scripting. This category allows you to test the status of files and directories on the Linux filesystem. Table 12-3 lists these comparisons.

**TABLE 12-3 The test File Comparisons**

| Comparison | Description |
|---|---|
| -d *file* | Checks if *file* exists and is a directory. |
| -e *file* | Checks if *file* exists. |
| -f *file* | Checks if *file* exists and is a file. |
| -r *file* | Checks if *file* exists and is readable. |
| -s *file* | Checks if *file* exists and is not empty. |
| -w *file* | Checks if *file* exists and is writable. |
| -x *file* | Checks if *file* exists and is executable. |
| -O *file* | Checks if *file* exists and is owned by the current user. |
| -G *file* | Checks if *file* exists and the default group is the same as the current user. |
| *file1* -nt *file2* | Checks if *file1* is newer than *file2*. |
| *file1* -ot *file2* | Checks if *file1* is older than *file2*. |

These conditions give you the ability to check filesystem files within shell scripts. They are often used in scripts that access files. Because they're used so often, let's look at each of these individually.

### Checking directories

The -d test checks to see if a specified directory exists on the system. This is usually a good thing to do if you're trying to write a file to a directory or before you try to change to a directory location:

```
$ cat jump_point.sh
#!/bin/bash
# Look before you leap
#
jump_directory=/home/Torfa
#
if [ -d $jump_directory ]
then
      echo "The $jump_directory directory exists."
      cd $jump_directory
      ls
else
```

```
            echo "The $jump_directory directory does NOT exist."
    fi
    $
    $ ./jump_point.sh
    The /home/Torfa directory does NOT exist.
    $
```

The -d test condition checks to see if the jump_directory variable's directory exists. If it does, it proceeds to use the cd command to change to the current directory and performs a directory listing. If it does not, the script emits a warning message and exits the script.

### Checking whether an object exists

The -e comparison allows you to check if either a file or directory object exists before you attempt to use it in your script:

```
$ cat update_file.sh
#!/bin/bash
# Check if either a directory or file exists
#
location=$HOME
file_name="sentinel"
#
if [ -d $location ]
then
      echo "OK on the $location directory"
      echo "Now checking on the file, $file_name..."
      if [ -e $location/$file_name ]
      then
            echo "OK on the file, $file_name."
            echo "Updating file's contents."
            date >> $location/$file_name
      #
      else
            echo "File, $location/$file_name, does NOT exist."
            echo "Nothing to update."
      fi
#
else
      echo "Directory, $location, does NOT exist."
      echo "Nothing to update."
fi
$
$ ./update_file.sh
OK on the /home/christine directory
Now checking on the file, sentinel...
File, /home/christine/sentinel, does NOT exist.
Nothing to update.
```

*(Continues)*

321

*(continued)*

```
$
$ touch /home/christine/sentinel
$
$ ./update_file.sh
OK on the /home/christine directory
Now checking on the file, sentinel...
OK on the file, sentinel.
Updating file's contents.
$
```

The first check uses the -e comparison to determine whether the user has a $HOME directory. If so, the next -e comparison checks to determine whether the sentinel file exists in the $HOME directory. If the file doesn't exist, the shell script notes that the file is missing and that there is nothing to update.

To ensure that the update will work, the sentinel file was created and the shell script was run a second time. This time when the conditions are tested, both the $HOME and the sentinel file are found, and the current date and time is appended to the file.

## Checking for a file

The -e comparison works for both files and directories. To ensure that the object specified is a file and not a directory, you must use the -f comparison:

```
$ cat dir-or-file.sh
#!/bin/bash
# Check if object exists and is a directory or a file
#
object_name=$HOME
echo
echo "The object being checked: $object_name"
echo
#
if [ -e $object_name ]
then
      echo "The object, $object_name, does exist,"
      #
      if [ -f $object_name ]
      then
            echo "and $object_name is a file."
      #
      else
            echo "and $object_name is a directory."
      fi
#
else
      echo "The object, $object_name, does NOT exist."
fi
$
```

```
$ ./dir-or-file.sh

The object being checked: /home/christine

The object, /home/christine, does exist,
and /home/christine is a directory.
$
```

First, this script uses the -e comparison to test whether $HOME exists. If it does, it uses -f to test whether it's a file. If it isn't a file (which of course it isn't), a message is displayed stating that it is a directory.

A slight modification to the variable object_name, replacing the directory $HOME with a file, $HOME/sentinel, causes a different outcome:

```
$ nano dir-or-file.sh
$
$ cat dir-or-file.sh
#!/bin/bash
# Check if object exists and is a directory or a file
#
object_name=$HOME/sentinel
echo
echo "The object being checked: $object_name"
echo
#
if [ -e $object_name ]
then
     echo "The object, $object_name, does exist,"
     #
     if [ -f $object_name ]
     then
          echo "and $object_name is a file."
     #
     else
          echo "and $object_name is a directory."
     fi
#
else
     echo "The object, $object_name, does NOT exist."
fi
$
$ ./dir-or-file.sh

The object being checked: /home/christine/sentinel

The object, /home/christine/sentinel, does exist,
and /home/christine/sentinel is a file.
$
```

Now when the script is run, the -f test on $HOME/sentinel exits with a zero status, triggering the then statement, which in turn outputs the message and /home/christine/sentinel is a file.

### Checking for read access

Before trying to read data from a file, it's usually a good idea to test whether you can read from the file first. You do this with the -r comparison:

```
$ cat can-I-read-it.sh
#!/bin/bash
# Check if you can read a file
#
pwfile=/etc/shadow
echo
echo "Checking if you can read $pwfile..."
#
# Check if file exists and is a file.
#
if [ -f $pwfile ]
then
      # File does exist. Check if can read it.
      #
      if [ -r $pwfile ]
      then
            echo "Displaying end of file..."
            tail $pwfile
      #
      else
            echo "Sorry, read access to $pwfile is denied."
      fi
#
else
      echo "Sorry, the $pwfile file does not exist."
fi
$
$ ./can-I-read-it.sh

Checking if you can read /etc/shadow...
Sorry, read access to /etc/shadow is denied.
$
```

The /etc/shadow file contains the encrypted passwords for system users, so it's not readable by normal users on the system. The -r comparison determined that read access to the file wasn't allowed, so the test command failed and the Bash shell executed the else section of the if-then statement.

### Checking for empty files

You should use -s comparison to check whether a file is empty, especially if you don't want to remove a non-empty file. Be careful because when the -s comparison succeeds, it indicates that a file has data in it:

```
$ cat is-it-empty.sh
#!/bin/bash
# Check if a file is empty
#
file_name=$HOME/sentinel
echo
echo "Checking if $file_name file is empty..."
echo
#
# Check if file exists and is a file.
#
if [ -f $file_name ]
then
      # File does exist. Check if it is empty.
      #
      if [ -s $file_name ]
      then
            echo "The $file_name file exists and has data in it."
            echo "Will not remove this file."
      #
      else
            echo "The $file_name file exits, but is empty."
            echo "Deleting empty file..."
            rm $file_name
      fi
#
else
      echo "The $file_name file does not exist."
fi
$
$ ls -sh $HOME/sentinel
4.0K /home/christine/sentinel
$
$ ./is-it-empty.sh

Checking if /home/christine/sentinel file is empty...

The /home/christine/sentinel file exists and has data in it.
Will not remove this file.
$
```

First, the -f comparison tests whether the file exists. If it does exist, the -s comparison is triggered to determine whether the file is empty. An empty file will be deleted. You can see from the `ls -sh` command that the `sentinel` file is not empty (4.0 K), and therefore the script does not delete it.

### Checking whether you can write to a file

The `-w` comparison determines whether you have permission to write to a file. The `can-I-write-to-it.sh` script is simply an update of the `can-I-read-it.sh` script. Now instead of checking if you can read the `item_name` file, this script checks to see whether you have permission to write to the file:

```
$ cat can-I-write-to-it.sh
#!/bin/bash
# Check if a file is writable
#
item_name=$HOME/sentinel
echo
echo "Checking if you can write to $item_name..."
#
# Check if file exists and is a file.
#
if [ -f $item_name ]
then
        # File does exist. Check if can write to it.
        #
        if [ -w $item_name ]
        then
                echo "Writing current time to $item_name"
                date +%H%M >> $item_name
        #
        else
                echo "Sorry, write access to $item_name is denied."
        fi
#
else
        echo "Sorry, the $item_name does not exist"
        echo "or is not a file."
fi
$
$ ls -o $HOME/sentinel
-rw-rw-r-- 1 christine 32 May 25 17:08 /home/christine/sentinel
$
$ ./can-I-write-to-it.sh

Checking if you can write to /home/christine/sentinel...
Writing current time to /home/christine/sentinel
$
```

The `item_name` variable is set to `$HOME/sentinel`, and this file allows user write access (see Chapter 7, "Understanding Linux File Permissions," for more information on file permissions). Thus, when the script is run, the -w test expression returns a non-zero exit status and the then code block is executed, which writes a time stamp into the sentinel file.

When the sentinel file user's write access is removed via chmod, the -w test expression returns a non-zero status, and a time stamp is not written to the file:

```
$ chmod u-w $HOME/sentinel
$
$ ls -o $HOME/sentinel
-r--rw-r-- 1 christine 37 May 29 12:07 /home/christine/sentinel
$
$ ./can-I-write-to-it.sh

Checking if you can write to /home/christine/sentinel...
Sorry, write access to /home/christine/sentinel is denied.
$
```

The chmod command could be used again to grant the write permission back for the user. This would make the write test expression return a zero exit status and allow a write attempt to the file.

### Checking whether you can run a file

The -x comparison is a handy way to determine whether you have execute permission for a specific file. Although this may not be needed for most commands, if you run lots of scripts from your shell scripts, it could be useful:

```
$ cat can-I-run-it.sh
#!/bin/bash
# Check if you can run a file
#
item_name=$HOME/scripts/can-I-write-to-it.sh
echo
echo "Checking if you can run $item_name..."
#
# Check if file is executable.
#
if [ -x $item_name ]
then
        echo "You can run $item_name."
        echo "Running $item_name..."
        $item_name
#
else
        echo "Sorry, you cannot run $item_name."
#
fi
$
$ ./can-I-run-it.sh
```

*(Continues)*

(continued)
```
        Checking if you can run /home/christine/scripts/can-I-write-to-it.sh...
        You can run /home/christine/scripts/can-I-write-to-it.sh.
        Running /home/christine/scripts/can-I-write-to-it.sh...
        [...]
        $
        $ chmod u-x can-I-write-to-it.sh
        $
        $ ./can-I-run-it.sh

        Checking if you can run /home/christine/scripts/can-I-write-to-it.sh...
        Sorry, you cannot run /home/christine/scripts/can-I-write-to-it.sh.
        $
```

This example shell script uses the -x comparison to test whether you have permission to
execute the can-I-write-to-it.sh script. If so, it runs the script. After successfully
running the can-I-write-to-it.sh script the first time, the permissions were changed.
This time, the -x comparison failed, because the execute permission had been removed for
the can-I-write-to-it.sh script.

## Checking ownership

The -O comparison allows you to easily test whether you're the owner of a file:

```
        $ cat do-I-own-it.sh
        #!/bin/bash
        # Check if you own a file
        #
        if [ -O /etc/passwd ]
        then
              echo "You are the owner of the /etc/passwd file."
        #
        else
              echo "Sorry, you are NOT /etc/passwd file's owner."
        #
        fi
        $
        $ whoami
        christine
        $
        $ ls -o /etc/passwd
        -rw-r--r-- 1 root 2842 Apr 23 15:25 /etc/passwd
        $
        $ ./do-I-own-it.sh
        Sorry, you are NOT /etc/passwd file's owner.
        $
```

The script uses the -O comparison to test whether the user running the script is the owner of the /etc/passwd file. The script is run under a user account other than root, so the test fails.

### Checking default group membership

The -G comparison checks the group of a file, and it succeeds if it matches the default group for the user. This can be somewhat confusing because the -G comparison checks only the script user's default group and not all the groups to which the user belongs. Here's an example:

```
$ cat check_default_group.sh
#!/bin/bash
# Compare file and script user's default groups
#
if [ -G $HOME/TestGroupFile ]
then
     echo "You are in the same default group as"
     echo "the $HOME/TestGroupFile file's group."
#
else
     echo "Sorry, your default group and $HOME/TestGroupFile"
     echo "file's group are different."
#
fi
$
$ touch $HOME/TestGroupFile
$
$ ls -g $HOME/TestGroupFile
-rw-rw-r-- 1 christine 0 May 29 13:58 /home/christine/TestGroupFile
$
$ ./check_default_group.sh
You are in the same default group as
the /home/christine/TestGroupFile file's group.
$
$ groups
christine adm cdrom sudo dip plugdev lpadmin lxd sambashare
$
$ chgrp adm $HOME/TestGroupFile
$
$ ls -g $HOME/TestGroupFile
-rw-rw-r-- 1 adm 0 May 29 13:58 /home/christine/TestGroupFile
$
$ ./check_default_group.sh
Sorry, your default group and /home/christine/TestGroupFile
file's group are different.
$
```

The first time the script is run, the $HOME/TestGroupFile file is in the christine group and the -G comparison succeeds. Next, the group is changed to the adm group, of which the user is also a member. However, the -G comparison failed, because it compares only the user's default group, not any additional group memberships.

### Checking file date

The last set of comparisons deal with comparing the creation times of two files. This comes in handy when writing scripts to install software. Sometimes, you don't want to install a file that is older than a file already installed on the system.

The -nt comparison determines whether a file is newer than another file. If a file is newer, it has a more recent file creation time. The -ot comparison determines whether a file is older than another file. If the file is older, it has an older file creation time:

```
$ cat check_file_dates.sh
#!/bin/bash
# Compare two file's creation dates/times
#
if [ $HOME/Downloads/games.rpm -nt $HOME/software/games.rpm ]
then
      echo "The $HOME/Downloads/games.rpm file is newer"
      echo "than the $HOME/software/games.rpm file."
#
else
      echo "The $HOME/Downloads/games.rpm file is older"
      echo "than the $HOME/software/games.rpm file."
#
fi
$
$ ./check_file_dates.sh
The /home/christine/Downloads/games.rpm file is newer
than the /home/christine/software/games.rpm file.
$
```

Neither of these comparisons in the script checks whether the files exist first. That's a problem. Try this test:

```
$ rm $HOME/Downloads/games.rpm
$
$ ./check_file_dates.sh
The /home/christine/Downloads/games.rpm file is older
than the /home/christine/software/games.rpm file.
$
```

This little example demonstrates that if one of the files doesn't exist, the -nt comparison returns incorrect information. It's imperative to ensure that the files exist before trying to use them in the -nt or -ot comparison.

# Considering Compound Testing

The if-then statement allows you to use Boolean logic to combine tests. You can use these two Boolean operators:

- [ condition1 ] && [ condition2 ]
- [ condition1 ] || [ condition2 ]

The first Boolean operation uses the AND Boolean operator to combine two conditions. Both conditions must be met for the then section to execute.

**NOTE** Boolean logic is a method that reduces potential returned values to either TRUE or FALSE.

12

The second Boolean operation uses the OR Boolean operator to combine two conditions. If either condition evaluates to a TRUE condition, the then section is executed.

The following shows the AND Boolean operator in use:

```
$ cat AndBoolean.sh
#!/bin/bash
# Testing an AND Boolean compound condition
#
if [ -d $HOME ] && [ -w $HOME/newfile ]
then
     echo "The file exists and you can write to it."
#
else
     echo "You cannot write to the file."
#
fi
$
$ ls -l $HOME/newfile
ls: cannot access '/home/christine/newfile': No such file or directory
$
$ ./AndBoolean.sh
You cannot write to the file.
$
$ touch $HOME/newfile
$
$ ./AndBoolean.sh
The file exists and you can write to it.
$
```

Using the AND Boolean operator, both of the comparisons must be met. The first comparison checks to see if the $HOME directory exists for the user. The second comparison checks to see if there's a file called newfile in the user's $HOME directory and if the user has write permissions for the file. If either of these comparisons fails, the if statement fails and the shell executes the else section. If both of the comparisons succeed, the if statement succeeds, and the shell executes the then section.

# Working with Advanced *if-then* Features

Three additions to the Bash shell provide advanced features that you can use in if-then statements:

- Single parentheses for running the command in a subshell
- Double parentheses for mathematical expressions
- Double square brackets for advanced string handling functions

The following sections describe each of these features in more detail.

## Using single parentheses

Single parentheses allow you to use subshells in your if statement comparisons. Subshells were covered in Chapter 5, "Understanding the Shell." This is the format of the single parentheses test command:

```
(command)
```

Before the Bash shell executes the *command*, it creates a subshell in which to run the command. If the command completes its task successfully, the exit status (covered in Chapter 11) is set to zero, and the commands listed under the then section are executed. If the exit status of the command is anything else, the then commands aren't executed. Here's a script to test using subshells:

```
$ cat SingleParentheses.sh
#!/bin/bash
# Testing a single parentheses condition
#
echo $BASH_SUBSHELL
#
if (echo $BASH_SUBSHELL)
then
      echo "The subshell command operated successfully."
#
else
      echo "The subshell command was NOT successful."
#
fi
$
$ ./SingleParentheses.sh
0
1
The subshell command operated successfully.
$
```

When the script runs the echo $BASH_SUBSHELL command the first time (prior to the if statement), it completes the operation within the current shell. The command displays a 0, indicating there is no subshell in use. (The $BASH_SUBSHELL environment variable was covered in Chapter 5.) Within the if statement, the script performs the command in a subshell and the echo $BASH_SUBSHELL command shows a 1, indicating a subshell was used. This subshell operation completes successfully, triggering the then command.

> **WARNING**
>
> While you can use process lists (covered in Chapter 5) within the if test statement, unexpected results may occur. If all the process list's commands fail except the **last** command, the subshell will set the exit status to zero, and the commands listed under the then section will run.

Modifying the script slightly, here's an example of an unsuccessful command run in a subshell:

```
$ cat SingleParentheses.sh
#!/bin/bash
# Testing a single parentheses condition
#
#echo $BASH_SUBSHELL
#
if (cat /etc/PASSWORD)
then
     echo "The subshell command operated successfully."
#
else
     echo "The subshell command was NOT successful."
#
fi
$
$ ./SingleParentheses.sh
cat: /etc/PASSWORD: No such file or directory
The subshell command was NOT successful.
$
```

Because the subshell command contained an incorrect filename in its operation, the exit status was not set to zero. Thus, the else command was triggered instead of the then command.

## Using double parentheses

The *double parentheses* command allows you to incorporate advanced mathematical formulas in your comparisons. The test command allows for only simple arithmetic operations in the comparison. The double parentheses command provides more mathematical symbols, which programmers who have used other programming languages may be familiar with using. Here's the format of the double parentheses command:

```
(( expression ))
```

The *expression* term can be any mathematical assignment or comparison expression. Besides the standard mathematical operators that the test command uses, the additional operators shown in Table 12-4 are available for use in the double parentheses command.

**TABLE 12-4** **The Double Parentheses Command Symbols**

| Symbol | Description |
|--------|-------------|
| val++ | Post-increment |
| val-- | Post-decrement |
| ++val | Pre-increment |
| --val | Pre-decrement |
| ! | Logical negation |
| ~ | Bitwise negation |
| ** | Exponentiation |
| << | Left bitwise shift |
| >> | Right bitwise shift |
| & | Bitwise Boolean AND |
| \| | Bitwise Boolean OR |
| && | Logical AND |
| \|\| | Logical OR |

You can use the double parentheses command in an if statement, as well as in a normal command in the script for assigning values:

```
$ cat DoubleParentheses.sh
#!/bin/bash
# Testing a double parentheses command
#
val1=10
#
if (( $val1 ** 2 > 90 ))
then
     (( val2 = $val1 ** 2 ))
     echo "The square of $val1 is $val2,"
     echo "which is greater than 90."
#
fi
$
$ ./DoubleParentheses.sh
The square of 10 is 100,
which is greater than 90.
$
```

Notice that you don't need to escape the greater-than symbol in the expression within the double parentheses. This is yet another advanced feature besides the double parentheses command.

## Using double brackets

The *double bracket* command provides advanced features for string comparisons. Here's the double bracket command format:

```
[[ expression ]]
```

The double bracketed *expression* uses the standard string comparison used in the test evaluations. However, it provides an additional feature that the test evaluations don't — *pattern matching*.

**12**

In pattern matching, you can define a regular expression (discussed in detail in Chapter 20, "Regular Expressions") that's matched against the string value:

```
$ cat DoubleBrackets.sh
#!/bin/bash
# Using double brackets for pattern matching
#
#
if [[ $BASH_VERSION == 5.* ]]
then
     echo "You are using the Bash Shell version 5 series."
fi
$
$ ./DoubleBrackets.sh
You are using the Bash Shell version 5 series.
$
```

Notice in the preceding script that double equal signs (==) are used. These double equal signs designate the string to the right (5.*) as a pattern, and pattern matching rules are applied. The double bracket command matches the $BASH_VERSION environment variable to see whether it starts with a 5. string. If so, the comparison succeeds, and the shell executes the then section commands.

# Considering the *case* Command

Often, you'll find yourself trying to evaluate a variable's value, looking for a specific value within a set of possible values. In this scenario, you end up having to write a lengthy if-then-else statement, like this:

```
$ cat LongIf.sh
#!/bin/bash
```

*(Continues)*

```
(continued)
      # Using a tedious and long if statement
      #
      if [ $USER == "rich" ]
      then
            echo "Welcome $USER"
            echo "Please enjoy your visit."
      elif [ $USER == "barbara" ]
      then
            echo "Hi there, $USER"
            echo "We're glad you could join us."
      elif [ $USER == "christine" ]
      then
            echo "Welcome $USER"
            echo "Please enjoy your visit."
      elif [ $USER == "tim" ]
      then
            echo "Hi there, $USER"
            echo "We're glad you could join us."
      elif [ $USER = "testing" ]
      then
            echo "Please log out when done with test."
      else
            echo "Sorry, you are not allowed here."
      fi
$
$ ./LongIf.sh
Welcome christine
Please enjoy your visit.
$
```

The `elif` statements continue the `if-then` checking, looking for a specific value for the single comparison variable.

Instead of having to write all the `elif` statements to continue checking the same variable value, you can use the `case` command. The `case` command checks multiple values of a single variable in a list-oriented format:

```
case variable in
pattern1 | pattern2) commands1;;
pattern3) commands2;;
*) default commands;;
esac
```

The `case` command compares the variable specified against the different patterns. If the variable matches the pattern, the shell executes the commands specified for the pattern. You can list more than one pattern on a line, using the bar operator to separate the patterns. The asterisk symbol is the catch-all for values that don't match any of the listed patterns. Here's an example of converting the if-then-else program to using the case command:

```
$ cat ShortCase.sh
#!/bin/bash
# Using a short case statement
#
case $USER in
rich | christine)
    echo "Welcome $USER"
    echo "Please enjoy your visit.";;
barbara | tim)
    echo "Hi there, $USER"
    echo "We're glad you could join us.";;
testing)
    echo "Please log out when done with test.";;
*)
    echo "Sorry, you are not allowed here."
esac
$
$ ./ShortCase.sh
Welcome christine
Please enjoy your visit.
$
```

The case command provides a much cleaner way of specifying the various options for each possible variable value.

# Working through a Practical Example

In this section, we'll describe a script that puts the structure commands we've covered in this chapter to a practical use — determining what package managers are available on the current system. It also takes a guess on which Linux distribution the current system is based, using the installed package managers as a guide.

For its analysis, the script first checks for standard Red Hat–based package managers (rpm, dnf, and flatpak). It uses the which command for each package manager and uses single parentheses in the if condition statement. If the package manager is found, a special Boolean variable for that particular manager is set to TRUE (1), and if not found, it is set to FALSE (0), as shown snipped here:

```
$ cat PackageMgrCheck.sh
#!/bin/bash
 [...]
if (which rpm &> /dev/null)
then
    item_rpm=1
    echo "You have the basic rpm utility."
```

*(Continues)*

```
(continued)
    #
    else
        item_rpm=0
    #
    fi
    [...]
    if (which flatpak &> /dev/null)
    then
        item_flatpak=1
        echo "You have the flatpak application container."
    #
    else
        item_flatpak=0
    #
    fi
    [...]
$
```

There is special handling for dnf and yum (covered in Chapter 9, "Installing Software") in case you are running the script on an older Red Hat–based distro that doesn't yet have the dnf utility. Notice that an elif statement is employed to check for yum if dnf is not found:

```
$ cat PackageMgrCheck.sh
[...]
if (which dnf &> /dev/null)
then
    item_dnfyum=1
    echo "You have the dnf package manager."
#
elif (which yum &> /dev/null)
then
    item_dnfyum=1
    echo "You have the yum package manager."
else
    item_dnfyum=0
#
fi
[...]
$
```

> **NOTE**
>
> Output redirection is used after the which command within the single parentheses. Building off what was covered in Chapter 10, "Working with Editors," regular (standard) output and any error messages from the which command are redirected via the &> symbols. They go to /dev/null, which is humorously called the *black hole*, because things put into it never come out. This action cleans up the script's output significantly but does not adversely affect its integrity. Error redirection is covered more thoroughly in Chapter 15.

After the script finishes its package manager analysis of the system, it calculates a score (redhatscore). This score is used later to make a hypothesis concerning this system's distribution base:

```
$ cat PackageMgrCheck.sh
[...]
redhatscore=$[$item_rpm + $item_dnfyum + $item_flatpak]
[...]
$
```

When the Red Hat package manager audit is completed, a Debian analysis starts. It is very similar to the Red Hat assessment, except it covers Debian package managers (dpkg, apt, snap), and determines a Debian score, shown snipped here:

```
$ cat PackageMgrCheck.sh
[...]
if (which dpkg &> /dev/null)
then
      item_dpkg=1
      echo "You have the basic dpkg utility."
#
else
      item_dpkg=0
#
fi
[...]
debianscore=$[$item_dpkg + $item_aptaptget + $item_snap]
[...]
$
```

The two scores, redhatscore and debianscore, are compared, and a distribution determination is declared:

```
$ cat PackageMgrCheck.sh
[...]
if [ $debianscore -gt $redhatscore ]
then
    echo "Most likely your Linux distribution is Debian-based."
    #
elif [ $redhatscore -gt $debianscore ]
then
    echo "Most likely your Linux distribution is Red Hat-based."
else
    echo "Unable to determine Linux distribution base."
fi
[...]
$
```

Here is the entire script for your perusal. As you read through, think of different ways to accomplish these tasks using modified if-then statements or even case structures. Getting your creative juices flowing is all part of learning:

```
$ cat PackageMgrCheck.sh
#!/bin/bash
# Checks system for popular package managers
#
#################### User Introduction ####################
echo "#######################################################"
echo
echo "     This script checks your Linux system for popular"
echo "package managers and application containers, lists"
echo "what's available, and makes an educated guess on your"
echo "distribution's base distro (Red Hat or Debian)."
echo
echo "#######################################################"
#
#################### Red Hat Checks ####################
#
echo
echo "Checking for Red Hat-based package managers &"
echo "application containers..."
#####
if (which rpm &> /dev/null)
then
     item_rpm=1
     echo "You have the basic rpm utility."
#
else
     item_rpm=0
#
fi
####
if (which dnf &> /dev/null)
then
     item_dnfyum=1
     echo "You have the dnf package manager."
#
elif (which yum &> /dev/null)
then
     item_dnfyum=1
     echo "You have the yum package manager."
else
     item_dnfyum=0
#
fi
####
if (which flatpak &> /dev/null)
then
```

```
          item_flatpak=1
          echo "You have the flatpak application container."
#
else
          item_flatpak=0
#
fi
####
redhatscore=$[$item_rpm + $item_dnfyum + $item_flatpak]
#
##################### Debian Checks #####################
#
echo
echo "Checking for Debian-based package managers &"
echo "application containers..."
#####
if (which dpkg &> /dev/null)
then
          item_dpkg=1
          echo "You have the basic dpkg utility."
#
else
          item_dpkg=0
#
fi
####
if (which apt &> /dev/null)
then
          item_aptaptget=1
          echo "You have the apt package manager."
#
elif (which apt-get &> /dev/null)
then
          item_aptaptget=1
          echo "You have the apt-get/apt-cache package manager."
#
else
          item_aptaptget=0
fi
####
if (which snap &> /dev/null)
then
          item_snap=1
          echo "You have the snap application container."
#
else
          item_snap=0
#
fi
####
```

*(Continues)*

*(continued)*

```
#
debianscore=$[$item_dpkg + $item_aptaptget + $item_snap]
#
#
##################### Determine Distro ######################
#
echo
if [ $debianscore -gt $redhatscore ]
then
    echo "Most likely your Linux distribution is Debian-based."
    #
elif [ $redhatscore -gt $debianscore ]
then
    echo "Most likely your Linux distribution is Red Hat-based."
else
    echo "Unable to determine Linux distribution base."
fi
#
echo
#
############################################################
#
exit
$
```

Here's the script in action on an Ubuntu system:

```
$ ./PackageMgrCheck.sh
######################################################

        This script checks your Linux system for popular
package managers and application containers, lists
what's available, and makes an educated guess on your
distribution's base distro (Red Hat or Debian).

######################################################

Checking for Red Hat-based package managers &
application containers...

Checking for Debian-based package managers &
application containers...
You have the basic dpkg utility.
You have the apt package manager.
You have the snap application container.

Most likely your Linux distribution is Debian-based.

$
```

Hopefully you are thinking of your own ways to accomplish this script's tasks differently using the topics covered in this chapter. And possibly you have some ideas for additional scripts.

## Summary

Structured commands allow you to alter the normal flow of shell script execution. The most basic structured command is the `if-then` statement. This statement provides a command evaluation and performs other commands based on the evaluated command's output.

You can expand the `if-then` statement to include a set of commands the Bash shell executes if the specified command fails as well. The `if-then-else` statement executes commands only if the command being evaluated returns a non-zero exit status code.

You can also link `if-then-else` statements together, using the `elif` statement. The `elif` is equivalent to using an `else if` statement, providing for additional checking of whether the original command that was evaluated failed.

In most scripts, instead of evaluating a command, you'll want to evaluate a condition, such as a numeric value, the contents of a string, or the status of a file or directory. The `test` command provides an easy way for you to evaluate all these conditions. If the condition evaluates to a TRUE condition, the `test` command produces a zero exit status code for the `if-then` statement. If the condition evaluates to a FALSE condition, the `test` command produces a non-zero exit status code for the `if-then` statement.

The square bracket is a special Bash command that is a synonym for the `test` command. You can enclose a test condition in square brackets in the `if-then` statement to test for numeric, string, and file conditions.

The double parentheses command provides advanced mathematical evaluations using additional operators. The double square bracket command allows you to perform advanced string pattern-matching evaluations.

Finally, we discussed the `case` command, which is a shorthand way of performing multiple `if-then-else` commands, checking the value of a single variable against a list of values.

The next chapter continues the discussion of structured commands by examining the shell looping commands. The `for` and `while` commands let you create loops that iterate through commands for a given period of time.

**12**

# More Structured Commands

## IN THIS CHAPTER

I n the previous chapter, you saw how to manipulate the flow of a shell script program by checking the output of commands and the values of variables. In this chapter, we continue to look at structured commands that control the flow of your shell scripts. You'll see how you can perform repeating processes, commands that can loop through a set of commands until an indicated condition has been met. This chapter discusses and demonstrates the for, while, and until Bash shell looping commands.

## Looking at the *for* Command

Iterating through a series of commands is a common programming practice. Often, you need to repeat a set of commands until a specific condition has been met, such as processing all the files in a directory, all the users on a system, or all the lines in a text file.

The Bash shell provides the for command to allow you to create a loop that iterates through a series of values. Each iteration performs a defined set of commands using one of the values in the series. Here's the basic format of the Bash shell for command:

```
for var in list
do
    commands
done
```

You supply the series of values used in the iterations in the *list* parameter. You can specify the values in the list in several ways.

In each iteration, the variable *var* contains the current value in the list. The first iteration uses the first item in the list, the second iteration the second item, and so on, until all the items in the list have been used.

The *commands* entered between the do and done statements can be one or more standard Bash shell commands. Within the *commands*, the $var variable contains the current list item value for the iteration.

We mentioned that there are several ways to specify the values in the list. The following sections show the various ways.

## Reading values in a list

The most basic use of the for command is to iterate through a list of values defined within the for command itself:

```
$ cat test1
#!/bin/bash
# basic for command

for test in Alabama Alaska Arizona Arkansas California Colorado
do
    echo The next state is $test
done
$ ./test1
The next state is Alabama
The next state is Alaska
The next state is Arizona
The next state is Arkansas
The next state is California
The next state is Colorado
$
```

Each time the for command iterates through the list of values provided, it assigns the $test variable the next value in the list. The $test variable can be used just like any other script variable within the for command statements. After the last iteration, the $test variable remains valid throughout the remainder of the shell script. It retains the last iteration value (unless you change its value):

```
$ cat test1b
#!/bin/bash
# testing the for variable after the looping
```

```
for test in Alabama Alaska Arizona Arkansas California Colorado
do
    echo "The next state is $test"
done
echo "The last state we visited was $test"
test=Connecticut
echo "Wait, now we're visiting $test"
$ ./test1b
The next state is Alabama
The next state is Alaska
The next state is Arizona
The next state is Arkansas
The next state is California
The next state is Colorado
The last state we visited was Colorado
Wait, now we're visiting Connecticut
$
```

The $test variable retained its value and allowed us to change the value and use it outside of the for command loop, as any other variable would.

## Reading complex values in a list

Things aren't always as easy as they seem with the for loop. There are times when you run into data that causes problems. Here's a classic example of what can cause problems for shell script programmers:

```
$ cat badtest1
#!/bin/bash
# another example of how not to use the for command

for test in I don't know if this'll work
do
    echo "word:$test"
done
$ ./badtest1
word:I
word:dont know if thisll
word:work
$
```

Ouch, that hurts. The shell saw the single quotation marks within the list values and attempted to use them to define a single data value, and it really messed things up in the process.

You have two ways to solve this problem:

- Use the escape character (the backslash) to escape the single quotation mark.
- Use double quotation marks to define the values that use single quotation marks.

Neither solution is all that fantastic, but each one helps solve the problem:

```
$ cat test2
#!/bin/bash
# solutions to the quote problem

for test in I don\'t know if "this'll" work
do
    echo "word:$test"
done
$ ./test2
word:I
word:don't
word:know
word:if
word:this'll
word:work
$
```

In the first problem value, you added the backslash character to escape the single quotation mark in the don't value. In the second problem value, you enclosed the this'll value in double quotation marks. Both methods worked fine to distinguish the value.

Another problem you may run into is multiword values. Remember that the for loop assumes that each value is separated with a space. If you have data values that contain spaces, you run into yet another problem:

```
$ cat badtest2
#!/bin/bash
# another example of how not to use the for command

for test in Nevada New Hampshire New Mexico New York North Carolina
do
    echo "Now going to $test"
done
$ ./badtest2
Now going to Nevada
Now going to New
Now going to Hampshire
Now going to New
Now going to Mexico
Now going to New
Now going to York
Now going to North
Now going to Carolina
$
```

Oops, that's not exactly what we wanted. The `for` command separates each value from the others in the list with a space. If there are spaces in the individual data values, you must accommodate them using double quotation marks:

```
$ cat test3
#!/bin/bash
# an example of how to properly define values

for test in Nevada "New Hampshire" "New Mexico" "New York"
do
    echo "Now going to $test"
done
$ ./test3
Now going to Nevada
Now going to New Hampshire
Now going to New Mexico
Now going to New York
$
```

Now the `for` command can properly distinguish between the different values. Also, notice that when you use double quotation marks around a value, the shell doesn't include the quotation marks as part of the value.

## Reading a list from a variable

Often what happens in a shell script is that you accumulate a list of values stored in a variable and then need to iterate through the list. You can do this using the `for` command as well:

```
$ cat test4
#!/bin/bash
# using a variable to hold the list

list="Alabama Alaska Arizona Arkansas Colorado"
list=$list" Connecticut"

for state in $list
do
    echo "Have you ever visited $state?"
done
$ ./test4
Have you ever visited Alabama?
Have you ever visited Alaska?
Have you ever visited Arizona?
Have you ever visited Arkansas?
Have you ever visited Colorado?
Have you ever visited Connecticut?
$
```

13

The $list variable contains the standard text list of values to use for the iterations. Notice that the code also uses another assignment statement to add (or concatenate) an item to the existing list contained in the $list variable. This is a common method for adding text to the end of an existing text string stored in a variable.

## Reading values from a command

Another way to generate values for inclusion in the list is to use the output of a command. You use command substitution to execute any command that produces output and then use the output of the command in the for command:

```
$ cat test5
#!/bin/bash
# reading values from a file

file="states.txt"

for state in $(cat $file)
do
    echo "Visit beautiful $state"
done
$ cat states.txt
Alabama
Alaska
Arizona
Arkansas
Colorado
Connecticut
Delaware
Florida
Georgia
$ ./test5
Visit beautiful Alabama
Visit beautiful Alaska
Visit beautiful Arizona
Visit beautiful Arkansas
Visit beautiful Colorado
Visit beautiful Connecticut
Visit beautiful Delaware
Visit beautiful Florida
Visit beautiful Georgia
$
```

This example uses the cat command in the command substitution to display the contents of the file states.txt. Notice that the states.txt file includes each state on a separate line, not separated by spaces. The for command still iterates through the output of the cat command one line at a time, assuming that each state is on a separate line. However, this doesn't solve the problem of having spaces in data. If you list a state with a space in it, the `for` command still takes each word as a separate value. There's a reason for this, which we look at in the next section.

> **NOTE**
> The `test5` code example assigned the filename to the variable using just the filename without a path. This requires that the file be in the same directory as the script. If this isn't the case, you need to use a full pathname (either absolute or relative) to reference the file location.

## Changing the field separator

The cause of this problem is the special environment variable IFS, the *internal field separator*. The IFS environment variable defines a list of characters the Bash shell uses as field separators. By default, the Bash shell considers the following characters as field separators:

- A space
- A tab
- A newline

If the Bash shell sees any of these characters in the data, it assumes that you're starting a new data field in the list. When working with data that can contain spaces (such as filenames), this can be annoying, as you saw in the previous script example.

To solve this problem, you can temporarily change the IFS environment variable values in your shell script to restrict the characters the Bash shell recognizes as field separators. For example, if you want to change the IFS value to recognize only the newline character, you need to do this:

```
IFS=$'\n'
```

Adding this statement to your script tells the Bash shell to ignore spaces and tabs in data values. Applying this technique to the previous script yields the following:

```
$ cat test5b
#!/bin/bash
# reading values from a file

file="states.txt"

IFS=$'\n'
for state in $(cat $file)
do
    echo "Visit beautiful $state"
done
$ ./test5b
Visit beautiful Alabama
Visit beautiful Alaska
Visit beautiful Arizona
```

*(Continues)*

*(continued)*

```
        Visit beautiful Arkansas
        Visit beautiful Colorado
        Visit beautiful Connecticut
        Visit beautiful Delaware
        Visit beautiful Florida
        Visit beautiful Georgia
        Visit beautiful New York
        Visit beautiful New Hampshire
        Visit beautiful North Carolina
        $
```

Now the shell script can use values in the list that contain spaces.

### WARNING

When working on long scripts, you may change the IFS value in one place and then forget about it and assume the default value elsewhere in the script. A safe practice to get into is to save the original IFS value before changing it and then restore it when you're finished.

This technique can be coded like this:

```
IFS.OLD=$IFS
IFS=$'\n'
<use the new IFS value in code>
IFS=$IFS.OLD
```

This ensures that the IFS value is returned to the default value for future operations within the script.

Other excellent applications of the IFS environment variable are possible. Suppose you want to iterate through values in a file that are separated by a colon (such as in the /etc/passwd file). You just need to set the IFS value to a colon:

```
IFS=:
```

If you want to specify more than one IFS character, just string them together on the assignment line:

```
IFS=$'\n':;"
```

This assignment uses the newline, colon, semicolon, and double quotation mark characters as field separators. There's no limit to how you can parse your data using the IFS characters.

## Reading a directory using wildcards

Finally, you can use the for command to automatically iterate through a directory of files. To do this, you must use a wildcard character in the file or pathname. This forces the shell to use *file globbing*. File globbing is the process of producing filenames or pathnames that match a specified wildcard character.

This feature is great for processing files in a directory when you don't know all the filenames:

```
$ cat test6
#!/bin/bash
# iterate through all the files in a directory

for file in /home/rich/test/*
do

    if [ -d "$file" ]
    then
        echo "$file is a directory"
    elif [ -f "$file" ]
    then
        echo "$file is a file"
    fi
done
$ ./test6
/home/rich/test/dir1 is a directory
/home/rich/test/myprog.c is a file
/home/rich/test/myprog is a file
/home/rich/test/myscript is a file
/home/rich/test/newdir is a directory
/home/rich/test/newfile is a file
/home/rich/test/newfile2 is a file
/home/rich/test/testdir is a directory
/home/rich/test/testing is a file
/home/rich/test/testprog is a file
/home/rich/test/testprog.c is a file
$
```

The for command iterates through the results of the /home/rich/test/* listing. The code tests each entry using the test command (using the square bracket method) to see if it's a directory, using the -d parameter, or a file, using the -f parameter (see Chapter 11, "Basic Script Building").

Notice in this example that we did something different in the if statement tests:

```
if [ -d "$file" ]
```

In Linux, it's perfectly legal to have directory and filenames that contain spaces. To accommodate that, you should enclose the $file variable in double quotation marks. If you don't, you'll get an error if you run into a directory or filename that contains spaces:

```
./test6: line 6: [: too many arguments
./test6: line 9: [: too many arguments
```

The Bash shell interprets the additional words as arguments within the test command, causing an error.

13

You can also combine both the directory search method and the list method in the same `for` statement by listing a series of directory wildcards in the `for` command:

```
$ cat test7
#!/bin/bash
# iterating through multiple directories

for file in /home/rich/.b* /home/rich/badtest
do
   if [ -d "$file" ]
   then
      echo "$file is a directory"
   elif [ -f "$file" ]
   then
      echo "$file is a file"
   else
      echo "$file doesn't exist"
   fi
done
$ ./test7
/home/rich/.backup.timestamp is a file
/home/rich/.bash_history is a file
/home/rich/.bash_logout is a file
/home/rich/.bash_profile is a file
/home/rich/.bashrc is a file
/home/rich/badtest doesn't exist
$
```

The `for` statement first uses file globbing to iterate through the list of files that result from the wildcard character; then it iterates through the next file in the list. You can combine any number of wildcard entries in the list to iterate through.

> **WARNING**
>
> Notice that you can enter anything in the list data. Even if the file or directory doesn't exist, the `for` statement attempts to process whatever you place in the list. This can be a problem when you're working with files and directories. You have no way of knowing if you're trying to iterate through a nonexistent directory. It's always a good idea to test each file or directory before trying to process it.

## Trying the C-Style *for* Command

If you've done any programming using the C programming language, you're probably surprised by the way the Bash shell uses the `for` command. In the C language, a `for` loop normally defines a variable, which it then alters automatically during each iteration. Typically, programmers use this variable as a counter and either increment or decrement the counter by 1 in each iteration. The Bash for command can also provide this functionality. This section shows you how to use a C-style for command in a Bash shell script.

## The C language *for* command

The C language for command has a method for specifying a variable, a condition that must remain true for the iterations to continue, and a method for altering the variable for each iteration. When the specified condition becomes false, the for loop stops. The condition equation is defined using standard mathematical symbols. For example, consider the following C language code:

```
for (i = 0; i < 10; i++)
{
    printf("The next number is %d\n", i);
}
```

This code produces a simple iteration loop, where the variable i is used as a counter. The first section assigns a default value to the variable. The middle section defines the condition under which the loop will iterate. When the defined condition becomes false, the for loop stops iterations. The last section defines the iteration process. After each iteration, the expression defined in the last section is executed. In this example, the i variable is incremented by 1 after each iteration.

The Bash shell also supports a version of the for loop that looks similar to the C-style for loop, although it does have some subtle differences, including a couple of things that will confuse shell script programmers. Here's the basic format of the C-style Bash for loop:

```
for (( variable assignment ; condition ; iteration process ))
```

The format of the C-style for loop can be confusing for Bash shell script programmers, because it uses C-style variable references instead of the shell-style variable references. Here's what a C-style for command looks like:

```
for (( a = 1; a < 10; a++ ))
```

Notice that there are a couple of things that don't follow the standard Bash shell for method:

- The assignment of the variable value can contain spaces.
- The variable in the condition isn't preceded with a dollar sign.
- The equation for the iteration process doesn't use the expr command format.

The shell developers created this format to more closely resemble the C-style for command. Although this is great for C programmers, it can throw even expert shell programmers into a tizzy. Be careful when using the C-style for loop in your scripts.

Here's an example of using the C-style for command in a Bash shell program:

```
$ cat test8
#!/bin/bash
# testing the C-style for loop

for (( i=1; i <= 10; i++ ))
```

*(Continues)*

**13**

*(continued)*

```
    do
        echo "The next number is $i"
    done
$ ./test8
The next number is 1
The next number is 2
The next number is 3
The next number is 4
The next number is 5
The next number is 6
The next number is 7
The next number is 8
The next number is 9
The next number is 10
$
```

The for loop iterates through the commands using the variable defined in the for loop (the letter *i* in this example). In each iteration, the $i variable contains the value assigned in the for loop. After each iteration, the loop iteration process is applied to the variable, which in this example increments the variable by 1.

## Using multiple variables

The C-style for command also allows you to use multiple variables for the iteration. The loop handles each variable separately, allowing you to define a different iteration process for each variable. Although you can have multiple variables, you can define only one condition in the for loop:

```
$ cat test9
#!/bin/bash
# multiple variables

for (( a=1, b=10; a <= 10; a++, b-- ))
do
    echo "$a - $b"
done
$ ./test9
1 - 10
2 - 9
3 - 8
4 - 7
5 - 6
6 - 5
7 - 4
8 - 3
9 - 2
10 - 1
$
```

The a and b variables are each initialized with different values and different iteration processes are defined. While the loop increases the a variable, it decreases the b variable for each iteration.

# Exploring the *while* Command

The while command is somewhat of a cross between the if-then statement and the for loop. The while command allows you to define a command to test and then loop through a set of commands for as long as the defined test command returns a zero exit status. It tests the test command at the start of each iteration. When the test command returns a non-zero exit status, the while command stops executing the set of commands.

## Basic *while* format

Here's the format of the while command:

```
while test command
do
 other commands
done
```

The *test command* defined in the while command is the exact same format as in if-then statements (see Chapter 11). As in the if-then statement, you can use any normal Bash shell command, or you can use the *test command* to test for conditions, such as variable values.

The key to the while command is that the exit status of the *test command* specified must change, based on the commands run during the loop. If the exit status never changes, the while loop will get stuck in an infinite loop.

The most common use of the *test command* is to use brackets to check a value of a shell variable that's used in the loop commands:

```
$ cat test10
#!/bin/bash
# while command test

var1=10
while [ $var1 -gt 0 ]
do
    echo $var1
    var1=$[ $var1 - 1 ]
done
$ ./test10
10
9
8
7
```

*(Continues)*

*(continued)*
```
6
5
4
3
2
1
$
```

The `while` command defines the test condition to check for each iteration:

```
while [ $var1 -gt 0 ]
```

As long as the test condition is true, the `while` command continues to loop through the commands defined. Within the commands, the variable used in the test condition must be modified, or you'll have an infinite loop. In this example, we use shell arithmetic to decrease the variable value by 1:

```
var1=$[ $var1 - 1 ]
```

The `while` loop stops when the test condition is no longer true.

## Using multiple test commands

The `while` command allows you to define multiple test commands on the `while` statement line. Only the exit status of the last test command is used to determine when the loop stops. This can cause some interesting results if you're not careful. Here's an example of what we mean:

```
$ cat test11
#!/bin/bash
# testing a multicommand while loop

var1=10

while echo $var1
      [ $var1 -ge 0 ]
do
    echo "This is inside the loop"
    var1=$[ $var1 - 1 ]
done
$ ./test11
10
This is inside the loop
9
This is inside the loop
8
This is inside the loop
7
This is inside the loop
6
```

```
This is inside the loop
5
This is inside the loop
4
This is inside the loop
3
This is inside the loop
2
This is inside the loop
1
This is inside the loop
0
This is inside the loop
-1
$
```

Pay close attention to what happened in this example. Two test commands were defined in the while statement:

```
while echo $var1
      [ $var1 -ge 0 ]
```

The first test simply displays the current value of the var1 variable. The second test uses brackets to determine the value of the var1 variable. Inside the loop, an echo statement displays a simple message, indicating that the loop was processed. Notice when you run the example how the output ends:

```
This is inside the loop
-1
$
```

The while loop executed the echo statement when the var1 variable was equal to 0 and then decreased the var1 variable value. The test commands were then executed for the next iteration. The echo test command was executed, displaying the value of the var1 variable, which is now less than 0. It's not until the shell executes the test command that the while loop terminates.

This demonstrates that in a multicommand while statement, all the test commands are executed in each iteration, including the last iteration when the last test command fails. Be careful of this. Another thing to be careful of is how you specify the multiple test commands. Note that each test command is on a separate line!

## Using the *until* Command

The until command works in exactly the opposite way from the while command. The until command requires that you specify a test command that normally produces a non-zero exit status. As long as the exit status of the test command is non-zero, the Bash shell executes the commands listed in the loop. When the test command returns a zero exit status, the loop stops.

As you would expect, the format of the until command is

```
until test commands
do
    other commands
done
```

Similar to the while command, you can have more than one *test command* in the until command statement. Only the exit status of the last command determines if the Bash shell executes the *other commands* defined.

The following is an example of using the until command:

```
$ cat test12
#!/bin/bash
# using the until command

var1=100

until [ $var1 -eq 0 ]
do
    echo $var1
    var1=$[ $var1 - 25 ]
done
$ ./test12
100
75
50
25
$
```

This example tests the var1 variable to determine when the until loop should stop. As soon as the value of the variable is equal to 0, the until command stops the loop. The same caution we warned you about for the while command applies when you use multiple test commands with the until command:

```
$ cat test13
#!/bin/bash
# using the until command

var1=100

until echo $var1
      [ $var1 -eq 0 ]
do
    echo Inside the loop: $var1
    var1=$[ $var1 - 25 ]
```

```
done
$ ./test13
100
Inside the loop: 100
75
Inside the loop: 75
50
Inside the loop: 50
25
Inside the loop: 25
0
$
```

The shell executes the test commands specified and stops only when the last command is true.

# Nesting Loops

A loop statement can use any other type of command within the loop, including other loop commands. This is called a *nested loop*. Care should be taken when using nested loops, because you're performing an iteration within an iteration, which multiplies the number of times commands are being run. If you don't pay close attention to this, it can cause problems in your scripts.

Here's a simple example of nesting a for loop inside another for loop:

```
$ cat test14
#!/bin/bash
# nesting for loops

for (( a = 1; a <= 3; a++ ))
do
    echo "Starting loop $a:"
    for (( b = 1; b <= 3; b++ ))
    do
        echo "   Inside loop: $b"
    done
done
$ ./test14
Starting loop 1:
   Inside loop: 1
   Inside loop: 2
   Inside loop: 3
Starting loop 2:
   Inside loop: 1
   Inside loop: 2
   Inside loop: 3
Starting loop 3:
```

*(Continues)*

*(continued)*

```
        Inside loop: 1
        Inside loop: 2
        Inside loop: 3
$
```

The nested loop (also called the *inner loop*) iterates through its values for each iteration of the outer loop. Notice that there's no difference between the do and done commands for the two loops. The Bash shell knows when the first done command is executed that it refers to the inner loop and not the outer loop.

The same applies when you mix loop commands, such as placing a for loop inside a while loop:

```
$ cat test15
#!/bin/bash
# placing a for loop inside a while loop

var1=5

while [ $var1 -ge 0 ]
do
    echo "Outer loop: $var1"
    for (( var2 = 1; $var2 < 3; var2++ ))
    do
        var3=$[ $var1 * $var2 ]
        echo "  Inner loop: $var1 * $var2 = $var3"
    done
    var1=$[ $var1 - 1 ]
done
$ ./test15
Outer loop: 5
  Inner loop: 5 * 1 = 5
  Inner loop: 5 * 2 = 10
Outer loop: 4
  Inner loop: 4 * 1 = 4
  Inner loop: 4 * 2 = 8
Outer loop: 3
  Inner loop: 3 * 1 = 3
  Inner loop: 3 * 2 = 6
Outer loop: 2
  Inner loop: 2 * 1 = 2
  Inner loop: 2 * 2 = 4
Outer loop: 1
  Inner loop: 1 * 1 = 1
  Inner loop: 1 * 2 = 2
Outer loop: 0
  Inner loop: 0 * 1 = 0
  Inner loop: 0 * 2 = 0
$
```

Again, the shell distinguished between the do and done commands of the inner for loop from the same commands in the outer while loop.

If you really want to test your brain, you can even combine until and while loops:

```
$ cat test16
#!/bin/bash
# using until and while loops

var1=3

until [ $var1 -eq 0 ]
do
    echo "Outer loop: $var1"
    var2=1
    while [ $var2 -lt 5 ]
    do
        var3=$(echo "scale=4; $var1 / $var2" | bc)
        echo "   Inner loop: $var1 / $var2 = $var3"
        var2=$[ $var2 + 1 ]
    done
    var1=$[ $var1 - 1 ]
done
$ ./test16
Outer loop: 3
    Inner loop: 3 / 1 = 3.0000
    Inner loop: 3 / 2 = 1.5000
    Inner loop: 3 / 3 = 1.0000
    Inner loop: 3 / 4 = .7500
Outer loop: 2
    Inner loop: 2 / 1 = 2.0000
    Inner loop: 2 / 2 = 1.0000
    Inner loop: 2 / 3 = .6666
    Inner loop: 2 / 4 = .5000
Outer loop: 1
    Inner loop: 1 / 1 = 1.0000
    Inner loop: 1 / 2 = .5000
    Inner loop: 1 / 3 = .3333
    Inner loop: 1 / 4 = .2500
$
```

13

The outer until loop starts with a value of 3 and continues until the value equals 0. The inner while loop starts with a value of 1 and continues as long as the value is less than 5. Each loop must change the value used in the test condition, or the loop will get stuck infinitely.

## Looping on File Data

Often, you must iterate through items stored inside a file. This requires combining two of the techniques covered:

- Using nested loops
- Changing the IFS environment variable

By changing the IFS environment variable, you can force the for command to handle each line in the file as a separate item for processing, even if the data contains spaces. After you've extracted an individual line in the file, you may have to loop again to extract data contained within it.

The classic example of this is processing data in the /etc/passwd file. This requires that you iterate through the /etc/passwd file line by line and then change the IFS variable value to a colon so that you can separate the individual components in each line.

The following is an example of doing just that:

```
#!/bin/bash
# changing the IFS value

IFS.OLD=$IFS
IFS=$'\n'
for entry in $(cat /etc/passwd)
do
    echo "Values in $entry -"
    IFS=:
    for value in $entry
    do
        echo "    $value"
    done
done
$
```

This script uses two different IFS values to parse the data. The first IFS value parses the individual lines in the /etc/passwd file. The inner for loop next changes the IFS value to the colon, which allows you to parse the individual values within the /etc/passwd lines.

When you run this script, you get output something like this:

```
Values in rich:x:501:501:Rich Blum:/home/rich:/bin/bash -
    rich
    x
    501
    501
    Rich Blum
    /home/rich
    /bin/bash
```

```
Values in katie:x:502:502:Katie Blum:/home/katie:/bin/bash -
    katie
    x
    502
    502
    Katie Blum
    /home/katie
    /bin/bash
```

The inner loop parses each individual value in the /etc/passwd entry. This is also a great way to process comma-separated data, a common way to import spreadsheet data.

# Controlling the Loop

You might be tempted to think that after you start a loop, you're stuck until the loop finishes all its iterations. This is not true. A couple of commands help us control what happens inside a loop:

- The break command
- The continue command

Each command has a different use in controlling the operation of a loop. The following sections describe how you can use these commands to control the operation of your loops.

## The *break* command

The break command is a simple way to escape a loop in progress. You can use the break command to exit any type of loop, including while and until loops.

You can use the break command in several situations. This section shows each of these methods.

### Breaking out of a single loop

When the shell executes a break command, it attempts to break out of the loop that's currently processing:

```
$ cat test17
#!/bin/bash
# breaking out of a for loop

for var1 in 1 2 3 4 5 6 7 8 9 10
do
    if [ $var1 -eq 5 ]
    then
        break
    fi
    echo "Iteration number: $var1"
```

*(Continues)*

(continued)

```
      done
      echo "The for loop is completed"
$ ./test17
Iteration number: 1
Iteration number: 2
Iteration number: 3
Iteration number: 4
The for loop is completed
$
```

The for loop should normally have iterated through all the values specified in the list. However, when the if-then condition was satisfied, the shell executed the break command, which stopped the for loop.

This technique also works for while and until loops:

```
$ cat test18
#!/bin/bash
# breaking out of a while loop

var1=1

while [ $var1 -lt 10 ]
do
    if [ $var1 -eq 5 ]
    then
        break
    fi
    echo "Iteration: $var1"
    var1=$[ $var1 + 1 ]
done
echo "The while loop is completed"
$ ./test18
Iteration: 1
Iteration: 2
Iteration: 3
Iteration: 4
The while loop is completed
$
```

The while loop terminated when the if-then condition was met, executing the break command.

### Breaking out of an inner loop

When you're working with multiple loops, the break command automatically terminates the innermost loop you're in:

```
$ cat test19
#!/bin/bash
# breaking out of an inner loop
```

```
for (( a = 1; a < 4; a++ ))
do
   echo "Outer loop: $a"
   for (( b = 1; b < 100; b++ ))
   do
      if [ $b -eq 5 ]
      then
         break
      fi
      echo "   Inner loop: $b"
   done
done
$ ./test19
Outer loop: 1
   Inner loop: 1
   Inner loop: 2
   Inner loop: 3
   Inner loop: 4
Outer loop: 2
   Inner loop: 1
   Inner loop: 2
   Inner loop: 3
   Inner loop: 4
Outer loop: 3
   Inner loop: 1
   Inner loop: 2
   Inner loop: 3
   Inner loop: 4
$
```

13

The for statement in the inner loop specifies to iterate until the b variable is equal to 100. However, the if-then statement in the inner loop specifies that when the b variable value is equal to 5, the break command is executed. Notice that even though the inner loop is terminated with the break command, the outer loop continues working as specified.

### Breaking out of an outer loop

There may be times when you're in an inner loop but need to stop the outer loop. The break command includes a single command-line parameter value:

```
break n
```

where n indicates the level of the loop to break out of. By default, n is 1, indicating to break out of the current loop. If you set n to a value of 2, the break command stops the next level of the outer loop:

```
$ cat test20
#!/bin/bash
# breaking out of an outer loop
```

*(Continues)*

*(continued)*

```
      for (( a = 1; a < 4; a++ ))
      do
          echo "Outer loop: $a"
          for (( b = 1; b < 100; b++ ))
          do
              if [ $b -gt 4 ]
              then
                  break 2
              fi
              echo "    Inner loop: $b"
          done
      done
$ ./test20
Outer loop: 1
    Inner loop: 1
    Inner loop: 2
    Inner loop: 3
    Inner loop: 4
$
```

Now when the shell executes the break command, the outer loop stops.

## The *continue* command

The continue command is a way to prematurely stop processing commands inside of a loop but not terminate the loop completely. This allows you to set conditions within a loop where the shell won't execute commands. Here's a simple example of using the continue command in a for loop:

```
$ cat test21
#!/bin/bash
# using the continue command

for (( var1 = 1; var1 < 15; var1++ ))
do
    if [ $var1 -gt 5 ] && [ $var1 -lt 10 ]
    then
        continue
    fi
    echo "Iteration number: $var1"
done
$ ./test21
Iteration number: 1
Iteration number: 2
Iteration number: 3
Iteration number: 4
Iteration number: 5
Iteration number: 10
Iteration number: 11
Iteration number: 12
```

```
Iteration number: 13
Iteration number: 14
$
```

When the conditions of the `if-then` statement are met (the value is greater than 5 and less than 10), the shell executes the `continue` command, which skips the rest of the commands in the loop but keeps the loop going. When the `if-then` condition is no longer met, things return to normal.

You can use the `continue` command in `while` and `until` loops, but be extremely careful with what you're doing. Remember that when the shell executes the `continue` command, it skips the remaining commands. If you're incrementing your test condition variable in one of those conditions, bad things happen:

```
$ cat badtest3
#!/bin/bash
# improperly using the continue command in a while loop

var1=0

while echo "while iteration: $var1"
      [ $var1 -lt 15 ]
do
   if [ $var1 -gt 5 ] && [ $var1 -lt 10 ]
   then
      continue
   fi
   echo "   Inside iteration number: $var1"
   var1=$[ $var1 + 1 ]
done
$ ./badtest3 | more
while iteration: 0
   Inside iteration number: 0
while iteration: 1
   Inside iteration number: 1
while iteration: 2
   Inside iteration number: 2
while iteration: 3
   Inside iteration number: 3
while iteration: 4
   Inside iteration number: 4
while iteration: 5
   Inside iteration number: 5
while iteration: 6
while iteration: 6
while iteration: 6
while iteration: 6
while iteration: 6
while iteration: 6
```

*(Continues)*

*(continued)*

```
    while iteration: 6
    while iteration: 6
    while iteration: 6
    while iteration: 6
    while iteration: 6
    $
```

You'll want to make sure you redirect the output of this script to the more command so that you can stop things. Everything seems to be going just fine until the if-then condition is met and the shell executes the continue command. When the shell executes the continue command, it skips the remaining commands in the while loop. Unfortunately, that's where the $var1 counter variable that is tested in the while test command is incremented. That means that the variable isn't incremented, as you can see from the continually displaying output.

As with the break command, the continue command allows you to specify what level of loop to continue with a command-line parameter:

```
continue n
```

where *n* defines the loop level to continue. Here's an example of continuing an outer for loop:

```
$ cat test22
#!/bin/bash
# continuing an outer loop

for (( a = 1; a <= 5; a++ ))
do
    echo "Iteration $a:"
    for (( b = 1; b < 3; b++ ))
    do
        if [ $a -gt 2 ] && [ $a -lt 4 ]
        then
            continue 2
        fi
        var3=$[ $a * $b ]
        echo "   The result of $a * $b is $var3"
    done
done
$ ./test22
Iteration 1:
    The result of 1 * 1 is 1
    The result of 1 * 2 is 2
Iteration 2:
    The result of 2 * 1 is 2
    The result of 2 * 2 is 4
Iteration 3:
Iteration 4:
    The result of 4 * 1 is 4
```

```
    The result of 4 * 2 is 8
Iteration 5:
    The result of 5 * 1 is 5
    The result of 5 * 2 is 10
$
```

The if-then statement

```
if [ $a -gt 2 ] && [ $a -lt 4 ]
then
    continue 2
fi
```

uses the continue command to stop processing the commands inside the loop but continue the outer loop. Notice in the script output that the iteration for the value 3 doesn't process any inner loop statements because the continue command stopped the processing, but it continues with the outer loop processing.

## Processing the Output of a Loop

Finally, you can either pipe or redirect the output of a loop within your shell script. You do this by adding the processing command to the end of the done command:

```
for file in /home/rich/*
do
   if [ -d "$file" ]
   then
       echo "$file is a directory"
   elif
       echo "$file is a file"
   fi
done > output.txt
```

Instead of displaying the results on the monitor, the shell redirects the results of the for command to the file output.txt.

Consider the following example of redirecting the output of a for command to a file:

```
$ cat test23
#!/bin/bash
# redirecting the for output to a file

for (( a = 1; a < 10; a++ ))
do
    echo "The number is $a"
done > test23.txt
echo "The command is finished."
$ ./test23
The command is finished.
```

*(Continues)*

*(continued)*

```
$ cat test23.txt
The number is 1
The number is 2
The number is 3
The number is 4
The number is 5
The number is 6
The number is 7
The number is 8
The number is 9
$
```

The shell creates the file `test23.txt` and redirects the output of the `for` command only to the file. The shell displays the `echo` statement after the `for` command as usual.

The same technique also works for piping the output of a loop to another command:

```
$ cat test24
#!/bin/bash
# piping a loop to another command

for state in "North Dakota" Connecticut Illinois Alabama Tennessee
do
    echo "$state is the next place to go"
done | sort
echo "This completes our travels"
$ ./test24
Alabama is the next place to go
Connecticut is the next place to go
Illinois is the next place to go
North Dakota is the next place to go
Tennessee is the next place to go
This completes our travels
$
```

The state values aren't listed in any particular order in the `for` command list. The output of the `for` command is piped to the `sort` command, which changes the order of the `for` command output. Running the script indeed shows that the output was properly sorted within the script.

# Working through a Few Practical Examples

Now that you've seen how to use the different ways to create loops in shell scripts, let's look at some practical examples of how to use them. Looping is a common way to iterate through data on the system, whether it's files in folders or data contained in a file. Here are a couple of examples that demonstrate using simple loops to work with data.

## Finding executable files

When you run a program from the command line, the Linux system searches a series of folders looking for that file. Those folders are defined in the PATH environment variable. If you want to find out what executable files are available on your system for you to use, just scan all the folders in the PATH environment variable. That may take some time to do manually, but it's a breeze working out a small shell script to do that.

The first step is to create a for loop to iterate through the folders stored in the PATH environment variable. When you do that, don't forget to set the IFS separator character:

```
IFS=:
for folder in $PATH
do
```

Now that you have the individual folders in the $folder variable, you can use another for loop to iterate through all the files inside that particular folder:

```
for file in $folder/*
do
```

The last step is to check whether the individual files have the executable permission set, which you can do using the if-then test feature:

```
if [ -x $file ]
then
    echo "    $file"
fi
```

And there you have it! Putting all the pieces together into a script looks like this:

```
$ cat test25
#!/bin/bash
# finding files in the PATH

IFS=:
for folder in $PATH
do
    echo "$folder:"
    for file in $folder/*
    do
        if [ -x $file ]
        then
            echo "    $file"
        fi
    done
done
$
```

When you run the code, you get a listing of the executable files that you can use from the command line:

```
$ ./test25 | more
/usr/local/bin:
/usr/bin:
    /usr/bin/Mail
    /usr/bin/Thunar
    /usr/bin/X
    /usr/bin/Xorg
    /usr/bin/[
    /usr/bin/a2p
    /usr/bin/abiword
    /usr/bin/ac
    /usr/bin/activation-client
    /usr/bin/addr2line
...
```

The output shows all the executable files found in all the folders defined in the PATH environment variable, which is quite a few!

## Creating multiple user accounts

The goal of shell scripts is to make life easier for the system administrator. If you happen to work in an environment with lots of users, one of the most boring tasks can be creating new user accounts. Fortunately, you can use the while loop to make your job a little easier.

Instead of having to manually enter useradd commands for every new user account you need to create, you can place the new user accounts in a text file and create a simple shell script to do that work for you. The format of the text file we'll use looks like this:

```
loginname, name
```

The first entry is the login name you want to use for the new user account. The second entry is the full name of the user. The two values are separated by a comma, making this a comma-separated values (CSV) file format. This is a very common file format used in spreadsheets, so you can easily create the user account list in a spreadsheet program and save it in CSV format for your shell script to read and process.

To read the file data, we're going to use a little shell scripting trick. We'll set the IFS separator character to a comma as the test part of the while statement. Then to read the individual lines, we'll use the read command. That looks like this:

```
while IFS=',' read -r userid name
```

The read command does the work of moving on to the next line of text in the CSV text file, so we don't need another loop to do that. The while command exits when the read command returns a FALSE value, which happens when it runs out of lines to read in the file. Tricky!

To feed the data from the file into the while command, you just use a redirection symbol at the end of the while command.

Putting everything together results in this script:

```
$ cat test26
#!/bin/bash
# process new user accounts

input="users.csv"
while IFS=',' read -r loginname name
do
   echo "adding $loginname"
   useradd -c "$name" -m $loginname
done < "$input"
$
```

The $input variable points to the data file and is used as the redirect data for the while command. The users.csv file looks like this:

```
$ cat users.csv
rich,Richard Blum
christine,Christine Bresnahan
barbara,Barbara Blum
tim,Timothy Bresnahan
$
```

To run the program, you must be the root user account, because the useradd command requires root privileges:

```
# ./test26
adding rich
adding christine
adding barbara
adding tim
#
```

Then, by taking a quick look at the /etc/passwd file, you can see that the accounts have been created:

```
# tail /etc/passwd
rich:x:1001:1001:Richard Blum:/home/rich:/bin/bash
christine:x:1002:1002:Christine Bresnahan:/home/christine:/bin/bash
barbara:x:1003:1003:Barbara Blum:/home/barbara:/bin/bash
tim:x:1004:1004:Timothy Bresnahan:/home/tim:/bin/bash
#
```

Congratulations, you've saved yourself lots of time in adding user accounts!

# Summary

Looping is an integral part of programming. The Bash shell provides three looping commands that you can use in your scripts.

The `for` command allows you to iterate through a list of values — supplied within the command line, contained in a variable, or obtained by using file globbing — to extract file and directory names from a wildcard character.

The `while` command provides a method to loop based on the condition of a command, using either ordinary commands or the `test` command, which allows you to test conditions of variables. As long as the command (or condition) produces a zero exit status, the `while` loop continues to iterate through the specified set of commands.

The `until` command also provides a method to iterate through commands, but it bases its iterations on a command (or condition) producing a non-zero exit status. This feature allows you to set a condition that must be met before the iteration stops.

You can combine loops in shell scripts, producing multiple layers of loops. The Bash shell provides the `continue` and `break` commands, which allow you to alter the flow of the normal loop process based on different values within the loop.

The Bash shell also allows you to use standard command redirection and piping to alter the output of a loop. You can use redirection to redirect the output of a loop to a file or piping to redirect the output of a loop to another command. This provides a wealth of features with which you can control your shell script execution.

The next chapter explores how to interact with your shell script user. Often, shell scripts aren't completely self-contained. They require some sort of external data that must be supplied at the time you run them. The next chapter discusses different methods with which you can provide real-time data to your shell scripts for processing.

# Handling User Input

S o far you've seen how to write scripts that interact with data, variables, and files on the Linux system. Sometimes, you need to write a script that has to interact with the person running the script. The Bash shell provides a few different methods for retrieving data from people, including command-line parameters (data values added after the command), command-line options (single-letter values that modify the behavior of the command), and the capability to read input directly from the keyboard. This chapter discusses how to incorporate these various methods into your Bash shell scripts to obtain data from the person running your script.

## Passing Parameters

The most basic method of passing data to your shell script is to use *command-line parameters*. Command-line parameters allow you to add data values to the command line when you execute the script:

```
$ ./addem 10 30
```

This example passes two command-line parameters (10 and 30) to the script addem. The script handles the command-line parameters using special variables. The following sections describe how to use command-line parameters in your Bash shell scripts.

### Reading parameters

The Bash shell assigns special variables, called *positional parameters*, to all of the command-line parameters entered. This includes the name of the script the shell is executing. The positional parameter variables are standard numbers, with $0 being the script's name, $1 being the first parameter, $2 being the second parameter, and so on, up to $9 for the ninth parameter.

Here's a simple example of using one command-line parameter in a shell script:

```
$ cat positional1.sh
#!/bin/bash
# Using one command-line parameter
#
factorial=1
for (( number = 1; number <= $1; number++ ))
do
        factorial=$[ $factorial * $number ]
done
echo The factorial of $1 is $factorial
exit
$
$ ./positional1.sh 5
The factorial of 5 is 120
$
```

You can use the $1 variable just like any other variable in the shell script. The shell script automatically assigns the value from the command-line parameter to the variable, so you don't need to do anything special.

If you want to enter more command-line parameters for your script, each parameter must be separated by a space on the command line. And the shell assigns each parameter to the appropriate variable:

```
$ cat positional2.sh
#!/bin/bash
# Using two command-line parameters
#
product=$[ $1 * $2 ]
echo The first parameter is $1.
echo The second parameter is $2.
echo The product value is $product.
exit
$
$ ./positional2.sh 2 5
The first parameter is 2.
The second parameter is 5.
The product value is 10.
$
```

In the preceding example, the command-line parameters used were both numerical values. You can also use text strings as parameters:

```
$ cat stringparam.sh
#!/bin/bash
# Using one command-line string parameter
```

```
#
echo Hello $1, glad to meet you.
exit
$
$ ./stringparam.sh world
Hello world, glad to meet you.
$
```

The shell passes the string value entered into the command line to the script. However, you'll have a problem if you try to do this with a text string that contains spaces:

```
$ ./stringparam.sh big world
Hello big, glad to meet you.
$
```

Remember that the parameters are separated by spaces, so the shell interpreted the space as just separating the two values. To include a space as a parameter value, you must use quotation marks (either single or double quotation marks):

```
$ ./stringparam.sh 'big world'
Hello big world, glad to meet you.
$
$ ./stringparam.sh "big world"
Hello big world, glad to meet you.
$
```

> **NOTE**
>
> The quotation marks used when you pass text strings as parameters are not part of the data. They just delineate the beginning and the end of the data.

If your script needs more than nine command-line parameters, you can continue, but the variable names change slightly. After the ninth variable, you must use braces around the variable number, such as ${10}. Here's an example of doing that:

```
$ cat positional10.sh
#!/bin/bash
# Handling lots of command-line parameters
#
product=$[ ${10} * ${11} ]
echo The tenth parameter is ${10}.
echo The eleventh parameter is ${11}.
echo The product value is $product.
exit
$
$ ./positional10.sh 1 2 3 4 5 6 7 8 9 10 11 12
The tenth parameter is 10.
The eleventh parameter is 11.
The product value is 110.
$
```

14

This technique allows you to add as many command-line parameters to your scripts as you could possibly need.

## Reading the script name

You can use the $0 parameter to determine the script name the shell started from the command line. This can come in handy if you're writing a utility that has multiple functions or that produces log messages.

```
$ cat positional0.sh
#!/bin/bash
# Handling the $0 command-line parameter
#
echo This script name is $0.
exit
$
$ bash positional0.sh
This script name is positional0.sh.
$
```

However, there is a potential problem. When using a different command to run the shell script, the command becomes entangled with the script name in the $0 parameter:

```
$ ./positional0.sh
This script name is ./positional0.sh.
$
```

An additional issue occurs when the actual string passed is the full script path, and not just the script's name. In this case, the $0 variable gets set to the full script path and name:

```
$ $HOME/scripts/positional0.sh
This script name is /home/christine/scripts/positional0.sh.
$
```

If you want to write a script that only uses the script's name, you'll have to do a little work in order to strip off whatever path is used to run the script or any entangled commands. Fortunately, there's a handy little command available that does just that. The basename command returns just the script's name without the path:

```
$ cat posbasename.sh
#!/bin/bash
# Using basename with the $0 command-line parameter
#
name=$(basename $0)
#
echo This script name is $name.
exit
$
$ ./posbasename.sh
This script name is posbasename.sh.
$
```

Now that's much better. You can use this technique to write a script that produces log messages identifying when it ran:

```
$ cat checksystem.sh
#!/bin/bash
# Using the $0 command-line parameter in messages
#
scriptname=$(basename $0)
#
echo The $scriptname ran at $(date) >> $HOME/scripttrack.log
exit
$
$ ./checksystem.sh
$ cat $HOME/scripttrack.log
The checksystem.sh ran at Thu 04 Jun 2020 10:01:53 AM EDT
$
```

Having a script that identifies itself is useful for tracking down script problems, auditing the system, and producing log messages.

## Testing parameters

Be careful when using command-line parameters in your shell scripts. If the script is run without the needed parameters, bad things can happen:

```
$ ./positional1.sh
./positional1.sh: line 5: ((: number <= : syntax error:
operand expected (error token is "<= ")
The factorial of is 1
$
```

When the script assumes there is data in a parameter variable and no data is present, most likely you'll get an error message from your script. This is a poor way to write scripts. Always check your parameters to make sure the data is there before using it:

```
$ cat checkpositional1.sh
#!/bin/bash
# Using one command-line parameter
#
if [ -n "$1" ]
then
      factorial=1
      for (( number = 1; number <= $1; number++ ))
      do
            factorial=$[ $factorial * $number ]
      done
      echo The factorial of $1 is $factorial
else
      echo "You did not provide a parameter."
```

14

```
fi
exit
$
$ ./checkpositional1.sh
You did not provide a parameter.
$
$ ./checkpositional1.sh 3
The factorial of 3 is 6
$
```

In this example, the -n test evaluation was used to check for data in the $1 command-line parameter. In the next section, you'll learn another way to check command-line parameters.

# Using Special Parameter Variables

A few special Bash shell variables track command-line parameters. This section describes what they are and how to use them.

## Counting parameters

As you saw in the last section, you should verify command-line parameters before using them in your script. For scripts that use multiple command-line parameters, this checking can get tedious.

Instead of testing each parameter, you can count how many parameters were entered on the command line. The Bash shell provides a special variable for this purpose.

The $# variable contains the number of command-line parameters included when the script was run. You can use this special variable anywhere in the script, just like a normal variable:

```
$ cat countparameters.sh
#!/bin/bash
# Counting command-line parameters
#
if [ $# -eq 1 ]
then
    fragment="parameter was"
else
    fragment="parameters were"
fi
echo $# $fragment supplied.
exit
$
$ ./countparameters.sh
0 parameters were supplied.
$
$ ./countparameters.sh Hello
```

```
1 parameter was supplied.
$
$ ./countparameters.sh Hello World
2 parameters were supplied.
$

$ ./countparameters.sh "Hello World"
1 parameter was supplied.
$
```

Now you have the ability to test the number of parameters present before trying to use them:

```
$ cat addem.sh
#!/bin/bash
# Adding command-line parameters
#
if [ $# -ne 2 ]
then
     echo Usage: $(basename $0) parameter1 parameter2
else
     total=$[ $1 + $2 ]
     echo $1 + $2 is $total
fi
exit
$
$ ./addem.sh
Usage: addem.sh parameter1 parameter2
$
$ ./addem.sh 17
Usage: addem.sh parameter1 parameter2
$
$ ./addem.sh 17 25
17 + 25 is 42
$
```

The if-then statement uses the -ne evaluation to perform a numeric test of the command-line parameters supplied. If the correct number of parameters isn't present, an error message displays showing the correct usage of the script.

This variable also provides a cool way of grabbing the last parameter on the command line without having to know how many parameters were used. However, you need to use a little trick to get there.

If you think this through, you might think that because the $# variable contains the value of the number of parameters, using the variable ${$#} would represent the last command-line parameter variable. Try that and see what happens:

```
$ cat badlastparamtest.sh
#!/bin/bash
# Testing grabbing the last parameter
```

*(Continues)*

*(continued)*

```
#
echo The number of parameters is $#
echo The last parameter is ${$#}
exit
$
$ ./badlastparamtest.sh one two three four
The number of parameters is 4
The last parameter is 2648
$
```

Obviously, something went wrong. It turns out that you can't use the dollar sign within the braces. Instead, you must replace the dollar sign with an exclamation mark. Odd, but it works:

```
$ cat goodlastparamtest.sh
#!/bin/bash
# Testing grabbing the last parameter
#
echo The number of parameters is $#
echo The last parameter is ${!#}
exit
$
$ ./goodlastparamtest.sh one two three four
The number of parameters is 4
The last parameter is four
$
$ ./goodlastparamtest.sh
The number of parameters is 0
The last parameter is ./goodlastparamtest.sh
$
```

Perfect. It's important to notice that, when there weren't any parameters on the command line, the $# value was 0, but the ${!#} variable returns the script name used on the command line.

## Grabbing all the data

In some situations you want to grab all the parameters provided on the command line. Instead of having to mess with using the $# variable to determine how many parameters are on the command line and having to loop through them all, you can use a couple of other special variables.

The $* and $@ variables provide easy access to all your parameters. Both of these variables include all the command-line parameters within a single variable.

The $* variable takes all the parameters supplied on the command line as a single word. The word contains each of the values as they appear on the command line. Basically, instead of treating the parameters as multiple objects, the $* variable treats them all as one parameter.

The $@ variable, on the other hand, takes all the parameters supplied on the command line as separate words in the same string. It allows you to iterate through the values, separating out each parameter supplied. This is most often accomplished using a for loop.

It can easily get confusing trying to figure out how these two variables operate. Let's look at the difference between the two:

```
$ cat grabbingallparams.sh
#!/bin/bash
# Testing different methods for grabbing all the parameters
#
echo
echo "Using the \$* method: $*"
echo
echo "Using the \$@ method: $@"
echo
exit
$
$ ./grabbingallparams.sh alpha beta charlie delta

Using the $* method: alpha beta charlie delta

Using the $@ method: alpha beta charlie delta

$
```

Notice that on the surface, both variables produce the same output, showing all the command-line parameters provided at once. The following example demonstrates where the differences are:

```
$ cat grabdisplayallparams.sh
#!/bin/bash
# Exploring different methods for grabbing all the parameters
#
echo
echo "Using the \$* method: $*"
count=1
for param in "$*"
do
      echo "\$* Parameter #$count = $param"
      count=$[ $count + 1 ]
done
#
echo
echo "Using the \$@ method: $@"
count=1
for param in "$@"
do
      echo "\$@ Parameter #$count = $param"
      count=$[ $count + 1 ]
```

*(Continues)*

```
(continued)
      done
      echo
      exit
      $
      $ ./grabdisplayallparams.sh alpha beta charlie delta

      Using the $* method: alpha beta charlie delta
      $* Parameter #1 = alpha beta charlie delta

      Using the $@ method: alpha beta charlie delta
      $@ Parameter #1 = alpha
      $@ Parameter #2 = beta
      $@ Parameter #3 = charlie
      $@ Parameter #4 = delta

      $
```

Now we're getting somewhere. By using the for command to iterate through the special variables, you can see how they each treat the command-line parameters differently. The $* variable treated all the parameters as a single parameter, whereas the $@ variable treated each parameter separately. This is a great way to iterate through command-line parameters.

# Being Shifty

Another tool you have in your Bash shell tool belt is the shift command. The Bash shell provides the shift command to help you manipulate command-line parameters. The shift command literally shifts the command-line parameters in their relative positions.

When you use the shift command, it moves each parameter variable one position to the left by default. Thus, the value for variable $3 is moved to $2, the value for variable $2 is moved to $1, and the value for variable $1 is discarded (note that the value for variable $0, the program name, remains unchanged).

This is another great way to iterate through command-line parameters. You can just operate on the first parameter, shift the parameters over, and then operate on the first parameter again.

Here's a short demonstration of how this works:

```
$ cat shiftparams.sh
#!/bin/bash
# Shifting through the parameters
#
echo
echo "Using the shift method:"
count=1
while [ -n "$1" ]
do
```

```
        echo "Parameter #$count = $1"
        count=$[ $count + 1 ]
        shift
done
echo
exit
$
$ ./shiftparams.sh alpha bravo charlie delta

Using the shift method:
Parameter #1 = alpha
Parameter #2 = bravo
Parameter #3 = charlie
Parameter #4 = delta

$
```

The script performs a while loop, testing the length of the first parameter's value. When the first parameter's length is 0, the loop ends. After testing the first parameter, the shift command is used to shift all the parameters one position.

> **NOTE**
>
> Be careful when working with the shift command. When a parameter is shifted out, its value is lost and can't be recovered.

Alternatively, you can perform a multiple location shift by providing a parameter to the shift command. Just provide the number of places you want to shift:

```
$ cat bigshiftparams.sh
#!/bin/bash
# Shifting multiple positions through the parameters
#
echo
echo "The original parameters: $*"
echo "Now shifting 2..."
shift 2
echo "Here's the new first parameter: $1"
echo
exit
$
$ ./bigshiftparams.sh alpha bravo charlie delta

The original parameters: alpha bravo charlie delta
Now shifting 2...
Here's the new first parameter: charlie

$
```

14

387

By using values in the `shift` command, you can easily skip over parameters you don't need in certain situations.

# Working with Options

If you've been following along in the book, you've seen several Bash commands that provide both parameters and options. *Options* are single letters preceded by a dash that alter the behavior of a command. This section shows three methods for working with options in your shell scripts.

## Finding your options

On the surface, there's nothing all that special about command-line options. They appear on the command line immediately after the script name, just the same as command-line parameters. In fact, if you want, you can process command-line options the same way you process command-line parameters.

### Processing simple options

In the `shiftparams.sh` script earlier, you saw how to use the `shift` command to work your way down the command-line parameters provided with the script program. You can use the same technique to process command-line options.

As you extract each individual parameter, use the `case` statement (see Chapter 12, "Using Structured Commands") to determine when a parameter is formatted as an option:

```
$ cat extractoptions.sh
#!/bin/bash
# Extract command-line options
#
echo
while [ -n "$1" ]
do
    case "$1" in
        -a) echo "Found the -a option" ;;
        -b) echo "Found the -b option" ;;
        -c) echo "Found the -c option" ;;
        *) echo "$1 is not an option" ;;
    esac
    shift
done
echo
exit
$
$ ./extractoptions.sh -a -b -c -d

Found the -a option
Found the -b option
```

```
Found the -c option
-d is not an option

$
```

The `case` statement checks each parameter for valid options. When one is found, the appropriate commands are run in the `case` statement.

This method works, no matter in what order the options are presented on the command line:

```
$ ./extractoptions.sh -d -c -a

-d is not an option
Found the -c option
Found the -a option

$
```

The `case` statement processes each option as it finds it in the command-line parameters. If any other parameters are included on the command line, you can include commands in the catch-all part of the `case` statement to process them.

### Separating options from parameters

Often you'll run into situations where you'll want to use both options and parameters for a shell script. The standard way to do this in Linux is to separate the two with a special character code that tells the script when the options are finished and when the normal parameters start.

For Linux, this special character is the double dash (--). The shell uses the double dash to indicate the end of the option list. After seeing the double dash, your script can safely process the remaining command-line parameters as parameters and not options.

To check for the double dash, simply add another entry in the `case` statement:

```
$ cat extractoptionsparams.sh
#!/bin/bash
# Extract command-line options and parameters
#
echo
while [ -n "$1" ]
do
      case "$1" in
            -a) echo "Found the -a option" ;;
            -b) echo "Found the -b option" ;;
            -c) echo "Found the -c option" ;;
            --) shift
                break;;
            *) echo "$1 is not an option" ;;
```

14

*(Continues)*

*(continued)*

```
        esac
        shift
done
#
echo
count=1
for param in $@
do
        echo "Parameter #$count: $param"
        count=$[ $count + 1 ]
done
echo
exit
$
```

This script uses the break command to break out of the while loop when it encounters the double dash. Because we're breaking out prematurely, we need to ensure that we stick in another shift command to get the double dash out of the parameter variables.

For the first test, try running the script using a normal set of options and parameters:

```
$ ./extractoptionsparams.sh -a -b -c test1 test2 test3

Found the -a option
Found the -b option
Found the -c option
test1 is not an option
test2 is not an option
test3 is not an option

$
```

The results show that the script assumed that all the command-line parameters were options when it processed them. Next, try the same thing, only this time using the double dash to separate the options from the parameters on the command line:

```
$ ./extractoptionsparams.sh -a -b -c -- test1 test2 test3

Found the -a option
Found the -b option
Found the -c option

Parameter #1: test1
Parameter #2: test2
Parameter #3: test3

$
```

When the script reaches the double dash, it stops processing options and assumes that any remaining parameters are command-line parameters.

### Processing options with values

Some options require an additional parameter value. In these situations, the command line looks something like this:

```
$ ./testing.sh -a test1 -b -c -d test2
```

Your script must be able to detect when your command-line option requires an additional parameter and be able to process it appropriately. Here's an example of how to do that:

```
$ cat extractoptionsvalues.sh
#!/bin/bash
# Extract command-line options and values
#
echo
while [ -n "$1" ]
do
      case "$1" in
            -a) echo "Found the -a option" ;;
            -b) param=$2
                echo "Found the -b option with parameter value $param"
                shift;;
            -c) echo "Found the -c option" ;;
            --) shift
                break;;
            *) echo "$1 is not an option" ;;
      esac
      shift
done
#
echo
count=1
for param in $@
do
      echo "Parameter #$count: $param"
      count=$[ $count + 1 ]
done
exit
$
$ ./extractoptionsvalues.sh -a -b BValue -d

Found the -a option
Found the -b option with parameter value BValue
-d is not an option
$
```

In this example, the case statement defines three options that it processes. The -b option also requires an additional parameter value. Because the parameter being processed is $1, you know that the additional parameter value is located in $2 (because all the parameters are shifted after they are processed). Just extract the parameter value from

the $2 variable. Of course, because we used two parameter spots for this option, you also
need to run the shift command to shift one additional position.

Just as with the basic feature, this process works no matter what order you place the
options in (just remember to include the appropriate option parameter with each option):

```
$ ./extractoptionsvalues.sh -c -d -b BValue -a

Found the -c option
-d is not an option
Found the -b option with parameter value BValue
Found the -a option
$
```

Now you have the basic ability to process command-line options in your shell scripts, but
there are limitations. For example, this doesn't work if you try to combine multiple options
in one parameter:

```
$ ./extractoptionsvalues.sh -ac

-ac is not an option
$
```

It is a common practice in Linux to combine options, and if your script is going to be user-
friendly, you'll want to offer this feature for your users as well. Fortunately, there's another
method for processing options that can help you.

## Using the *getopt* command

The getopt command is a great tool to have handy when processing command-line options
and parameters. It reorganizes the command-line parameters to make parsing them in your
script easier.

### Looking at the command format

The getopt command can take a list of command-line options and parameters, in
any form, and automatically turn them into the proper format. It uses the following
command format:

```
getopt optstring parameters
```

The *optstring* is the key to the process. It defines the valid option letters that can be
used in the command line. It also defines which option letters require a parameter value.

First, list each command-line option letter you're going to use in your script in the
*optstring*. Then place a colon after each option letter that requires a parameter value.
The getopt command parses the supplied parameters based on the *optstring*
you define.

Here's a simple example of how getopt works:

```
$ getopt ab:cd -a -b BValue -cd test1 test2
 -a -b BValue -c -d -- test1 test2
$
```

The *optstring* defines four valid option letters: a, b, c, and d. A colon (:) is placed after the letter b in order to require option b to have a parameter value. When the getopt command runs, it examines the provided parameter list (-a -b BValue -cd test2 test3) and parses it based on the supplied *optstring*. Notice that it automatically separated the -cd options into two options and inserted the double dash to separate the additional parameters on the line.

If you specify a parameter option not in the *optstring*, by default the getopt command produces an error message:

```
$ getopt ab:cd -a -b BValue -cde test1 test2
getopt: invalid option -- 'e'
 -a -b BValue -c -d -- test1 test2
$
```

If you prefer to just ignore the error messages, use getopt with the -q option:

```
$ getopt -q ab:cd -a -b BValue -cde test1 test2
 -a -b 'BValue' -c -d -- 'test1' 'test2'
$
```

Note that the getopt command options must be listed before the *optstring*. Now you should be ready to use this command in your scripts to process command-line options.

### Using *getopt* in your scripts

You can use the getopt command in your scripts to format any command-line options or parameters entered for your script. It's a little tricky, however, to use.

The trick is to replace the existing command-line options and parameters with the formatted version produced by the getopt command. The way to do that is to use the set command.

You saw the set command back in Chapter 6, "Using Linux Environment Variables." The set command works with the different variables in the shell.

One of the set command options is the double dash (--). The double dash instructs set to replace the command-line parameter variables with the values on the set command's command line.

14

The trick then is to feed the original script's command-line parameters to the getopt command and then feed the output of the getopt command to the set command to replace the original command-line parameters with the nicely formatted ones from getopt. It looks something like this:

```
set -- $(getopt -q ab:cd "$@")
```

Now the values of the original command-line parameter variables are replaced with the output from the getopt command, which formats the command-line parameters for us.

Using this technique, we can now write scripts that handle our command-line parameters for us:

```
$ cat extractwithgetopt.sh
#!/bin/bash
# Extract command-line options and values with getopt
#
set -- $(getopt -q ab:cd "$@")
#
echo
while [ -n "$1" ]
do
      case "$1" in
            -a) echo "Found the -a option" ;;
            -b) param=$2
                echo "Found the -b option with parameter value $param"
                shift;;
            -c) echo "Found the -c option" ;;
            --) shift
                break;;
            *) echo "$1 is not an option" ;;
      esac
      shift
done
#
echo
count=1
for param in $@
do
      echo "Parameter #$count: $param"
      count=$[ $count + 1 ]
done
exit
$
```

You'll notice that this is basically the same script as in extractoptionsvalues.sh. The only thing that changed is the addition of the getopt command to help format our command-line parameters.

Now when you run the script with complex options, things work much better:

```
$ ./extractwithgetopt.sh -ac

Found the -a option
Found the -c option
$
```

And of course, all the original features work just fine as well:

```
$ ./extractwithgetopt.sh -c -d -b BValue -a test1 test2

Found the -c option
-d is not an option
Found the -b option with parameter value 'BValue'
Found the -a option

Parameter #1: 'test1'
Parameter #2: 'test2'
$
```

Now things are looking pretty fancy. However, there's still one small bug that lurks in the `getopt` command. Check out this example:

```
$ ./extractwithgetopt.sh -c -d -b BValue -a "test1 test2" test3

Found the -c option
-d is not an option
Found the -b option with parameter value 'BValue'
Found the -a option

Parameter #1: 'test1
Parameter #2: test2'
Parameter #3: 'test3'
$
```

The `getopt` command isn't good at dealing with parameter values with spaces and quotation marks. It interpreted the space as the parameter separator, instead of following the double quotation marks and combining the two values into one parameter. Fortunately, this problem has another solution.

## Advancing to *getopts*

The `getopts` command (notice that it is plural) is built into the Bash shell. It looks much like its `getopt` cousin but has some expanded features.

Unlike `getopt`, which produces one output for all the processed options and parameters found in the command line, the `getopts` command works on the existing shell parameter variables sequentially.

14

It processes the parameters it detects in the command line one at a time each time it's called. When it runs out of parameters, it exits with an exit status greater than zero. This makes it great for using in loops to parse all the parameters on the command line.

Here's the format of the getopts command:

```
getopts optstring variable
```

The *optstring* value is similar to the one used in the getopt command. Valid option letters are listed in the *optstring*, along with a colon if the option letter requires a parameter value. To suppress error messages, start the *optstring* with a colon. The getopts command places the current parameter in the *variable* defined in the command line.

The getopts command uses two environment variables. The OPTARG environment variable contains the value to be used if an option requires a parameter value. The OPTIND environment variable contains the value of the current location within the parameter list where getopts left off. This allows you to continue processing other command-line parameters after finishing the options.

Let's look at a simple example that uses the getopts command:

```
$ cat extractwithgetopts.sh
#!/bin/bash
# Extract command-line options and values with getopts
#
echo
while getopts :ab:c opt
do
      case "$opt" in
            a) echo "Found the -a option" ;;
            b) echo "Found the -b option with parameter value $OPTARG";;
            c) echo "Found the -c option" ;;
            *) echo "Unknown option: $opt" ;;
      esac
done
exit
$
$ ./extractwithgetopts.sh -ab BValue -c

Found the -a option
Found the -b option with parameter value BValue
Found the -c option
$
```

The while statement defines the getopts command, specifying what command-line options for which to look, along with the variable name (*opt*) to store them in for each iteration.

You'll notice something different about the case statement in this example. When the getopts command parses the command-line options, it strips off the leading dash, so you don't need leading dashes in the case definitions.

The getopts command offers several nice features. For starters, you can include spaces in your parameter values:

```
$ ./extractwithgetopts.sh -b "BValue1 BValue2" -a

Found the -b option with parameter value BValue1 BValue2
Found the -a option
$
```

Another nice feature is that you can run the option letter and the parameter value together without a space:

```
$ ./extractwithgetopts.sh -abBValue

Found the -a option
Found the -b option with parameter value BValue
$
```

The getopts command correctly parsed the BValue value from the -b option. In addition, the getopts command bundles any undefined option it finds in the command line into a single output, the question mark:

```
$ ./extractwithgetopts.sh -d

Unknown option: ?
$
$ ./extractwithgetopts.sh -ade

Found the -a option
Unknown option: ?
Unknown option: ?
$
```

Any option letter not defined in the *optstring* value is sent to your code as a question mark.

The getopts command knows when to stop processing options and leave the parameters for you to process. As getopts processes each option, it increments the OPTIND environment variable by 1. When you've reached the end of the getopts processing, you can use the OPTIND value with the shift command to move to the parameters:

```
$ cat extractoptsparamswithgetopts.sh
#!/bin/bash
# Extract command-line options and parameters with getopts
#
echo
```

14

*(Continues)*

```
(continued)
      while getopts :ab:cd opt
      do
           case "$opt" in
                a) echo "Found the -a option" ;;
                b) echo "Found the -b option with parameter value $OPTARG";;
                c) echo "Found the -c option" ;;
                d) echo "Found the -d option" ;;
                *) echo "Unknown option: $opt" ;;
           esac
      done
      #
      shift $[ $OPTIND - 1 ]
      #
      echo
      count=1
      for param in "$@"
      do
           echo "Parameter $count: $param"
           count=$[ $count + 1 ]
      done
      exit
$
$ ./extractoptsparamswithgetopts.sh -db BValue test1 test2

Found the -d option
Found the -b option with parameter value BValue

Parameter 1: test1
Parameter 2: test2
$
```

Now you have a full-featured command-line option and parameter processing utility you can use in all your shell scripts!

# Standardizing Options

When you create your shell script, obviously you're in control of what happens. It's completely up to you as to which letter options you select to use and how you select to use them.

However, a few letter options have achieved a somewhat standard meaning in the Linux world. If you leverage these options in a shell script, your scripts will be more user-friendly.

Table 14-1 shows some of the common meanings for command-line options used in Linux.

You'll probably recognize most of these option meanings just from working with the various bash commands throughout the book. Using the same meaning for your options helps users interact with your script without having to worry about determining what options to use when.

**TABLE 14-1** **Common Linux Command-Line Options**

| Option | Description |
|--------|-------------|
| -a | Shows all objects. |
| -c | Produces a count. |
| -d | Specifies a directory. |
| -e | Expands an object. |
| -f | Specifies a file to read data from. |
| -h | Displays a help message for the command. |
| -i | Ignores text case. |
| -l | Produces a long format version of the output. |
| -n | Uses a non-interactive (batch) mode. |
| -o | Specifies a file to which all output is redirected. |
| -q | Runs in quiet mode. |
| -r | Processes directories and files recursively. |
| -s | Runs in silent mode. |
| -v | Produces verbose output. |
| -x | Excludes an object. |
| -y | Answers yes to all questions. |

# Getting User Input

Although providing command-line options and parameters is a great way to get data from your script users, sometimes your script needs to be more interactive. You may need to ask a question while the script is running, and wait for a response from the person running your script. The Bash shell provides the read command just for this purpose.

## Reading basics

The read command accepts input either from standard input (such as from the keyboard) or from another file descriptor. After receiving the input, the read command places the data into a variable. Here's the read command at its simplest:

```
$ cat askname.sh
#!/bin/bash
# Using the read command
#
echo -n "Enter your name: "
read name
echo "Hello $name, welcome to my script."
exit
```

*(Continues)*

*(continued)*

```
$
$ ./askname.sh
Enter your name: Richard Blum
Hello Richard Blum, welcome to my script.
$
```

That's pretty simple. Notice that the echo command that produced the prompt uses the -n option. This suppresses the newline character at the end of the string, allowing the script user to enter data immediately after the string, instead of on the next line. This gives your scripts a more form-like appearance.

In fact, the read command includes the -p option, which allows you to specify a prompt directly in the read command line:

```
$ cat askage.sh
#!/bin/bash
# Using the read command with the -p option
#
read -p "Please enter your age: " age
days=$[ $age * 365 ]
echo "That means you are over $days days old!"
exit
$
$ ./askage.sh
Please enter your age: 30
That means you are over 10950 days old!
$
```

You'll notice in the first example that when a name was entered, the read command assigned both the first name and last name to the same variable. The read command assigns all data entered at the prompt to a single variable, or you can specify multiple variables. Each data value entered is assigned to the next variable in the list. If the list of variables runs out before the data does, the remaining data is assigned to the last variable:

```
$ cat askfirstlastname.sh
#!/bin/bash
# Using the read command for multiple variables
#
read -p "Enter your first and last name: " first last
echo "Checking data for $last, $first..."
exit
$
$ ./askfirstlastname.sh
Enter your first and last name: Richard Blum
Checking data for Blum, Richard...
$
```

You can also specify no variables on the `read` command line. If you do that, the `read` command places any data it receives in the special environment variable REPLY:

```
$ cat asknamereply.sh
#!/bin/bash
# Using the read command with REPLY variable
#
read -p "Enter your name: "
echo
echo "Hello $REPLY, welcome to my script."
exit
$
$ ./asknamereply.sh
Enter your name: Christine Bresnahan

Hello Christine Bresnahan, welcome to my script.
$
```

The REPLY environment variable contains all the data entered in the input, and it can be used in the shell script like any other variable.

## Timing Out

Be careful when using the `read` command. Your script may get stuck waiting for the script user to enter data. If the script must go on regardless of whether any data was entered, you can use the -t option to specify a timer. The -t option specifies the number of seconds for the `read` command to wait for input. When the timer expires, the `read` command returns a non-zero exit status:

```
$ cat asknametimed.sh
#!/bin/bash
# Using the read command with a timer
#
if read -t 5 -p "Enter your name: " name
then
    echo "Hello $name, welcome to my script."
else
    echo
    echo "Sorry, no longer waiting for name."
fi
exit
$
$ ./asknametimed.sh
Enter your name: Christine
Hello Christine, welcome to my script.
$
$ ./asknametimed.sh
Enter your name:
Sorry, no longer waiting for name.
$
```

14

Because the `read` command exits with a non-zero exit status if the timer expires, it's easy to use the standard structured statements, such as an `if-then` statement or a `while` loop, to track what happened. In this example, when the timer expires, the `if` statement fails, and the shell executes the commands in the `else` section.

Instead of timing the input, you can also set the `read` command to count the input characters. When a preset number of characters has been entered, the script automatically continues (the user does not have to press the Enter key), assigning the entered data to the variable:

```
$ cat continueornot.sh
#!/bin/bash
# Using the read command for one character
#
read -n 1 -p "Do you want to continue [Y/N]? " answer
#
case $answer in
Y | y) echo
       echo "Okay. Continue on...";;
N | n) echo
       echo "Okay. Goodbye"
       exit;;
esac
echo "This is the end of the script."
exit
$
$ ./continueornot.sh
Do you want to continue [Y/N]? Y
Okay. Continue on...
This is the end of the script.
$
$ ./continueornot.sh
Do you want to continue [Y/N]? n
Okay. Goodbye
$
```

This example uses the -n option with the value of 1, instructing the `read` command to accept only a single character before continuing. As soon as you press the single character to answer, the `read` command accepts the input and passes it to the variable. You don't need to press the Enter key.

## Reading with no display

Sometimes you need input from the script user, but you don't want that input to display on the monitor. The classic example is when entering passwords, but there are plenty of other types of data that you need to hide.

The -s option prevents the data entered in the `read` command from being displayed on the monitor; actually, the data is displayed, but the `read` command sets the text color to the same as the background color. Here's an example of using the -s option in a script:

```
$ cat askpassword.sh
#!/bin/bash
# Hiding input data
#
read -s -p "Enter your password: " pass
echo
echo "Your password is $pass"
exit
$
$ ./askpassword.sh
Enter your password:
Your password is Day31Bright-Test
$
```

The data typed at the input prompt doesn't appear on the monitor but is assigned to the variable for use in the script.

## Reading from a file

Finally, you can also use the read command to read data stored in a file on the Linux system. Each call to the read command reads a single line of text from the file. When no more lines are left in the file, the read command exits with a non-zero exit status.

The tricky part is getting the data from the file to the read command. The most common method is to pipe (|) the result of the cat command of the file directly to a while command that contains the read command. Here's an example:

```
$ cat readfile.sh
#!/bin/bash
# Using the read command to read a file
#
count=1
cat $HOME/scripts/test.txt | while read line
do
      echo "Line $count: $line"
      count=$[ $count + 1 ]
done
echo "Finished processing the file."
exit
$
$ cat $HOME/scripts/test.txt
The quick brown dog jumps over the lazy fox.
This is a test. This is only a test.
O Romeo, Romeo! Wherefore art thou Romeo?
$
$ ./readfile.sh
Line 1: The quick brown dog jumps over the lazy fox.
Line 2: This is a test. This is only a test.
Line 3: O Romeo, Romeo! Wherefore art thou Romeo?
Finished processing the file.
$
```

14

The while command loop continues processing lines of the file with the read command, until the read command exits with a non-zero exit status.

# Working through a Practical Example

In this section is a practical script that handles user input from what we've covered in this chapter, and employs the ping or ping6 command to test connectivity to other local systems. The ping (or ping6) command is a quick way to determine if a system is up and operating on the network. It's a useful command and is often employed as a first check. If you have only one system to check, just use the command directly. But if you have two or three or possibly even hundreds of systems to check, a shell script can help.

This example script has two methods to select the systems to check — through command-line options or via a file. Here's the script in action on an Ubuntu system using the command-line options:

```
$ ./CheckSystems.sh -t IPv4 192.168.1.102 192.168.1.104

Checking system at 192.168.1.102...
[...]
--- 192.168.1.102 ping statistics ---
3 packets transmitted, 3 received, 0% packet loss,[...]

Checking system at 192.168.1.104...
[...]
--- 192.168.1.104 ping statistics ---
3 packets transmitted, 0 received, +3 errors, 100% packet loss,[...]

$
```

If the IP address parameters are accidentally not included, the script produces a message for the user and exits:

```
$ ./CheckSystems.sh -t IPv4

IP Address(es) parameters are missing.

Exiting script...
$
```

In this example, the script asks for a filename (filled with IP addresses), which is provided by the user, when no command-line options are entered:

```
$ cat /home/christine/scripts/addresses.txt
192.168.1.102
IPv4
192.168.1.103
IPv4
```

```
192.168.1.104
IPv4
$
$ ./CheckSystems.sh

Please enter the file name with an absolute directory reference...

Enter name of file: /home/christine/scripts/addresses.txt
/home/christine/scripts/addresses.txt is a file, is readable,
and is not empty.

Checking system at 192.168.1.102...
[...]
--- 192.168.1.102 ping statistics ---
3 packets transmitted, 3 received, 0% packet loss,[...]

Checking system at 192.168.1.103...
[...]
Checking system at 192.168.1.104...
[...]
Finished processing the file. All systems checked.
$
```

And here is the script. Notice that getopts is used to grab the provided command-line option, value, and parameter(s). But if none are entered, the script instead asks the user for the file's name, which contains the systems' IP addresses and types. The file is processed using the read command:

```
$ cat CheckSystems.sh
#!/bin/bash
# Check systems on local network allowing for
# a variety of input methods.
#
#
########## Determine Input Method ##################
#
# Check for command-line options here using getopts.
# If none, then go on to File Input Method
#
while getopts t: opt
do
    case "$opt" in
        t) # Found the -t option
            if [ $OPTARG = "IPv4" ]
            then
                    pingcommand=$(which ping)
            #
            elif [ $OPTARG = "IPv6" ]
            then
```

*(Continues)*

*(continued)*

```
                    pingcommand=$(which ping6)
            #
            else
                echo "Usage: -t IPv4 or -t IPv6"
                echo "Exiting script..."
                exit
            fi
            ;;
        *) echo "Usage: -t IPv4 or -t IPv6"
            echo "Exiting script..."
            exit;;
    esac
    #
    shift $[ $OPTIND - 1 ]
    #
    if [ $# -eq 0 ]
    then
        echo
        echo "IP Address(es) parameters are missing."
        echo
        echo "Exiting script..."
        exit
    fi
    #
    for ipaddress in "$@"
    do
        echo
        echo "Checking system at $ipaddress..."
        echo
        $pingcommand -q -c 3 $ipaddress
        echo
    done
    exit
done
#
########## File Input Method ##################
#
echo
echo "Please enter the file name with an absolute directory
reference..."
echo
choice=0
while [ $choice -eq 0 ]
do
    read -t 60 -p "Enter name of file: " filename
    if [ -z $filename ]
    then
        quitanswer=""
        read -t 10 -n 1 -p "Quit script [Y/n]? " quitanswer
```

```
                    #
                    case $quitanswer in
                    Y | y)  echo
                            echo "Quitting script..."
                            exit;;
                    N | n)  echo
                            echo "Please answer question: "
                            choice=0;;
                    *)      echo
                            echo "No response. Quitting script..."
                            exit;;
                    esac
            else
                    choice=1
            fi
    done
    #
    if [ -s $filename ] && [ -r $filename ]
            then
                    echo "$filename is a file, is readable, and is not empty."
                    echo
                    cat $filename | while read line
                    do
                            ipaddress=$line
                            read line
                            iptype=$line
                            if [ $iptype = "IPv4" ]
                            then
                                    pingcommand=$(which ping)
                            else
                                    pingcommand=$(which ping6)
                            fi
                            echo "Checking system at $ipaddress..."
                            $pingcommand -q -c 3 $ipaddress
                            echo
                    done
                    echo "Finished processing the file. All systems checked."
            else
                    echo
                    echo "$filename is either not a file, is empty, or is"
                    echo "not readable by you. Exiting script..."
    fi
    #
    ################### Exit Script ###################
    #
    exit
    $
```

14

You may notice some repeated code within this script. It would be nice to use functions in order to eliminate the repeated code, but we'll have to wait until Chapter 17, "Creating Functions," which covers that topic. Another script improvement to consider is checking for correct formatting of the user-provided file (ensuring the file line under an IP address has either IPv4 or IPv6). Also, this script doesn't have a help option (-h), which is another nice addition you can make. What are some additional user input improvements you thought about when reading through this script?

# Summary

This chapter showed three methods for retrieving data from the script user. Command-line parameters allow users to enter data directly on the command line when they run the script. The script uses positional parameters to retrieve the command-line parameters and assign them to variables.

The shift command allows you to manipulate the command-line parameters by rotating them within the positional parameters. This command allows you to easily iterate through the parameters without knowing how many parameters are available.

You can use three special variables when working with command-line parameters. The shell sets the $# variable to the number of parameters entered on the command line. The $* variable contains all the parameters as a single string, and the $@ variable contains all the parameters as separate words. These variables come in handy when you're trying to process long parameter lists.

Besides parameters, your script users can use command-line options to pass information to your script. Command-line options are single letters preceded by a dash. Different options can be assigned to alter the behavior of your script.

The Bash shell provides three ways to handle command-line options. You can iterate through the options using the positional parameter variables, processing each option as it appears on the command line. Use the getopt command to convert command-line options and parameters into a standard format that you can process in your script. Or you can use the getopts command, which provides more advanced processing of the command-line parameters.

An interactive method to obtain data from your script users is the read command. The read command allows your scripts to query users for information and wait. The read command places any data entered by the script user into one or more variables, which you can use within the script.

Several options are available for the read command that allow you to customize the data input into your script, such as using hidden data entry, applying timed data entry, and requesting a specific number of input characters.

In the next chapter, we look further into how Bash shell scripts output data. So far, you've seen how to display data on the monitor and redirect it to a file. Next, we explore a few other options that you have available, not only to direct data to specific locations but also to direct specific types of data to specific locations. This will help make your shell scripts look professional!

14

# Presenting Data

S o far the scripts shown in this book display information either by echoing data to the monitor or by redirecting data to a file. Chapter 11, "Basic Script Building," demonstrated how to redirect the output of a command to a file. This chapter expands on that topic by showing you how you can redirect the output of your script to different locations on your Linux system.

## Understanding Input and Output

So far, you've seen two methods for displaying the output from your scripts:

- Displaying output on the monitor screen
- Redirecting output to a file

Both methods produced an all-or-nothing approach to data output. There are times, however, when it would be nice to display some data on the monitor and other data in a file. For these instances, it comes in handy to know how Linux handles input and output so that you can get your script output to the right place.

The following sections describe how to use the standard Linux input and output system to your advantage, to help direct script output to specific locations.

## Standard file descriptors

The Linux system handles every object as a file. This includes the input and output process. Linux identifies each file object using a *file descriptor*. The file descriptor is a non-negative integer that uniquely identifies open files in a session. Each process is allowed to have up to nine open file descriptors at a time. The Bash shell reserves the first three file descriptors (0, 1, and 2) for special purposes. These are shown in Table 15-1.

**TABLE 15-1**    **Linux Standard File Descriptors**

| File Descriptor | Abbreviation | Description |
| --- | --- | --- |
| 0 | STDIN | Standard input |
| 1 | STDOUT | Standard output |
| 2 | STDERR | Standard error |

These three special file descriptors handle the input and output from your script. The shell uses them to direct the default input and output in the shell to the appropriate location, which by default is usually your monitor. The following sections describe each of these standard file descriptors in greater detail.

### STDIN

The STDIN file descriptor references the standard input to the shell. For a terminal interface, the standard input is the keyboard. The shell receives input from the keyboard on the STDIN file descriptor and processes each character as you type it.

When you use the input redirect symbol (<), Linux replaces the standard input file descriptor with the file referenced by the redirection. It reads the file and retrieves data just as if it were typed on the keyboard.

Many Bash commands accept input from STDIN, especially if no files are specified on the command line. Here's an example of using the cat command with data entered from STDIN:

```
$ cat
this is a test
this is a test
this is a second test.
this is a second test.
```

When you enter the cat command on the command line by itself, it accepts input from STDIN. As you enter each line, the cat command echoes the line to the display.

However, you can also use the STDIN redirect symbol to force the cat command to accept input from another file other than STDIN:

```
$ cat < testfile
This is the first line.
```

```
This is the second line.
This is the third line.
$
```

Now the `cat` command uses the lines that are contained in the `testfile` file as the input. You can use this technique to input data to any shell command that accepts data from STDIN.

### STDOUT

The STDOUT file descriptor references the standard output for the shell. On a terminal interface, the standard output is the terminal monitor. All output from the shell (including programs and scripts you run in the shell) is directed to the standard output, which is the monitor.

Most Bash commands direct their output to the STDOUT file descriptor by default. As shown in Chapter 11, you can change that using output redirection:

```
$ ls -l > test2
$ cat test2
total 20
-rw-rw-r-- 1 rich rich 53 2020-06-20 11:30 test
-rw-rw-r-- 1 rich rich  0 2020-06-20 11:32 test2
-rw-rw-r-- 1 rich rich 73 2020-06-20 11:23 testfile
$
```

With the output redirection symbol, all the output that normally would go to the monitor is instead redirected to the designated redirection file by the shell.

You can also append data to a file. You do this using the >> symbol:

```
$ who >> test2
$ cat test2
total 20
-rw-rw-r-- 1 rich rich 53 2020-06-20 11:30 test
-rw-rw-r-- 1 rich rich  0 2020-06-20 11:32 test2
-rw-rw-r-- 1 rich rich 73 2020-06-20 11:23 testfile
rich      pts/0         2020-06-20 15:34 (192.168.1.2)
$
```

The output generated by the `who` command is appended to the data already in the test2 file.

However, if you use the standard output redirection for your scripts, you can run into a problem. Here's an example of what can happen in your script:

```
$ ls -al badfile > test3
ls: cannot access badfile: No such file or directory
$ cat test3
$
```

15

When a command produces an error message, the shell doesn't redirect the error message to the output redirection file. The shell created the output redirection file, but the error message appeared on the monitor screen, not in the file. Notice that there isn't an error when trying to display the contents of the test3 file. The test3 file was created just fine, but it's empty.

The shell handles error messages separately from the normal output. If you're creating a shell script that runs in background mode, often you must rely on the output messages being sent to a log file. Using this technique, if any error messages occur, they don't appear in the log file. You need to do something different.

### STDERR

The shell handles error messages using the special STDERR file descriptor. The STDERR file descriptor references the standard error output for the shell. This is the location where the shell sends error messages generated by the shell or programs and scripts running in the shell.

By default, the STDERR file descriptor points to the same place as the STDOUT file descriptor (even though they are assigned different file descriptor values). This means that, by default, all error messages go to the monitor display.

However, as you saw in the example, when you redirect STDOUT, this doesn't automatically redirect STDERR. When working with scripts, you'll often want to change that behavior, especially if you're interested in logging error messages to a log file.

## Redirecting errors

You've already seen how to redirect the STDOUT data by using the redirection symbol. Redirecting the STDERR data isn't much different; you just need to define the STDERR file descriptor when you use the redirection symbol. You can do this in a couple of ways.

### Redirecting errors only

As you saw in Table 15-1, the STDERR file descriptor is set to the value 2. You can select to redirect only error messages by placing this file descriptor value immediately before the redirection symbol. The value must appear immediately before the redirection symbol or it doesn't work:

```
$ ls -al badfile 2> test4
$ cat test4
ls: cannot access badfile: No such file or directory
$
```

Now when you run the command, the error message doesn't appear on the monitor. Instead, the output file contains any error messages that are generated by the command. Using this method, the shell redirects the error messages only, not the normal data. Here's another example of mixing STDOUT and STDERR messages in the same output:

```
$ ls -al test badtest test2 2> test5
-rw-rw-r-- 1 rich rich 158 2020-06-20 11:32 test2
```

```
$ cat test5
ls: cannot access test: No such file or directory
ls: cannot access badtest: No such file or directory
$
```

The `ls` command tries to find information on three files—test, `badtest`, and `test2`. The normal `STDOUT` output from the `ls` command went to the default `STDOUT` file descriptor, which is the monitor. Because the command redirects file descriptor 2 output (`STDERR`) to an output file, the shell sent any error messages generated directly to the specified redirection file.

### Redirecting errors and data

If you want to redirect both errors and the normal output, you need to use two redirection symbols. You need to precede each with the appropriate file descriptor for the data you want to redirect and then have them point to the appropriate output file for holding the data:

```
$ ls -al test test2 test3 badtest 2> test6 1> test7
$ cat test6
ls: cannot access test: No such file or directory
ls: cannot access badtest: No such file or directory
$ cat test7
-rw-rw-r-- 1 rich rich 158 2020-06-20 11:32 test2
-rw-rw-r-- 1 rich rich   0 2020-06-20 11:33 test3
$
```

The shell redirects the normal output of the `ls` command that would have gone to `STDOUT` to the `test7` file using the `1>` symbol. Any error messages that would have gone to `STDERR` were redirected to the `test6` file using the `2>` symbol.

You can use this technique to separate normal script output from any error messages that occur in the script. This allows you to easily identify errors without having to wade through thousands of lines of normal output data.

Alternatively, if you want, you can redirect both `STDERR` and `STDOUT` output to the same output file. The Bash shell provides a special redirection symbol just for this purpose, the `&>` symbol:

```
$ ls -al test test2 test3 badtest &> test7
$ cat test7
ls: cannot access test: No such file or directory
ls: cannot access badtest: No such file or directory
-rw-rw-r-- 1 rich rich 158 2020-06-20 11:32 test2
-rw-rw-r-- 1 rich rich   0 2020-06-20 11:33 test3
$
```

When you use the `&>` symbol, all the output generated by the command is sent to the same location, both data and errors. Notice that one of the error messages is out of order from what you'd expect. The error message for the `badtest` file (the last file to be listed)

15

415

appears second in the output file. The Bash shell automatically gives error messages a higher priority than the standard output. This allows you to view the error messages together, rather than having them scattered throughout the output file.

# Redirecting Output in Scripts

You can use the STDOUT and STDERR file descriptors in your scripts to produce output in multiple locations simply by redirecting the appropriate file descriptors. There are two methods for redirecting output in the script:

- Temporarily redirecting each line
- Permanently redirecting all commands in the script

The following sections describe how each of these methods works.

## Temporary redirections

If you want to purposely generate error messages in your script, you can redirect an individual output line to STDERR. You just need to use the output redirection symbol to redirect the output to the STDERR file descriptor. When you redirect to a file descriptor, you must precede the file descriptor number with an ampersand (&):

```
echo "This is an error message" >&2
```

This line displays the text wherever the STDERR file descriptor for the script is pointing, instead of the normal STDOUT. The following is an example of a script that uses this feature:

```
$ cat test8
#!/bin/bash
# testing STDERR messages

echo "This is an error" >&2
echo "This is normal output"
$
```

If you run the script as normal, you don't notice any difference:

```
$ ./test8
This is an error
This is normal output
$
```

Remember that, by default, Linux directs the STDERR output to STDOUT. However, if you redirect STDERR when running the script, any text directed to STDERR in the script is redirected:

```
$ ./test8 2> test9
This is normal output
$ cat test9
```

```
This is an error
$
```

Perfect! The text displayed using STDOUT appears on the monitor, whereas the echo statement text sent to STDERR is redirected to the output file.

This method is great for generating error messages in your scripts. If someone uses your scripts, they can easily redirect the error messages using the STDERR file descriptor, as shown.

## Permanent redirections

If you have lots of data that you're redirecting in your script, it can get tedious having to redirect every echo statement. Instead, you can tell the shell to redirect a specific file descriptor for the duration of the script by using the exec command:

```
$ cat test10
#!/bin/bash
# redirecting all output to a file
exec 1>testout

echo "This is a test of redirecting all output"
echo "from a script to another file."
echo "without having to redirect every individual line"
$ ./test10
$ cat testout
This is a test of redirecting all output
from a script to another file.
without having to redirect every individual line
$
```

The exec command starts a new shell and redirects the STDOUT file descriptor to a file. All output in the script that goes to STDOUT is instead redirected to the file.

You can also redirect the STDOUT in the middle of a script:

```
$ cat test11
#!/bin/bash
# redirecting output to different locations

exec 2>testerror

echo "This is the start of the script"
echo "now redirecting all output to another location"

exec 1>testout

echo "This output should go to the testout file"
echo "but this should go to the testerror file" >&2
$
```

*(Continues)*

**15**

*(continued)*

```
$ ./test11
This is the start of the script
now redirecting all output to another location
$ cat testout
This output should go to the testout file
$ cat testerror
but this should go to the testerror file
$
```

The script uses the `exec` command to redirect any output going to STDERR to the file `testerror`. Next, the script uses the `echo` statement to display a few lines to STDOUT. After that, the `exec` command is used again to redirect STDOUT to the `testout` file. Notice that even when STDOUT is redirected, you can still specify the output from an `echo` statement to go to STDERR, which in this case is still redirected to the `testerror` file.

This feature can come in handy when you want to redirect the output of just parts of a script to an alternative location, such as an error log. There's just one problem you run into when using this.

After you redirect STDOUT or STDERR, you can't easily redirect them back to their original location. If you need to switch back and forth with your redirection, you need to learn a trick. The "Creating Your Own Redirection" section later in this chapter discusses this trick and how to use it in your shell scripts.

# Redirecting Input in Scripts

You can use the same technique used to redirect STDOUT and STDERR in your scripts to redirect STDIN from the keyboard. The `exec` command allows you to redirect STDIN from a file on the Linux system:

```
exec 0< testfile
```

This command informs the shell that it should retrieve input from the file `testfile` instead of STDIN. This redirection applies any time the script requests input. Here's an example of this in action:

```
$ cat test12
#!/bin/bash
# redirecting file input

exec 0< testfile
count=1

while read line
do
    echo "Line #$count: $line"
    count=$[ $count + 1 ]
```

```
done
$ ./test12
Line #1: This is the first line.
Line #2: This is the second line.
Line #3: This is the third line.
$
```

Chapter 14, "Handling User Input," showed you how to use the read command to read data entered from the keyboard by a user. By redirecting STDIN from a file, when the read command attempts to read from STDIN, it retrieves data from the file instead of the keyboard.

This is an excellent technique to read data in files for processing in your scripts. A common task for Linux system administrators is to read data from log files for processing. This is the easiest way to accomplish that task.

# Creating Your Own Redirection

When you redirect input and output in your script, you're not limited to the three default file descriptors. I mentioned that you could have up to nine open file descriptors in the shell. The other six file descriptors are numbered from 3 through 8 and are available for you to use as either input or output redirection. You can assign any of these file descriptors to a file and then use them in your scripts as well. This section shows you how to use the other file descriptors in your scripts.

## Creating output file descriptors

You assign a file descriptor for output by using the exec command. As with the standard file descriptors, after you assign an alternative file descriptor to a file location, that redirection stays permanent until you reassign it. Here's a simple example of using an alternative file descriptor in a script:

```
$ cat test13
#!/bin/bash
# using an alternative file descriptor

exec 3>test13out

echo "This should display on the monitor"
echo "and this should be stored in the file" >&3
echo "Then this should be back on the monitor"
$ ./test13
This should display on the monitor
Then this should be back on the monitor
$ cat test13out
and this should be stored in the file
$
```

The script uses the `exec` command to redirect file descriptor 3 to an alternative file location. When the script executes the `echo` statements, they display on STDOUT as you would expect. However, the `echo` statements that you redirect to file descriptor 3 go to the alternative file. This allows you to keep normal output for the monitor and redirect special information to files, such as log files.

You can also use the `exec` command to append data to an existing file instead of creating a new file:

```
exec 3>>test13out
```

Now the output is appended to the `test13out` file instead of creating a new file.

## Redirecting file descriptors

Here's the trick to help you bring back a redirected file descriptor. You can assign an alternative file descriptor to a standard file descriptor, and vice versa. This means that you can redirect the original location of STDOUT to an alternative file descriptor and then redirect that file descriptor back to STDOUT. This might sound somewhat complicated, but in practice it's fairly straightforward. This example will clear things up for you:

```
$ cat test14
#!/bin/bash
# storing STDOUT, then coming back to it

exec 3>&1
exec 1>test14out

echo "This should store in the output file"
echo "along with this line."

exec 1>&3

echo "Now things should be back to normal"
$
$ ./test14
Now things should be back to normal
$ cat test14out
This should store in the output file
along with this line.
$
```

This example is a little crazy, so let's walk through it piece by piece. First, the script redirects file descriptor 3 to the current location of file descriptor 1, which is STDOUT. This means that any output sent to file descriptor 3 goes to the monitor.

The second `exec` command redirects STDOUT to a file. The shell now redirects any output sent to STDOUT directly to the output file. However, file descriptor 3 still points to the original location of STDOUT, which is the monitor. If you send output data to file descriptor 3 at this point, it still goes to the monitor, even though STDOUT is redirected.

After sending some output to STDOUT, which points to a file, the script then redirects STDOUT to the current location of file descriptor 3, which is still set to the monitor. This means that now STDOUT points to its original location, the monitor.

This method can get confusing, but it's a common way to temporarily redirect output in script files and then set the output back to the normal settings.

## Creating input file descriptors

You can redirect input file descriptors exactly the same way as output file descriptors. Save the STDIN file descriptor location to another file descriptor before redirecting it to a file; when you're finished reading the file, you can restore STDIN to its original location:

```
$ cat test15
#!/bin/bash
# redirecting input file descriptors

exec 6<&0

exec 0< testfile

count=1
while read line
do
    echo "Line #$count: $line"
    count=$[ $count + 1 ]
done
exec 0<&6
read -p "Are you done now? " answer
case $answer in
Y|y) echo "Goodbye";;
N|n) echo "Sorry, this is the end.";;
esac
$ ./test15
Line #1: This is the first line.
Line #2: This is the second line.
Line #3: This is the third line.
Are you done now? y
Goodbye
$
```

In this example, file descriptor 6 is used to hold the location for STDIN. The script then redirects STDIN to a file. All the input for the read command comes from the redirected STDIN, which is now the input file.

When all the lines have been read, the script returns STDIN to its original location by redirecting it to file descriptor 6. The script tests to make sure that STDIN is back to normal by using another read command, which this time waits for input from the keyboard.

15

## Creating a read/write file descriptor

As odd as it may seem, you can also open a single file descriptor for both input and output. You can then use the same file descriptor to both read data from a file and write data to the same file.

You need to be especially careful with this method, however. As you read and write data to and from a file, the shell maintains an internal pointer, indicating where it is in the file. Any reading or writing occurs where the file pointer last left off. This can produce some interesting results if you're not careful. Look at this example:

```
$ cat test16
#!/bin/bash
# testing input/output file descriptor

exec 3<> testfile
read line <&3
echo "Read: $line"
echo "This is a test line" >&3
$ cat testfile
This is the first line.
This is the second line.
This is the third line.
$ ./test16
Read: This is the first line.
$ cat testfile
This is the first line.
This is a test line
ine.
This is the third line.
$
```

This example uses the `exec` command to assign file descriptor 3 for both input and output sent to and from the file `testfile`. Next, it uses the `read` command to read the first line in the file, using the assigned file descriptor, and then it displays the read line of data in STDOUT. After that, it uses the `echo` statement to write a line of data to the file opened with the same file descriptor.

When you run the script, at first things look just fine. The output shows that the script read the first line in the `testfile` file. However, if you display the contents of the `testfile` file after running the script, you see that the data written to the file overwrote the existing data.

When the script writes data to the file, it starts where the file pointer is located. The `read` command reads the first line of data, so it left the file pointer pointing to the first character in the second line of data. When the `echo` statement outputs data to the file, it places the data at the current location of the file pointer, overwriting whatever data was there.

## Closing file descriptors

If you create new input or output file descriptors, the shell automatically closes them when the script exits. There are situations, however, when you need to manually close a file descriptor before the end of the script.

To close a file descriptor, redirect it to the special symbol &-. This is how it looks in the script:

```
exec 3>&-
```

This statement closes file descriptor 3, preventing it from being used any more in the script. Here's an example of what happens when you try to use a closed file descriptor:

```
$ cat badtest
#!/bin/bash
# testing closing file descriptors

exec 3> test17file

echo "This is a test line of data" >&3

exec 3>&-

echo "This won't work" >&3
$ ./badtest
./badtest: 3: Bad file descriptor
$
```

After you close the file descriptor, you can't write any data to it in your script or the shell produces an error message.

There's yet another thing to be careful of when closing file descriptors. If you open the same output file later on in your script, the shell replaces the existing file with a new file. This means that if you output any data, it overwrites the existing file. Consider the following example of this problem:

```
$ cat test17
#!/bin/bash
# testing closing file descriptors

exec 3> test17file
echo "This is a test line of data" >&3
exec 3>&-

cat test17file
```

*(Continues)*

15

*(continued)*

```
    exec 3> test17file
    echo "This'll be bad" >&3
$ ./test17
This is a test line of data
$ cat test17file
This'll be bad
$
```

After sending a data string to the test17file file and closing the file descriptor, the script uses the cat command to display the contents of the file. So far, so good. Next, the script reopens the output file and sends another data string to it. When you display the contents of the output file, all you see is the second data string. The shell overwrote the original output file.

# Listing Open File Descriptors

With only nine file descriptors available to you, you'd think that it wouldn't be hard to keep things straight. Sometimes, however, it's easy to get lost when trying to keep track of which file descriptor is redirected where. To help you keep your sanity, the Bash shell provides the lsof command.

The lsof command lists all the open file descriptors on the entire Linux system. This includes files open by all the processes running in the background, as well as any user accounts logged in to the system.

Plenty of command-line parameters and options are available to help filter out the lsof output. The most commonly used are -p, which allows you to specify a process ID (PID), and -d, which allows you to specify the file descriptor numbers to display, separated by commas.

To easily determine the current PID of the process, you can use the special environment variable $$, which the shell sets to the current PID. The -a option is used to perform a Boolean AND of the results of the other two options, to produce the following:

```
$ /usr/sbin/lsof -a -p $$ -d 0,1,2
COMMAND  PID USER    FD    TYPE DEVICE SIZE NODE NAME
bash    3344 rich    0u    CHR  136,0       2 /dev/pts/0
bash    3344 rich    1u    CHR  136,0       2 /dev/pts/0
bash    3344 rich    2u    CHR  136,0       2 /dev/pts/0
$
```

This shows the default file descriptors (0, 1, and 2) for the current process (the Bash shell). The default output of lsof contains several columns of information, described in Table 15-2.

**TABLE 15-2    Default lsof Output**

| Column | Description |
|---|---|
| COMMAND | The first nine characters of the name of the command in the process |
| PID | The process ID of the process |
| USER | The login name of the user who owns the process |
| FD | The file descriptor number and access type (r — [read], w — [write], u — [read/write]) |
| TYPE | The type of file (CHR — [character], BLK — [block], DIR — [directory], REG — [regular file]) |
| DEVICE | The device numbers (major and minor) of the device |
| SIZE | If available, the size of the file |
| NODE | The node number of the local file |
| NAME | The name of the file |

The file type associated with STDIN, STDOUT, and STDERR is character mode. Because the STDIN, STDOUT, and STDERR file descriptors all point to the terminal, the name of the output file is the device name of the terminal. All three standard files are available for both reading and writing (although it does seem odd to be able to write to STDIN and read from STDOUT).

Now, let's look at the results of the lsof command from inside a script that's opened a couple of alternative file descriptors:

```
$ cat test18
#!/bin/bash
# testing lsof with file descriptors

exec 3> test18file1
exec 6> test18file2
exec 7< testfile

/usr/sbin/lsof -a -p $$ -d0,1,2,3,6,7
$ ./test18
COMMAND  PID USER    FD    TYPE DEVICE SIZE    NODE NAME
test18  3594 rich     0u    CHR  136,0            2 /dev/pts/0
test18  3594 rich     1u    CHR  136,0            2 /dev/pts/0
test18  3594 rich     2u    CHR  136,0            2 /dev/pts/0
18  3594 rich      3w    REG  253,0      0 360712 /home/rich/test18file1
18  3594 rich      6w    REG  253,0      0 360715 /home/rich/test18file2
18  3594 rich      7r    REG  253,0     73 360717 /home/rich/testfile
$
```

The script creates three alternative file descriptors, two for output (3 and 6) and one for input (7). When the script runs the lsof command, you can see the new file descriptors in the output. We truncated the first part of the output so that you could see the results of the filename. The filename shows the complete pathname for the files used in the file descriptors. It shows each of the files as type REG, which indicates that they are regular files on the filesystem.

## Suppressing Command Output

Sometimes, you may not want to display any output from your script. This often occurs if you're running a script as a background process (see Chapter 16, "Script Control"). If any error messages occur from the script while it's running in the background, the shell emails them to the owner of the process. This can get tedious, especially if you run scripts that generate minor nuisance errors.

To solve that problem, you can redirect STDERR to a special file called the *null file*. The null file is pretty much what it says it is—a file that contains nothing. Any data that the shell outputs to the null file is not saved, thus the data is lost.

The standard location for the null file on Linux systems is /dev/null. Any data you redirect to that location is thrown away and doesn't appear:

```
$ ls -al > /dev/null
$ cat /dev/null
$
```

This is a common way to suppress any error messages without actually saving them:

```
$ ls -al badfile test16 2> /dev/null
-rwxr--r--    1 rich      rich           135 Jun 20 19:57 test16*
$
```

You can also use the /dev/null file for input redirection as an input file. Because the /dev/null file contains nothing, it is often used by programmers to quickly remove data from an existing file without having to remove the file and re-create it:

```
$ cat testfile
This is the first line.
This is the second line.
This is the third line.
$ cat /dev/null > testfile
$ cat testfile
$
```

The file testfile still exists on the system, but now it is empty. This is a common method used to clear out log files that must remain in place for applications to operate.

# Using Temporary Files

The Linux system contains a special directory location reserved for temporary files. Linux uses the /tmp directory for files that don't need to be kept indefinitely. Most Linux distributions configure the system to automatically remove any files in the /tmp directory at bootup.

Any user account on the system has privileges to read and write files in the /tmp directory. This feature provides an easy way for you to create temporary files that you don't necessarily have to worry about cleaning up.

There's even a specific command to use for creating a temporary file. The mktemp command allows you to easily create a unique temporary file in the /tmp folder. The shell creates the file but doesn't use your default umask value (see Chapter 7, "Understanding Linux File Permissions"). Instead, it only assigns read and write permissions to the file's owner and makes you the owner of the file. After you create the file, you have full access to read and write to and from it from your script, but no one else can access it (other than the root user, of course).

## Creating a local temporary file

By default, mktemp creates a file in the local directory. To create a temporary file in a local directory with the mktemp command, you just need to specify a filename template. The template consists of any text filename, plus six X's appended to the end of the filename:

```
$ mktemp testing.XXXXXX
$ ls -al testing*
-rw-------   1 rich     rich          0 Jun 20 21:30 testing.UfIi13
$
```

The mktemp command replaces the six X's with a six-character code to ensure that the filename is unique in the directory. You can create multiple temporary files and be assured that each one is unique:

```
$ mktemp testing.XXXXXX
testing.1DRLuV
$ mktemp testing.XXXXXX
testing.1VBtkW
$ mktemp testing.XXXXXX
testing.PgqNKG
$ ls -l testing*
-rw-------   1 rich     rich          0 Jun 20 21:57 testing.1DRLuV
-rw-------   1 rich     rich          0 Jun 20 21:57 testing.PgqNKG
-rw-------   1 rich     rich          0 Jun 20 21:30 testing.UfIi13
-rw-------   1 rich     rich          0 Jun 20 21:57 testing.1VBtkW
$
```

15

As you can see, the output of the mktemp command is the name of the file that it creates. When you use the mktemp command in a script, you'll want to save that filename in a variable so that you can refer to it later on in the script:

```
$ cat test19
#!/bin/bash
# creating and using a temp file

tempfile=$(mktemp test19.XXXXXX)

exec 3>$tempfile

echo "This script writes to temp file $tempfile"

echo "This is the first line" >&3
echo "This is the second line." >&3
echo "This is the last line." >&3
exec 3>&-

echo "Done creating temp file. The contents are:"
cat $tempfile
rm -f $tempfile 2> /dev/null
$ ./test19
This script writes to temp file test19.vCHoya
Done creating temp file. The contents are:
This is the first line
This is the second line.
This is the last line.
$ ls -al test19*
-rwxr--r--    1 rich      rich             356 Jun 20 22:03 test19
$
```

The script uses the mktemp command to create a temporary file and assigns the filename to the $tempfile variable. It then uses the temporary file as the output redirection file for file descriptor 3. After displaying the temporary filename on STDOUT, it writes a few lines to the temporary file, and then it closes the file descriptor. Finally, it displays the contents of the temporary file and then uses the rm command to remove it.

## Creating a temporary file in /tmp

The -t option forces mktemp to create the file in the temporary directory of the system. When you use this feature, the mktemp command returns the full pathname used to create the temporary file, not just the filename:

```
$ mktemp -t test.XXXXXX
/tmp/test.xG3374
$ ls -al /tmp/test*
-rw------- 1 rich rich 0 2020-06-20 18:41 /tmp/test.xG3374
$
```

Because the `mktemp` command returns the full pathname, you can then reference the temporary file from any directory on the Linux system, no matter where it places the temporary directory:

```
$ cat test20
#!/bin/bash
# creating a temp file in /tmp

tempfile=$(mktemp -t tmp.XXXXXX)

echo "This is a test file." > $tempfile
echo "This is the second line of the test." >> $tempfile

echo "The temp file is located at: $tempfile"
cat $tempfile
rm -f $tempfile
$ ./test20
The temp file is located at: /tmp/tmp.Ma3390
This is a test file.
This is the second line of the test.
$
```

When `mktemp` creates the temporary file, it returns the full pathname to the environment variable. You can then use that value in any command to reference the temporary file.

## Creating a temporary directory

The -d option tells the `mktemp` command to create a temporary directory instead of a file. You can then use that directory for whatever purposes you need, such as creating additional temporary files:

```
$ cat test21
#!/bin/bash
# using a temporary directory

tempdir=$(mktemp -d dir.XXXXXX)
cd $tempdir
tempfile1=$(mktemp temp.XXXXXX)
tempfile2=$(mktemp temp.XXXXXX)
exec 7> $tempfile1
exec 8> $tempfile2

echo "Sending data to directory $tempdir"
echo "This is a test line of data for $tempfile1" >&7
echo "This is a test line of data for $tempfile2" >&8
$ ./test21
Sending data to directory dir.ouT8S8
$ ls -al
total 72
```

*(Continues)*

```
(continued)
    drwxr-xr-x    3 rich      rich           4096 Jun 21 22:20 ./
    drwxr-xr-x    9 rich      rich           4096 Jun 21 09:44 ../
    drwx------    2 rich      rich           4096 Jun 21 22:20 dir.ouT8S8/
    -rwxr--r--    1 rich      rich            338 Jun 21 22:20 test21
    $ cd dir.ouT8S8
    [dir.ouT8S8]$ ls -al
    total 16
    drwx------    2 rich      rich           4096 Jun 21 22:20 ./
    drwxr-xr-x    3 rich      rich           4096 Jun 21 22:20 ../
    -rw-------    1 rich      rich             44 Jun 21 22:20 temp.N5F3O6
    -rw-------    1 rich      rich             44 Jun 21 22:20 temp.SQslb7
    [dir.ouT8S8]$ cat temp.N5F3O6
    This is a test line of data for temp.N5F3O6
    [dir.ouT8S8]$ cat temp.SQslb7
    This is a test line of data for temp.SQslb7
    [dir.ouT8S8]$
```

The script creates a directory in the current directory and uses the cd command to change
to that directory before creating two temporary files. The two temporary files are then
assigned to file descriptors and used to store output from the script.

# Logging Messages

Sometimes, it's beneficial to send output both to the monitor and to a file for logging.
Instead of having to redirect output twice, you can use the special tee command.

The tee command is like a T-connector for pipes. It sends data from STDIN to two desti-
nations at the same time. One destination is STDOUT. The other destination is a filename
specified on the tee command line:

```
tee filename
```

Because tee redirects data from STDIN, you can use it with the pipe command to redirect
output from any command:

```
$ date | tee testfile
Sun Jun 21 18:56:21 EDT 2020
$ cat testfile
Sun Jun 21 18:56:21 EDT 2020
$
```

The output appears in STDOUT and is written to the file specified. Be careful; by default,
the tee command overwrites the output file on each use:

```
$ who | tee testfile
rich     pts/0           2020-06-20 18:41 (192.168.1.2)
$ cat testfile
rich     pts/0           2020-06-20 18:41 (192.168.1.2)
$
```

If you want to append data to the file, you must use the -a option:

```
$ date | tee -a testfile
Sun Jun 21 18:58:05 EDT 2020
$ cat testfile
rich      pts/0          2020-06-201 18:41 (192.168.1.2)
Sun Jun 21 18:58:05 EDT 2020
$
```

Using this technique, you can both save data in files and display the data on the monitor for your users:

```
$ cat test22
#!/bin/bash
# using the tee command for logging

tempfile=test22file

echo "This is the start of the test" | tee $tempfile
echo "This is the second line of the test" | tee -a $tempfile
echo "This is the end of the test" | tee -a $tempfile
$ ./test22
This is the start of the test
This is the second line of the test
This is the end of the test
$ cat test22file
This is the start of the test
This is the second line of the test
This is the end of the test
$
```

Now you can save a permanent copy of your output at the same time as you're displaying it to your users.

# Working through a Practical Example

File redirection is very common, both when reading files into scripts and when outputting data from a script into a file. This example script does both of those things. It reads a CSV-formatted data file and outputs SQL INSERT statements to insert the data into a database.

The shell script uses a command-line parameter to define the name of the CSV file from which to read the data. The CSV format is used to export data from spreadsheets, so you can place the database data into a spreadsheet, save the spreadsheet in CSV format, read the file, and create INSERT statements to insert the data into a MySQL database.

15

Here's what the script looks like:

```
$cat test23
#!/bin/bash
# read file and create INSERT statements for MySQL

outfile='members.sql'
IFS=','
while read lname fname address city state zip
do
    cat >> $outfile << EOF
    INSERT INTO members (lname,fname,address,city,state,zip) VALUES
('$lname', '$fname', '$address', '$city', '$state', '$zip');
EOF
done < ${1}
$
```

That's a pretty short script, thanks to the file redirection that goes on! There are three redirection operations happening in the script. The while loop uses the read statement (discussed in Chapter 14) to read text from the data file. Notice in the done statement the redirection symbol:

```
done < ${1}
```

The $1 represents the first command-line parameter when you run the test23 program. That specifies the data file from which to read the data. The read statement parses the text using the IFS character, which we specify as a comma.

The other two redirection operations in the script both appear in the same statement:

```
cat >> $outfile << EOF
```

This one statement has one output append redirection (the double greater-than symbol) and one input append redirection (the double less-than symbol). The output redirection appends the cat command output to the file specified by the $outfile variable. The input to the cat command is redirected from the standard input to use the data stored inside the script. The EOF symbol marks the start and end delimiter of the data that's appended to the file:

```
INSERT INTO members (lname,fname,address,city,state,zip) VALUES
('$lname', '$fname',
  '$address', '$city', '$state', '$zip');
```

The text creates a standard SQL INSERT statement. Notice that the data values are replaced with the variables for the data read from the read statement.

So, basically the while loop reads the data one line at a time, plugs those data values into the INSERT statement template, and then outputs the result to the output file.

For this experiment, we used this as the input data file:

```
$ cat members.csv
Blum,Richard,123 Main St.,Chicago,IL,60601
```

```
Blum,Barbara,123 Main St.,Chicago,IL,60601
Bresnahan,Christine,456 Oak Ave.,Columbus,OH,43201
Bresnahan,Timothy,456 Oak Ave.,Columbus,OH,43201
$
```

When you run the script, nothing appears in the output on the monitor:

```
$ ./test23 < members.csv
$
```

But when you look at the members.sql output file, you should see the output data:

```
$ cat members.sql
   INSERT INTO members (lname,fname,address,city,state,zip)
VALUES ('Blum',
 'Richard', '123 Main St.', 'Chicago', 'IL', '60601');
   INSERT INTO members (lname,fname,address,city,state,zip)
VALUES ('Blum',
 'Barbara', '123 Main St.', 'Chicago', 'IL', '60601');
   INSERT INTO members (lname,fname,address,city,state,zip) VALUES
('Bresnahan',
 'Christine', '456 Oak Ave.', 'Columbus', 'OH', '43201');
   INSERT INTO members (lname,fname,address,city,state,zip) VALUES
('Bresnahan',
 'Timothy', '456 Oak Ave.', 'Columbus', 'OH', '43201');
$
```

The script worked exactly as expected! Now you can easily import the members.sql file
into a MySQL database table.

# Summary

Understanding how the Bash shell handles input and output can come in handy when creating your scripts. You can manipulate both how the script receives data and how it displays data, to customize your script for any environment. You can redirect the input of a
script from the standard input (STDIN) to any file on the system. You can also redirect the
output of the script from the standard output (STDOUT) to any file on the system.

Besides the STDOUT, you can redirect any error messages your script generates by redirecting the STDERR output. This is accomplished by redirecting the file descriptor associated
with the STDERR output, which is file descriptor 2. You can redirect STDERR output to the
same file as the STDOUT output or to a completely separate file. This enables you to separate normal script messages from any error messages generated by the script.

The Bash shell allows you to create your own file descriptors for use in your scripts. You can
create file descriptors 3 through 8 and assign them to any output file you desire. After you
create a file descriptor, you can redirect the output of any command to it, using the standard redirection symbols.

15

The bash shell also allows you to redirect input to a file descriptor, providing an easy way to read data contained in a file into your script. You can use the `lsof` command to display the active file descriptors in your shell.

Linux systems provide a special file, called /dev/null, to allow you to redirect output that you don't want. The Linux system discards anything redirected to the /dev/null file. You can also use this file to produce an empty file by redirecting the contents of the /dev/ null file to the file.

The `mktemp` command is a handy feature of the Bash shell that allows you to easily create temporary files and directories. Simply specify a template for the `mktemp` command, and it creates a unique file each time you call it, based on the file template format. You can also create temporary files and directories in the /tmp directory on the Linux system, which is a special location that isn't preserved between system boots.

The `tee` command is a convenient way to send output both to the standard output and to a log file. This enables you to display messages from your script on the monitor and store them in a log file at the same time.

In Chapter 16, you'll see how to control and run your scripts. Linux provides several different methods for running scripts other than directly from the command-line interface prompt. You'll see how to schedule your scripts to run at a specific time, as well as learn how to pause them while they're running.

# Script Control

A s you start building advanced scripts, you'll probably wonder how to run and control them on your Linux system. So far in this book, the only way we've run scripts is directly from the command-line interface in real-time mode. This isn't the only way to execute scripts in Linux. Quite a few options are available for running your shell scripts. There are also options for controlling your scripts. Various control methods include sending signals to your script, modifying a script's priority, and switching the run mode while a script is running. This chapter examines the various ways you can control your shell scripts.

## Handling Signals

Linux uses signals to communicate with processes running on the system. Chapter 4, "More Bash Shell Commands," described the different Linux signals and how the Linux system uses these signals to stop, start, and kill processes. You can control the operation of your shell script by programming the script to perform certain commands when it receives specific signals.

### Signaling the Bash shell

There are more than 30 Linux signals that can be generated by the system and applications. Table 16-1 lists the most common Linux system signals that you'll run across in your shell script writing.

435

**TABLE 16-1  Linux Signals**

| Signal | Value | Description |
|--------|---------|-------------|
| 1 | SIGHUP | Hangs up the process |
| 2 | SIGINT | Interrupts the process |
| 3 | SIGQUIT | Stops the process |
| 9 | SIGKILL | Unconditionally terminates the process |
| 15 | SIGTERM | Terminates the process if possible |
| 18 | SIGCONT | Continues a stopped process |
| 19 | SIGSTOP | Unconditionally stops, but doesn't terminate, the process |
| 20 | SIGTSTP | Stops or pauses the process, but doesn't terminate |

By default, the Bash shell ignores any SIGQUIT (3) and SIGTERM (15) signals it receives (so an interactive shell cannot be accidentally terminated). However, the Bash shell does not ignore any received SIGHUP (1) and SIGINT (2) signals.

If the Bash shell receives a SIGHUP signal, such as when you leave an interactive shell, it exits. Before it exits, however, it passes the SIGHUP signal to any processes started by the shell, including any running shell scripts.

With a SIGINT signal, the shell is just interrupted. The Linux kernel stops giving the shell processing time on the CPU. When this happens, the shell passes the SIGINT signal to any processes started by the shell to notify them of the situation.

As you probably have noticed, the shell passes these signals on to your shell script program for processing. However, a shell script's default behavior does not govern these signals, which may have an adverse effect on the script's operation. To avoid this situation, you can program your script to recognize signals and perform commands to prepare the script for the consequences of the signal.

## Generating signals

The Bash shell allows you to generate two basic Linux signals using key combinations on the keyboard. This feature comes in handy if you need to stop or pause a runaway script.

### Interrupting a process

The Ctrl+C key combination generates a SIGINT signal and sends it to any processes currently running in the shell. You can test this by running a command that normally takes a long time to finish and pressing the Ctrl+C key combination:

```
$ sleep 60
^C
$
```

The `sleep` command pauses the shell's operation for the specified number of seconds and returns the shell prompt. The Ctrl+C key combination sends a `SIGINT` signal, which simply stops the current process running in the shell. By pressing the Ctrl+C key combination before the time passed (60 seconds), you permanently terminated the `sleep` command.

## Pausing a process

Instead of terminating a process, you can pause it in the middle of whatever it's doing. Sometimes, this can be a dangerous thing (for example, if a script has a file lock open on a crucial system file), but often it allows you to peek inside what a script is doing without actually terminating the process.

The Ctrl+Z key combination generates a `SIGTSTP` signal, stopping any processes running in the shell. Stopping a process is different than terminating the process. Stopping the process leaves the program in memory and able to continue running from where it left off. In the "Controlling the Job" section later in this chapter, you learn how to restart a process that's been stopped.

When you use the Ctrl+Z key combination, the shell informs you that the process has been stopped:

```
$ sleep 60
^Z
[1]+  Stopped                 sleep 60
$
```

The number in the square brackets is the *job number* assigned by the shell. The shell refers to each process running in the shell as a *job* and assigns each job a unique number within the current shell. It assigns the first started process job number 1, the second job number 2, and so on.

If you have a stopped job assigned to your shell session, Bash warns you the first time you try to exit the shell:

```
$ sleep 70
^Z
[2]+  Stopped                 sleep 70
$
$ exit
logout
There are stopped jobs.
$
```

You can view the stopped jobs using the `ps` command:

```
$ ps -l
F S   UID     PID    PPID  [...] TTY          TIME CMD
0 S  1001    1509    1508  [...] pts/0    00:00:00 bash
0 T  1001    1532    1509  [...] pts/0    00:00:00 sleep
```

*(Continues)*

*(continued)*

```
0 T  1001    1533    1509  […] pts/0    00:00:00 sleep
0 R  1001    1534    1509  […] pts/0    00:00:00 ps
$
```

In the S column (process state), the ps command shows the stopped job's state as T. This indicates the command is either being traced or is stopped.

If you really want to exit the shell with a stopped job (or jobs) still active, just type the exit command again. The shell exits, terminating the stopped job.

Alternately, now that you know the PID of the stopped job(s), you can use the kill command to send a SIGKILL (9) signal to terminate it:

```
$ kill -9 1532
[1]-  Killed                sleep 60
$ kill -9 1533
[2]+  Killed                sleep 70
$
```

Each time the shell produces a prompt, it also displays the status of any jobs that have changed states in the shell. After you kill a job, the shell displays a message showing that the job was killed while running, and then provides the prompt.

> **NOTE**
>
> On some Linux systems, when you kill the job, you initially don't get any response. However, the next time you do something that produces a shell prompt (such as pressing the Enter key), you'll see a message indicating that the job was killed.

## Trapping signals

Instead of allowing your script to leave signals ungoverned, you can trap them when they appear and perform other commands. The trap command allows you to specify which Linux signals your shell script can watch for and intercept from the shell. If the script receives a signal listed in the trap command, it prevents it from being processed by the shell and instead handles it locally.

The format of the trap command is

```
trap commands signals
```

On the trap command line, you just list the *commands* you want the shell to execute, along with a space-separated list of *signals* you want to trap. You can specify the *signals* either by their numeric value or by their Linux signal name.

Here's a simple example of using the trap command to capture the SIGINT signal and govern the script's behavior when the signal is sent:

```
$ cat trapsignal.sh
#!/bin/bash
```

```
#Testing signal trapping
#
trap "echo ' Sorry! I have trapped Ctrl-C'" SIGINT
#
echo This is a test script.
#
count=1
while [ $count -le 5 ]
do
      echo "Loop #$count"
      sleep 1
      count=$[ $count + 1 ]
done
#
echo "This is the end of test script."
exit
$
```

The trap command used in this example displays a simple text message each time it
detects the SIGINT signal. Trapping this signal makes this script impervious to the user
attempting to stop the program by using the Bash shell keyboard Ctrl+C command:

```
$ ./trapsignal.sh
This is a test script.
Loop #1
Loop #2
^C Sorry! I have trapped Ctrl-C
Loop #3
^C Sorry! I have trapped Ctrl-C
Loop #4
Loop #5
This is the end of test script.
$
```

Each time the Ctrl+C key combination was used, the script executed the echo statement
specified in the trap command instead of not managing the signal and allowing the shell
to stop the script.

---

**WARNING**

If a command in your script is interrupted by a signal, using trap with a specified command will not necessarily
allow the interrupted command to continue where it left off. To keep critical operations flowing in your scripts, use
trap with a null specification along with a list of the signals to trap, such as

```
trap "" SIGINT
```

Using trap in this way allows the script to completely ignore signal interruptions and continue its important work.

## Trapping a script exit

Besides trapping signals in your shell script, you can trap them when the shell script exits. This is a convenient way to perform commands just as the shell finishes its job.

To trap the shell script exiting, just add the EXIT signal to the trap command:

```
$ cat trapexit.sh
#!/bin/bash
#Testing exit trapping
#
trap "echo Goodbye..." EXIT
#
count=1
while [ $count -le 5 ]
do
      echo "Loop #$count"
      sleep 1
      count=$[ $count + 1 ]
done
#
exit
$
$ ./trapexit.sh
Loop #1
Loop #2
Loop #3
Loop #4
Loop #5
Goodbye...
$
```

When the script gets to the normal exit point, the trap is triggered, and the shell executes the command you specify on the trap command line. The EXIT trap also works if you prematurely exit the script:

```
$ ./trapexit.sh
Loop #1
Loop #2
Loop #3
^CGoodbye...

$
```

Because the SIGINT signal isn't in the trap command list, when the Ctrl+C key combination is used to send that signal the script exits. However, before the script exits, because the EXIT is trapped, the shell executes the trap command.

## Modifying or removing a trap

To handle traps differently in various sections of your shell script, you simply reissue the
trap command with new options:

```
$ cat trapmod.sh
#!/bin/bash
#Modifying a set trap
#
trap "echo ' Sorry...Ctrl-C is trapped.'" SIGINT
#
count=1
while [ $count -le 3 ]
do
      echo "Loop #$count"
      sleep 1
      count=$[ $count + 1 ]
done
#
trap "echo ' I have modified the trap!'" SIGINT
#
count=1
while [ $count -le 3 ]
do
      echo "Second Loop #$count"
      sleep 1
      count=$[ $count + 1 ]
done
#
exit
$
```

After the signal trap is modified, the script manages the signal or signals differently. However, if a signal is received before the trap is modified, the script processes it per the original trap command:

```
$ ./trapmod.sh
Loop #1
^C Sorry...Ctrl-C is trapped.
Loop #2
Loop #3
Second Loop #1
Second Loop #2
^C I have modified the trap!
Second Loop #3
$
```

You can also remove a set trap. Add two dashes after the `trap` command and a list of the signals you want to return to default behavior:

```
$ cat trapremoval.sh
#!/bin/bash
#Removing a set trap
#
trap "echo ' Sorry...Ctrl-C is trapped.'" SIGINT
#
count=1
while [ $count -le 3 ]
do
      echo "Loop #$count"
      sleep 1
      count=$[ $count + 1 ]
done
#
trap -- SIGINT
echo "The trap is now removed."
#
count=1
while [ $count -le 3 ]
do
      echo "Second Loop #$count"
      sleep 1
      count=$[ $count + 1 ]
done
#
exit
$
```

After the signal trap is removed, the script handles the SIGINT signal in its default manner, terminating the script. However, if a signal is received before the trap is removed, the script processes it per the original `trap` command:

```
$ ./trapremoval.sh
Loop #1
Loop #2
^C Sorry...Ctrl-C is trapped.
```

```
Loop #3
The trap is now removed.
Second Loop #1
Second Loop #2
^C
$
```

In this example, the first Ctrl+C key combination was used to attempt to terminate the script prematurely. Because the signal was received before the trap was removed, the script executed the command specified in the trap. After the script executed the trap removal, Ctrl+C could prematurely terminate the script.

# Running Scripts in Background Mode

Sometimes, running a shell script directly from the command line is inconvenient. Some scripts can take a long time to process, and you may not want to tie up the command-line interface as it executes. While the script is running, you can't do anything else in your terminal session. Fortunately, there's a simple solution to that problem.

When you use the ps  -e command, you see a whole bunch of different processes running on the Linux system:

```
$ ps -e
    PID TTY          TIME CMD
      1 ?        00:00:02 systemd
      2 ?        00:00:00 kthreadd
      3 ?        00:00:00 rcu_gp
      4 ?        00:00:00 rcu_par_gp
[…]
   2585 pts/0    00:00:00 ps
$
```

Obviously, all these processes are not running on your terminal. In fact, many are not running on any terminal — they are running in the *background*. In background mode, a process runs without being associated with a STDIN, STDOUT, and STDERR on a terminal session (Chapter 15, "Presenting Data").

You can exploit this feature with your shell scripts as well, allowing them to run behind the scenes and not lock up your terminal session. The following sections describe how to run your scripts in background mode on your Linux system.

## Running in the background

Running a shell script in background mode is a fairly easy thing to do. To run a shell script in background mode from the command-line interface, just place an ampersand symbol (&) after the command:

```
$ cat backgroundscript.sh
#!/bin/bash
```

*(Continues)*

443

(continued)

```
#Test running in the background
#
count=1
while [ $count -le 5 ]
do
     sleep 1
     count=$[ $count + 1 ]
done
#
exit
$
$ ./backgroundscript.sh &
[1] 2595
$
```

When you place the ampersand symbol after a command, it separates the command from the current shell and runs it as a separate background process on the system. The first thing that displays is the line

```
[1] 2595
```

The number in the square brackets is the job number (1) assigned by the shell to the background process. The next number is the process ID (PID) the Linux system assigns to the process. Every process running on the Linux system must have a unique PID.

As soon as the system displays these items, a new command-line interface prompt appears. You are returned to the current shell, and the command you executed runs safely in background mode. At this point, you can enter new commands at the prompt.

When the background process finishes, it displays a message on the terminal:

```
[1]+   Done                      ./backgroundscript.sh
```

This shows the job number and the status of the job (Done), along with the command used to start the job (minus the &).

Be aware that while the background process is running, it still uses your terminal monitor for STDOUT and STDERR messages:

```
$ cat backgroundoutput.sh
#!/bin/bash
#Test running in the background
#
echo "Starting the script..."
count=1
while [ $count -le 5 ]
do
     echo "Loop #$count"
     sleep 1
     count=$[ $count + 1 ]
done
#
echo "Script is completed."
```

```
exit
$
$ ./backgroundoutput.sh &
[1] 2615
$ Starting the script...
Loop #1
Loop #2
Loop #3
Loop #4
Loop #5
Script is completed.

[1]+  Done                    ./backgroundoutput.sh
$
```

You'll notice from the example that the output from the backgroundoutput.sh script displays. The output intermixes with the shell prompt, which is why Starting the script appears next to the $ prompt.

You can still issue commands while this output is occurring:

```
$ ./backgroundoutput.sh &
[1] 2719
$ Starting the script...
Loop #1
Loop #2
Loop #3
pwd
/home/christine/scripts
$ Loop #4
Loop #5
Script is completed.

[1]+  Done                    ./backgroundoutput.sh
$
```

While the backgroundoutput.sh script is running in the background, the command pwd was entered. The script's output, the typed command, and the command's output all intermixed with each other's output display. This can be confusing! It is a good idea to redirect STDOUT and STDERR (Chapter 15) for scripts you will be running in the background to avoid this messy display.

## Running multiple background jobs

You can start any number of background jobs at the same time from the command-line prompt:

```
$ ./testAscript.sh &
[1] 2753
$ This is Test Script #1.
```

*(Continues)*

*(continued)*

```
$ ./testBscript.sh &
[2] 2755
$ This is Test Script #2.

$ ./testCscript.sh &
[3] 2757
$ And... another Test script.

$ ./testDscript.sh &
[4] 2759
$ Then...there was one more Test script.

$
```

Each time you start a new job, the Linux system assigns it a new job number and PID. You can see that all the scripts are running using the ps command:

```
$ ps
    PID TTY          TIME CMD
   1509 pts/0    00:00:00 bash
   2753 pts/0    00:00:00 testAscript.sh
   2754 pts/0    00:00:00 sleep
   2755 pts/0    00:00:00 testBscript.sh
   2756 pts/0    00:00:00 sleep
   2757 pts/0    00:00:00 testCscript.sh
   2758 pts/0    00:00:00 sleep
   2759 pts/0    00:00:00 testDscript.sh
   2760 pts/0    00:00:00 sleep
   2761 pts/0    00:00:00 ps
$
```

You must be careful when using background processes from a terminal session. Notice in the output from the ps command that each of the background processes is tied to the terminal session (pts/0) terminal. If the terminal session exits, the background process also exits.

> **NOTE**
>
> Earlier in this chapter we mentioned that when you attempt to exit a terminal session, a warning is issued if there are stopped processes. However, with background processes, only some terminal emulators remind you that a background job is running, before you attempt to exit the terminal session.

If you want your script to continue running in background mode after you have logged off the console, there's something else you need to do. The next section discusses that process.

# Running Scripts without a Hang-up

Sometimes, you may want to start a shell script from a terminal session and let the script run in background mode until it finishes, even if you exit the terminal session. You can do this by using the nohup command.

## 16

The nohup command blocks any SIGHUP signals that are sent to the process it is protecting. This prevents the process from exiting when you exit your terminal session.

The format used for the nohup command is as follows:

```
nohup command
```

Here's an example using a shell script launched into the background as the command:

```
$ nohup ./testAscript.sh &
[1] 1828
$ nohup: ignoring input and appending output to 'nohup.out'

$
```

As with a normal background process, the shell assigns the command a job number, and the Linux system assigns a PID number. The difference is that when you use the nohup command, the script ignores any SIGHUP signals sent by the terminal session if you close the session.

Because the nohup command disassociates the process from the terminal, the process loses the STDOUT and STDERR output links. To accommodate any output generated by the command, the nohup command automatically redirects STDOUT and STDERR messages to a file called nohup.out.

> **NOTE**
> If possible, the nohup.out file is created in your current working directory. Otherwise, it is created in your $HOME directory.

The nohup.out file contains all the output that would normally be sent to the terminal monitor. After the process finishes running, you can view the nohup.out file for the output results:

```
$ cat nohup.out
This is Test Script #1.
$
```

The output appears in the nohup.out file just as if the process ran on the command line.

---

With the use of nohup, you can run scripts in the background, log out of your terminal session to accomplish other tasks without stopping the script process, and check on its output later. There's even more flexibility to managing your background jobs, which is covered next.

# Controlling the Job

Earlier in this chapter, you saw how to use the Ctrl+C key combination to stop a job running in the shell. After you stop a job, the Linux system lets you either kill or restart it. You can kill the process by using the kill command. Restarting a stopped process requires that you send it a SIGCONT signal.

The function of starting, stopping, killing, and resuming jobs is called *job control*. With job control, you have full control over how processes run in your shell environment. This section describes the commands used to view and control jobs running in your shell.

## Viewing jobs

The key command for job control is the jobs command. The jobs command allows you to view the current jobs being handled by the shell. Though it doesn't contain the jobs command, the following script will help us demonstrate the command's power:

```
$ cat jobcontrol.sh
#!/bin/bash
#Testing job control
#
echo "Script Process ID: $$"
#
count=1
while [ $count -le 5 ]
do
     echo "Loop #$count"
     sleep 10
     count=$[ $count + 1 ]
done
#
echo "End of script..."
exit
$
```

The script uses the $ variable to display the PID that the Linux system assigns to the script; then it goes into a loop, sleeping for 10 seconds at a time for each iteration.

You can start the script from the command-line interface and then stop it using the Ctrl+Z key combination:

```
$ ./jobcontrol.sh
Script Process ID: 1580
Loop #1
Loop #2
Loop #3
^Z
[1]+  Stopped                 ./jobcontrol.sh
$
```

Using the same script, another job is started as a background process, using the ampersand symbol. To make life a little easier, the output of that script is redirected to a file so that it doesn't appear on the screen:

```
$ ./jobcontrol.sh > jobcontrol.out &
[2] 1603
$
```

The jobs command enables you to view the jobs assigned to the shell, as shown here:

```
$ jobs
[1]+  Stopped                 ./jobcontrol.sh
[2]-  Running                 ./jobcontrol.sh > jobcontrol.out &
$
```

The jobs command shows both the stopped and the running jobs, along with their job numbers and the commands used in the jobs.

> **NOTE**
> You probably noticed the plus and minus signs in the jobs command output. The job with the plus sign is considered the *default job*. It would be the job referenced by any job control commands, if a job number wasn't specified in the command line.
>
> The job with the minus sign is the job that would become the default job when the current default job finishes processing. There will be only one job with the plus sign and one job with the minus sign at any time, no matter how many jobs are running in the shell.

You can view the various jobs' PIDs by adding the -l parameter (lowercase L) to the jobs command:

```
$ jobs -l
[1]+  1580 Stopped               ./jobcontrol.sh
[2]-  1603 Running               ./jobcontrol.sh > jobcontrol.out &
$
```

The jobs command uses a few different command-line parameters, including the ones shown in Table 16-2.

**TABLE 16-2** **The jobs Command Parameters**

| Parameter | Description |
|-----------|-------------|
| -1 | Lists the PID of the process along with the job number |
| -n | Lists only jobs that have changed their status since the last notification from the shell |
| -p | Lists only the PIDs of the jobs |
| -r | Lists only the running jobs |
| -s | Lists only stopped jobs |

If you need to remove stopped jobs, use the kill command to send a SIGKILL (9) signal to the correct PID. It's a good idea to double-check that you've got an accurate process number to avoid stopping processes that need to keep running:

```
$ jobs -1
[1]+  1580 Stopped            ./jobcontrol.sh
$
$ kill -9 1580
[1]+  Killed             ./jobcontrol.sh
$
```

It's a little tedious to check and recheck for correct PIDs. So in the next section, you learn how to use commands to interact with the default process using no PID or job number.

## Restarting stopped jobs

Under Bash job control, you can restart any stopped job as either a background process or a foreground process. A foreground process takes over control of the terminal you're working on, so be careful about using that feature.

To restart a job in background mode, use the bg command:

```
$ ./restartjob.sh
^Z
[1]+  Stopped            ./restartjob.sh
$
$ bg
[1]+ ./restartjob.sh &
$
$ jobs
[1]+  Running            ./restartjob.sh &
$
```

Because the job was the default job, indicated by the plus sign, only the bg command was needed to restart it in background mode. Notice that no PID is listed when the job is moved into background mode.

If you have additional jobs, you need to use the job number along with the bg command to control the ones that are not the default job:

```
$ jobs
$
$ ./restartjob.sh
^Z
[1]+  Stopped                 ./restartjob.sh
$
$ ./newrestartjob.sh
^Z
[2]+  Stopped                 ./newrestartjob.sh
$
$ bg 2
[2]+ ./newrestartjob.sh &
$
$ jobs
[1]+  Stopped                 ./restartjob.sh
[2]-  Running                 ./newrestartjob.sh &
$
```

The command bg 2 was used to send the second job into background mode. Notice that when the jobs command was used, it listed both jobs with their status, even though the default job is not currently in background mode.

To restart a job in foreground mode, use the fg command, along with the job number:

```
$ jobs
[1]+  Stopped                 ./restartjob.sh
[2]-  Running                 ./newrestartjob.sh &
$
$ fg 2
./newrestartjob.sh
This is the script's end.
$
```

Because the job is running in foreground mode, the command-line prompt does not appear until the script finishes.

# Being Nice

In a multitasking operating system (which Linux is), the kernel is responsible for assigning CPU time for each process running on the system. The *scheduling priority* is the amount of CPU time the kernel assigns to the process relative to the other processes. By default, all user processes started from the shell have the same scheduling priority on the Linux system.

The scheduling priority, also called the *nice value*, is an integer value. It ranges from −20 (the highest priority) to +19 (the lowest priority). By default, the Bash shell starts all user processes with a scheduling priority of 0.

> **TIP**
>
> It's confusing to remember that -20 (the lowest value) is the highest priority, and +19 (the highest value) is the lowest priority. Just remember the phrase, "Nice guys finish last." The "nicer" or higher you are in value, the lower your chance of getting the CPU.

Sometimes, you want to change the scheduling priority of a shell script — lowering its priority so that it doesn't take as much processing power away from other running programs or giving it a higher priority so that it gets more CPU time. You can do this by using the nice command.

## Using the *nice* command

The nice command allows you to set the scheduling priority of a command as you start it. To make a command run with less priority, just use the -n command-line option for nice to specify a new priority level:

```
$ nice -n 10 ./jobcontrol.sh > jobcontrol.out &
[2] 16462
$
$ ps -p 16462 -o pid,ppid,ni,cmd
    PID    PPID  NI CMD
  16462    1630  10 /bin/bash ./jobcontrol.sh
$
```

Notice that you must use the nice command on the same line as the command you are starting. The output from the ps command confirms that the *nice* value (column NI) has been set to 10.

The nice command causes the script to run at a lower priority. However, if you try to increase the priority of one of your commands, you might be in for a surprise:

```
$ nice -n -5 ./jobcontrol.sh > jobcontrol.out &
[2] 16473
$ nice: cannot set niceness: Permission denied

$ ps -p 16473 -o pid,ppid,ni,cmd
    PID    PPID  NI CMD
  16473    1630   0 /bin/bash ./jobcontrol.sh
$
```

The `nice` command prevents normal system users from increasing the priority of their commands. Notice that the job does run, even though the attempt to raise its priority with the `nice` command failed. Only the `root` user or users with super user privileges can elevate a job's priority.

You don't have to use the -n option with the `nice` command. You can simply type the priority, preceded by a dash:

```
$ nice -10 ./jobcontrol.sh > jobcontrol.out &
[2] 16520
$
$ ps -p 16520 -o pid,ppid,ni,cmd
    PID    PPID  NI CMD
  16520    1630  10 /bin/bash ./jobcontrol.sh
$
```

However, this can get confusing when the priority is a negative number, because a double-dash is required. It's best just to use the -n option to avoid confusion.

## Using the *renice* command

Sometimes, you'd like to change the priority of a command that's already running on the system. The `renice` command helps in this situation. It allows you to specify the PID of a running process to change its priority:

```
$ ./jobcontrol.sh > jobcontrol.out &
[2] 16642
$
$ ps -p 16642 -o pid,ppid,ni,cmd
    PID    PPID  NI CMD
  16642    1630   0 /bin/bash ./jobcontrol.sh
$
$ renice -n 10 -p 16642
16642 (process ID) old priority 0, new priority 10
$
$ ps -p 16642 -o pid,ppid,ni,cmd
    PID    PPID  NI CMD
  16642    1630  10 /bin/bash ./jobcontrol.sh
$
```

The `renice` command automatically updates the scheduling priority of the running process. As with the `nice` command, the `renice` command has some limitations for those without super user privileges — you can only `renice` processes that you own, and only to a lower priority. However, the root user account and those users with super user privileges can use the `renice` command to change any process to any priority.

# Running like Clockwork

When you start working with scripts, you may want to run a script at some time in the future — usually at a time when you're not there. The Linux system provides ways to run a script at a preselected future time: the at command, the cron table, and anacron. Each method uses a different technique for scheduling when and how often to run scripts. The following sections describe each of these methods.

## Scheduling a job using the *at* command

The at command allows you to specify one future time when the Linux system will run a script. The at command submits a job to a queue with directions for when the shell should run the job.

The at daemon, atd, runs in the background and checks the job queue for jobs to run. Many Linux distributions start this daemon automatically at boot time, but some don't even have the package installed. If your distribution doesn't have it, and you'd like to install it (Chapter 9, "Installing Software"), the package name is, as you might suppose, at.

The atd daemon checks a special directory on the system (usually /var/spool/at or /var/spool/cron/atjobs) for jobs submitted using the at command. By default, the atd daemon checks this directory every 60 seconds. When a job is present, the atd daemon checks the time the job is set to be run. If the time matches the current time, the atd daemon runs the job.

The following sections describe how to use the at command to submit jobs to run and how to manage these jobs.

### Understanding the *at* command format

The basic at command format is pretty simple:

```
at [-f filename] time
```

By default, the at command submits input from STDIN to the queue. You can specify a filename used to read commands (your script file) using the -f parameter.

The *time* parameter specifies when you want the Linux system to run the job. If you specify a time that has already passed, the at command runs the job at that time on the next day.

You can get pretty creative with how you specify the time. The at command recognizes lots of different time formats:

- A standard hour and minute, such as 10:15
- An a.m./p.m. indicator, such as 10:15PM
- A specific named time, such as now, noon, midnight, or teatime (4:00 p.m.)

In addition to specifying the time to run the job, you can include a specific date, using a few different date formats:

- A standard date format, such as *MMDDYY*, *MM/DD/YY*, or *DD.MM.YY*
- A text date, such as Jul 4 or Dec 25, with or without the year
- A time increment:
  - Now + 25 minutes
  - 10:15PM tomorrow
  - 10:15 + 7 days

> **TIP**
>
> Several different date and time formats are available for use with the at utility. All of them are conveniently described in the /usr/share/doc/at/timespec file.

When you use the at command, the job is submitted to a *job queue*. The job queue holds the jobs submitted by the at command for processing. There are 52 different job queues available for different priority levels. Job queues are referenced using lowercase letters, a through z, and uppercase letters A through Z, with A queue being a different queue than a queue.

> **NOTE**
>
> A few years ago, the batch command was another method that allowed a script to be run at a later time. The batch command was unique because you could schedule a script to run when the system was at a lower usage level. Nowadays the batch command is simply a script, /usr/bin/batch, that calls the at command and submits your job to the b queue.

The higher alphabetically the job queue letter, the lower the priority (higher nice value) the job will run under. By default, at jobs are submitted to the at job a queue. If you want to run a job at a lower priority, you can specify a different queue letter using the -q parameter. And if you want your jobs to consume as little CPU as possible compared to other current processes, you'll want to put your job into the z (lowercase Z) queue.

### Retrieving job output

When an at job runs on the Linux system, there's no monitor associated with the job. Instead, the Linux system uses the email address of the user who submitted the at job as STDOUT and STDERR. Any output destined to STDOUT or STDERR is mailed to the user via the mail system.

Here's a simple example using the at command to schedule a job to run on a CentOS distribution:

```
$ cat tryat.sh
#!/bin/bash
```

*(Continues)*

*(continued)*

```
# Trying out the at command
#
echo "This script ran at $(date +%B%d,%T)"
echo
echo "This script is using the $SHELL shell."
echo
sleep 5
echo "This is the script's end."
#
exit
$
$ at -f tryat.sh now
warning: commands will be executed using /bin/sh
job 3 at Thu Jun 18 16:23:00 2020
$
```

The at command displays the job number assigned to the job along with the time the job is scheduled to run. The -f option tells what script file to use, and the now time designation directs at to run the script immediately.

> **NOTE**
>
> Don't let that warning message from the at command cause you concern. Because this script has #!/bin/bash as its first line, the commands in this shell script will be executed by the Bash shell.

Using email for the at command's output is inconvenient at best. The at command sends email via the sendmail application. If your system does not use sendmail, you won't get any output! Therefore, it's best to redirect STDOUT and STDERR in your scripts (Chapter 15) when using the at command, as the following example shows:

```
$ cat tryatout.sh
#!/bin/bash
# Trying out the at command redirecting output
#
outfile=$HOME/scripts/tryat.out
#
echo "This script ran at $(date +%B%d,%T)" > $outfile
echo >> $outfile
echo "This script is using the $SHELL shell." >> $outfile
echo >> $outfile
sleep 5
echo "This is the script's end." >> $outfile
#
exit
$
$ at -M -f tryatout.sh now
warning: commands will be executed using /bin/sh
job 4 at Thu Jun 18 16:48:00 2020
```

```
$
$ cat $HOME/scripts/tryat.out
This script ran at June18,16:48:21

This script is using the /bin/bash shell.

This is the script's end.
$
```

If you don't want to use email or redirection with at, it is best to add the -M option to suppress any output generated by jobs using the at command.

## Listing pending jobs

The atq command allows you to view what jobs are pending on the system:

```
$ at -M -f tryatout.sh teatime
warning: commands will be executed using /bin/sh
job 5 at Fri Jun 19 16:00:00 2020
$
$ at -M -f tryatout.sh tomorrow
warning: commands will be executed using /bin/sh
job 6 at Fri Jun 19 16:53:00 2020
$
$ at -M -f tryatout.sh 20:30
warning: commands will be executed using /bin/sh
job 7 at Thu Jun 18 20:30:00 2020
$
$ at -M -f tryatout.sh now+1hour
warning: commands will be executed using /bin/sh
job 8 at Thu Jun 18 17:54:00 2020
$
$ atq
1          Thu Jun 18 16:11:00 2020 a christine
5          Fri Jun 19 16:00:00 2020 a christine
6          Fri Jun 19 16:53:00 2020 a christine
7          Thu Jun 18 20:30:00 2020 a christine
8          Thu Jun 18 17:54:00 2020 a christine
$
```

The job listing from the atq command shows the job number, the date and time the system will run the job, and the job queue in which the job is stored.

## Removing jobs

After you know the information about what jobs are pending in the job queues, you can use the atrm command to remove a pending job. Just specify the job number you want to remove:

```
$ atq
1          Thu Jun 18 16:11:00 2020 a christine
```

*(Continues)*

```
(continued)
    5           Fri Jun 19 16:00:00 2020 a christine
    6           Fri Jun 19 16:53:00 2020 a christine
    7           Thu Jun 18 20:30:00 2020 a christine
    8           Thu Jun 18 17:54:00 2020 a christine
$
$ atrm 5
$
$ atq
    1           Thu Jun 18 16:11:00 2020 a christine
    6           Fri Jun 19 16:53:00 2020 a christine
    7           Thu Jun 18 20:30:00 2020 a christine
    8           Thu Jun 18 17:54:00 2020 a christine
$
```

You can only remove jobs that you submit for execution. Jobs submitted by others to at are off-limits for removal by you.

## Scheduling regular scripts

Using the at command to schedule a script to run at a future preset time is great, but what if you need that script to run at the same time every day or once a week or once a month? Instead of having to continually submit at jobs, you can use another feature of the Linux system.

The Linux system uses the cron program to allow you to schedule jobs that need to run on a regular basis. The cron program runs in the background and checks special tables, called *cron tables,* for jobs that are scheduled to run.

### Looking at the *cron* table

The cron table uses a special format for allowing you to specify when a job should be run. The format for the cron table is

```
minutepasthour hourofday dayofmonth month dayofweek command
```

The cron table allows you to specify entries as values, as ranges of values (such as 1–5), or as a wildcard character (the asterisk). For example, if you want to run a command at 10:15 every day, you would use this cron table entry:

```
15 10 * * * command
```

The wildcard character used in the *dayofmonth*, *month*, and *dayofweek* fields indicates that cron will execute the command every day of every month at 10:15. To specify a command to run at 4:15 p.m. every Monday, you would use military time (1:00 p.m. is 13, 2:00 p.m. is 14, 3:00 p.m. is 15, and so on), as in the following:

```
15 16 * * 1 command
```

You can specify the *dayofweek* entry as either a three-character text value (mon, tue, wed, thu, fri, sat, sun) or as a numeric value, with 0 and 7 representing Sunday and 6 being Saturday.

Here's another example. To execute a command at 12:00 noon on the first day of every month, you would use the following format:

```
00 12 1 * * command
```

The *dayofmonth* entry specifies a date value (1–31) for the month.

> **TIP**
>
> The astute reader might be wondering just how you would be able to set a command to execute on the last day of every month because you can't set the *dayofmonth* value to cover every month's last day. A common method is to add an if-then statement that uses the date command to check if tomorrow's date is the first day of the month (01):
>
> ```
> 00 12 28-31 * * if [ "$(date +%d -d tomorrow)" = 01 ] ; then command ; fi
> ```
>
> This line checks on the potential last days of a month (28-31) at 12:00 noon to see if it is indeed the last day of the month, and if so, cron runs *command*.
>
> Another method replaces *command* with a controlling script and runs it on potential last days of the month. The controlling script contains an if-then statement to check if tomorrow's date is the first day of the month. When tomorrow is the 1st, the controlling script issues the command to execute the script that must run on the month's last day.

The command list must specify the full command pathname or shell script to run. You can add any command-line parameters or redirection symbols you like, as a regular command line:

```
15 10 * * * /home/christine/backup.sh > backup.out
```

The cron program runs the script using the user account that submitted the job. Thus, you must have the proper permissions to access the script (or command) and output files specified in the command listing.

### Building the *cron* table

Each system user can have their own cron table (including the root user) for running scheduled jobs. Linux provides the crontab command for handling the cron table. To list an existing cron table, use the -l parameter:

```
$ crontab -l
no crontab for christine
$
```

By default, each user's cron table file doesn't exist. To add entries to your cron table, use the -e parameter. When you do that, the crontab command starts a text editor (Chapter 10, "Working with Editors") with the existing cron table (or an empty file if it doesn't yet exist).

### Viewing *cron* directories

When you create a script that has less precise execution time needs, it is easier to use one of the preconfigured `cron` script directories. There are four basic directories: hourly, daily, monthly, and weekly.

```
$ ls /etc/cron.*ly
/etc/cron.daily:
0anacron   apt-compat     cracklib-runtime   logrotate   [...]
apport     bsdmainutils   dpkg               man-db      [...]

/etc/cron.hourly:

/etc/cron.monthly:
0anacron

/etc/cron.weekly:
0anacron   man-db   update-notifier-common
$
```

Thus, if you have a script that needs to be run one time per day, just copy the script to the daily directory and `cron` executes it each day.

### Looking at the *anacron* program

The only problem with the `cron` program is that it assumes that your Linux system is operational 24 hours a day, 7 days a week. Unless you're running Linux in a server environment, this may not necessarily be true.

If the Linux system is turned off at the time a job is scheduled to run in the `cron` table, the job doesn't run. The `cron` program doesn't retroactively run missed jobs when the system is turned back on. To resolve this issue, many Linux distributions include the anacron program.

If anacron determines that a job has missed a scheduled running, it runs the job as soon as possible. This means that if your Linux system is turned off for a few days, when it starts back up any jobs scheduled to run during the time it was off are automatically run. With anacron, you're guaranteed that a job is run, which is why it is often used instead of cron for managing scheduled jobs.

The anacron program deals only with programs located in the cron directories, such as /etc/cron.monthly. It uses time stamps to determine if the jobs have been run at the proper scheduled intervals. A time stamp file exists for each cron directory and is located in /var/spool/anacron:

```
$ ls /var/spool/anacron
cron.daily  cron.monthly  cron.weekly
$
```

```
$ sudo cat /var/spool/anacron/cron.daily
[sudo] password for christine:
20200619
$
```

The anacron program has its own table (usually located at /etc/anacrontab) to check
the job directories:

```
$ cat /etc/anacrontab
# /etc/anacrontab: configuration file for anacron

# See anacron(8) and anacrontab(5) for details.

SHELL=/bin/sh
PATH=/usr/local/sbin:/usr/local/bin:/sbin:/bin:/usr/sbin:/usr/bin
HOME=/root
LOGNAME=root

# These replace cron's entries
1        5         cron.daily      run-parts --report /etc/cron.daily
7        10        cron.weekly     run-parts --report /etc/cron.weekly
@monthly 15        cron.monthly    run-parts --report /etc/cron.monthly
$
```

The basic format of the anacron table is slightly different from that of the cron table:

*period delay identifier command*

The *period* entry defines how often the jobs should be run, specified in days. The anacron program uses this entry to check against the jobs' time stamp file. The *delay* entry
specifies how many minutes after the system starts the anacron program should run
missed scripts.

**NOTE**

The anacron utility does not run scripts located in the /etc/cron.hourly directory. This is because the anacron program does not deal with scripts that have execution time needs of less than daily.

The *identifier* entry is a unique non-blank character string — for example, cron.
weekly. It is used to uniquely identify the job in log messages and error emails. The
*command* entry contains the run-parts program and a cron script directory name. The
run-parts program is responsible for running any script in the directory passed to it.

The at, cron, and anacron utilities all have their place in keeping your scripts running
at their scheduled times. However, you may want a script's execution triggered when a user
starts a new Bash shell instead of at a particular time on the clock. We'll look at that next.

## Starting scripts with a new shell

The ability to run a script every time a user starts a new Bash shell (even just when a specific user starts a Bash shell) can come in handy. Sometimes, you want to set shell features for a shell session or ensure that a specific file has been set.

Recall that the user's startup files run when they log into the Bash shell (covered in detail in Chapter 6, "Using Linux Environment Variables"). Also, remember that not every distribution has all the startup files. Essentially, the first file found in the following ordered list is run and the rest are ignored:

- $HOME/.bash _ profile
- $HOME/.bash _ login
- $HOME/.profile

Therefore, you should place any scripts you want run at login time in the first file listed for your distribution.

The Bash shell runs the .bashrc file any time a new shell is started. You can test this by adding a simple echo statement to the .bashrc file in your home directory and starting a new shell:

```
$ cat $HOME/.bashrc
# .bashrc

# Source global definitions
if [ -f /etc/bashrc ]; then
        . /etc/bashrc
fi

# User specific environment
PATH="$HOME/.local/bin:$HOME/bin:$PATH"
export PATH

# Uncomment the following line if you don't like systemctl's auto-
paging feature:
# export SYSTEMD_PAGER=

# User specific aliases and functions
echo "I'm in a new shell!"
$
$ bash
I'm in a new shell!
$
$ exit
exit
$
```

The .bashrc file is also typically run from one of the Bash startup files. Because the .bashrc file runs both when you log into the Bash shell and when you start a Bash shell, if you need a script to run in both instances place your shell script or the call to execute your script inside this file.

## Working through a Practical Example

In this section, we'll describe a script that puts a few of the script control commands we've covered in this chapter to a practical use — trapping signals for a script, and then running it in the background. This particular script works best for executing small scripts you already use that need protection from interrupting signals while they run.

For ease of use, the controlling script accepts signals to trap as script options, as well as a parameter naming the script to run by employing getopts (Chapter 14, "Handling User Input"). The script option to denote signals is handled here in the script:

```
while getopts S: opt    #Signals to trap listed with -S option
do
     case "$opt" in
         S) # Found the -S option
            signalList="" #Set signalList to null
            #
            for arg in $OPTARG
            do
                 case $arg in
                 1)    #SIGHUP signal is handled
                       signalList=$signalList"SIGHUP "
                 ;;
                 2)    #SIGINT signal is handled
                       signalList=$signalList"SIGINT "
                 ;;
                 20)   #SIGTSTP signal is handled
                       signalList=$signalList"SIGTSTP "
                 ;;
                 *)    #Unknown or unhandled signal
                       echo "Only signals 1 2 and/or 20 are allowed."
                       echo "Exiting script..."
                       exit
                 ;;
                 esac
            done
         ;;
         *) echo 'Usage: -S "Signal(s)" script-to-run-name'
            echo 'Exiting script...'
            exit
         ;;
     esac
     #
done
```

Notice that this code section uses while and for loops (Chapter 13, "More Structured Commands"), as well as a case statement (Chapter 12, "Using Structured Commands") to process through the -S option and its accompanying signal numbers. The only signals allowed for trapping with this script are SIGHUP (1), SIGINT (2), and SIGTSTP (20). If an option besides -S is used or incorrect signals to trap are listed, "error" messages are provided to the script user.

After the -S option and its parameters are processed, the script determines if a script name was provided using $@ stored in the $OPTIND environment variable:

```
shift $[ $OPTIND - 1 ] #Script name should be in parameter
#
if [ -z $@ ]
then
      echo
      echo 'Error: Script name not provided.'
      echo 'Usage: -S "Signal(s)"  script-to-run-name'
      echo 'Exiting script...'
      exit
elif [ -O $@ ] && [ -x $@ ]
then
      scriptToRun=$@
      scriptOutput="$@.out"
else
      echo
      echo "Error: $@ is either not owned by you or not executable."
      echo "Exiting..."
      exit
fi
```

If the script name parameter is provided, a few additional checks are done to ensure that the script file is owned by the script user and that it is executable via if-then and elif statements (Chapter 12). If all is well, the script's name is stored in another variable, scriptToRun, which is not essential but adds to the code's clarity. Additionally, an output file is created that contains the script's name and tacks on .out.

Now that we have the script's name we need to run and the signals to block, we're ready to trap signals and kick off the script:

```
trap "" $signalList  #Ignore these signals
#
source $scriptToRun > $scriptOutput &  #Run script in background
#
trap -- $signalList  #Set to default behavior
#
```

First notice we're being a little fancy in how we run our script. Instead of using bash or ./ to execute the file, we're employing the source utility. This is another method for running Bash scripts called *sourcing*. It operates just like using bash to run a script but doesn't create a subshell. However, source does not deal well with any commands listed in trap besides null (""). That's not a problem, because using null causes the source executed script to simply ignore any signals listed in the trap command. Our running script will disregard any sent $signalList signals. Once $scriptToRun is kicked off into the background to execute, its output is saved to the scriptOutput file.

Another item to notice in this script segment is the second trap command. Immediately after sending $scriptToRun into the background, the signal traps are removed. This is considered good form — trapping signals before the code that needs the traps, and then removing the signal traps immediately afterward.

Before we test this practical script, let's look at a script that was created specifically to test this code. Nothing too exciting here, but you'll want to familiarize yourself with the script's output so that the test's output file will make sense:

```
$ cat testTandR.sh
#!/bin/bash
#Test script to use with trapandrun.sh
#
echo "This is a test script."
#
count=1
while [ $count -le 5 ]
do
      echo "Loop #$count"
      sleep 10
      count=$[ $count + 1 ]
done
#
echo "This is the end of test script."
#exit
$
```

Now we'll run the test and send the trapped signals to the running script process to see if they are ignored or processed in a default manner. First, we'll use the proper syntax for specifying to our script (trapandrun.sh) the signals to ignore (1, 2, and 20) and the name of our script for it to execute (testTandR.sh):

```
$ ./trapandrun.sh -S "1 2 20" testTandR.sh

Running the testTandR.sh script in background
while trapping signal(s): SIGHUP SIGINT SIGTSTP
Output of script sent to: testTandR.sh.out

$
```

Now that the script (`testTandR.sh`) is running, we'll use the `ps` command to find its PID and the `kill` command to send a signal to it:

```
$ ps
    PID TTY          TIME CMD
   1637 pts/0    00:00:00 bash
   1701 pts/0    00:00:00 trapandrun.sh
   1702 pts/0    00:00:00 sleep
   1703 pts/0    00:00:00 ps
$
$ kill -1 1701
$
$ cat testTandR.sh.out
This is a test script.
Loop #1
Loop #2
$
$ ps
    PID TTY          TIME CMD
   1637 pts/0    00:00:00 bash
   1701 pts/0    00:00:00 trapandrun.sh
   1704 pts/0    00:00:00 sleep
   1706 pts/0    00:00:00 ps
$
```

You can tell from the script's output file as well as the second `ps` command that the script just ignored our SIGHUP (1) signal and didn't hang up. This time, let's try to interrupt the script using the SIGINT (2) signal:

```
$ kill -2 1701
$
$ cat testTandR.sh.out
This is a test script.
Loop #1
Loop #2
Loop #3
$
$ ps
    PID TTY          TIME CMD
   1637 pts/0    00:00:00 bash
   1701 pts/0    00:00:00 trapandrun.sh
   1709 pts/0    00:00:00 sleep
   1711 pts/0    00:00:00 ps
$
```

The script ignored this signal too! So far it is running as we planned. Let's try sending our last trapped signal, SIGTSTP (20):

```
$ kill -20 1701
$
```

```
$ ps
    PID TTY          TIME CMD
   1637 pts/0    00:00:00 bash
   1701 pts/0    00:00:00 trapandrun.sh
   1712 pts/0    00:00:00 sleep
   1714 pts/0    00:00:00 ps
$
$ cat testTandR.sh.out
This is a test script.
Loop #1
Loop #2
Loop #3
Loop #4
Loop #5
$
$ cat testTandR.sh.out
This is a test script.
Loop #1
Loop #2
Loop #3
Loop #4
Loop #5
This is the end of test script.
$
$ ps
    PID TTY          TIME CMD
   1637 pts/0    00:00:00 bash
   1718 pts/0    00:00:00 ps
$
```

It worked perfectly. All three designated signals were ignored, and the script ran in the background without interruption. Here's the controlling script in its entirety for your perusal:

```
$ cat trapandrun.sh
#!/bin/bash
# Set specified signal traps; then run script in background
#
##################### Check Signals to Trap #####################
#
while getopts S: opt    #Signals to trap listed with -S option
do
     case "$opt" in
          S) # Found the -S option
             signalList="" #Set signalList to null
             #
             for arg in $OPTARG
             do
```

(Continues)

*(continued)*

```
                        case $arg in
                        1)   #SIGHUP signal is handled
                             signalList=$signalList"SIGHUP "
                        ;;
                        2)   #SIGINT signal is handled
                             signalList=$signalList"SIGINT "
                        ;;
                        20)  #SIGTSTP signal is handled
                             signalList=$signalList"SIGTSTP "
                        ;;
                        *)   #Unknown or unhandled signal
                             echo "Only signals 1 2 and/or 20 are allowed."
                             echo "Exiting script..."
                             exit
                        ;;
                        esac
                done
                ;;
            *) echo 'Usage: -S "Signal(s)" script-to-run-name'
               echo 'Exiting script...'
               exit
               ;;
        esac
        #
done
#
##################### Check Script to Run #####################
#
shift $[ $OPTIND - 1 ] #Script name should be in parameter
#
if [ -z $@ ]
then
     echo
     echo 'Error: Script name not provided.'
     echo 'Usage: -S "Signal(s)"  script-to-run-name'
     echo 'Exiting script...'
     exit
elif [ -O $@ ] && [ -x $@ ]
then
     scriptToRun=$@
     scriptOutput="$@.out"
else
     echo
     echo "Error: $@ is either not owned by you or not executable."
     echo "Exiting..."
     exit
fi
#
####################### Trap and Run #########################
#
```

```
echo
echo "Running the $scriptToRun script in background"
echo "while trapping signal(s): $signalList"
echo "Output of script sent to: $scriptOutput"
echo
trap "" $signalList  #Ignore these signals
#
source $scriptToRun > $scriptOutput &  #Run script in background
#
trap -- $signalList  #Set to default behavior
#
##################### Exit script #####################
#
exit
$
```

One item we hope you caught in reading through this controlling script is that checking whether or not you have execute permission on the file is not needed. When using the source command to run a script, just as with bash, you don't need execute permissions set on the file.

What improvements did you consider while reading through this script's code? How about modifying it so that the script user has the option of running the script in the future using the at utility? You might consider allowing the user to choose between running the script at the default priority or a lower one. You could trap all the controlling script's exits so that all the exit messages are consistent. There are so many things you can do to fine-tune the control of your scripts!

# Summary

The Linux system allows you to control your shell scripts by using signals. The Bash shell accepts signals and passes them on to any process running under the shell process. Linux signals allow you to easily kill a runaway process or temporarily pause a long-running process.

You can use the trap statement in your scripts to catch signals and perform commands. This feature provides a simple way to control whether a user can interrupt your script while it's running.

By default, when you run a script in a terminal session shell, the interactive shell is suspended until the script completes. You can cause a script or command to run in background mode by adding an ampersand sign (&) after the command name. When you run a script or command in background mode, the interactive shell returns, allowing you to continue entering more commands.

Any background processes you start are still tied to your terminal session. If you exit the terminal session, the background processes also exit. To prevent this from happening, use the nohup command. This command intercepts any signals intended for the command that would stop it — for example, when you exit the terminal session. This allows scripts to continue running in background mode even if you exit the terminal session.

When you move a process to background mode, you can still control what happens to it. The jobs command allows you to view processes started from the shell session. After you know the job ID of a background process, you can use the kill command to send Linux signals to the process or use the fg command to bring the process back to the foreground in the shell session. You can suspend a running foreground process by using the Ctrl+Z key combination and place it back in background mode by using the bg command.

The nice and renice commands allow you to change the priority level of a process. By giving a process a lower priority, you give other, higher-priority processes more time from the CPU. This comes in handy when running long processes that can take lots of CPU time.

In addition to controlling processes while they're running, you can determine when a process starts on the system. Instead of running a script directly from the command-line interface prompt, you can schedule the process to run at an alternative time. You can accomplish this in several different ways. The at command enables you to run a script once at a preset time. The cron program provides an interface that can run scripts at a regularly scheduled interval. And the anacron utility ensures scripts that need to run are executed in a timely manner.

Finally, the Linux system provides script files for you to use for scheduling your scripts to run whenever a user starts a new Bash shell. Similarly, the startup files, such as .bashrc, are located in every user's home directory to provide a location to place scripts and commands that run with a new shell.

In the next chapter, where we're introducing the Part III: Advanced Shell Scripting section, we look at how to write script functions. Script functions allow you to write code blocks once and then use them in multiple locations throughout your script. This keeps your code cleaner and makes script updates much easier.

# Part III

# Advanced Shell Scripting

## IN THIS PART

# Creating Functions

O ften while writing shell scripts, you'll find yourself using the same code in multiple locations. If it's just a small code snippet, it's usually not that big a deal. However, rewriting large chunks of code multiple times in your shell script can get tiring. The Bash shell provides a way to help you out by supporting user-defined functions. You can encapsulate your shell script code into a function and use it as many times as you want, anywhere in your script. This chapter walks you through the process of creating your own shell script functions and demonstrates how to use them in other shell script applications.

## Exploring Basic Script Functions

As you start writing more complex shell scripts, you'll find yourself reusing parts of code that perform specific tasks. Sometimes, it's something simple, such as displaying a text message and retrieving an answer from the script users. Other times, it's a complicated calculation that's used multiple times in your script as part of a larger process.

In each of these situations, it can get tiresome writing the same blocks of code over and over in your script. It would be nice to just write the block of code once and be able to refer to that block of code anywhere in your script without having to rewrite it.

The Bash shell provides a feature allowing you to do just that. *Functions* are blocks of script code that you assign a name to and reuse anywhere in your code. Whenever you need to use that block of code in your script, you simply use the function name you assigned it (referred to as *calling* the function). This section describes how to create and use functions in your shell scripts.

## Creating a function

You can use one of two formats to create functions in Bash shell scripts. The first format uses the keyword `function`, along with the function name you assign to the block of code:

```
function name {
    commands
}
```

The *name* attribute defines a unique name assigned to the function. Each function you define in your script must be assigned a unique name.

The *commands* are one or more Bash shell commands that make up your function. When you call the function, the Bash shell executes each of the commands in the order in which they appear in the function, just as in a normal script.

The second format for defining a function in a Bash shell script more closely follows how functions are defined in other programming languages:

```
name() {
commands
}
```

The empty parentheses after the function name indicate that you're defining a function. The same naming rules apply in this format as in the original shell script function format.

## Using functions

To use a function in your script, specify the function name on a line, just as you would any other shell command:

```
$ cat test1
#!/bin/bash
# using a function in a script

function func1 {
    echo "This is an example of a function"
}

count=1
while [ $count -le 5 ]
do
    func1
    count=$[ $count + 1 ]
done
```

```
echo "This is the end of the loop"
func1
echo "Now this is the end of the script"
$
$ ./test1
This is an example of a function
This is an example of a function
This is an example of a function
This is an example of a function
This is an example of a function
This is the end of the loop
This is an example of a function
Now this is the end of the script
$
```

Each time you reference the `func1` function name, the Bash shell returns to the `func1` function definition and executes any commands you defined there.

The function definition doesn't have to be the first thing in your shell script, but be careful. If you attempt to use a function before it's defined, you'll get an error message:

```
$ cat test2
#!/bin/bash
# using a function located in the middle of a script

count=1
echo "This line comes before the function definition"

function func1 {
    echo "This is an example of a function"
}

while [ $count -le 5 ]
do
    func1
    count=$[ $count + 1 ]
done
echo "This is the end of the loop"
func2
echo "Now this is the end of the script"

function func2 {
    echo "This is an example of a function"
}
$
$ ./test2
This line comes before the function definition
This is an example of a function
This is an example of a function
```

(Continues)

*(continued)*

```
This is an example of a function
This is an example of a function
This is an example of a function
This is the end of the loop
./test2: func2: command not found
Now this is the end of the script
$
```

The first function, func1, was defined after a couple of statements in the script, which is perfectly fine. When the func1 function was used in the script, the shell knew where to find it.

However, the script attempted to use the func2 function before it was defined. Because the func2 function wasn't defined, when the script reached the place where we used it, it produced an error message.

You also need to be careful about your function names. Remember, each function name must be unique, or you'll have a problem. If you redefine a function, the new definition overrides the original function definition, without producing any error messages:

```
$ cat test3
#!/bin/bash
# testing using a duplicate function name

function func1 {
echo "This is the first definition of the function name"
}

func1

function func1 {
    echo "This is a repeat of the same function name"
}

func1
echo "This is the end of the script"
$
$ ./test3
This is the first definition of the function name
This is a repeat of the same function name
This is the end of the script
$
```

The original definition of the func1 function works fine, but after the second definition of the func1 function, any subsequent uses of the function utilize the second definition.

# Returning a Value from a Function

The Bash shell treats functions like mini-scripts, complete with an exit status (see Chapter 11, "Basic Script Building"). There are three different ways you can generate an exit status for your functions.

## The default exit status

By default, the exit status of a function is the exit status returned by the last command in the function. After the function executes, you use the standard *$?* variable to determine the exit status of the function:

```
$ cat test4
#!/bin/bash
# testing the exit status of a function

func1() {
   echo "trying to display a non-existent file"
   ls -l badfile
}

echo "testing the function: "
func1
echo "The exit status is: $?"
$
$ ./test4
testing the function:
trying to display a non-existent file
ls: badfile: No such file or directory
The exit status is: 1
$
```

The exit status of the function is 1 because the last command in the function failed. However, you have no way of knowing whether or not any of the other commands in the function completed successfully. Look at this example:

```
$ cat test4b
#!/bin/bash
# testing the exit status of a function

func1() {
   ls -l badfile
   echo "This was a test of a bad command"
}
```

*(Continues)*

477

```
(continued)
      echo "testing the function:"
      func1
      echo "The exit status is: $?"
$
$ ./test4b
testing the function:
ls: badfile: No such file or directory
This was a test of a bad command
The exit status is: 0
$
```

This time, because the function ended with an `echo` statement that completed successfully, the exit status of the function is 0, even though one of the commands in the function failed. Using the default exit status of a function can be a dangerous practice. Fortunately, we have a couple of other solutions.

## Using the *return* command

The Bash shell uses the `return` command to exit a function with a specific exit status. The `return` command allows you to specify a single integer value to define the function exit status, providing an easy way for you to programmatically set the exit status of your function:

```
$ cat test5
#!/bin/bash
# using the return command in a function

function dbl {
    read -p "Enter a value: " value
    echo "doubling the value"
    return $[ $value * 2 ]
}

dbl
echo "The new value is $?"
$
```

The `dbl` function doubles the integer value contained in the *$value* variable provided by the user input. It then returns the result using the `return` command, which the script displays using the *$?* variable.

You must be careful, however, when using this technique to return a value from a function. Keep the following two tips in mind to avoid problems:

- Remember to retrieve the return value as soon as the function completes.
- Remember that an exit status must be in the range of 0 to 255.

If you execute any other commands before retrieving the value of the function using the *$?* variable, the return value from the function is lost. Remember that the *$?* variable returns the exit status of the last executed command.

The second problem defines a limitation for using this return value technique. Because an exit status must be less than 256, the result of your function must produce an integer value less than 256. Any value over that returns an error value:

```
$ ./test5
Enter a value: 200
doubling the value
The new value is 1
$
```

You cannot use this return value technique if you need to return either larger integer values or a string value. Instead, you need to use another method, demonstrated in the next section.

## Using function output

Just as you can capture the output of a command to a shell variable, you can also capture the output of a function to a shell variable. You can use this technique to retrieve any type of output from a function to assign to a variable:

```
result=$(dbl)
```

This command assigns the output of the dbl function to the $result shell variable. Here's an example of using this method in a script:

```
$ cat test5b
#!/bin/bash
# using the echo to return a value

function dbl {
   read -p "Enter a value: " value
   echo $[ $value * 2 ]
}

result=$(dbl)
echo "The new value is $result"
$
$ ./test5b
Enter a value: 200
The new value is 400
$
$ ./test5b
Enter a value: 1000
The new value is 2000
$
```

The new function now uses an echo statement to display the result of the calculation. The script just captures the output of the dbl function instead of looking at the exit status for the answer.

*(Continues)*

There's a subtle trick that this example demonstrates. You'll notice that the db1 function really outputs two messages. The read command outputs a short message querying the user for the value. The Bash shell script is smart enough to not consider this as part of the STDOUT output and ignores it. If you had used an echo statement to produce this query message to the user, it would have been captured by the shell variable as well as the output value.

> **NOTE**
>
> Using this technique, you can also return floating-point and string values, making this an extremely versatile method for returning values from functions.

# Using Variables in Functions

You might have noticed in the test5 example in the previous section that we used a variable called $value within the function to hold the value that it processed. When you use variables in your functions, you need to be somewhat careful about how you define and handle them. This is a common cause of problems in shell scripts. This section goes over a few techniques for handling variables both inside and outside your shell script functions.

## Passing parameters to a function

As mentioned earlier in the "Returning a Value from a Function" section, the Bash shell treats functions just like mini-scripts. This means that you can pass parameters to a function just like a regular script (see Chapter 14, "Handling User Input").

Functions can use the standard parameter environment variables to represent any parameters passed to the function on the command line. For example, the name of the function is defined in the $0 variable, and any parameters on the function command line are defined using the variables $1, $2, and so on. You can also use the special variable $# to determine the number of parameters passed to the function.

When specifying the function in your script, you must provide the parameters on the same command line as the function, like this:

```
func1 $value1 10
```

The function can then retrieve the parameter values using the parameter environment variables. Here's an example of using this method to pass values to a function:

```
$ cat test6
#!/bin/bash
# passing parameters to a function

function addem {
    if [ $# -eq 0 ] || [ $# -gt 2 ]
    then
```

```
        echo -1
    elif [ $# -eq 1 ]
    then
        echo $[ $1 + $1 ]
    else
        echo $[ $1 + $2 ]
    fi
}

echo -n "Adding 10 and 15: "
value=$(addem 10 15)
echo $value
echo -n "Let's try adding just one number: "
value=$(addem 10)
echo $value
echo -n "Now try adding no numbers: "
value=$(addem)
echo $value
echo -n "Finally, try adding three numbers: "
value=$(addem 10 15 20)
echo $value
$
$ ./test6
Adding 10 and 15: 25
Let's try adding just one number: 20
Now try adding no numbers: -1
Finally, try adding three numbers: -1
$
```

The addem function in the text6 script first checks the number of parameters passed to it by the script. If there aren't any parameters, or if there are more than two parameters, addem returns a value of -1. If there's just one parameter, addem adds the parameter to itself for the result. If there are two parameters, addem adds them together for the result.

Because the function uses the special parameter environment variables for its own parameter values, it can't directly access the script parameter values from the command line of the script. The following example fails:

```
$ cat badtest1
#!/bin/bash
# trying to access script parameters inside a function

function badfunc1 {
    echo $[ $1 * $2 ]
}

if [ $# -eq 2 ]
then
```

*(Continues)*

**481**

*(continued)*

```
      value=$(badfunc1)
      echo "The result is $value"
   else
      echo "Usage: badtest1 a b"
   fi
   $
   $ ./badtest1
   Usage: badtest1 a b
   $ ./badtest1 10 15
   ./badtest1: *  : syntax error: operand expected (error token is "*
   ")
   The result is
   $
```

Even though the function uses the *$1* and *$2* variables, they aren't the same *$1* and *$2* variables available in the main part of the script. Instead, if you want to use those values in your function, you have to manually pass them when you call the function:

```
$ cat test7
#!/bin/bash
# trying to access script parameters inside a function

function func7 {
   echo $[ $1 * $2 ]
}

if [ $# -eq 2 ]
then
   value=$(func7 $1 $2)
   echo "The result is $value"
else
   echo "Usage: badtest1 a b"
fi
$
$ ./test7
Usage: badtest1 a b
$ ./test7 10 15
The result is 150
$
```

When we pass the *$1* and *$2* variables to the function, they become available for the function to use, just like any other parameter.

## Handling variables in a function

One thing that causes problems for shell script programmers is the *scope* of a variable. The scope is where the variable is visible. Variables defined in functions can have a different scope than regular variables—that is, they can be hidden from the rest of the script.

Functions use two types of variables:

- Global
- Local

The following sections describe how to use both types of variables in your functions.

### Global variables

*Global variables* are variables that are valid anywhere within the shell script. If you define a global variable in the main section of a script, you can retrieve its value inside a function. Likewise, if you define a global variable inside a function, you can retrieve its value in the main section of the script.

By default, any variables you define in the script are global variables. Variables defined outside a function can be accessed within the function just fine:

```
$ cat test8
#!/bin/bash
# using a global variable to pass a value

function dbl {
    value=$[ $value * 2 ]
}

read -p "Enter a value: " value
dbl
echo "The new value is: $value"
$
$ ./test8
Enter a value: 450
The new value is: 900
$
```

The *$value* variable is defined outside the function and assigned a value outside the function. When the dbl function is called, the variable and its value are still valid inside the function. When the variable is assigned a new value inside the function, that new value is still valid when the script references the variable.

This practice can be dangerous, however, especially if you intend to use your functions in different shell scripts. It requires that you know exactly what variables are used in the function, including any variables used to calculate values not returned to the script. Here's an example of how things can go bad:

```
$ cat badtest2
#!/bin/bash
# demonstrating a bad use of variables
```

*(Continues)*

17

```
(continued)
    function func1 {
        temp=$[ $value + 5 ]
        result=$[ $temp * 2 ]
    }

    temp=4
    value=6

    func1
    echo "The result is $result"
    if [ $temp -gt $value ]
    then
        echo "temp is larger"
    else
        echo "temp is smaller"
    fi
    $
    $ ./badtest2
    The result is 22
    temp is larger
    $
```

Because the $temp variable was used in the function, its value is compromised in the script, producing a result that you may not have intended. There's an easy way to solve this problem in your functions, as shown in the next section.

## Local variables

Instead of using global variables in functions, any variables that the function uses internally can be declared as local variables. To do that, just use the `local` keyword in front of the variable declaration:

```
local temp
```

You can also use the `local` keyword in an assignment statement while assigning a value to the variable:

```
local temp=$[ $value + 5 ]
```

The `local` keyword ensures that the variable is limited to within the function. If a variable with the same name appears outside the function in the script, the shell keeps the two variable values separate. That means you can easily keep your function variables separate from your script variables and share only the ones you want to share:

```
$ cat test9
#!/bin/bash
# demonstrating the local keyword

function func1 {
    local temp=$[ $value + 5 ]
    result=$[ $temp * 2 ]
}
```

```
temp=4
value=6

func1
echo "The result is $result"
if [ $temp -gt $value ]
then
    echo "temp is larger"
else
    echo "temp is smaller"
fi
$
$ ./test9
The result is 22
temp is smaller
$
```

Now when you use the *$temp* variable within the func1 function, it doesn't affect the value assigned to the *$temp* variable in the main script.

# Investigating Array Variables and Functions

Chapter 5, "Understanding the Shell," discussed an advanced way of allowing a single variable to hold multiple values by using arrays. Using array variable values with functions is a little tricky, and there are some special considerations. This section describes a technique that allows you to do that.

## Passing arrays to functions

The art of passing an array variable to a script function can be confusing. If you try to pass the array variable as a single parameter, it doesn't work:

```
$ cat badtest3
#!/bin/bash
# trying to pass an array variable

function testit {
    echo "The parameters are: $@"
    thisarray=$1
    echo "The received array is ${thisarray[*]}"
}

myarray=(1 2 3 4 5)
echo "The original array is: ${myarray[*]}"
testit $myarray
$
$ ./badtest3
The original array is: 1 2 3 4 5
```

*(Continues)*

*(continued)*

```
The parameters are: 1
The received array is 1
$
```

If you try using the array variable as a function parameter, the function only picks up the first value of the array variable.

To solve this problem, you must disassemble the array variable into its individual values and use the values as function parameters. Inside the function, you can reassemble all the parameters into a new array variable. Here's an example of doing this:

```
$ cat test10
#!/bin/bash
# array variable to function test

function testit {
   local newarray
   newarray=(`echo "$@"`)
   echo "The new array value is: ${newarray[*]}"
}

myarray=(1 2 3 4 5)
echo "The original array is ${myarray[*]}"
testit ${myarray[*]}
$
$ ./test10
The original array is 1 2 3 4 5
The new array value is: 1 2 3 4 5
$
```

The script uses the *$myarray* variable to hold all the individual array values to place them all on the command line for the function. The function then rebuilds the array variable from the command-line parameters. Once inside the function, the array can be used just like any other array:

```
$ cat test11
#!/bin/bash
# adding values in an array

function addarray {
   local sum=0
   local newarray
   newarray=(`echo "$@"`)
   for value in ${newarray[*]}
   do
      sum=$[ $sum + $value ]
   done
   echo $sum
}
```

```
    myarray=(1 2 3 4 5)
    echo "The original array is: ${myarray[*]}"
    arg1=$(echo ${myarray[*]})
    result=$(addarray $arg1)
    echo "The result is $result"
    $
    $ ./test11
    The original array is: 1 2 3 4 5
    The result is 15
    $
```

The `addarray` function iterates through the array values, adding them together. You can put any number of values in the *myarray* array variable, and the `addarray` function adds them.

## Returning arrays from functions

Passing an array variable from a function back to the shell script uses a similar technique. The function uses an `echo` statement to output the individual array values in the proper order, and the script must reassemble them into a new array variable:

```
    $ cat test12
    #!/bin/bash
    # returning an array value

    function arraydblr {
        local origarray
        local newarray
        local elements
        local i
        origarray=($(echo "$@"))
        newarray=($(echo "$@"))
        elements=$[ $# - 1 ]
        for (( i = 0; i <= $elements; i++ ))
        {
            newarray[$i]=$[ ${origarray[$i]} * 2 ]
        }
        echo ${newarray[*]}
    }

    myarray=(1 2 3 4 5)
    echo "The original array is: ${myarray[*]}"
    arg1=$(echo ${myarray[*]})
    result=($(arraydblr $arg1))
    echo "The new array is: ${result[*]}"
    $
    $ ./test12
    The original array is: 1 2 3 4 5
    The new array is: 2 4 6 8 10
```

The script passes the array value, using the *$arg1* variable to the `arraydblr` function. The `arraydblr` function reassembles the array into a new array variable, and it makes a copy for the output array variable. It then iterates through the individual array variable values, doubles each value, and places it into the copy of the array variable in the function.

The `arraydblr` function then uses the `echo` statement to output the individual values of the array variable values. The script uses the output of the `arraydblr` function to reassemble a new array variable with the values.

# Considering Function Recursion

One feature that local function variables provide is *self-containment*. A self-contained function doesn't use any resources outside the function, other than the variables that the script passes to it in the command line.

This feature enables the function to be called *recursively*, which means that the function calls itself to reach an answer. Usually, a recursive function has a base value that it eventually iterates down to. Many advanced mathematical algorithms use recursion to reduce a complex equation down one level repeatedly, until they get to the level defined by the base value.

The classic example of a recursive algorithm is calculating factorials. A factorial of a number is the value of the preceding numbers multiplied with the number. Thus, to find the factorial of 5, you'd perform the following equation:

```
5! = 1 * 2 * 3 * 4 * 5 = 120
```

Using recursion, the equation is reduced down to the following format:

```
x! = x * (x-1)!
```

or in English, the factorial of $x$ is equal to $x$ times the factorial of $x-1$. This can be expressed in a simple recursive script:

```
function factorial {
   if [ $1 -eq 1 ]
   then
      echo 1
   else
      local temp=$[ $1 - 1 ]
      local result=`factorial $temp`
      echo $[ $result * $1 ]
   fi
}
```

The factorial function uses itself to calculate the value for the factorial:

```
$ cat test13
#!/bin/bash
# using recursion
```

```
function factorial {
   if [ $1 -eq 1 ]
   then
      echo 1
   else
      local temp=$[ $1 - 1 ]
      local result=$(factorial $temp)
      echo $[ $result * $1 ]
   fi
}

read -p "Enter value: " value
result=$(factorial $value)
echo "The factorial of $value is: $result"
$
$ ./test13
Enter value: 5
The factorial of 5 is: 120
$
```

Using the factorial function is easy. Having created a function like this, you may want to use it in other scripts. Next, let's look at how to do that efficiently.

## Creating a Library

It's easy to see how functions can help save typing in a single script, but what if you just happen to use the same single code block between scripts? It's obviously challenging if you have to define the same function in each script, only to use it one time in each script.

There's a solution for that problem! The Bash shell allows you to create a *library file* for your functions and then reference that single library file in as many scripts as you need to.

The first step in the process is to create a common library file that contains the functions you need in your scripts. Here's a simple library file called myfuncs that defines three simple functions:

```
$ cat myfuncs
# my script functions

function addem {
   echo $[ $1 + $2 ]
}

function multem {
   echo $[ $1 * $2 ]
}

function divem {
```

*(Continues)*

*(continued)*

```
      if [ $2 -ne 0 ]
      then
          echo $[ $1 / $2 ]
      else
          echo -1
      fi
}
$
```

The next step is to include the myfuncs library file in your script files that want to use any of the functions. This is where things get tricky.

The problem is with the scope of shell functions. As with environment variables, shell functions are valid only for the shell session in which you define them. If you run the myfuncs shell script from your shell command-line interface prompt, the shell creates a new shell and runs the script in that new shell. This defines the three functions for that shell, but when you try to run another script that uses those functions, they aren't available.

This applies to scripts as well. If you try to just run the library file as a regular script file, the functions don't appear in your script:

```
$ cat badtest4
#!/bin/bash
# using a library file the wrong way
./myfuncs

result=$(addem 10 15)
echo "The result is $result"
$
$ ./badtest4
./badtest4: addem: command not found
The result is
$
```

The key to using function libraries is the source command. The source command executes commands within the current shell context instead of creating a new shell to execute them. You use the source command to run the library file script inside your shell script. Doing so makes the functions available to the script.

The source command has a shortcut alias, called the *dot operator*. To source the myfuncs library file in a shell script, you just need to add the following line:

```
. ./myfuncs
```

This example assumes that the myfuncs library file is located in the same directory as the shell script. If not, you need to use the appropriate path to access the file. Here's an example of creating a script that uses the myfuncs library file:

```
$ cat test14
#!/bin/bash
```

```
# using functions defined in a library file
. ./myfuncs

value1=10
value2=5
result1=$(addem $value1 $value2)
result2=$(multem $value1 $value2)
result3=$(divem $value1 $value2)
echo "The result of adding them is: $result1"
echo "The result of multiplying them is: $result2"
echo "The result of dividing them is: $result3"
$
$ ./test14
The result of adding them is: 15
The result of multiplying them is: 50
The result of dividing them is: 2
$
```

The script successfully uses the functions defined in the myfuncs library file.

## Using Functions on the Command Line

You can use script functions to create some pretty complex operations. Sometimes, it would be nice to be able to use these functions directly on the command-line interfacet.

Just as you can use a script function as a command in a shell script, you can also use a script function as a command in the command-line interface. This is a nice feature because after you define the function in the shell, you can use it from any directory on the system; you don't have to worry about a script being in your PATH environment variable. The trick is to get the shell to recognize the function. You can do that in a couple of ways.

### Creating functions on the command line

Because the shell interprets commands as you type them, you can define a function directly on the command line. You can do that in two ways.

The first method defines the function all on one line:

```
$ function divem { echo $[ $1 / $2 ];  }
$ divem 100 5
20
$
```

When you define the function on the command line, you must remember to include a semi-colon at the end of each command so that the shell knows where to separate commands:

```
$ function doubleit { read -p "Enter value: " value; echo $[
  $value * 2 ]; }
$
```

*(Continues)*

*(continued)*

```
$ doubleit
Enter value: 20
40
$
```

The other method is to use multiple lines to define the function. When you do that, the Bash shell uses the secondary prompt to ask you for more commands. Using this method, you don't need to place a semicolon at the end of each command; just press the Enter key.

```
$ function multem {
> echo $[ $1 * $2 ]
> }
$ multem 2 5
10
$
```

When you use the brace at the end of the function, the shell knows that you're finished defining the function.

---

**WARNING**

Be extremely careful when creating functions on the command line. If you use a function with the same name as a built-in command or another command, the function overrides the original command.

---

## Defining functions in the *.bashrc* file

The obvious downside to defining shell functions directly on the command line is that when you exit the shell, your function disappears. For complex functions, this can become a problem.

A much simpler method is to define the function in a place where it is reloaded by the shell each time you start a new shell.

The best place to do that is the .bashrc file. The Bash shell looks for this file in your home directory each time it starts, whether interactively or as the result of starting a new shell from within an existing shell.

### Directly defining functions

You can define the functions directly in the .bashrc file in your home directory. Most Linux distributions already define some things in the .bashrc file, so be careful not to remove those items. Just add your functions to the bottom of the existing file. Here's an example of doing that:

```
$ cat .bashrc
# .bashrc

# Source global definitions
if [ -r /etc/bashrc ]; then
```

```
        . /etc/bashrc
fi

function addem {
    echo $[ $1 + $2 ]
}
$
```

The function doesn't take effect until the next time you start a new Bash shell. After you do that, you can use the function anywhere on the system.

### Sourcing function files

Just as in a shell script, you can use the source command (or its alias, the dot operator) to add functions from an existing library file to your .bashrc script:

```
$ cat .bashrc
# .bashrc

# Source global definitions
if [ -r /etc/bashrc ]; then
        . /etc/bashrc
fi

. /home/rich/libraries/myfuncs
$
```

Make sure that you include the proper pathname to reference the library file for the Bash shell to find. The next time you start a shell, all the functions in your library are available at the command-line interface:

```
$ addem 10 5
15
$ multem 10 5
50
$ divem 10 5
2
$
```

Even better, the shell also passes any defined functions to child shell processes so that your functions are automatically available for any shell scripts you run from your shell session. You can test this by writing a script that uses the functions without defining or sourcing them:

```
$ cat test15
#!/bin/bash
# using a function defined in the .bashrc file

value1=10
value2=5
result1=$(addem $value1 $value2)
```

*(Continues)*

```
(continued)
    result2=$(multem $value1 $value2)
    result3=$(divem $value1 $value2)
    echo "The result of adding them is: $result1"
    echo "The result of multiplying them is: $result2"
    echo "The result of dividing them is: $result3"
    $
    $ ./test15
    The result of adding them is: 15
    The result of multiplying them is: 50
    The result of dividing them is: 2
    $
```

Even without sourcing the library file, the functions worked perfectly in the shell script.

# Working Through a Practical Example

There's much more to using functions than just creating your own functions to work with. In the open source world, code sharing is essential, and that also applies to shell script functions. Quite a few different shell script functions are available for you to download and use in your own applications.

This section walks through downloading, installing, and using the GNU shtool shell script function library. The shtool library provides some simple shell script functions for performing everyday shell functions, such as working with temporary files and folders or formatting output to display.

## Downloading and installing

The first step in the process is to download and install the GNU shtool library to your system so that you can use the library functions in your own shell scripts. To do that, you need to use an FTP client program or a browser in a graphical desktop. Use this URL to download the shtool package:

```
ftp://ftp.gnu.org/gnu/shtool/shtool-2.0.8.tar.gz
```

This downloads the file shtool-2.0.8.tar.gz to your download folder. From there, you can use the cp command-line tool or the graphical file manager tool in your Linux distribution (such as Files in Ubuntu) to copy the file to your home directory.

After you copy the file to your home directory, you can extract it using the tar command:

```
tar -zxvf shtool-2.0.8.tar.gz
```

This extracts the package files into a folder named shtool-2.0.8. Use the cd command to change to the newly created folder:

```
cd shtool-2.0.8
```

Now you're ready to build the shell script library file.

## Building the library

The shtool distribution file must be configured for your specific Linux environment. To do that, it uses standard `configure` and `make` commands, commonly used in the C programming environment. To build the library file, you just need to run two commands:

```
$ ./configure
$ make
```

The `configure` command checks the software necessary to build the shtool library file. As it finds the tools it needs, it modifies the configuration file with the proper paths to the tools.

The `make` command runs through the steps to build the shtool library file. The resulting file (`shtool`) is the full library package file. You can test the library file using the `make` command as well:

```
$ make test
Running test suite:
echo..........ok
mdate.........ok
table.........ok
prop..........ok
move..........ok
install.......ok
mkdir.........ok
mkln..........ok
mkshadow......ok
fixperm.......ok
rotate........ok
tarball.......ok
subst.........ok
platform......ok
arx...........ok
slo...........ok
scpp..........ok
version.......ok
path..........ok
OK: passed: 19/19
$
```

The test mode tests all the functions available in the shtool library. If all pass, then you're ready to install the library into a common location on your Linux system so that all your scripts can use it. To do so, you can use the `install` option of the `make` command. However, you need to be logged in as the `root` user account to run it:

```
# make install
Password:
```

*(Continues)*

*(continued)*

```
./shtool mkdir -f -p -m 755 /usr/local
./shtool mkdir -f -p -m 755 /usr/local/bin
./shtool mkdir -f -p -m 755 /usr/local/share/man/man1
./shtool mkdir -f -p -m 755 /usr/local/share/aclocal
./shtool mkdir -f -p -m 755 /usr/local/share/shtool
...
./shtool install -c -m 644 sh.version /usr/local/share/shtool/
sh.version
./shtool install -c -m 644 sh.path /usr/local/share/shtool/sh.path
#
```

Now you're ready to start using the functions in your own shell scripts!

## The shtool library functions

The shtool library provides quite a few functions that can come in handy when you're working with shell scripts. Table 17.1 shows the functions available in the library.

**TABLE 17.1  The shtool Library Functions**

| Function | Description |
| --- | --- |
| arx | Creates an archive with extended features |
| echo | Displays the string value with construct expansion |
| fixperm | Changes file permissions inside a folder tree |
| install | Installs a script or file |
| mdate | Displays modification time of a file or directory |
| mkdir | Creates one or more directories |
| mkln | Creates a link using relative paths |
| mkshadow | Creates a shadow tree |
| move | Moves files with substitution |
| path | Works with program paths |
| platform | Displays the platform identity |
| rop | Displays an animated progress propeller |
| rotate | Rotates logfiles |
| scpp | The sharing C preprocessor |
| slo | Separates linker options by library class |
| subst | Uses sed substitution operations |
| table | Displays field-separated data in a table format |
| tarball | Creates tar files from files and folders |
| version | Creates a version information file |

Each of the shtool functions has lots of options and arguments that you can use to modify how it works. Here's the format to use a shtool function:

```
shtool [options] [function [options] [args]]
```

## Using the library

You can use the `shtool` functions directly from the command line or from within your shell scripts. Here's an example of using the `platform` function inside a shell script:

```
$ cat test16
#!/bin/bash

shtool platform
$ ./test16
Ubuntu 20.04 (AMD64)
$
```

The `platform` function returns the Linux distribution and the CPU hardware that the host system is using. One of our favorites is the `prop` function. It creates a spinning propeller from alternating the \, |, /, and – characters while something is processing. That's a great tool to help show your shell script users that something is happening in the background while the script is running.

To use the `prop` function, you just pipe the output of the function you want to monitor to the `shtool` script:

```
$ ls -al /usr/bin | shtool prop -p "waiting....."
waiting...
$
```

The `prop` function alternates between the propeller characters to indicate that something is happening. In this case, it's the output from the `ls` command. How much of that you see depends on how fast your CPU can list all the files in the /usr/bin folder! The –p option allows you to customize the output text that appears before the propeller characters. Now that's getting fancy!

# Summary

Shell script functions allow you to place script code that's repeated throughout the script in a single place. Instead of having to rewrite blocks of code, you can create a function containing the code block and then just reference the function name in your script. The Bash shell jumps to the function code block whenever it sees the function name used in the script.

You can even create script functions that return values. This allows you to create functions that interact with the script, returning both numeric and character data. Script functions can return numeric data by using the exit status of the last command in the function or by

497

using the `return` command. The `return` command lets you programmatically set the exit status of your function to a specific value based on the results of the function.

Functions can also return values using the standard `echo` statement. You can capture the output data using the backtick character as you would any other shell command. This enables you to return any type of data from a function, including strings and floating-point numbers.

You can use shell variables within your functions, assigning values to variables and retrieving values from existing variables. This allows you to pass any type of data both into and out of a script function from the main script program. Functions also allow you to define local variables, which are accessible only from within the function code block. Local variables let you create self-contained functions, which don't interfere with any variables or processes used in the main shell script.

Functions can also call other functions, including themselves. When a function calls itself, it is called recursion. A recursive function often has a base value that is the terminal value of the function. The function continues to call itself with a decreasing parameter value until the base value is reached.

If you use lots of functions in your shell scripts, you can create library files of script functions. The library files can be included in any shell script file by using the source command, or its alias, the dot operator. This approach is called sourcing the library file. The shell doesn't run the library file but makes the functions available within the shell that runs the script. You can use this same technique to create functions that you can use on the normal shell command line. You can either define functions directly on the command line or add them to your `.bashrc` file so that they are available for each new shell session you start. This is a handy way to create utilities that can be used no matter what your `PATH` environment variable is set to.

The next chapter discusses the use of text graphics in your scripts. In this day of modern graphical interfaces, sometimes a plain-text interface just doesn't cut it. The Bash shell provides some easy ways for you to incorporate simple graphics features in your scripts to help spice things up.

# Writing Scripts for Graphical Desktops

O ver the years, shell scripts have acquired a reputation for being dull and boring. This doesn't have to be the case, however, if you plan on running your scripts in a graphical environment. There are plenty of ways to interact with your script user that don't rely on the read and echo statements. This chapter dives into a few methods you can use to add life to your interactive scripts so that they don't look so old-fashioned.

## Creating Text Menus

The most common way to create an interactive shell script is to utilize a menu. Offering your users a choice of various options helps guide them through what the script can and can't do.

Menu scripts usually clear the display area and then show a list of available options. The user can select an option by pressing an associated letter or number assigned to each option. Figure 18-1 shows the layout of a sample menu.

The core of a shell script menu is the case command (see Chapter 12, "Using Structured Commands"). The case command performs specific commands, depending on what character your user selects from the menu.

The following sections walk you through the steps you should follow to create a menu-based shell script.

### Create the menu layout

The first step in creating a menu is, obviously, to determine what elements you want to appear in the menu and lay them out the way that you want them to appear.

**FIGURE 18-1**

Displaying a menu from a shell script

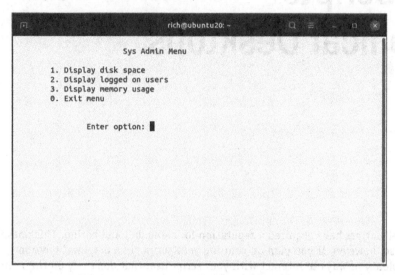

Before creating the menu, it's usually a good idea to clear the monitor display. Doing so enables you to display your menu in a clean environment without distracting text.

The `clear` command uses the terminal settings information of your terminal session (see Chapter 2, "Getting to the Shell") to clear any text that appears on the monitor. After the `clear` command, you can use the `echo` command to display your menu elements.

By default, the `echo` command can display only printable text characters. When you're creating menu items, it's often helpful to use nonprintable items, such as the tab and new-line characters. To include these characters in your `echo` command, you must use the `-e` option. Thus, the command

```
echo -e "1.\tDisplay disk space"
```

results in the output line

```
1.          Display disk space
```

This greatly helps in formatting the layout of the menu items. With just a few `echo` commands, you can create a reasonable-looking menu:

```
clear
echo
echo -e "\t\t\tSys Admin Menu\n"
echo -e "\t1. Display disk space"
echo -e "\t2. Display logged on users"
echo -e "\t3. Display memory usage"
```

```
echo -e "\t0. Exit menu\n\n"
echo -en "\t\tEnter option: "
```

The -en option on the last line displays the line without adding the newline character at the end. This gives the menu a more professional look, because the cursor stays at the end of the line waiting for the user's input.

The last part of creating the menu is to retrieve the input from the user. This is done using the read command (see Chapter 14, "Handling User Input"). Because we expect only single-character input, the nice thing to do is to use the -n option in the read command to retrieve only one character. Doing so allows the user to enter a number without having to press the Enter key:

```
read -n 1 option
```

Next, you need to create your menu functions.

## Create the menu functions

Shell script menu options are easier to create as a group of separate functions. This approach enables you to create a simple, concise case command that is easy to follow.

To do that, you must create separate shell functions for each of your menu options. The first step in creating a menu shell script is to determine what functions you want your script to perform and lay them out as separate functions in your code.

It is common practice to create *stub functions* for functions that aren't implemented yet. A stub function is a function that doesn't contain any commands yet or possibly just an echo statement indicating what should be there eventually:

```
function diskspace {
   clear
   echo "This is where the diskspace commands will go"
}
```

The stub function enables your menu to operate smoothly while you work on the individual functions. You don't have to code all the functions for your menu to work. You'll notice that the function starts out with the clear command. This enables you to start the function on a clean monitor screen, without the menu showing.

One thing that helps out in the shell script menu is to create the menu layout itself as a function:

```
function menu {
   clear
   echo
   echo -e "\t\t\tSys Admin Menu\n"
   echo -e "\t1. Display disk space"
   echo -e "\t2. Display logged on users"
   echo -e "\t3. Display memory usage"
   echo -e "\t0. Exit program\n\n"
```

*(Continues)*

**501**

*(continued)*

```
        echo -en "\t\tEnter option: "
        read -n 1 option
    }
```

This strategy enables you to easily redisplay the menu at any time just by calling the menu function.

## Add the menu logic

Now that you have your menu layout and your functions, you just need to create the programming logic to put the two together. As mentioned earlier, this requires the case command.

The case command should call the appropriate function according to the character selection expected from the menu. It's always a good idea to use the default case command character (the asterisk) to catch any incorrect menu entries.

The following code illustrates the use of the case command in a typical menu:

```
menu
case $option in
0)
    break ;;
1)
    diskspace ;;
2)
    whoseon ;;
3)
    memusage ;;
*)
    clear
    echo "Sorry, wrong selection";;
esac
```

This code first uses the menu function to clear the monitor screen and display the menu. The read command in the menu function pauses until the user presses a character on the keyboard. After that's been done, the case command takes over. The case command calls the appropriate function based on the returned character. After the function completes, the case command exits.

## Putting it all together

Now that you've seen all the parts that make up a shell script menu, let's put them together and see how they all interoperate. Here's an example of a full menu script:

```
$ cat menu1
#!/bin/bash
# simple script menu

function diskspace {
```

```
   clear
   df -k
}

function whoseon {
   clear
   who
}

function memusage {
   clear
   cat /proc/meminfo
}

function menu {
   clear
   echo
   echo -e "\t\t\tSys Admin Menu\n"
   echo -e "\t1. Display disk space"
   echo -e "\t2. Display logged on users"
   echo -e "\t3. Display memory usage"
   echo -e "\t0. Exit program\n\n"
   echo -en "\t\tEnter option: "
   read -n 1 option
}

while [ 1 ]
do
   menu
   case $option in
   0)
      break ;;
   1)
      diskspace ;;
   2)
      whoseon ;;
   3)
      memusage ;;
   *)
      clear
      echo "Sorry, wrong selection";;
   esac
   echo -en "\n\n\t\t\tHit any key to continue"
   read -n 1 line
done
clear
$
```

This menu creates three functions to retrieve administrative information about the Linux system using common commands. It uses a `while` loop to continually loop through the menu until the user selects option 0, which uses the `break` command to break out of the while loop.

You can use this template to create any shell script menu interface. It provides a simple way to interact with your users.

## Using the *select* command

You may have noticed that half the challenge of creating a text menu is just creating the menu layout and retrieving the answer that you enter. The Bash shell provides a handy little utility for you that does all this work automatically.

The `select` command allows you to create a menu from a single command line and then retrieve the entered answer and automatically process it. The format of the `select` command is as follows:

```
select variable in list
do
     commands
done
```

The `list` parameter is a space-separated list of text items that build the menu. The `select` command displays each item in the list as a numbered option and then displays a special prompt, defined by the PS3 environment variable, for the selection.

Here's a simple example of the `select` command in action:

```
$ cat smenu1
#!/bin/bash
# using select in the menu

function diskspace {
   clear
   df -k
}

function whoseon {
   clear
   who
}

function memusage {
   clear
   cat /proc/meminfo
}

PS3="Enter option: "
```

```
select option in "Display disk space" "Display logged on users" ~CA
"Display memory usage" "Exit program"
do
    case $option in
    "Exit program")
            break ;;
    "Display disk space")
            diskspace ;;
    "Display logged on users")
            whoseon ;;
    "Display memory usage")
            memusage ;;
    *)
            clear
            echo "Sorry, wrong selection";;
    esac
done
clear
$
```

The `select` statement must all be on one line in the code file. That's indicated by the continuation character in the listing. When you run the program, it automatically produces the following menu:

```
$ ./smenu1
1) Display disk space     3) Display memory usage
2) Display logged on users  4) Exit program
Enter option:
```

When you use the `select` command, remember that the result value stored in the variable is the entire text string and not the number associated with the menu item. The text string values are what you need to compare in your `case` statements.

# Doing Windows

Using text menus is a step in the right direction, but there's still so much missing in our interactive scripts, especially if we try to compare them to the graphical Windows world. Fortunately for us, some resourceful people out in the open source world have helped us out.

The *dialog* package is a nifty little tool originally created by Savio Lam and currently maintained by Thomas E. Dickey. This package re-creates standard Windows dialogs in a text environment using ANSI escape control codes. You can easily incorporate these dialogs in your shell scripts to interact with your script users. This section describes the dialog package and demonstrates how to use it in shell scripts.

**NOTE**

The dialog package isn't installed in all Linux distributions by default. If it's not installed by default, because of its popularity it's almost always included in the software repository. Check your specific Linux distribution documentation for how to load the dialog package. For the Ubuntu Linux distribution, the following is the command to install it:

```
sudo apt-get install dialog
```

To install the dialog package in Red Hat–based systems, such as CentOS, use the `dnf` command:

```
sudo dnf install dialog
```

The package installer installs the dialog package plus any required libraries for it to work on your system.

## The dialog package

The `dialog` command uses command-line parameters to determine what type of Windows *widget* to produce. A widget is the dialog package term for a type of Windows element. The dialog package currently supports the types of widgets shown in Table 18.1.

**TABLE 18.1 The dialog Widgets**

| Widget | Description |
|---|---|
| calendar | Provides a calendar from which to select a date |
| checklist | Displays multiple entries where each entry can be turned on or off |
| form | Allows you to build a form with labels and text fields to be filled out |
| fselect | Provides a file selection window to browse for a file |
| gauge | Displays a meter showing a percentage of completion |
| infobox | Displays a message without waiting for a response |
| inputbox | Displays a single text form box for text entry |
| inputmenu | Provides an editable menu |
| menu | Displays a list of selections from which to choose |
| msgbox | Displays a message and requires the user to click an OK button |
| pause | Displays a meter showing the status of a specified pause period |
| passwordbox | Displays a single text box that hides entered text |
| passwordform | Displays a form with labels and hidden text fields |
| radiolist | Provides a group of menu items where only one item can be selected |
| tailbox | Displays text from a file in a scroll window using the `tail` command |
| tailboxbg | Same as `tailbox`, but operates in background mode |
| textbox | Displays the contents of a file in a scroll window |
| timebox | Provides a window to select an hour, minute, and second |
| yesno | Provides a simple message with Yes and No buttons |

As you can see from Table 18.1, you can choose from lots of different widgets to give your scripts a professional look with little effort.

To specify a specific widget on the command line, use the double dash format:

```
dialog --widget parameters
```

where *widget* is the widget name as seen in Table 18.1 and *parameters* defines the size of the widget window and any text required for the widget.

Each dialog widget provides output in two forms:

- Using STDERR
- Using the exit code status

The exit code status of the dialog command determines the button selected by the user. If an OK or Yes button is selected, the dialog command returns a 0 exit status. If a Cancel or No button is selected, the dialog command returns a 1 exit status. You can use the standard $? variable to determine which button was clicked in the dialog widget.

If a widget returns any data, such as a menu selection, the dialog command sends the data to STDERR. You can use the standard Bash shell technique of redirecting the STDERR output to another file or file descriptor:

```
dialog --inputbox "Enter your age:" 10 20 2>age.txt
```

This command redirects the text entered in the text box to the age.txt file.

The following sections look at some examples of the more common dialog widgets you'll use in your shell scripts.

### The *msgbox* widget

The msgbox widget is the most common type of dialog. It displays a simple message in a window and waits for the user to click an OK button before disappearing. The following format is required to use a msgbox widget:

```
dialog --msgbox text height width
```

The *text* parameter is any string you want to place in the window. The dialog command automatically wraps the text to fit the size of the window you create, using the *height* and *width* parameters. If you want to place a title at the top of the window, you can also use the --title parameter, along with the text of the title. Here's an example of using the msgbox widget:

```
$ dialog --title Testing --msgbox "This is a test" 10 20
```

After you enter this command, the message box appears on the screen of the terminal emulator session you're using. Figure 18-2 shows what this looks like.

FIGURE 18-2

Using the msgbox widget in the dialog command

If your terminal emulator supports the mouse, you can click the OK button to close the dialog. You can also use keyboard commands to simulate a click — just press the Enter key.

### The *yesno* widget

The yesno widget takes the msgbox widget one step further, allowing the user to answer a yes/no question displayed in the window. It produces two buttons at the bottom of the window — one for Yes and another for No. The user can switch between buttons by using the mouse, the Tab key, or the keyboard arrow keys. To select the button, the user can press either the spacebar or the Enter key.

Here's an example of using the yesno widget:

```
$ dialog --title "Please answer" --yesno "Is this thing on?" 10 20
$ echo $?
1
$
```

This code produces the widget shown in Figure 18-3.

The exit status of the dialog command is set depending on which button the user selects. If the No button is clicked, the exit status is 1, and if the Yes button is clicked, the exit status is 0.

### The *inputbox* widget

The inputbox widget provides a simple text box area for the user to enter a text string. The dialog command sends the value of the text string to STDERR. You must redirect that to retrieve the answer. Figure 18-4 shows what the inputbox widget looks like.

**FIGURE 18-3**

Using the yesno widget in the dialog command

**FIGURE 18-4**

The inputbox widget

As you can see in Figure 18-4, the `inputbox` provides two buttons — OK and Cancel. If the Cancel button is clicked, the exit status of the command is 1; otherwise, the exit status is 0:

```
$ dialog --inputbox "Enter your age:" 10 20 2>age.txt
$ echo $?
0
$ cat age.txt
12$
```

You'll notice that when you use the `cat` command to display the contents of the text file there's no newline character after the value. This way, you can easily redirect the file contents to a variable in a shell script to extract the string entered by the user.

### The *textbox* widget

The `textbox` widget is a great way to display lots of information in a window. It produces a scrollable window containing the text from a file specified in the parameters:

```
$ dialog --textbox /etc/passwd 15 45
```

The contents of the /etc/passwd file are shown within the scrollable text window, as illustrated in Figure 18-5.

**FIGURE 18-5**

The `textbox` widget

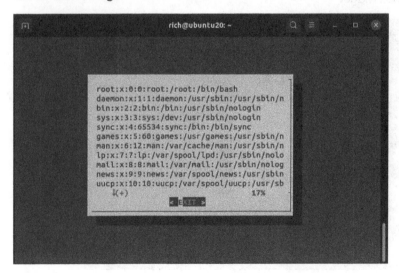

You can use the arrow keys to scroll left and right, as well as up and down in the text file. The bottom line in the window shows the location percentage within the file that you're viewing. The textbox widget contains only a single Exit button, which should be selected to exit the widget.

### The *menu* widget

The menu widget allows you to create a window version of the text menu we created earlier in this chapter. You simply provide a selection tag and the text for each item:

```
$ dialog --menu "Sys Admin Menu" 20 30 10 1 "Display disk space"
2 "Display users" 3 "Display memory usage" 4 "Exit" 2> test.txt
```

The first parameter defines a title for the menu. The next two parameters define the height and width of the menu window, and the third parameter defines the number of menu items that appear in the window at one time. If there are more menu items, you can scroll through them using the arrow keys.

Following those parameters, you must add menu item pairs. The first element is the tag used to select the menu item. Each tag should be unique for each menu item and can be selected by pressing the appropriate key on the keyboard. The second element is the text used in the menu. Figure 18-6 demonstrates the menu produced by the sample command.

**FIGURE 18-6**

The menu widget with menu items

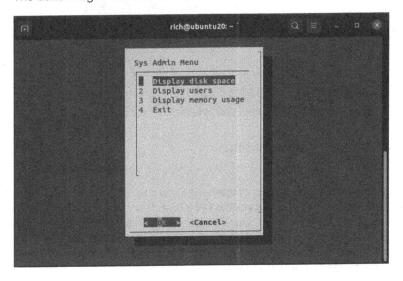

If the user selects a menu item by pressing the appropriate key for the tag, that menu item is highlighted but not selected. A selection isn't made until the OK button is selected by using either the mouse or the Enter key. The dialog command sends the selected menu item text to STDERR, which you can redirect as needed.

### The *fselect* widget

There are several fancy built-in widgets provided by the dialog command. The fselect widget is extremely handy when working with filenames. Instead of forcing the user to type a filename, you can allow them to use the fselect widget to browse to the file location and select the file, as shown in Figure 18-7.

**FIGURE 18-7**

The fselect widget

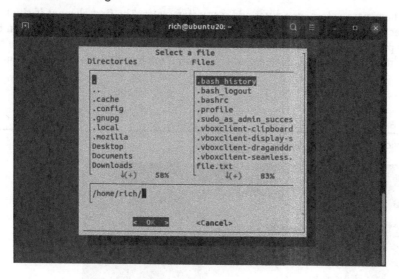

The fselect widget format looks like this:

```
$ dialog --title "Select a file" --fselect $HOME/ 10 50 2>file.txt
```

The first parameter after the fselect option is the starting folder location used in the window. The fselect widget window consists of a directory listing on the left side, a file listing on the right side that shows all the files in the selected directory, and a simple text box that contains the currently selected file or directory. You can manually type a filename in the text box, or you can use the directory and file listings to select one (use the space-bar to select a file to add to the text box).

## The *dialog* options

In addition to the standard widgets, you can customize lots of different options in the dialog command. You've already seen the --title parameter in action. This parameter allows you to set a title for the widget that appears at the top of the window.

**TABLE 18.2** **The** dialog **Command Options**

| Option | Description |
|---|---|
| --add-widget | Proceeds to the next dialog unless the Esc key has been pressed or the Cancel button clicked |
| --aspect *ratio* | Specifies the width/height aspect ratio of the window |
| --backtitle *title* | Specifies a title to display on the background, at the top of the screen |
| --begin *x y* | Specifies the starting location of the top-left corner of the window |
| --cancel-label *label* | Specifies an alternative label for the Cancel button |
| --clear | Clears the display using the default dialog background color |
| --colors | Embeds ANSI color codes in dialog text |
| --cr-wrap | Allows newline characters in dialog text and forces a line wrap |
| --create-rc *file* | Dumps a sample configuration file to the specified file |
| --defaultno | Makes the default of a yes/no dialog No |
| --default-item *string* | Sets the default item in a checklist, form, or menu dialog |
| --exit-label *label* | Specifies an alternative label for the Exit button |
| --extra-button | Displays an extra button between the OK and Cancel buttons |
| --extra-label *label* | Specifies an alternative label for the Extra button |
| --help | Displays the dialog command help message |
| --help-button | Displays a Help button after the OK and Cancel buttons |
| --help-label *label* | Specifies an alternative label for the Help button |
| --help-status | Writes the checklist, radiolist, or form information after the help information if the Help button was clicked |
| --ignore | Ignores options that dialog does not recognize |
| --input-fd *fd* | Specifies a file descriptor other than STDIN |
| --insecure | Changes the password widget to display asterisks when typing |
| --item-help | Adds a help column at the bottom of the screen for each tag in a checklist, radiolist, or menu for the tag item |
| --keep-window | Doesn't clear old widgets from the screen |
| --max-input *size* | Specifies a maximum string size for the input; default is 2048 |

*(Continues)*

18

**TABLE 18.2**  *(continued)*

| Option | Description |
|---|---|
| `--nocancel` | Suppresses the Cancel button |
| `--no-collapse` | Doesn't convert tabs to spaces in dialog text |
| `--no-kill` | Places the `tailboxbg` dialog in background and disables `SIGHUP` for the process |
| `--no-label` *label* | Specifies an alternative label for the No button |
| `--no-shadow` | Doesn't display shadows for dialog windows |
| `--ok-label` *label* | Specifies an alternative label for the OK button |
| `--output-fd` *fd* | Specifies an output file descriptor other than `STDERR` |
| `--print-maxsize` | Prints the maximum size of dialog windows allowed to the output |
| `--print-size` | Prints the size of each dialog window to the output |
| `--print-version` | Prints the dialog version to output |
| `--separate-output` | Outputs the result of a `checklist` widget one line at a time with no quoting |
| `--separator` *string* | Specifies a string that separates the output for each widget |
| `--separate-widget` *string* | Specifies a string that separates the output for each widget |
| `--shadow` | Draws a shadow to the right and bottom of each window |
| `--single-quoted` | Uses single quoting if needed for the checklist output |
| `--sleep` *sec* | Delays for the specified number of seconds after processing the dialog window |
| `--stderr` | Sends output to `STDERR` — the default behavior |
| `--stdout` | Sends output to `STDOUT` |
| `--tab-correct` | Converts tabs to spaces |
| `--tab-len` *n* | Specifies the number of spaces a tab character uses; default is 8 |
| `--timeout` *sec* | Specifies the number of seconds before exiting with an error code if no user input |
| `--title` *title* | Specifies the title of the dialog window |
| `--trim` | Removes leading spaces and newline characters from dialog text |
| `--visit-items` | Modifies the tab stops in the dialog window to include the list of items |
| `--yes-label` *label* | Specifies an alternative label for the Yes button |

Lots of other options allow you to completely customize both the appearance and the behavior of your windows. Table 18.2 shows the options available for the `dialog` command.

The `--backtitle` option is a handy way to create a common title for your menu through the script. If you specify it for each dialog window, it persists throughout your application, creating a professional look for your script.

As you can tell from Table 18.2, you can overwrite any of the button labels in your dialog window. This feature allows you to create just about any window situation you need.

## Using the *dialog* command in a script

Using the `dialog` command in your scripts is a snap. Just remember two things:

- Check the exit status of the `dialog` command if a Cancel or No button is available.
- Redirect STDERR to retrieve the output value.

If you follow these two rules, you'll have a professional-looking interactive script in no time. Here's an example using dialog widgets to reproduce the system admin menu created earlier in the chapter:

```
$ cat menu3
#!/bin/bash
# using dialog to create a menu

temp=$(mktemp -t test.XXXXXX)
temp2=$(mktemp -t test2.XXXXXX)

function diskspace {
    df -k > $temp
    dialog --textbox $temp 20 60
}

function whoseon {
    who > $temp
    dialog --textbox $temp 20 50
}

function memusage {
    cat /proc/meminfo > $temp
    dialog --textbox $temp 20 50
}

while [ 1 ]
do
dialog --menu "Sys Admin Menu" 20 30 10 1 "Display disk space" 2
    "Display users" 3 "Display memory usage" 0 "Exit" 2> $temp2
if [ $? -eq 1 ]
then
    break
fi
```

*(Continues)*

```
(continued)
    selection=$(cat $temp2)

    case $selection in
    1)
       diskspace ;;
    2)
       whoseon ;;
    3)
       memusage ;;
    0)
       break ;;
    *)
       dialog --msgbox "Sorry, invalid selection" 10 30
    esac
    done
    rm -f $temp 2> /dev/null
    rm -f $temp2 2> /dev/null
    $
```

The script uses the while loop with a constant true value to create an endless loop displaying the menu dialog. This means that, after every function, the script returns to displaying the menu.

The menu dialog includes a Cancel button, so the script checks the exit status of the dialog command in case the user presses the Cancel button to exit. Because it's in a while loop, exiting is as easy as using the break command to jump out of the while loop.

The script uses the mktemp command to create two temporary files for holding data for the dialog commands. The first one, $temp, is used to hold the output of the df, who, and meminfo commands so that they can be displayed in the textbox dialog (see Figure 18-8). The second temporary file, $temp2, is used to hold the selection value from the main menu dialog.

Now this is starting to look like a real application that you can show off to people!

# Getting Graphic

If you're looking for even more graphics for your interactive scripts, you can go one step further. Both the KDE and GNOME desktop environments (see Chapter 1, "Starting with Linux Shells") have expanded on the dialog command idea and include commands that produce X Windows graphical widgets for their respective environments.

This section describes the kdialog and zenity packages, which provide graphical window widgets for the KDE and GNOME desktops, respectively.

**FIGURE 18-8**

The `meminfo` command output displayed using the `textbox` dialog option

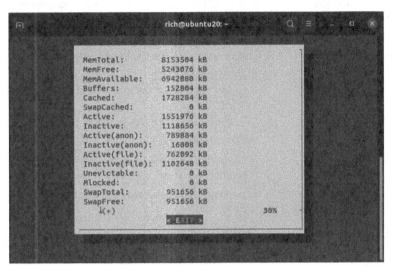

## The KDE environment

18

The KDE graphical environment includes the kdialog package by default. The kdialog package uses the `kdialog` command to generate standard windows, similar to the dialog-style widgets, within your KDE desktop. However, instead of having the clunky feel to them, these windows blend right in with the rest of your KDE application windows. This allows you to produce Windows-quality user interfaces directly from your shell scripts.

**NOTE**

Just because your Linux distribution uses the KDE desktop doesn't necessarily mean it has the kdialog package installed by default. You may need to manually install it from the distribution repository.

### kdialog widgets

Just like the `dialog` command, the `kdialog` command uses command-line options to specify what type of window widget to use. Here is the format of the kdialog command:

```
kdialog display-options window-options arguments
```

The *display-options* options allow you to customize the window widget, such as add a title or change the colors. The *window-options* options are what allow you to specify what type of window widget to use. The available options are shown in Table 18.3.

**TABLE 18.3    kdialog Window Options**

| Option | Description |
| --- | --- |
| --checklist *title* *[tag item status]* | A checklist menu, with status specifying whether or not the item is checked |
| --error *text* | Error message box |
| --inputbox *text* *[init]* | Input text box where you can specify the default value using the *init* value |
| --menu *title* *[tag item]* | Menu selection box title and a list of items identified by a tag |
| --msgbox *text* | Simple message box with specified text |
| --password *text* | Password input text box that hides user input |
| --radiolist *title* *[tag item status]* | A radiolist menu, with status specifying whether or not the item is selected |
| --separate-output | Returns items on separate lines for checklist and radiolist menus |
| --sorry *text* | Sorry message box |
| --textbox *file* *[width]* *[height]* | Text box displaying the contents of file, alternatively specified by *width* and *height* |
| --title *title* | Specifies a title for the TitleBar area of the dialog window |
| --warningyesno *text* | Warning message box with Yes and No buttons |
| --warningcontinue-cancel *text* | Warning message box with Continue and Cancel buttons |
| --warningyesnocancel *text* | Warning message box with Yes, No, and Cancel buttons |
| --yesno *text* | Question box with Yes and No buttons |
| --yesnocancel *text* | Question box with Yes, No, and Cancel buttons |

As you can see from Table 18.3, all the standard window dialog types are represented. However, when you use a kdialog window widget, it appears as a separate window in the KDE desktop, not inside the terminal emulator session.

The checklist and radiolist widgets allow you to define individual items in the lists and whether they are selected by default:

```
$kdialog --checklist "Items I need" 1 "Toothbrush" on 2 "Toothpaste"
    off 3 "Hairbrush" on 4 "Deodorant" off 5 "Slippers" off
```

The resulting checklist window is shown in Figure 18-9.

**FIGURE 18-9**

A kdialog checklist dialog window

The items specified as "on" are highlighted in the checklist. To select or deselect an item in the checklist, just click it. If you click the OK button, the kdialog sends the tag values to STDOUT:

```
"1" "3"
$
```

When you press the Enter key, the kdialog box appears with the selections. When you click the OK or Cancel button, the kdialog command returns each tag as a string value to STDOUT (these are the "1" and "3" values you see in the output). Your script must be able to parse the resulting values and match them with the original values.

### Using kdialog

You can use the kdialog window widgets in your shell scripts similarly to how you use the dialog widgets. The big difference is that the kdialog window widgets output values using STDOUT instead of STDERR.

Here's a script that converts the system admin menu created earlier into a KDE application:

```
$ cat menu4
#!/bin/bash
# using kdialog to create a menu

temp=$(mktemp -t temp.XXXXXX)
temp2=$(mktemp -t temp2.XXXXXX)
```

*(Continues)*

*(continued)*

```
function diskspace {
    df -k > $temp
    kdialog --textbox $temp 1000 10
}

function whoseon {
    who > $temp
    kdialog --textbox $temp 500 10
}

function memusage {
    cat /proc/meminfo > $temp
    kdialog --textbox $temp 300 500
}

while [ 1 ]
do
kdialog --menu "Sys Admin Menu" "1" "Display disk space" "2" "Display
users" "3" "Display memory usage" "0" "Exit" > $temp2
if [ $? -eq 1 ]
then
    break
fi

selection=$(cat $temp2)

case $selection in
1)
    diskspace ;;
2)
    whoseon ;;
3)
    memusage ;;
0)
    break ;;
*)
    kdialog --msgbox "Sorry, invalid selection"
esac
done
$
```

The script using the kdialog command isn't much different from the one using the dialog command. The resulting main menu is shown in Figure 18-10.

Now your simple shell script looks just like a real KDE application! There's no limit to what you can do with your interactive scripts now.

**FIGURE 18-10**

The sys admin menu script using `kdialog`

## The GNOME environment

The GNOME graphical environment supports two popular packages that can generate standard windows:

- gdialog
- zenity

By far, zenity is the most commonly available package found in most GNOME desktop Linux distributions (it's installed by default in both Ubuntu and CentOS). This section describes the features of zenity and demonstrates how to use it in your shell scripts.

### zenity Widgets

As you would expect, zenity allows you to create different window widgets by using command-line options. Table 18.4 shows the various widgets that zenity can produce.

**TABLE 18.4  The zenity Window Widgets**

| Option | Description |
| --- | --- |
| `--calendar` | Displays a full month calendar |
| `--entry` | Displays a text entry dialog window |
| `--error` | Displays an error message dialog window |
| `--file-selection` | Displays a full pathname and filename dialog window |
| `--info` | Displays an informational dialog window |
| `--list` | Displays a checklist or radiolist dialog window |
| `--notification` | Displays a notification icon |

*(Continues)*

**TABLE 18.4** *(continued)*

| Option | Description |
| --- | --- |
| --progress | Displays a progress bar dialog window |
| --question | Displays a yes/no question dialog window |
| --scale | Displays a scale dialog window with a sliding bar to select the value within a range |
| --text-info | Displays a text box containing text |
| --warning | Displays a warning dialog window |

The zenity command-line program works somewhat differently than the kdialog and dialog programs. Many of the widget types are defined using additional options on the command line, instead of including them as arguments to an option.

The zenity command does offer some pretty cool advanced dialog windows. The --calendar option produces a full month calendar, as shown in Figure 18-11.

**FIGURE 18-11**

The zenity calendar dialog window

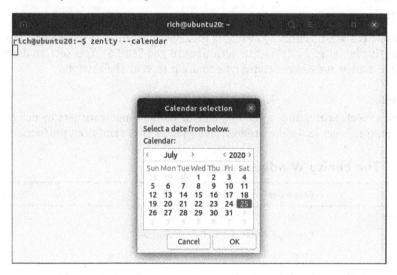

When you select a date from the calendar, the zenity command returns the value to STDOUT, just like kdialog:

```
$ zenity --calendar
12/25/2011
$
```

**FIGURE 18-12**

The zenity file selection dialog window

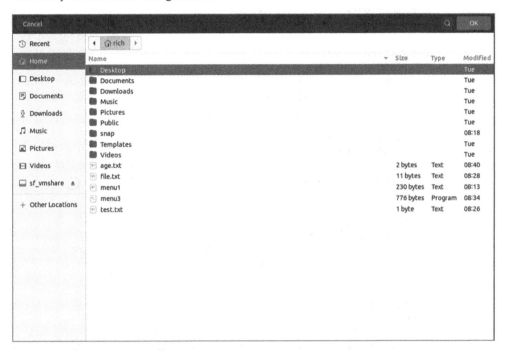

Another pretty cool window in `zenity` is the file selection option, shown in Figure 18-12.

You can use the dialog window to browse to any directory location on the system (as long as you have the privileges to view the directory) and select a file. When you select a file, the `zenity` command returns the full file and pathname:

```
$ zenity --file-selection
/home/ubuntu/menu5
$
```

With tools like that at your disposal, the sky's the limit with your shell script creations!

### Using zenity in scripts

As you would expect, zenity performs well in shell scripts. Unfortunately, the creators of zenity chose not to follow the option convention used in `dialog` and `kdialog`, so converting any existing interactive scripts to zenity may prove challenging.

In converting the system admin menu from kdialog to zenity, we had to do quite a bit of manipulation of the widget definitions:

```
$cat menu5
#!/bin/bash
# using zenity to create a menu

temp=$(mktemp -t temp.XXXXXX)
temp2=$(mktemp -t temp2.XXXXXX)

function diskspace {
    df -k > $temp
    zenity --text-info --title "Disk space" --filename=$temp
--width 750 --height 10
}

function whoseon {
    who > $temp
    zenity --text-info --title "Logged in users" --filename=$temp
--width 500 --height 10
}

function memusage {
    cat /proc/meminfo > $temp
    zenity --text-info --title "Memory usage" --filename=$temp
--width 300 --height 500
}

while [ 1 ]
do
zenity --list --radiolist --title "Sys Admin Menu" --column "Select"
--column "Menu Item" FALSE "Display disk space" FALSE "Display users"
FALSE "Display memory usage" FALSE "Exit" > $temp2
if [ $? -eq 1 ]
then
    break
fi

selection=$(cat $temp2)
case $selection in
"Display disk space")
    diskspace ;;
"Display users")
    whoseon ;;
"Display memory usage")
    memusage ;;
Exit)
    break ;;
*)
    zenity --info "Sorry, invalid selection"
esac
done
$
```

Because zenity doesn't support the menu dialog window, we used a radiolist type window for the main menu, as shown in Figure 18-13.

**FIGURE 18-13**

The system admin menu using zenity

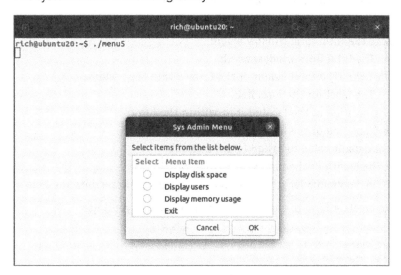

The radiolist uses two columns, each with a column heading. The first column includes the radio buttons, and the second column is the item text. The radiolist also doesn't use tags for the items. When you select an item, the full text of the item is returned to STDOUT. This makes life a little more interesting if you use the case command. You must use the full text from the items in the case options. If there are any spaces in the text, you need to use quotation marks around the text.

Using the zenity package, you can add a Windows feel to your interactive shell scripts in the GNOME desktop.

# Working Through a Practical Example

The one downside to each of these graphical packages is that there isn't a way to create a window with multiple entries, such as combining several text box inputs along with a calendar input, as you can do in a true graphical environment. That limitation does make querying for multiple data items a bit clunky, but it's still manageable. The trick is to keep track of each data query using appropriately named variables.

The dialog package does include a form feature, but it's fairly elementary. It only allows you to combine several text boxes into a single window to enter multiple data items. The format for the --form option is

```
--form text height width formheight [ label y x item y x flen
ilen ] ...
```

The parameters used by the --form option are as follows:

- *text*: A title that appears at the top of the form
- *height*: The total form window height
- *width*: The total form window width
- *formheight*: The total height of the form within the window
- *label*: The label for the form field
- *y*: The Y position of the label or item within the form
- *x*: The X position of the label or item within the form
- *item*: A default value to assign to a form field
- *flen*: The length of the form field to display
- *ilen*: The maximum length of the data that can be entered into the field

For example, to create a form to enter employee information, you'd use

```
dialog --form "Enter new employee" 19 50 0 \
    "Last name " 1 1 "" 1 15 30 0 \
    "First name " 3 1 "" 3 15 30 0 \
    "Address " 5 1 "" 5 15 30 0 \
    "City " 7 1 "" 7 15 30 0 \
    "State " 9 1 "" 9 15 30 0 \
    "Zip " 11 1 "" 11 15 30 0 2>data.txt
```

This code produces the form window shown in Figure 18-14.

When you enter data into the form fields and click the OK button, the form sends the data to the data.txt file. The data.txt file places each data item in order on a separate line in the file:

```
$ cat data.txt
Test
Ima
123 Main Street
Chicago
Illinois
60601
$
```

**FIGURE 18-14**

The dialog form feature

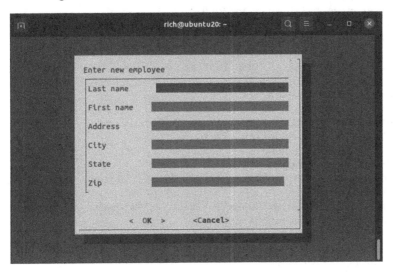

Your script can then retrieve the form data from the file by reading the file line by line. The head and tail commands are an easy way to retrieve specific lines in the file:

```
last=$(cat data.txt | head -1)
first=$(cat data.txt | head -2 | tail -1)
address=$(cat data.txt | head -3 | tail -1)
city=$(cat data.txt | head -4 | tail -1)
state=$(cat data.txt | head -5 | tail -1)
zip=$(cat data.txt | tail -1)
```

Now you have all of the data from the form stored in variables that you can use anywhere in your script:

```
record="INSERT INTO employees (last, first, address, city, state,
zip) VALUES
('$last', '$first', '$address', '$city', '$state', '$zip');"
echo $record >> newrecords.txt
```

The newrecords.txt file will contain the INSERT statements for each new form record so that you can easily import them all into a database. You can then create a simple front-end menu for the scripts and put everything together:

```
#!/bin/bash
temp=$(mktemp -t record.XXXX)
```

*(Continues)*

*(continued)*

```
function newrecord {
dialog --form "Enter new employee" 19 50 0 \
    "Last name " 1 1 "" 1 15 30 0 \
    "First name " 3 1 "" 3 15 30 0 \
    "Address " 5 1 "" 5 15 30 0 \
    "City " 7 1 "" 7 15 30 0 \
    "State " 9 1 "" 9 15 30 0 \
    "Zip " 11 1 "" 11 15 30 0 2>$temp

last=$(cat $temp | head -1)
first=$(cat $temp | head -2 | tail -1)
address=$(cat $temp | head -3 | tail -1)
city=$(cat $temp | head -4 | tail -1)
state=$(cat $temp | head -5 | tail -1)
zip=$(cat $temp | head -6 | tail -1)
record="INSERT INTO employees (last, first, address, city, state,
zip) VALUES
('$last', '$first', '$address', '$city', '$state', '$zip');"
echo $record >> newrecords.txt
}

function listrecords {
dialog --title "New Data" --textbox data.txt 20 50
}

while [ 1 ]
do
dialog --menu "Employee Data" 20 30 5 \
    1 "Enter new employee" \
    2 "Display records" \
    3 "Exit" 2>$temp

if [ $? -eq 1 ]
then
    break
fi

selection=$(cat $temp)

case $selection in
1)
    newrecord ;;
2)
    listrecords ;;
3)
    break ;;
*)
```

```
        dialog --msgbox "Invalid selection" 10 30
    esac
    done
    rm -f $temp 2> /dev/null
```

This script creates a simple graphical front end that allows you to quickly enter employee data to create an SQL file that you can easily import into a database.

## Summary

Interactive shell scripts have a reputation for being dull and boring. You can change that by using a few techniques and tools available on most Linux systems. First, you can create menu systems for your interactive scripts by using the case command and shell script functions.

The menu command allows you to paint a menu, using the standard echo command, and read a response from the user, using the read command. The case command then selects the appropriate shell script function based on the value entered.

The dialog program provides several prebuilt text widgets for creating Windows-like objects on a text-based terminal emulator. You can create dialogs for displaying text, entering text, and choosing files and dates by using the dialog program. Doing so brings even more life to your shell script.

If you're running your shell scripts in a graphical X Windows environment, you can utilize even more tools in your interactive scripts. For the KDE desktop, there's the kdialog program. This program provides simple commands to create window widgets for all the basic window functions. For the GNOME desktop, there are the gdialog and zenity programs. Each of these programs provides window widgets that blend into the GNOME desktop just like a real Windows application.

The next chapter dives into the subject of editing and manipulating text data files. Often the biggest use of shell scripts revolves around parsing and displaying data in text files such as log and error files. The Linux environment includes two very useful tools, sed and gawk, for working with text data in your shell scripts. The next chapter introduces you to these tools and shows the basics of how to use them.

18

# Introducing *sed* and *gawk*

B y far, one of the most common functions for which people use shell scripts is to work with text files. Between examining log files, reading configuration files, and handling data elements, shell scripts can help automate the mundane tasks of manipulating any type of data contained in text files. However, trying to manipulate the contents of text files using just shell script commands is somewhat awkward. If you perform any type of data manipulation in your shell scripts, you want to become familiar with the sed and gawk tools available in Linux. These tools can greatly simplify any data-handling tasks you need to perform.

## Manipulating Text

Chapter 10, "Working with Editors," demonstrated how to edit text files using different editor programs available in the Linux environment. These editors enable easy manipulation of text contained in a text file by using simple commands or clicks of the mouse.

There are times, however, when you'll find yourself wanting to manipulate text in a text file on the fly, without having to pull out a full-fledged interactive text editor. In these situations, it's useful to have a simple command-line editor that can easily format, insert, modify, or delete text elements automatically.

The Linux system provides two common tools for doing just that. We describe in this section the two most popular command-line editors used in the Linux world, sed and gawk.

## Getting to know the *sed* editor

The sed editor is called a *stream editor,* as opposed to a normal interactive text editor. In an interactive text editor, such as vim, keyboard commands are used interactively to insert, delete, or replace text in the data. A stream editor edits a stream of data based on a set of rules supplied ahead of time.

The sed editor can manipulate data in a stream based on commands either entered into the command line or stored in a command text file. The sed editor operates as follows:

1. Read one data line from the input.
2. Match that data with the supplied editor commands.
3. Change data in the stream as specified in the commands.
4. Output the new data to STDOUT.

After the stream editor matches and enacts all the commands against a line of data, it reads the next line of data and repeats the process. After the stream editor processes all the lines of data in the stream, it terminates.

Because the commands are applied sequentially line by line, the sed editor makes only one pass through the data stream to make the edits. This feature makes the sed editor much faster than an interactive editor and provides the ability to make quick changes to file data.

Here's the format for using the sed command:

```
sed options script file
```

The *options* parameter allows you to customize the behavior of the sed command and includes the options shown in Table 19.1.

**TABLE 19.1   The *sed* Command Options**

| Option | Description |
| --- | --- |
| -e *commands* | Adds additional sed commands to run while processing the input |
| -f *file* | Adds the commands specified in the file to the commands run while processing the input |
| -n | Doesn't produce output for each command, but waits for the print (p) command |

The *script* parameter specifies a single command to apply against the data stream. If more than one command is required, you must use either the -e option to specify them in the command line or the -f option to specify them in a separate file. Numerous commands are available for manipulating data. We examine some of the basic commands used by the sed editor in this chapter and then look at some of the more advanced commands in Chapter 21, "Advanced *sed.*"

### Defining an editor command in the command line

By default, the sed editor applies the specified commands to the STDIN input stream. This allows you to pipe data directly to the sed editor for processing. Here's a quick example demonstrating how to do this:

```
$ echo "This is a test" | sed 's/test/big test/'
This is a big test
$
```

This example uses the s command in the sed editor. The s command substitutes a second text string for the first text string pattern specified between the forward slashes. In this example, the words big test were substituted for the word test.

When you run this example, it should display the results almost instantaneously. That's the power of using the sed editor. You can make multiple edits to data in about the same time it takes for some of the interactive editors just to start up!

Of course, this simple test demonstrated an edit of one data line. The same speedy results occur when editing complete files of data, as shown here:

```
$ cat data1.txt
The quick brown fox jumps over the lazy dog.
The quick brown fox jumps over the lazy dog.
The quick brown fox jumps over the lazy dog.
The quick brown fox jumps over the lazy dog.
$
$ sed 's/dog/cat/' data1.txt
The quick brown fox jumps over the lazy cat.
The quick brown fox jumps over the lazy cat.
The quick brown fox jumps over the lazy cat.
The quick brown fox jumps over the lazy cat.
$
```

The sed command executes and returns the data very quickly. As it processes each line of data, the results are displayed. You'll start seeing results before the sed editor completes processing the entire file.

It's important to note that the sed editor *doesn't* modify the data in the text file itself; it only sends the modified text to STDOUT. If you look at the text file, it still contains the original data:

```
$ cat data1.txt
The quick brown fox jumps over the lazy dog.
The quick brown fox jumps over the lazy dog.
The quick brown fox jumps over the lazy dog.
The quick brown fox jumps over the lazy dog.
$
```

19

### Using multiple editor commands in the command line

To execute more than one command from the sed command line, use the -e option:

```
$ sed -e 's/brown/red/; s/dog/cat/' data1.txt
The quick red fox jumps over the lazy cat.
The quick red fox jumps over the lazy cat.
The quick red fox jumps over the lazy cat.
The quick red fox jumps over the lazy cat.
$
```

Both commands are applied to each line of data in the file. The commands must be separated with a semicolon (;), and there shouldn't be any spaces between the end of the first command and the semicolon.

Instead of using a semicolon to separate the commands, you can use the secondary prompt in the Bash shell. Just enter the first single quotation mark to open the sed program script (also called the sed editor command list), and Bash continues to prompt you for more commands until you enter the closing quotation mark:

```
$ sed -e '
> s/brown/green/
> s/fox/toad/
> s/dog/cat/' data1.txt
The quick green toad jumps over the lazy cat.
The quick green toad jumps over the lazy cat.
The quick green toad jumps over the lazy cat.
The quick green toad jumps over the lazy cat.
$
```

You must remember to finish the command on the same line where the closing single quotation mark appears. After the Bash shell detects the closing quotation mark, it processes the command. After it starts, the sed command applies each command you specified to each data line in the text file.

### Reading editor commands from a file

Finally, if you have lots of sed commands you want to process, it is often easier to just store them in a separate file. Use the -f option to specify the file in the sed command:

```
$ cat script1.sed
s/brown/green/
s/fox/toad/
s/dog/cat/
$
$ sed -f script1.sed data1.txt
The quick green toad jumps over the lazy cat.
The quick green toad jumps over the lazy cat.
The quick green toad jumps over the lazy cat.
The quick green toad jumps over the lazy cat.
$
```

In this case, a semicolon is *not* placed after each command. The sed editor knows that each line contains a separate command. As with entering commands on the command line, the sed editor reads the commands from the specified file and applies them to each line in the data file.

> **TIP**
>
> It's easy to confuse sed editor script files with Bash shell scripts or other text files. To eliminate confusion, it is considered good form to use the .sed file extension on any sed script files.

We'll look at some other sed editor commands that come in handy for manipulating data in the "Looking at the *sed* Editor Basic Commands" section. Before that, let's quickly look at the other Linux data editor.

## Getting to know the *gawk* program

Although the sed editor is a handy tool for modifying text files on the fly, it has its limitations. Often, a more advanced tool is needed for manipulating data in a file, one that provides a more programming-like environment allowing the modification and reorganization of data in a file. This is where gawk comes in.

> **NOTE**
>
> The gawk program is not installed by default on all distributions. If your Linux distribution does not have the gawk program, install the gawk package using Chapter 9, "Installing Software," as a guide.

The gawk program is the GNU version of the original awk program in Unix. The gawk program takes stream editing one step further than the sed editor by providing a programming language instead of just editor commands. Within the gawk programming language, the following is possible:

- Define variables to store data.
- Use arithmetic and string operators to operate on data.
- Use structured programming concepts, such as if-then statements and loops, to add logic to your data processing.
- Generate formatted reports by extracting data elements within the data file and repositioning them in another order or format.

The gawk program's report-generating capabilities are often used for extracting data elements from large, bulky text files and formatting them into a readable report. The perfect example of this is formatting program log files. Trying to dig through lines of errors in a log file can be difficult. The gawk program allows the filtering of data elements you want to view from the log file, and then formats them in a manner that makes reading the important data easier.

19

### Visiting the *gawk* command format

Here's the basic format of the gawk program:

```
gawk options program file
```

Table 19.2 shows a few options available with the gawk program.

**TABLE 19.2 The *gawk* Options**

| Option | Description |
| --- | --- |
| -F *fs* | Specifies a file separator for delineating data fields in a line |
| -f *file* | Specifies a filename to read the program from |
| -v *var=value* | Defines a variable and default value used in the gawk program |
| -L [*keyword*] | Specifies the compatibility mode or warning level for gawk |

The command-line options provide an easy way to customize features in the gawk program. We'll look more closely at some of these as we explore gawk basics.

The power of gawk is in the program script. You can write scripts to read the data within a text line and then manipulate and display the data to create any type of output report.

### Reading the program script from the command line

A gawk program script is defined by opening and closing braces. You must place script commands between the two braces ({}). If you incorrectly use a parenthesis instead of a brace to enclose your gawk script, error messages, similar to the following, are generated:

```
$ gawk '(print "Hello World!")'
gawk: cmd. line:1: (print "Hello World!")
gawk: cmd. line:1:    ^ syntax error
gawk: cmd. line:2: (print "Hello World!")
gawk: cmd. line:2:                          ^ unexpected newline or
 end of string
$
```

Because the gawk command line assumes that the script is a single text string, you must also enclose your script in single quotation marks. Here's an example of a simple gawk program script specified on the command line:

```
$ gawk '{print "Hello World!"}'
```

The program script defines a single command, the print command. The print command does what it says: it prints text to STDOUT. If you try running this command, you'll be somewhat disappointed, because nothing happens right away. Because no filename was defined in the command line, the gawk program retrieves data from STDIN. When you run the program, it just waits for text to come in via STDIN.

If you type a line of text and press the Enter key, gawk runs the text through the program script. Just like the sed editor, the gawk program executes the program script on each line of text available in the data stream. Because the program script is set to display a fixed text string, no matter what text you enter in the data stream, you get the same text output:

```
$ gawk '{print "Hello World!"}'
This is a test
Hello World!
hello
Hello World!
Goodbye
Hello World!
This is another test
Hello World!
```

To terminate the gawk program, you must signal that the data stream has ended. The Bash shell provides a key combination to generate an end-of-file (EOF) character. The Ctrl+D key combination generates an EOF character in Bash. Using that key combination terminates the gawk program and returns you to a command-line interface prompt.

### Using data field variables

One of the primary features of gawk is its ability to manipulate data in the text file. It does this by automatically assigning a variable to each data element in a line. By default, gawk assigns the following variables to each data field it detects in the line of text:

- $0 represents the entire line of text.
- $1 represents the first data field in the line of text.
- $2 represents the second data field in the line of text.
- $n represents the *n*th data field in the line of text.

Each data field is determined in a text line by a *field separation character*. When gawk reads a line of text, it delineates each data field using the defined field separation character. The default field separation character in gawk is any whitespace character (such as the tab or space characters).

Here's an example gawk program that reads a text file and displays only the first data field value:

```
$ cat data2.txt
One line of test text.
Two lines of test text.
Three lines of test text.
$
$ gawk '{print $1}' data2.txt
One
Two
Three
$
```

This program uses the $1 field variable to display only the first data field for each line of text.

For reading a file that uses a different field separation character, specify the character by using the -F option:

```
$ gawk -F: '{print $1}' /etc/passwd
root
daemon
bin
[...]
christine
sshd
$
```

This short program displays the first data field in the password file on the system. Because the /etc/passwd file uses a colon (:) to separate the data fields, to separate each data element, we used the field separation character (-F:) in the gawk options.

### Using multiple commands in the program script

A programming language wouldn't be very useful if you could only execute one command. The gawk programming language allows the combination of commands into a normal program. To use multiple commands in the program script specified on the command line, just place a semicolon between each command:

```
$ echo "My name is Rich" | gawk '{$4="Christine"; print $0}'
My name is Christine
$
```

The first command assigns a value to the $4 field variable. The second command then prints the entire data field. Notice from the output that the gawk program replaced the fourth data field in the original text with the new value.

You can also use the secondary prompt to enter your program script commands one line at a time:

```
$ gawk '{
> $4="Christine";
> print $0}'
My name is Rich
My name is Christine
$
```

After we opened with a single quotation mark, the Bash shell provided the secondary prompt to prompt us for more data. We added our commands one at a time on each line until we entered the closing single quotation mark. Because no filename was defined in the command line, the gawk program retrieves data from STDIN. When we ran the program, it waited for text to come in via STDIN. To exit the program, we pressed the Ctrl+D key combination to signal the end of the data and get back to a shell prompt.

### Reading the program from a file

Like the `sed` editor, the `gawk` editor allows you to store your programs in a file and refer to them in the command line:

```
$ cat script2.gawk
{print $1 "'s home directory is " $6}
$
$ gawk -F: -f script2.gawk /etc/passwd
root's home directory is /root
daemon's home directory is /usr/sbin
bin's home directory is /bin
[...]
christine's home directory is /home/christine
sshd's home directory is /run/sshd
$
```

The `script2.gawk` program script uses the `print` command again to print the /etc /passwd file's home directory data field (field variable `$6`) and the user name data field (field variable `$1`).

You can specify multiple commands in the program file. To do so, just place each command on a separate line. You don't need to use semicolons:

```
$ cat script3.gawk
{
text = "'s home directory is "
print $1 text $6
}
$
$ gawk -F: -f script3.gawk /etc/passwd
root's home directory is /root
daemon's home directory is /usr/sbin
bin's home directory is /bin
[...]
christine's home directory is /home/christine
sshd's home directory is /run/sshd
$
```

The `script3.gawk` program script defines a variable, `text`, to hold a text string used in the `print` command. Notice that `gawk` programs don't use a dollar sign when referencing a variable's value, as a shell script does.

### Running scripts before processing data

The `gawk` program also allows you to specify when the program script is run. By default, `gawk` reads a line of text from the input and then executes the program script on the data in the line of text. Sometimes, you may need to run a script before processing data, such as to create a header section for a report. The `BEGIN` keyword is used to accomplish this.

It forces gawk to execute the program script specified after the BEGIN keyword, before gawk reads the data:

```
$ gawk 'BEGIN {print "Hello World!"}'
Hello World!
$
```

This time the print command displays the text before reading any data. However, after it displays the text, it quickly exits without waiting for any data.

The reason for this is that the BEGIN keyword only applies the specified script before it processes any data. If you want to process data with a normal program script, you must define the program using another script section:

```
$ cat data3.txt
Line 1
Line 2
Line 3
$
$ gawk 'BEGIN {print "The data3 File Contents:"}
> {print $0}' data3.txt
The data3 File Contents:
Line 1
Line 2
Line 3
$
```

Now after gawk executes the BEGIN script, it uses the second script to process any file data. Be careful when doing this — both of the scripts are still considered one text string on the gawk command line. You need to place your single quotation marks accordingly.

### Running scripts after processing data

Like the BEGIN keyword, the END keyword allows you to specify a program script that gawk executes after reading the data:

```
$ gawk 'BEGIN {print "The data3 File Contents:"}
> {print $0}
> END {print "End of File"}' data3.txt
The data3 File Contents:
Line 1
Line 2
Line 3
End of File
$
```

When the gawk program is finished printing the file contents, it executes the commands in the END script. This is a great technique to use to add footer data to reports after all the normal data has been processed.

You can put all these elements together into a nice little program script file to create a full report from a simple data file:

```
$ cat script4.gawk
BEGIN {
print "The latest list of users and shells"
print "UserID  \t Shell"
print "------- \t -------"
FS=":"
}

{
print $1 "        \t "  $7
}

END {
print "This concludes the listing"
}
$
```

This script uses the BEGIN script to create a header section for the report. It also defines a special variable called FS. This is yet another way to define the field separation character. This way, you don't have to depend on the script's user to define the field separation character in the command-line options.

Here's a somewhat truncated output from running this gawk program script:

```
$ gawk -f script4.gawk /etc/passwd
The latest list of users and shells
UserID          Shell
-------         -------
root            /bin/bash
daemon          /usr/sbin/nologin
[...]
christine       /bin/bash
sshd            /usr/sbin/nologin
This concludes the listing
$
```

As expected, the BEGIN script created the header text, the program script processed the information from the specified data file (the /etc/passwd file), and the END script produced the footer text. The \t within the print command produces some nicely formatted tabbed output.

This gives you a small taste of the power available through using simple gawk scripts. Chapter 22, "Advanced *gawk*," describes some more basic programming principles available for your gawk scripts, along with some even more advanced programming concepts you can use in your gawk program scripts to create professional-looking reports from even the most cryptic data files.

19

# Looking at the *sed* Editor Basic Commands

The key to successfully using the `sed` editor is to know its myriad of commands and formats, which help you to customize your text editing. This section describes some of the basic commands and features you can incorporate into your script to start using the `sed` editor.

## Introducing more substitution options

We've already covered how to use the `s` command to substitute new text for the text in a line. However, a few additional options are available for the `s` command that can help make your life easier.

### Substituting flags

There's a caveat to how the `s` command replaces matching patterns in the text string. Watch what happens in this example:

```
$ cat data4.txt
This is a test of the test script.
This is the second test of the test script.
$
$ sed 's/test/trial/' data4.txt
This is a trial of the test script.
This is the second trial of the test script.
$
```

The `s` command works fine in replacing text in multiple lines, but by default, it replaces only the first occurrence in each line. To get the `s` command to work on different occurrences of the text, you must use a *substitution flag*. The substitution flag is set after the substitution command strings:

```
s/pattern/replacement/flags
```

Four types of substitution flags are available:

- A number, indicating the pattern occurrence for which new text should be substituted
- g, indicating that new text should be substituted for all occurrences of the existing text
- p, indicating that the contents of the original line should be printed
- w *file*, which means to write the results of the substitution to a file

In the first type of substitution, you can specify which occurrence of the matching pattern the `sed` editor should substitute new text for:

```
$ sed 's/test/trial/2' data4.txt
This is a test of the trial script.
This is the second test of the trial script.
$
```

As a result of specifying a 2 as the substitution flag, the sed editor replaces the pattern only in the *second* occurrence in each line. The g substitution flag enables you to replace every occurrence (global) of the pattern in the text:

```
$ sed 's/test/trial/g' data4.txt
This is a trial of the trial script.
This is the second trial of the trial script.
$
```

The p substitution flag prints a line that contains a matching pattern in the substitute command. This is most often used in conjunction with the -n sed option:

```
$ cat data5.txt
This is a test line.
This is a different line.
$
$ sed -n 's/test/trial/p' data5.txt
This is a trial line.
$
```

The -n option suppresses output from the sed editor. However, the p substitution flag outputs any line that has been modified. Using the two in combination produces output only for lines that have been modified by the substitute command.

The w substitution flag produces the same output but stores the output in the specified file:

```
$ sed 's/test/trial/w test.txt' data5.txt
This is a trial line.
This is a different line.
$
$ cat test.txt
This is a trial line.
$
```

The normal output of the sed editor appears in STDOUT, but only the lines that include the matching pattern are stored in the specified output file.

### Replacing characters

Sometimes, you run across characters in text strings that aren't easy to use in the substitution pattern. One popular example in the Linux world is the forward slash (/).

Substituting pathnames in a file can get awkward. For example, if you wanted to substitute the C shell for the Bash shell in the /etc/passwd file, you'd have to do this:

```
$ sed 's/\/bin\/bash/\/bin\/csh/' /etc/passwd
```

Because the forward slash is used as the string delimiter, you must use a backslash to escape it if it appears in the pattern text. This often leads to confusion and mistakes.

19

To solve this problem, the sed editor allows you to select a different character for the string delimiter in the substitute command:

```
$ sed 's!/bin/bash!/bin/csh!' /etc/passwd
```

In this example, the exclamation point (!) is used for the string delimiter, making the pathnames much easier to read and understand.

## Using addresses

By default, the commands you use in the sed editor apply to all lines of the text data. If you want to apply a command only to a specific line or a group of lines, you must use *line addressing*.

There are two forms of line addressing in the sed editor:

- A numeric range of lines
- A text pattern that matches text within a line

Both forms use the same format for specifying the address:

```
[address] command
```

You can also group more than one command together for a specific address:

```
address {
    command1
    command2
    command3
}
```

The sed editor applies each of the commands you specify only to lines that match the address specified. This section demonstrates using both of these addressing techniques in your sed editor scripts.

### Addressing the numeric line

When using numeric line addressing, you reference lines using their line position in the text stream. The sed editor assigns the first line in the text stream as line number 1 and continues sequentially for each new line.

The address you specify in the command can be a single line number or a range of lines specified by a starting line number, a comma, and an ending line number. Here's an example of specifying a line number to which the sed command will be applied:

```
$ cat data1.txt
The quick brown fox jumps over the lazy dog.
The quick brown fox jumps over the lazy dog.
The quick brown fox jumps over the lazy dog.
The quick brown fox jumps over the lazy dog.
$
$ sed '2s/dog/cat/' data1.txt
The quick brown fox jumps over the lazy dog.
```

```
The quick brown fox jumps over the lazy cat.
The quick brown fox jumps over the lazy dog.
The quick brown fox jumps over the lazy dog.
$
```

The sed editor modified the text only in line 2 per the address specified. Here's another example, this time using a range of line addresses (lines 2 through 3):

```
$ sed '2,3s/dog/cat/' data1.txt
The quick brown fox jumps over the lazy dog.
The quick brown fox jumps over the lazy cat.
The quick brown fox jumps over the lazy cat.
The quick brown fox jumps over the lazy dog.
$
```

If you want to apply a command to a group of lines starting at some point within the text but continuing to the end of the text, you can use a dollar sign in place of the last address range number:

```
$ sed '2,$s/dog/cat/' data1.txt
The quick brown fox jumps over the lazy dog.
The quick brown fox jumps over the lazy cat.
The quick brown fox jumps over the lazy cat.
The quick brown fox jumps over the lazy cat.
$
```

Because you may not know how many lines of data are in the text, the dollar sign often comes in handy.

### Using text pattern filters

The other method of restricting to which lines a command is applied is a bit more complicated. The sed editor allows the specification of a text pattern, and uses it as a filter to determine to which lines the command is applied. This is the format:

```
/pattern/command
```

You must encapsulate the *pattern* you specify in forward slashes. The sed editor applies the command only to lines that contain the text pattern you specify.

For example, if you want to change the default shell for only the user rich, you'd use the sed command:

```
$ grep /bin/bash /etc/passwd
root:x:0:0:root:/root:/bin/bash
christine:x:1001:1001::/home/christine:/bin/bash
rich:x:1002:1002::/home/rich:/bin/bash
$
$ sed '/rich/s/bash/csh/' /etc/passwd
root:x:0:0:root:/root:/bin/bash
daemon:x:1:1:daemon:/usr/sbin:/usr/sbin/nologin
[...]
```

*(Continues)*

*(continued)*
```
christine:x:1001:1001::/home/christine:/bin/bash
sshd:x:126:65534::/run/sshd:/usr/sbin/nologin
rich:x:1002:1002::/home/rich:/bin/csh
$
```

The command was applied only to the line with the matching text pattern. Although using a fixed text pattern may be useful for filtering specific values, as in the previous example, it's somewhat limited in what you can do with it. The sed editor uses a feature called *regular expressions* in text patterns to allow you to create patterns that get pretty involved.

Regular expressions allow you to create advanced text pattern–matching formulas to match all sorts of data. These formulas combine a series of wildcard characters, special characters, and fixed text characters to produce a concise pattern that can match just about any text situation. Regular expressions are one of the trickier parts of shell script programming, and Chapter 20, "Regular Expressions," covers them in great detail.

### Grouping commands

If you need to perform more than one command on an individual line, group the commands together using braces. The sed editor processes each command listed on the address line(s):

```
$ sed '2{
> s/fox/toad/
> s/dog/cat/
> }' data1.txt
The quick brown fox jumps over the lazy dog.
The quick brown toad jumps over the lazy cat.
The quick brown fox jumps over the lazy dog.
The quick brown fox jumps over the lazy dog.
$
```

Both commands are processed only against the address. And of course, you can specify an address range before the grouped commands:

```
$ sed '3,${
> s/brown/green/
> s/fox/toad/
> s/lazy/sleeping/
> }' data1.txt
The quick brown fox jumps over the lazy dog.
The quick brown fox jumps over the lazy dog.
The quick green toad jumps over the sleeping dog.
The quick green toad jumps over the sleeping dog.
$
```

The sed editor applies all the commands to all the lines in the address range.

## Deleting lines

The text substitution command isn't the only command available in the sed editor. If you need to delete specific lines of text in a text stream, you can use the delete command.

The delete (d) command pretty much does what it says. It deletes any text lines that match the addressing scheme supplied. Be careful with the d command, because if you forget to include an addressing scheme, all the lines are deleted from the stream:

```
$ cat data1.txt
The quick brown fox jumps over the lazy dog.
The quick brown fox jumps over the lazy dog.
The quick brown fox jumps over the lazy dog.
The quick brown fox jumps over the lazy dog.
$
$ sed 'd' data1.txt
$
```

The d command is obviously most helpful when used in conjunction with a specified address. This allows you to remove specific lines of text from the data stream, either by line number:

```
$ cat data6.txt
This is line number 1.
This is line number 2.
This is the 3rd line.
This is the 4th line.
$
$ sed '3d' data6.txt
This is line number 1.
This is line number 2.
This is the 4th line.
$
```

or by a specific range of lines:

```
$ sed '2,3d' data6.txt
This is line number 1.
This is the 4th line.
$
```

or by using the special end-of-file character:

```
$ sed '3,$d' data6.txt
This is line number 1.
This is line number 2.
$
```

The pattern-matching feature of the sed editor also applies to the delete (d) command:

```
$ sed '/number 1/d' data6.txt
This is line number 2.
This is the 3rd line.
This is the 4th line.
$
```

The sed editor removes the line containing text that matches the pattern you specify.

> **NOTE**
> Remember that the sed editor doesn't touch the original file. Any lines you delete are only gone from the sed editor's output. The original file still contains the "deleted" lines.

You can also delete a range of lines using two text patterns, but be careful if you do this. The first pattern you specify "turns on" the line deletion, and the second pattern "turns off" the line deletion. The sed editor deletes any lines between the two specified lines (including the specified lines):

```
$ sed '/1/,/3/d' data6.txt
This is the 4th line.
$
```

In addition, you must be careful because the delete feature "turns on" whenever the sed editor detects the start pattern in the data stream. This may produce an unexpected result:

```
$ cat data7.txt
This is line number 1.
This is line number 2.
This is the 3rd line.
This is the 4th line.
This is line number 1 again; we want to keep it.
This is more text we want to keep.
Last line in the file; we want to keep it.
$
$ sed '/1/,/3/d' data7.txt
This is the 4th line.
$
```

The second occurrence of a line with the number 1 in it triggered the delete (d) command again, deleting the rest of the lines in the data stream, because the stop pattern wasn't recognized. Of course, the other obvious problem occurs if you specify a stop pattern that never appears in the text:

```
$ sed '/3/,/5/d' data7.txt
This is line number 1.
This is line number 2.
$
```

Because the delete feature "turned on" at the first pattern match but never found the end pattern match, it didn't "turn off." And the entire rest of the data stream was deleted.

## Inserting and appending text

As you would expect, like any other editor, the sed editor allows you to insert and append text lines to the data stream. However, the difference between the two actions can be confusing:

- The insert (i) command adds a new line *before* the specified line.
- The append (a) command adds a new line *after* the specified line.

What is confusing about these two commands is their formats. You can't always use these commands on a single command line. You sometimes must specify the line to insert or append the line to insert on a separate line. Here's the format for doing this:

```
sed '[address]command\
new line'
```

The text in *new line* appears in the sed editor output in the place you specify. Remember that when you use the insert (i) command, the text appears *before* the data stream text:

```
$ echo "Test Line 2" | sed 'i\Test Line 1'
Test Line 1
Test Line 2
$
```

And when you use the append (a) command, the text appears *after* the data stream text:

```
$ echo "Test Line 2" | sed 'a\Test Line 1'
Test Line 2
Test Line 1
$
```

When you use the sed editor from the command-line interface prompt, you get the secondary prompt to enter the new line of data. You must complete the sed editor command on this line. After you enter the ending single quotation mark, the Bash shell processes the command:

```
$ echo "Test Line 2" | sed 'i\
> Test Line 1'
Test Line 1
Test Line 2
$
```

This works well for adding text before or after the text in the data stream, but what about adding text inside the data stream?

To insert or append data inside the data stream lines, you must use addressing to tell the sed editor where you want the data to appear. You can specify only a single line address when using these commands. You can match either a numeric line number or a text pattern, but you cannot use a range of addresses. This is logical, because you can only insert or append before or after a single line, and not a range of lines.

Here's an example of inserting a new line before line 3 in the data stream:

```
$ cat data6.txt
This is line number 1.
This is line number 2.
This is the 3rd line.
This is the 4th line.
$
$ sed '3i\
> This is an inserted line.
> ' data6.txt
This is line number 1.
This is line number 2.
This is an inserted line.
This is the 3rd line.
This is the 4th line.
$
```

Here's an example of appending a new line after line 3 in the data stream:

```
$ sed '3a\
> This is an appended line.
> ' data6.txt
This is line number 1.
This is line number 2.
This is the 3rd line.
This is an appended line.
This is the 4th line.
$
```

This uses the same process as the insert (i) command; it just places the new text line after the specified line number. If you have a multiline data stream and you want to append a new line of text to the end of a data stream, just use the dollar sign, which represents the last line of data:

```
$ sed '$a\
> This line was added to the end of the file.
> ' data6.txt
This is line number 1.
This is line number 2.
This is the 3rd line.
This is the 4th line.
This line was added to the end of the file.
$
```

The same idea applies if you want to add a new line at the beginning of the data stream. Just insert (i) a new line before line number 1.

To insert or append more than one line of text, you must use a backslash on each line of new text until you reach the last text line where you want to insert or append text:

```
$ sed '1i\
> This is an inserted line.\
> This is another inserted line.
> ' data6.txt
This is an inserted line.
This is another inserted line.
This is line number 1.
This is line number 2.
This is the 3rd line.
This is the 4th line.
$
```

Both of the specified lines are added to the data stream.

## Changing lines

The change (c) command allows you to change the contents of an entire line of text in the data stream. It works the same way as the insert and append commands in that you must specify the new line separately from the rest of the sed command:

```
$ sed '2c\
> This is a changed line of text.
> ' data6.txt
This is line number 1.
This is a changed line of text.
This is the 3rd line.
This is the 4th line.
$
```

In the preceding example, the sed editor changes the text in line number 2. You can also use a text pattern for the address:

```
$ sed '/3rd line/c\
> This is a changed line of text.
> ' data6.txt
This is line number 1.
This is line number 2.
This is a changed line of text.
This is the 4th line.
$
```

The text pattern change (c) command changes any line of text in the data stream that it matches.

```
$ cat data8.txt
I have 2 Infinity Stones
I need 4 more Infinity Stones
I have 6 Infinity Stones!
```

*(Continues)*

```
(continued)
      I need 4 Infinity Stones
      I have 6 Infinity Stones...
      I want 1 more Infinity Stone
      $
      $ sed '/have 6 Infinity Stones/c\
      > Snap! This is changed line of text.
      > ' data8.txt
      I have 2 Infinity Stones
      I need 4 more Infinity Stones
      Snap! This is changed line of text.
      I need 4 Infinity Stones
      Snap! This is changed line of text.
      I want 1 more Infinity Stone
      $
```

You can use an address range in the change command, but the results may not be what you expect:

```
      $ cat data6.txt
      This is line number 1.
      This is line number 2.
      This is the 3rd line.
      This is the 4th line.
      $
      $ sed '2,3c\
      > This is a changed line of text.
      > ' data6.txt
      This is line number 1.
      This is a changed line of text.
      This is the 4th line.
      $
```

Instead of changing both lines with the text, the sed editor uses the single line of text to replace both lines.

## Transforming characters

The transform (y) command is the only sed editor command that operates on a single character. The transform command uses the format

```
[address]y/inchars/outchars/
```

The transform command performs a one-to-one mapping of the *inchars* and the *outchars* values. The first character in *inchars* is converted to the first character in *outchars*. The second character in *inchars* is converted to the second character in *outchars*. This mapping continues throughout the length of the specified characters. If the *inchars* and *outchars* are not the same length, the sed editor produces an error message.

Here's a simple example of using the transform (y) command:

```
$ cat data9.txt
This is line 1.
This is line 2.
This is line 3.
This is line 4.
This is line 5.
This is line 1 again.
This is line 3 again.
This is the last file line.
$
$ sed 'y/123/789/' data9.txt
This is line 7.
This is line 8.
This is line 9.
This is line 4.
This is line 5.
This is line 7 again.
This is line 9 again.
This is the last file line.
$
```

As you can see from the output, each instance of the characters specified in the *inchars* pattern has been replaced by the character in the same position in the *outchars* pattern.

The transform (y) command is a global command; that is, it performs the transformation on any character found in the text line automatically, without regard to the occurrence:

```
$ echo "Test #1 of try #1." | sed 'y/123/678/'
Test #6 of try #6.
$
```

The sed editor transformed both instances of the matching character 1 in the text line. You can't limit the transformation to a specific occurrence of the character.

## Printing revisited

The "Introducing more substitution options" section showed how to use the p flag with the substitution (s) command to display lines that the sed editor changed. In addition, three commands can be used to print information from the data stream:

- The print (p) command to print a text line
- The equal sign (=) command to print line numbers
- The list (l) command to list a line

The following sections look at these three printing commands in the sed editor.

### Printing lines

Like the p flag in the substitution (s) command, the print (p) command prints a line in the sed editor output. On its own, this command doesn't offer much excitement:

```
$ echo "This is a test." | sed 'p'
This is a test.
This is a test.
$
```

All it does is print the data text that you already know is there. The most common use for the print command is printing lines that contain matching text from a text pattern:

```
$ cat data6.txt
This is line number 1.
This is line number 2.
This is the 3rd line.
This is the 4th line.
$
$ sed -n '/3rd line/p' data6.txt
This is the 3rd line.
$
```

By using the -n option on the command line, you can suppress all the other lines and print only the line that contains the matching text pattern.

You can also use this as a quick way to print a subset of lines in a data stream:

```
$ sed -n '2,3p' data6.txt
This is line number 2.
This is the 3rd line.
$
```

You can also use the print (p) command when you need to see a line before it gets altered, such as with the substitution (s) or change (c) command. You can create a script that displays the line before it's changed:

```
$ sed -n '/3/{
> p
> s/line/test/p
> }' data6.txt
This is the 3rd line.
This is the 3rd test.
$
```

This sed editor command searches for lines that contain the number 3 and executes two commands. First, the script uses the p command to print the original version of the line; then it uses the s command to substitute text, along with the p flag to print the resulting text. The output shows both the original line text and the new line text.

### Printing line numbers

The equal sign (=) command prints the current line number for the line within the data stream. Line numbers are determined by using the newline character in the data stream. Each time a newline character appears in the data stream, the sed editor assumes that it terminates a line of text:

```
$ cat data1.txt
The quick brown fox jumps over the lazy dog.
The quick brown fox jumps over the lazy dog.
The quick brown fox jumps over the lazy dog.
The quick brown fox jumps over the lazy dog.
$
$ sed '=' data1.txt
1
The quick brown fox jumps over the lazy dog.
2
The quick brown fox jumps over the lazy dog.
3
The quick brown fox jumps over the lazy dog.
4
The quick brown fox jumps over the lazy dog.
$
```

The sed editor prints the line number before the actual line of text. The = command comes in handy if you're searching for a specific text pattern in the data stream:

```
$ cat data7.txt
This is line number 1.
This is line number 2.
This is the 3rd line.
This is the 4th line.
This is line number 1 again; we want to keep it.
This is more text we want to keep.
Last line in the file; we want to keep it.
$
$ sed -n '/text/{
> =
> p
> }' data7.txt
6
This is more text we want to keep.
$
```

By using the -n option, you can have the sed editor display both the line number and text for the line that contains the matching text pattern.

### Listing lines

The list (l) command allows you to print both the text and nonprintable characters in a data stream. Any nonprintable characters are shown using either their octal values, proceeded by a backslash, or the standard C-style nomenclature for common nonprintable characters, such as \t for tab characters:

```
$ cat data10.txt
This     line     contains          tabs.
This line does contain tabs.
$
$ sed -n 'l' data10.txt
This\tline\tcontains\ttabs.$
This line does contain tabs.$
$
```

The tab character locations are shown with the \t. The dollar sign at the end of each line indicates the newline character. If you have a data stream that contains an escape character, the list (l) command displays it (using the octal code if necessary):

```
$ cat data11.txt
This line contains an escape character.
$
$ sed -n 'l' data11.txt
This line contains an escape character. \a$
$
```

The data11.txt file contains an escape control code, which generates a bell sound. When the cat command is used to display the text file, the escape control code isn't shown; only the sound is generated (if the computer's sound is turned on). However, using the list command, the escape control code used is displayed.

## Using files with *sed*

The substitution (s) command contains flags that allow you to work with files. There are also regular sed editor commands that let you do that without having to substitute text.

### Writing to a file

The write (w) command is used to write lines to a file. Here's the format for the write command:

```
[address]w filename
```

The *filename* can be specified as either a relative or absolute pathname, but in either case, the person running the sed editor must have write permissions for the file. The address can be any type of addressing method used in sed, such as a single line number, a text pattern, or a range of line numbers or text patterns.

Here's an example that prints only the first two lines of a data stream to a text file:

```
$ sed '1,2w test.txt' data6.txt
This is line number 1.
This is line number 2.
This is the 3rd line.
This is the 4th line.
```

```
$
$ cat test.txt
This is line number 1.
This is line number 2.
$
```

Of course, if you don't want the lines to display on STDOUT, you can use the -n option for the sed command.

This is a great tool to use if you need to create a data file from a master file on the basis of common text values, such as those in a mailing list:

```
$ cat data12.txt
Blum, R         Browncoat
McGuiness, A    Alliance
Bresnahan, C    Browncoat
Harken, C       Alliance
$
$ sed -n '/Browncoat/w Browncoats.txt' data12.txt
$
$ cat Browncoats.txt
Blum, R         Browncoat
Bresnahan, C    Browncoat
$
```

The sed editor writes to a destination file only the data lines that contain the text pattern.

### Reading data from a file

You've already seen how to insert data into and append text to a data stream from the sed command line. The read (r) command allows you to insert data contained in a separate file.

Here's the format of the read command:

```
[address]r filename
```

The `filename` parameter specifies either an absolute or relative pathname for the file that contains the data. You can't use a range of addresses for the read (r) command. You can only specify a single line number or text pattern address. The sed editor inserts the text from the file after the address.

```
$ cat data13.txt
This is an added line.
This is a second added line.
$
$ sed '3r data13.txt' data6.txt
This is line number 1.
This is line number 2.
This is the 3rd line.
This is an added line.
```

*(Continues)*

*(continued)*

```
      This is a second added line.
      This is the 4th line.
      $
```

The `sed` editor inserts into the data stream all the text lines in the data file. The same technique works when using a text pattern address:

```
$ sed '/number 2/r data13.txt' data6.txt
This is line number 1.
This is line number 2.
This is an added line.
This is a second added line.
This is the 3rd line.
This is the 4th line.
$
```

If you want to add text to the end of a data stream, just use the dollar sign address symbol:

```
$ sed '$r data13.txt' data6.txt
This is line number 1.
This is line number 2.
This is the 3rd line.
This is the 4th line.
This is an added line.
This is a second added line.
$
```

A cool application of the read (r) command is to use it in conjunction with a delete (d) command to replace a placeholder in a file with data from another file. For example, suppose that you had a form stored in a text file that looked like this:

```
$ cat notice.std
Would the following people:
LIST
please report to the ship's captain.
$
```

The form letter uses the generic placeholder LIST in place of a list of people. To insert the list of people after the placeholder, you just use the read (r) command. However, this still leaves the placeholder text in the output. To remove that, just use the delete (d) command. The result looks like this:

```
$ sed '/LIST/{
> r data12.txt
> d
> }' notice.std
Would the following people:
Blum, R        Browncoat
McGuiness, A  Alliance
Bresnahan, C  Browncoat
```

```
Harken, C      Alliance
please report to the ship's captain.
$
```

Now the placeholder text is replaced with the list of names from the data file.

# Working Through a Practical Example

In this section, we'll describe a script that puts both `sed` and `gawk` into action. Before looking at the script, let's describe a situation where the script is useful. First, we need to discuss the shebang. In Chapter 11, "Basic Script Building," we covered the first line of a shell script file:

```
#!/bin/bash
```

This first line is sometimes referred to as the *shebang* and traditionally looks like this for shell scripts in Unix:

```
#!/bin/sh
```

Often the tradition was carried over to Bash shell scripts on Linux, which wasn't a problem in the past — most distributions had /bin/sh linked to the Bash shell (/bin/bash). Thus, if /bin/sh was used as the shebang in a shell script, it was as if /bin/bash had been written:

```
$ ls -l /bin/sh
lrwxrwxrwx 1 root root 4 Nov 8 2019 /bin/sh -> bash
$
```

Somewhere along the way this changed on some Linux distributions, such as Ubuntu. And on these Linux systems, the /bin/sh file is now linked to a different file than the Bash shell:

```
$ ls -l /bin/sh
lrwxrwxrwx 1 root root 4 Apr 23 14:33 /bin/sh -> dash
$
```

If a shell script that has /bin/sh as its shebang runs on this system, the script will be run in the Dash shell instead of the Bash shell. This may cause many of the shell script commands to fail.

Now let's look at our real-world scenario for the practical script: a particular company uses only RHEL, and the Bash shell scripts on their systems use the old-fashioned /bin/sh shebang. This is not a problem, because on that distribution, the /bin/sh file still links to /bin/bash. But now, the company wants to bring in servers that run Ubuntu, and the shell scripts must be converted to use the /bin/bash shebang so that they run properly on these new servers.

How can this problem be solved? Do you spend hours with a text editor fixing every shebang by hand? Could the new IT intern be forced into such terrible manual labor? This type of situation is where `sed` and `gawk` shine, so we'll put them to use for this problem.

First, we'll use sed to create a listing of all the shell scripts in a particular directory that contain /bin/sh as the shebang in their first line. We can start the process by using the substitute (s) command along with addressing only the first line of a shell script:

```
$ sed '1s!/bin/sh!/bin/bash!' OldScripts/testAscript.sh
#!/bin/bash
[...]
echo "This is Test Script #1."
[...]
#
exit
$
```

This provides the substitution, so the testAScript.sh script *does* contain #!/bin/sh as its shebang. But we need to check all the files in the directory, and we don't want to see the script's contents, so we'll modify the command slightly. Using the -s option (which we haven't covered yet in this chapter) will tell sed to treat every file within the directory as an individual stream, and thus we can check the first line in each file. The -n option will suppress any output, so we don't have to view all the scripts' contents:

```
$ sed -sn '1s!/bin/sh!/bin/bash!' OldScripts/*.sh
$
```

Well, that worked, but it's not quite what we want. We need to see the script file's names, so we know which scripts have the old shebang.

We'll introduce another useful sed command — F. This command tells sed to print the current data file's name on which it is operating, even if the -n option is used. We only need to see the name one time, so we'll put a one (1) in front of the command (otherwise we'd see the name for every line processed in every file). Now we get the listing we desire:

```
$ sed -sn '1F;
> 1s!/bin/sh!/bin/bash!' OldScripts/*.sh
OldScripts/backgroundoutput.sh
OldScripts/backgroundscript.sh
[...]
OldScripts/tryat.sh
$
```

Now let's get gawk in on this act to pretty up the report. By redirecting (|) the output from sed into gawk, we can make the information a little nicer to view:

```
$ sed -sn '1F;
> 1s!/bin/sh!/bin/bash!' OldScripts/*.sh |
> gawk 'BEGIN {print ""
> print "The following scripts have /bin/sh as their shebang:"
> print ""}
> {print $0}
> END {print "End of Report"}'
```

The following scripts have /bin/sh as their shebang:

```
OldScripts/backgroundoutput.sh
OldScripts/backgroundscript.sh
[...]
OldScripts/tryat.sh
End of Report
$
```

Now that we've produced a report, we'll verify that we want to update these scripts to use a more modern shebang. Once the decision is made to update the scripts, we can make the needed changes. But we'll let sed do all the updating work for us along with a for loop:

```
$ mkdir TestScripts
$
$ for filename in $(grep -l "bin/sh" OldScripts/*.sh)
> do
> newFilename=$(basename $filename)
> cat $filename |
> sed '1c\#!/bin/bash' > TestScripts/$newFilename
> done
$
$ grep "/bin/bash" TestScripts/*.sh
TestScripts/backgroundoutput.sh:#!/bin/bash
TestScripts/backgroundscript.sh:#!/bin/bash
[...]
TestScripts/tryat.sh:#!/bin/bash
$
```

Success! Next we need to take this basic sed and gawk functionality and put it into our practical script. Here is the script in its entirety for your perusal:

```
$ cat ChangeScriptShell.sh
#!/bin/bash
# Change the shebang used for a directory of scripts
#
################## Function Declarations #########################
#
function errorOrExit {
        echo
        echo $message1
        echo $message2
        echo "Exiting script..."
        exit
}
#
function modifyScripts {
        echo
        read -p "Directory name in which to store new scripts? " newScriptDir
```

*(Continues)*

*(continued)*

```
        #
        echo "Modifying the scripts started at $(date +%N) nanoseconds"
        #
        count=0
        for filename in $(grep -l "/bin/sh" $scriptDir/*.sh)
        do
                newFilename=$(basename $filename)
                cat $filename |
                sed '1c\#!/bin/bash' > $newScriptDir/$newFilename
                count=$[$count + 1]
        done
        echo "$count modifications completed at $(date +%N) nanoseconds"
}
#
############### Check for Script Directory ####################
if [ -z $1 ]
then
        message1="The name of the directory containing scripts to check"
        message2="is missing. Please provide the name as a parameter."
        errorOrExit
else
        scriptDir=$1
fi
#
############### Create Shebang Report #########################
#
sed -sn '1F;
1s!/bin/sh!/bin/bash!' $scriptDir/*.sh |
gawk 'BEGIN {print ""
print "The following scripts have /bin/sh as their shebang:"
print "===================================================="}
{print $0}
END {print ""
print "End of Report"}'
#
################ Change Scripts? ##############################
#
#
echo
read -p "Do you wish to modify these scripts' shebang? (Y/n)? " answer
#
case $answer in
Y | y)
        modifyScripts
        ;;
```

```
N | n)
        message1="No scripts will be modified."
        message2="Run this script later to modify, if desired."
        errorOrExit
        ;;
*)
        message1="Did not answer Y or n."
        message2="No scripts will be modified."
        errorOrExit
        ;;
esac
$
```

Notice that we added a few time stamps around the running of the sed to modify the scripts. Let's look at the script in action:

```
$ mkdir NewScripts
$ ./ChangeScriptShell.sh OldScripts

The following scripts have /bin/sh as their shebang:
=====================================================
OldScripts/backgroundoutput.sh
OldScripts/backgroundscript.sh
[...]
OldScripts/tryat.sh

End of Report

Do you wish to modify these scripts' shebang? (Y/n)? Y

Directory name in which to store new scripts? NewScripts
Modifying the scripts started at 168687219 nanoseconds
18 modifications completed at 266043476 nanoseconds
$
```

That was fast! If you have hundreds of old shell scripts to modify, imagine how much time this script will save you.

A few improvements to this script include

- Checking to ensure the new directory location of the modified Bash shell scripts exists
- Checking to see if the file being saved does not already reside in the directory so that no files are accidentally overwritten
- Allowing the new directory location to be passed as a parameter, and possibly saving the report produced by sed and gawk

What modifications did you come up with?

# Summary

Shell scripts can do lots of work on their own, but it's often difficult to manipulate data with just a shell script. Linux provides two handy utilities to help with handling text data. The sed editor is a stream editor that quickly processes data on the fly as it reads it. You must provide the sed editor with a list of editing commands, which it applies to the data.

The gawk program is a utility from the GNU organization that mimics and expands on the functionality of the Unix awk program. The gawk program contains a built-in programming language that you can use to write scripts to handle and process data. You can use the gawk program to extract data elements from large data files and output them in just about any format you desire. This makes processing large log files a snap, as well as creating custom reports from data files.

A crucial element of using both the sed and gawk programs is knowing how to use regular expressions. Regular expressions are key to creating customized filters for extracting and manipulating data in text files. The next chapter dives into the often misunderstood world of regular expressions, showing you how to build regular expressions for manipulating all types of data.

# Regular Expressions

The key to successfully working with sed and gawk in your shell script is your comfort using regular expressions. This is not always an easy thing to do, because trying to filter specific data from a large batch of data can (and often does) get complicated. This chapter describes how to create regular expressions in both sed and gawk that can filter out just the data you need.

## Exploring Regular Expressions

The first step to understanding regular expressions is to define just exactly what they are. This section explains what a regular expression is and describes how Linux uses regular expressions.

### A definition

A regular expression is a pattern template you define that a Linux utility uses to filter text. A Linux utility (such as sed or gawk) matches the regular expression pattern against data as that data flows into the utility. If the data matches the pattern, it's accepted for processing. If the data doesn't match the pattern, it's rejected. This is illustrated in Figure 20-1.

The regular expression pattern makes use of wildcard characters to represent one or more characters in the data stream. There are plenty of instances in Linux where you can specify a wildcard character to represent data you don't know about. You've already seen an example of using wildcard characters with the Linux ls command for listing files and directories (see Chapter 3, "Basic Bash Shell Commands").

**FIGURE 20-1**

Matching data against a regular expression pattern

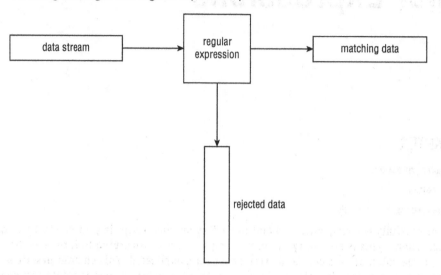

The asterisk wildcard character allows you to list only files that match a certain criterion. For example:

```
$ ls -al da*
-rw-r--r--    1 rich      rich               45 Nov 26 12:42 data
-rw-r--r--    1 rich      rich               25 Dec  4 12:40 data.tst
-rw-r--r--    1 rich      rich              180 Nov 26 12:42 data1
-rw-r--r--    1 rich      rich               45 Nov 26 12:44 data2
-rw-r--r--    1 rich      rich               73 Nov 27 12:31 data3
-rw-r--r--    1 rich      rich               79 Nov 28 14:01 data4
-rw-r--r--    1 rich      rich              187 Dec  4 09:45 datatest
$
```

The da* parameter instructs the ls command to list only the files whose name starts with "da." There can be any number of characters after the "da" in the filename (including none). The ls command reads the information regarding all the files in the directory but displays only the ones that match the wildcard character.

Regular expression wildcard patterns work in a similar way. The regular expression pattern contains text and/or special characters that define a template for sed and gawk to follow when matching data. You can use different special characters in a regular expression to define a specific pattern for filtering data.

## Types of regular expressions

The biggest problem with using regular expressions is that there isn't just one set of them. Several different applications use different types of regular expressions in the Linux environment. These include such diverse applications as programming languages (Java, Perl, and Python), Linux utilities (such as sed, gawk, and the grep utility), and mainstream applications (such as the MySQL and PostgreSQL database servers).

A regular expression is implemented using a *regular expression engine*. A regular expression engine is the underlying software that interprets regular expression patterns and uses those patterns to match text.

While there are many different regular expression engines in the Linux world, the two most popular ones are

- The POSIX Basic Regular Expression (BRE) engine
- The POSIX Extended Regular Expression (ERE) engine

Most Linux utilities at a minimum conform to the POSIX BRE engine specifications, recognizing all the pattern symbols it defines. Unfortunately, some utilities (such as sed) conform only to a subset of the BRE engine specifications. This is due to speed constraints, because sed attempts to process text in the data stream as quickly as possible.

The POSIX ERE engine is often found in programming languages that rely on regular expressions for text filtering. It provides advanced pattern symbols as well as special symbols for common patterns, such as matching digits, words, and alphanumeric characters. Gawk uses the ERE engine to process its regular expression patterns.

Because there are so many different ways to implement regular expressions, it's hard to present a single, concise description of all the possible regular expressions. The following sections discuss the most commonly found regular expressions and demonstrate how to use them in sed and gawk.

# Defining BRE Patterns

The most basic BRE pattern is matching text characters in a data stream. This section demonstrates how you can define text in the regular expression pattern and what to expect from the results.

## Plain text

Chapter 18, "Writing Scripts for Graphical Desktops," demonstrated how to use standard text strings in sed and gawk to filter data. Here's an example to refresh your memory:

```
$ echo "This is a test" | sed -n '/test/p'
This is a test
```

*(Continues)*

**20**

```
(continued)
$ echo "This is a test" | sed -n '/trial/p'
$
$ echo "This is a test" | gawk '/test/{print $0}'
This is a test
$ echo "This is a test" | gawk '/trial/{print $0}'
$
```

The first pattern defines a single word, "test." Sed and gawk scripts each use their own version of the print command to print any lines that match the regular expression pattern. Because the echo statement contains the word "test" in the text string, the data stream text matches the defined regular expression pattern, and sed displays the line.

The second pattern again defines just a single word, this time the word "trial." Because the echo statement text string doesn't contain that word, the regular expression pattern doesn't match, so neither sed nor gawk prints the line.

You probably already noticed that the regular expression doesn't care where in the data stream the pattern occurs. It also doesn't matter how many times the pattern occurs. After the regular expression can match the pattern anywhere in the text string, it passes the string along to the Linux utility that's using it.

The key is matching the regular expression pattern to the data stream text. It's important to remember that regular expressions are extremely picky about matching patterns. The first rule to remember is that regular expression patterns are case sensitive. This means they'll match only those patterns with the proper case of characters:

```
$ echo "This is a test" | sed -n '/this/p'
$
$ echo "This is a test" | sed -n '/This/p'
This is a test
$
```

The first attempt failed to match because the word "this" doesn't appear in all lowercase in the text string, whereas the second attempt, which uses the uppercase letter in the pattern, worked just fine.

You don't have to limit yourself to whole words in the regular expression. If the defined text appears anywhere in the data stream, the regular expression matches the following:

```
$ echo "The books are expensive" | sed -n '/book/p'
The books are expensive
$
```

Even though the text in the data stream is "books," the data in the stream contains the regular expression "book", so the regular expression pattern matches the data. Of course, if you try the opposite, the regular expression fails:

```
$ echo "The book is expensive" | sed -n '/books/p'
$
```

The complete regular expression text didn't appear in the data stream, so the match failed and sed didn't display the text.

You also don't have to limit yourself to single text words in the regular expression. You can include spaces and numbers in your text string as well:

```
$ echo "This is line number 1" | sed -n '/ber 1/p'
This is line number 1
$
```

Spaces are treated just like any other character in the regular expression:

```
$ echo "This is line number1" | sed -n '/ber 1/p'
$
```

If you define a space in the regular expression, it must appear in the data stream. You can even create a regular expression pattern that matches multiple contiguous spaces:

```
$ cat data1
This is a normal line of text.
This is  a line with too many spaces.
$ sed -n '/  /p' data1
This is  a line with too many spaces.
$
```

The line with two spaces between words matches the regular expression pattern. This is a great way to catch spacing problems in text files!

## Special characters

As you use text strings in your regular expression patterns, there's something you need to be aware of. There are a few exceptions when defining text characters in a regular expression. Regular expression patterns assign a special meaning to a few characters. If you try to use these characters in your text pattern, you won't get the results you were expecting.

These special characters are recognized by regular expressions:

```
.*[]^${}\+?|()
```

As the chapter progresses, you'll find out just what these special characters do in a regular expression. For now, however, just remember that you can't use these characters by themselves in your text pattern.

If you want to use one of the special characters as a text character, you need to *escape* it. When you escape the special characters, you add a special character in front of it to indicate to the regular expression engine that it should interpret the next character as a normal text character. The special character that does this is the backslash character (\).

For example, if you want to search for a dollar sign in your text, just precede it with a backslash character:

```
$ cat data2
The cost is $4.00
```

20

*(Continues)*

*(continued)*

```
$ sed -n '/\$/p' data2
The cost is $4.00
$
```

Because the backslash is a special character, if you need to use it in a regular expression pattern, you need to escape it as well, producing a double backslash:

```
$ echo "\ is a special character" | sed -n '/\\/p'
\ is a special character
$
```

Finally, although the forward slash isn't a regular expression special character, if you use it in your regular expression pattern in sed or gawk, you get an error:

```
$ echo "3 / 2" | sed -n '///p'
sed: -e expression #1, char 2: No previous regular expression
$
```

To use a forward slash, you need to escape that as well:

```
$ echo "3 / 2" | sed -n '/\//p'
3 / 2
$
```

Now sed can properly interpret the regular expression pattern, and all is well.

## Anchor characters

As shown in the "Plain text" section, by default, when you specify a regular expression pattern, if the pattern appears anywhere in the data stream, it matches. You can use two special characters to anchor a pattern to either the beginning or the end of lines in the data stream.

### Starting at the beginning

The caret character (^) defines a pattern that starts at the beginning of a line of text in the data stream. If the pattern is located any place other than the start of the line of text, the regular expression pattern fails.

To use the caret character, you must place it before the pattern specified in the regular expression:

```
$ echo "The book store" | sed -n '/^book/p'
$
$ echo "Books are great" | sed -n '/^Book/p'
Books are great
$
```

The caret anchor character checks for the pattern at the beginning of each new line of data, as determined by the newline character:

```
$ cat data3
This is a test line.
```

```
this is another test line.
A line that tests this feature.
Yet more testing of this
$ sed -n '/^this/p' data3
this is another test line.
$
```

As long as the pattern appears at the start of a new line, the caret anchor catches it.

If you position the caret character in any place other than at the beginning of the pattern, it acts like a normal character and not as a special character:

```
$ echo "This ^ is a test" | sed -n '/s ^/p'
This ^ is a test
$
```

Because the caret character is listed last in the regular expression pattern, sed uses it as a normal character to match text.

> **NOTE**
> If you need to specify a regular expression pattern using only the caret character, you don't have to escape it with a backslash. However, if you specify the caret character first, followed by additional text in the pattern, you need to use the escape character before the caret character.

### Looking for the ending

The opposite of looking for a pattern at the start of a line is looking for it at the end of a line. The dollar sign ($) special character defines the end anchor. Add this special character after a text pattern to indicate that the line of data must end with the text pattern:

```
$ echo "This is a good book" | sed -n '/book$/p'
This is a good book
$ echo "This book is good" | sed -n '/book$/p'
$
```

The problem with an ending text pattern is that you must be careful what you're looking for:

```
$ echo "There are a lot of good books" | sed -n '/book$/p'
$
```

Making the word "book" plural at the end of the line means that it no longer matches the regular expression pattern, even though "book" is in the data stream. The text pattern must be the last thing on the line for the pattern to match.

20

### Combining anchors

In some common situations, you can combine both the start and the end anchors on the same line. In the first situation, suppose you want to look for a line of data containing only a specific text pattern:

```
$ cat data4
this is a test of using both anchors
I said this is a test
this is a test
I'm sure this is a test.
$ sed -n '/^this is a test$/p' data4
this is a test
$
```

Sed ignores the lines that include other text besides the specified text.

The second situation may seem a little odd at first but is extremely useful. By combining both anchors in a pattern with no text, you can filter blank lines from the data stream. Consider this example:

```
$ cat data5
This is one test line.

This is another test line.
$ sed '/^$/d' data5
This is one test line.
This is another test line.
$
```

The regular expression pattern that is defined looks for lines that have nothing between the start and the end of the line. Because blank lines contain no text between the two newline characters, they match the regular expression pattern. Sed uses the d command to delete lines that match the regular expression pattern, thus removing all blank lines from the text. This is an effective way to remove blank lines from documents.

## The dot character

The dot special character is used to match any single character except a newline character. The dot character must match a character, however; if there's no character in the place of the dot, then the pattern fails.

Let's look at a few examples of using the dot character in a regular expression pattern:

```
$ cat data6
This is a test of a line.
The cat is sleeping.
That is a very nice hat.
This test is at line four.
at ten o'clock we'll go home.
$ sed -n '/.at/p' data6
```

```
The cat is sleeping.
That is a very nice hat.
This test is at line four.
$
```

You should be able to figure out why the first line in the data file failed to match, and why the second and third lines in the data file passed. The fourth line is a little tricky. Notice that we matched the at, but there's no character in front of it to match the dot character. Ah, but there is! In regular expressions, spaces count as characters, so the space in front of the at matches the pattern. The fifth line proves this, by putting the at in the front of the line, which fails to match the pattern.

## Character classes

The dot special character is great for matching a character position against any character, but what if you want to limit what characters to match? This is called a *character class* in regular expressions.

You can define a class of characters that would match a position in a text pattern. If one of the characters from the character class is in the data stream, it matches the pattern.

To define a character class, you use square brackets. The brackets should contain any character you want to include in the class. You then use the entire class within a pattern just like any other wildcard character. This takes a little getting used to at first, but after you catch on, it can generate some pretty amazing results.

The following is an example of creating a character class:

```
$ sed -n '/[ch]at/p' data6
The cat is sleeping.
That is a very nice hat.
$
```

Using the same data file as in the dot special character example, we came up with a different result. This time we managed to filter out the line that just contained the word at. The only words that match this pattern are "cat" and "hat." Also notice that the line that started with "at" didn't match as well. There must be a character in the character class that matches the appropriate position.

Character classes come in handy if you're not sure which case a character is in:

```
$ echo "Yes" | sed -n '/[Yy]es/p'
Yes
$ echo "yes" | sed -n '/[Yy]es/p'
yes
$
```

You can use more than one character class in a single expression:

```
$ echo "Yes" | sed -n '/[Yy][Ee][Ss]/p'
Yes
```

*(Continues)*

20

*(continued)*
```
$ echo "yEs" | sed -n '/[Yy][Ee][Ss]/p'
yEs
$ echo "yeS" | sed -n '/[Yy][Ee][Ss]/p'
yeS
$
```

The regular expression used three character classes to cover both lower and upper cases for all three character positions.

Character classes don't have to contain just letters; you can use numbers in them as well:

```
$ cat data7
This line doesn't contain a number.
This line has 1 number on it.
This line a number 2 on it.
This line has a number 4 on it.
$ sed -n '/[0123]/p' data7
This line has 1 number on it.
This line a number 2 on it.
$
```

The regular expression pattern matches any lines that contain the numbers 0, 1, 2, or 3. Any other numbers are ignored, as are lines without numbers in them.

You can combine character classes to check for properly formatted numbers, such as phone numbers and ZIP codes. However, when you're trying to match a specific format, you must be careful. Here's an example of a ZIP code match gone wrong:

```
$ cat data8
60633
46201
223001
4353
22203
$ sed -n '
>/[0123456789][0123456789][0123456789][0123456789][0123456789]/p
>' data8
60633
46201
223001
22203
$
```

This might not have produced the result you were thinking of. It did a fine job of filtering out the number that was too short to be a ZIP code, because the last character class didn't have a character to match against. However, it still passed the six-digit number, even though we only defined five character classes.

Remember that the regular expression pattern can be found anywhere in the text of the data stream. You may always have additional characters besides the matching pattern characters. If you want to ensure that you match against only five numbers, you need to delineate them somehow, either with spaces, or as in this example, by showing that they're at the start and end of the line:

```
$ sed -n '
> /^[0123456789] [0123456789] [0123456789] [0123456789] [0123456789]$/p
> ' data8
60633
46201
22203
$
```

Now that's much better! Later in this chapter, we'll look at how to simplify this even further.

One extremely popular use for character classes is parsing words that might be misspelled, such as data entered from a user form. You can easily create regular expressions that can accept common misspellings in data:

```
$ cat data9
I need to have some maintenence done on my car.
I'll pay that in a seperate invoice.
After I pay for the maintenance my car will be as good as new.
$ sed -n '
/maint[ea]n[ae]nce/p
/sep[ea]r[ea]te/p
' data9
I need to have some maintenence done on my car.
I'll pay that in a seperate invoice.
After I pay for the maintenance my car will be as good as new.
$
```

The two sed print commands in this example utilize regular expression character classes to help catch the misspelled words, "maintenance" and "separate," in the text. The same regular expression pattern also matches the properly spelled occurrence of "maintenance."

## Negating character classes

In regular expression patterns, you can also reverse the effect of a character class. Instead of looking for a character contained in the class, you can look for any character that's not in the class. To do that, just place a caret character at the beginning of the character class range:

```
$ sed -n '/[^ch]at/p' data6
This test is at line four.
$
```

By negating the character class, the regular expression pattern matches any character that's neither a "c" nor an "h", along with the text pattern. Because the space character fits

20

this category, it passed the pattern match. However, even with the negation, the character class must still match a character, so the line with the "at" in the start of the line still doesn't match the pattern.

## Using ranges

You may have noticed when I showed the ZIP code example earlier that it was somewhat awkward having to list all the possible digits in each character class. Fortunately, you can use a shortcut so you don't have to do that.

You can use a range of characters within a character class by using the dash symbol. Just specify the first character in the range, a dash, and then the last character in the range. The regular expression includes any character that's within the specified character range, according to the character set used by the Linux system (see Chapter 2, "Getting to the Shell").

Now you can simplify the ZIP code example by specifying a range of digits:

```
$ sed -n '/^[0-9][0-9][0-9][0-9][0-9]$/p' data8
60633
46201
45902
$
```

That saved lots of typing! Each character class matches any digit from 0 to 9. The pattern fails if a letter is present anywhere in the data:

```
$ echo "a8392" | sed -n '/^[0-9][0-9][0-9][0-9][0-9]$/p'
$
$ echo "1839a" | sed -n '/^[0-9][0-9][0-9][0-9][0-9]$/p'
$
$ echo "18a92" | sed -n '/^[0-9][0-9][0-9][0-9][0-9]$/p'
$
```

The same technique works with letters:

```
$ sed -n '/[c-h]at/p' data6
The cat is sleeping.
That is a very nice hat.
$
```

The new pattern "[c-h]at" matches words where the first letter is between the letter "c" and the letter "h." In this case, the line with only the word "at" failed to match the pattern.

You can also specify multiple, noncontinuous ranges in a single character class:

```
$ sed -n '/[a-ch-m]at/p' data6
The cat is sleeping.
That is a very nice hat.
$
```

The character class allows the ranges "a" through "c", and "h" through "m" to appear before the at text. This range would reject any letters between "d" and "g":

```
$ echo "I'm getting too fat." | sed -n '/[a-ch-m]at/p'
$
```

This pattern rejected the "fat" text, as it wasn't in the specified range.

## Special character classes

In addition to defining your own character classes, the BRE contains special character classes you can use to match against specific types of characters. Table 20.1 describes the BRE special characters you can use.

**TABLE 20.1** **BRE Special Character Classes**

| Class | Description |
|---|---|
| [[:alpha:]] | Matches any alphabetical character, either upper or lower case |
| [[:alnum:]] | Matches any alphanumeric character 0–9, A–Z, or a–z |
| [[:blank:]] | Matches a space or Tab character |
| [[:digit:]] | Matches a numerical digit from 0 through 9 |
| [[:lower:]] | Matches any lowercase alphabetical character a–z |
| [[:print:]] | Matches any printable character |
| [[:punct:]] | Matches a punctuation character |
| [[:space:]] | Matches any whitespace character: space, Tab, NL (newline), FF (formfeed), VT (vertical tab), CR (carriage return) |
| [[:upper:]] | Matches any uppercase alphabetical character A–Z |

You use the special character classes just as you would a normal character class in your regular expression patterns:

```
$ echo "abc" | sed -n '/[[:digit:]]/p'
$
$ echo "abc" | sed -n '/[[:alpha:]]/p'
abc
$ echo "abc123" | sed -n '/[[:digit:]]/p'
abc123
$ echo "This is, a test" | sed -n '/[[:punct:]]/p'
This is, a test
$ echo "This is a test" | sed -n '/[[:punct:]]/p'
$
```

Using the special character classes is an easy way to define ranges. Instead of having to use a range [0–9], you can just use [[:digit:]].

## The asterisk

Placing an asterisk after a character signifies that the character must appear zero or more times in the text to match the pattern:

```
$ echo "ik" | sed -n '/ie*k/p'
ik
$ echo "iek" | sed -n '/ie*k/p'
iek
$ echo "ieek" | sed -n '/ie*k/p'
ieek
$ echo "ieeek" | sed -n '/ie*k/p'
ieeek
$ echo "ieeeek" | sed -n '/ie*k/p'
ieeeek
$
```

This pattern symbol is commonly used for handling words that have a common misspelling or variations in language spellings. For example, if you need to write a script that may be used in either American or British English, you could write:

```
$ echo "I'm getting a color TV" | sed -n '/colou*r/p'
I'm getting a color TV
$ echo "I'm getting a colour TV" | sed -n '/colou*r/p'
I'm getting a colour TV
$
```

The u* in the pattern indicates that the letter *u* may or may not appear in the text to match the pattern. Similarly, if you know of a word that is commonly misspelled, you can accommodate it by using the asterisk:

```
$ echo "I ate a potatoe with my lunch." | sed -n '/potatoe*/p'
I ate a potatoe with my lunch.
$ echo "I ate a potato with my lunch." | sed -n '/potatoe*/p'
I ate a potato with my lunch.
$
```

Placing an asterisk next to the possible extra letter allows you to accept the misspelled word.

Another handy feature is combining the dot special character with the asterisk special character. This combination provides a pattern to match any number of any characters. It's often used between two text strings that may or may not appear next to each other in the data stream:

```
$ echo "this is a regular pattern expression" | sed -n '
> /regular.*expression/p'
this is a regular pattern expression
$
```

Using this pattern, you can easily search for multiple words that may appear anywhere in a line of text in the data stream.

The asterisk can also be applied to a character class. Doing so allows you to specify a group or range of characters that can appear more than once in the text:

```
$ echo "bt" | sed -n '/b[ae]*t/p'
bt
$ echo "bat" | sed -n '/b[ae]*t/p'
bat
$ echo "bet" | sed -n '/b[ae]*t/p'
bet
$ echo "btt" | sed -n '/b[ae]*t/p'
btt
$ echo "baat" | sed -n '/b[ae]*t/p'
baat
$ echo "baaeeet" | sed -n '/b[ae]*t/p'
baaeeet
$ echo "baeeaeeat" | sed -n '/b[ae]*t/p'
baeeaeeat
$ echo "baakeeet" | sed -n '/b[ae]*t/p'
$
```

As long as the *a* and *e* characters appear in any combination between the *b* and *t* characters (including not appearing at all), the pattern matches. If any other character outside of the defined character class appears, the pattern match fails.

# Trying Out Extended Regular Expressions

The POSIX ERE patterns include a few additional symbols that are used by some Linux applications and utilities. Gawk recognizes the ERE patterns, but sed doesn't.

> **CAUTION**
> Remember that the regular expression engines in sed and gawk are different. Gawk can use most of the extended regular expression pattern symbols, and it can provide some additional filtering capabilities that sed doesn't have. However, because of this, it is often slower in processing data streams.

This section describes the more commonly found ERE pattern symbols that you can use in your gawk program scripts.

## The question mark

The question mark is similar to the asterisk, but with a slight twist. The question mark indicates that the preceding character can appear zero or one time, but that's all. It doesn't match repeating occurrences of the character:

```
$ echo "bt" | gawk '/be?t/{print $0}'
bt
```

*(Continues)*

*(continued)*

```
$ echo "bet" | gawk '/be?t/{print $0}'
bet
$ echo "beet" | gawk '/be?t/{print $0}'
$
$ echo "beeet" | gawk '/be?t/{print $0}'
$
```

If the *e* character doesn't appear in the text, or as long as it appears only once in the text, the pattern matches.

As with the asterisk, you can use the question mark symbol along with a character class:

```
$ echo "bt" | gawk '/b[ae]?t/{print $0}'
bt
$ echo "bat" | gawk '/b[ae]?t/{print $0}'
bat
$ echo "bot" | gawk '/b[ae]?t/{print $0}'
$
$ echo "bet" | gawk '/b[ae]?t/{print $0}'
bet
$ echo "baet" | gawk '/b[ae]?t/{print $0}'
$
$ echo "beat" | gawk '/b[ae]?t/{print $0}'
$
$ echo "beet" | gawk '/b[ae]?t/{print $0}'
$
```

If zero or one character from the character class appears, the pattern match passes. However, if both characters appear, or if one of the characters appears twice, the pattern match fails.

## The plus sign

The plus sign is another pattern symbol that's similar to the asterisk, but with a different twist than the question mark. The plus sign indicates that the preceding character can appear one or more times but must be present at least once. The pattern doesn't match if the character is not present:

```
$ echo "beeet" | gawk '/be+t/{print $0}'
beeet
$ echo "beet" | gawk '/be+t/{print $0}'
beet
$ echo "bet" | gawk '/be+t/{print $0}'
bet
$ echo "bt" | gawk '/be+t/{print $0}'
$
```

If the *e* character is not present, the pattern match fails. The plus sign also works with character classes, the same way the asterisk and question mark do:

```
$ echo "bt" | gawk '/b[ae]+t/{print $0}'
$
```

```
$ echo "bat" | gawk '/b[ae]+t/{print $0}'
bat
$ echo "bet" | gawk '/b[ae]+t/{print $0}'
bet
$ echo "beat" | gawk '/b[ae]+t/{print $0}'
beat
$ echo "beet" | gawk '/b[ae]+t/{print $0}'
beet
$ echo "beeat" | gawk '/b[ae]+t/{print $0}'
beeat
$
```

This time, if either character defined in the character class appears, the text matches the specified pattern.

## Using braces

Curly braces are available in ERE to allow you to specify a limit on a repeatable regular expression. This is often referred to as an *interval*. You can express the interval in two formats:

- m—The regular expression appears exactly *m* times.
- m,n—The regular expression appears at least *m* times, but no more than *n* times.

This feature allows you to fine-tune exactly how many times you allow a character (or character class) to appear in a pattern.

> **CAUTION**
>
> By default, gawk doesn't recognize regular expression intervals. You must specify the --re-interval command-line option for gawk to recognize regular expression intervals.

Here's an example of using a simple interval of one value:

```
$ echo "bt" | gawk --re-interval '/be{1}t/{print $0}'
$
$ echo "bet" | gawk --re-interval '/be{1}t/{print $0}'
bet
$ echo "beet" | gawk --re-interval '/be{1}t/{print $0}'
$
```

By specifying an interval of 1, you restrict the number of times the character can be present for the string to match the pattern. If the character appears more times, the pattern match fails.

Often, specifying the lower and upper limits comes in handy:

```
$ echo "bt" | gawk --re-interval '/be{1,2}t/{print $0}'
$
$ echo "bet" | gawk --re-interval '/be{1,2}t/{print $0}'
```

*(Continues)*

20

(continued)

```
bet
$ echo "beet" | gawk --re-interval '/be{1,2}t/{print $0}'
beet
$ echo "beeet" | gawk --re-interval '/be{1,2}t/{print $0}'
$
```

In this example, the *e* character can appear once or twice for the pattern match to pass; otherwise, the pattern match fails.

The interval pattern match also applies to character classes:

```
$ echo "bt" | gawk --re-interval '/b[ae]{1,2}t/{print $0}'
$
$ echo "bat" | gawk --re-interval '/b[ae]{1,2}t/{print $0}'
bat
$ echo "bet" | gawk --re-interval '/b[ae]{1,2}t/{print $0}'
bet
$ echo "beat" | gawk --re-interval '/b[ae]{1,2}t/{print $0}'
beat
$ echo "beet" | gawk --re-interval '/b[ae]{1,2}t/{print $0}'
beet
$ echo "beeat" | gawk --re-interval '/b[ae]{1,2}t/{print $0}'
$
$ echo "baeet" | gawk --re-interval '/b[ae]{1,2}t/{print $0}'
$
$ echo "baeaet" | gawk --re-interval '/b[ae]{1,2}t/{print $0}'
$
```

This regular expression pattern matches if there are exactly one or two instances of the letter *a* or *e* in the text pattern, but it fails if there are any more in any combination.

## The pipe symbol

The pipe symbol allows you to specify two or more patterns that the regular expression engine uses in a logical OR formula when examining the data stream. If any of the patterns match the data stream text, the text passes. If none of the patterns match, the data stream text fails.

Here's the format for using the pipe symbol:

```
expr1|expr2|...
```

Here's an example:

```
$ echo "The cat is asleep" | gawk '/cat|dog/{print $0}'
The cat is asleep
$ echo "The dog is asleep" | gawk '/cat|dog/{print $0}'
The dog is asleep
$ echo "The sheep is asleep" | gawk '/cat|dog/{print $0}'
$
```

This example looks for the regular expression "cat" or "dog" in the data stream. You can't place any spaces within the regular expressions and the pipe symbol, or they're added to the regular expression pattern.

The regular expressions on either side of the pipe symbol can use any regular expression pattern, including character classes, to define the text:

```
$ echo "He has a hat." | gawk '/[ch]at|dog/{print $0}'
He has a hat.
$
```

This example would match "cat", "hat", or "dog" in the data stream text.

## Grouping expressions

Regular expression patterns can also be grouped by using parentheses. When you group a regular expression pattern, the group is treated like a standard character. You can apply a special character to the group just as you would to a regular character. For example:

```
$ echo "Sat" | gawk '/Sat(urday)?/{print $0}'
Sat
$ echo "Saturday" | gawk '/Sat(urday)?/{print $0}'
Saturday
$
```

The grouping of the "urday" ending along with the question mark allows the pattern to match either the full day name "Saturday" or the abbreviated name "Sat."

It's common to use grouping along with the pipe symbol to create groups of possible pattern matches:

```
$ echo "cat" | gawk '/(c|b)a(b|t)/{print $0}'
cat
$ echo "cab" | gawk '/(c|b)a(b|t)/{print $0}'
cab
$ echo "bat" | gawk '/(c|b)a(b|t)/{print $0}'
bat
$ echo "bab" | gawk '/(c|b)a(b|t)/{print $0}'
bab
$ echo "tab" | gawk '/(c|b)a(b|t)/{print $0}'
$
$ echo "tac" | gawk '/(c|b)a(b|t)/{print $0}'
$
```

The pattern (c|b)a(b|t) matches any combination of the letters in the first group along with any combination of the letters in the second group.

20

# Working Through Some Practical Examples

Now that you've seen the rules and a few simple demonstrations of using regular expression patterns, it's time to put that knowledge into action. The following sections demonstrate some common regular expression examples within shell scripts.

## Counting directory files

To start things out, let's look at a shell script that counts the executable files that are present in the directories defined in your PATH environment variable. To do that, you need to parse out the PATH variable into separate directory names. Chapter 6, "Using Linux Environment Variables," showed you how to display the PATH environment variable:

```
$ echo $PATH
/usr/local/sbin:/usr/local/bin:/usr/sbin:/usr/bin:/sbin:/bin:/usr/
games:/usr/
local/games
$
```

Your PATH environment variable will differ, depending on where the applications are located on your Linux system. The key is to recognize that each directory in the PATH is separated by a colon. To get a listing of directories that you can use in a script, you must replace each colon with a space. You now recognize that sed can do just that using a simple regular expression:

```
$ echo $PATH | sed 's/:/ /g'
/usr/local/sbin /usr/local/bin /usr/sbin /usr/bin /sbin /bin
/usr/games /usr/local/games
$
```

After you have the directories separated out, you can use them in a standard for statement (see Chapter 13, "More Structured Commands") to iterate through each directory:

```
mypath=`echo $PATH | sed 's/:/ /g'`
for directory in $mypath
do
...
done
```

After you have each directory, you can use the ls command to list each file in each directory and use another for statement to iterate through each file, incrementing a counter for each file.

The final version of the script looks like this:

```
$ cat countfiles
#!/bin/bash
# count number of files in your PATH
mypath=$(echo $PATH | sed 's/:/ /g')
```

```
count=0
for directory in $mypath
do
   check=$(ls $directory)
   for item in $check
   do
        count=$[ $count + 1 ]
   done
   echo "$directory - $count"
   count=0
done
$ ./countfiles /usr/local/sbin - 0
/usr/local/bin - 2
/usr/sbin - 213
/usr/bin - 1427
/sbin - 186
/bin - 152
/usr/games - 5
/usr/local/games - 0
$
```

Now we're starting to see some of the power behind regular expressions!

## Validating a phone number

The previous example showed how to incorporate the simple regular expression along with sed to replace characters in a data stream to process data. Often, regular expressions are used to validate data to ensure that data is in the correct format for a script.

A common data validation application checks phone numbers. Often, data entry forms request phone numbers, and often customers fail to enter a properly formatted phone number. People in the United States use several common ways to display a phone number:

```
(123)456-7890
(123) 456-7890
123-456-7890
123.456.7890
```

This leaves four possibilities for how customers can enter their phone number in a form. The regular expression must be robust enough to handle any of these situations.

When building a regular expression, it's best to start on the left side and build your pattern to match the possible characters you'll run into. In this example, there may or may not be a left parenthesis in the phone number. This can be matched by using the pattern

```
^\(?
```

The caret is used to indicate the beginning of the data. Because the left parenthesis is a special character, you must escape it to use it as a normal character. The question mark indicates that the left parenthesis may or may not appear in the data to match.

20

585

Next is the three-digit area code. In the United States, area codes start with the number 2 (no area codes start with the digits 0 or 1) and can go to 9. To match the area code, you'd use the following pattern:

```
[2-9][0-9]{2}
```

This requires that the first character be a digit between 2 and 9, followed by any two digits. After the area code, the ending right parenthesis may or may not appear:

```
\)?
```

After the area code, there can be a space, no space, a dash, or a dot. You can group those using a character group along with the pipe symbol:

```
(| |-|\.)
```

The very first pipe symbol appears immediately after the left parenthesis to match the no space condition. You must use the escape character for the dot; otherwise, it is interpreted to match any character.

Next is the three-digit phone exchange number. Nothing special is required here:

```
[0-9]{3}
```

After the phone exchange number, you must match a space, a dash, or a dot (this time you don't have to worry about matching no space because there must be at least a space between the phone exchange number and the rest of the number):

```
( |-|\.)
```

Then to finish things off, you must match the four-digit local phone extension at the end of the string:

```
[0-9]{4}$
```

Putting the entire pattern together results in this:

```
^\(?[2-9][0-9]{2}\)?(| |-|\.)[0-9]{3}( |-|\.)[0-9]{4}$
```

You can use this regular expression pattern in gawk to filter out bad phone numbers. Now you just need to create a simple script using the regular expression in gawk and filter your phone list through the script. Remember that when you use regular expression intervals in gawk, you must use the --re-interval command-line option or you won't get the correct results.

Here's the script:

```
$ cat isphone
#!/bin/bash
# script to filter out bad phone numbers
gawk --re-interval '/^\(?[2-9][0-9]{2}\)?(| |-|\.)
[0-9]{3}( |-|\.)[0-9]{4}/{print $0}'
$
```

Although you can't tell from this listing, the `gawk` command is on a single line in the shell script. You can then redirect phone numbers to the script for processing:

```
$ echo "317-555-1234" | ./isphone
317-555-1234
$ echo "000-555-1234" | ./isphone
$ echo "312 555-1234" | ./isphone
312 555-1234
$
```

Or you can redirect an entire file of phone numbers to filter out the invalid ones:

```
$ cat phonelist
000-000-0000
123-456-7890
212-555-1234
(317)555-1234
(202) 555-9876
33523
1234567890
234.123.4567
$ cat phonelist | ./isphone
212-555-1234
(317)555-1234
(202) 555-9876
234.123.4567
$
```

Only the valid phone numbers that match the regular expression pattern appear.

## Parsing an email address

These days, email has become a crucial form of communication. Trying to validate email addresses has become quite a challenge for script builders because of the myriad ways to create an email address. This is the basic form of an email address:

*username@hostname*

The *username* value can use any alphanumeric character, along with several special characters:

- Dot
- Dash
- Plus sign
- Underscore

These characters can appear in any combination in a valid email UserID. The *hostname* portion of the email address consists of one or more domain names and a server name. The

**20**

server and domain names must also follow strict naming rules, allowing only alphanumeric characters, along with these special characters:

- Dot
- Underscore

The server and domain names are each separated by a dot, with the server name specified first, any subdomain names specified next, and finally, the top-level domain name without a trailing dot.

At one time, the top-level domains were fairly limited, and regular expression pattern builders attempted to add them all in patterns for validation. Unfortunately, as the Internet grew, so did the possible top-level domains. This technique is no longer a viable solution.

Let's start building the regular expression pattern from the left side. We know that there can be multiple valid characters in the username. This should be fairly easy:

```
^([a-zA-Z0-9_\-\.\+]+)@
```

This grouping specifies the allowable characters in the username and the plus sign to indicate that at least one character must be present. The next character obviously is the @ symbol—no surprises there.

The hostname pattern uses the same technique to match the server name and the subdomain names:

```
([a-zA-Z0-9_\-\.]+)
```

This pattern matches the text

```
server
server.domain
server.subdomain.domain
```

There are special rules for the top-level domain. Top-level domains are only alphabetic characters, and they must be no fewer than two characters (used in country codes) and no more than five characters in length. The following is the regular expression pattern for the top-level domain:

```
\.([a-zA-Z]{2,5})$
```

Putting the entire pattern together results in the following:

```
^([a-zA-Z0-9_\-\.\+]+)@([a-zA-Z0-9_\-\.]+)\.([a-zA-Z]{2,5})$
```

This pattern filters out poorly formatted email addresses from a data list. Now you can create your script to implement the regular expression:

```
$ echo "rich@here.now" | ./isemail
rich@here.now
$ echo "rich@here.now." | ./isemail
$
```

```
$ echo "rich@here.n" | ./isemail
$
$ echo "rich@here-now" | ./isemail
$
$ echo "rich.blum@here.now" | ./isemail
rich.blum@here.now
$ echo "rich_blum@here.now" | ./isemail
rich_blum@here.now
$ echo "rich/blum@here.now" | ./isemail
$
$ echo "rich#blum@here.now" | ./isemail
$
$ echo "rich*blum@here.now" | ./isemail
$
```

This is a great example of not only the power of regular expressions, but also their simplicity. At first glance, the regular expression for filtering out email addresses looks pretty complicated, but walking through the patterns one at a time makes understanding what's going on much easier.

# Summary

If you manipulate data files in shell scripts, you need to become familiar with regular expressions. Regular expressions are implemented in Linux utilities, programming languages, and applications using regular expression engines. A host of different regular expression engines is available in the Linux world. The two most popular are the POSIX Basic Regular Expression (BRE) engine and the POSIX Extended Regular Expression (ERE) engine. Sed conforms mainly to the BRE engine, whereas gawk utilizes most features found in the ERE engine.

A regular expression defines a pattern template that's used to filter text in a data stream. The pattern consists of a combination of standard text characters and special characters. The special characters are used by the regular expression engine to match a series of one or more characters, similar to how wildcard characters work in other applications.

By combining characters and special characters, you can define a pattern to match almost any type of data. You can then use sed or gawk to filter specific data from a larger data stream, or for validating data received from data entry applications.

The next chapter digs deeper into using sed to perform advanced text manipulation. Lots of advanced features are available in sed that make it useful for handling large data streams and filtering out just what you need.

20

# Advanced *sed*

C hapter 19, "Introducing sed and gawk," showed you how to use the basics of the sed editor to manipulate text in data streams. The basic sed editor commands are capable of handling most of your everyday text-editing requirements. This chapter looks at the more advanced features that the sed editor has to offer. These are features that you might not use as often. But when you need them, it's nice to know that they're available as well as how to use them.

## Looking at Multiline Commands

When using the basic sed editor commands, you may have noticed a limitation. All the sed editor commands perform functions on a single line of data. As the sed editor reads a data stream, it divides the data into lines based on the presence of newline characters. The sed editor handles the data lines one at a time, processing the defined script commands on the data line and then moving on to the next line and repeating the processing.

Sometimes, you need to perform actions on data that spans more than one line. This is especially true if you're trying to find or replace a phrase.

For example, if you're looking for the phrase Linux System Administrators Group in your data, it's quite possible that the phrase's words can be split onto two lines. If you processed the text using a normal sed editor command, it would be impossible to detect the split phrase.

Fortunately, the designers behind the sed editor thought of that situation and devised a solution. The sed editor includes three special commands that you can use to process multiline text:

- N adds the next line in the data stream to create a multiline group for processing.
- D deletes a single line in a multiline group.
- P prints a single line in a multiline group.

The following sections examine these multiline commands more closely and demonstrate how you can use them in your scripts.

## Navigating the next command

Before you can examine the multiline next (N) command, you first need to look at how the single-line version of the next command works. After you know what that command does, it's much easier to understand how the multiline version of the next command operates.

### Using the single-line next command

The single-line next (n) command tells the sed editor to move to the next line of text in the data stream, without going back to the beginning of the commands. Remember that normally the sed editor processes all the defined commands on a line before moving to the next line of text in the data stream. The single-line next (n) command alters this flow.

This may sound somewhat complicated, and sometimes it is. In this example, we have a data file that contains five lines, two of which are blank. The goal is to remove the first blank line, which is after the header line, but leave the second blank line intact. If we write a sed script to delete blank lines, *both* blank lines are removed, which is not what we wanted:

```
$ cat data1.txt
Header Line

Data Line #1

End of Data Lines
$
$ sed '/^$/d' data1.txt
Header Line
Data Line #1
End of Data Lines
$
```

Because the line we want to remove is blank, there is no text we can search for to uniquely identify the line. The solution is to use the single-line next (n) command. In this next example, the script looks for a unique line that contains the word Header. After the script identifies that line, the n command moves the sed editor to the next line of text, which is the blank line.

```
$ sed '/Header/{n ; d}' data1.txt
Header Line
Data Line #1

End of Data Lines
$
```

At that point, the sed editor continues processing the command list, which uses the d command to delete the empty line. When the sed editor reaches the end of the command script, it reads the next line of text from the data stream and starts processing commands from the top of the command script. The sed editor does not find another line with the word Header; thus, no further lines are deleted.

### Combining lines of text

Now that you've seen the single-line next (n) command, we can look at the multiline version. The single-line next command moves the next line of text from the data stream into the processing space (called the *pattern space*) of the sed editor. The multiline version of the next command (which uses a capital N) adds the next line of text to the text already in the pattern space.

This has the effect of combining two lines of text from the data stream into the same pattern space. The lines of text are still separated by a newline character, but the sed editor can now treat both lines of text as *one* line.

Here's a demonstration of how the multiline (N) command operates:

```
$ cat data2.txt
Header Line
First Data Line
Second Data Line
End of Data Lines
$
$ sed '/First/{ N ; s/\n/ / }' data2.txt
Header Line
First Data Line Second Data Line
End of Data Lines
$
```

The sed editor script searches for the line of text that contains the word First in it. When it finds the line, it uses the N command to combine the next line with that line in the pattern space. It then uses the substitution (s) command to replace the newline character (\n) with a space. The result is that the two lines in the text file appear as one line in the sed editor output.

This has a practical application if you're searching for a text phrase that may be split between two lines in the data file. Here's an example:

```
$ cat data3.txt
On Tuesday, the Linux System
```

*(Continues)*

*(continued)*

```
        Admin group meeting will be held.
        All System Admins should attend.
        Thank you for your cooperation.
        $
        $ sed 's/System Admin/DevOps Engineer/' data3.txt
        On Tuesday, the Linux System
        Admin group meeting will be held.
        All DevOps Engineers should attend.
        Thank you for your cooperation.
        $
```

The substitution (s) command is looking for the specific two-word phrase System Admin in the text file. In the single line where the phrase appears, everything is fine; the substitution command can replace the text. But in the situation where the phrase is split between two lines, the substitution command doesn't recognize the matching pattern.

The N command helps solve this problem:

```
        $ sed 'N ; s/System.Admin/DevOps Engineer/' data3.txt
        On Tuesday, the Linux DevOps Engineer group meeting will be held.
        All DevOps Engineers should attend.
        Thank you for your cooperation.
        $
```

By using the multiline (N) command to combine the next line with the line where the first word is found, you can detect when a line split occurs in the phrase.

Notice that the substitution (s) command uses a wildcard pattern (.) between the word System and the word Admin to match both the space and the newline situation. However, when it matched the newline character, it removed it from the string, causing the two lines to merge into one line. This may not be exactly what you want.

To solve this problem, you can use two substitution commands in the sed editor script, one to match the multiline occurrence and one to match the single-line occurrence:

```
        $ sed 'N
        > s/System\nAdmin/DevOps\nEngineer/
        > s/System Admin/DevOps Engineer/
        > ' data3.txt
        On Tuesday, the Linux DevOps
        Engineer group meeting will be held.
        All DevOps Engineers should attend.
        Thank you for your cooperation.
        $
```

The first substitution command specifically looks for the newline character between the two search words and includes it in the replacement string. This allows you to add the newline character in the same place in the new text.

There's still one subtle problem with this script, however. The script always reads the next line of text into the pattern space before executing the sed editor commands. When it reaches the last line of text, there isn't a next line of text to read, so the N command causes the sed editor to stop. If the matching text is on the last line in the data stream, the commands don't catch the matching data:

```
$ cat data4.txt
On Tuesday, the Linux System
Admin group meeting will be held.
All System Admins should attend.
$
$ sed 'N
> s/System\nAdmin/DevOps\nEngineer/
> s/System Admin/DevOps Engineer/
> ' data4.txt
On Tuesday, the Linux DevOps
Engineer group meeting will be held.
All System Admins should attend.
$
```

Because the System Admin text appears in the last line in the data stream, the multiline (N) command misses it, as there isn't another line to read into the pattern space to combine. We can easily resolve this problem by moving our single-line editing commands before the multiline command and having only the editing commands for the multiple lines appear after the N, like this:

```
$ sed '
> s/System Admin/DevOps Engineer/
> N
> s/System\nAdmin/DevOps\nEngineer/
> ' data4.txt
On Tuesday, the Linux DevOps
Engineer group meeting will be held.
All DevOps Engineers should attend.
$
```

Now, the substitution (s) command that looks for the phrase in a single line works just fine on the last line in the data stream, and the substitution command after the multiline (N) command covers the occurrence in the middle of the data stream.

## Navigating the multiline delete command

In Chapter 19, "Introducing sed and gawk," we touched on the topic of the single-line delete (d) command. The sed editor uses it to delete the current line in the pattern space. If you're working with the N command, however, you must be careful when using the single-line delete command:

```
$ sed 'N ; /System\nAdmin/d' data4.txt
All System Admins should attend.
$
```

The delete (d) command looked for the words System and Admin in separate lines and deleted both of the lines in the pattern space. This may or may not have been what you intended.

The sed editor provides the multiline delete (D) command, which deletes only the first line in the pattern space. It removes all characters up to and including the newline character:

```
$ sed 'N ; /System\nAdmin/D' data4.txt
Admin group meeting will be held.
All System Admins should attend.
$
```

The second line of text, added to the pattern space by the N command, remains intact. This comes in handy if you need to remove a line of text that appears before a line that you find a data string in.

Here's an example of removing a blank line that appears before the first line in a data stream:

```
$ cat data5.txt

Header Line
First Data Line

End of Data Lines
$
$ sed '/^$/{N ; /Header/D}' data5.txt
Header Line
First Data Line

End of Data Lines
$
```

This sed editor script looks for blank lines and then uses the N command to add the next line of text into the pattern space. If the new pattern space contents contain the word Header, the D command removes the first line in the pattern space. Without the combination of the N and D commands, it would be impossible to remove the first blank line without removing all other blank lines.

## Navigating the multiline print command

By now, you're probably catching on to the difference between the single-line and multiline versions of the commands. The multiline print command (P) follows along using the same technique. It prints only the first line in a multiline pattern space. This includes all characters up to the newline character in the pattern space. It is used in much the same way as the single-line p command to display text when you use the -n option to suppress output from the script.

```
$ sed -n 'N ; /System\nAdmin/P' data3.txt
On Tuesday, the Linux System
$
```

When the multiline match occurs, the P command prints only the first line in the pattern space. The power of the multiline P command comes into play when you combine it with the N and D multiline commands.

The D command has a unique feature in that after deleting the first line from the pattern space, it forces the sed editor to return to the beginning of the script and repeat the commands on the current pattern space (it doesn't read a new line of text from the data stream). By including the N command in the command script, you can effectively single-step through the pattern space, matching multiple lines together.

Next, by using the P command, you can print the first line, and then using the D command, you can delete the first line and loop back to the beginning of the script. When you are back at the script's beginning, the N command reads in the next line of text and starts the process all over again. This loop continues until you reach the end of the data stream, as shown in removing the data corruption in this file:

```
$ cat corruptData.txt
Header Line#
@
Data Line #1
Data Line #2#
@
End of Data Lines#
@
$
$ sed -n '
> N
> s/#\n@//
> P
> D
> ' corruptData.txt
Header Line
Data Line #1
Data Line #2
End of Data Lines
$
```

The data file has been corrupted with # at some lines' ends followed by @ on the next line. To fix this issue, using sed the Header Line# line is loaded into the pattern space, and then the multiline next (N) command loads the second line (@), appending it to the first line within the space. The substitution (s) command removes the offending data (#\n@) by replacing it with a null. Next, the P command prints only the now cleaned-up first line within the pattern space. The delete (D) command removes this first line from the space and goes back to the beginning of the script, where the next N command reads the third line (Data Line #1) of text into the pattern space and the editing loop continues.

# Holding Space

The *pattern space* is an active buffer area that holds the text examined by the sed editor while it processes commands. However, it isn't the only space available in the sed editor for storing text.

The sed editor utilizes another buffer area called the *hold space*. You can use the hold space to temporarily hold lines of text while working on other lines in the pattern space. The five commands associated with operating with the hold space are shown in Table 21.1.

**TABLE 21.1  The** sed **Editor Hold Space Commands**

| Command | Description |
|---------|-------------|
| h | Copies pattern space to hold space |
| H | Appends pattern space to hold space |
| g | Copies hold space to pattern space |
| G | Appends hold space to pattern space |
| x | Exchanges contents of pattern and hold spaces |

These commands let you copy text from the pattern space to the hold space. This frees up the pattern space to load another string for processing.

Usually, after using the h or H command to move a string to the hold space, eventually you want to use the g, G, or x command to move the stored string back into the pattern space (otherwise, you wouldn't have cared about saving them in the first place).

With two buffer areas, trying to determine what line of text is in which buffer area can sometimes get confusing. Here's a short example that demonstrates how to use the h and g commands to move data back and forth between the sed editor buffer spaces:

```
$ cat data2.txt
Header Line
First Data Line
Second Data Line
End of Data Lines
$
$ sed -n '/First/ {
> h ; p ;
> n ; p ;
> g ; p }
> ' data2.txt
First Data Line
Second Data Line
First Data Line
$
```

Let's look at the preceding code example step by step:

1. The sed script uses a regular expression in the address to filter the line containing the word First.

2. When the line containing the word First appears, the initial command in {}, the h command, copies the line in the pattern space to the hold space. At this point, the pattern space and the hold space have the same data.

3. The p command then prints the contents of the pattern space (First Data Line), which is still the line that was copied into the hold space.

4. The n command retrieves the next line in the data stream (Second Data Line) and places it in the pattern space. Now the pattern space has *different* data than the hold space.

5. The p command prints the contents of the pattern space (Second Data Line).

6. The g command places the contents of the hold space (First Data Line) back into the pattern space, replacing the current text. The pattern space and the hold space now have the same data again.

7. The p command prints the current contents of the pattern space (First Data Line).

By shuffling the text lines around using the hold space, we can force the First Data Line to appear after the Second Data Line in the output. If we just drop the first p command, we can output the two lines in reverse order:

```
$ sed -n '/First/ {
> h ;
> n ; p
> g ; p }
> ' data2.txt
Second Data Line
First Data Line
$
```

This is the start of something useful. You can use this technique to create a sed script that reverses an entire file of text data! To do that, however, you need to see the negating feature of the sed editor, which is what the next section is all about.

## Negating a Command

Chapter 19 showed that the sed editor applies commands either to every text line in the data stream or to lines specifically indicated by either a single address or an address range. You can also configure a command to *not* apply to a specific address or address range in the data stream.

The exclamation mark (!) command is used to negate a command. This means in situations where the command would normally have been activated, it isn't. Here's an example demonstrating this feature:

```
$ sed -n '/Header/!p' data2.txt
First Data Line
Second Data Line
End of Data Lines
$
```

The normal p command would have printed only the line in the data2 file that contained the word Header. By adding the exclamation mark, the opposite happens — all lines in the file are printed except the one that contained the word Header.

Using the exclamation mark comes in handy in several applications. Recall that earlier in the chapter, the "Navigating the Next Command" section showed a situation where a sed editor command wouldn't operate on the last line of text in the data stream because there wasn't a line after it. You can use the exclamation point to fix that problem:

```
$ cat data4.txt
On Tuesday, the Linux System
Admin group meeting will be held.
All System Admins should attend.
$
$ sed 'N;
> s/System\nAdmin/DevOps\nEngineer/
> s/System Admin/DevOps Engineer/
> ' data4.txt
On Tuesday, the Linux DevOps
Engineer group meeting will be held.
All System Admins should attend.
$
$ sed '$!N;
> s/System\nAdmin/DevOps\nEngineer/
> s/System Admin/DevOps Engineer/
> ' data4.txt
On Tuesday, the Linux DevOps
Engineer group meeting will be held.
All DevOps Engineers should attend.
$
```

This example shows the exclamation mark used with the N command, along with the dollar sign ($) special address. The dollar sign represents the last line of text in the data stream, so when the sed editor reaches the last line, it doesn't execute the N command. However, for all other lines, it does execute the command.

Using this technique, you can reverse the order of text lines in a data stream. To reverse the order of the lines as they appear in the text stream (display the last line first and the first line last), you need to do some fancy footwork using the hold space.

To accomplish this, use sed to

1. Place a text line in the pattern space.
2. Copy the line in the pattern space into the hold space.
3. Put the next line of text in the pattern space.
4. Append the hold space to the pattern space.
5. Copy everything in the pattern space into the hold space.
6. Repeat steps 3 through 5 until you've put all the lines in reverse order in the hold space.
7. Retrieve the lines, and print them.

Figure 21-1 diagrams what this looks like in more detail.

**FIGURE 21-1**

Reversing the order of a text file using the hold space

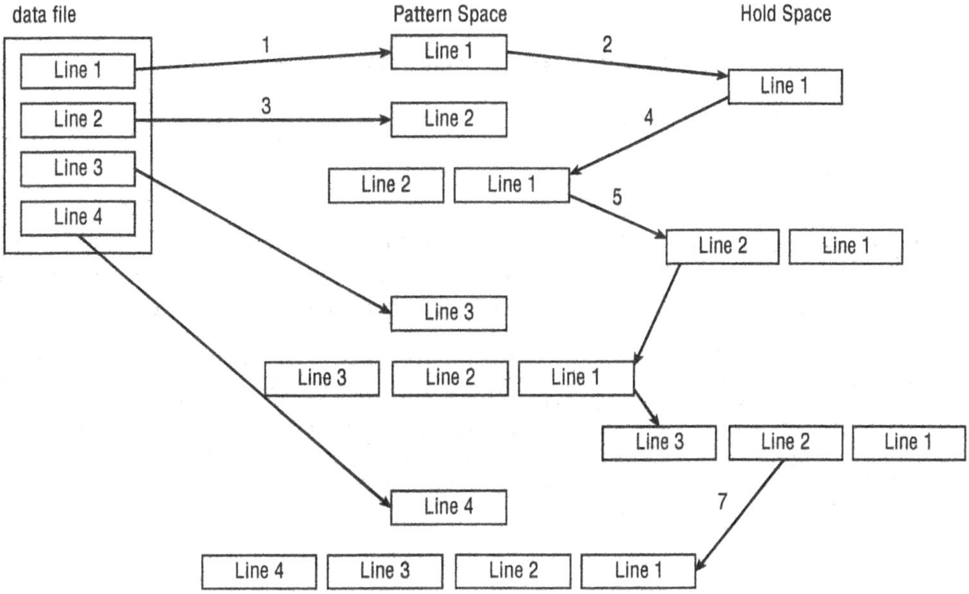

When using this technique, you do not want to print lines as they are processed. This means using the -n command-line option for sed. The next thing to determine is how to append the hold space text to the pattern space text. This is done by using the G command.

The only problem is that you don't want to append the hold space to the first line of text processed. This is easily solved by using the exclamation mark command:

```
1!G
```

The next step is to copy the new pattern space (the text line with the appended reverse lines) into the hold space. This is simple enough; just use the h command.

When you've got the entire data stream in the pattern space in reverse order, you just need to print the results. You know you have the entire data stream in the pattern space when you've reached the last line in the data stream. To print the results, just use the following command:

```
$p
```

Those are the pieces we need to create our line-reversing sed editor script. Now we'll try it out in a test run:

```
$ cat data2.txt
Header Line
First Data Line
Second Data Line
End of Data Lines
$
$ sed -n '{1!G ; h ; $p }' data2.txt
End of Data Lines
Second Data Line
First Data Line
Header Line
$
```

The sed editor script performed as expected. The output from the script reverses the original lines in the text file. This demonstrates the power of using the hold space in your sed scripts. It provides an easy way to manipulate the order of lines in the script output.

> **NOTE**
> In case you're wondering, a Bash shell command can perform the function of reversing a text file. The tac command displays a text file in reverse order. You probably noticed the clever name of the command because it performs the reverse function of the cat command.

## Changing the Flow

Normally, the sed editor processes commands starting at the top and proceeding toward the end of the script (the exception is the D command, which forces the sed editor to return to the top of the script without reading a new line of text). The sed editor provides a method for altering the flow of the command script, producing a result similar to that of a structured programming environment.

# Branching

In the previous section, you saw how the exclamation mark command is used to negate the effect of a command on a line of text. The sed editor provides a way to negate an entire section of commands, based on an address, an address pattern, or an address range. This allows you to perform a group of commands only on a specific subset within the data stream.

Here's the format of the branch (b) command:

```
[address]b [label]
```

The *address* parameter determines which line or lines of data trigger the branch (b) command. The *label* parameter defines the location within the script to which to branch. If the *label* parameter is not present, the branch (b) command skips the line or lines of data that triggered the branch, and goes on to process the other text lines.

Here is an example using the *address* parameter with the branch command but no *label*:

```
$ cat data2.txt
Header Line
First Data Line
Second Data Line
End of Data Lines
$
$ sed '{2,3b ;
> s/Line/Replacement/}
> ' data2.txt
Header Replacement
First Data Line
Second Data Line
End of Data Replacements
$
```

The branch (b) command skips the substitution commands for the second and third lines in the data stream.

Instead of going to the end of the script, you can define a *label* providing a location for the branch command to jump. Labels start with a colon and can be up to seven characters in length:

```
:label2
```

To specify the *label*, just add it after the b command. Using labels allows you to provide alternative commands to process data that match the branch *address* but still process other text lines using the original commands in the script:

```
$ sed '{/First/b jump1 ;
> s/Line/Replacement/
> :jump1
> s/Line/Jump Replacement/}
> ' data2.txt
```

*(Continues)*

*(continued)*

```
    Header Replacement
    First Data Jump Replacement
    Second Data Replacement
    End of Data Replacements
    $
```

The branch (b) command specifies that the program should jump to the script line labeled jump1 if the matching text First appears in the line. If the branch command *address* doesn't match, the sed editor continues processing commands in the script, including the command *after* the branch label, jump1. (Thus, both substitution commands are processed on lines that don't match the branch *address*.)

If a line matches the branch *address*, the sed editor branches to the labeled line, jump1. Thus, only the last substitution command is executed for lines matching the branch *address*.

The example shows branching to a label further down in the sed script. You can also branch to a label that appears earlier in the script, thus creating a looping effect:

```
$ echo "This, is, a, test, to, remove, commas." |
> sed -n {'
> :start
> s/,//1p
> b start
> }'
This is, a, test, to, remove, commas.
This is a, test, to, remove, commas.
This is a test, to, remove, commas.
This is a test to, remove, commas.
This is a test to remove, commas.
This is a test to remove commas.
^C
$
```

Each script iteration removes the first occurrence of a comma from the text string and prints the string. There's one catch to this script — it never ends. This situation creates an endless loop, searching for commas until you manually stop it by sending a signal with the Ctrl+C key combination.

To prevent this problem, specify an address pattern for the branch (b) command. If the pattern isn't present, the branching stops:

```
$ echo "This, is, a, test, to, remove, commas." |
> sed -n {'
> :start
> s/,//1p
> /,/b start
> }'
This is, a, test, to, remove, commas.
This is a, test, to, remove, commas.
```

```
This is a test, to, remove, commas.
This is a test to, remove, commas.
This is a test to remove, commas.
This is a test to remove commas.
$
```

Now the branch command branches only if there's a comma in the line. After the last comma has been removed, the branch (b) command doesn't execute, allowing the script to properly finish.

## Testing

Similar to the branch command, the test (t) command is also used to modify the flow of the sed editor script. Instead of jumping to a *label* based on an *address*, the test (t) command jumps to a *label* based on the outcome of a preceding substitution command.

If the substitution command successfully matches and substitutes a pattern, the test command branches to the specified label. If the substitution command doesn't match the specified pattern, the test command doesn't branch.

The test (t) command uses the same format as the branch command:

```
[address]t [label]
```

As with the branch command, if you don't specify a *label*, sed jumps to the end of the script's commands, but only if the test succeeds.

The test (t) command provides a cheap way to perform a basic if-then statement on the text in the data stream. For example, if you don't need to make a substitution if another substitution was made, the test command, without a specified label, can help:

```
$ sed '{s/First/Matched/ ; t
> s/Line/Replacement/}
> ' data2.txt
Header Replacement
Matched Data Line
Second Data Replacement
End of Data Replacements
$
```

The first substitution command looks for the pattern text First. If it matches the pattern in the line, it replaces the text, and the test (t) command jumps over the second substitution command. If the first substitution command doesn't match the text pattern, the second substitution command is processed.

Using the test command, we can clean up the loop we tried using the branch command:

```
$ echo "This, is, a, test, to, remove, commas." |
> sed -n '{
> :start
> s/,//1p
```

*(Continues)*

*(continued)*

```
> t start
> }'
This is, a, test, to, remove, commas.
This is a, test, to, remove, commas.
This is a test, to, remove, commas.
This is a test to, remove, commas.
This is a test to remove, commas.
This is a test to remove commas.
$
```

When there are no more comma substitutions to make, the test command doesn't branch, and the processing ends.

# Replacing via a Pattern

We've covered how to use patterns in the sed commands to replace text in the data stream. However, when using wildcard characters it's not easy to know exactly what text will match the pattern.

For example, say that you want to place double quotation marks around a word you match in a line. That's simple enough if you're just looking for one word in the pattern to match:

```
$ echo "The cat sleeps in his hat." |
> sed 's/cat/"cat"/'
The "cat" sleeps in his hat.
$
```

But what if you use a wildcard character (.) in the pattern to match more than one word?

```
$ echo "The cat sleeps in his hat." |
> sed 's/.at/".at"/g'
The ".at" sleeps in his ".at".
$
```

The substitution string used the dot wildcard character to match any occurrence of a letter followed by "at". Unfortunately, the replacement string doesn't match the wildcard character value of the matching word.

## Using the ampersand

The sed editor has a solution for you. The ampersand symbol (&) is used to represent the matching pattern in the substitution command. Whatever text matches the pattern defined, you can use the ampersand symbol to recall it in the replacement pattern. This lets you manipulate whatever word matches the pattern defined:

```
$ echo "The cat sleeps in his hat." |
> sed 's/.at/"&"/g'
The "cat" sleeps in his "hat".
$
```

When the pattern matches the word cat, "cat" appears in the substituted word. When it matches the word hat, "hat" appears in the substituted word.

## Replacing individual words

The ampersand symbol retrieves the entire string that matches the pattern you specify in the substitution command. Sometimes, you'll want to retrieve only a subset of the string. You can do that, too, but it's a little tricky.

The sed editor uses parentheses to define a substring component within the substitution pattern. You can then reference each substring component using a special character in the replacement pattern. The replacement character consists of a backslash and a number. The number indicates the substring component's position. The sed editor assigns the first component the character \1, the second component the character \2, and so on.

> **NOTE**
> When you use parentheses in the substitution command, you must use the escape character to identify them as grouping characters and not normal parentheses. This is the reverse of when you escape other special characters.

Look at an example of using this feature in a sed editor script:

```
$ echo "The Guide to Programming" |
> sed '
> s/\(Guide to\) Programming/\1 DevOps/'
The Guide to DevOps
$
```

This substitution command uses one set of parentheses around Guide To identifying it as a substring component. It then uses the \1 in the replacement pattern to recall the first identified component. This isn't too exciting, but it can really be useful when working with wildcard patterns.

Suppose you need to replace a phrase with just a single word that's a substring of the phrase, but that substring just happens to be using a wildcard character. In such cases, using substring components is a lifesaver:

```
$ echo "That furry cat is pretty." |
> sed 's/furry \(.at\)/\1/'
That cat is pretty.
$
$ echo "That furry hat is pretty." |
> sed 's/furry \(.at\)/\1/'
That hat is pretty.
$
```

In this situation, you can't use the ampersand symbol, because it would replace the entire matching pattern. The substring component provides the answer, allowing you to select just which part of the pattern to use as the replacement pattern.

This feature can be especially helpful when you need to insert text between two or more substring components. Here's a script that uses substring components to insert a comma in long numbers:

```
$ echo "1234567" | sed '{
> :start
> s/\(.*[0-9]\)\([0-9]\{3\}\)/\1,\2/
> t start}'
1,234,567
$
```

The script divides the matching pattern into two components:

```
.*[0-9]
[0-9]{3}
```

This pattern looks for two substrings. The first substring is any number of characters ending in a digit. The second substring is a series of three digits (see Chapter 20, "Regular Expressions," for information about how to use braces in a regular expression). If this pattern is found in the text, the replacement text puts a comma between the two components, each identified by its component position. The script uses the test (t) command to iterate through the number until all commas have been put in their proper place.

# Placing *sed* Commands in Scripts

Now that you've seen the various parts of the sed editor, it's time to put them together and use them in your shell scripts. This section demonstrates some of the features that you should know about when using the sed editor in your Bash shell scripts.

## Using wrappers

You may have noticed that trying to implement a sed editor script can be cumbersome, especially if the script is long. Instead of having to retype the entire script each time you want to use it, you can place the sed editor command in a shell script *wrapper*. The wrapper acts as a go-between for the sed editor script and the command line. A shell script wrapper, ChangeScriptShell.sh, was used back in Chapter 19 as a practical example.

Once inside the shell script, you can use normal shell variables and parameters with your sed editor scripts. Here's an example of using the command-line parameter variable as the input to a sed script:

```
$ cat reverse.sh
#!/bin/bash
# Shell wrapper for sed editor script
# to reverse test file lines.
#
sed -n '{1!G; h; $p}' $1
#
exit
$
```

The shell script called `reverse.sh` uses the sed editor script to reverse text lines in a data stream. It uses the $1 shell parameter to retrieve the first parameter from the command line, which should be the name of the file to reverse:

```
$ cat data2.txt
Header Line
First Data Line
Second Data Line
End of Data Lines
$
$ ./reverse.sh data2.txt
End of Data Lines
Second Data Line
First Data Line
Header Line
$
```

Now you can easily use the sed editor script on any file without having to constantly retype the entire sed command line.

## Redirecting *sed* output

By default, the sed editor outputs the results of the script to STDOUT. You can employ all the standard methods of redirecting the output of the sed editor in your shell scripts.

You can use dollar sign/parenthesis, $(), to redirect the output of your sed editor command to a variable for use later in the script. The following is an example of using the sed script to add commas to the result of a numeric computation:

```
$ cat fact.sh
#!/bin/bash
# Shell wrapper for sed editor script
# to calculate a factorial, and
# format the result with commas.
#
factorial=1
counter=1
number=$1
#
while [ $counter -le $number ]
do
    factorial=$[ $factorial * $counter ]
    counter=$[ $counter + 1 ]
done
#
result=$(echo $factorial |
sed '{
:start
s/\(.*[0-9]\)\([0-9]\{3\}\)/\1,\2/
t start
```

*(Continues)*

21

```
(continued)
    }')
#
echo "The result is $result"
#
exit
$
$ ./fact.sh 20
The result is 2,432,902,008,176,640,000
$
```

After you use the normal factorial calculation script, the result of that script is used as the input to the sed editor script, which adds commas. This value is then used in the echo statement to produce the result. And how nice to now have that long sed script within a Bash shell script so that you can use it without typing all the sed commands in again!

# Creating *sed* Utilities

As you've seen in the short examples presented so far in this chapter, you can do lots of cool data-formatting things with the sed editor. This section shows a few handy well-known sed editor scripts for performing common data-handling functions.

## Spacing with double lines

To start things off, look at a simple sed script to insert a blank line between lines in a text file:

```
$ sed 'G' data2.txt
Header Line

First Data Line

Second Data Line

End of Data Lines

$
```

That was pretty simple! The key to this trick is the default value of the hold space. Recall that the G command simply appends the contents of the hold space to the current pattern space contents. When you start the sed editor, the hold space contains an empty line. By appending that to an existing line, you create a blank line after the existing line.

You may have noticed that this script also adds a blank line to the last line in the data stream, producing a blank line at the end of the file. If you want to get rid of this, you can use the negate symbol and the last line symbol to ensure that the script doesn't add the blank line to the last line of the data stream:

```
$ sed '$!G' data2.txt
Header Line
```

```
    First Data Line

    Second Data Line

    End of Data Lines
    $
```

Now that looks a little better. As long as the line isn't the last line, the G command appends the contents of the hold space. When the sed editor gets to the last line, it skips the G command.

## Spacing files that may have blanks

To take double spacing one step further, what if the text file already has a few blank lines but you want to double-space all the lines? If you use the previous script, you'll get some areas that have too many blank lines, because each existing blank line gets doubled:

```
$ cat data6.txt
Line one.
Line two.

Line three.
Line four.
$
$ sed '$!G' data6.txt
Line one.

Line two.



Line three.

Line four.
$
```

Now we have three blank lines where the original blank line was located. The solution to this problem is to first delete any blank lines from the data stream and then use the G command to insert new blank lines after all the lines. To delete existing blank lines, we just need to use the d command with a pattern that matches a blank line:

```
/^$/d
```

This pattern uses the start line tag (the caret) and the end line tag (the dollar sign). Adding this pattern to the script produces the desired results:

```
$ sed '/^$/d ; $!G' data6.txt
Line one.

Line two.
```

*(Continues)*

*(continued)*
```
    Line three.

    Line four.
    $
```

Perfect! It works just as desired.

## Numbering lines in a file

Chapter 19 showed you how to use the equal sign to display the line numbers of lines in the data stream:

```
$ sed '=' data2.txt
1
Header Line
2
First Data Line
3
Second Data Line
4
End of Data Lines
$
```

This can be a little awkward to read, because the line number is on a line above the actual line in the data stream. A better solution is to place the line number on the same line as the text.

Now that you've seen how to combine lines using the N command, it shouldn't be too hard to utilize that information in the sed editor script. The trick to this utility, however, is that you can't combine the two commands in the same script.

After you have the output for the equal sign command, you can pipe the output to another sed editor script that uses the N command to combine the two lines. You also need to use the substitution (s) command to replace the newline character with either a space or a tab character. Here's what the final solution looks like:

```
$ sed '=' data2.txt | sed 'N; s/\n/ /'
1 Header Line
2 First Data Line
3 Second Data Line
4 End of Data Lines
$
```

Now that looks much better. This is a great little utility to have around when you're working on programs where you need to see the line numbers used in error messages.

There are Bash shell commands that can also add line numbers. However, they add some additional (and potentially unwanted) spacing:

```
$ nl data2.txt
     1  Header Line
```

```
        2  First Data Line
        3  Second Data Line
        4  End of Data Lines
$
$ cat -n data2.txt
        1  Header Line
        2  First Data Line
        3  Second Data Line
        4  End of Data Lines
$
$ nl data2.txt | sed 's/      //; s/\t/ /'
1 Header Line
2 First Data Line
3 Second Data Line
4 End of Data Lines
$
```

The sed editor script handles the output without any additional spacing. But if you want to use these utilities, sed is there to help you remove any unwanted spacing!

## Printing last lines

So far, we've covered how to use the p command to print all the lines in a data stream or just lines that match a specific pattern. What if you just need to work with the last few lines of a long listing, such as a log file?

The dollar sign represents the last line of a data stream, so it's easy to display just the last line:

```
$ sed -n '$p' data2.txt
End of Data Lines
$
```

Now, how can you use the dollar sign symbol to display a set number of lines at the end of the data stream? The answer is to create a *rolling window*.

A rolling window is a common way to examine blocks of text lines in the pattern space by combining them using the N command. The N command appends the next line of text to the text already in the pattern space. After you have a block of 10 text lines in the pattern space, you can check to see if you're at the end of the data stream using the dollar sign. If you're not at the end, continue adding more lines to the pattern space while removing the original lines (remember the D command, which deletes the first line in the pattern space).

By looping through the N and D commands, you add new lines to the block of lines in the pattern space while removing old lines. The branch (b) command is the perfect fit for the loop. To end the loop, just identify the last line and use the q command to quit.

Here's what the final sed editor script looks like:

```
$ cat data7.txt
Line1
```

*(Continues)*

```
(continued)
      Line2
      Line3
      Line4
      Line5
      Line6
      Line7
      Line1
      Line2
      Line3
      Line4
      Line5
      Line6
      Line7
      Line8
      Line9
      Line10
      Line11
      Line12
      Line13
      Line14
      Line15
$
$ sed '{
> :start
> $q ; N ; 11,$D
> b start
> }' data7.txt
Line6
Line7
Line8
Line9
Line10
Line11
Line12
Line13
Line14
Line15
$
```

The script first checks whether the line is the last line in the data stream. If it is, the quit (q) command stops the loop. The N command appends the next line to the current line in the pattern space. The 11,$D command deletes the first line in the pattern space if the current line is after line 10. This creates the sliding window effect in the pattern space. Thus, the sed program script displays only the last 10 lines of the data7.txt file.

## Deleting lines

Another useful utility for the sed editor is to remove unwanted blank lines in a data stream. It's easy to remove all the blank lines from a data stream, but it takes a little ingenuity to selectively remove blank lines. This section shows you three quick sed editor scripts that you can use to help remove unwanted blank lines from your data.

### Deleting consecutive blank lines

It can be a nuisance when extra blank lines crop up in data files. Often you have a data file that contains blank lines, but sometimes a data line is missing and produces too many blank lines (as you saw in the double-spacing example earlier).

The easiest way to remove consecutive blank lines is to check the data stream using a range address. In Chapter 19 we covered how to use ranges in addresses, including how to incorporate patterns in the address range. The sed editor executes the command for all lines that match within the specified address range.

The key to removing consecutive blank lines is to create an address range that includes a non-blank line and a blank line. If the sed editor comes across this range, it shouldn't delete the line. However, for lines that don't match that range (two or more blank lines in a row), it should delete the lines.

Here's the script to do this:

```
/./,/^$/!d
```

The range is /./ to /^$/. The start address in the range matches any line that contains at least one character. The end address in the range matches a blank line. Lines within this range aren't deleted.

Here's the script in action:

```
$ cat data8.txt
Line one.


Line two.

Line three.



Line four.
$
$ sed '/./,/^$/!d' data8.txt
Line one.

Line two.

Line three.

Line four.
$
```

No matter how many blank lines appear between lines of data in the file, the output places only one blank line between the lines.

### Deleting leading blank lines

It is also a nuisance when data files contain multiple blank lines at the start of the file. Often when you are trying to import data from a text file into a database, the blank lines create null entries, throwing off any calculations using the data.

Removing blank lines from the top of a data stream is not a difficult task. Here's the script that accomplishes that function:

```
/./,$!d
```

The script uses an address range to determine what lines are deleted. The range starts with a line that contains a character and continues to the end of the data stream. Any line within this range is not deleted from the output. This means that any lines before the first line that contain a character are deleted.

Look at this simple script in action:

```
$ cat data9.txt


Line one.

Line two.
$
$ sed '/./,$!d' data9.txt
Line one.

Line two.
$
```

The test file contains two blank lines before the data lines. The script successfully removes both of the leading blank lines while keeping the blank line within the data intact.

### Deleting trailing blank lines

Unfortunately, deleting trailing blank lines is not as simple as deleting leading blank lines. Just like printing the end of a data stream, deleting blank lines at the end of a data stream requires a little ingenuity and looping.

Before we start the discussion, let's see what the script looks like:

```
sed '{
:start
/^\n*$/{$d; N; b start }
}'
```

This may look a little odd to you at first. Notice that there are braces within the normal script braces. This allows you to group commands together within the overall command script. The group of commands applies to the specified address pattern. The address pattern matches any line that contains only a newline character. When one is found, if it's the last line, the d command deletes it. If it's not the last line, the N command appends the next line to it, and the branch (b) command loops to the beginning to start over.

Here's the script in action:

```
$ cat data10.txt
Line one.
Line two.


$
$ sed '{
> :start
> /^\n*$/{$d; N; b start}
> }' data10.txt
Line one.
Line two.
$
```

The script successfully removed the blank lines from the end of the text file.

## Removing HTML tags

These days, it's not uncommon to download text from a website to save or use as data in an application. Sometimes, however, when you download text from the website, you also get the HTML tags used to format the data. This can be a problem when all you want to see is the data.

A standard HTML web page contains several different types of HTML tags, identifying formatting features required to properly display the page information. Here's a sample of what an HTML file looks like:

```
$ cat data11.txt
<html>
<head>
<title>This is the page title</title>
</head>
<body>
<p>
This is the <b>first</b> line in the Web page.
This should provide some <i>useful</i>
information to use in our sed script.
</body>
</html>
$
```

HTML tags are identified by the less-than and greater-than symbols. Most HTML tags come in pairs. One tag starts the formatting process (for example, <b> for bolding), and another tag stops the formatting process (for example, </b> to turn off bolding).

Removing HTML tags creates a problem, however, if you're not careful. At first glance, you'd think that the way to remove HTML tags would be to just look for a text string that starts with a less-than symbol (<), ends with a greater-than symbol (>), and has data in between the symbols:

```
s/<.*>//g
```

Unfortunately, this command has some unintended consequences:

```
$ sed 's/<.*>//g' data11.txt




This is the  line in the Web page.
This should provide some
information to use in our sed script.



$
```

Notice that the title text is missing, along with the text that was bolded and italicized. The sed editor literally interpreted the script to mean any text between the less-than and greater-than sign, including other less-than and greater-than signs! Each time the text was enclosed in HTML tags (such as <b>first</b>), the sed script removed the entire text.

The solution to this problem is to have the sed editor ignore any embedded greater-than signs between the original tags. To do that, you can create a character class that negates the greater-than sign. This changes the script to

```
s/<[^>]*>//g
```

This script now works properly, displaying the data you need to see from the web page HTML code:

```
$ sed 's/<[^>]*>//g' data11.txt


This is the page title



This is the first line in the Web page.
This should provide some useful
information to use in our sed script.


$
```

That's a little better. To clean things up some, we can add a delete command to get rid of those pesky blank lines:

```
$ sed 's/<[^>]*>//g ; /^$/d' data11.txt
This is the page title
This is the first line in the Web page.
This should provide some useful
information to use in our sed script.
$
```

Now that's much more compact; there's only the data you need to see.

# Working Through a Practical Example

For our practical example in this chapter, we'll use sed to scan Bash shell scripts. The purpose of this scan is to find commands that may be better off located within a function.

Back in Chapter 17, "Creating Functions," we covered how to set up functions that can be called multiple times within a script. It's considered good form to put any duplicated code blocks within a function. That way, if a change is needed for the commands in the code block, you need to make those changes in only one place. Not only is this approach a time-saver, but it also reduces the chances of introducing errors that may occur if you change one block of code but not the others strewn about the script.

To keep things simple, we'll just look for three repeating lines of code within a file. Consider the following text file:

```
$ cat ScriptData.txt
Line 1
Line 2
Line 3
Line 4
Line 5
Line 6
Line 3
Line 4
Line 5
Line 7
Line 8
Line 3
Line 4
Line 5
Line 9
Line 10
Line 11
Line 12
$
```

If you look carefully, you'll notice that Line 3, Line 4, and Line 5 are repeated three times throughout this file. To find those repeated lines, we'll merge each text line together with the next two following lines:

1. Read in the next line, but only if processing the text file's first line, using the multiline N command.

2. Read in the next line (this is the second read for the text file's first line) using the multiline N command. Now we have three lines within the pattern space.

3. Print the pattern space to STDOUT.

4. Delete the first line in the pattern space using the D command, which deletes the text within the pattern space up to and including the first newline, and then starts processing the sed script commands from the beginning.

The following command shows this process:

```
$ sed -n '{
> 1N
> N
> P
> D}
> ' ScriptData.txt
Line 1
Line 2
Line 3
Line 2
Line 3
Line 4
Line 3
Line 4
Line 5
Line 4
Line 5
Line 6
Line 5
Line 6
Line 3
Line 6
Line 3
Line 4
Line 3
Line 4
Line 5
Line 4
Line 5
[...]
Line 9
```

```
Line 10
Line 9
Line 10
Line 11
Line 10
Line 11
Line 12
$
```

The problem with this method is that it is hard for a human to differentiate what lines have been merged together. Because the lines still contain the newline character (\n), the output is nearly impossible to interpret.

To fix this issue, we'll replace the newline character at the end of each text line with a bell sound character (\a) using the substitute (s) command:

```
$ sed -n '{
> 1N
> N
> s/\n/\a/g
> p
> s/\a/\n/
> D}
> ' ScriptData.txt
Line 1Line 2Line 3
Line 2Line 3Line 4
Line 3Line 4Line 5
Line 4Line 5Line 6
Line 5Line 6Line 3
Line 6Line 3Line 4
Line 3Line 4Line 5
Line 4Line 5Line 7
Line 5Line 7Line 8
Line 7Line 8Line 3
Line 8Line 3Line 4
Line 3Line 4Line 5
Line 4Line 5Line 9
Line 5Line 9Line 10
Line 9Line 10Line 11
Line 10Line 11Line 12
$
```

Now, we're getting somewhere! Notice that although we replaced the newline characters with a bell sound character (globally) in the third line of the sed script, after printing the pattern space we had to switch the first bell sound character back to a newline. This is due to the delete (D) command, which needs the newline character after the first text line so that it won't delete the entire pattern space.

While it may be tempting to forge ahead to comparing the lines and finding duplicates, there is one more consideration. Shell script lines often have spaces or tabs within each line, as shown in this test text file:

```
$ cat ScriptDataB.txt
Line 1
Line 2
Line 3
Line 4
 Line 5
Line 6
      Line 3
      Line 4
   Line 5
Line 7
Line 8
        Line 3
        Line 4
        Line 5
Line 9
Line 10
Line 11
Line 12
$
```

These spaces and tabs will disrupt the matching process. But it's fairly easy to handle this situation. We'll just eliminate the spaces and tabs via a global (g) substitute (s) command:

```
$ sed -n '{
> 1N
> N
> s/ //g
> s/\t//g
> s/\n/\a/g
> p
> s/\a/\n/
> D}
> ' ScriptDataB.txt
Line1Line2Line3
Line2Line3Line4
Line3Line4Line5
Line4Line5Line6
Line5Line6Line3
Line6Line3Line4
Line3Line4Line5
Line4Line5Line7
Line5Line7Line8
Line7Line8Line3
Line8Line3Line4
Line3Line4Line5
```

```
Line4Line5Line9
Line5Line9Line10
Line9Line10Line11
Line10Line11Line12
$
```

Now we'll employ two other Bash shell commands to help us sort the file (sort) and find any duplicates (uniq -d):

```
$ sed -n '{
> 1N;
> N;
> s/ //g;
> s/\t//g;
> s/\n/\a/g;
> p
> s/\a/\n/;
> D}
> ' ScriptDataB.txt |
> sort | uniq -d |
> sed 's/\a/\n/g'
Line3
Line4
Line5
$
```

Perfect! The commands scanned the file and found three repeating lines. Now we can pretty this up, and store it in a shell wrapper. Here's one way to do it:

```
$ cat NeededFunctionCheck.sh
#!/bin/bash
# Checks for 3 duplicate lines in scripts.
# Suggest these lines be possibly replaced
# by a function.
#
tempfile=$2
#
#
sed -n '{
1N; N;
s/ //g; s/\t//g;
s/\n/\a/g; p;
s/\a/\n/; D}' $1 >> $tempfile
#
sort $tempfile | uniq -d | sed 's/\a/\n/g'
#
rm -i $tempfile
#
exit
$
```

Notice that this script takes two parameters — the first ($1) for which file to scan, and the second ($2) to designate a temporary file to store the merged file lines. The reason we redirected STDOUT to a file, instead of directly into the sort command, is that it gives you the ability to keep the temporary file to see if your sed merging process (and any tweaks you make to it) are working correctly.

Before you start diving into modifying this script to try out variations, let's scan our test text file with it:

```
$ ./NeededFunctionCheck.sh ScriptDataB.txt TempFile.txt
Line3
Line4
Line5
rm: remove regular file 'TempFile.txt'? Y
$
```

This is exactly what we are wanting. Now, let's try scanning a real script and see how it does:

```
$ ./NeededFunctionCheck.sh CheckMe.sh TempFile.txt
echo"Usage:./CheckMe.shparameter1parameter2"
echo"Exitingscript..."
exit
rm: remove regular file 'TempFile.txt'? Y
$
```

This is a little harder to read, because we eliminated *all* the spaces within each script line. (One script improvement you can make is to only remove multiple spaces between characters.) However, it gives us enough of a shove in the right direction. We know that these three lines are repeated within the script. And the script needs to be reviewed to possibly replace the repeated commands with a function.

You can make lots of potential improvements within this script. Once you've got your modifications in place and working, remove that temporary file to make it faster. How about producing line numbers to show where the code is located within the script? You could even make the information into a fancy report. . .but we recommend you wait until you read through the next chapter, "Advanced gawk," before you try that script improvement.

# Summary

The sed editor provides some advanced features that allow you to work with text patterns across multiple lines. This chapter showed you how to use the multiline next (N) command to retrieve the next line in a data stream and place it in the pattern space. Once it's in the pattern space, you can perform complex substitution (s) commands to replace phrases that span more than one line of text.

The multiline delete (D) command allows you to remove the first line when the pattern space contains two or more lines. This is a convenient way to iterate through multiple lines in the data stream. Similarly, the multiline print (P) command allows you to print just the first line when the pattern space contains two or more lines of text. The combination of the multiline commands allows you to iterate through the data stream and create a multiline substitution system.

Next, we covered the hold space. The hold space allows you to set aside a line of text while processing more lines of text. You can recall the contents of the hold space at any time and either replace the text in the pattern space or append the contents of the hold space to the text in the pattern space. Using the hold space allows you to sort through data streams, reversing the order of text lines as they appear in the data.

Next we reviewed the various sed editor flow control commands. The branch (b) command provides a way for you to alter the normal flow of sed editor commands in the script, creating loops or skipping commands under certain conditions. The test (t) command provides an if-then type of statement for your sed editor command scripts. The test (t) command branches only if a prior substitution (s) command succeeds in replacing text in a line.

The chapter continued with a discussion of how to use sed scripts in your shell scripts. A common technique for large sed scripts is to place the script in a shell wrapper. You can use command-line parameter variables within the sed script to pass shell command-line values. This creates an easy way to utilize your sed editor scripts directly from the command line, or even from other shell scripts.

We concluded the chapter with a look at creating common sed utilities, which allow you to do lots of processing of text files. Some features include numbering lines in a file in a more human-readable format, printing last text file lines, and removing HTML tags.

The next chapter digs deeper into the gawk world. The gawk program supports many features of higher-level programming languages. You can create some pretty involved data manipulation and reporting programs just by using gawk. The chapter describes the various programming features and demonstrates how to use them to generate your own fancy reports from simple data.

# Advanced *gawk*

C hapter 19, "Introducing *sed* and *gawk*" introduced the gawk program and demonstrated
the basics of using it to produce formatted reports from raw data files. This chapter
dives more deeply into customizing gawk to produce reports. The gawk program is a
full-fledged programming language, providing features that allow you to write advanced programs
to manipulate data. If you are jumping into the shell script world from another programming
language, you should feel right at home with gawk. In this chapter, you'll see how to use the
gawk programming language to write programs to handle just about any data-formatting task
you'll run into.

## Using Variables

One important feature of any programming language is the ability to store and recall values using
variables. The gawk programming language supports two different types of variables:

- Built-in variables
- User-defined variables

Several built-in variables are available for you to use in gawk. The built-in variables contain information used in handling the data fields and records in the data file. You can also create your own
variables in your gawk programs. The following sections walk you through how to use variables in
your gawk programs.

**TABLE 22.1   The *gawk* Data Field and Record Variables**

| Variable | Description |
| --- | --- |
| FIELDWIDTHS | A space-separated list of numbers defining the exact width (in spaces) of each data field |
| FS | Input field separator character |
| RS | Input record separator character |
| OFS | Output field separator character |
| ORS | Output record separator character |

## Built-in variables

The gawk program uses built-in variables to reference specific features within the program data. This section describes the built-in variables available for you to use in your gawk programs and demonstrates how to use them.

### The field and record separator variables

Chapter 19 demonstrated one type of built-in variable available in gawk, the *data field variables*. The data field variables allow you to reference individual data fields within a data record using a dollar sign and the numerical position of the data field in the record. Thus, to reference the first data field in the record, you use the $1 variable. To reference the second data field, you use the $2 variable, and so on.

Data fields are delineated by a field separator character. By default, the field separator character is a whitespace character, such as a space or a tab. Chapter 19 showed how to change the field separator character either on the command line by using the -F command-line parameter or within the gawk program by using the special FS built-in variable.

The FS built-in variable belongs to a group of built-in variables that control how gawk handles fields and records in both input data and output data. Table 22.1 lists the built-in variables contained in this group.

The FS and OFS variables define how your gawk program handles data fields in the data stream. You've already seen how to use the FS variable to define what character separates data fields in a record. The OFS variable performs the same function but for the output by using the print command.

By default, gawk sets the OFS variable to a space, so when you use the command

```
print $1,$2,$3
```

you see the output as

```
field1 field2 field3
```

You can see this in the following example:

```
$ cat data1
data11,data12,data13,data14,data15
data21,data22,data23,data24,data25
data31,data32,data33,data34,data35
$ gawk 'BEGIN{FS=","} {print $1,$2,$3}' data1
data11 data12 data13
data21 data22 data23
data31 data32 data33
$
```

The print command automatically places the value of the OFS variable between each data field in the output. By setting the OFS variable, you can use any string to separate data fields in the output:

```
$ gawk 'BEGIN{FS=","; OFS="-"} {print $1,$2,$3}' data1
data11-data12-data13
data21-data22-data23
data31-data32-data33
$ gawk 'BEGIN{FS=","; OFS="--"} {print $1,$2,$3}' data1
data11--data12--data13
data21--data22--data23
data31--data32--data33
$ gawk 'BEGIN{FS=","; OFS="<-->"} {print $1,$2,$3}' data1
data11<-->data12<-->data13
data21<-->data22<-->data23
data31<-->data32<-->data33
$
```

The FIELDWIDTHS variable allows you to read records without using a field separator character. In some applications, instead of using a field separator character, data is placed in specific columns within the record. In these instances, you must set the FIELDWIDTHS variable to the match the layout of the data in the records.

Once you set the FIELDWIDTHS variable, gawk ignores the FS and calculates data fields based on the provided field width sizes. Here's an example using field widths instead of field separator characters:

```
$ cat data1b
1005.3247596.37
115-2.349194.00
05810.1298100.1
$ gawk 'BEGIN{FIELDWIDTHS="3 5 2 5"}{print $1,$2,$3,$4}' data1b
100 5.324 75 96.37
115 -2.34 91 94.00
058 10.12 98 100.1
$
```

The FIELDWIDTHS variable defines four data fields, and gawk parses the data record accordingly. The string of numbers in each record is split based on the defined field width values.

The RS and ORS variables define how your gawk program handles records in the data stream. By default, gawk sets the RS and ORS variables to the newline character. The default RS variable value indicates that each new line of text in the input data stream is a new record.

Sometimes you run into situations where data fields are spread across multiple lines in the data stream. A classic example of this is data that includes an address and phone number, each on a separate line:

```
Ima Test
123 Main Street
Chicago, IL 60601
(312)555-1234
```

If you try to read this data using the default FS and RS variable values, gawk will read each line as a separate record and interpret each space in the record as a field separator. This isn't what you intended.

To solve this problem, you need to set the FS variable to the newline character. This indicates that each line in the data stream is a separate field and that all of the data on a line belongs to the data field. However, when you do that, you don't know where a new record starts.

To solve this problem, set the RS variable to an empty string and then leave a blank line between data records in the data stream. The gawk program will interpret each blank line as a record separator.

The following is an example of using this technique:

```
$ cat data2
Ima Test
123 Main Street
Chicago, IL  60601
(312)555-1234

Frank Tester
456 Oak Street
Indianapolis, IN  46201
(317)555-9876
```

```
Haley Example
4231 Elm Street
Detroit, MI 48201
(313)555-4938
$ gawk 'BEGIN{FS="\n"; RS=""} {print $1,$4}' data2
Ima Test (312)555-1234
Frank Tester (317)555-9876
Haley Example (313)555-4938
$
```

Perfect—the gawk program interpreted each line in the file as a data field and the blank lines as record separators.

### Data variables

Besides the field and record separator variables, gawk provides some other built-in variables to help you know what's going on with your data and to extract information from the shell environment. Table 22.2 shows the other built-in variables in gawk.

**TABLE 22.2** **More *gawk* Built-in Variables**

| Variable | Description |
|---|---|
| ARGC | The number of command-line parameters present. |
| ARGIND | The index in ARGV of the current file being processed. |
| ARGV | An array of command-line parameters. |
| CONVFMT | The conversion format for numbers (see the printf statement). The default value is %.6 g. |
| ENVIRON | An associative array of the current shell environment variables and their values. |
| ERRNO | The system error if an error occurs when reading or closing input files. |
| FILENAME | The filename of the data file used for input to the gawk program. |
| FNR | The current record number in the data file. |
| IGNORECASE | If set to a non-zero value, ignore the case of characters in strings used in the gawk command. |
| NF | The total number of data fields in the data file. |
| NR | The number of input records processed. |
| OFMT | The output format for displaying numbers. The default is %.6g., which displays the value in either floating-point or scientific notation, whichever is shorter, using up to six decimal places. |
| RLENGTH | The length of the substring matched in the match function. |
| RSTART | The start index of the substring matched in the match function. |

You should recognize a few of these variables from your shell script programming. The ARGC and ARGV variables allow you to retrieve the number of command-line parameters and their values from the shell. This can be a little tricky, however, since gawk doesn't count the program script as part of the command-line parameters:

```
$ gawk 'BEGIN{print ARGC,ARGV[1]}' data1
2 data1
$
```

The ARGC variable indicates that there are two parameters on the command line. This includes the gawk command and the data1 parameter (remember, the program script doesn't count as a parameter). The ARGV array starts with an index of 0, which represents the command. The first array value is the first command-line parameter after the gawk command.

**TIP**

Note that unlike shell variables, when you reference a gawk variable in the script, you don't add a dollar sign before the variable name.

The ENVIRON variable may seem a little odd to you. It uses an *associative array* to retrieve shell environment variables. An associative array uses text for the array index values instead of numeric values.

The text in the array index is the shell environment variable. The value of the array is the value of the shell environment variable. The following is an example of this:

```
$ gawk '
> BEGIN{
> print ENVIRON["HOME"]
> print ENVIRON["PATH"]
> }'
/home/rich
/usr/local/sbin:/usr/local/bin:/usr/sbin:/usr/bin:/sbin:/bin:/usr/
games:/usr/local/games:/snap/bin
$
```

The ENVIRON["HOME"] variable retrieves the HOME environment variable value from the shell. Likewise, the ENVIRON["PATH"] variable retrieves the PATH environment variable value. You can use this technique to retrieve any environment variable value from the shell to use in your gawk programs.

The FNR, NF, and NR variables come in handy when you're trying to keep track of data fields and records in your gawk program. Sometimes you're in a situation where you don't know exactly how many data fields are in a record. The NF variable allows you to specify the last data field in the record without having to know its position:

```
$ gawk 'BEGIN{FS=":"; OFS=":"} {print $1,$NF}' /etc/passwd
root:/bin/bash
```

```
daemon:/usr/sbin/nologin
bin:/usr/sbin/nologin
sys:/usr/sbin/nologin
sync:/bin/sync
games:/usr/sbin/nologin
man:/usr/sbin/nologin
...
rich:/bin/bash
$
```

The NF variable contains the numerical value of the last data field in the data file. You can then use it as a data field variable by placing a dollar sign in front of it.

The FNR and NR variables are similar to each other but slightly different. The FNR variable contains the number of records processed in the current data file. The NR variable contains the total number of records processed. Let's look at a couple of examples to see this difference:

```
$ gawk 'BEGIN{FS=","}{print $1,"FNR="FNR}' data1 data1
data11 FNR=1
data21 FNR=2
data31 FNR=3
data11 FNR=1
data21 FNR=2
data31 FNR=3
$
```

In this example, the gawk program command line defines two input files. (It specifies the same input file twice.) The script prints the first data field value and the current value of the FNR variable. Notice that the FNR value was reset back to 1 when the gawk program processed the second data file.

Now, let's add the NR variable and see what that produces:

```
$ gawk '
> BEGIN {FS=","}
> {print $1,"FNR="FNR,"NR="NR}
> END{print "There were",NR,"records processed"}' data1 data1
data11 FNR=1 NR=1
data21 FNR=2 NR=2
data31 FNR=3 NR=3
data11 FNR=1 NR=4
data21 FNR=2 NR=5
data31 FNR=3 NR=6
There were 6 records processed
$
```

The FNR variable value was reset when gawk processed the second data file, but the NR variable maintained its count into the second data file. The bottom line is that if you're using only one data file for input, the FNR and NR values will be the same. If you're using multiple data files for input, the FNR value will be reset for each data file, and the NR value will keep count throughout all the data files.

## User-defined variables

Just like any other self-respecting programming language, gawk allows you to define your own variables for use within the program code. A gawk user-defined variable name can be any number of letters, digits, and underscores, but it can't begin with a digit. It is also important to remember that gawk variable names are case sensitive.

### Assigning variables in scripts

Assigning values to variables in gawk programs is similar to doing so in a shell script, using an *assignment statement*:

```
$ gawk '
> BEGIN{
> testing="This is a test"
> print testing
> }'
This is a test
$
```

The output of the print statement is the current value of the testing variable. Like shell script variables, gawk variables can hold either numeric or text values:

```
$ gawk '
> BEGIN{
> testing="This is a test"
> print testing
> testing=45
> print testing
> }'
This is a test
45
$
```

In this example, the value of the testing variable is changed from a text value to a numeric value.

Assignment statements can also include mathematical algorithms to handle numeric values:

```
$ gawk 'BEGIN{x=4; x= x * 2 + 3; print x}'
11
$
```

As you can see from this example, the `gawk` programming language includes the standard mathematical operators for processing numerical values. These can include the remainder symbol (%) and the exponentiation symbol (using either ^ or **).

### Assigning variables on the command line

You can also use the `gawk` command line to assign values to variables for the `gawk` program. This allows you to set values outside of the normal code, changing values on the fly. Here's an example of using a command-line variable to display a specific data field in the file:

```
$ cat script1
BEGIN{FS=","}
{print $n}
$ gawk -f script1 n=2 data1
data12
data22
data32
$ gawk -f script1 n=3 data1
data13
data23
data33
$
```

This feature allows you to change the behavior of the script without necessitating that you change the actual script code. The first example displays the second data field in the file, whereas the second example displays the third data field, just by setting the value of the n variable in the command line.

There's one problem with using command-line parameters to define variable values. When you set the variable, the value isn't available in the BEGIN section of the code:

```
$ cat script2
BEGIN{print "The starting value is",n; FS=","}
{print $n}
$ gawk -f script2 n=3 data1
The starting value is
data13
data23
data33
$
```

You can solve this by using the -v command line parameter. This allows you to specify variables that are set before the BEGIN section of code. The -v command-line parameter must be placed before the script code in the command line:

```
$ gawk -v n=3 -f script2 data1
The starting value is 3
data13
data23
data33
$
```

Now the n variable contains the value set in the command line during the BEGIN section of code.

# Working with Arrays

Many programming languages provide arrays for storing multiple values in a single variable. The gawk programming language provides the array feature using *associative arrays*.

Associative arrays are different from numerical arrays in that the index value can be any text string. You don't have to use sequential numbers to identify data elements contained in the array. Instead, an associative array consists of a hodgepodge of strings referencing values. Each index string must be unique and uniquely identifies the data element that's assigned to it. If you're familiar with other programming languages, this is the same concept as hash maps or dictionaries.

The following sections walk you through using associative array variables in your gawk programs.

## Defining array variables

You can define an array variable using a standard assignment statement. The format of the array variable assignment is

```
var[index] = element
```

where *var* is the variable name, *index* is the associative array index value, and *element* is the data element value. Here are some examples of array variables in gawk:

```
capital["Illinois"] = "Springfield"
capital["Indiana"] = "Indianapolis"
capital["Ohio"] = "Columbus"
```

When you reference an array variable, you must include the index value to retrieve the appropriate data element value:

```
$ gawk 'BEGIN{
> capital["Illinois"] = "Springfield"
> print capital["Illinois"]
> }'
Springfield
$
```

When you reference the array variable, the data element value appears. This also works with numeric data element values:

```
$ gawk 'BEGIN{
> var[1] = 34
> var[2] = 3
> total = var[1] + var[2]
> print total
> }'
37
$
```

As you can see from this example, you can use array variables just as you would any other variable in the gawk program.

## Iterating through array variables

The problem with associative array variables is that you might not have any way of knowing what the index values are. Unlike numeric arrays, which use sequential numbers for index values, an associative array index can be anything.

If you need to iterate through an associate array in gawk, you can use a special format of the for statement:

```
for (var in array)
{
    statements
}
```

The for statement loops through the statements, each time assigning the variable *var* the next index value from the *array* associative array. It's important to remember that the variable is the value of the index and not the data element value. You can easily extract the data element value by using the variable as the array index:

```
$ gawk 'BEGIN{
> var["a"] = 1
> var["g"] = 2
> var["m"] = 3
> var["u"] = 4
> for (test in var)
> {
>    print "Index:",test," - Value:",var[test]
> }
> }'
Index: u  - Value: 4
Index: m  - Value: 3
Index: a  - Value: 1
Index: g  - Value: 2
$
```

Notice that the index values aren't returned in any particular order, but they each reference the appropriate data element value. This is somewhat important to know, since you can't count on the returned values being in the same order, just that the index and data values match.

## Deleting array variables

Removing an array index from an associative array requires a special command:

```
delete array[index]
```

The `delete` command removes the associative index value and the associated data element value from the array:

```
$ gawk 'BEGIN{
> var["a"] = 1
> var["g"] = 2
> for (test in var)
> {
>    print "Index:",test," - Value:",var[test]
> }
> delete var["g"]
> print "---"
> for (test in var)
>    print "Index:",test," - Value:",var[test]
> }'
Index: a  - Value: 1
Index: g  - Value: 2
---
Index: a  - Value: 1
$
```

Once you delete an index value from the associative array, you can't retrieve it.

# Considering Patterns

The `gawk` program supports several types of matching patterns to filter data records, in much the same way as the `sed` editor. Chapter 19 already showed two special patterns in action. The BEGIN and END keywords are special patterns that execute statements before or after the data stream data has been read. Similarly, you can create other patterns to execute statements when matching data appears in the data stream.

This section demonstrates how to use matching patterns in your `gawk` scripts to limit what records a program script applies to.

## Regular expressions

Chapter 20, "Regular Expressions," showed how to use regular expressions as matching patterns. You can use either a basic regular expression (BRE) or an extended regular expression (ERE) to filter which lines in the data stream the program script applies to.

When you're using a regular expression, the regular expression must appear before the left brace of the program script that it controls:

```
$ gawk 'BEGIN{FS=","} /11/{print $1}' data1
data11
$
```

The regular expression /11/ matches records that contain the string 11 anywhere in the data fields. The gawk program matches the defined regular expression against all the data fields in the record, including the field separator character:

```
$ gawk 'BEGIN{FS=","} /,d/{print $1}' data1
data11
data21
data31
$
```

This example matches the comma used as the field separator in the regular expression. This is not always a good thing. It can lead to problems trying to match data specific to one data field that may also appear in another data field. If you need to match a regular expression to a specific data instance, you should use the matching operator.

## The matching operator

The *matching operator* allows you to restrict a regular expression to a specific data field in the records. The matching operator is the tilde symbol (~). You specify the matching operator, along with the data field variable, and the regular expression to match:

```
$1 ~ /^data/
```

The $1 variable represents the first data field in the record. This expression filters records where the first data field starts with the text data. The following is an example of using the matching operator in a gawk program script:

```
$ gawk 'BEGIN{FS=","} $2 ~ /^data2/{print $0}' data1
data21,data22,data23,data24,data25
$
```

The matching operator compares the second data field with the regular expression /^data2/, which indicates the string starts with the text data2.

This is a powerful tool that is commonly used in gawk program scripts to search for specific data elements in a data file:

```
$ gawk -F: '$1 ~ /rich/{print $1,$NF}' /etc/passwd
rich /bin/bash
$
```

This example searches the first data field for the text rich. When it finds the pattern in a record, it prints the first and last data field values of the record.

You can also negate the regular expression match by using the ! symbol:

```
$1 !~ /expression/
```

If the regular expression isn't found in the record, the program script is applied to the record data:

```
$ gawk -F: '$1 !~ /rich/{print $1,$NF}' /etc/passwd
root /bin/bash
daemon /bin/nologin
bin /bin/nologin
sys /bin/nologin
--- output truncated ---
$
```

In this example, the gawk program script prints the user ID and shell for all of the entries in the /etc/passwd file that don't match the user ID rich!

## Mathematical expressions

In addition to regular expressions, you can use mathematical expressions in the matching pattern. This feature comes in handy when matching numerical values in data fields. For example, if you want to display all the system users who belong to the root users group (group number 0), you could use this script:

```
$ gawk -F: '$4 == 0{print $1}' /etc/passwd
root
$
```

The script checks for records where the fourth data field contains the value 0. On this Linux system there's just one user account that belongs to the root user group.

You can use any of the normal mathematical comparison expressions:

- $x == y$: Value $x$ is equal to $y$.
- $x <= y$: Value $x$ is less than or equal to $y$.
- $x < y$: Value $x$ is less than $y$.
- $x >= y$: Value $x$ is greater than or equal to $y$.
- $x > y$: Value $x$ is greater than $y$.

You can also use expressions with text data, but you must be careful. Unlike regular expressions, expressions are an exact match. The data must match exactly with the pattern:

```
$ gawk -F, '$1 == "data"{print $1}' data1
$
$ gawk -F, '$1 == "data11"{print $1}' data1
data11
$
```

The first test doesn't match any records because the first data field value isn't data in any of the records. The second test matches one record with the value data11.

# Structured Commands

The gawk programming language supports the usual cast of structured programming commands. This section describes each of these commands and demonstrates how to use them within a gawk programming environment.

## The *if* statement

The gawk programming language supports the standard if-then-else format of the if statement. You must define a condition for the if statement to evaluate, enclosed in parentheses. If the condition evaluates to a TRUE condition, the statement immediately following the if statement is executed. If the condition evaluates to a FALSE condition, the statement is skipped. This can use the format

```
if (condition)
    statement1
```

or you can place it on one line, like this:

```
if (condition) statement1
```

Here's a simple example demonstrating this format:

```
$ cat data4
10
5
13
50
34
$ gawk '{if ($1 > 20) print $1}' data4
50
34
$
```

Not too complicated. If you need to execute multiple statements in the if statement, you must enclose them with braces:

```
$ gawk '{
> if ($1 > 20)
```

*(Continues)*

```
(continued)
> {
>    x = $1 * 2
>    print x
> }
> }' data4
100
68
$
```

Be careful that you don't confuse the if statement braces with the braces used to start and stop the program script. The gawk program can detect missing braces and will produce an error message if you mess up:

```
$ gawk '{
> if ($1 > 20)
> {
>    x = $1 * 2
>    print x
> }' data4
gawk: cmd. line:7: (END OF FILE)
gawk: cmd. line:7: parse error
$
```

The gawk if statement also supports the else clause, allowing you to execute one or more statements if the if statement condition fails. Here's an example of using the else clause:

```
$ gawk '{
> if ($1 > 20)
> {
>    x = $1 * 2
>    print x
> } else
> {
>    x = $1 / 2
>    print x
> }}' data4
5
2.5
6.5
100
68
$
```

You can use the else clause on a single line, but you must use a semicolon after the if statement section:

```
if (condition) statement1; else statement2
```

Here's the same example using the single-line format:

```
$ gawk '{if ($1 > 20) print $1 * 2; else print $1 / 2}' data4
5
2.5
6.5
100
68
$
```

This format is more compact but can be harder to follow.

## The *while* statement

The while statement provides a basic looping feature for gawk programs. The following is the format of the while statement:

```
while (condition)
{
   statements
}
```

The while loop allows you to iterate over a set of data, checking a condition that stops the iteration. This is useful if you have multiple data values in each record that you must use in calculations:

```
$ cat data5
130 120 135
160 113 140
145 170 215
$ gawk '{
> total = 0
> i = 1
> while (i < 4)
> {
>    total += $i
>    i++
> }
> avg = total / 3
> print "Average:",avg
> }' data5
Average: 128.333
Average: 137.667
Average: 176.667
$
```

The while statement iterates through the data fields in the record, adding each value to the total variable and then incrementing the counter variable, i. When the counter value is equal to 4, the while condition becomes FALSE, and the loop terminates, dropping through to the next statement in the script. That statement calculates the average; then the average is printed. This process is repeated for each record in the data file.

The gawk programming language supports using the break and continue statements in while loops, allowing you to jump out of the middle of the loop:

```
$ gawk '{
> total = 0
> i = 1
> while (i < 4)
> {
>    total += $i
>    if (i == 2)
>       break
>    i++
> }
> avg = total / 2
> print "The average of the first two data elements is:",avg
> }' data5
The average of the first two data elements is: 125
The average of the first two data elements is: 136.5
The average of the first two data elements is: 157.5
$
```

The break statement is used to break out of the while loop if the value of the i variable is 2.

## The *do-while* statement

The do-while statement is similar to the while statement but performs the statements before checking the condition statement. The following is the format for the do-while statement:

```
do
{
  statements
} while (condition)
```

This format guarantees that the statements are executed at least one time before the condition is evaluated. This comes in handy when you need to perform statements before evaluating the condition:

```
$ gawk '{
> total = 0
> i = 1
> do
> {
>    total += $i
>    i++
> } while (total < 150)
```

```
> print total }' data5
250
160
315
$
```

The script reads the data fields from each record and totals them until the cumulative value reaches 150. If the first data field is over 150 (as seen in the second record), the script is guaranteed to read at least the first data field before evaluating the condition.

## The *for* statement

The for statement is a common method used in many programming languages for looping. The gawk programming language supports the C-style of for loops:

```
for( variable assignment; condition; iteration process)
```

This helps simplify the loop by combining several functions in one statement:

```
$ gawk '{
> total = 0
> for (i = 1; i < 4; i++)
> {
>    total += $i
> }
> avg = total / 3
> print "Average:",avg
> }' data5
Average: 128.333
Average: 137.667
Average: 176.667
$
```

By defining the iteration counter in the for loop, you don't have to worry about incrementing it yourself as you did when using the while statement.

# Printing with Formats

You may have noticed that the print statement doesn't exactly give you much control over how gawk displays your data. About all you can do is control the output field separator character (OFS). If you're creating detailed reports, often you'll need to place data in a specific format and location.

The solution is to use the formatted printing command, called printf. If you're familiar with C programming, the printf command in gawk performs the same way, allowing you to specify detailed instructions on how to display data.

The following is the format of the printf command:

```
printf "format string", var1, var2
```

The *format string* is the key to the formatted output. It specifies exactly how the formatted output should appear, using both text elements and *format specifiers*. A format specifier is a special code that indicates what type of variable is displayed and how to display it. The gawk program uses each format specifier as a placeholder for each variable listed in the command. The first format specifier matches the first variable listed, the second matches the second variable, and so on.

The format specifiers use the following format:

```
%[modifier] control-letter
```

where `control-letter` is a one-character code that indicates what type of data value will be displayed, and `modifier` defines an optional formatting feature.

Table 22.3 lists the control letters that can be used in the format specifier.

**TABLE 22.3  Format Specifier Control Letters**

| Control letter | Description |
| --- | --- |
| c | Displays a number as an ASCII character |
| d | Displays an integer value |
| i | Displays an integer value (same as d) |
| e | Displays a number in scientific notation |
| f | Displays a floating-point value |
| g | Displays either scientific notation or floating point, whichever is shorter |
| o | Displays an octal value |
| s | Displays a text string |
| x | Displays a hexadecimal value |
| X | Displays a hexadecimal value, but using capital letters for A through F |

Thus, if you need to display a string variable, you'd use the format specifier %s. If you need to display an integer variable, you'd use either %d or %i (%d is the C-style for decimals). If you want to display a large value using scientific notation, you'd use the %e format specifier:

```
$ gawk 'BEGIN{
> x = 10 * 100
> printf "The answer is: %e\n", x
> }'
The answer is: 1.000000e+03
$
```

In addition to the control letters, there are three modifiers that you can use for even more control over your output:

- width: A numeric value that specifies the minimum width of the output field. If the output is shorter, printf pads the output with spaces with spaces, using right justification for the text. If the output is longer than the specified width, it overrides the width value.
- prec: A numeric value that specifies the number of digits to the right of the decimal place in floating-point numbers, or the maximum number of characters displayed in a text string.
- - (minus sign): The minus sign indicates that left justification should be used instead of right justification when placing data in the formatted space.

When using the printf statement, you have complete control over how your output appears. For example, in the "Built-in Variables" section, we used the print command to display data fields from our records:

```
$ gawk 'BEGIN{FS="\n"; RS=""} {print $1,$4}' data2
Ima Test (312)555-1234
Frank Tester (317)555-9876
Haley Example (313)555-4938
$
```

You can use the printf command to help format the output so that it looks better. First, let's convert the print command to a printf command and see what that does:

```
$ gawk 'BEGIN{FS="\n"; RS=""} {printf "%s %s\n", $1, $4}' data2
Ima Test   (312)555-1234
Frank Tester   (317)555-9876
Haley   (313)555-4938
$
```

That produces the same output as the print command. The printf command uses the %s format specifier as a placeholder for the two string values.

Notice that you have to manually add the newline character at the end of the printf command to force a new line. Without it, the printf command will continue to use the same line on subsequent prints.

This is useful if you need to print multiple things on the same line but using separate printf commands:

```
$ gawk 'BEGIN{FS=","} {printf "%s ", $1} END{printf "\n"}' data1
data11 data21 data31
$
```

Each of the printf outputs appears on the same line. To be able to terminate the line, the END section prints a single newline character.

Next, let's use a modifier to format the first string value:

```
$ gawk 'BEGIN{FS="\n"; RS=""} {printf "%16s  %s\n", $1, $4}' data2
       Ima Test  (312)555-1234
    Frank Tester  (317)555-9876
   Haley Example  (313)555-4938
$
```

By adding the 16 modifier value, we force the output for the first string to use 16 spaces. By default, the printf command uses right justification to place the data in the format space. To make it left justified, just add a minus sign to the modifier:

```
$ gawk 'BEGIN{FS="\n"; RS=""} {printf "%-16s  %s\n", $1, $4}' data2
Ima Test          (312)555-1234
Frank Tester      (317)555-9876
Haley Example     (313)555-4938
$
```

Now that looks pretty professional!

The printf command also comes in handy when dealing with floating-point values. By specifying a format for the variable, you can make the output look more uniform:

```
$ gawk '{
> total = 0
> for (i = 1; i < 4; i++)
> {
>    total += $i
> }
> avg = total / 3
> printf "Average: %5.1f\n",avg
> }' data5
Average: 128.3
Average: 137.7
Average: 176.7
$
```

By using the %5.1f format specifier, you can force the printf command to round the floating-point values to a single decimal place.

# Using Built-in Functions

The gawk programming language provides quite a few built-in functions that perform common mathematical, string, and even time functions. You can utilize these functions in your gawk programs to help cut down on the coding requirements in your scripts. This section walks you through the different built-in functions available in gawk.

## Mathematical functions

If you've done programming in any type of language, you're probably familiar with using built-in functions in your code to perform common mathematical functions. The gawk programming language doesn't disappoint those looking for advanced mathematical features.

Table 22.4 shows the mathematical built-in functions available in gawk.

**TABLE 22.4  The *gawk* Mathematical Functions**

| Function | Description |
|---|---|
| atan2(x, y) | The arctangent of x / y, with x and y specified in radians. |
| cos(x) | The cosine of x, with x specified in radians. |
| exp(x) | The exponential of x. |
| int(x) | The integer part of x, truncated toward 0. |
| log(x) | The natural logarithm of x. |
| rand() | A random floating-point value larger than 0 and less than 1. |
| sin(x) | The sine of x, with x specified in radians. |
| sqrt(x) | The square root of x. |
| srand(x) | Specify a seed value for calculating random numbers. |

22

Although gawk does not have an extensive list of mathematical functions, it does provide some of the basic elements you need for standard mathematical processing. The int() function produces the integer portion of a value, but it doesn't round the value. It behaves much like a floor function found in other programming languages. It produces the nearest integer to a value between the value and 0.

This means that the int() function of the value 5.6 will return 5, while the int() function of the value –5.6 will return –5.

The rand() function is great for creating random numbers, but you'll need to use a trick to get meaningful values. The rand() function returns a random number, but only between the values 0 and 1 (not including 0 or 1). To get a larger number, you'll need to scale the returned value.

A common method for producing larger integer random numbers is to create an algorithm that uses the rand() function, along with the int() function:

```
x = int(10 * rand())
```

This returns a random integer value between (and including) 0 and 9. Just substitute the 10 in the equation with the upper limit value for your application, and you're ready to go.

Be careful when using some of the mathematical functions, because the gawk programming language does have a limited range of numeric values it can work with. If you go over that range, you'll get an error message:

```
$ gawk 'BEGIN{x=exp(100); print x}'
26881171418161356094253400435962903554686976
$ gawk 'BEGIN{x=exp(1000); print x}'
gawk: warning: exp argument 1000 is out of range
inf
$
```

The first example calculates the exponential of 100, which is a very large number but within the range of the system. The second example attempts to calculate the exponential of 1000, which goes over the numerical range limit of the system and produces an error message.

Besides the standard mathematical functions, gawk also provides a few functions for bitwise manipulating of data:

- and(v1, v2): Performs a bitwise AND of values v1 and v2
- compl(val): Performs the bitwise complement of val
- lshift(val, count): Shifts the value val count number of bits left
- or(v1, v2): Performs a bitwise OR of values v1 and v2
- rshift(val, count): Shifts the value val count number of bits right
- xor(v1, v2): Performs a bitwise XOR of values v1 and v2

The bit manipulation functions are useful when working with binary values in your data.

## String functions

The gawk programming language also provides several functions you can use to manipulate string values, shown in Table 22.5.

**TABLE 22.5** **The *gawk* String Functions**

| Function | Description |
|---|---|
| asort(s [,d]) | Sort an array s based on the data element values. The index values are replaced with sequential numbers indicating the new sort order. Alternatively, the new sorted array is stored in array d if specified. |
| asorti(s [,d]) | Sort an array s based on the index values. The resulting array contains the index values as the data element values, with sequential number indexes indicating the sort order. Alternatively, the new sorted array is stored in array d if specified. |

| Function | Description |
|---|---|
| gensub (r, s, h [, t]) | Search either the variable $0, or the target string *t* if supplied, for matches of the regular expression *r*. If *h* is a string beginning with either *g* or *G*, replaces the matching text with *s*. If *h* is a number, it represents which occurrence of *r* to replace. |
| gsub(r, s [,t]) | Search either the variable $0, or the target string *t* if supplied, for matches of the regular expression *r*. If found, substitute the string *s* globally. |
| index(s, t) | Returns the index of the string *t* in string *s*, or 0 if not found. |
| length([s]) | Returns the length of string *s*, or if not specified, the length of $0. |
| match(s, r [,a]) | Returns the index of the string *s* where the regular expression *r* occurs. If array *a* is specified, it contains the portion of *s* that matches the regular expression. |
| split(s, a [,r]) | Splits *s* into array *a* using either the FS (field separator) character, or the regular expression *r* if supplied. Returns the number of fields. |
| sprintf(*format*, *variables*) | Returns a string similar to the output of printf using the *format* and *variables* supplied. |
| sub(r, s [,t]) | Search either the variable $0, or the target string *t*, for matches of the regular expression *r*. If found, substitutes the string *s* for the first occurrence. |
| substr(s, i [,n]) | Returns the *n*th character substring of *s*, starting at index *i*. If *n* is not supplied, the rest of *s* is used. |
| tolower(s) | Converts all characters in *s* to lowercase. |
| toupper(s) | Converts all characters in *s* to uppercase. |

Some of the string functions are relatively self-explanatory:

```
$ gawk 'BEGIN{x = "testing"; print toupper(x); print length(x) }'
TESTING
7
$
```

However, some of the string functions can get pretty complicated. The asort and asorti functions are new gawk functions that allow you to sort an array variable based on either the data element values (asort) or the index values (asorti). Here's an example of using asort:

```
$ gawk 'BEGIN{
> var["a"] = 1
> var["g"] = 2
> var["m"] = 3
```

*(Continues)*

*(continued)*

```
> var["u"] = 4
> asort(var, test)
> for (i in test)
>     print "Index:",i," - value:",test[i]
> }'
Index: 4  - value: 4
Index: 1  - value: 1
Index: 2  - value: 2
Index: 3  - value: 3
$
```

The new array, test, contains the newly sorted data elements of the original array, but the index values are now changed to numerical values, indicating the proper sort order.

The split function is a great way to push data fields into an array for further processing:

```
$ gawk 'BEGIN{ FS=","}{
> split($0, var)
> print var[1], var[5]
> }' data1
data11 data15
data21 data25
data31 data35
$
```

The new array uses sequential numbers for the array index, starting with index value 1 containing the first data field.

## Time functions

The gawk programming language contains a few functions to help you deal with time values, shown in Table 22.6.

### TABLE 22.6  The *gawk* Time Functions

| Function | Description |
| --- | --- |
| mktime(*datespec*) | Converts a date specified in the format YYYY MM DD HH MM SS [DST] into a timestamp value |
| strftime(*format* [, *timestamp*]) | Formats either the current time of day timestamp, or timestamp if provided, into a formatted day and date, using the date() shell function format |
| systime() | Returns the timestamp for the current time of day |

The time functions are often used when working with log files that contain dates that you need to compare. By converting the text representation of a date to the epoch time (the number of seconds since midnight, January 1, 1970), you can easily compare dates.

The following is an example of using the time functions in a gawk program:

```
$ gawk 'BEGIN{
> date = systime()
> day = strftime("%A, %B %d, %Y", date)
> print day
> }'
Friday, December 26, 2014
$
```

This example uses the systime function to retrieve the current epoch timestamp from the system and then uses the strftime function to convert it into a human-readable format using the shell command's date format characters.

# Trying Out User-Defined Functions

You're not limited to just using the built-in functions available in gawk. You can create your own functions for use in your gawk programs. This section shows you how to define and use your own functions in your gawk programs.

## Defining a function

To define your own function, you must use the function keyword:

```
function name([variables])
{
    statements
}
```

The function name must uniquely identify your function. You can pass one or more variables into the function from the calling gawk program:

```
function printthird()
{
    print $3
}
```

This function will print the third data field in the record.

The function can also return a value using the return statement:

```
return value
```

The value can be a variable, or an equation that evaluates to a value:

```
function myrand(limit)
{
    return int(limit * rand())
}
```

You can assign the value returned from the function to a variable in the gawk program:

```
x = myrand(100)
```

The variable will contain the value returned from the function.

## Using your functions

When you define a function, it must appear by itself before you define any programming sections (including the BEGIN section). This may look a little odd at first, but it helps keep the function code separate from the rest of the gawk program:

```
$ gawk '
> function myprint()
> {
>      printf "%-16s - %s\n", $1, $4
> }
> BEGIN{FS="\n"; RS=""}
> {
>      myprint()
> }' data2
Ima Test        - (312)555-1234
Frank Tester    - (317)555-9876
Haley Example   - (313)555-4938
$
```

The function defines the myprint() function, which formats the first and fourth data fields in the record for printing. The gawk program then uses the function to display the data from the data file.

Once you define a function, you can use it as often as necessary in the program section of the code. This saves lots of work when using long algorithms.

## Creating a function library

Obviously, having to rewrite your gawk functions every time you need them is not all that pleasant of an experience. However, gawk provides a way for you to combine your functions into a single library file that you can use in all your gawk programming.

First, you need to create a file that contains all your gawk functions:

```
$ cat funclib
function myprint()
{
  printf "%-16s - %s\n", $1, $4
}
function myrand(limit)
{
```

```
   return int(limit * rand())
}
function printthird()
{
   print $3
}
$
```

The `funclib` file contains three function definitions. To use them, you need to use the -f command-line parameter. Unfortunately, you can't combine the -f command-line parameter with an inline `gawk` script, but you can use multiple -f parameters on the same command line.

Thus, to use your library, just create a file that contains your `gawk` program, and specify both the library file and your program file on the command line:

```
$ cat script4
BEGIN{ FS="\n"; RS="" }
{
    myprint()
}
$ gawk -f funclib -f script4 data2
Ima Test          - (312)555-1234
Frank Tester      - (317)555-9876
Haley Example     - (313)555-4938
$
```

Now all you need to do is add the `funclib` file to your `gawk` command line whenever you need to use a function defined in the library.

## Working Through a Practical Example

The advanced `gawk` features come in handy if you have to handle data values in a data file, such as tabulating sales figures or calculating bowling scores. When you work with data files, the key is to first group related data records together and then perform any calculations required on the related data.

For example, let's work with a data file that contains the bowling scores from a game between two teams, each with two players:

```
$ cat scores.txt
Rich Blum,team1,100,115,95
Barbara Blum,team1,110,115,100
Christine Bresnahan,team2,120,115,118
Tim Bresnahan,team2,125,112,116
$
```

Each player has scores from three separate games in the data file, and each player is identified by a team name in the second column. Here's the shell script to sort out the data for each team and calculate the totals and averages:

```
$ cat bowling.sh
$!/bin/sh

for team in $(gawk -F, '{print $2}' scores.txt | uniq)
do
    gawk -v team=$team 'BEGIN{FS=","; total=0}
    {
        if ($2==team)
        {
            total += $3 + $4 + $5;
        }
    }
    END {
        avg = total / 6;
        print "Total for", team, "is", total, ",the average is",avg
    }' scores.txt
done
$
```

The first gawk statement inside the for loop filters out the team names in the data file and then uses the uniq function to return one value for each separate team name. The for loop then iterates for each separate team name.

The gawk statement inside the for loop is what's doing the calculations. For each data record it first determines if the team name matches the team value currently in the loop iteration. That's done by using the -v option in gawk, which allows us to pass a shell variable inside the gawk program. If the team name matches, the code keeps a running sum of the three scores in the data record, adding each data record's values, as long as that data record matches the team name.

At the end of each loop iteration, the gawk code displays the score totals as well as the average of the scores. The output should look like this:

```
$ ./bowling.sh
Total for team1 is 635, the average is 105.833
Total for team2 is 706, the average is 117.667
$
```

Now you have a handy shell script to calculate the results of all your bowling tournaments; you just need to plug the data from each player into the data text file and run the script!

## Summary

This chapter walked you through the more advanced features of the gawk programming language. Every programming language requires using variables, and gawk is no different. The gawk programming language includes some built-in variables that you can use to reference specific data field values and retrieve information about the number of data fields and records processed in the data file. You can also create your own variables for use in your scripts.

The gawk programming language also provides many of the standard structured commands you'd expect from a programming language. You can easily create fancy programs using if-then logic, while, do-while, and for loops. Each of these commands allows you to alter the flow of your gawk program script to iterate through data field values to create detailed data reports.

The printf command is a great tool to have if you need to customize your report output. It allows you to specify the exact format for displaying data from the gawk program script. You can easily create formatted reports, placing data elements in exactly the correct position.

Finally, this chapter discussed the many built-in functions available in the gawk programming language and showed you how to create your own functions. The gawk program contains many useful functions for handling mathematical features, such as standard square roots and logarithms, as well as trigonometric functions. There are also several string-related functions that make extracting substrings from larger strings a breeze.

You aren't limited to the built-in functions in the gawk program. If you're working on an application that uses lots of specialized algorithms, you can create your own functions to process the algorithms and then use those functions in your own code. You can also set up a library file containing all the functions you use in your gawk programs, saving you time and effort in all your coding.

The next chapter switches gears a little. It examines a few other shell environments you may run into in your Linux shell-scripting endeavors. Although the Bash shell is the most common shell used in Linux, it's not the only shell. It helps to know a little about some of the other shells available and how they differ from the Bash shell.

22

# Working with Alternative Shells

A lthough the Bash shell is the most widely used shell in Linux distributions, it's not the only one. Now that you've seen the ins and outs of the standard Linux Bash shell and what you can do with it, it's time to examine a few other shells available in the Linux world. This chapter describes two other popular shells that you may run into in your Linux journey and shows how they differ from the Bash shell.

## Considering the Dash Shell

The Debian Linux distribution, like many of its derivatives, such as Ubuntu, uses the Dash shell as a replacement for the standard Linux Bash shell. The Dash shell has had an interesting past. It's a direct descendant of the ash shell, a simple copy of the Bourne shell available on Unix systems (see Chapter 1, "Starting with Linux Shells"). Kenneth Almquist created a small-scale version of the Bourne shell for Unix systems and called it the Almquist shell, which was then shortened to ash. This original version of the ash shell was extremely small and fast but lacked many advanced features, such as command-line editing and history features, making it difficult to use as an interactive shell.

The NetBSD Unix operating system adopted the ash shell and still uses it today as the default shell. The NetBSD developers customized the ash shell by adding several new features, making it closer to the Bourne shell. The new features include command-line editing using both Emacs and vi editor commands, as well as a history command to recall previously entered commands. This version of the ash shell is also used by the FreeBSD operating system as the default login shell.

The Debian Linux distribution created its own version of the ash shell (called Debian ash, or *Dash*) for inclusion in its version of Linux. For the most part, Dash copies the features of the NetBSD version of the ash shell, providing the advanced command-line editing capabilities.

However, to add to the shell confusion, the Dash shell is not actually the default user shell in many Debian-based Linux distributions. Because of the popularity of the Bash shell in Linux, most Debian-based Linux distributions use the Bash shell as the normal login shell, and only use the Dash shell as a quick-start shell for the installation script to install the distribution files.

To check this out on your system, just take a peek at the /etc/passwd file entry for your user account; you can see the default interactive shell assigned to your account. Here's an example:

```
$ cat /etc/passwd | grep rich
rich:x:1000:1000:Rich,,,:/home/rich:/bin/bash
$
```

This Ubuntu system uses the Bash shell as the default for the interactive user shell. To check out the default system shell, use the ls command to look at the /bin directory for the sh file:

```
$ ls -al /bin/sh
lrwxrwxrwx 1 root root 4 Jul 21 08:10 /bin/sh -> dash
$
```

Sure enough, this Ubuntu system uses the Dash shell as the default system shell. This is where problems can come in.

As you saw in Chapter 11, "Basic Script Building," every shell script must start with a line that declares the shell used for the script. In our Bash shell scripts, we've been using the following:

```
#!/bin/bash
```

This tells the shell to use the shell program located at /bin/bash to execute the script. In the Unix world, the default shell was always located at /bin/sh. Many shell script programmers familiar with the Unix environment use this in their Linux shell scripts:

```
#!/bin/sh
```

On most Linux distributions, the /bin/sh file is a symbolic link (see Chapter 3, "Basic Bash Shell Commands") to the /bin/bash shell program. This allows you to easily port shell scripts designed for the Unix Bourne shell to the Linux environment without having to modify them.

But as you saw in the example, the Ubuntu Linux distribution links the /bin/sh file to the /bin/dash shell program. Because the Dash shell contains only a subset of the commands available in the original Bourne shell, this can (and often does) cause some shell scripts to not work properly.

The next section walks you through the basics of the Dash shell and how it differs from the Bash shell. This is especially important to know if you write Bash shell scripts that may need to be run in an Ubuntu environment.

# Looking at the Dash Shell Features

Although both the Bash shell and the Dash shell are modeled after the Bourne shell, they have some differences. This section walks you through the features found in the Dash shell to acquaint you with how it works before we dive into the shell scripting features.

## The Dash command-line parameters

The Dash shell uses command-line parameters to control its behavior. Table 23.1 lists these parameters and describes what each does.

**TABLE 23.1   The Dash Command-Line Parameters**

| Parameter | Description |
| --- | --- |
| -a | Export all variables assigned to the shell. |
| -c | Read commands from a specified command string. |
| -e | If not interactive, exit immediately if any untested command fails. |
| -f | Display pathname wildcard characters. |
| -n | If not interactive, read commands but don't execute them. |
| -u | Write an error message to STDERR when attempting to expand a variable that is not set. |
| -v | Write input to STDERR as it is read. |
| -x | Write each command to STDERR as it's executed. |
| -I | Ignore EOF characters from the input when in interactive mode. |
| -i | Force the shell to operate in interactive mode. |
| -m | Turn on job control (enabled by default in interactive mode). |
| -s | Read commands from STDIN (the default behavior if no file arguments are present). |
| -E | Enable the Emacs command-line editor. |
| -V | Enable the vi command-line editor. |

There are just a few additional command-line parameters that Debian added to the original ash shell command-line parameter list. The -E and -V command-line parameters enable the special command-line editing features of the Dash shell.

The -E command-line parameter allows you to use the Emacs editor commands for editing command-line text (see Chapter 10, "Working with Editors"). You can use all of the

Emacs commands for manipulating text on a single line by using the Ctrl and Alt key combinations.

The -V command-line parameter allows you to use the vi editor commands for editing command-line text (again, see Chapter 9, "Installing Software"). This feature allows you to switch between normal mode and vi editor mode on the command line by pressing the Esc key. When you're in vi editor mode, you can use all of the standard vi editor commands (such as x to delete a character and i to insert text). Once you are finished editing the command line, you must press the Esc key again to exit vi editor mode.

## The Dash environment variables

There are quite a few default environment variables that the Dash shell uses to track information, and you can create your own environment variables as well. This section describes the environment variables and how Dash handles them.

### Default environment variables

The Dash environment variables are very similar to the environment variables used in Bash (see Chapter 5, "Understanding the Shell"). This is not by accident. Remember that both the Dash and Bash shells are extensions of the Bourne shell, so they both incorporate many of its features. However, because of its goal of simplicity, the Dash shell contains significantly fewer environment variables than Bash. You need to take this fact into consideration when creating shell scripts in a Dash shell environment.

The Dash shell uses the set command to display environment variables:

```
$set
COLORTERM=''
DESKTOP_SESSION='default'
DISPLAY=':0.0'
DM_CONTROL='/var/run/xdmctl'
GS_LIB='/home/atest/.fonts'
HOME='/home/atest'
IFS='
'
KDEROOTHOME='/root/.kde'
KDE_FULL_SESSION='true'
KDE_MULTIHEAD='false'
KONSOLE_DCOP='DCOPRef(konsole-5293,konsole)'
KONSOLE_DCOP_SESSION='DCOPRef(konsole-5293,session-1)'
LANG='en_US'
LANGUAGE='en'
LC_ALL='en_US'
LOGNAME='atest'
OPTIND='1'
PATH='/usr/local/sbin:/usr/local/bin:/usr/sbin:/usr/bin:/sbin:/bin'
PPID='5293'
```

```
PS1='$ '
PS2='> '
PS4='+ '
PWD='/home/atest'
SESSION_MANAGER='local/testbox:/tmp/.ICE-unix/5051'
SHELL='/bin/dash'
SHLVL='1'
TERM='xterm'
USER='atest'
XCURSOR_THEME='default'
_='ash'
$
```

Your default Dash shell environment will most likely differ, since different Linux distributions assign different default environment variables at login.

### Positional parameters

In addition to the default environment variables, the Dash shell assigns special variables to any parameters defined in the command line. Here are the positional parameter variables available for use in the Dash shell:

- $0: The name of the shell script
- $n: The $n$th position parameter
- $*: A single value with the contents of all the parameters, separated by the first character in the IFS environment variable, or a space if IFS isn't defined
- $@: Expands to multiple arguments consisting of all the command-line parameters
- $#: The number of positional parameters
- $?: The exit status of the most recent command
- $-: The current option flags
- $$: The process ID (PID) of the current shell
- $!: The process ID (PID) of the most recent background command

All of the Dash positional parameters mimic the same positional parameters available in the Bash shell. You can use each of the positional parameters in your shell scripts just as you would in the Bash shell.

### User-defined environment variables

The Dash shell also allows you to set your own environment variables. As with Bash, you can define a new environment variable on the command line by using the assignment statement:

```
$ testing=10 ; export testing
$ echo $testing
10
$
```

23

Without the `export` command, user-defined environment variables are visible only in the current shell or process.

> **WARNING**
>
> There's one huge difference between Dash variables and Bash variables. The Dash shell doesn't support variable arrays. This small feature causes all sorts of problems for advanced shell script writers.

## The Dash built-in commands

Just as with the Bash shell, the Dash shell contains a set of built-in commands that it recognizes. You can use these commands directly from the command-line interface, or you can incorporate them in your shell scripts. Table 23.2 lists the Dash shell built-in commands.

**TABLE 23.2   The Dash Shell Built-in Commands**

| Command | Description |
| --- | --- |
| alias | Create an alias string to represent a text string. |
| bg | Continue the specified job in background mode. |
| cd | Switch to the specified directory. |
| echo | Display a text string and environment variables. |
| eval | Concatenate all arguments with a space. |
| exec | Replace the shell process with the specified command. |
| exit | Terminate the shell process. |
| export | Export the specified environment variable for use in all child shells. |
| fc | List, edit, or reexecute commands previously entered on the command line. |
| fg | Continue the specified job in foreground mode. |
| getopts | Obtain options and arguments from a list of parameters. |
| hash | Maintain and retrieve a hash table of recent commands and their locations. |
| pwd | Display the value of the current working directory. |
| read | Read a line from STDIN and assign the value to a variable. |
| readonly | Read a line from STDIN to a variable that can't be changed. |
| printf | Display text and variables using a formatted string. |
| set | List or set option flags and environment variables. |
| shift | Shift the positional parameters a specified number of times. |
| test | Evaluate an expression and return 0 if true or 1 if false. |
| times | Display the accumulated user and system times for the shell and all shell processes. |

| Command | Description |
|---------|-------------|
| trap | Parse and execute an action when the shell receives a specified signal. |
| type | Interpret the specified name and display the resolution (alias, built-in, command, keyword). |
| ulimit | Query or set limits on processes. |
| umask | Set the value of the default file and directory permissions. |
| unalias | Remove the specified alias. |
| unset | Remove the specified variable or option flag from the exported variables. |
| wait | Wait for the specified job to complete and return the exit status. |

You probably recognize all of these built-in commands from the Bash shell. The Dash shell supports many of the same built-in commands as the Bash shell. You'll notice that there aren't any commands for the command history file or the directory stack. The Dash shell doesn't support these features.

# Scripting in Dash

Unfortunately, the Dash shell doesn't recognize all of the scripting features of the Bash shell. Shell scripts written for the Bash environment often fail when run in the Dash shell, causing all sorts of grief for shell script programmers. This section describes the differences you'll need to be aware of to get your shell scripts to run properly in a Dash shell environment.

## Creating Dash scripts

You probably guessed by now that creating shell scripts for the Dash shell is pretty similar to creating shell scripts for the Bash shell. You should always specify which shell you want to use in your script to ensure that the script runs with the proper shell.

You do this on the first line of the shell:

```
#!/bin/dash
```

You can also specify a shell command-line parameter on this line, as was demonstrated earlier in "The Dash command-line parameters" section.

## Things that won't work

Unfortunately, because the Dash shell is only a subset of the Bourne shell features, there are a few things in Bash shell scripts that won't work in the Dash shell. These are often called Bash*isms*. This section is a quick summary of Bash shell features you may be used to using in your Bash shell scripts that won't work if you're in a Dash shell environment.

### Using arithmetic

Chapter 11 showed three ways to express a mathematical operation in the Bash shell script:

- Using the expr command: expr operation
- Using square brackets: $[ operation ]
- Using double parentheses: $(( operation ))

The Dash shell supports the expr command and the double parentheses method but doesn't support the square brackets method. This can be a problem if you have lots of mathematical operations that use the square brackets.

The proper format for performing mathematical operations in Dash shell scripts is to use the double parentheses method:

```
$ cat test1
#!/bin/dash
# testing mathematical operations

value1=10
value2=15

value3=$(( $value1 * $value2 ))
echo "The answer is $value3"
$ ./test1
The answer is 150
$
```

Now the shell can perform the calculation properly.

### The *test* command

While the Dash shell supports the test command, you must be careful how you use it. The Bash shell version of the test command is slightly different from the Dash shell version.

The Bash shell test command allows you to use the double equal sign (==) to test if two strings are equal. This is an add-on to accommodate programmers familiar with using this format in other programming languages.

However, the test command available in the Dash shell doesn't recognize the == symbol for text comparisons. Instead, it only recognizes the = symbol. If you use the == symbol in your Bash scripts, you'll need to change the text comparison symbol to just a single equal sign:

```
$ cat test2
#!/bin/dash
# testing the = comparison

test1=abcdef
test2=abcdef
```

```
if [ $test1 = $test2 ]
then
    echo "They're the same!"
else
    echo "They're different"
fi
$ ./test2
They're the same!
$
```

This little Bashism is responsible for many hours of frustration for shell programmers!

### The *function* command

Chapter 17, "Creating Functions," showed you how to define your own functions in your shell scripts. The Bash shell supports two methods for defining functions:

- Using the function statement
- Using the function name only

The Dash shell doesn't support the function statement. Instead, you must define a function using the function name followed by parentheses.

If you're writing shell scripts that may be used in the Dash environment, always define functions using the function name and not the function statement:

```
$ cat test3
#!/bin/dash
# testing functions

func1() {
    echo "This is an example of a function"
}

count=1
while [ $count -le 5 ]
do
    func1
    count=$(( $count + 1 ))
done
echo "This is the end of the loop"
func1
echo "This is the end of the script"
$ ./test3
This is an example of a function
This is an example of a function
This is an example of a function
This is an example of a function
This is an example of a function
This is the end of the loop
```

*(Continues)*

*(continued)*

```
This is an example of a function
This is the end of the script
$
```

Now the Dash shell recognized the function defined in the script just fine and was able to use it within the script.

# Exploring the zsh Shell

Another popular shell that you may run into is the Z shell (called zsh). The zsh shell is an open source Unix shell developed by Paul Falstad. It takes ideas from all of the existing shells and adds many unique features to create a full-blown advanced shell designed for programmers.

The following are some of the features that make the zsh shell unique:

- Improved shell option handling
- Shell compatibility modes
- Loadable modules

Of all these features, the loadable module is the most advanced feature in shell design. As you've seen in the Bash and Dash shells, each shell contains a set of built-in commands that are available without the need for external utility programs. The benefit of built-in commands is execution speed. The shell doesn't have to load a utility program into memory before running it; the built-in commands are already in the shell memory, ready to go.

The zsh shell provides a core set of built-in commands, plus the capability to add additional *command modules*. Each command module provides a set of additional built-in commands for specific circumstances, such as network support and advanced math functions. You can add only the modules you think you need for your specific situation.

This feature provides a great way either to limit the size of the zsh shell for situations that require a small shell size and few commands or to expand the number of available built-in commands for situations that require faster execution speeds.

> **TIP**
>
> The Z shell is usually not installed by default in most Linux distributions. However, due to its popularity, you can easily install it from the standard repository in just about every Linux distribution (see Chapter 9).

# Viewing Parts of the zsh Shell

This section walks you through the basics of the zsh shell, showing the built-in commands that are available (or that can be added by installing modules) as well as the command-line parameters and environment variables used by the zsh shell.

## Shell options

Most shells use command-line parameters to define the behavior of the shell. The zsh shell uses a few command-line parameters to define the operation of the shell, but mostly it uses *options* to customize the behavior of the shell. You can set shell options either on the command line or within the shell itself by using the set command.

Table 23.3 lists the command-line parameters available for the zsh shell.

**TABLE 23.3  The zsh Shell Command-Line Parameters**

| Parameter | Description |
| --- | --- |
| -c | Execute only the specified command and exit. |
| -i | Start as an interactive shell, providing a command-line interface prompt. |
| -s | Force the shell to read commands from STDIN. |
| -o | Specify command-line options. |

Although this may seem like a small set of command-line parameters, the -o parameter is somewhat misleading. It allows you to set shell options that define features within the shell. By far the zsh shell is the most customizable shell available. There are lots of features that you can alter for your shell environment. The different options fit into several general categories:

- **Changing directories:** Options that control how the cd and dirs commands handle directory changes
- **Completion:** Options that control command-completion features
- **Expansion and globbing:** Options that control file expansion in commands
- **History:** Options that control command history recall
- **Initialization:** Options that control how the shell handles variables and startup files when started
- **Input/Output:** Options that control command handling
- **Job Control:** Options that dictate how the shell handles and starts jobs
- **Prompting:** Options that define how the shell works with command-line prompts
- **Scripts and functions:** Options that control how the shell processes shell scripts and defines shell functions
- **Shell emulation:** Options that allow you to set the behavior of the zsh shell to mimic the behavior of other shell types
- **Shell state:** Options that define what type of shell to start
- **zle:** Options for controlling the zsh line editor (zle) feature
- **Option aliases:** Special options that can be used as aliases for other option names

23

With this many different categories of shell options, you can imagine just how many actual options the zsh shell supports.

## Built-in commands

The zsh shell is unique in that it allows you to expand the built-in commands available in the shell. This provides for a wealth of speedy utilities at your fingertips for a host of different applications.

This section describes the core built-in commands, along with the various modules available as of this writing.

### Core built-in commands

The core of the zsh shell contains the basic built-in commands you're used to seeing in other shells. Table 23.4 describes the built-in commands available for you.

**TABLE 23.4 The zsh Core Built-in Commands**

| Command | Description |
| --- | --- |
| alias | Define an alternate name for a command and arguments. |
| autoload | Preload a shell function into memory for quicker access. |
| bg | Execute a job in background mode. |
| bindkey | Bind keyboard combinations to commands. |
| builtin | Execute the specified built-in command instead of an executable file of the same name. |
| bye | The same as exit. |
| cd | Change the current working directory. |
| chdir | Change the current working directory. |
| command | Execute the specified command as an external file instead of a function or built-in command. |
| declare | Set the data type of a variable (same as typeset). |
| dirs | Display the contents of the directory stack. |
| disable | Temporarily disable the specified hash table elements. |
| disown | Remove the specified job from the job table. |
| echo | Display variables and text. |
| emulate | Set zsh to emulate another shell, such as the Bourne, Korn, or C shell. |
| enable | Enable the specified hash table elements. |
| eval | Execute the specified command and arguments in the current shell process. |
| exec | Execute the specified command and arguments replacing the current shell process. |

| Command | Description |
|---------|-------------|
| exit | Exit the shell with the specified exit status. If none specified, use the exit status of the last command. |
| export | Allow the specified environment variable names and values to be used in child shell processes. |
| false | Return an exit status of 1. |
| fc | Select a range of commands from the history list. |
| fg | Execute the specified job in foreground mode. |
| float | Set the specified variable for use as a floating-point variable. |
| functions | Set the specified name as a function. |
| getln | Read the next value in the buffer stack and place it in the specified variable. |
| getopts | Retrieve the next valid option in the command-line arguments and place it in the specified variable. |
| hash | Directly modify the contents of the command hash table. |
| history | List the commands contained in the history file. |
| integer | Set the specified variable for use as an integer value. |
| jobs | List information about the specified job, or all jobs assigned to the shell process. |
| kill | Send a signal (Default SIGTERM) to the specified process or job. |
| let | Evaluate a mathematical operation and assign the result to a variable. |
| limit | Set or display resource limits. |
| local | Set the data features for the specified variable. |
| log | Display all users currently logged in who are affected by the watch parameter. |
| logout | Same as exit, but only works when the shell is a login shell. |
| popd | Remove the next entry from the directory stack. |
| print | Display variables and text. |
| printf | Display variables and text using C-style format strings. |
| pushd | Change the current working directory, and put the previous directory in the directory stack. |
| pushln | Place the specified arguments into the editing buffer stack. |
| pwd | Display the full pathname of the current working directory. |
| read | Read a line and assign data fields to the specified variables using the IFS characters. |
| readonly | Assign a value to a variable that can't be changed. |
| rehash | Rebuild the command hash table. |

*(Continues)*

23

**TABLE 23.4** *(continued)*

| Command | Description |
| --- | --- |
| set | Set options or positional parameters for the shell. |
| setopt | Set the options for a shell. |
| shift | Read and delete the first positional parameter, and then shift the remaining ones down one position. |
| source | Find the specified file and copy its contents into the current location. |
| suspend | Suspend the execution of the shell until it receives a SIGCONT signal. |
| test | Return an exit status of 0 if the specified condition is TRUE. |
| times | Display the cumulative user and system times for the shell and processes that run in the shell. |
| trap | Block the specified signals from being processed by the shell, and execute the specified commands if the signals are received. |
| true | Return a zero exit status. |
| ttyctl | Lock and unlock the display. |
| type | Display how the specified command would be interpreted by the shell. |
| typeset | Set or display attributes of variables. |
| ulimit | Set or display resource limits of the shell or processes running in the shell. |
| umask | Set or display the default permissions for creating files and directories. |
| unalias | Remove the specified command alias. |
| unfunction | Remove the specified defined function. |
| unhash | Remove the specified command from the hash table. |
| unlimit | Remove the specified resource limit. |
| unset | Remove the specified variable attribute. |
| unsetopt | Remove the specified shell option. |
| wait | Wait for the specified job or process to complete. |
| whence | Display how the specified command would be interpreted by the shell. |
| where | Display the pathname of the specified command if found by the shell. |
| which | Display the pathname of the specified command using the csh shell-style output. |
| zcompile | Compile the specified function or script for faster autoloading. |
| zmodload | Perform operations on loadable zsh modules. |

The zsh shell is no slouch when it comes to providing built-in commands! You should recognize most of these commands from their Bash counterparts. The most important features of the zsh shell built-in commands are modules.

### Add-in modules

There's a long list of modules that provide additional built-in commands for the zsh shell, and the list continues to grow as resourceful programmers create new modules. Table 23.5 shows some popular modules.

**TABLE 23.5    The zsh Modules**

| Module | Description |
| --- | --- |
| zsh/datetime | Additional date and time commands and variables |
| zsh/files | Commands for basic file handling |
| zsh/mapfile | Access to external files via associative arrays |
| zsh/mathfunc | Additional scientific functions |
| zsh/pcre | The extended regular expression library |
| zsh/net/socket | Unix domain socket support |
| zsh/stat | Access to the stat system call to provide system statistics |
| zsh/system | Interface for various low-level system features |
| zsh/net/tcp | Access to TCP sockets |
| zsh/zftp | A specialized FTP client command |
| zsh/zselect | Block and return when file descriptors are ready |
| zsh/zutil | Various shell utilities |

The zsh shell modules cover a wide range of topics, from providing simple command-line editing features to advanced networking functions. The idea behind the zsh shell is to provide a basic minimum shell environment and let you add on the pieces you need to accomplish your programming job.

### Viewing, adding, and removing modules

The zmodload command is the interface to the zsh modules. You use this command to view, add, and remove modules from the zsh shell session.

Using the zmodload command without any command-line parameters displays the currently installed modules in your zsh shell:

```
% zmodload
zsh/complete
zsh/files
zsh/main
zsh/parameter
zsh/stat
zsh/terminfo
zsh/zle
zsh/zutil
%
```

23

Different zsh shell implementations include different modules by default. To add a new module, just specify the module name on the `zmodload` command line:

```
% zmodload zsh/net/tcp
%
```

Nothing indicates that the module loaded. You can perform another `zmodload` command, and the new module should appear in the list of installed modules. Once you load a module, the commands associated with the module are available as built-in commands.

> **Tip**
> It's a common practice to place `zmodload` commands in the `$HOME/.zshrc` startup file so that your favorite functions load automatically when the zsh shell starts.

# Scripting with zsh

The main purpose of the zsh shell was to provide an advanced programming environment for shell programmers. With that in mind, it's no surprise that the zsh shell offers many features that make shell scripting easier.

## Mathematical operations

As you would expect, the zsh shell allows you to perform mathematical functions with ease. In the past, the Korn shell has led the way in supporting mathematical operations by providing support for floating-point numbers. The zsh shell has full support for floating-point numbers in all of its mathematical operations!

### Performing calculations

The zsh shell supports two methods for performing mathematical operations:

- The `let` command
- Double parentheses

When you use the `let` command, you should enclose the operation in double quotation marks to allow for spaces:

```
% let value1=" 4 * 5.1 / 3.2 "
% echo $value1
6.3749999999999991
%
```

Notice that using floating-point numbers introduces a precision problem. To solve this, it's always a good idea to use the `printf` command and specify the decimal precision needed to correctly display the answer:

```
% printf "%6.3f\n" $value1
6.375
%
```

Now that's much better!

The second method is to use the double parentheses. This method incorporates two techniques for defining the mathematical operation:

```
% value1=$(( 4 * 5.1 ))
% (( value2 = 4 * 5.1 ))
% printf "%6.3f\n" $value1 $value2
20.400
20.400
%
```

Notice that you can place the double parentheses either around just the operation (preceded by a dollar sign) or around the entire assignment statement. Both methods produce the same results.

If you don't use the typeset command to declare the data type of a variable beforehand, the zsh shell attempts to automatically assign the data type. This can be dangerous when working with both integer and floating-point numbers. Take a look at this example:

```
% value=10
% value2=$(( $value1 / 3 ))
% echo $value2
3
%
```

Now that's probably not the answer you want to come out from the calculation. When you specify numbers without decimal places, the zsh shell interprets them as integer values and performs integer calculations. To ensure that the result is a floating-point number, you must specify the numbers with decimal places:

```
% value=10.
% value2=$(( $value1 / 3. ))
% echo $value2
3.3333333333333335
%
```

Now the result is in the floating-point format.

## Mathematical functions

With the zsh shell, built-in mathematical functions are either feast or famine. The default zsh shell doesn't include any special mathematical function. However, if you install the zsh/mathfunc module, you'll have more math functions than you'll most likely ever need:

```
% value1=$(( sqrt(9) ))
zsh: unknown function: sqrt
% zmodload zsh/mathfunc
% value1=$(( sqrt(9) ))
% echo $value1
3.
%
```

That was simple! Now you have an entire math library of functions at your fingertips.

> **TIP**
>
> Lots of mathematical functions are supported in zsh. For a complete listing of all the math functions that the `zsh/mathfunc` module provides, look at the manual page for `zshmodules`.

## Structured commands

The zsh shell provides the usual set of structured commands for your shell scripts:

- `if-then-else` statements
- `for` loops (including the C-style)
- `while` loops
- `until` loops
- `select` statements
- `case` statements

The zsh shell uses the same syntax for each of these structured commands that you're used to from the Bash shell. The zsh shell also includes a different structured command called `repeat`. The `repeat` command uses the following format:

```
repeat param
do
    commands
done
```

The `param` parameter must be a number or a mathematical operation that equates to a number. The `repeat` command then performs the specified commands that number of times:

```
% cat test4
#!/bin/zsh
# using the repeat command

value1=$(( 10 / 2 ))
repeat $value1
do
    echo "This is a test"
done
$ ./test4
This is a test
This is a test
This is a test
This is a test
This is a test
%
```

This command allows you to repeat sections of code for a set number of times based on a calculation.

## Functions

The zsh shell supports the creation of your own functions either by using the `function` command or by defining the function name followed by parentheses:

```
% function functest1 {
> echo "This is the test1 function"
}
% functest2() {
> echo "This is the test2 function"
}
% functest1
This is the test1 function
% functest2
This is the test2 function
%
```

As with Bash shell functions (see Chapter 17), you can define functions within your shell script and then either use global variables or pass parameters to your functions.

# Working Through a Practical Example

A very useful module in the zsh shell is the `tcp` module. It allows you to create a TCP socket, listen for incoming connections, and then establish a connection with a remote system. This is a great way to transfer data between shell applications!

To demonstrate, here's a quick example. First, you'll want to open a shell window to act as the server. Start zsh, load the `tcp` module, and then define a TCP socket number to listen for incoming connections. Do that with these commands:

```
server$ zsh
server% zmodload zsh/net/tcp
server% ztcp -l 8000
server% listen=$REPLY
server% ztcp -a $listen
```

The `ztcp` command with the -l option listens on the specified TCP port (8000 in this example) for incoming network connections. The special `$REPLY` variable contains the file handle associated with the network socket. The `ztcp` command with the -a option waits until an incoming connection is established.

Now open another shell window on your system (or you can even do this on another Linux system on the same network) to act as the client, and enter these commands to connect to the other shell:

```
client$ zsh
client% zmodload zsh/net/tcp
client% ztcp localhost 8000
client% remote=$REPLY
client%
```

When the connection is established, you'll see a zsh shell prompt appear on in the server shell window. You can then save the new connection handle on the server to a variable:

```
server% remote=$REPLY
```

Now you're ready to send and receive data! To send a message from one system to the other, use the print statement, sending the text to the $remote connection handle:

```
client% print 'This is a test message' >&$remote
client%
```

Then, in the other shell window use the read command to retrieve the data received on the $remote connection handle and the print command to display it:

```
server% read -r data <&$remote; print -r $data
This is a test message
server%
```

Congratulations, you've just sent data from one shell to another! You can use the same technique to send data in the opposite direction. When you're done, use the -c option to close out the appropriate handles on each system. For the server, use the following:

```
server% ztcp -c $listen
server% ztcp -c $remote
```

And for the client, use this:

```
client% ztcp -c $remote
```

Now you have networking features available for your shell scripts, taking them to a new level!

# Summary

This chapter discussed two popular alternative Linux shells that you may run into. The Dash shell was developed as part of the Debian Linux distribution and is mainly found in the Ubuntu Linux distribution. It's a smaller version of the Bourne shell, so it doesn't support as many features as the Bash shell, which can cause problems for script writing.

The zsh shell is often found in programming environments, since it provides lots of cool features for shell script programmers. It uses loadable modules to load separate code libraries, which make using advanced functions as easy as running command-line commands. Loadable modules are available for lots of different functions, from complex mathematical algorithms to network applications such as FTP and HTTP.

The next section of this book dives into some specific scripting applications you might encounter in the Linux environment. In the next chapter you'll see how to put your scripting skills to use to help with Linux system administration.

# Part IV

# Creating and Managing Practical Scripts

# Writing Simple Script Utilities

S hell scripts are all about automating tasks, making your life easier, and letting the system handle the boring jobs.

We've included several sample useful scripts throughout the book, and this chapter adds some additional ones. Learning how to write Bash script utilities will pay you back many times over. And the beauty of shell scripts is that they are easily customized for your particular needs — especially now that you are almost a Bash script-writing guru!

## Performing Backups

Whether you're responsible for a Linux system in a large corporate environment or a small mom-and-pop shop, or you're just using it at home, the loss of data can be catastrophic. To help prevent bad things from happening, it's always a good idea to perform regular *backups* (also called *archives*).

However, what's a good idea and what's practical are often two separate things. Trying to arrange a backup schedule to store important project files can be a challenge. This is another place where shell scripts often come to the rescue.

> **NOTE**
> There are several fancy GUI and/or web-based programs you can use to conduct and manage backups, such as Amanda, Bacula, and Duplicity. However, at their core are Bash shell commands. If don't want or need anything that flashy, or you'd like to understand the engine within these programs, this chapter section is for you.

If you desire to write your own backup scripts, we demonstrate two methods for using shell scripts so that you can archive specific data on your Linux systems.

## Backing up files daily

If you're using your Linux system to work on an important project, you can create a shell script that automatically takes backups of specific directories. Doing so helps avoid a time-consuming restore process from your main archive files. Designating these directories in a configuration file allows you to change them when a particular project changes and/or reuse the script's configuration file for a different project.

Here we show you how to create an automated shell script that can take backups of specified directories and keep a record of your data's past versions.

### Obtaining the required functions

The workhorse for backing up data in the Linux world is the `tar` command (Chapter 4, "More Bash Shell Commands"). The `tar` command is used to archive entire directories into a single file. Here's an example of creating an archive file of a working directory using the `tar` command:

```
$ ls -1 /home/christine/Project
addem.sh
AndBoolean.sh
askage.sh
[…]
update_file.sh
variable_content_eval.sh
$
$ tar -cf archive.tar /home/christine/Project/*.*
tar: Removing leading `/' from member names
tar: Removing leading `/' from hard link targets
$
$ ls -og archive.tar
-rw-rw-r-- 1 112640 Aug  6 13:33 archive.tar
$
```

Notice the `tar` command responds with a warning message that it's removing the leading forward slash from member names. This means that the pathname is converted from an absolute pathname to a relative pathname (Chapter 3, "Basic Bash Shell Commands"), which allows you to extract the `tar` archived files anywhere you want in your filesystem. You'll probably want to get rid of any output messages in your script. We can accomplish this by redirecting STDERR to the /dev/null file (Chapter 15, "Presenting Data"):

```
$ pwd
/home/christine
$
$ tar -cf archive.tar Project/*.* 2>/dev/null
$
$ ls -og archive.tar
-rw-rw-r-- 1 112640 Aug  6 13:38 archive.tar
$
```

Because a `tar` archive file can consume lots of disk space, it's a good idea to compress the file. You can do so by simply adding the `-z` option (Chapter 4). This compresses the `tar` archive file into a gzipped `tar` file, which is called a *tarball*. Be sure to use the proper file extensions to denote that the file is a tarball. Either `.tar.gz` or `.tgz` is fine. Here's an example of creating a tarball of a project directory:

```
$ tar -zcf archive.tgz Project/*.* 2>/dev/null
$
$ ls -hog archive.tgz
-rw-rw-r-- 1 11K Aug  6 13:40 archive.tgz
$
$ ls -hog archive.tar
-rw-rw-r-- 1 110K Aug  6 13:38 archive.tar
$
```

Notice that due to compression `archive.tgz` is about 99 KB smaller than the `archive.tar` file. Now we have the main component for our backup script completed.

Instead of modifying or creating a new archive script for every new directory of files we want to back up, we can use a configuration file. The configuration file should contain each directory's absolute directory reference we want included in the archive.

```
$ cat Files_To_Backup.txt
/home/christine/BackupScriptProject/
/home/christine/Downloads/
/home/christine/Does_not_exist/
/home/christine/PythonConversion/
$
```

Notice the `Does_not_exist` directory. We'll use that particular directory (which doesn't exist) to test a script feature later.

> **NOTE**
>
> If you're using a Linux distribution that includes a graphical desktop, be careful about backing up your entire $HOME directory. Although this may be tempting, the $HOME directory contains lots of configuration and temporary files related to the graphical desktop. It creates a much larger archive file than you probably intended. Pick a subdirectory (or two) in which to store your working files, and use that subdirectory in your archive configuration file.

**24**

To have our script read through the configuration file and add the names of each directory to an archive list, we'll use the simple `read` command (Chapter 14, "Handling User Input"). But instead of using the `cat` command piped into a `while` loop (Chapter 13, "More Structured Commands"), this script redirects standard input (STDIN) using the `exec` command (see Chapter 15). Here's how it looks in the script:

```
exec 0 < $config_file

read file_name
```

Notice that a variable is used for the archive configuration file, config_file. Each record is read in from the configuration file. As long as the read command finds a new configuration file record to read, it returns an exit value of 0 for success in the ? variable (Chapter 11, "Basic Script Building"). You can use this as a test in a while loop in order to read all the records from the configuration file:

```
while [ $? -eq 0 ]
do
[...]
read file_name
done
```

When the read command hits the end of the configuration file, it returns a non-zero status in the ? variable. At that point, the while loop is exited.

In the while loop, two things need to happen. First, we must add the directory name to our archive list. Even more important is to check if that directory even exists! It would be very easy to remove a directory from the filesystem and forget to update the archive configuration file. We can check a directory's existence using a simple if statement (see Chapter 12, "Using Structured Commands"). If the directory does exist, it is added to the list of directories to archive, file_list. Otherwise, a warning message is issued. Here is what this if statement looks like:

```
if [ -f $file_name -o -d $file_name ]
then
        file_list="$file_list $file_name"
else
        echo
        echo "$file_name, does not exist."
        echo "Obviously, I will not include it in this archive."
        echo "It is listed on line $file_no of the config file."
        echo "Continuing to build archive list..."
        echo
fi
#
file_no=$[$file_no + 1]
```

Because a record in our archive configuration file can be a filename or a directory, the if statement tests for the existence of both, using the -f and the -d options. The or option, -o, allows for either the file's or the directory's existence test to return a non-zero status for the entire if statement to be treated as true.

To provide a little extra help in tracking down nonexistent directories and files, the variable file_no is added. Thus, the script can tell you exactly what line number in the archive configuration file contains the incorrect or missing file or directory.

### Creating a daily archive location

If you are just backing up a few files, it's fine to keep the archive in your personal directory. However, if several directories are backed up, it is best to create a central repository archive directory:

```
$ sudo mkdir /archive
  [sudo] password for christine:
$
$ ls -ld /archive
drwxr-xr-x 2 root root 4096 Aug  6 14:20 /archive
$
```

After you have your central repository archive directory created, you need to grant access to it for certain users. If you do not do this, trying to create files in this directory fails, as shown here:

```
$ mv Files_To_Backup.txt /archive/
mv: cannot move 'Files_To_Backup.txt' to
'/archive/Files_To_Backup.txt': Permission denied
$
```

You could grant the users needing to create files in this directory permission via sudo or create a user group. In this case, a special user group is created, Archivers:

```
$ sudo groupadd Archivers
$
$ sudo chgrp Archivers /archive
$
$ ls -ld /archive
drwxr-xr-x 2 root Archivers 4096 Aug  6 14:20 /archive
$
$ sudo usermod -aG Archivers christine
$
$ sudo chmod 775 /archive
$
$ ls -ld /archive
drwxrwxr-x 2 root Archivers 4096 Aug  6 14:20 /archive
$
```

After a user has been added to the Archivers group, the user must log out and log back in for the group membership to take effect. Now files can be created by this group's members without the use of super user privileges:

```
$ mv Files_To_Backup.txt /archive/
$
$ ls /archive/
Files_To_Backup.txt
$
```

24

Keep in mind that all Archivers group members can add and delete files from this directory. It may be best to add the sticky bit (Chapter 7, "Understanding Linux File Permissions") to the directory, in order to keep group members from deleting each other's tarballs. To keep things organized, consider creating subdirectories within the /archive directory for each user.

You should now have enough information to start building the script. The next section walks you through creating this daily project backup script.

### Creating a daily backup script

The Daily_Archive.sh script automatically creates an archive to a designated location, using the current date to uniquely identify the file. Here's the code for that portion of the script:

```
today=$(date +%y%m%d)
#
# Set Archive File Name
#
backupFile=archive$today.tar.gz
#
# Set Configuration and Destination File
#
config_file=/archive/Files_To_Backup
destination=/archive/$backupFile
#
```

The destination variable appends the full pathname for the archived file. The config_ file variable points to the archive configuration file containing the directories to be archived. These both are easily changed to alternate directories and files if needed.

The Daily_Archive.sh script, all put together, now looks like this:

```
$ cat Daily_Archive.sh
#!/bin/bash
#
# Daily_Archive - Archive designated files & directories
##########################################################
#
# Gather Current Date
#
today=$(date +%y%m%d)
#
# Set Archive File Name
#
backupFile=archive$today.tar.gz
#
# Set Configuration and Destination File
#
config_file=/archive/Files_To_Backup.txt
```

```
destination=/archive/$backupfile
#
######### Main Script #########################
#
# Check Backup Config file exists
#
if [ -f $config_file ] # Make sure the config file still exists.
then            # If it exists, do nothing but continue on.
     echo
else            # If it doesn't exist, issue error & exit script.
     echo
     echo "$config_file does not exist."
     echo "Backup not completed due to missing Configuration File"
     echo
     exit
fi
#
# Build the names of all the files to backup
#
file_no=1             # Start on Line 1 of Config File.
exec 0< $config_file  # Redirect Std Input to name of Config File
#
read file_name        # Read 1st record
#
while [ $? -eq 0 ]    # Create list of files to backup.
do
        # Make sure the file or directory exists.
     if [ -f $file_name -o -d $file_name ]
     then
          # If file exists, add its name to the list.
          file_list="$file_list $file_name"
     else
          # If file doesn't exist, issue warning
          echo
          echo "$file_name, does not exist."
          echo "Obviously, I will not include it in this archive."
          echo "It is listed on line $file_no of the config file."
          echo "Continuing to build archive list..."
          echo
     fi
#
     file_no=$[$file_no + 1]  # Increase Line/File number by one.
     read file_name           # Read next record.
done
#
######################################
#
# Backup the files and Compress Archive
#
```

*(Continues)*

*(continued)*

```
    echo "Starting archive..."
    echo
    #
    tar -czf $destination $file_list 2> /dev/null
    #
    echo "Archive completed"
    echo "Resulting archive file is: $destination"
    echo
    #
    exit
    $
```

Hopefully, you saw a few potential needed improvements for this script. For example, what if there are *no* existing files or directories to back up and $file_list is empty? You can use an if-then statement to check for that problem. How about using the -v option on the tar command and redirecting STDOUT to create a report or log? You can make this script as rigorous as you need.

### Running the daily archive script

Before you attempt to test the script, remember that we need to change permissions on the script file (Chapter 11). The file's owner must be given execute (x) privilege before the script can be run:

```
$ ls -og Daily_Archive.sh
-rw-r--r-- 1 2039 Aug  6 14:13 Daily_Archive.sh
$
$ chmod u+x Daily_Archive.sh
$
$ ls -og Daily_Archive.sh
-rwxr--r-- 1 2039 Aug  6 14:13 Daily_Archive.sh
$
```

Testing the Daily_Archive.sh script is straightforward:

```
$ ./Daily_Archive.sh


/home/christine/Does_not_exist/, does not exist.
Obviously, I will not include it in this archive.
It is listed on line 3 of the config file.
Continuing to build archive list...

Starting archive...

Archive completed
Resulting archive file is: /archive/archive200806.tar.gz

$
```

You can see that the script caught one directory that does not exist, /home/christine/ Does_not_exist. It lets you know what line number in the configuration file this erroneous directory is on and continues making a list and archiving the data.

Our special project data (and other files) is now safely archived in a tarball file:

```
$ ls /archive/
archive200806.tar.gz  Files_To_Backup.txt
$
```

Since this is an important script, consider using anacron (Chapter 16, "Script Control") so that it is run on a daily basis without you needing to remember to launch the script.

> **TIP**
>
> Keep in mind that tar is one way to perform backups on your system using Bash shell commands. There are several other utilities (or combinations of commands) that may better meet your needs, such as rsync. To see various utility names that may assist in this backup endeavor, type man -k archive and then man -k copy at the command-line prompt.

## Creating an hourly archive script

If you are in a high-volume production environment where files are changing rapidly, a daily archive might not meet your needs. If you want to increase the archiving frequency to hourly, you need to take another item into consideration.

When you're backing up files hourly and trying to use the date command to time stamp each tarball, things can get ugly rather quickly. Sifting through a directory of tarballs with filenames looking like this is tedious:

```
archive200806110233.tar.gz
```

Instead of placing all the archive files in the same folder, you can create a directory hierarchy for your archived files. Figure 24.1 demonstrates this principle.

The archive directory contains directories for each month of the year, using the month number as the directory name. Each month's directory in turn contains folders for each day of the month (using the day's numerical value as the directory name). This allows you to just time stamp the individual tarballs and place them in the appropriate directory for the day and month.

First, the new directory /archive/hourly must be created, along with the appropriate permissions set upon it. Remember from early in this chapter that members of the Archivers group are granted permission to create archives in this directory area. Thus, the newly created directory must have its primary group and group permissions changed:

24

**FIGURE 24.1**

Creating an archive directory hierarchy

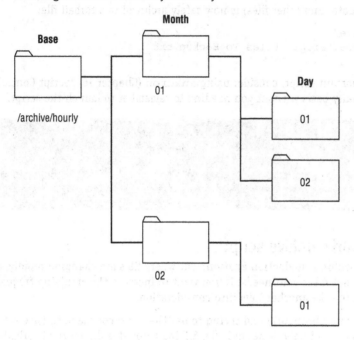

```
$ sudo mkdir /archive/hourly
[sudo] password for christine:
$
$ sudo chgrp Archivers /archive/hourly
$
$ ls -ogd /archive/hourly/
drwxr-xr-x 2 4096 Aug  7 15:56 /archive/hourly/
$
$ sudo chmod 775 /archive/hourly
$
$ ls -ogd /archive/hourly/
drwxrwxr-x 2 4096 Aug  7 15:56 /archive/hourly/
$
```

After the new directory is set up, the Files_To_Backup configuration file for the hourly archives can be moved to the new directory:

```
$ cat Files_To_Backup.txt
/usr/local/Production/Machine_Errors/
/home/Development/Simulation_Logs/
$
$ mv Files_To_Backup.txt /archive/hourly/
$
```

Now, there is a new challenge to solve. The script must create the individual month and day directories automatically. However, if these directories already exist and the script tries to create them, an error is generated. This is not a desirable outcome!

If you look at the command-line options for the mkdir command (Chapter 3), you'll find the -p command-line option. This option allows you to create directories and subdirectories in a single command. Plus, the added benefit is that it doesn't produce an error message if the directory already exists. Perfect fit for what is needed in the script!

We're now ready to create the Hourly_Archive.sh script. Here is the top half of the script:

```
$ cat Hourly_Archive.sh
#!/bin/bash
#
# Hourly_Archive - Every hour create an archive
###############################################
#
# Set Configuration File
#
config_file=/archive/hourly/Files_To_Backup.txt
#
# Set Base Archive Destination Location
#
basedest=/archive/hourly
#
# Gather Current Day, Month & Time
#
day=$(DATE +%D)
month=$(DATE +%M)
time=$(DATE +%K%M)
#
# Create Archive Destination Directory
#
mkdir -p $basedest/$month/$day
#
# Build Archive Destination File Name
#
destination=$basedest/$month/$day/archive$time.tar.gz
#
######### Main Script #####################
[…]
```

When Hourly_Archive.sh reaches the "Main Script" section, the rest of the code is an exact duplicate of what is in the Daily_Archive.sh script. Lots of the work was already done!

Hourly_Archive.sh retrieves the day and month values from the date command, along with the time stamp used to uniquely identify the archive file. It then uses that information to create the archive directory for the day (or to silently continue if it already exists). Finally, the script uses the tar command to create the archive and compress it into a tarball.

### Running the hourly archive script

As with the Daily_Archive.sh script, it's a good idea to test the Hourly_Archive.sh script before putting it in the cron table. But first the permissions need modification. Also, it's a good idea to get the current hour and minute via the date command before testing the script. Having this information allows verification of final archive's filename for correctness:

```
$ chmod u+x Hourly_Archive.sh
$
$ date +%k%M
1610
$
$ ./Hourly_Archive.sh

Starting archive...

Archive completed
Resulting archive file is:
/archive/hourly/08/07/archive1610.tar.gz

$
$ ls /archive/hourly/08/07/
/archive/hourly/08/07/archive1610.tar.gz
$
```

The script worked fine the first time, creating the appropriate month and day directories, and then creating the properly named archive file. Notice that the archive file has the appropriate hour (16) and minute (10) in its name, archive1610.tar.gz.

> **TIP**
>
> If you run the Hourly_Archive.sh script during the day, when the hour is in single digits, your archive file's name will have only three digits. For example, if you run the script at 1:15 a.m., the archive file's name is archive115.tar.gz. If you prefer to always have four digits in the archive filename, modify the script line, TIME=$(date +%k%M) to TIME=$(date +%k0%M). By adding a zero (0) after the %k, any single-digit hours are padded to two digits with a leading zero. Thus, archive115.tar.gz is instead named archive0115.tar.gz.

Just to test things out, the script is run a second time to see if it has a problem with the existing directory, /archive/hourly/08/07/:

```
$ date +%k%M
1615
$
$ ./Hourly_Archive.sh

Starting archive...

Archive completed
Resulting archive file is:
/archive/hourly/08/07/archive1615.tar.gz

$
$ ls /archive/hourly/08/07/
archive1610.tar.gz  archive1615.tar.gz
$
```

No problems with the existing directory! The script again ran fine and created a second archive file. It's now ready for the cron table.

# Managing Account Deletion

Managing local user accounts is much more than just adding, modifying, and deleting accounts. You must also consider security issues, the need to preserve work, and the accurate deletion of accounts. This can be a time-consuming task. Here is another instance when writing script utilities is a real time saver!

## Obtaining the required functions

Deleting a local account is the more complicated task of accounts management, because at least four separate actions are required:

1. Obtain the correct user account name to delete.
2. Kill any processes currently running on the system that belong to the account.
3. Determine all files on the system belonging to the account.
4. Remove the user account.

It's easy to miss a step. The shell script utility in this section helps you (or your system admin interns) avoid making such mistakes.

### Getting the correct account name

The first step in the account deletion process is the most important: obtaining the correct user account name to delete. Because this is an interactive script, we use the read command (Chapter 14) to obtain the account name. Since the script user may get interrupted and leave the question hanging, we added the -t option on the read command and timeout after giving the script user 60 seconds to answer the question:

```
echo "Please enter the username of the user "
echo -e "account you wish to delete from system: \c"
read -t 60 answer
```

Because interruptions are part of life, it's best to give users three chances to answer the question. This is accomplished by using a while loop (Chapter 13) with the -z option, to test whether the answer variable is empty. The answer variable is empty when the script first enters the while loop on purpose. The question to fill the answer variable is at the end of the loop:

```
while [ -z "$answer" ]
do
[...]
echo "Please enter the username of the user "
echo -e "account you wish to delete from system: \c"
read -t 60 answer
done
```

A way to communicate with the script user is needed when the first question timeout occurs, when there is another chance to answer the question. The case statement (Chapter 12) is the structured command that works perfectly here. Using an incremented variable (ask_count), different messages are set up to communicate with the script user. The code for this section looks like this:

```
case $ask_count in
2)
    echo
    echo "Please answer the question."
    echo
;;
3)
    echo
    echo "One last try...please answer the question."
    echo
;;
4)
    echo
    echo "Since you refuse to answer the question..."
    echo "exiting program."
    echo
    #
    exit
;;
esac
#
```

Now the script has all the structure it needs to ask the user what account to delete. There are several more questions in this script to ask the user, and asking just that one question was lots of code! Therefore, we'll turn this piece of code into a function (Chapter 17, "Creating Functions") in order to use it in multiple locations within the Delete_User. sh script.

### Creating a function to get the correct account name

The first thing we did was to declare the function's name, get_answer. Next, we clear out any previous answers to questions the script user gave, using the unset command (Chapter 6, "Using Linux Environment Variables"). The code to do these two items looks like this:

```
function get_answer {
#
unset answer
```

The other original code item we need to change is the question to the script user. The script doesn't ask the same question each time, so two new variables are created, line1 and line2, to handle question lines:

```
echo $line1
echo -e $line2" \c"
```

However, not every question has two lines to display. Some have only one line. An if statement (Chapter 12) assists with this problem. The function tests if line2 is empty and only uses line1 if it is:

```
if [ -n "$line2" ]
then
     echo $line1
     echo -e $line2" \c"
else
     echo -e $line1" \c"
fi
```

Finally, the function needs to clean up after itself by clearing out the line1 and line2 variables. The function now looks like this:

```
function get_answer {
#
unset answer
$ask_count=0
#
while [ -z "$answer" ]
do
     ask_count=$[ $ask_count + 1 ]
#
     case $ask_count in
     2)
```

*(Continues)*

```
(continued)
                        echo
        [...]
              esac
    #
              echo
              if [ -n "$line2" ]
              then                      #Print 2 lines
                    echo $line1
                    echo -e $line2" \c"
              else                        #Print 1 line
                    echo -e $line1" \c"
              fi
    #
              read -t 60 answer
    done
    #
    unset line1
    unset line2
    #
    }   #End of get_answer function
```

To ask the script user what account to delete, a few variables are set and the `get_answer` function is called. Using this function makes the script code cleaner:

```
line1="Please enter the username of the user "
line2="account you wish to delete from system:"
get_answer
user_account=$answer
```

### Verifying the entered account name

Because of potential typographical errors, the user account name entered needs verification. Doing so is easy because the code is already in place to handle asking questions:

```
line1="Is $user_account the user account "
line2="you wish to delete from the system? [y/n]"
get_answer
```

After the question is asked, the script must process the answer. The variable `answer` again carries the script user's answer to the question. If the user answers "yes," the correct user account to delete has been entered and the script can continue. A case statement (see Chapter 12) is used to process the answer, and it is coded in a way to check for the multiple ways the answer "yes" can be entered.

```
case $answer in
y|Y|YES|yes|Yes|yEs|yeS|YEs|yES )
#
;;
*)
        echo
```

```
        echo "Because the account, $user_account, is not "
        echo "the one you wish to delete, we are leaving the
script..."
        echo
        exit
    ;;
    esac
```

That's tedious! Since we plan on only continuing the processing if the user answers a variation of "yes" to our question, we can simplify the case statement by stripping down the answer variable. To accomplish this task, we employ command substitution (Chapter 11), a pipe, and the cut command, which will allow us to reduce the characters in the answer variable. Specifically, the cut command's -c1 option strips everything from answer but the first character:

```
answer=$(echo $answer | cut -c1)
```

Now that we have to deal with only the first character, our case statement is more compact:

```
case $answer in
y|Y)
#
    ;;
[...]
esac
```

**24**

In different locations, this script handles multiple yes/no answers from the user. Thus, again, it makes sense to create a function to handle this task, and only a few changes are made to the preceding code: the function's name is declared and the variables exit_line1 and exit_line2 are added to the case statement. These changes, along with some variable cleanup at the end, result in the process_answer function:

```
function process_answer {
#
answer=$(echo $answer | cut -c1)
#
case $answer in
y|Y)
    ;;
*)
```

*(Continues)*

*(continued)*

```
            echo
            echo $exit_line1
            echo $exit_line2
            echo
            exit
    ;;
    esac
    #
    unset exit_line1
    unset exit_line2
    #
    } #End of process_answer function
```

A simple function call now processes the answer:

```
exit_line1="Because the account, $user_account, is not "
exit_line2="the one you wish to delete, we are leaving the script..."
process_answer
```

### Determining whether the account exists

The user has given us the name of the account to delete and has verified it. Now is a good time to double-check that the user account really exists on the system. Also, just to be safe, we'll show the full account record to the script user to check one more time that this is the account to delete. To accomplish these items, a variable, user_account_record, is set to the outcome of a grep (Chapter 4) search for the account through the /etc/ passwd file. The -w option allows an exact word match for this particular user account:

```
user_account_record=$(cat /etc/passwd | grep -w $user_account)
```

If no user account record is found in /etc/passwd, the account has already been deleted or never existed in the first place. In either case, the script user needs notification of this situation and the script exited. The exit status of the grep command helps here. If the account record is not found, the ? variable is set to 1:

```
if [ $? -eq 1 ]
then
    echo
    echo "Account, $user_account, not found. "
    echo "Leaving the script..."
    echo
    exit
fi
```

If the record was found, we still need to verify with the script user that this is the correct account. Here is where all the work to set up the functions really pays off! We just set the proper variables and call the functions:

```
echo "I found this record:"
echo $user_account_record
```

```
echo
#
line1="Is this the correct User Account? [y/n]"
get_answer
#
exit_line1="Because the account, $user_account, is not"
exit_line2="the one you wish to delete, we are leaving the script..."
process_answer
```

### Removing any account processes

So far, the script has obtained and verified the correct name of the user account to be deleted. In order to remove the user account from the system, the account cannot own any processes currently running. Thus, the next step is to find and kill off those processes. This is going to get a little complicated!

Finding the user processes is the easy part. Here the script can use the ps command (Chapter 4) and the -u option to locate any running processes owned by the account. By redirecting the output to /dev/null, the user doesn't see any display. This is handy, because if there are no processes, the ps command shows only a header, which may confuse the script user:

```
ps -u $user_account >/dev/null
```

The ps command's exit status and a case structure are used to determine the next step to take:

```
case $? in
1)    # No processes running for this User Account
      #
      echo "There are no processes for this account currently running."
      echo
;;
0)    # Processes running for this User Account.
      # Ask Script User if wants us to kill the processes.
      #
      echo "$user_account has the following process(es) running:"
      ps -u $user_account
      #
      line1="Would you like me to kill the process(es)? [y/n]"
      get_answer
      #
[...]
;;
esac
```

If the ps command's exit status returns a 1, there are no processes running on the system that belong to the user account. However, if the exit status returns a 0, processes owned by this account are running on the system. In this case, the script needs to ask the script user if they would like to have these processes killed. This task can be accomplished by using the get_answer function.

You might think that the next action the script does is to call the process_answer function. Unfortunately, the next item is too complicated for process_answer. Thus, another case statement is embedded to process the script user's answer. The first part of the case statement looks very similar to the process_answer function:

```
answer=$(echo $answer | cut -c1)
#
case $answer in
y|Y)      # If user answers "yes",
          # kill User Account processes.
[…]
;;
*)    # If user answers anything but "yes", do not kill.
      echo
      echo "Will not kill the process(es)"
      echo
#
;;
esac
```

As you can see, there is nothing interesting in the case statement itself. However, things get intriguing within the "yes" section of the case statement, where the user account processes are killed. To build the command necessary to kill off one or more processes, three commands are needed. The first command is the ps command again. It is needed to gather up the process IDs (PIDs) of the currently running user account processes. The necessary ps command is assigned to the variable, command_1:

```
command_1="ps -u $user_account --no-heading"
```

The second command strips off just the PIDs. This simple gawk command (Chapter 19, "Introducing *sed* and *gawk*") strips off the first field from the ps command's output, which happens to be the PIDs:

```
gawk '{print $1}'
```

The third command, xargs, has not yet been introduced in this book. The xargs command builds and executes commands from standard input, STDIN (Chapter 15). It is a great command to use at the end of a pipe, building and executing commands from each STDIN item produced. The xargs command is actually killing off each process via its PID using the absolute directory reference of the kill command and sudo:

```
command_3="xargs -d \\n /usr/bin/sudo /bin/kill -9"
```

The xargs command is assigned to the variable command _ 3. It uses the -d option to denote what is considered a delimiter. In other words, because the xargs command can accept multiple items as input, what separates one item from another item? In this case, \n (newline) is used to set the delimiter. Thus, when each PID is sent to xargs, it treats the

PID as a separate item to process. Because the xargs command is being assigned to a variable, the backslash (\) in the \n must be escaped with an additional backslash (\).

Notice that xargs uses the full pathname of the commands it is using on each PID. Both the sudo and kill (Chapter 4) commands are used to kill any of the user account's running processes. Also notice that the kill signal -9 is used.

> **NOTE**
>
> Modern implementations of the xargs command *do not* require the absolute directory reference of commands, such as sudo and kill. However, Linux distributions that are only a few years older may have the earlier version of the xargs command, so we kept the absolute directory references.

All three commands are hooked together via a pipe. The ps command produces a list of the user's running processes, which include the PID of each process. The ps command passes its standard output (STDOUT) as STDIN to the gawk command. The gawk command, in turn, strips off only the PIDs from the ps command's STDOUT (Chapter 15). The xargs command takes each PID the gawk command produces as STDIN. It creates and executes the kill command for each PID to kill all the user's running processes. The entire command pipe looks like this:

```
$command_1 | gawk '{print $1}' | $command_3
```

Thus, the complete case statement for killing off any of the user account's running processes is as follows:

```
case $answer in
y|Y)    # If user answers "yes",
        # kill User Account processes.
        #
        echo
        echo "Killing off process(es)..."
        #
        # List user process running code in command_1
        command_1="ps -u $user_account --no-heading"
        #
        # Create command_3 to kill processes in variable
        command_3="xargs -d \\n /usr/bin/sudo /bin/kill -9"
        #
        # Kill processes via piping commands together
        $command_1 | gawk '{print $1}' | $command_3
        #
        echo
        echo "Process(es) killed."
;;
*)      #If user answers anything but "yes", do not kill.
        echo
        echo "Will not kill process(es)."
;;
esac
```

24

By far, this is the most complicated piece of the script! However, now with any user account–owned processes gone, the script can move on to the next step: finding all the user account's files.

### Finding account files

When a user account is deleted from the system, it is a good practice to back up all the files that belonged to that account. Along with that practice, it is also important to remove the files or assign their ownership to another account. If the account you delete has a User ID of 1003, and you don't remove or reassign those files, then the next account that is created with a User ID of 1003 owns those files! You can see the security disasters that can occur in this scenario.

The `Delete_User.sh` script doesn't do all that for you; instead, it creates a report that can be slightly modified and used in a backup script as an archive configuration file. Also, you can use the report to help you remove or reassign the files.

To find the user's files, we use another new-to-this-book command: the `find` command. In this case, the `find` command searches the entire virtual directory (/) with the `-user` option, which pinpoints any files owned by the `user_account`. The command looks like the following:

```
find / -user $user_account > $report_file
```

That was pretty simple compared to dealing with the user account processes. It gets even easier in the next step of the `Delete_User.sh` script: actually removing the user account.

### Removing the account

A little caution is always a good idea when removing a user account from the system. Therefore, we ask *one* more time if the script user really wants to remove the account:

```
line1="Remove $user_account's account from system? [y/n]"
get_answer
#
exit_line1="Since you do not wish to remove the user account,"
exit_line2="$user_account at this time, exiting the script..."
process_answer
```

Finally, we get to the main purpose of our script: actually removing the user account from the system. Here the `userdel` command (Chapter 7) is used:

```
userdel $user_account
```

Now that we have all the script's pieces, we are ready to put them together into a whole, useful script utility.

## Creating the script

The Delete_User.sh script is highly interactive with the script's user. Therefore, it is important to include lots of verbiage to keep the script user informed about what is going on during the script's execution.

At the top of the script, the two functions get_answer and process_answer are declared. The script then goes to the four steps of removing the user account:

1. Obtaining and confirming the user account name

2. Finding and killing any user processes

3. Creating a report of all files owned by the user account

4. Removing the user account

Here's the entire Delete_User.sh script:

```
$ cat Delete_User.sh
#!/bin/bash
#
#Delete_User - Automates the 4 steps to remove an account
#
###############################################################
# Define Functions
#
###################################################
function get_answer {
#
unset answer
ask_count=0
#
while [ -z "$answer" ]    #While no answer is given, keep asking.
do
      ask_count=$[ $ask_count + 1 ]
#
      case $ask_count in   #If user gives no answer in time allotted
      2)
          echo
          echo "Please answer the question."
          echo
      ;;
      3)
          echo
          echo "One last try...please answer the question."
          echo
      ;;
      4)
```

*(Continues)*

**24**

*(continued)*

```
            echo
            echo "Since you refuse to answer the question..."
            echo "exiting program."
            echo
            #
            exit
    ;;
    esac
#
    if [ -n "$line2" ]
    then                    #Print 2 lines
            echo $line1
            echo -e $line2" \c"
    else                            #Print 1 line
            echo -e $line1" \c"
    fi
#
#    Allow 60 seconds to answer before time-out
    read -t 60 answer
done
# Do a little variable clean-up
unset line1
unset line2
#
}  #End of get_answer function
#
#######################################################
function process_answer {
#
answer=$(echo $answer | cut -c1)
#
case $answer in
y|Y)
# If user answers "yes", do nothing.
;;
*)
# If user answers anything but "yes", exit script
        echo
        echo $exit_line1
        echo $exit_line2
        echo
        exit
;;
esac
#
# Do a little variable clean-up
#
unset exit_line1
unset exit_line2
```

```
#
} #End of process_answer function
#
###############################################
# End of Function Definitions
#
############## Main Script ###################
# Get name of User Account to check
#
echo "Step #1 - Determine User Account name to Delete "
echo
line1="Please enter the username of the user "
line2="account you wish to delete from system:"
get_answer
user_account=$answer
#
# Double check with script user that this is the correct User Account
#
line1="Is $user_account the user account "
line2="you wish to delete from the system? [y/n]"
get_answer
#
# Call process_answer funtion:
#     if user answers anything but "yes", exit script
#
exit_line1="Because the account, $user_account, is not "
exit_line1="the one you wish to delete, we are leaving the script..."
process_answer
#
################################################################
# Check that user_account is really an account on the system
#
user_account_record=$(cat /etc/passwd | grep -w $user_account)
#
if [ $? -eq 1 ]          # If the account is not found, exit script
then
     echo
     echo "Account, $user_account, not found. "
     echo "Leaving the script..."
     echo
     exit
fi
#
echo
echo "I found this record:"
echo $user_account_record
echo
#
line1="Is this the correct User Account? [y/n]"
```

24

*(Continues)*

*(continued)*

```
get_answer
#
#
# Call process_answer function:
#       if user answers anything but "yes", exit script
#
exit_line1="Because the account, $user_account, is not "
exit_line2="the one you wish to delete, we are leaving the script..."
process_answer
#
###############################################################
# Search for any running processes that belong to the User Account
#
echo
echo "Step #2 - Find process on system belonging to user account"
echo
#
ps -u $user_account > /dev/null  #List user processes running.

case $? in
1)     # No processes running for this User Account
       #
     echo "There are no processes for this account
currently running."
     echo
;;
0)     # Processes running for this User Account.
       # Ask Script User if wants us to kill the processes.
       #
     echo "$user_account has the following process(es) running:"
     ps -u $user_account
     #
     line1="Would you like me to kill the process(es)? [y/n]"
     get_answer
     #
     answer=$(echo $answer | cut -c1)
     #
     case $answer in
     y|Y)   # If user answers "yes",
            # kill User Account processes.
            #
            echo
            echo "Killing off process(es)..."
            #
            # List user process running code in command_1
            command_1="ps -u $user_account --no-heading"
            #
            # Create command_3 to kill processes in variable
            command_3="xargs -d \\n /usr/bin/sudo /bin/kill -9"
```

```
                    #
                    # Kill processes via piping commands together
                    $command_1 | gawk '{print $1}' | $command_3
                    #
                    echo
                    echo "Process(es) killed."
        ;;
        *)      #If user answers anything but "yes", do not kill.
                    echo
                    echo "Will not kill process(es)."

        ;;
        esac
;;
esac
##################################################################
# Create a report of all files owned by User Account
#
echo
echo "Step #3 - Find files on system belonging to user account"
echo
echo "Creating a report of all files owned by $user_account."
echo
echo "It is recommended that you backup/archive these files,"
echo "and then do one of two things:"
echo "  1) Delete the files"
echo "  2) Change the files' ownership to a current user account."
echo
echo "Please wait. This may take a while..."
#
report_date=$(date +%y%m%d)
report_file="$user_account"_Files_"$report_date".rpt
#
find / -user $user_account > $report_file 2>/dev/null
#
echo
echo "Report is complete."
echo "Name of report:      $report_file"
echo -n "Location of report: "; pwd
echo
####################################
#  Remove User Account
echo
echo "Step #4 - Remove user account"
echo
#
line1="Do you wish to remove $user_account's account from system? [y/n] "
get_answer
#
```

(Continues)

*(continued)*

```
# Call process_answer function:
#       if user answers anything but "yes", exit script
#
exit_line1="Since you do not wish to remove the user account,"
exit_line2="$user_account at this time, exiting the script..."
process_answer
#
userdel $user_account          #delete user account
echo
echo "User account, $user_account, has been removed"
echo
#
exit
$
```

That was lots of work! However, the Delete_User.sh script is a great time-saver and helps you avoid lots of nasty problems when deleting local user accounts.

## Running the script

Because it is intended to function as an interactive script, the Delete_User.sh script should not be placed in the cron table. However, it is still important to ensure that it works as expected.

Before the script is tested, the appropriate permissions are set on the script's file:

```
$ chmod u+x Delete_User.sh
$
$ ls -og Delete_User.sh
-rwxr-xr-x 1 6111 Aug 12 14:18 Delete_User.sh
$
```

> **NOTE**
>
> To run this type of script, you must either be logged in as the root user account or use the sudo command to run the script with super user privileges.

The script is tested by removing an account, consultant, that was set up for a company's temporary consultant on this system:

```
$ sudo ./Delete_User.sh
[sudo] password for christine:
Step #1 - Determine User Account name to Delete

Please enter the username of the user
account you wish to delete from system: consultant
Is consultant the user account
you wish to delete from the system? [y/n] yes
```

```
I found this record:
consultant:x:1003:1004::/home/consultant:/bin/bash

Is this the correct User Account? [y/n] y

Step #2 - Find process on system belonging to user account

consultant has the following process(es) running:
    PID TTY          TIME CMD
   5781 ?        00:00:00 systemd
[…]
   5884 ?        00:00:00 trojanhorse.sh
   5885 ?        00:00:00 sleep
   5886 ?        00:00:00 badjuju.sh
   5887 ?        00:00:00 sleep
Would you like me to kill the process(es)? [y/n] y

Killing off process(es)...

Process(es) killed.

Step #3 - Find files on system belonging to user account

Creating a report of all files owned by consultant.

It is recommended that you backup/archive these files,
and then do one of two things:
  1) Delete the files
  2) Change the files' ownership to a current user account.

Please wait. This may take a while...

Report is complete.
Name of report:       consultant_Files_200812.rpt
Location of report: /home/christine/scripts


Step #4 - Remove user account

Do you wish to remove consultant's account from system? [y/n] yes

User account, consultant, has been removed

$ ls *.rpt
consultant_Files_200812.rpt
$
$ grep ^consultant /etc/passwd
$
```

That worked great! Notice the script was run using sudo, because super user privileges are needed for deleting accounts. And notice that the Consultant user's files were found and put into a report file, and then the account was deleted.

Now you have a script utility that assists you when you need to delete user accounts. Even better, you can modify it to meet your organization's needs.

# Monitoring Your System

Mistakes happen. But you don't want those mistakes to compromise the security of your Linux system. One thing you can do to keep an eye on things is monitor your system with an audit script. In this section, we'll delve into a script that allows you to monitor two particularly tricky areas within your Linux systems — system account shells and potentially dangerous file permissions.

## Obtaining the default shell audit functions

System accounts (Chapter 7) are accounts that provide services or perform special tasks. Typically, they need an account record within the /etc/passwd file but are blocked from logging into the system. (A classic exception to this rule is the root account.)

The way to prevent anyone from logging into these accounts is to set their default shell to /bin/false, /usr/sbin/nologin, or some variation (such as /sbin/nologin). The problem occurs when a system account's default shell is changed from its current setting to /bin/bash. Although a nefarious person (called a *bad actor* in modern security terminology) cannot log in to that account unless a password is set for it, it still is a step toward weakened security. Thus, these account settings need auditing and any incorrect default shell situations rectified.

One way to audit this potential issue is to determine how many accounts have false or nologin set as their default shell, and then periodically check this number. If the number decreases, it's worth further investigation.

First, to grab the default shell from each account within the /etc/passwd file, we'll use the cut command. With this command, we can denote the field delimiter used by the file, and tell it what field we want from each record. In the case of the /etc/passwd file, the delimiter is a colon (:), and we want to see what is in the default shell field, which happens to be the seventh field in each record:

```
$ cut -d: -f7 /etc/passwd
/bin/bash
/usr/sbin/nologin
/usr/sbin/nologin
/usr/sbin/nologin
[…]
/bin/false
/bin/bash
```

```
/usr/sbin/nologin
/bin/bash
/usr/sbin/nologin
/bin/bash
$
```

Now that we're able to grab the right field, we need to filter out the results. The only items we are interested in are `false` and `nologin` shells. Here, `grep` (Chapter 4) can help us. One of the neat things about `grep` is that we can use regular expressions (Chapter 20, "Regular Expressions") as our pattern for which to search. In this case, because we need to search for both `false` and `nologin`, we'll need an extended regular expression (ERE). And `grep` can handle those, too, as long as we tack on its `-E` option. We'll pipe the `cut` command's findings into the `grep` command and filter out any default shells that don't match what we're looking for:

```
$ cut -d: -f7 /etc/passwd |
> grep -E "(false|nologin)"
/usr/sbin/nologin
/usr/sbin/nologin
/usr/sbin/nologin
/usr/sbin/nologin
[...]
/bin/false
/bin/false
/usr/sbin/nologin
/usr/sbin/nologin
$
```

That works perfectly! Notice in our `grep` command, the two choices to find are `false` and `nologin`. In order to act as an extended regular expression, these either/or choices are placed into parentheses and separated by a pipe (|) symbol. One more item is required for this `grep` filter to work: *shell quoting*. Due to the fact that parentheses and pipes have special meaning to the Bash shell, we must encase this ERE syntax in shell quotes to protect them from incorrect interpretation by the shell.

Now we have almost all the pieces of the puzzle in place. Still needed is the ability to count the number of accounts that have these special default shells. Thus, we'll include the `wc` command (Chapter 11). Because the only item we are interested in is the number of accounts that have these shells, we will use the `-l` (lowercase L) option to count the lines produced by the `grep` command. Now our code looks like this:

```
$ cut -d: -f7 /etc/passwd |
> grep -E "(false|nologin)" | wc -l
44
$
```

Thus, we have 44 accounts on this system that have either `false` or `nologin` as their default shell. We still need to send this number to a report file, but we want it to display to the script user too. To accomplish this task, we'll use the `tee` command (Chapter 15).

```
$ cut -d: -f7 /etc/passwd |
> grep -E "(false|nologin)" | wc -l |
> tee mydefaultshell.rpt
44
$
$ cat mydefaultshell.rpt
44
$
```

Now we're getting somewhere. However, because we need to keep multiple copies of the produced report for later comparison, a name better than `mydefaultshell.rpt` is essential. It's typically a good idea to include the current date into the file's name in situations like this. To grab the date and some additional time identification information, we'll use the date command. The needed format of the date command looks like this:

```
$ date +%F%s
2020-08-141597420127
$
```

So that we can use it in a filename, we set the format to one that displays the current date with dashes (`%F`). Because this audit may run multiple times per day, we tacked onto the time stamp additional time identification information (`%s`): the number of seconds since January 1, 1970.

> **NOTE**
>
> Unix Epoch time, which is also called POSIX time, is the number of seconds since January 1, 1970. It is used within Linux systems for a variety of purposes, such as recording the last time your password was changed.

Now we can create an absolute directory reference to our uniquely named file for use in our tee command:

```
reportDir="/home/christine/scripts/AuditReports"
reportDate="$(date +%F%s)"
accountReport=$reportDir/AccountAudit$reportDate.rpt
cat /etc/passwd | cut -d: -f7 |
grep -E "(nologin|false)" | wc -l |
tee $accountReport
```

There is another problem to handle before we move on to the second audit of this script: protecting the newly created report. Once this system account default shell count is recorded, you don't want anyone to modify the report or delete it, because the script will need it later for a count comparison.

To protect the report, we'll enlist the *immutable attribute*. This setting is so named because, once set on a file, no one can modify the file or remove it (as well as some additional features.) To set this attribute, super user privileges are required, and the chattr command is used:

```
$ sudo chattr +i mydefaultshell.rpt
[sudo] password for christine:
```

```
$
$ rm -i mydefaultshell.rpt
rm: cannot remove 'mydefaultshell.rpt': Operation not permitted
$
$ sudo rm -i mydefaultshell.rpt
rm: remove regular file 'mydefaultshell.rpt'? y
rm: cannot remove 'mydefaultshell.rpt': Operation not permitted
$
$ echo "Hello" >> mydefaultshell.rpt
-bash: mydefaultshell.rpt: Operation not permitted
$
```

Once the immutable attribute (sometimes called the immutable bit) is set, no one can remove or modify the file, including those with super user privileges! To see if this attribute is set, use the lsattr command and look for the i in the output. To remove the attribute, you again need super user privileges for use the chattr command. Once removed, the file can be modified or deleted:

```
$ lsattr mydefaultshell.rpt
----i---------e----- mydefaultshell.rpt
$
$ sudo chattr -i mydefaultshell.rpt
$
$ lsattr mydefaultshell.rpt
--------------e----- mydefaultshell.rpt
$
$ echo "Hello" >> mydefaultshell.rpt
$
$ cat mydefaultshell.rpt
44
Hello
$
$ rm -i mydefaultshell.rpt
rm: remove regular file 'mydefaultshell.rpt'? y
$
```

Now that we can protect our audit report, only one last issue remains: comparing the current report to the last report. In order to do this, we'll employ the ls command and two new options: -1 (the number one) and -t. Using these options, the ls command will list out the files in a single column in the order of newest report to oldest:

```
$ reportDate="$(date +%F%s)"
$ touch AccountAudit$reportDate.rpt
$
$ reportDate="$(date +%F%s)"
$ touch AccountAudit$reportDate.rpt
```

(Continues)

*(continued)*

```
$
$ ls -1t AccountAudit*.rpt
AccountAudit2020-08-141597422307.rpt
AccountAudit2020-08-141597422296.rpt
$
```

The reason for listing the files in a single-column format is so that we can employ sed to help us grab the filename of the second oldest report for comparison, as such:

```
$ prevReport="$(ls -1t AccountAudit*.rpt |
> sed -n '2p')"
$
$ echo $prevReport
AccountAudit2020-08-141597422296.rpt
$
```

That worked just as we were expecting. But what if the second report doesn't exist? We'll get unexpected results, which may result in problems within our script. To handle this last audit report issue, we'll bring in the if-then statement:

```
prevReport="$(ls -1t $reportDir/AccountAudit*.rpt |
sed -n '2p')"
#
if [ -z $prevReport ]
then
    echo
    echo "No previous false/nologin report exists to compare."
else
    echo
    echo "Previous report's false/nologin shells: "
    cat $prevReport
    fi
```

Now that we've got all the default shell audit functionality determined, we can start taking a look at the permission audit side of our script.

> **NOTE**
>
> This script is handy for conducting audits. However, it is not an intrusion detection system (IDS). An IDS application monitors the network and/or applications running on your system, looking for suspicious behavior. It provides various features, such as blocking attacks and reporting anything it finds potentially malicious. If you are concerned about bad actors compromising your system, an IDS application is the way to go. There are several from which to choose, such as Snort, DenyHosts, and Fail2ban.

## Obtaining the permission audit functions

The set user ID (SUID) and set group ID (SGID) are handy permissions that are used by several programs within the Linux virtual directory system (Chapter 7). However, problems arise if these permissions are unintentionally or even maliciously set on programs, causing them to run under a different grouping of permissions. Thus, these two potentially "dangerous" permissions are worthwhile to audit on your system to ensure they are set only where they belong.

To locate the files and directories that have these two permissions, we'll employ the `find` command. Since we need to audit all files and directories residing on this system, the starting point for this search will be the top of the virtual directory structure (/). To designate to the `find` command what permissions we are searching for, the `-perm` option (permissions) will work. This particular option allows us to use an octal value (Chapter 7) to designate the particular permission settings we need to find. We'll also use super user privileges to examine all the various files and directories. And to keep the display clean, we'll throw errors (2) into the black hole (/dev/null):

```
$ sudo find / -perm /6000 2>/dev/null
[sudo] password for christine:
/var/local
/var/crash
/var/metrics
/var/log/journal
[...]
/usr/bin/umount
/usr/bin/sudo
/usr/bin/chsh
[...]
/run/log/journal
$
```

Notice that the value after -perm is /6000. The octal value of 6 designates `find` to search for both SUID and SGID permissions. The forward slash (/) and the 000 octal values tell the `find` command to *ignore* the rest of a file's or directory's permissions. If the forward slash (/) was not used, `find` would look for files with the SUID and SGID permissions, and all other permissions set to *nothing* (000), which is not what we want.

**NOTE**

In older versions of the `find` command, the plus symbol was used (+), instead of the forward slash (/) to ignore certain permissions. If you are using an older version of Linux, you may need to swap out the forward slash for the plus symbol.

24

You can redirect STDOUT from the `find` command into a file to leisurely review later. It is also useful to save this report to compare with later audits of these permissions:

```
reportDir="/home/christine/scripts/AuditReports"
reportDate="$(date +%F%s)"
permReport=$reportDir/PermissionAudit$reportDate.rpt
#
sudo find / -perm /6000 >$permReport 2>/dev/null
```

Now that the permission audit report is saved, we can compare earlier versions of the report to the current one to notify the script user of any differences between the two. Changes to file permissions indicate either new software was installed that needed these settings or that a file has been erroneously (or maliciously) set with these permissions.

To perform this comparison, we can use the `diff` command. This utility allows us to compare files, and it displays any differences between the two to STDOUT.

> **WARNING**
>
> The `diff` command compares files only on a line-by-line basis. Thus, for these reports it will compare line 1 of the first report to line 1 of the second report, line 2 to line 2, line 3 to line 3, and so on. If a new file or set of files is added, due to say a software installation, and the files need the SUID or SGID permissions, when the next audit is run, `diff` will display many differences! To solve this potential problem, you can use the `-q` or the `--brief` option on the `diff` command, and it will only display the message that the two reports are different.

We'll also need verification that another report exists before we try this comparison. Here's what this code looks like:

```
prevReport="$(ls -1t $reportDir/PermissionAudit*.rpt |
sed -n '2p')"
#
if [ -z $prevReport ]
then
    echo
    echo "No previous permission report exists to compare."
else
    echo
    echo "Differences between this report and the last: "
    #
    differences=$(diff $permReport $prevReport)
    #
    if [ -z "$differences" ]
    then
        echo "No differences exist."
    else
        echo $differences
        fi
    fi
```

Notice that checks are done not only for another report but also to see if there are truly any differences between the two reports. If there are no differences, only `No differences exist` is displayed.

## Creating the script

Now that we have all the primary features figured out for this audit script, we can start putting it together. For this particular Bash shell script, we decided to use `getopts`

(Chapter 14) and offer the use of the -A option to run only the account audit, and the -p option to execute only the permission audit. Although you can run both audits by combining the two options (-Ap), we included the flexibility of running both audits if no options were provided. This allows easier incorporation of this script into an automated environment via cron or anacron.

Here's the entire Audit_System.sh script for your review:

```
$ cat Audit_System.sh
#!/bin/bash
#
# Audit_System.sh - Audit system files and accounts
#####################################################
#
### Initialize variables ######################
#
runAccountAudit="false"
runPermAudit="false"
#
reportDir="/home/christine/scripts/AuditReports"
#
### Get options (if provided) ################
#
while getopts :Ap opt
do
     case "$opt" in
          A) runAccountAudit="true" ;;
          p) runPermAudit="true" ;;
          *) echo "Not a valid option."
             echo "Valid options are: -A, -p, or -Ap"
             exit
          ;;
     esac
done
#
### Determine if no options #################
#
if [ $OPTIND -eq 1 ]
then
     # No options were provided; set&#x00A0;all to "true"
     runAccountAudit="true"
     runPermAudit="true"
fi
#
### Run selected audits ######################
#
## Account Audit #################
#
if [ $runAccountAudit = "true" ]
```

*(Continues)*

*(continued)*

```
    then
        echo
        echo "****** Account Audit *****"
        echo
#
# Determine current false/nologin shell count
#
        echo "Number of current false/nologin shells: "
#
        reportDate="$(date +%F%s)"
        accountReport=$reportDir/AccountAudit$reportDate.rpt
#
        # Create current report
        cat /etc/passwd | cut -d: -f7 |
        grep -E "(nologin|false)" | wc -l |
        tee $accountReport
#
        # Change report's attributes:
        sudo chattr +i  $accountReport
#
# Show past false/nologin shell count
#
        prevReport="$(ls -1t $reportDir/AccountAudit*.rpt |
        sed -n '2p')"
        if [ -z $prevReport ]
        then
            echo
            echo "No previous false/nologin report exists to compare."
        else
            echo
            echo "Previous report's false/nologin shells: "
            cat $prevReport
        fi
    fi
#
## Permissions Audit #############
#
if [ $runPermAudit = "true" ]
then
    echo
    echo "****** SUID/SGID Audit *****"
    echo
    reportDate="$(date +%F%s)"
    permReport=$reportDir/PermissionAudit$reportDate.rpt
#
    # Create current report
    echo "Creating report. This may take a while..."
    sudo find / -perm /6000 >$permReport 2>/dev/null
```

```
#
    # Change report's attributes:
    sudo chattr +i  $permReport
#
# Compare to last permission report
#
    #
    prevReport="$(ls -1t $reportDir/PermissionAudit*.rpt |
    sed -n '2p')"
    #
    if [ -z $prevReport ]
    then
        echo
        echo "No previous permission report exists to compare."
    else
        echo
        echo "Differences between this report and the last: "
        #
        differences=$(diff $permReport $prevReport)
        #
        if [ -z "$differences" ]
        then
            echo "No differences exist."
        else
            echo $differences
        fi
    fi
fi
#
exit
$
```

There is a lot of high-level scripting going on in this file. And now that you've reached Bash shell scripting guru status, you may be tempted to start thinking about tweaks, but hold on. We've got to test the script first.

## Running the script

Before we run the script, we need to create the audit report directory. The directory will hold the audit reports, so choose your directory location carefully.

```
$ mkdir AuditReports
$ ls AuditReports/
$
```

Once the audit report directory is created, you can start running the script. Our first time through, we'll run only the account default shell audit by using the -A option:

```
$ ./Audit_System.sh -A

****** Account Audit *****

Number of current false/nologin shells:
44

No previous false/nologin report exists to compare.
$
```

That worked perfectly. Notice that there are 44 accounts on this system that use `false` or `nologin` as their default shells. Also notice that since no other account audit reports exist, the script properly let us know there was nothing with which to compare this report.

Now let's try out the permission audit portion of the script by employing the `-p` option:

```
$ ./Audit_System.sh -p

****** SUID/SGID Audit *****

Creating report. This may take a while...

No previous permission report exists to compare.
$
$ ls -1 AuditReports/
AccountAudit2020-08-141597427922.rpt
PermissionAudit2020-08-141597428079.rpt
$
```

It worked as expected. Now we have two audit reports stored in our `AuditReports` directory.

> **NOTE**
>
> You may have noticed that the `sudo` command is used two times within this script. The reason the script didn't ask for our password when running the script is due to our recent use of the `sudo` command. If you haven't used `sudo` in a while, it will come up and ask for your password. If you don't want this type of behavior within your script, remove the `sudo` commands from it and run the script like this: `sudo ./Audit_System.sh`, along with the options you choose to use.

Now, let's add a bogus file that has SUID permissions and see if the script catches it. We'll try running it with both options (so that both audits are conducted) this time too:

```
$ touch sneakyFile.exe
$ chmod u+xs sneakyFile.exe
$
$ ./Audit_System.sh -Ap

****** Account Audit *****

Number of current false/nologin shells:
44
```

```
Previous report's false/nologin shells:
44

****** SUID/SGID Audit *****

Creating report. This may take a while...

Differences between this report and the last:
82d81 < /home/christine/scripts/sneakyFile.exe
$
```

Not only did both audits run, but the permission audit caught our sneakyFile.exe SUID permission. Now that we know the script runs correctly, it's time to start thinking about modifications and improvements. Here are a few for you to consider:

- Add additional audits to the script, such as reports on newly added accounts or failed login attempts.
- Limit the number of reports stored in the AuditReports directory.
- Use checksums (type **man SHA512sum** to learn more) to add an additional layer that helps ensure reports have not been modified.

What additional functionality or tweaks would you like to add to this script? Now that you are a Linux Bash shell scripting ninja, we bet you have a lot of great ideas.

# Summary

This chapter put some of the shell-scripting information presented in the book to good use for creating additional Linux utilities. When you're responsible for a Linux system, whether it's a large multiuser system or your own system, you need to watch lots of things. Instead of manually running commands, you can create shell script utilities to do the work for you.

The first section walked you through using shell scripts for archiving and backing up data files on the Linux system. The tar command is a popular command for archiving data. The chapter showed you how to use it in shell scripts to create archive files and how to manage the archive files in an archive directory.

The next section covered using a shell script for the four steps needed to delete user accounts. Creating functions for shell code that is repeated within a script makes the code easier to read and modify. This script combined many of the different structured commands, such as the case and while commands. The chapter demonstrated the difference in script structure for a script destined for the cron tables versus an interactive script.

The chapter ended with a script that helps to audit some potential problems: misuse of the SUID and SGID permissions, and incorrect default shells for system accounts. This script is easily expanded to add many additional audits. It is also rather simple to modify the script so that it can be run automatically on a daily or a weekly basis by anacron.

Next, we'll look at how to manage all these shell scripts you now have, as well as the additional ones you'll write along your Bash shell scripting career path.

24

# Getting Organized

Writing complex and useful shell scripts saves lots of time, but you can quickly lose that saved time through script mismanagement. Tracking updates to scripts, working with other team members involved in modifying the scripts, and distributing the scripts to your various systems all add to the complexity of script management. Fortunately, there is a utility that can help you properly manage your Bash shell scripts. In this chapter, we take you through the concept of version control and the popular Git utility that implements it.

## Understanding Version Control

Imagine a system admin team whose members all write scripts for the various Linux systems in the company. A backup script is managed by this team, and it is deployed on nearly all of the company's servers. A few special versions of this backup script exist that use encryption due to files being transferred over public networks.

One day, it's determined that the backup script needs an update to improve its processing speed and reliability. The team starts the backup script update project. They begin the process of modifying the backup script and testing the modifications. Through this process, each project team member has to make sure they get the latest version of the script to modify and/or test. Adding more complexity to this matter, the team is not located in the same building. In fact, they are located around the world. To keep everything straight, the backup script update project requires a lot of text messages, emails, and sometimes online meetings. In addition, the special versions of the backup script that use encryption also must be modified with the latest changes and tested. This script update project quickly becomes bogged down with complications and required extra communication.

The backup script update project team can get help through version control. *Version control* (also known as *source control* or *revision control*) is a method or system that organizes various project files and tracks updates to them.

A version control system (VCS) provides a common central place to store and merge Bash script files so that the latest version is easily accessed. It protects the files so that a script is not accidentally overwritten by another script writer. And it eliminates extra communications concerning who is currently modifying what.

Additional benefits include situations around new team members of a script project. For example, a new script writer team member can get a copy of the latest backup script version through the version control system and immediately start work on the backup script update project.

*Distributed VCSs* make script projects even easier. The script writers can perform their development or modification work on their own Linux system. Once they've reach a modification goal, they send a copy of their modified files and VCS metadata to the remote central system, and other team members can download this latest project version and conduct tests or work on their modification goal. A side benefit is that now the work is backed up to a central location, which is easily accessible from around the world.

Git is a distributed VCS, which is often employed in agile and continuous software development environments. But it is also used for managing Bash shell scripts. To understand Git's underlying principles, you need to know a few terms related to its configuration. Figure 25-1 shows a conceptual depiction of the Git environment.

Each location within the Git environment is important. The following sections cover the details of these areas and highlight a few special Git features.

## Working directory

The *working directory* is where all the scripts are created, modified, and reviewed. It is typically a subdirectory within the script writer's home directory, similar to

**FIGURE 25-1**

Conceptual depiction of the Git environment

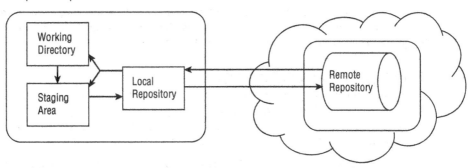

`/home/christine/scripts`. It is best to create a new subdirectory for every project, because Git places files within that location for tracking purposes.

The script writer's Linux system, where the working directory resides, is typically a local server or laptop, depending on workplace requirements. You could even set up your working environment within a local virtual machine that mimics the script's destination system(s). This is also a wonderful method for testing modified or new scripts, because it protects the destination Linux systems from disruption.

## Staging area

A *staging area* is also called the *index*. This area is located on the same system as the working directory. Bash scripts in the working directory are *registered* into the staging area via a Git command (`git add`). The staging area employs a hidden subdirectory in the working directory named .git. This required location is created via the `git init` command.

When scripts are cataloged into the staging area, Git creates or updates script information in an index file, `.git/index`. The data recorded includes checksums (Chapter 24, "Writing Simple Script Utilities"), time stamps, and associated script filenames.

Besides updating the index file, Git compresses the script file(s) and stores these compressed files as an object(s), also called a *blob*, in a `.git/objects/` directory. If a script has been modified, it is compressed and stored as a *new* object in the `.git/objects/` directory. Git does not just store script modifications; it keeps a compressed copy of *each* modified script.

## Looking at the local repository

The local repository contains each script file's history. It uses the working directory's `.git` subdirectory as well. Relationships between the script file versions (called a *project tree*)

25

and commit information are stored as objects in the `.git/objects/` directory via a Git command (`git commit`).

Together the project tree and commit data are called a *snapshot*. Every commit creates a *new* snapshot. However, old snapshots are kept, and they are viewable. Another nice feature is that you can return to a previous snapshot if needed.

## Exploring a remote repository

In the Git configuration, the remote repository is typically a cloud-based location that provides a code hosting service. However, you can set up a code hosting site on another server within your local network to serve as the remote repository. What you use really depends on your project's needs as well as your script management team members' locations.

Prominent remote repositories include GitHub, GitLab, BitBucket, and Launchpad. However, by far, GitHub is the most popular. We use GitHub for our remote repository examples in this book.

## Branching

An additional feature provided by Git, called a *branch*, can help in your various script projects. A branch is an area within a local repository for a particular project section. For example, you can have the primary branch in your script project named `main`, and when you make a modification to the script in the `main` branch, it's best practice to create a new branch, called something like `modification`, and make the changes to the script there. Once the script changes have been tested, the script in the `modification` branch is often merged back into the primary branch.

The advantage to using this method is that your scripts that reside in the `main` branch stay production-worthy, since the Bash shell scripts that are being modified and tested reside in a different branch. Only when the modified scripts are successfully tested are the scripts merged into the `main` branch.

## Cloning

Another nice feature of Git is that you can copy a project. This process is called *cloning*. If your team brings on a new member, that individual can clone the script and tracking files from the remote repository and have all they need to start participating in modifying the script.

This feature is also useful for specialized versions of a script. In our earlier scenario, the backup script was modified on a few Linux systems to include encryption. When the backup script update project has completed its modifications, merged them into the primary branch, and pushed the local repository to a remote repository, the team responsible for making the special backup script versions can clone the project. Then they'll have all the pieces needed to add encryption to the improved backup script.

> **NOTE**
>
> With Git, cloning and forking are different but closely related activities. A project clone occurs when the files are downloaded from a remote repository to your local system using the `git clone` command. *Forking* happens when you copy from one remote repository to another one.

## Using Git for VCS

In case you are not yet sold on the idea of using Git as your version control system for your script projects, we'll try to make our case a little stronger. Using Git as your VCS includes the following benefits:

**Performance**    Git uses only local files to operate, making it faster to employ. The exceptions to this include sending and retrieving files to and from a remote repository.

**History**    Git captures all the files' contents at the moment the file is registered with the index. When a commit is completed to the local repository, Git creates and stores a reference to that snapshot in time.

**Accuracy**    Git employs checksums to protect file integrity.

**Decentralization**    Script writers can work on the same project, but they don't have to be on the same network or system.

Older VCSs required script writers to be on the same network, which didn't provide a great deal of flexibility. They were also slower in operation, which is one reason Linus Torvalds decided to create Git.

Now that, hopefully, we have convinced you to consider Git, we'll cover the basics of using it for your next script writing or modification project.

## Setting Up Your Git Environment

The Git utility typically is not installed by default. Thus, you'll need to install the `git` package prior to setting up your Git environment. See Chapter 9, "Installing Software," for details on package installation.

Here's an installation of Git on a CentOS Linux distribution:

```
$ sudo dnf install git
[sudo] password for christine:
[...]
Dependencies resolved.
```

*(Continues)*

*(continued)*

```
=========================================================================
 Package                Arch         Version
Repository       Size
=========================================================================
Installing:
 git                    x86_64       2.18.4-2.el8_2
AppStream        186 k
Installing dependencies:
 git-core               x86_64       2.18.4-2.el8_2
AppStream        4.0 M
 git-core-doc           noarch       2.18.4-2.el8_2
AppStream        2.3 M
 perl-Error             noarch       1:0.17025-2.el8
AppStream        46 k
 perl-Git               noarch       2.18.4-2.el8_2
AppStream        77 k
 perl-TermReadKey       x86_64       2.37-7.el8
AppStream        40 k

Transaction Summary
=========================================================================
Install  6 Packages

Total download size: 6.6 M
Installed size: 36 M
Is this ok [y/N]: y
Downloading Packages:
[...]
Running transaction check
Transaction check succeeded.
Running transaction test
Transaction test succeeded.
[...]
Installed:
  git-2.18.4-2.el8_2.x86_64            git-core-2.18.4-2.
el8_2.x86_64
  git-core-doc-2.18.4-2.el8_2.noarch   perl-Error-1:0.17025-2.
el8.noarch
  perl-Git-2.18.4-2.el8_2.noarch       perl-TermReadKey-2.37-7.
el8.x86_64

Complete!
$
$ which git
/usr/bin/git
$
```

And here's an installation of Git on an Ubuntu Linux distribution:

```
$ sudo apt install git
[sudo] password for christine:
```

```
Reading package lists... Done
Building dependency tree
Reading state information... Done
The following additional packages will be installed:
  git-man liberror-perl
[...]
After this operation, 38.4 MB of additional disk space will be used.
Do you want to continue? [Y/n] Y
[...]
Fetched 5,464 kB in 1min 33s (58.9 kB/s)
Selecting previously unselected package liberror-perl.
(Reading database ... 202052 files and directories currently
installed.)
[...]
Unpacking git (1:2.25.1-1ubuntu3) ...
Setting up liberror-perl (0.17029-1) ...
Setting up git-man (1:2.25.1-1ubuntu3) ...
Setting up git (1:2.25.1-1ubuntu3) ...
Processing triggers for man-db (2.9.1-1) ...
$
$ which git
/usr/bin/git
$
```

Nothing was too difficult with this process. As long as you have super user privileges, installing Git is fairly easy.

After you have the `git` package installed on your system, setting up your Git environment for a new script writing project involves four basic steps:

1. Create a working directory.

2. Initialize the .git/ directory.

3. Set up the local repository options.

4. Establish your remote repository location.

To begin the process, create a working directory. A subdirectory in your local home folder will suffice:

```
$ mkdir MWGuard
$
$ cd MWGuard/
$
$ pwd
/home/christine/MWGuard
$
```

A simple subdirectory MWGuard was created for the script writing project. After the working directory is created, use the cd command to move your present working directory into it.

25

Within the working directory, initialize the .git/ directory. This task employs the git init command:

```
$ git init
Initialized empty Git repository in /home/christine/MWGuard/.git/
$
$ ls -ld .git
drwxrwxr-x 7 christine christine 4096 Aug 24 14:49 .git
$
```

The git init command creates the .git/ subdirectory. Because the directory name is preceded with a dot (.), it is hidden from regular ls commands. Use the ls -la command or add the directory name as an argument to the ls -ld command, as we did earlier, in order to view its metadata.

If this is the first time you have built a .git/ subdirectory on your system, add a name and email address to the global Git repository's configuration file. This identification data helps in tracking file changes, especially if you have several people involved in the project. To perform this task, use the git config command:

```
$ git config --global user.name "Christine Bresnahan"
$
$ git config --global user.email "cbresn1723@gmail.com"
$
$ git config --get user.name
Christine Bresnahan
$
$ git config --get user.email
cbresn1723@gmail.com
$
```

By including --global on the git config command, the user.name and user.email data is stored in the global Git configuration file. Notice that you can view this information using the --get option and passing it the data's name as an argument.

Git global configuration information is stored in the .gitconfig file within your home directory and the local repository, which is the *working-directory*/.git/config configuration file. Be aware that some systems have a system-level configuration file, which is /etc/gitconfig.

To view all the various configurations stored in these files, use the git config --list command:

```
$ git config --list
user.name=Christine Bresnahan
user.email=cbresn1723@gmail.com
core.repositoryformatversion=0
core.filemode=true
core.bare=false
core.logallrefupdates=true
$
$ ls /home/christine/.gitconfig
/home/christine/.gitconfig
$
$ cat /home/christine/.gitconfig
[user]
        name = Christine Bresnahan
        email = cbresn1723@gmail.com
$
$ ls /home/christine/MWGuard/.git/config
/home/christine/MWGuard/.git/config
$
$ cat /home/christine/MWGuard/.git/config
[core]
        repositoryformatversion = 0
        filemode = true
        bare = false
        logallrefupdates = true
$
```

The settings that are displayed via the --list option use a *file-section.name* format. Notice that when the two Git configuration files (global and the project's local repository) are displayed to STDOUT with the cat command, the section names are shown along with the data they hold.

After your local Git environment is configured, it is time to establish your project's remote repository. For demonstration purposes, we chose the cloud-based remote repository GitHub. If you want to follow along, you can set up a free remote repository through the github.com/join link.

**NOTE**

Though Git can work with any file type, its tools are primarily aimed at plain-text files, such as Bash shell scripts. Therefore, be aware that you are not able to use all the git utilities on any nontext files.

25

After you have your project's remote repository established, you'll need to record the web address it provides. This address is used for sending your project files to the remote repository, which is covered later in this chapter.

# Committing with Git

When you have your Git environment established, you can begin employing its various organizational features. There are basic four steps, as follows:

1. Create or modify the script(s).
2. Add the script(s) to the staging area (index).
3. Commit the script(s) to the local repository.
4. Push the script(s) to the remote repository.

Depending on your workflow, you may repeat certain steps before progressing to the next one. For example, in a single day, a Linux admin works on writing Bash shell scripts and, as they are completed, moves them to the staging area. At the end of the day, the script writer commits the entire project to the local repository. After that, they push the project work to the remote repository for nonlocal team members to access.

Here, a simple shell script, `MyGitExampleScript.sh`, was created to use as a project example with Git:

```
$ cat MyGitExampleScript.sh
#!/bin/bash
# Git example script
#
echo "Hello Git World"
exit
$
```

After the script is created, it is added to the staging area (index). This is accomplished through the `git add` command. Since the script was not currently in our working directory, /home/christine/MWGuard, we copied it there first. Now that our script is in the correct location, we'll perform the `git add` command while our present working directory (displayed via the `pwd` command) is also in the correct location, /home/christine/MWGuard:

```
$ pwd
/home/christine/scripts
$
$ cp MyGitExampleScript.sh /home/christine/MWGuard/
$
$ cd /home/christine/MWGuard/
$
$ pwd
/home/christine/MWGuard
```

```
$
$ ls *.sh
MyGitExampleScript.sh
$
$ git add MyGitExampleScript.sh
$
$ git status
[&hellip;]
No commits yet

Changes to be committed:
  (use "git rm --cached <file>..." to unstage)
        new file:   MyGitExampleScript.sh

$
```

The git add command does not provide any output when it is executed. Thus, to see if it worked as desired, we used the git status command. The git status command shows that a new file, MyGitExampleScript.sh, was added to the index. This is just what we wanted to happen.

> **TIP**
>
> If you want, you can add *all* your scripts in the current working directory to the staging area's index at the same time. To accomplish this, issue the git add . command. Notice the period (.) at the end of the command! It is effectively a wildcard, telling Git to add *all* the working directory's files to the index.
>
> However, if you have files in your working directory that you do not want added to the staging area index, create a .gitignore file in the working directory. Next, add the names of files and directories you do not want included in the index into this file via your favorite text editor. The git add . command will now ignore those files but move the rest of the script files to the staging area's index.

The staging area's index filename is .git/index, and when the file command is used on it, the file type is shown as a Git index. This is the file that Git uses to track changes.

```
$ file .git/index
.git/index: Git index, version 2, 1 entries
$
```

The next step in the process is to commit the project to the local repository. The commit is accomplished via the git commit command. We added the -m option to add a comment, which is useful for documenting commits:

```
$ git commit -m "Initial Commit"
[&hellip;] Initial Commit
 1 file changed, 5 insertions(+)
 create mode 100644 MyGitExampleScript.sh
$
$ cat .git/COMMIT_EDITMSG
```

25

*(Continues)*

*(continued)*

```
Initial Commit
$
$ git status
[&hellip;]
nothing to commit, working tree clean
$
```

After you have issued **git commit**, the git status command will display the message nothing to commit, working directory clean. This tells you that Git now considers all the scripts in the working directory as committed to the local repository.

Now that the script project is committed to the local repository, it can be shared with other script project team members by pushing it to the remote repository. If the script(s) is completed, you can also share it with select others or the whole world.

If this is a new script project, after the remote repository account is established, create a special file called a *Markdown file*. The file's content displays on the remote repository's web page and describes the repository. It uses what is called *Markdown* language. You'll need to name the file **README.md**. Here is an example of creating this file, adding it to the staging area index, and committing it to the local repository:

```
$ pwd
/home/christine/MWGuard
$
$ ls
MyGitExampleScript.sh
$
$ echo "# Milky Way Guardian" > README.md
$ echo "## Script Project" >> README.md
$
$ cat README.md
# Milky Way Guardian
## Script Project
```

```
$
$
$ git add README.md
$
$ git status
[...]
Changes to be committed:
  (use "git restore --staged <file>..." to unstage)
        new file:    README.md

$
$ git commit -m "README.md commit"
[...] README.md commit
 1 file changed, 2 insertions(+)
 create mode 100644 README.md
$
$ git status
[...]
nothing to commit, working tree clean
$
```

> **NOTE**
> You can get really fancy with your README.md file by using various features of the Markdown language. Find out more about Markdown at guides.github.com/features/mastering-markdown.

At any time you can review the Git log, but it's always a good idea to do so before pushing your script project to a remote repository. Each commit is given a hash number to identify it, which is shown in the log. Also, notice the various comment lines along with dates and author information.

```
$ git log
commit 898330bd0b01e0b6eee507c5eeb3c72f9544f506[...]
Author: Christine Bresnahan <cbresn1723@gmail.com>
Date:   Mon Aug 24 15:58:52 2020 -0400

    README.md commit

commit 3b484638bc6e391d0a1b816946cba8c5f4bbc8e6
Author: Christine Bresnahan <cbresn1723@gmail.com>
Date:   Mon Aug 24 15:46:56 2020 -0400

    Initial Commit
$
```

Before you can push your project to the remote repository, you need to configure its address on your system. This address is provided to you when you set up your remote repository with a Git service provider, such as GitHub.

25

To add the address, use the `git remote add origin` *URL* command, where *URL* is the remote repository's address:

```
$ git remote add origin https://github.com/C-Bresnahan/MWGuard.git
$
$ git remote -v
origin  https://github.com/C-Bresnahan/MWGuard.git (fetch)
origin  https://github.com/C-Bresnahan/MWGuard.git (push)
$
```

Notice that we checked the status of the remote address via the `git remote -v` command. It's a good idea to check the address before pushing a project. If you've got the wrong address or you made a typographical error, the push will not work. So review everything carefully!

> **TIP**
>
> If you make a mistake, such as a typographical error, in the address, you can remove the remote repository's address via the `git remote rm origin` command. After it is removed, set up the remote address again using the correct address.

After the remote repository address is configured, we can push our script project up to its location. However, before we do that, to keep things simple we're going to rename the primary branch to `main` using the `git branch` command:

```
$ git branch -m main
$
$ git branch --show-current
main
$
```

Notice that you can see the current branch name using the `git branch --show-current` command. It's is a good idea to do this before a push to ensure you've got the correct branch name, which we need in the `push` command.

Now to copy our script up to the remote repository, we need the `-u origin` option tacked onto the `push` command to denote the location of the repository, and the name of the branch, `main`, that we are currently using:

```
$ git push -u origin main
Username for 'https://github.com': C-Bresnahan
Password for 'https://C-Bresnahan@github.com':
Enumerating objects: 6, done.
Counting objects: 100% (6/6), done.
Compressing objects: 100% (4/4), done.
Writing objects: 100% (6/6), 604 bytes | 60.00 KiB/s, done.
Total 6 (delta 0), reused 0 (delta 0)
To https://github.com/C-Bresnahan/MWGuard.git
```

```
 *  [new branch]        main -> main
Branch 'main' set up to track remote branch 'main' from 'origin'.
$
```

Typically the remote repository will demand a username and password. When the project is pushed to the remote repository, you should be able to view it using your favorite web browser. If it is a private repository, you'll have to log into the remote repository service in order to see your work.

Figure 25-2 shows the remote repository on GitHub for this project. Keep in mind that different Git remote repository providers will have different user interfaces for your script projects.

FIGURE 25-2

MWGuard remote repository

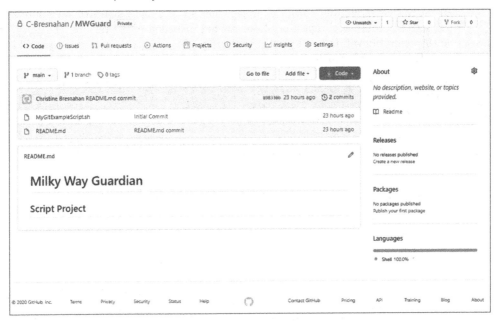

What is really nice about the remote repository is that anyone on your Linux admin team who is working on the project can pull down the latest script versions using the `git pull` command. You'll need to either set up access for them to the remote repository or make it public.

```
$ whoami
rich
$
$ pwd
```

*(Continues)*

*(continued)*

```
/home/rich/MWGuard
$
$ git remote add origin https://github.com/C-Bresnahan/MWGuard.git
$
$ git pull origin main
remote: Enumerating objects: 6, done.
remote: Counting objects: 100% (6/6), done.
remote: Compressing objects: 100% (4/4), done.
remote: Total 6 (delta 0), reused 6 (delta 0), pack-reused 0
Unpacking objects: 100% (6/6), 584 bytes | 58.00 KiB/s, done.
From https://github.com/C-Bresnahan/MWGuard
 * branch            main        -> FETCH_HEAD
 * [new branch]      main        -> origin/main
$
```

If the individual pulling down the project files already has a modified version of a particular script in their local repository that was not uploaded to the remote repository, the `git pull` command will fail and protect that script. However, the error message will instruct how to rectify this problem.

> **WARNING**
>
> Keep in mind that if anyone wants the latest script versions, and they weren't already working on the project, they'll get an error message similar to `fatal: not a git repository` when they attempt to issue the `git remote add origin` command. It would be best for them to clone the project, which is covered next.

A new development team member can copy the *entire* script project to their local system from the remote repository using the `git clone` command:

```
$ whoami
tim
$
$ ls
$
$ git clone https://github.com/C-Bresnahan/MWGuard.git
Cloning into 'MWGuard'...
remote: Enumerating objects: 6, done.
remote: Counting objects: 100% (6/6), done.
remote: Compressing objects: 100% (4/4), done.
remote: Total 6 (delta 0), reused 6 (delta 0), pack-reused 0
Unpacking objects: 100% (6/6), 584 bytes | 58.00 KiB/s, done.
$
$ ls
MWGuard
$
$ cd MWGuard/
$
$ ls -a
```

```
.   ..   .git  MyGitExampleScript.sh  README.md
$
$ git log
commit [...](HEAD -> main, origin/main, origin/HEAD)
Author: Christine Bresnahan <cbresn1723@gmail.com>
Date:   Mon Aug 24 15:58:52 2020 -0400

    README.md commit

commit 3b484638bc6e391d0a1b816946cba8c5f4bbc8e6
Author: Christine Bresnahan <cbresn1723@gmail.com>
Date:   Mon Aug 24 15:46:56 2020 -0400

    Initial Commit
$
```

When the project is cloned from the remote repository, the working directory is automatically created, along with the .git/ directory, the Git staging area (index), and the local repository. The git log command shows the project's history. This is an easy way for a new team member to grab everything needed to begin working on the project.

The distributed VCS utility Git is useful in many ways beyond the needs of script writers. There are many more useful project features available with Git. The ones covered in this chapter will get you started down the right path for managing all the amazing Bash shell scripts you are going to write in your lifetime.

# Summary

In this chapter, we first set the stage for Git by covering concepts such as VCS. Created by Linus Torvalds, Git provides an amazing distributed VCS that is useful for many things, including managing Bash shell scripts. We also took a look at important Git locations, such as the working directory; the staging area, which is also called the index; and the local and remote repositories. In addition, we touched on the branches and cloning features of Git.

Because many Linux distributions do not have Git installed by default, we stepped through installing the git package on both CentOS and Ubuntu. Setting up a working directory for the project was done first for the local configuration. The next part covered how to use the git init command, which creates a hidden subdirectory, .git/, within the working directory. After that, we demonstrated how to configure local repository options for tracking purposes. Finally, we touched on the remote repository, using GitHub as our example.

The chapter ended with using Git in a practical way. Using a sample Bash shell script, we moved it to the working directory, and then added it to the staging area (index) using the git add command. The sample script was next committed to the local repository. This was accomplished by using the git commit command. The last step in this process was

25

to move the project files to the remote repository. We used GitHub as our remote repository and sent the project there through the `git push` command.

Thanks for joining us on this journey through the Linux command line and shell scripting. We hope you've enjoyed the expedition and have learned how to get around on the command line, and how to create and manage shell scripts to save time. But don't stop your command-line education here! There's always something new being developed in the open source world, whether it's a new command-line utility or a full-blown shell. Stay in touch with the Linux community and follow along with new advances and features.

# Quick Guide to Bash Commands

## IN THIS APPENDIX

**Reviewing built-in commands**

**Looking at common Bash commands**

**Assessing environment variables**

A s you've seen throughout this book, the Bash shell contains lots of features and thus has lots of commands available. This appendix provides a concise guide to allow you to quickly look up a feature or command that you can use from the Bash command line or from a Bash shell script.

## Reviewing Built-In Commands

The Bash shell includes many popular commands built into the shell. You can use these commands to achieve faster processing times. Table A.1 shows the built-in commands available directly from the Bash shell.

**TABLE A.1   Bash Built-In Commands**

| Command | Description |
| --- | --- |
| & | Starts a job in background mode |
| ((x)) | Evaluates the $x$ mathematical expression |
| not: | Reads and executes commands from a designated file in the current shell |
| : | Does nothing, and always exits successfully |
| [ t ] | Evaluates the $t$ conditional expression |
| [[ e ]] | Evaluates the $e$ conditional expression |
| alias | Defines an alias for the specified command |
| bg | Resumes a job in background mode |

*(Continues)*

**TABLE A.1**  *(continued)*

| Command | Description |
|---|---|
| bind | Binds a keyboard sequence to a readline function or macro |
| break | Exits from a for, while, select, or until loop |
| builtin | Executes the specified shell built-in command |
| caller | Returns the context of any active subroutine call |
| case | Selectively executes commands based on pattern |
| cd | Changes the current directory to the specified directory |
| command | Executes the specified command without the normal shell lookup |
| compgen | Generates possible completion matches for the specified word |
| complete | Displays how the specified words would be completed |
| compopt | Changes options for how the specified words would be completed |
| continue | Resumes the next iteration of a for, while, select, or until loop |
| coproc | Executes a coprocess |
| declare | Declares a variable or variable type |
| dirs | Displays a list of currently remembered directories |
| disown | Removes the specified jobs from the jobs table for the process |
| echo | Displays the specified string to STDOUT |
| enable | Enables or disables the specified built-in shell command |
| eval | Concatenates the specified arguments into a single command, and executes the command |
| exec | Replaces the shell process with the specified command |
| exit | Forces the shell to exit with the specified exit status |
| export | Sets the specified variables to be available for child shell processes |
| false | Sets a result to failed status |
| fc | Selects a list of commands from the history list |
| fg | Resumes a job in foreground mode |
| for | Executes set commands for every item in the list |
| function | Defines a shell script function |
| getopts | Parses the specified positional parameters |
| hash | Finds and remembers the full pathname of the specified command |
| help | Displays a help file |
| history | Displays the command history |
| if | Executes set commands based on conditional expression |
| jobs | Lists the active jobs |

| Command | Description |
|---|---|
| kill | Sends a system signal to the specified process ID (PID) |
| let | Evaluates each argument in a mathematical expression |
| local | Creates a limited-scope variable in a function |
| logout | Exits a login shell |
| mapfile | Reads STDIN lines and puts them into an indexed array |
| popd | Removes entries from the directory stack |
| printf | Displays text using formatted strings |
| pushd | Adds a directory to the directory stack |
| pwd | Displays the pathname of the current working directory |
| read | Reads one line of data from STDIN, and assigns it to a variable |
| readarray | Reads STDIN lines, and puts them into an indexed array |
| readonly | Reads one line of data from STDIN, and assigns it to a variable that can't be changed |
| return | Forces a function to exit with a value that can be retrieved by the calling script |
| select | Displays list of words with numbers allowing selection |
| set | Sets and displays environment variable values and shell attributes |
| shift | Rotates positional parameters down one position |
| shopt | Toggles the values of variables controlling optional shell behavior |
| source | Reads and executes commands from a designated file in the current shell |
| suspend | Suspends the execution of the shell until a SIGCONT signal is received |
| test | Returns an exit status of 0 or 1 based on the specified condition |
| time | Displays the accumulated real, user, and system times executing command(s) |
| times | Displays the accumulated user and system shell times |
| trap | Executes the specified command if the specified system signal is received |
| true | Sets a result to successful status |
| type | Displays how the specified word would be interpreted if used as a command |
| typeset | Declares a variable or variable type |
| ulimit | Sets a limit on the specified resource for system users |
| umask | Sets default permissions for newly created files and directories |
| unalias | Removes the specified alias |

*(Continues)*

A

**TABLE A.1** *(continued)*

| Command | Description |
| --- | --- |
| unset | Removes the specified environment variable or shell attribute |
| until | Executes set commands until condition statement returns true |
| wait | Waits for the specified process to complete, and returns the exit status |
| while | Executes set commands while condition statement returns true |
| { c; } | Group commands to execute within current shell |

The built-in commands provide higher performance than external commands, but the more built-in commands that are added to a shell, the more memory it consumes with commands that you may never use. The Bash shell also contains external commands that provide extended functionality for the shell. These are discussed in the following section.

# Looking at Common Bash Commands

In addition to the built-in commands, the Bash shell utilizes external commands to allow you to maneuver around the filesystem and manipulate files and directories. Table A.2 shows the common external commands you'll want to use when working in the Bash shell.

**TABLE A.2    The Bash Shell External Commands**

| Command | Description |
| --- | --- |
| at | Executes designated script or command to run at set future time |
| atq | Displays jobs in the at utility queue |
| atrm | Removes designated job from the at utility queue |
| bash | Interprets commands from standard input or from a file, or starts a subshell using the Bourne Again Shell command language |
| bc | Performs calculations via its programming language |
| bzip2 | Compresses using the Burrows–Wheeler block sorting text compression algorithm and Huffman coding |
| cat | Lists the contents of the specified file |
| chage | Changes the password expiration date for the specified system user account |
| chfn | Changes the specified user account's current information |
| chgrp | Changes the default group of the specified file or directory |
| chmod | Changes system security permissions for the specified file or directory |
| chown | Changes the default owner of the specified file or directory |
| chpasswd | Reads a file of login name and password pairs and updates the passwords |

| Command | Description |
|---|---|
| chsh | Changes the specified user account's default shell |
| clear | Removes text from a terminal emulator or virtual console terminal |
| compress | Original Unix file compression utility |
| coproc | Spawns a subshell in background mode and executes the designated command |
| cp | Copies the specified files to an alternate location |
| crontab | Initiates the editor for the user's cron table file, if allowed |
| cut | Removes a designated portion of each specified file's lines |
| date | Displays the date in various formats |
| df | Displays current disk space statistics for all mounted devices |
| dialog | Creates window dialogs in a text environment |
| du | Displays disk usage statistics for the specified file path |
| emacs | Invokes the Emacs text editor |
| env | Executes the designated program in a modified environment or displays the value of all the environment variables |
| exit | Performs a normal termination of current process |
| expr | Evaluates the designated expression |
| fdisk | Organizes and creates the specified disk's partition table |
| file | Displays the file type of the specified file |
| find | Performs a recursive search for files |
| free | Checks available and used memory on the system |
| fsck | Checks and optionally repairs designated filesystem |
| gawk | Streams editing using programming language commands |
| grep | Searches a file for the specified pattern |
| gedit | Invokes the GNOME Desktop editor |
| getopt | Parses command options, including long options |
| gdialog | Creates window dialogs for GNOME Shell |
| groups | Displays group membership of the designated user |
| groupadd | Creates a new system group |
| groupmod | Modifies an existing system group |
| gunzip | The GNU Project's reversal of compression using Lempel–Ziv compression |
| gzcat | The GNU Project's utility for displaying contents of compressed files using Lempel–Ziv compression |
| gzip | The GNU Project's compression using Lempel–Ziv compression |
| head | Displays the first portion of the specified file's contents |

*(Continues)*

A

**TABLE A.2** *(continued)*

| Command | Description |
|---------|-------------|
| help | Displays the help pages for Bash built-in commands |
| kdialog | Creates window dialogs for KDE |
| killall | Sends a system signal to a running process based on process name |
| kwrite | Invokes the KWrite text editor |
| less | Advanced viewing of file contents |
| link | Creates a link to a file using an alias name |
| ln | Creates a symbolic or hard link to a designated file |
| ls | Lists directory contents and/or file information |
| lvcreate | Creates a Logical Volume Manager (LVM) volume |
| lvdisplay | Displays an LVM volume |
| lvextend | Increases the size of an LVM volume |
| lvreduce | Decreases the size of an LVM volume |
| mandb | Creates the database allowing man page keyword searches |
| man | Displays the man pages for the designated command or topic |
| mkdir | Creates the specified directory |
| mkfs | Formats a partition with specified filesystem |
| mktemp | Creates a temporary file or directory |
| more | Lists the contents of the specified file, pausing after each screen of data |
| mount | Displays or mounts disk devices into the virtual filesystem |
| mv | Renames a file or directory |
| nano | Invokes the nano text editor |
| nice | Runs a command using a different priority level on the system |
| nohup | Executes designated command while ignoring SIGHUP signal |
| passwd | Changes the password for a system user account |
| printenv | Displays the value of the specified environment variable or displays the value of all the environment variables |
| ps | Displays information about the running processes on the system |
| pvcreate | Creates a physical LVM volume |
| pvdisplay | Displays a physical LVM volume |
| pwd | Displays the current working directory |
| renice | Changes the priority of a running application on the system |
| rm | Deletes the specified file or directory |
| rmdir | Deletes the specified empty directory |

| Command | Description |
|---|---|
| sed | Streams line editing using editor commands |
| setterm | Modifies terminal settings |
| sleep | Pauses Bash shell operation for a specified amount of time |
| sort | Organizes data in a data file based on the specified order |
| stat | Views the file statistics of the specified file |
| sudo | Runs an application as the root user account |
| tail | Displays the last portion of the specified file's contents |
| tar | Archives data and directories into a single file |
| tee | Sends information to both STDOUT and STDIN |
| top | Displays the active processes, showing vital system statistics |
| touch | Creates a new empty file or updates the time stamp on an existing file |
| umount | Removes a mounted disk device from the virtual filesystem |
| uptime | Displays information on how long the system has been running |
| useradd | Creates a new system user account |
| userdel | Removes an existing system user account |
| usermod | Modifies an existing system user account |
| vgchange | Activates or deactivates an LVM volume group |
| vgcreate | Creates an LVM volume group |
| vgdisplay | Displays an LVM volume group |
| vgextend | Increases the size of an LVM volume group |
| vgreduce | Decreases the size of an LVM volume group |
| vgremove | Deletes an LVM volume group |
| vi | Invokes the vim text editor |
| vim | Invokes the vim text editor |
| vmstat | Produces a detailed report on memory and CPU usage on the system |
| wc | Displays text file statistics |
| whereis | Displays a designated command's files, including binary, source code, and man pages |
| which | Finds the location of an executable file |
| who | Displays users currently logged into system |
| whoami | Displays the current user's username |
| xargs | Takes items from STDIN, builds commands, and executes the commands |
| xterm | Invokes the xterm terminal emulator |
| zenity | Creates window widgets for GNOME Shell |
| zip | Unix version of the Windows PKZIP program |

A

You can accomplish just about any task you need to on the command line by using these commands.

# Assessing Environment Variables

The Bash shell also utilizes many environment variables. Although environment variables aren't commands, they often affect how shell commands operate, so it's important to know some of the shell environment variables. Table A.3 shows several of the environment variables available in the Bash shell.

**TABLE A.3  Bash Shell Environment Variables**

| Variable | Description |
| --- | --- |
| * | Contains all the command-line parameters as a single text value |
| @ | Contains all the command-line parameters as separate text values |
| # | The number of command-line parameters |
| ? | The exit status of the most recently used foreground process |
| - | The current command-line option flags |
| $ | The process ID (PID) of the current shell |
| ! | The PID of the most recently executed background process |
| 0 | The name of the command from the command line |
| _ | The absolute pathname of the shell |
| BASH | The full filename used to invoke the shell |
| BASHOPTS | Enabled shell options in a colon-separated list |
| BASHPID | The current Bash shell's PID |
| BASH_ALIASES | An array containing the currently used aliases |
| BASH_ARGC | The number of parameters in the current subroutine |
| BASH_ARGV | An array containing all the command-line parameters specified |
| BASH_CMDS | An array containing the internal hash table of commands |
| BASH_COMMAND | The name of the command currently being executed |
| BASH_ENV | When set, each Bash script attempts to execute a startup file defined by this variable before running. |
| BASH_EXECU-TION_STRING | The command used in the -c command-line option |
| BASH_LINENO | An array containing the line numbers of each command in the script |
| BASH_REMATCH | An array containing text elements that match a specified regular expression |

| Variable | Description |
| --- | --- |
| BASH_SOURCE | An array containing source filenames for the declared functions in the shell |
| BASH_SUBSHELL | The number of subshells spawned by the current shell |
| BASH_VERSINFO | A variable array that contains the individual major and minor version numbers of the current instance of the Bash shell |
| BASH_VERSION | The version number of the current instance of the Bash shell |
| BASH_XTRACEFD | When set to a valid file descriptor integer, trace output is generated and separated from diagnostic and error messages. The file descriptor must have set -x enabled. |
| BROWSER | The absolute pathname of the preferred web browser |
| COLUMNS | Contains the terminal width of the terminal used for the current instance of the Bash shell |
| COMP_CWORD | An index into the variable COMP_WORDS, which contains the current cursor position |
| COMP_KEY | The completion invocation character keyboard key |
| COMP_LINE | The current command line |
| COMP_POINT | The index of the current cursor position relative to the beginning of the current command |
| COMP_TYPE | The completion type integer value |
| COM_WORDBREAKS | A set of characters used as word separators when performing word completion |
| COMP_WORDS | A variable array that contains the individual words on the current command line |
| COMPREPLY | A variable array that contains the possible completion codes generated by a shell function |
| COPROC | A variable array that holds file descriptors for an unnamed coprocess's I/O |
| DBUS_SESSION_BUS_ADDRESS | The current login session's D-Bus address that provides a map for connections |
| DE | A variable that contains the current login session's desktop environment |
| DESKTOP_SESSION | Within an LXDE environment, a variable that contains the current login session's desktop environment |
| DIRSTACK | A variable array that contains the current contents of the directory stack |
| DISPLAY | A variable that contains a map for graphical applications for where to display the graphical user interface |

*(Continues)*

A

**TABLE A.3** *(continued)*

| Variable | Description |
|---|---|
| EDITOR | When set, defines the default editor used by some shell commands |
| EMACS | When set, the shell assumes it's running in an Emacs shell buffer and disables line editing. |
| ENV | When the shell is invoked in POSIX mode, each Bash script attempts to execute a startup file defined by this variable before running. |
| EUID | The numeric effective user ID of the current user |
| FCEDIT | The default editor used by the `fc` command |
| FIGNORE | A colon-separated list of suffixes to ignore when performing filename completion |
| FUNCNAME | The name of the currently executing shell function |
| FUNCNEST | The maximum level for nesting functions |
| GLOBIGNORE | A colon-separated list of patterns defining the set of filenames to be ignored by filename expansion |
| GROUPS | A variable array containing the list of groups of which the current user is a member |
| histchars | Up to three characters that control history expansion |
| HISTCMD | The history number of the current command |
| HISTCONTROL | Controls what commands are entered in the shell history list |
| HISTFILE | The name of the file to save the shell history list (~/.bash _ history by default) |
| HISTFILESIZE | The maximum number of lines to save in the history file |
| HISTIGNORE | A colon-separated list of patterns used to decide which commands are ignored for the history file |
| HISTSIZE | The maximum number of commands stored in the history file |
| HISTTIMEFORMAT | When set, determines the format string for the history file entries' time stamps |
| HOME | Current login session's home directory name |
| HOSTALIASES | Contains the name of the file that holds aliases for various host names used by some shell commands |
| HOSTFILE | Contains the name of the file that should be read when the shell needs to complete a host name |
| HOSTNAME | The name of the current host |
| HOSTTYPE | A string describing the machine the Bash shell is running on |
| IFS | Contains a list of characters used to separate files, when the words are split as part of an expansion |

| Variable | Description |
|---|---|
| IGNOREEOF | The number of consecutive EOF characters the shell must receive before exiting. If this value doesn't exist, the default is 1. |
| INFODIR | A colon-separated list of info page directories searched by the `info` command |
| INPUTRC | The name of the readline initialization file. The default is ~/.inputrc. |
| INVOCATION_ID | A random and unique 128-bit identifier used to identify login shells (and other units) by `systemd` |
| JOURNAL_STREAM | A colon-separated list of a file descriptor's device and inode number (in decimal format). This is set only when STDOUT or STDERR are connected to the journaling system. |
| LANG | The locale category for the shell |
| LC_ALL | Overrides the LANG variable, defining a locale category |
| LC_ADDRESS | Determines how address information is displayed |
| LC_COLLATE | Sets the collation order used when sorting string values |
| LC_CTYPE | Determines the interpretation of characters used in filename expansion and pattern matching |
| LC_IDENTIFICATION | Contains locale metadata information |
| LC_MEASUREMENT | Sets the locale to use for units of measurement |
| LC_MESSAGES | Determines the locale setting used when interpreting double-quoted strings preceded by a dollar sign |
| LC_MONETARY | Defines the format of monetary numeric values |
| LC_NAME | Sets the format of names |
| LC_NUMERIC | Determines the locale setting used when formatting numbers |
| LC_PAPER | Defines the locale setting used for paper standards and formats |
| LC_TELEPHONE | Sets the structure of telephone numbers |
| LD_LIBRARY_PATH | A colon-separated list of library directories searched prior to standard library directories |
| LINENO | The line number in a script currently executing |
| LINES | Defines the number of lines available on the terminal |
| LOGNAME | Username of current login session |
| LS_COLORS | Determines the colors used to display filenames |
| MACHTYPE | A string defining the system type in *cpu-company-system* format |
| MAIL | If set, defines the mail file of the current login session intermittently searched by some mail programs for new mail |
| MAILCHECK | Sets how often (in seconds) the shell should check for new mail (the default is 60) |

*(Continues)*

A

**TABLE A.3**  *(continued)*

| Variable | Description |
| --- | --- |
| MAILPATH | A colon-separated list of mail filenames intermittently searched by some mail programs for new mail |
| MANPATH | A colon-separated list of man page directories searched by the `man` command |
| MAPFILE | Array variable containing the `mapfile` command's read text; used only when no variable name is given |
| OLDPWD | The previous working directory used in the shell |
| OPTARG | Contains the value to use if an option requires a parameter value, and is set by the `getopts` command |
| OPTERR | If set to 1, the Bash shell displays errors generated by the `getopts` command. |
| OPTIND | Contains the value of the current location within a parameter list where the `getopts` command left off |
| OSTYPE | A string defining the operating system the shell is running on |
| PAGER | Determines the pager utility to use for viewing files with some shell commands |
| PATH | A colon-separated list of directories searched by the shell for commands |
| PIPESTATUS | A variable array containing a list of exit status values from the processes in the foreground process |
| POSIXLY_CORRECT | If set, Bash starts in POSIX mode. |
| PPID | The PID of the Bash shell's parent process |
| PROMPT_COMMAND | If set, the command to execute before displaying the primary prompt |
| PS1 | The primary command-line prompt string |
| PS2 | The secondary command-line prompt string |
| PS3 | The prompt to use for the `select` command |
| PS4 | The prompt displayed before the command line is echoed if the Bash -x parameter is used |
| PWD | The current working directory |
| RANDOM | Returns a random number between 0 and 32767. Assigning a value to this variable seeds the random number generator. |
| READLINE_LINE | The readline line buffer contents |
| READLINE_POINT | The current readline line buffer's insertion point position |
| REPLY | The default variable for the `read` command |
| SECONDS | The number of seconds since the shell was started. Assigning a value resets the timer to the value. |

| Variable | Description |
|---|---|
| SHELL | The shell's full pathname |
| SHELLOPTS | A colon-separated list of enabled Bash shell options |
| SHLVL | Indicates the shell level, incremented by 1 each time a new Bash shell is started |
| TERM | Terminal type currently in use by login session, where the information is provided from a file pointed to by the variable |
| TERMCAP | Terminal type currently in use by login session, where the information is provided within the variable |
| TIMEFORMAT | A format specifying how the shell displays time values |
| TMOUT | The value of how long (in seconds) the select and read commands should wait for input. The default of 0 indicates to wait indefinitely. |
| TMPDIR | When set to a directory name, the shell uses the directory as a location for temporary shell files. |
| TZ | If set, specifies the system's time zone |
| TZDIR | Defines the directory where time zone files are located |
| UID | The numeric real user ID of the current user |
| USER | Username of current login session |
| VISUAL | When set, defines the default screen-based editor used by some shell commands |

You can display the currently defined environment variables using the printenv command. Shell environment variables established at boot time can (and often do) vary between different Linux distributions.

A

# Quick Guide to *sed* and *gawk*

## IN THIS APPENDIX

The basics for using sed

What you need to know about gawk

I f you do any type of data handling in your shell scripts, most likely you'll need to use either the sed program or the gawk program (and sometimes both). This appendix provides a quick reference for sed and gawk commands that come in handy when working with data in your shell scripts.

## The sed Editor

The sed editor can manipulate data in a data stream based on commands you either enter into the command line or store in a command text file. It reads one line of data at a time from the input and matches that data with the supplied editor commands, changes data in the stream as specified in the commands, and then outputs the new data to STDOUT.

### Starting the *sed* editor

Here's the format for using the sed command:

```
sed options script file
```

The *options* parameters allow you to customize the behavior of the sed command and include the options shown in Table B.1.

**TABLE B.1  The sed Command Options**

| Option | Description |
| --- | --- |
| -e *script* | Adds commands specified in *script* to the commands run while processing the input |
| -f *file* | Adds the commands specified in the file *file* to the commands run while processing the input |
| -n | Doesn't produce output for each command but waits for the print command |

The *script* parameter specifies a single command to apply against the stream data. If more than one command is required, you must use either the -e option, to specify them in the command line, or the -f option, to specify them in a separate file.

## *sed* commands

The sed editor script contains commands that sed processes for each line of data in the input stream. This section describes some of the more common sed commands you'll want to use.

### Substitution

The s command substitutes text in the input stream. Here's the format of the s command:

```
s/pattern/replacement/flags
```

*pattern* is the text to replace, and *replacement* is the new text that sed inserts in its place.

The *flags* parameter controls how the substitution takes place. Four types of substitution flags are available:

- A number indicates the pattern occurrence that should be replaced.
- g indicates that all occurrences of the text should be replaced.
- p indicates that the contents of the original line should be printed.
- w *file* indicates that the results of the substitution should be written to a file.

In the first type of substitution, you can specify which occurrence of the matching pattern the sed editor should replace. For example, you use the number 2 to replace only the second occurrence of the pattern.

### Addressing

By default, the commands you use in the sed editor apply to all lines of the text data. If you want to apply a command to only a specific line, or a group of lines, you must use *line addressing*.

There are two forms of line addressing in the sed editor:

- A numeric range of lines
- A text pattern that filters out a line

Both forms use the same format for specifying the address:

```
[address] command
```

When using numeric line addressing, you reference lines by their line position in the text stream. The sed editor assigns the first line in the text stream as line number 1 and continues sequentially for each new line. To replace the word "dog" with the word "cat" but only if it appears on lines 2 or 3 in the data file, you'd use this:

```
$ sed '2,3s/dog/cat/' data1
```

The other method of restricting which lines a command applies to is a bit more complicated. The sed editor allows you to specify a text pattern that it uses to filter lines for the command. Here's the format for this:

> /pattern/command

You must encapsulate the *pattern* you specify in forward slashes. The sed editor applies the command only to lines that contain the text pattern that you specify.

```
$ sed '/rich/s/bash/csh/' /etc/passwd
```

This filter finds the line that contains the text rich and replaces the text bash with csh.

You can also group more than one command together for a specific address:

> address {
>         command1
>         command2
>         command3 }

The sed editor applies each of the commands you specify only to lines that match the address specified. The sed editor processes each command listed on the address line(s):

```
$ sed '2{
> s/fox/elephant/
> s/dog/cat/
> }' data1
```

The sed editor applies each of the substitutions to the second line in the data file.

### Deleting lines

The delete command, d, pretty much does what it says. It deletes any text lines that match the addressing scheme supplied. Be careful with the delete command, because if you forget to include an addressing scheme, all the lines are deleted from the stream:

```
$ sed 'd' data1
```

The delete command is obviously most useful when used in conjunction with a specified address. This allows you to delete specific lines of text from the data stream, either by line number:

```
$ sed '3' data1
```

or by a specific range of lines:

```
$ sed '2,3d' data1
```

The pattern-matching feature of the sed editor also applies to the delete command:

```
$ sed '/number 1/d' data1
```

Only lines matching the specified text are deleted from the stream.

B

### Inserting and appending text

As you would expect, like any other editor, the sed editor allows you to insert and append text lines to the data stream. The difference between the two actions can be confusing:

- The insert command (i) adds a new line before the specified line.
- The append command (a) adds a new line after the specified line.

The format of these two commands can be confusing; you can't use these commands on a single command line. You must specify the line to insert or append on a separate line by itself. Here's the format for doing this:

```
sed '[address]command\
new line'
```

The text in *new line* appears in the sed editor output in the place you specify. Remember that when you use the insert command, the text appears before the data stream text:

```
$ echo "testing" | sed 'i\
> This is a test'
This is a test
testing
$
```

And when you use the append command, the text appears after the data stream text:

```
$ echo "testing" | sed 'a\
> This is a test'
testing
This is a test
$
```

This allows you to insert text at the end of the normal text.

### Changing lines

The change command (c) allows you to change the contents of an entire line of text in the data stream. It works the same as the insert and append commands, in that you must specify the new line separately from the rest of the sed command:

```
$ sed '3c\
> This is a changed line of text.' data1
```

The backslash character is used to indicate the new line of data in the script.

### Transform command

The transform command (y) is the only sed editor command that operates on a single character. The transform command uses this format:

```
[address]y/inchars/outchars/
```

The transform command performs a one-to-one mapping of the *inchars* and the *outchars* values. The first character in *inchars* is converted to the first character in *outchars*. The second character in *inchars* is converted to the second character in *outchars*. This mapping continues throughout the length of the specified characters. If the *inchars* and *outchars* are not the same length, the sed editor produces an error message.

### Printing lines

Similar to the p flag in the substitution command, the p command prints a line in the sed editor output. The most common use for the print command is for printing lines that contain matching text from a text pattern:

```
$ sed -n '/number 3/p' data1
This is line number 3.
$
```

The print command allows you to filter only specific lines of data from the input stream.

### Writing to a file

The w command is used to write lines to a file. Here's the format for the w command:

```
[address]w filename
```

The *filename* can be specified as either a relative or absolute pathname, but in either case, the person running the sed editor must have write permissions for the file. *address* can be any type of addressing method used in sed, such as a single line number, a text pattern, or a range of line numbers or text patterns.

Here's an example that prints only the first two lines of a data stream to a text file:

```
$ sed '1,2w test' data1
```

The output file test contains only the first two lines from the input stream.

### Reading from a file

You've already seen how to insert and append text into a data stream from the sed command line. The read command (r) allows you to insert data contained in a separate file.

Here's the format of the read command:

```
[address]r filename
```

The *filename* parameter specifies either an absolute or relative pathname for the file that contains the data. You can't use a range of addresses for the read command. You can specify only a single line number or text pattern address. The sed editor inserts the text from the file after the address.

```
$ sed '3r data' data1
```

The sed editor inserts the complete text from the data file into the data1 file, starting at line 3 of the data1 file.

B

# The *gawk* Program

The gawk program is the GNU version of the original awk program in Unix. The awk program takes stream editing one step further than the sed editor by providing a programming language instead of just editor commands. This section describes the basics of the gawk program as a quick reference to its abilities.

## The *gawk* command format

The basic format of the gawk program is as follows:

```
gawk options program file
```

Table B.2 shows the options available with the gawk program.

**TABLE B.2  The gawk Options**

| Option | Description |
| --- | --- |
| -F *fs* | Specifies a file separator for delineating data fields in a line |
| -f *file* | Specifies a filename to read the program from |
| -v var=value | Defines a variable and default value used in the gawk program |
| -mf *N* | Specifies the maximum number of fields to process in the data file |
| -mr *N* | Specifies the maximum record size in the data file |
| -W *keyword* | Specifies the compatibility mode or warning level for gawk. Use the help option to list all the available keywords. |

The command-line options provide an easy way to customize features in the gawk program.

## Using *gawk*

You can use gawk either directly from the command line or from within your shell scripts. This section demonstrates how to use the gawk program and how to enter scripts for gawk to process.

### Reading the program script from the command line

A gawk program script is defined by an opening and closing brace. You must place script commands between the two braces. Because the gawk command line assumes that the script is a single text string, you must also enclose your script in single quotation marks. Here's an example of a simple gawk program script specified on the command line:

```
$ gawk '{print $1}'
```

This script displays the first data field in every line of the input stream.

## Using multiple commands in the program script

A programming language wouldn't be very useful if you could execute only one command. The gawk programming language allows you to combine commands into a normal program. To use multiple commands in the program script specified on the command line, just place a semicolon between commands:

```
$ echo "My name is Rich" | gawk '{$4="Dave"; print $0}'
My name is Dave
$
```

The script performs two commands: it replaces the fourth data field with a different value, and then it displays the entire data line in the stream.

## Reading the program from a file

As with the sed editor, the gawk editor allows you to store your programs in a file and refer to them in the command line:

```
$ cat script1
{ print $5 "'s userid is " $1 }
$ gawk -F: -f script1 /etc/passwd
```

The gawk program processes all the commands specified in the file on the input stream data.

## Running scripts before processing data

The gawk program also allows you to specify when the program script is run. By default, gawk reads a line of text from the input and then executes the program script on the data in the line of text. Sometimes, you may need to run a script before processing data, such as to create a header section for a report. To do that, you use the BEGIN keyword. This forces gawk to execute the program script specified after the BEGIN keyword before reading the data:

```
$ gawk 'BEGIN {print "This is a test report"}'
This is a test report
$
```

You can place any type of gawk command in the BEGIN section, such as commands that assign default values to variables.

## Running scripts after processing data

Similar to the BEGIN keyword, the END keyword allows you to specify a program script that gawk executes after reading the data:

```
$ gawk 'BEGIN {print "Hello World!"} {print $0} END {print
    "byebye"}' data1
Hello World!
```

*(Continues)*

B

*(continued)*

```
This is a test
This is a test
This is another test.
This is another test.
byebye
$
```

The gawk program executes the code in the BEGIN section first, then processes any data in the input stream, and then executes the code in the END section.

## The *gawk* variables

The gawk program is more than just an editor; it's a complete programming environment. As such, lots of commands and features are associated with gawk. This section shows the main features you need to know for programming with gawk.

### Built-in variables

The gawk program uses built-in variables to reference specific features within the program data. This section describes the gawk built-in variables available for you to use in your gawk programs and demonstrates how to use them.

The gawk program defines data as records and data fields. A *record* is a line of data (delineated by the newline characters by default), and a *data field* is a separate data element within the line (delineated by a white space character, such as a space or tab, by default).

The gawk program uses data field variables to reference data elements within each record. Table B.3 describes these variables.

**TABLE B.3  The gawk Data Field and Record Variables**

| Variable | Description |
| --- | --- |
| $0 | The entire data record |
| $1 | The first data field in the record |
| $2 | The second data field in the record |
| $n | The *n*th data field in the record |
| FIELDWIDTHS | A space-separated list of numbers defining the exact width (in spaces) of each data field |
| FS | Input field separator character |
| RS | Input record separator character |
| OFS | Output field separator character |
| ORS | Output record separator character |

In addition to the field and record separator variables, gawk provides some other built-in variables to help you know what's going on with your data and to extract information from the shell environment. Table B.4 shows the other built-in variables in gawk.

**TABLE B.4  More gawk Built-In Variables**

| Variable | Description |
|---|---|
| ARGC | The number of command-line parameters present |
| ARGIND | The index in ARGV of the current file being processed |
| ARGV | An array of command-line parameters |
| CONVFMT | The conversion format for numbers (see the printf statement), with a default value of %.6g |
| ENVIRON | An associative array of the current shell environment variables and their values |
| ERRNO | The system error if an error occurs reading or closing input files |
| FILENAME | The filename of the data file used for input to the gawk program |
| FNR | The current record number in the data file |
| IGNORECASE | If set to a non-zero value, gawk ignores the case of all characters in all string functions (including regular expressions) |
| NF | The total number of data fields in the data file |
| NR | The number of input records processed |
| OFMT | The output format for displaying numbers, with a default of %.6g |
| RLENGTH | The length of the substring matched in the match function |
| RSTART | The start index of the substring matched in the match function |

You can use the built-in variables anywhere in the gawk program script, including the BEGIN and END sections.

### Assigning variables in scripts

Assigning values to variables in gawk programs is similar to how you assign values to variables in a shell script—using an *assignment statement*:

```
$ gawk '
> BEGIN{
> testing="This is a test"
> print testing
> }'
This is a test
$
```

After you assign a value to a variable, you can use that variable anywhere in your gawk script.

B

### Assigning variables in the command line

You can also use the gawk command line to assign values to variables for the gawk program. This allows you to set values outside of the normal code, changing values on the fly. Here's an example of using a command-line variable to display a specific data field in the file:

```
$ cat script1
BEGIN{FS=","}
{print $n}
$ gawk -f script1 n=2 data1
$ gawk -f script1 n=3 data1
```

This feature is a great way to process data from your shell scripts in the gawk script.

## The *gawk* program features

Some features of the gawk program make it handy for manipulating data, allowing you to create gawk scripts that can parse just about any type of text file, including log files.

### Regular expressions

You can use either a Basic Regular Expression (BRE) or an Extended Regular Expression (ERE) to filter the lines in the data stream to which the program script applies.

When using a regular expression, the regular expression must appear before the left brace of the program script that it controls:

```
$ gawk 'BEGIN{FS=","} /test/{print $1}' data1
This is a test
$
```

### The matching operator

The *matching operator* allows you to restrict a regular expression to a specific data field in the records. The matching operator is the tilde character (~). You specify the matching operator, along with the data field variable, and the regular expression to match:

```
$1 ~ /^data/
```

This expression filters records where the first data field starts with the text data.

### Mathematical expressions

In addition to regular expressions, you can use mathematical expressions in the matching pattern. This feature comes in handy when you're matching numerical values in data fields. For example, if you want to display all the system users who belong to the root users group (group number 0), you could use this script:

```
$ gawk -F: '$4 == 0{print $1}' /etc/passwd
```

This script displays the first data field value for all lines that contain the value 0 in the fourth data field.

### Structured commands

The gawk program supports the structured commands discussed in this section.

The if-then-else statement:

```
if (condition) statement1; else statement2
```

The while statement:

```
while (condition)
{
    statements
}
```

The do-while statement:

```
do {
    statements
} while (condition)
```

The for statement:

```
for (variable assignment; condition; iteration process)
```

This provides a wealth of programming opportunities for the gawk script programmer. You can write gawk programs that rival the functions of just about any higher-level language program.

B

# Index

## Symbols and Numerics

$#, 382–384
$@, 384–386
$*, 384–386
$?, 477, 478–479
$(), 609–610
$?, 663
$($#), 384–386
$() format, 283
$? special variable, 297
&>, 415
$0, 380, 480, 537
$1, 378, 537
1>, 415
$2, 537
2>, 415
& (ampersand), 443–444, 449, 606–607
* (asterisk), 64–65, 114, 502, 566, 578–579
\ (backslash character), 758
` (backtick character), 283
^ (caret character), 243, 570–571
' (closing quotation mark), 534
{} (curly braces), 127, 536, 581–582
$ (dollar sign), 48, 571–572, 600
. (dot) operator, 59, 68, 277, 490, 493, 572–573
-- (double dash), 389–390, 393
.. (double dot), 59–60
!! (double exclamation mark), 131
>> (double greater than), 285, 413
<< (double less-than symbol), 286
= (equal sign), 555
! (exclamation mark), 65, 600–602
/ (forward slash), 570
> (greater than), 285
< (less than), 285
+ (plus sign), 580–581
| (pipe character), 106, 582–583

# (pound sign), in shell scripts, 276
? (question mark), 64–65, 579–580
" (quotation marks), 141
; (semicolon), 121, 122, 127, 275, 276, 534
[] (square brackets), 573–575
~ (tilde), 639–640
| (vertical line), 287

## A

absolute directory references, 57–60, 67
access control list (ACL), 184–186
access permission triplets, 176–177
accounts
  creating multiple, 374–375
  managing
    creating script for, 703–708
    determining existence,
      698–699
    finding files, 702
    getting name, 693–696
    removing account, 702
    removing processes, 699–702
    running script for, 708–710
    verifying name, 696–698
  system, 164
  user, 163
Activities menu (GNOME 3 desktop), 14
add command, 732–733
address pattern, 604
addresses
  e-mail, 587–589
  range, 615
  sed
    about, 756–757
    grouping, 546
    numeric, 544–545
    text pattern filters, 545–546
Advanced Package Tool (APT) suite, 210

renaming files, 71–73
renice, 453
repairing filesystems, 201–202
repeat command, 676
replacement strings, 606–608
replace-string, 250
replacing, in Emacs editor, 249–250
Report Bug option (Help menu), 42
repositories
    about, 209–210
    aptitude, 218–220
    local, 725–726
    remote, 726
    rpm, 224
--reset option, 26
restarting jobs, 450–451
return command, 478–479
revision control. *See* version control
rf command, 76
RHEL, 27, 193, 194
rm, 73–74, 76
rmdir, 75–76
rolling window, 613
root directory, 54
root drive, 54
rpm, 210, 220, 287–289
RPM. *See* Red Hat Package Management system
rpmfusion.org, 224
rpm.list, 289
RS variable, 630
run level, 6–7
run-parts, 461
rxvt-unicode, 27

## S

s command, 593–594
Sakura, 27
SATA drives, 194
scale, 294
scheduling
    jobs, 454–458
    regular scripts, 458–461
scheduling priority, 451–452
scope, function, 482–483
script exits, trapping, 440

script name, reading, 380–381
scripting
    archiving data files
        about, 681–693
        configuration file, 682–684
        creating daily archive location, 685–686
        daily archive script, 686–688
        hourly archive script, 689–693
    background mode, 443–445
    bc, 295–297
    comment line, 276
    creating file, 276–278
    creating multiple user accounts, 374–375
    dash shell
        arithmetic, 666
        function command, 667–668
        test command, 666–667
    dialog command in, 515–516
    displaying messages, 278–279
    exiting, 297–300
    file descriptors
        closing, 424–425
        listing open, 424–426
        redirection, 419–424
    finding executable files, 373–374
    floating-point math, 293–297
    functions
        about, 473–476
        array variables, 485–488
        command line usage, 491–494
        creating, 474
        creating on command line, 491–492
        default exit status, 477–478
        defining in .bashrc file, 492–494
        global variables, 483–484
        libraries, 489–491
        local variables, 484–485
        parameter passing to, 480–482
        passing arrays, 485–487
        return command, 478–479
        returning arrays, 487–488
        returning values, 477–480
        scope, 482–483
        using, 474–476
        using output, 479–480
        variables in, 480–485
    gawk, assigning in scripts, 634–635